Parts of Speech and Grammar

Punctuation and Mechanics

The Business Writer's Handbook

About the Authors

Gerald J. Alred is Professor Emeritus of English at the University of Wisconsin–Milwaukee, where he is a teaching-award recipient and an adviser to the Professional Writing Program. He is the author of numerous scholarly articles and several standard bibliographies on business and technical communication, and he served as Associate Editor of the *Journal of Business Communication*. He is a recipient of the prestigious Jay R. Gould Award for "profound scholarly and textbook contributions to the teaching of business and technical writing." He developed and manages the Web site InlandChorus.com™.

Charles T. Brusaw served as a faculty member at NCR Corporation's Management College, where he developed and taught courses in professional writing, editing, and presentation skills for the corporation worldwide. Previously, he worked in advertising, technical writing, public relations, and curriculum development. He was also a communications consultant, an invited speaker at academic conferences, and a teacher of business writing at Sinclair Community College. He passed away in 2015.

Walter E. Oliu served as Chief of the Publishing Services Branch at the U.S. Nuclear Regulatory Commission, where he managed the agency's printing, graphics, editing, and publishing programs, as well as the daily operations of the agency's public Web site. He is the recipient of the agency's Meritorious Service Award. He has also taught at Miami University of Ohio, Slippery Rock State University, Montgomery College, and George Mason University.

Twelfth Edition

The Business Writer's Handbook

Gerald J. Alred

Charles T. Brusaw

Walter E. Oliu

bedford/st.martin's
Macmillan Learning

Boston | New York

For Bedford/St. Martin's

Vice President, Editorial, Macmillan Learning Humanities: Edwin Hill
Executive Program Director for English: Leasa Burton
Senior Program Manager: Laura Arcari
Marketing Manager: Laura Arrant
Director of Content Development: Jane Knetzger
Executive Development Editor: Jane Carter
Editorial Assistant: William Hwang
Content Project Manager: Louis C. Bruno Jr.
Senior Workflow Project Supervisor: Joe Ford
Production Supervisor: Robin Besofsky
Media Project Manager: Allison Hart
Director of Media Editoral, Humanities: Adam Whitehurst
Manager of Publishing Services: Andrea Cava
Project Management: Lumina Datamatics, Inc.
Editorial Services: Lumina Datamatics, Inc.
Composition: Lumina Datamatics, Inc.
Text Permission Manager: Kalina Ingham
Text Permissions Researcher: Claire Paschal
Photo Permissions Manager: Angela Boehler
Photo Permissions Researcher: Kerri Wilson, Lumina Datamatics, Inc.
Director of Design, Content Management: Diana Blume
Text Design: Books By Design, Inc.; Glenna Collett
Cover Design: William Boardman
Cover Image: Malorny / Getty Images
Printing and Binding: RR Donnelley, Shenzhen

1   2   3   4   5   6   23   22   21   20

For information, write: Bedford/St. Martin's, 75 Arlington Street, Boston, MA 02116

ISBN 978-1-319-36176-1

Acknowledgments

Copyrights appear on the same page as the art selections they cover; these copyrights constitute an extension of the copyright page.

Page 511, Kitty O. Locker. "'As Per Your Request': A History of Business Jargon," *Journal of Business and Technical Communication* 1, no. 1 (1987): 27–47. Reprinted by permission of SAGE Publications.

Contents

Preface

The Business Writer's Handbook is the text students and professionals need to land, navigate, and stand out on the job. Like previous editions, the twelfth edition is a comprehensive, easy-access guide that places business writing in a real-world context, with quick reference to hundreds of topics and scores of model documents and visuals.

Anticipating the needs of today's professionals and job seekers, this edition has been judiciously trimmed, while areas related to finding a job and using social media as a professional tool have been updated and expanded, based on expert advice. Further, *LaunchPad Solo for Professional Writing* provides online tutorials on today's most relevant digital writing topics, from content management to personal branding. This resource can be packaged with the text at no additional cost.

Helpful Features

The Business Writer's Handbook offers alphabetically arranged entries on an array of topics crucial to effective business writing, from "Abbreviations" and "Abstracts" through "Writing for the Web" and the "'You' Viewpoint." In its focus on the job search and résumé preparation, it provides up-to-date advice on how to network using professional and social media and offers tips on developing application materials that will spark the interest of prospective employers. Its concise yet comprehensive coverage of the writing process and in-depth treatment of grammar and usage provide detailed help for every stage of writing, from preparation, audience analysis, and research, to drafting, revising, and proofreading.

Real-world samples provide students with authentic models of business correspondence for a variety of workplace situations. Up-to-date instruction gives students the latest advice on writing and designing for the Web, using social media in business, conducting Internet research, and approaching new software. An emphasis on the latest workplace technologies stresses the importance of tailoring every message—from a formal business e-mail to a quick text—to its purpose, audience, and medium.

Quick reference features—including Contents by Topic (on the inside front cover), a comprehensive index, and a list of model documents and figures—make it easy to navigate. Checklists help writers tackle complex tasks such as proofreading and revising, communicating with international audiences, and evaluating sources. Throughout the text, "Ethics Notes" and "Professionalism Notes" highlight central concerns in today's business world and offer advice for dealing with those concerns. A thorough discussion of copyright and plagiarism clarifies what plagiarism is in the digital age and highlights the ethical aspects of using and documenting sources appropriately. Guidelines for online and interpersonal communication and tips on preparing important projects and presentations offer valuable advice on which students and professionals can rely.

New to This Edition

Our focus in revising the handbook for this edition has been on refining and updating existing entries to provide information that is especially relevant for securing a job in today's economy and for navigating the technologies needed to succeed on the job. We have made the following additions and improvements:

- **A new entry on creating an online professional profile** helps business writers select the appropriate forum and represent themselves and their accomplishments effectively on sites such as LinkedIn, AngelList, and Academia.edu.
- **A new entry on spreadsheets** explains how and why to use them and provides resources for up-to-date help.
- **A thorough updating of the job-search entry** includes new coverage of co-ops, service internships, and "gap year" opportunities—crucial information for students and professionals seeking a new career.
- **Updated coverage of interviewing for a job** offers more tips on what to do after the interview and includes a new model of a follow-up letter.
- **Updated coverage of documenting sources** provides current guidelines for citing sources in *CMS* and APA styles.
- **A new professionalism note on the etiquette of mobile devices** helps students move seamlessly between their personal and professional worlds.
- **New instructor support materials,** including advice on structuring the class and sample course plans, are available on the instructor's tab on the book's catalog page at macmillanlearning.com.

How to Use This Book

The Business Writer's Handbook is made up of alphabetically organized entries, with colored tabs delineating each letter section. Within each entry, underlined, boldfaced cross-references—for example, **proposals**—link readers to entries that contain further information. Many entries present advice and guidelines in the form of convenient "Writer's Checklists" and annotated model documents and figures.

The *Handbook*'s alphabetical organization enables readers to find specific topics quickly and easily; however, readers with general questions have several different ways to locate information in the book.

- **Contents by Topic.** The complete "Contents by Topic" on the inside front cover groups the alphabetical entries into topic categories. This topical key allows a writer focusing on a specific task or problem to browse all related entries; it also helps instructors correlate the *Handbook* to standard textbooks or to their own course materials.

- **Commonly Misused Words and Phrases.** The list of "Commonly Misused Words and Phrases" on pages 601–02 extends the "Contents by Topic" by listing all the usage entries, which appear in italics throughout the book—for example, *and/or*.

- **Model Documents and Figures by Topic.** The topically organized list of "Model Documents and Figures by Topic" on the inside back cover makes it easier to browse the book's most commonly referenced sample documents and visuals to find specific examples of business writing genres.

- **Checklist of the Writing Process.** The checklist on pages xxv–xxvi helps readers reference key entries in a sequence useful for planning and carrying out a writing project.

- **Comprehensive Index.** The user-friendly index lists all the topics covered in the book—including subtopics and model documents—in an alphabetical arrangement.

Acknowledgments

For their invaluable comments and suggestions for this edition of *The Business Writer's Handbook*, we thank the following reviewers who responded to our questionnaires: William Allegrezza, Indiana University Northwest; Jeanne Allison, University of Missouri–St. Louis; Stevens Amidon, Indiana University–Purdue University Fort Wayne; Greg Brecht, University of South Florida, St. Petersburg; Carol Davis, California State University, Monterey Bay; Sonia Khatchadourian, University of Wisconsin–Milwaukee; Nancy Nygaard, University of Wisconsin–Milwaukee; and Teeanna Rizkallah, California State University, Fullerton. Additional thanks go out to Sonia Khatchadourian, who kindly let us share her syllabus on our book's catalog page, so that other instructors could benefit from her experience with the book.

For this edition, we'd especially like to thank Richard C. Hay, founder and CEO of Twenty Six Design, LLC, for his advice on updating the figures and model documents throughout the book, and especially for his update of the brochure entry, including the new model brochure. We also owe special thanks to Traci Gardner, Virginia Tech, for her update of the entries on social media and for creating an online profile. Finally, we want to thank Saundra Williams, Human Resources Business Partner at Macmillan Learning, for her advice on updating the job search entries. We are indebted to Kenneth J. Cook, president of Ken Cook Co., for his ongoing support of this and earlier editions of the *Handbook* and for his continued permission to reprint the exemplary company newsletter.

We wish to thank Bedford/St. Martin's for supporting this book, especially Edwin Hill, Vice President, Humanities Editorial; Leasa Burton, Senior Program Director, English; Laura Arcari, Senior Program Manager, Rhetorics and Business and Technical Writing; and Lauren Arrant, Marketing Manager. We are grateful to Andrea Cava, Publishing Services Manager; Louis Bruno, Content Project Manager; and Robin Besofsky, Production Supervisor, for their patient management of the book's production. We thank Hilary Newman, Director of Rights and Permissions; Kalina Ingham, Permissions Manager; Angie Boehler, Permissions Editor; and Claire Paschal, Permissions Associate, for their help in managing the permissions process. We thank Billy Boardman, Senior Design Manager; Diana Blume, Design Director; and Diana's design team, as well as Rachel Comerford, Director of Content Standards, for helping make this book accessible to all readers. Our gratitude also goes out to William Hwang for his conscientious work on this project. Finally, we wish to thank Executive Development Editor Jane Carter for her editorial direction on this always-challenging project.

At Lumina Datamatics, we thank Jana Lewis, Bharathi Sriram, Sudheer Purushothaman, Kerri Wilson, Jamie Thaman, and Rebecca Roby for their help in the copyediting, proofreading, permissions, and production processes.

We offer our heartfelt gratitude to Barbara Brusaw for her patience and time spent preparing the manuscript for the first five editions. We also gratefully acknowledge the ongoing contributions of many students and instructors at the University of Wisconsin–Milwaukee. Finally, special thanks go to Janice Alred for her many hours of help in coordinating this project and for continuing to hold everything together.

With sorrow, we mark the 2015 passing of our esteemed coauthor, Charles "Ted" Brusaw, and dedicate this edition of *The Business Writer's Handbook* to his memory. Ted began his professional career as a freelance writer and moved on to a variety of positions in business and industry as a technical writer and corporate trainer. For many years, he was manager of technical publications at the NCR Corporation. Ted coauthored *Practical Writing*, *The Business Writer's Handbook*, *Handbook of Technical Writing*, *The Professional Writer*, *The Business Writer's Companion*, and *Writing That Works*. He also independently authored a well-reviewed book of World War II military history (a Book of the Month Club selection), a Civil War novel, a biography of Benedict Arnold, and a historical novel on the Lewis and Clark expedition. Ted was an accomplished writer, teacher, and mentor (most especially to both of us), whose standards were simply the highest. We are grateful to have had the good fortune to work with this consummate professional, who was also our friend.

Gerald J. Alred and Walter E. Oliu

We're All In. As Always.

Bedford/St. Martin's is as passionately committed to the discipline of English as ever, working hard to provide support and services that make it easier for you to teach your course your way.

Find **community support** at the Bedford/St. Martin's English Community (community.macmillan.com), where you can follow our *Bits* blog for new teaching ideas, download titles from our professional resource series, and review projects in the pipeline.

Choose **curriculum solutions** that offer flexible custom options, combining our carefully developed print and digital resources, acclaimed works from Macmillan's trade imprints, and your own course or program materials to provide the exact resources your students need. Our approach to customization makes it possible to create a customized project uniquely suited for your students, and based on your enrollment size, return money to your department, and raise your institutional profile with a high-impact author visit through the Macmillan Author Program ("MAP").

Rely on **outstanding service** from your Bedford/St. Martin's sales representative and editorial team. Contact us or visit macmillanlearning .com to learn more about any of the following options.

LaunchPad Solo for Professional Writing: *Where Students Learn.* Launch-Pad provides engaging content and new ways to get the most out of your book. Get an interactive e-book combined with assessment tools in a fully customizable course space, then assign and mix our resources with yours.

- **Sample documents** provide a wide range of effective professional writing models for students to emulate, including e-mails, résumés, cover letters, reports, proposals, brochures, and questionnaires.

- **Tutorials** show students how to maximize free online tools to access projects across platforms, design dynamic presentations, develop podcasts, manage their personal brand, and build common citations in APA and MLA styles.

- **Diagnostics** provide opportunities to assess areas for improvement and assign additional exercises based on students' needs. Visual reports show performance by topic, class, and student as well as improvement over time.

- **Prebuilt units**—including readings, videos, and quizzes—are easy to adapt by mixing your materials with our high-quality multimedia content and ready-made assessment options, such as **LearningCurve** adaptive quizzing and Exercise Central.

- Use LaunchPad on its own or **integrate it** with your school's learning management system so that your students are always on the same page.

LaunchPad Solo for Professional Writing can be purchased on its own or packaged with the print book at a significant discount. An activation code is required. To order *LaunchPad Solo for Professional Writing* with the print handbook, contact your Macmillan Learning representative. For more information, go to **launchpadworks.com**.

Choose from Alternative Formats of The Business Writer's Handbook. Bedford/St. Martin's offers a range of formats. Choose what works best for you and your students:

- *Spiral-bound edition* To order the spiral-bound edition, use ISBN 978-1-319-36176-1.
- *Popular e-book formats* For details of our e-book partners, visit **macmillanlearning.com/ebooks**.

Select Value Packages. Add value to your text by packaging Writer's Help 2.0 with *The Business Writer's Handbook* at a significant discount. Contact your sales representative for more information. **Writer's Help 2.0** is a powerful online writing resource that helps students find answers, whether they are searching for writing advice on their own or as part of an assignment.

- **Smart search.** Built on research with more than 1,600 student writers, the smart search in Writer's Help provides reliable results even when students use novice terms, such as *flow* and *unstuck.*
- **Trusted content from our best-selling handbooks.** Choose *Writer's Help 2.0, Hacker Version,* or *Writer's Help 2.0, Lunsford Version,* and ensure that students have clear advice and examples for all of their writing questions.
- **Diagnostics that help establish a baseline for instruction.** Assign diagnostics to identify areas of strength and areas for improvement and to help students plan a course of study. Use visual reports to track performance by topic, class, and student as well as improvement over time.
- **Adaptive exercises that engage students.** Writer's Help 2.0 includes LearningCurve, game-like online quizzing that adapts to what students already know and helps them focus on what they need to learn.

Student access is packaged with *The Business Writer's Handbook* at a significant discount. Contact your Macmillan Learning representative for packaging options to ensure that your students have easy access to online writing support. Students who rent or buy a used book can purchase access; instructors may request free access at **macmillanlearning.com/writershelp2**.

Instructor Resources. You have a lot to do in your course. We want to make it easy for you to find the support you need—and to find it quickly. Suggestions for structuring your course, including sample course plans, can be downloaded from macmillanlearning.com. Visit the instructor's tab for *The Business Writer's Handbook*.

Five Steps to Successful Writing

Successful writing on the job is not the product of inspiration, nor is it merely the spoken word converted to print; it is the result of knowing how to structure information using both text and design to achieve an intended purpose for a clearly defined audience. The best way to ensure that your writing will succeed—whether it is a proposal, a résumé, a Web page, or any other document—is to approach writing using the following steps:

1. Preparation
2. Research
3. Organization
4. Writing
5. Revision

You will no doubt need to follow those steps consciously at first. The same is true the first time you use new software, interview a job candidate, or chair a committee meeting. With practice, the steps become nearly automatic. This is not to suggest that writing becomes easy—it does not. However, the easiest and most efficient way to write effectively is to do it systematically.

As you master the five steps, keep in mind that they are interrelated and often overlap. For example, your readers' needs and your purpose, which you determine in step 1, will affect decisions you make in subsequent steps. You may also need to retrace steps. When you conduct research, for example, you may realize that you need to revise your initial impression of the document's purpose and audience. Similarly, when you begin to organize in step 3, you may discover the need to return to research (step 2) to gather more information.

The time required for each step varies with different writing tasks. When writing an informal memo, for example, you might accomplish the first three steps (preparation, research, and organization) by simply listing the points in the order you want to cover them. In such situations, you gather and organize information mentally as you consider your purpose and audience. For a formal report, the first three steps require well-organized research, careful note-taking, and detailed outlining. For a routine e-mail message to a coworker, the first four steps merge as you type the information onto the screen. In short, the five steps expand, contract, and at times must be repeated to fit the complexity or context of the writing task.

Dividing the writing process into steps is especially useful when you are writing as a part of a team. In that case, you typically divide work among team members, keep track of a project, and save time by not duplicating efforts. When you collaborate, you can use e-mail to share text and other files, suggest improvements to one an other's work, and generally keep everyone informed of your progress as you follow the steps in the writing process.

Preparation

Writing, like most professional tasks, requires solid **preparation**.* In fact, adequate preparation is as important as **writing a draft**. In preparation for writing, your goal is to accomplish the following four major tasks:

- Establish your primary **purpose**.
- Assess your **audience** (or readers) and the **context**.
- Determine the **scope** of your coverage.
- Select the appropriate medium. See **selecting the medium**.

Establishing Your Purpose.   To establish your primary purpose, simply ask yourself what you want your readers to know, to believe, or to be able to do after they have finished reading what you have written. Be precise. Often a writer states a purpose so broadly that it is almost useless. A purpose such as "to report on possible locations for a new research facility" is too general. However, "to compare the relative advantages of Paris, Singapore, and San Francisco as possible locations for a new research facility so that top management can choose the best one" is a purpose statement that can guide you throughout the writing process. In addition to your primary purpose, consider possible secondary purposes for your document. For example, a secondary purpose of the research-facility report might be to make corporate executive readers aware of the staffing needs of the new facility so that they can ensure its smooth operation in whichever location is selected.

Assessing Your Audience and Context.   The next task is to assess your audience. Again, be precise and ask key questions. Who exactly is your reader? Do you have multiple readers? Who needs to see or to use the document? What are your readers' needs in relation to your subject? What are your readers' attitudes about the subject? (Are they skeptical? Supportive? Anxious? Bored?) What do your readers already know about the subject? Should you define basic terminology, or will such definitions merely bore, or even impede, your readers? Are you

---

*Throughout this book, words and phrases shown as links—underlined and set in boldface type—refer to specific entries in the book.

communicating with international readers and therefore dealing with issues inherent in **global communication**? To be a successful writer in any language, you must understand the cultural values that underlie the language in which you are writing. In the United States, **conciseness**, **coherence**, and **clarity** characterize good writing. Make sure readers can follow your writing, and say only what is necessary to communicate your message.

For the research-facility report, the readers are described as "top management." Who is included in that category? Will one of the people evaluating the report be the human resources manager? That person would likely be interested in the availability of qualified professionals as well as in the presence of training, housing, and even recreational facilities available to potential employees in each city. The purchasing manager would be concerned with available sources for needed materials. The marketing manager would give priority to a facility's proximity to the primary markets and transportation to important clients. The chief financial officer would want to know about land and building costs and about each city's tax structure. The chief executive officer would be interested in all this information and perhaps more. As in this example, many workplace documents have audiences composed of multiple readers. You can accommodate their needs through one of a number of approaches described in the entry **audience**.

Part of knowing the needs and interests of your readers is learning as much as you can about the context. Simply put, context is the environment or circumstances in which writers produce documents and within which readers interpret their meanings. Everything is written within a context, as is illustrated in many of the entries and examples throughout this book. To determine the effect of context on the research-facility report, you might ask both specific and general questions about the situation and about your readers' backgrounds: Is this the company's first new facility, or has the company chosen locations for new facilities before? Have the readers visited all three cities? Have they already seen other reports on the three cities? What is the corporate culture in which your readers work, and what are its key values? What specific factors, such as competition, finance, and regulation, are recognized as important within the organization?

Determining the Scope.   Determining your purpose and assessing your readers and context will help you decide what to include and what not to include in your writing. Those decisions establish the **scope** of your writing project. If you do not clearly define the scope, you will spend needless hours on research because you will not be sure what kind of information you need or even how much. Given the purpose and audience established for the report on facility locations, the scope would include such information as land and building costs, available labor force, cultural issues, transportation options, and proximity to suppliers. However, it would probably not include the early history of the cities being considered or their climate and geological features, unless those aspects were directly related to your particular business.

Selecting the Medium. Finally, you need to determine the most appropriate medium for communicating your message. Professionals on the job face a wide array of options—from **e-mail**, **text messaging**, and videoconferencing to more traditional means, like **letters**, **memos**, **reports**, and face-to-face **meetings**.

The most important considerations in selecting the appropriate medium are the audience and the purpose of the communication. For example, if you need to collaborate with someone to solve a problem or if you need to establish rapport with someone, written exchanges would be far less efficient than a phone call or a face-to-face meeting. However, if you need to use precise wording or you need to provide a record of a complex message, communicating in writing would be best. If you need to make information that is frequently revised accessible to employees at a large company, the best choice might be to place the information on the company's intranet site. If reviewers need to make handwritten comments on a proposal, you may need to provide paper copies that can be faxed, or you can use collaborative software so that reviewers can insert comments electronically. The comparative advantages and primary characteristics of the most typical means of communication are discussed in **selecting the medium**.

Research

The only way to be sure that you can write about a complex subject is to thoroughly understand it. To do that, you must conduct adequate **research**, whether that means conducting an extensive investigation for a major proposal—through interviewing, library and Internet research, careful **note-taking**, and **documenting sources**—or simply checking a reputable Web site and jotting down points before you send an e-mail message to a colleague.

Methods of Research. Researchers frequently distinguish between primary and secondary research, depending on the types of sources consulted and the method of gathering information. *Primary research* refers to the gathering of raw data compiled from interviews, direct observation, surveys, experiments, **questionnaires**, audio and video recordings, and the like. In fact, direct observation and hands-on experience are the only ways to obtain certain kinds of information, such as the behavior of people and animals, certain natural phenomena, mechanical processes, and the operation of systems and equipment. *Secondary research* refers to gathering information that has been analyzed, assessed, evaluated, compiled, or otherwise organized into accessible form. Such forms or sources include books, articles, reports, Web documents, e-mail discussions, and brochures. Use the methods most appropriate to your needs, recognizing that some projects may require several types of research and that collaborative projects may require those research tasks to be distributed among team members.

Sources of Information.   As you conduct research, keep in mind all the sources of information that are available to you:

- Your own knowledge and that of your colleagues
- The knowledge of people outside your workplace, gathered through **interviewing for information**
- Internet sources, including Web sites, directories, archives, and discussion groups
- Library resources, including databases and indexes of articles as well as books and reference works
- Printed and electronic sources in the workplace, such as brochures, memos, e-mail, and Web documents

The amount of research you will need to do depends on the scope of your project.

Organization

Without organization, the material gathered during your research will be incoherent to your readers. To organize information effectively, you need to determine the best way to structure your ideas; that is, you must choose a primary **method of development**.

Methods of Development.   To choose the development method best suited to your document, consider your subject, your readers' needs, and your purpose. An appropriate method will help focus your information and make it easy for readers to follow your presentation.

For example, if you were writing instructions for assembling office equipment, you might naturally present the steps of the process in the order readers should perform them: the **sequential method of development**. If you were writing about the history of an organization, your account might naturally go from the beginning to the present: the **chronological method of development**. If your subject naturally lends itself to a certain method of development, use it—do not attempt to impose another method on it.

Often you will need to combine methods of development. For example, a persuasive brochure for a charitable organization might combine a specific-to-general method of development with a **cause-and-effect**

method of development. That is, you could begin with persuasive case histories of individual people in need and then move to general information about the positive effects of donations on recipients.

Outlining.   Once you have chosen a method of development, you are ready to prepare an outline. **Outlining** breaks large or complex subjects into manageable parts. It also enables you to emphasize key points by placing them in the positions of greatest importance. By structuring your thinking at an early stage, a well-developed outline ensures that your document will be complete and logically organized, allowing you to focus exclusively on writing when you begin the rough draft. An outline can be especially helpful for maintaining a collaborative writing team's focus throughout a large project. However, even a short letter or memo needs the logic and structure that an outline provides, whether the outline exists in your mind, on-screen, or on paper.

At this point, consider **layout and design** elements that will be helpful to your readers and appropriate to your subject and purpose. For example, if **visuals** such as photographs or tables will be useful, this is a good time to think about where they may be deployed and what kinds of visual elements will be effective, especially if they need to be prepared by someone else while you write and revise the draft. The outline can also suggest where **headings**, **lists**, and other special design features may be useful.

Writing

When you have established your purpose, your readers' needs, and your scope, and you have completed your research and your outline, you will be well prepared to write a first draft. Expand your outline into **paragraphs** without worrying about **grammar**, **usage**, or **punctuation**. Writing and revising are different activities; refinements come with **revision**.

Write the rough draft, concentrating entirely on converting your outline into sentences and paragraphs. You might try writing as though you were explaining your subject to a reader sitting across from you. Do not worry about a good opening. Just start. Do not be concerned in the rough draft about exact **word choice** unless it comes quickly and easily—concentrate instead on ideas.

Even with good preparation, writing the draft remains a chore for many writers. The most effective way to get started and keep going is to use your outline as a map for your first draft. Do not wait for inspiration—you need to treat writing a draft as you would any on-the-job task. The entry **writing a draft** describes tactics used by experienced writers; discover which ones are best suited to you and your task.

Consider writing the **introduction** last because then you will know more precisely what is in the body of the draft. Your opening should announce the subject and give readers essential background information, such as the document's primary purpose. For longer documents, an introduction should serve as a frame into which readers can fit the detailed information that follows.

Finally, you will need to write a **conclusion** that ties the main ideas together and emphatically makes a final, significant point. The final point may be to recommend a course of action, make a prediction or a judgment, or merely summarize your main points; the way you conclude depends on the purpose of your writing and your readers' needs.

Revision

The clearer a finished piece of writing seems to the reader, the more effort the writer has likely put into its **revision**. If you have followed the steps of the writing process to this point, you will have a rough draft that needs to be revised. Revising, however, requires a different frame of mind than does writing the draft. During revision, be eager to find and correct faults, and be honest. Be hard on yourself for the benefit of your readers. Read and evaluate the draft as if you were a reader seeing it for the first time.

Check your draft for accuracy, completeness, and effectiveness in achieving your purpose and meeting your readers' needs and expectations. Trim extraneous information: Your writing should give readers exactly what they need, but it should not burden them with unnecessary information or sidetrack them into loosely related subjects.

Do not try to revise for everything at once. Read your rough draft several times, each time looking for and correcting a different set of problems or errors. Concentrate first on larger issues, such as **unity** and **coherence**; save mechanical corrections, like **spelling** and punctuation, for later **proofreading**.

Finally, for important documents, consider having others review your writing and make suggestions for improvement. For collaborative writing, of course, team members must review one another's work on the various segments of the document as well as the final master draft. Use the "Checklist of the Writing Process" on pages xxv–xxvi to guide you not only as you revise but also throughout the writing process. See also **ethics in writing**.

◀ **PROFESSIONALISM NOTE**   **Style Guides and Standards** organizations and professional associations often follow such guides as *The Chicago Manual of Style*, *MLA Style Manual and Guide to Scholarly Publishing*, and *United States Government Publishing Office Style Manual* to ensure consistency in their publications on issues of usage, format, and documentation. Because this type of advice often varies from one guide to another, some organizations set their own standards for documents. Where such standards or specific style guides are recommended or required by regulation or policy, be sure to follow those style guidelines. ▶

Checklist of the Writing Process

This checklist arranges key entries of *The Business Writer's Handbook* according to the sequence presented in "Five Steps to Successful Writing," which begins on page xvii. This checklist is useful both for following the steps and for diagnosing writing problems.

Preparation   393

✔ Establish your **purpose**   434

✔ Identify your **audience** or **readers**   44, 447

✔ Consider the **context**   103

✔ Determine your **scope** of coverage   487

✔ **Select the medium**   488

Research   456

✔ **Brainstorm** to determine what you already know   54

✔ Conduct **research**   456

✔ Take notes (**note-taking**)   349

✔ **Interview for information**   273

✔ Create and use **questionnaires**   437

✔ Avoid **plagiarism**   384

✔ **Document sources**   133

Organization   363

✔ Choose the best **methods of development**   331

✔ **Outline** your notes and ideas   364

✔ Develop and integrate **visuals**   538

✔ Consider **layout and design**   305

logic errors   320

positive writing   390

voice   543

✔ Check for **ethics in writing**   179

biased language   49

copyrights, patents, and trademarks   106

plagiarism   384

✔ Check for appropriate **word choice**   549

abstract / concrete words   5

affectation, **buzzwords**, **jargon**, and **plain language**   21, 64, 291, 385

clichés   76

connotation / denotation   103

defining terms   122

✔ Eliminate problems with **grammar**   235

Writing a Draft   550

✔ Select an appropriate **point of view**   386

✔ Adopt an appropriate **style** and **tone**   510, 526

The Business
Writer's Handbook

a / an

A and *an* are indefinite **articles** because the **noun** designated by the article is not a specific person, place, or thing but one of a group.

▶ The insurance agent sold *a* policy. [This is not a specific policy but an unnamed policy.]

Use *a* before words or abbreviations beginning with a consonant or a vowel with a consonant sound. See also **adjectives**.

▶ We were awarded *a* DMV contract.

▶ It was *a* historic event for the organization. [*Historic* begins with the consonant *h*.]

▶ The year's activities are summarized in *a* one-page report. [*One* begins with the consonant sound "wuh."]

Use *an* before words or abbreviations beginning with a vowel or a consonant with a vowel sound.

▶ He seems *an* unlikely candidate for the job.

▶ The applicant arrived *an* hour early. [*Hour* begins with a silent *h*.]

▶ She received *an* SBA loan. [*SBA* begins with the vowel sound "ess."]

a lot

A lot is often incorrectly written as one word (*alot*). The phrase *a lot* is informal and often too vague for business writing. Use *many* or *numerous* for estimates, or give a specific number or amount.

▶ We received ~~a lot of~~ ^152^ e-mails supporting the new policy.

abbreviations

Abbreviations are shortened versions of words or combinations of the first letters of words (*Corp./Corporation*, *URL/Uniform Resource Locator*). If used appropriately, abbreviations can be convenient for both the reader and the writer. Like symbols, they can be important space savers in business writing.

Abbreviations that are formed by combining the initial letter of each word in a multiword term are called *initialisms*. Initialisms are pronounced as separate letters (*SEC/Securities and Exchange Commission*). Abbreviations that combine the first letter or letters of several words — and can be pronounced — are called *acronyms* (*PIN/personal identification number*, *LAN/local area network*).

Using Abbreviations

The most important consideration in the use of abbreviations is whether they will be understood by your **audience**. The same abbreviation, for example, can have two different meanings (*NEA* stands for both National Education Association and the National Endowment for the Arts). Like **jargon**, shortened forms are easily understood within a group of specialists; outside the group, however, shortened forms might be incomprehensible. In fact, abbreviations can be easily overused, either as an **affectation** or in a misguided attempt to make writing concise, even with **instant messaging** and **live chat**, where abbreviations are often appropriate. Remember that **memos**, **e-mail**, or **reports** addressed to specific people may be read by others, so consider those secondary audiences as well. A good rule to follow: "When in doubt, spell it out."

WRITER'S CHECKLIST **Using Abbreviations**

✔ Except for commonly used abbreviations (*U.S.*, *a.m.*), spell out a term to be abbreviated the first time it is used, followed by the abbreviation in **parentheses**. Thereafter, the abbreviation may be used alone.

(continued)

WRITER'S CHECKLIST   **Using Abbreviations** (*continued*)

✔ In long documents, repeat the full term in parentheses after the abbreviation at regular intervals to remind readers of the abbreviation's meaning. For digital texts, consider linking abbreviations to a glossary or providing a pop-up definition that appears when the cursor hovers over an abbreviation.

✔ Do not add an additional period at the end of a sentence that ends with an abbreviation. ("The official name of the company is DataBase, Inc.")

✔ For abbreviations specific to your profession or discipline, use a style guide recommended by your professional organization or company.

✔ Write acronyms in capital letters without periods. The only exceptions are acronyms that have become accepted as common nouns, such as *scuba* (*self-contained underwater breathing apparatus*).

✔ Generally, use periods for lowercase initialisms (*a.k.a.*, *p.m.*) but not for uppercase ones (*GDP*, *IRA*). Exceptions include geographic names (*U.S.*, *E.U.*) and the traditional expression of academic degrees (*B.A.*, *M.B.A.*).

✔ Form the plural of an acronym or initialism by adding a lowercase *s*. Do not use an **apostrophe** (*CARs*, *DVDs*).

✔ Do not follow an abbreviation with a word that repeats the final term in the abbreviation (*ATM location*, not *ATM machine location*).

✔ Avoid creating your own abbreviations; they will confuse readers.

Forming Abbreviations

Names of Organizations.   A company may include in its name a term such as *Brothers*, *Incorporated*, *Corporation*, *Company*, or *Limited Liability Company*. If the term is abbreviated in the official company name that appears on letterhead stationery or on its Web site, use the abbreviated form: *Bros.*, *Inc.*, *Corp.*, *Co.*, or *LLC*. If the term is not abbreviated in the official name, spell it out in writing, except in addresses, footnotes, **bibliographies**, and **lists** where abbreviations may be used. Likewise, use an **ampersand** (&) only if it appears in the official company name. For names of divisions within organizations, terms such as *Department* and *Division* should be abbreviated only when space is limited (*Dept.* and *Div.*).

Measurements.   Except for abbreviations that may be confused with words (*in.* for *inch* and *gal.* for *gallon*), abbreviations of measurement terms do not require periods (*yd* for *yard* and *qt* for *quart*). Abbreviations of units of measure are identical in the singular and plural: *1 cm* and *15 cm* (not *15 cms*). Some abbreviations can be used in combination with symbols (*°F* for *degrees Fahrenheit* and *ft²* for *square feet*).

For a listing of abbreviations for the basic units used in the International System of Units (SI), see http://physics.nist.gov/cuu/Units/units .html. For additional definitions and background, search the National Institute of Standards and Technology Web site at www.nist.gov and generally online for *units of information*. For information on abbreviating dates and time, see **numbers**.

Personal Names and Titles.   Personal names should generally not be abbreviated: *Thomas* (not *Thos.*) and *William* (not *Wm.*). An academic, civil, religious, or military title should be spelled out and lowercase when it does not precede a name. ("The *captain* checked the orders.") When preceding names, some titles are customarily abbreviated (*Dr. Smith, Mr. Mills, Ms. Katz*). See also **Ms. / Miss / Mrs.**

An abbreviation of a title may follow the name; however, be certain that it does not duplicate a title before the name (*Angeline Martinez, Ph.D.*, or *Dr. Angeline Martinez*). When addressing **correspondence** and including names in other documents, you should normally spell out titles (*The Honorable Mary J. Holt*; *Professor Charles Matlin*).

Common Scholarly Abbreviations and Terms.   The following is a partial list of abbreviations commonly used in reference books and for documenting sources in research papers and reports. Other than in such documents, generally avoid these abbreviations.

anon.	anonymous
bibliog.	bibliography, bibliographer, bibliographic
ca., c.	*circa*, "about" (used with approximate dates: *ca. 1756*)
cf.	*confer*, "compare"
chap.	chapter
diss.	dissertation
ed., eds.	edited by, editor(s), edition(s)
e.g.	*exempli gratia*, "for example" (see **e.g. / i.e.**)
esp.	especially
et al.	*et alii*, "and others"
etc.	*et cetera*, "and so forth" (see **etc.**)
f., ff.	and the following page(s) or line(s)
GPO	Government Printing Office, Washington, D.C.
i.e.	*id est*, "that is"
MS, MSS	manuscript, manuscripts
n., nn.	note, notes (used immediately after page number: *56n., 56n.3, 56nn.3–5*)
N.B., n.b.	*nota bene*, "take notice, mark well"
n.d.	no date (of publication)
n.p.	no place (of publication); no publisher; no page
p., pp.	page, pages

proc.	proceedings
pub.	published by, publisher, publication
rev.	revised by, revised, revision; review, reviewed by (spell out "review" where "rev." might be ambiguous)
rpt.	reprinted by, reprint
sec., secs.	section, sections
sic	so, thus; inserted after a misspelled or misused word in quotations ([*sic*]) (see **brackets**)
supp., suppl.	supplement
trans.	translated by, translator, translation
UP	University Press (used in MLA style, as in *Oxford UP*)
viz.	*videlicet*, "namely"
vol., vols.	volume, volumes
vs., v.	*versus*, "against" (*v.* preferred in titles of legal cases)

above

Avoid using *above* to refer to a preceding passage or **visual**, because its reference is vague and often an **affectation**. The same is true of *aforesaid* and *aforementioned*. (See also **former / latter**.) To refer to something previously mentioned, repeat the **noun** or **pronoun**, or construct your **paragraph** so that your reference is obvious.

▶ Please complete and submit ~~the above~~ *your travel voucher* by March 1.

absolutely

Absolutely means "definitely," "entirely," "completely," or "unquestionably." Avoid it as a redundant **intensifier** to mean "very" or "much."

▶ We are ~~absolutely~~ certain we can meet the deadline.

abstract / concrete words

Abstract words refer to general ideas, qualities, conditions, acts, or relationships—intangible things that cannot be detected by the five senses (sight, hearing, touch, taste, and smell), such as *learning*, *leadership*, and *technology*. *Concrete words* identify things that can be perceived by the five senses, such as *diploma*, *manager*, and *keyboard*.

Abstract words must often be further defined or described.

> The marketing team needs freedom. *to develop its own customer database*

Abstract words are best used with concrete words to help make intangible concepts specific and vivid.

> Public transportation [abstract] in Chicago includes *buses* [concrete] and *commuter trains* [concrete].

See also **context**, **purpose**, and **word choice**.

abstracts

An abstract summarizes and highlights the major points of a **formal report**, journal article, dissertation, or other long work. Its primary purpose is to enable readers to decide whether to read the work in full. For a discussion of how summaries differ from abstracts, see **executive summaries**.

Although abstracts, typically 200 to 250 words long, are published with the longer works they condense, they can also be published separately in periodical indexes, by abstracting services, and in introductory sections of online journals (see **research**). For this reason, an abstract should be readable apart from the original document and contain appropriate key search terms for researchers using online databases.

Types of Abstracts

Depending on the kind of information they contain, abstracts are often classified as descriptive or informative (see Figure A–1). A *descriptive abstract* summarizes the **purpose**, **scope**, and methods used to arrive at the reported findings. It is a slightly expanded **table of contents** in sentence and paragraph form. A descriptive abstract need not be longer than several sentences. An *informative abstract* is an expanded version of the descriptive abstract, including a summary of any results, **conclusions**, and recommendations. The informative abstract retains the **tone** and essential scope of the original work while omitting its details. The first two paragraphs of the abstract shown in Figure A–1 alone would be descriptive; with the addition of the paragraphs that detail the findings and conclusions of the report, the abstract becomes informative.

ABSTRACT

Purpose

This report investigates the long-term effects of long-distance running on the bones, joints, and general health of runners aged 50 to 72. The Sports Medicine Institute of Columbia Hospital sponsored this investigation, first to decide whether to add a geriatric unit to the institute, and second to determine whether physicians should recommend long-distance running for their older patients.

Descriptive section

Methods and scope

The investigation is based on recent studies conducted at Stanford University and the University of Florida. The Stanford study tested and compared male and female long-distance runners aged 50 to 72 with a control group of runners and nonrunners. The groups were matched by sex, race, education, and occupation. The Florida study used only male runners who had run at least 20 miles a week for five years and compared them with a group of runners and nonrunners. Both studies based findings on medical histories and on physical and X-ray examinations.

Findings

Both studies conclude that long-distance running is not associated with increased degenerative joint disease. Control groups were more prone to spur formation, sclerosis, and joint-space narrowing and showed more joint degeneration than runners. Female long-distance runners exhibited somewhat more sclerosis in knee joints and the lumbar spine area than matched control subjects. Both studies support the role of exercise in retarding bone loss with aging. The investigation concludes that the health risk factors are fewer for long-distance runners than for those less active aged 50 to 72.

Conclusions

The investigation recommends that the Sports Medicine Institute of Columbia Hospital consider the development of a geriatric unit a priority and that it inform physicians that an exercise program that includes long-distance running can be beneficial to their aging patients' health.

Recommendations

iii

FIGURE A–1. Informative Abstract (from a Report)

The type of abstract you should write depends on your **audience** and the organization or publication for which you are writing. Informative abstracts work best for wide audiences that need to know conclusions and recommendations; descriptive abstracts work best for compilations, such as proceedings and progress reports that do not contain conclusions or recommendations.

Writing Strategies

Write the abstract *after* finishing the report or document. Otherwise, the abstract may not accurately reflect the longer work. Begin with a topic sentence that announces the subject and scope of your original document. Then, using the major and minor headings of your outline or table of contents to distinguish primary ideas from secondary ones, decide what material is relevant to your abstract. (See **outlining**.) Write with **clarity** and **conciseness**, eliminating unnecessary words and ideas. Do not, however, become so terse that you omit articles (*a*, *an*, or *the*) and important transitional words and phrases (*however*, *therefore*, *but*, *next*). Write complete sentences, but avoid stringing together a group of short sentences end to end; instead, combine ideas by using **subordination** and **parallel structure**. Spell out all but the most common **abbreviations**. In a report, an abstract follows the title page and is numbered page iii.

accept / except

Accept is a **verb** meaning "consent to," "agree to take," or "admit willingly." ("I *accept* the responsibility.") *Except* is normally used as a **preposition** meaning "other than" or "excluding." ("We agreed on everything *except* the schedule.")

acceptances / refusals (for employment)

When you decide to accept a job offer, you can notify your new employer by telephone or in a meeting — but to make your decision official, you should send an acceptance in writing. What you include in your message and whether you send a **letter** or an **e-mail** depends on your previous conversations with your new employer. See also **correspondence**. Figure A–2 shows an example of a job acceptance written by a graduating student. (See his **résumé** in Figure R–8 on page 470.)

When you decide to reject a job offer (Figure A–3), send a written job refusal to make that decision official, even if you have already notified the employer during a meeting or on the phone. Writing to an employer is an important goodwill gesture. For general advice on handling refusals and negative messages, see **refusal letters**.

◀ **PROFESSIONALISM NOTE** Be especially tactful and courteous—the employer you are refusing has spent time and effort interviewing you and may have counted on your accepting the job. Remember, you may want to apply for another job at that company in the future. ▶

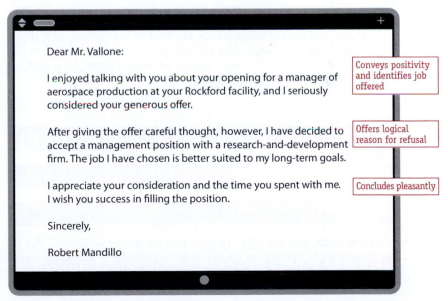

Dear Ms. Castro:

I am pleased to accept your offer of $47,500 per year as a Junior Graphic Designer with the Natural History Museum.

> Identifies job and salary accepted

After graduation, I plan to leave Pittsburgh on Tuesday, June 2. I should be able to find living accommodations and be ready to report for work on Monday, June 15. If you need to reach me prior to this date, please call me at 412-555-1212 (cell) or e-mail me at jgoodman@gmail.com.

> Confirms start date and contact information

I look forward to joining the marketing team and working with the excellent support staff I met during the interview.

> Conveys enthusiasm

Sincerely,

Joshua S. Goodman

FIGURE A–2. Acceptance (for Employment)

Dear Mr. Vallone:

I enjoyed talking with you about your opening for a manager of aerospace production at your Rockford facility, and I seriously considered your generous offer.

> Conveys positivity and identifies job offered

After giving the offer careful thought, however, I have decided to accept a management position with a research-and-development firm. The job I have chosen is better suited to my long-term goals.

> Offers logical reason for refusal

I appreciate your consideration and the time you spent with me. I wish you success in filling the position.

> Concludes pleasantly

Sincerely,

Robert Mandillo

FIGURE A–3. Refusal (for Employment)

↪ Send	✕ Cancel	📄 Save Draft	📎 Add Attachment	💬 Signature	Options ▶

TO Marsha Stein <stein39@macrofoods.com>

CC   Show BCC

Subject Check-out Reporting System

Dear Ms. Stein:

Your comprehensive report arrived today. When I finish studying it in detail, I'll send you our cost estimate for the installation of the Check-out Reporting System.

Thank you for preparing such a thorough analysis.

Regards,

Wilbur Kohn

FIGURE A–4. Acknowledgment

acknowledgments

When a colleague or client sends you something or makes a request, you should acknowledge what was sent, respond to the request, or explain that you cannot immediately respond to the request in a short, polite note. Send a message, like the one shown in Figure A–4, in the medium used or preferred by your reader, whether a **letter**, an **e-mail**, or a **text message**. See also **correspondence**.

acronyms and initialisms (*see* abbreviations)

active voice (*see* voice)

ad hoc

Ad hoc is Latin for "for this" or "for this particular occasion." An ad hoc committee is one set up temporarily to consider a particular issue. The term is not italicized. See **foreign words in English**.

adapt / adept / adopt

Adapt is a verb meaning "adjust to a new situation." *Adept* is an adjective meaning "highly skilled." *Adopt* is a verb meaning "take or use as one's own."

▶ The company will *adopt* a policy of finding executives who are *adept* managers and who can *adapt* to new situations.

adapting to new technologies

When faced with a new technology, ask "How much do I *need* to know about the specific technology to do my work?" What you need to learn will depend on your workplace **context**. Sometimes you may need only basic knowledge to accomplish specific and limited tasks. Other times, you may need much more in-depth knowledge—even expert knowledge—to serve as an adviser or as a resource for your colleagues. See also **selecting the medium**.

| **WRITER'S CHECKLIST** | **Strategies for Learning a New Technology** |

✔ *Experiment.* Acquaint yourself with a new technology simply by using it until it becomes familiar.

✔ *Conduct careful Internet searches.* Make terminology precise by including the name of the tool and keywords that describe your specific problem.

✔ *Consult IT staff and trusted colleagues.* Seek help from your organization's technology specialists and trainers as well as your tech-savvy colleagues.

✔ *Use built-in help and official help manuals.* Use tutorials, digital or printed instructional materials, and links to searchable online help sites.

✔ *Take product workshops and online tutorials.* Workshops teach everything from the basics to advanced functions of devices and software, and you benefit from the experiences of other attendees. Check for product vendor workshops and tutorials before looking for free and paid tutorials from such sites as Lynda.com, PCWorld, and YouTube.

✔ *Refer to third-party help manuals.* These documents often simplify information with full-color printing, photos, and a casual, friendly tone.

adjectives

An adjective is any word that modifies a **noun** or **pronoun**. *Descriptive adjectives* identify a quality of a noun or pronoun (*hot* surface). *Limiting adjectives* impose boundaries on the noun or pronoun (*three* phone lines).

Limiting Adjectives

Limiting adjectives include the following categories:

- Articles (*a, an, the*)
- Demonstrative adjectives (*this, that, these, those*)
- Possessive adjectives (*my, your, his, her, its, our, their*)
- Numeral adjectives (*two, first*)
- Indefinite adjectives (*all, none, some, any*)

Articles.   Articles (*a, an, the*) are traditionally classified as adjectives because they modify nouns by either limiting them or making them more specific. See also **a / an**, **articles**, and **English as a second language**.

Demonstrative Adjectives.   A demonstrative adjective points to the thing it modifies, specifying the object's position in space or time. *This* and *these* specify a closer position; *that* and *those* specify a more remote position.

▶ *This* version is more current than *that* version, which was produced last month.

▶ *These* test reports are more recent than *those* reported last week.

Demonstrative adjectives often cause problems when they modify the nouns *kind*, *type*, and *sort*. Demonstrative adjectives used with those nouns should agree with them in number.

▶ *this* kind, *these* kinds; *that* type, *those* types

Confusion often develops when the preposition *of* is added (*this kind of, these kinds of*) and the object of the preposition does not conform in number to the demonstrative adjective and its noun. See also **agreement** and **prepositions**.

> ▶ *This kind of* human resources ~~policies are~~ ^policy is^ standard.

> ▶ *These kinds of* human resources ~~policy is~~ ^policies are^ standard.

Avoid demonstrative adjectives like *kind*, *type*, and *sort* that can easily lead to vagueness. Be more specific. See also **kind of / sort of**.

Possessive Adjectives.   Because possessive adjectives (*my*, *your*, *his*, *her*, *its*, *our*, *their*) directly modify nouns, they function as adjectives, even though they are pronoun forms (*my* idea, *her* plans, *their* projects). See also **functional shift**.

Numeral Adjectives.   Numeral adjectives identify quantity, degree, or place in a sequence. They always modify count nouns. Numeral adjectives are divided into two subclasses: cardinal and ordinal. A *cardinal adjective* expresses an exact quantity (*one* pencil, *two* computers); an *ordinal adjective* expresses degree or sequence (*first* quarter, *second* edition).

In most writing, an ordinal adjective should be spelled out if it is a single word (*tenth*) and written in figures if it is more than one word (*312th*). Ordinal numbers can also function as adverbs. ("John arrived *first*.") See also **first / firstly** and **numbers**.

Indefinite Adjectives.   Indefinite adjectives do not designate anything specific about the nouns they modify (*some* monitors, *all* designers). The articles *a* and *an* are included among the indefinite adjectives (*a* chair, *an* application).

Comparison of Adjectives

Most adjectives in the positive form (for example, *long*) show the comparative form with the suffix *-er* (*longer*) for two items and the superlative form with the suffix *-est* (*longest*) for three or more items. Many two-syllable adjectives and most three-syllable adjectives are preceded by the word *more* or *most* to form the comparative or the superlative.

> ▶ The new media center is *more* impressive than the old one. It is the *most* impressive in the county.

A few adjectives have irregular forms of comparison (*much, more, most*; *little, less, least*). Some adjectives (*round, unique, exact, accurate*)—often called *absolute words* — are not logically subject to comparison. See also **equal / unique / perfect**.

Placement of Adjectives

When limiting and descriptive adjectives appear together, the limiting adjectives precede the descriptive adjectives, with the articles usually in the first position.

▶ *The ten yellow* taxis were sold at auction. [article (*The*), limiting adjective (*ten*), descriptive adjective (*yellow*)]

Within a sentence, adjectives may appear before the nouns they modify (the attributive position) or after the nouns they modify (the predicative position).

▶ The *small* jobs are given priority. [attributive position]

▶ The exposure is *brief*. [predicative position]

Use of Adjectives

Nouns often function as adjectives to clarify the meaning of other nouns.

▶ The *accident* report prompted a *product* redesign.

When adjectives modifying the same noun can be reversed and still make sense or when they can be separated by *and* or *or*, they should be separated by commas.

▶ The company seeks *bright, energetic, creative* managers.

Notice that there is no comma after *creative*. Never use a comma between a final adjective and the noun it modifies. When an adjective modifies a phrase, no comma is required.

▶ We need an *updated Web-page design*. [*Updated* modifies the phrase *Web-page design*.]

Writers sometimes string together a series of nouns used as adjectives to form a unit modifier, thereby creating stacked (jammed) **modifiers**, which can confuse readers.

▶ Your *staffing-level authorization reassessment* plan should result in a major improvement.

See also **word choice**.

Do not add *-s* or *-es* to an adjective to make it plural: the *long* trip, the *long* trips.

Capitalize adjectives of origin (city, state, nation, continent): *Venetian* canals, *Texas* longhorn steer, *French* government, *African* deserts.

In English, verbs of feeling (*bore, interest, surprise*) have two adjectival forms: the present participle (-*ing*) and the past participle (-*ed*). Use the present participle to describe what causes the feeling. Use the past participle to describe the person who experiences the feeling.

▶ We heard the *surprising* election results. [The *election results* cause the feeling.]

▶ Only the losing candidate was *surprised* by the election results. [The *candidate* experienced the feeling of surprise.]

Adjectives follow nouns in English in only two cases: when the adjective functions as a subjective complement ("That project is not *finished*") and when an adjective phrase or clause modifies the noun ("The project *that was suspended temporarily*"). In all other cases, adjectives are placed before the noun.

When a sentence has multiple adjectives, it is often difficult to know the right order. The guidelines illustrated in the following example would apply in most circumstances, but there are exceptions. (Normally, do not use a phrase with so many stacked **modifiers**.) See also **adverbs** and **articles**.

▶ The six extra-large rectangular brown cardboard take-out containers

determiner	number	comment	size	shape	color	material	qualifier	noun

adjustment messages

An adjustment **letter** or **e-mail** is written in response to a complaint and tells a customer or client what your organization intends to do about the complaint. Although sent in reply to a complaint, an adjustment message actually provides an excellent opportunity to build goodwill for your organization. An effective adjustment message, such as the examples shown in Figures A–5 and A–6, can not only repair any damage done but also restore the customer's confidence in your company. Consider that while an e-mail may allow you to respond more quickly, a printed or an attached letter with organizational letterhead may carry more weight.

No matter how unreasonable the complaint, the **tone** of your response should be positive and respectful. Avoid emphasizing the problem, but do take responsibility for it when appropriate. Focus your

A

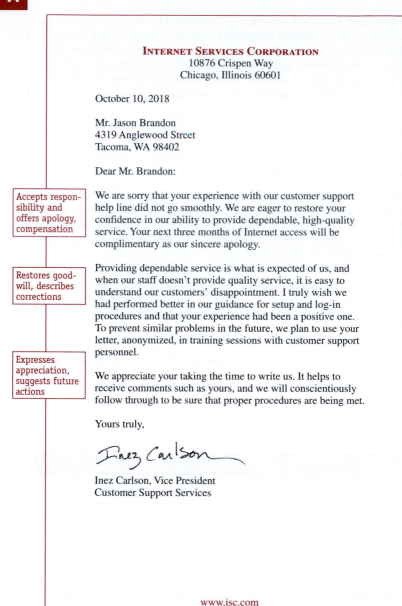

INTERNET SERVICES CORPORATION
10876 Crispen Way
Chicago, Illinois 60601

October 10, 2018

Mr. Jason Brandon
4319 Anglewood Street
Tacoma, WA 98402

Dear Mr. Brandon:

Accepts responsibility and offers apology, compensation

We are sorry that your experience with our customer support help line did not go smoothly. We are eager to restore your confidence in our ability to provide dependable, high-quality service. Your next three months of Internet access will be complimentary as our sincere apology.

Restores goodwill, describes corrections

Providing dependable service is what is expected of us, and when our staff doesn't provide quality service, it is easy to understand our customers' disappointment. I truly wish we had performed better in our guidance for setup and log-in procedures and that your experience had been a positive one. To prevent similar problems in the future, we plan to use your letter, anonymized, in training sessions with customer support personnel.

Expresses appreciation, suggests future actions

We appreciate your taking the time to write us. It helps to receive comments such as yours, and we will conscientiously follow through to be sure that proper procedures are being met.

Yours truly,

Inez Carlson

Inez Carlson, Vice President
Customer Support Services

www.isc.com

FIGURE A–5. Adjustment (When Company Takes Responsibility)

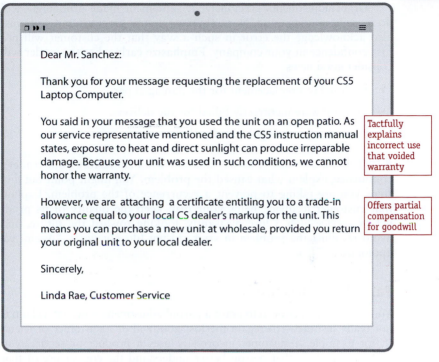

Dear Mr. Sanchez:

Thank you for your message requesting the replacement of your CS5 Laptop Computer.

You said in your message that you used the unit on an open patio. As our service representative mentioned and the CS5 instruction manual states, exposure to heat and direct sunlight can produce irreparable damage. Because your unit was used in such conditions, we cannot honor the warranty.

> Tactfully explains incorrect use that voided warranty

However, we are attaching a certificate entitling you to a trade-in allowance equal to your local CS dealer's markup for the unit. This means you can purchase a new unit at wholesale, provided you return your original unit to your local dealer.

> Offers partial compensation for goodwill

Sincerely,

Linda Rae, Customer Service

FIGURE A–6. Partial Adjustment

response on what you are doing to correct the problem. Settle such matters quickly and courteously, and lean toward giving the customer or client the benefit of the doubt at a reasonable cost to your organization. See also **refusal letters** and **"you" viewpoint**.

Full Adjustments

Before granting an adjustment to a claim for which your company is at fault, first determine what happened and what you can do to satisfy the customer. Be certain that you are familiar with your company's adjustment policy — and be careful with **word choice**.

▶ We have just received your letter of May 7 about our defective gas grill.

Saying something is "defective" could be ruled in a court of law as an admission that the product is in fact defective. When you are in doubt, seek legal advice.

Grant adjustments graciously: A settlement made grudgingly will do more harm than good. Not only must you be gracious, but you must also acknowledge the error in such a way that the customer will not lose confidence in your company. Emphasize early what the reader will consider good news.

▶ Enclosed is a replacement for the damaged part.

▶ Yes, you were incorrectly billed for the delivery.

▶ Please accept our apologies for the error in your account.

◖ **PROFESSIONALISM NOTE** If an explanation will help restore your reader's confidence, explain what caused the problem. You might point out any steps you are taking to prevent a recurrence of the problem. Explain that customer feedback helps your firm keep the quality of its product or service high. Close pleasantly, looking toward the future, and avoid recalling the problem in your closing (do not write, "Again, we apologize . . ."). ◗

Partial Adjustments

You may sometimes need to grant a partial adjustment—even if a claim is not really justified—to regain the lost goodwill of a customer or client. If, for example, a customer incorrectly uses a product or service, you may need to help that person better understand the correct use of that product or service. In such a circumstance, remember that your customer or client believes that his or her claim is justified. Therefore, you should give the explanation before granting the claim — otherwise, your reader may never get to the explanation. If your explanation establishes customer responsibility, do so tactfully. Figure A–6 is an example of a partial adjustment message. See also **correspondence**.

adverbs

An adverb modifies the action or condition expressed by a **verb**.

▶ The wrecking ball hit the side of the building *hard*. [The adverb tells *how* the wrecking ball hit the building.]

An adverb can also modify an **adjective**, another adverb, or a **clause**.

▶ The brochure design used *remarkably* bright colors. [*Remarkably* modifies the adjective *bright*.]

▶ The redesigned brake pad lasted *much* longer than the previous version. [*Much* modifies the adverb *longer*.]

▶ *Surprisingly*, the engine failed. [*Surprisingly* modifies the clause *the engine failed*.]

Use adverbs sparingly in business writing. Because they are often subjective (hot/cold, hard/soft, long/short), consider providing specifics that define them or provide context. How hot? (Give the temperature.) How fast? (State the speed or rate.) How short or long? (State the length.) How expensive or efficient? (Compare relative costs or provide data on time savings.)

Types of Adverbs

A simple adverb can answer one of the following questions:

Where? (adverb of place)

▶ Move the display *forward* slightly.

When? or *How often?* (adverb of time)

▶ Replace the thermostat *immediately*.

▶ I worked overtime *twice* this week.

How? (adverb of manner)

▶ Add the deductions *cautiously*.

How much? (adverb of degree)

▶ The *nearly* completed report was sent to the director.

An interrogative adverb can ask a question (*Where? When? Why? How?*).

▶ *How* many hours did you work last week?

▶ *Why* was the hard drive reformatted?

A conjunctive adverb can modify the clause that it introduces as well as join two independent clauses with a **semicolon**. The most common conjunctive adverbs are *however, nevertheless, moreover, therefore, further, then, consequently, besides, accordingly, also,* and *thus*.

▶ I rarely work on weekends; *however*, this weekend will be an exception.

In this example, note that a semicolon precedes and a comma follows *however*. The conjunctive adverb (*however*) introduces the independent clause (*this weekend will be an exception*) and indicates its relationship to the preceding independent clause (*I rarely work on weekends*). See also **transition**.

Comparison of Adverbs

Most one-syllable adverbs (such as *fast*) show comparison with the suffixes *-er* (*faster*, comparative form) and *-est* (*fastest*, superlative form). Most adverbs with two or more syllables end in *-ly*, and most adverbs ending in *-ly* are compared by inserting the comparative *more* or *less* or the superlative *most* or *least* in front of them.

▶ The patient recovered *more quickly* than the staff had expected.

▶ *Most surprisingly*, the engine failed during the final test phase.

A few irregular adverbs require a change in form to indicate comparison (*well, better, best*; *badly, worse, worst*; *far, farther, farthest*).

▶ The training program functions *well*.

▶ Our training program functions *better* than most others in the industry.

▶ Many consider our training program the *best* in the industry.

Placement of Adverbs

An adverb should usually be placed in front of the verb it modifies.

▶ The pilot *methodically* performed the preflight check.

An adverb may, however, follow the verb (or the verb and its object) that it modifies.

▶ The system failed *unexpectedly*.

▶ They replaced the battery *quickly*.

In a verb phrase, the adverb is typically placed between the helping verb and the main verb.

▶ In this temperature range, the pressure will *quickly* drop.

Adverbs such as *only, nearly, almost, just,* and *hardly* should be placed immediately before the words they limit. See also **modifiers** and **only**.

affect / effect

Affect is a **verb** that means "influence." ("The decision could *affect* the company's stock value.") *Effect* can function as a **noun** that means "result" ("The decision had a positive *effect*") or as a verb that means "bring about" or "cause." However, avoid using *effect* as a verb when you can replace it with a less formal word, such as *make* or *produce*.

▶ The new manager will ~~effect~~ *make* several changes to improve morale.

affectation

Affectation is the use of language that is more formal, technical, or showy than necessary to communicate information to the reader. Affectation is a widespread writing problem in the workplace because many people feel that it lends a degree of authority to their writing. In fact, affectation can alienate customers, clients, and colleagues because it forces readers to work harder to understand the writer's meaning.

Affected writing typically contains inappropriately abstract, highly technical, or foreign words and is often liberally sprinkled with trendy **buzzwords**.

❖ **ETHICS NOTE** **Jargon** and **euphemisms** can become affectation, especially if their purpose is to hide relevant facts or give a false impression of competence. See **ethics in writing**. ❖

Writers easily slip into affectation through the use of long variants—words created by adding prefixes and suffixes to simpler words (*orientate* for *orient*; *utilization* for *use*). Unnecessarily formal words (such as *penultimate* for *next to last*), created words using *-ese* (such as *managementese*), and outdated words (such as *aforesaid*) can produce affectation. (See also **above**.) Elegant variation — attempting to avoid repeating a word within a paragraph by substituting a pretentious synonym — is also a form of affectation. Either repeat the term or use a pronoun.

▶ The use of digital modules in the assembly process has increased

        and

   production. ~~Modular utilization has also~~ cut costs.
      ^

Another type of affectation is **gobbledygook**, which is wordy, roundabout writing with many legal- and technical-sounding terms (such as *wherein* and *morphing*). See also **clichés**, **conciseness**, **nominalizations**, and **word choice**.

affinity

Affinity refers to the attraction of two persons or things to each other. *Affinity* should not be used to mean "ability" or "aptitude."

      aptitude
▶ She has an ~~affinity~~ for problem solving.
    ^

agreement

Grammatical agreement is the correspondence in form between different elements of a sentence to indicate **number**, **person**, **gender**, and **case**.
A subject and its **verb** must agree in number.

▶ The *design is* acceptable. [The singular subject, *design*, requires the singular verb, *is*.]

▶ The new *products are* going into production soon. [The plural subject, *products*, requires the plural verb, *are*.]

A subject and its verb must agree in person.

▶ *I am* the designer. [The first-person singular subject, *I*, requires the first-person singular verb, *am*.]

▶ *They are* the designers. [The third-person plural subject, *they*, requires the third-person plural verb, *are*.]

A **pronoun** and its antecedent must agree in person, number, gender, and case.

▶ The *employees* report that *they* are more efficient in the new facility. [The third-person plural subject, *employees*, requires the third-person plural pronoun, *they*.]

▶ *Kaye McGuire* will meet with the staff on Friday, when *she* will assign duties. [The third-person singular subject, *Kaye McGuire*, requires *she*, the third-person feminine pronoun, in the subjective case.]

See also **sentence construction**.

Subject-Verb Agreement

Subject-verb agreement is not affected by intervening **phrases** and **clauses**.

▶ *One* in 20 hard drives we receive from our suppliers *is* faulty. [The verb, *is*, must agree in number with the subject, *one*, not *hard drives* or *suppliers*.]

The same is true when **nouns** fall between a subject and its verb.

▶ Only *one* of the emergency lights *was* functioning. [The subject of the verb is *one*, not *lights*.]

▶ *Each* of the managers *supervises* a very large region. [The subject of the verb is *each*, not *managers*.]

Note that *one* and *each* are normally singular.

Indefinite pronouns such as *some*, *none*, *all*, *more*, and *most* may be singular or plural, depending on whether they are used with a mass noun ("*Most* of the oil *has* been used") or with a count noun ("*Most* of the drivers *know* why they are here"). Mass nouns are singular, and count nouns are plural. Other words, such as *type*, *part*, *series*, and *portion*, take singular verbs even when they precede a phrase containing a plural noun.

▶ A *series* of meetings *was* held to develop a marketing strategy.

▶ A large *portion* of most annual reports *is* devoted to promoting the corporate image.

Modifying phrases can obscure a simple subject.

▶ The *advice* of two engineers, one lawyer, and three executives *was* obtained before making a commitment. [The subject of the verb *was* is *advice*.]

Inverted word order can cause problems with agreement.

▶ From this work *have come* several important *improvements*. [The subject of the verb is *improvements*, not *work*.]

The number of a subjective **complement** does not affect the number of the verb — the verb must always agree with the subject.

▶ The *topic* of his report *is* employee benefits. [The subject of the sentence is *topic*, not *benefits*.]

A subject that expresses measurement, weight, mass, or total often takes a singular verb even when the subject is plural in form. Such subjects are treated as a unit.

▶ *Four weeks is* the normal duration of the training program.

A verb following the relative pronoun *who* or *that* agrees in number with the noun to which the pronoun refers (its antecedent).

▶ This is one of those management *problems* that *require* careful analysis. [*That* refers to *problems*.]

▶ She is one of those *employees* who *are* rarely absent. [*Who* refers to *employees*.]

The word *number* sometimes causes confusion. When used to mean a specific number, it is singular.

▶ *The number* of committee members *was* six.

When used to mean an approximate number, it is plural.

▶ *A number* of people *were* waiting for the announcement.

Relative pronouns (*who*, *which*, and *that*) may take either singular or plural verbs, depending on whether the antecedent is singular or plural. See also **who / whom**.

▶ He is a manager *who seeks* the views of others.

▶ He is one of those managers *who seek* the views of others.

Some abstract nouns are singular in meaning but plural in form: *mathematics*, *news*, *physics*, and *economics*.

▶ *News* of the merger *is* on page 4 of the *Chronicle*.

Some words, such as the plural *jeans* and *scissors*, cause special problems.

▶ The *scissors were* ordered last week. [The subject is the plural *scissors*.]

▶ *A pair* of scissors *is* on order. [The subject is the singular *pair*.]

A book with a plural title takes a singular verb.

▶ *Accounting Essentials is* an essential resource.

A collective noun (*committee*, *faculty*, *class*, *jury*) used as a subject takes a singular verb when the group is thought of as a unit and a plural verb when the individuals in the group are thought of separately.

▶ The *committee is* unanimous in its decision.

▶ The *committee are* returning to their offices.

A clearer way to emphasize the individuals would be to use a phrase.

▶ The *committee members are* returning to their offices.

Compound Subjects

A compound subject is composed of two or more elements joined by a **conjunction** such as *and*, *or*, *nor*, *either . . . or*, or *neither . . . nor*. When the elements are connected by *and*, the subject is usually plural and requires a plural verb.

▶ *Writing skill and technical aptitude are* prerequisites for this position.

One exception occurs when the elements connected by *and* form a unit or refer to the same thing. In that case, the subject is regarded as singular and takes a singular verb.

▶ *Bacon and eggs is* a high-cholesterol meal.

▶ Our greatest *challenge and business opportunity is* the Internet.

A compound subject with a singular element and a plural element joined by *or* or *nor* requires that the verb agree with the closer element.

▶ Neither the director nor the *project assistants were* available.

▶ Neither the project assistants nor the *director was* available.

If *each* or *every* modifies the elements of a compound subject, use the singular verb.

▶ *Each* manager and supervisor *has* a production goal to meet.

▶ *Every* manager and supervisor *has* a production goal to meet.

Pronoun-Antecedent Agreement

Every pronoun must have an antecedent — a noun to which it refers. See also **pronoun reference**.

▶ When *employees* are hired, *they* must review the policy manual. [The pronoun *they* refers to the antecedent *employees*.]

Gender.   A pronoun must agree in gender with its antecedent.

▶ *Mr. Swivet* in the accounting department acknowledges *his* share of responsibility for the misunderstanding, just as *Ms. Barkley* in the research division must acknowledge *hers*.

Traditionally, a masculine, singular pronoun was used to agree with such indefinite antecedents as *anyone* and *person*. ("*Each* may stay or go as *he* chooses.") Because such usage ignores or excludes women, use alternatives when they are available. One solution is to use the plural. Another is to use both feminine and masculine pronouns, although that combination is clumsy when used too often.

▶ ~~Every employee~~ must sign ~~his~~ time ~~card~~.
  All employees   *their*   *cards*

▶ Every employee must sign his time card.
  or her

Do not attempt to avoid expressing gender by resorting to a plural pronoun when the antecedent is singular. An acceptable alternative is to avoid the pronoun entirely.

▶ Every employee must sign ~~their~~ *a* time card.

Avoid gender-related stereotypes in general references, as in "the nurse . . . *she*" or "the doctor . . . *he*." What if the nurse is male or the doctor female? See also **biased language**.

Number.   A pronoun must agree with its antecedent in number. Many problems of agreement are caused by expressions that are not clear in number.

▶ Although the typical engine runs well in moderate temperatures, ~~they~~ *it* often ~~stall~~ *stalls* in extreme cold.

Use singular pronouns with the antecedents *everybody* and *everyone* unless to do so would be illogical because the meaning is obviously plural. See also **everybody / everyone**.

▶ *Everyone* pulled *his or her* share of the load.

▶ *Everyone* thought my plan should be revised, and I really couldn't blame *them*.

Collective nouns may use a singular or plural pronoun, depending on the meaning.

▶ The *committee* agreed to the recommendations only after *it* had deliberated for days. [*committee* thought of as collective singular]

▶ The *committee* quit for the day and went to *their* respective offices. [*committee* thought of as plural]

Demonstrative **adjectives** sometimes cause problems with agreement of number. *This* and *that* are used with singular nouns, and *these* and *those* are used with plural nouns. Demonstrative adjectives often cause problems when they modify the nouns *kind*, *type*, and *sort*. When used with those nouns, demonstrative adjectives should agree with them in number.

▶ *this* kind, *these* kinds; *that* type, *those* types

Confusion often develops when the **preposition** *of* is added (*this kind of*, *these kinds of*) and the object of the preposition does not agree in number with the demonstrative adjective and its noun.

▶ This kind of retirement ~~plans are~~ *plan is* best.

Avoid that error by remembering to make the demonstrative adjective, the noun, and the object of the preposition — all three — agree in number. The agreement makes the sentence not only correct but also more precise. Using demonstrative adjectives with words like *kind*, *type*, and *sort* can easily lead to vagueness. See **kind of / sort of**.

Compound Antecedents.   A compound antecedent joined by *or* or *nor* is singular if both elements are singular and plural if both elements are plural.

▶ Neither the *engineer* nor the *technician* could do *his* job until *he* understood the new concept.

▶ Neither the *executives* nor the *directors* were pleased at the performance of *their* company.

When one of the antecedents connected by *or* or *nor* is singular and the other is plural, the pronoun agrees with the closer antecedent.

▶ Either the *computer* or the *printers* should have *their* serial numbers registered.

▶ Either the *printers* or the *computer* should have *its* serial number registered.

A compound antecedent with its elements joined by *and* requires a plural pronoun.

▶ *Seon Ju and Juanita* took *their* layout drawings with them.

If both elements refer to the same person, however, use the singular pronoun.

▶ The noted *economist and author* departed from *her* prepared speech.

allegedly / supposedly

Allegedly refers to an unproved assertion and is used appropriately for accusations or suspicions of illegal or undesirable behavior. ("He *allegedly* participated in the embezzlement.") *Supposedly* refers to something assumed to be true but for which there is some doubt. ("The new process will *supposedly* prevent delays.")

all ready / already

All ready is a two-word phrase meaning "completely prepared." *Already* is an **adverb** that means "before this time" or "previously." ("They were *all ready* to cancel the order; fortunately, we had *already* corrected the shipment.")

all right

All right means "all correct." ("The answers were *all right*.") In workplace writing, it should not be used to mean "good" or "acceptable." It is always written as two words; *alright* is nonstandard.

all together / altogether

All together means "all acting together" or "all in one place." ("The new employees were *all together* at the orientation.") *Altogether* means "entirely" or "completely." ("The trip was *altogether* unnecessary.")

allude / elude / refer

Allude means to make an indirect reference to something. ("The report simply *alluded* to the problem, rather than stating it explicitly.") *Elude* means to escape notice or detection. ("The discrepancy in the account *eluded* the auditor.") *Refer* is used to indicate a direct reference to something. ("She *referred* to the merger during her presentation.")

allusion / illusion

An *allusion* is an indirect reference to something not specifically mentioned. ("He made an *allusion* to metal fatigue in the airframe.") An *illusion* is a mistaken perception or a false image. ("The manager is under the *illusion* that the reorganization will cost very little.")

allusions

An allusion is an indirect reference to something from past or current events, literature, or other familiar sources. The use of allusion promotes economical writing because it is a shorthand way of referring to a body of material in a few words or of helping to explain a new and unfamiliar process in terms of one that is familiar. In the following example, the writer sums up a description with an allusion to a well-known story. The allusion, with its implicit reference to "right standing up to might," concisely emphasizes the writer's point.

▶ As it currently exists, the review process involves the consumer's attorney sitting alone, usually without adequate technical assistance, faced by two or three government attorneys, two or three attorneys from AccroSystems, and large teams of experts who support the government and the corporation. The process is a classic David versus Goliath confrontation.

Be sure, of course, that your reader is familiar with the material to which you allude. Allusions should be used with restraint, especially in **international correspondence**. If overdone, allusions can lead to **affectation** or can be viewed merely as **clichés**. See also **business writing style**.

also

Also is an **adverb** that means "additionally." ("Two 5,000-gallon tanks are on-site, and several 2,500-gallon tanks are *also* available.") *Also* should not be used as a connective in the sense of "and."

▶ He brought the reports, the specifications, ~~also~~ *and* the director's recommendations.

Avoid starting sentences with *also*. It is a weak transitional word that suggests an afterthought rather than planned writing.

▶ ~~Also,~~ *In addition* he brought a cost analysis to support his proposal.

▶ ~~Also, he~~ *He also* brought a cost analysis to support his proposal.

ambiguity

A word or passage is ambiguous when it can be interpreted in two or more ways yet provides the reader with no certain basis for choosing among the alternatives. Ambiguity can take many forms, as in ambiguous **pronoun reference**.

AMBIGUOUS	Inadequate quality-control procedures have resulted in more equipment failures. This is our most serious problem at present. [Does *this* refer to *inadequate quality-control procedures* or to *equipment failures*?]
SPECIFIC	Inadequate quality-control procedures have resulted in more equipment failures. *These failures* are our most serious problem at present.

SPECIFIC   Inadequate quality-control procedures have resulted in
more equipment failures. *Quality control* is our most
serious problem at present.

Incomplete **comparison** and missing or misplaced **modifiers** (including
dangling modifiers) cause ambiguity.

▶ Ms. Lee values rigid quality-control standards more than
does
Mr. Rosenblum. [Complete the comparison.]
^

also
▶ He lists his hobby as cooking. He is especially fond of cocker
^
spaniels. [Add the missing modifier.]

The placement of some modifiers enables them to be interpreted in
either of two ways.

▶ She volunteered *immediately* to deliver the bad news.

By moving the word *immediately*, the meaning can be clarified.

▶ She *immediately* volunteered to deliver the bad news.

▶ She volunteered to deliver the bad news *immediately*.

Imprecise **word choice** (including faulty **idioms**) can cause ambiguity.

▶ The general manager has denied reports that the plant's recent
rescinded
fuel-allocation cut will be ~~restored~~. [inappropriate word choice]
^

Various forms of **awkwardness** also can cause ambiguity.

amount / number

Amount is used with things that are thought of in bulk and that cannot
be counted (mass **nouns**), as in "the *amount* of electricity." *Number* is
used with things that can be counted as individual items (count nouns),
as in "the *number* of employees."

ampersands

The ampersand (&) is sometimes used to represent the word *and*,
especially in the names of organizations (*Rubin & Associates*). When
you are writing the name of an organization in sentences, addresses,

or references, spell out the word *and* unless the ampersand appears in the organization's official name on its letterhead stationery or Web site.

and / or

And/or means that either both circumstances are possible or only one of two circumstances is possible. This term is awkward and confusing because it makes the reader stop to puzzle over your distinction.

AWKWARD   Use A *and/or* B.

IMPROVED   Use A or B or both.

annual reports

The corporate annual report is, in effect, a state-of-the-company message, which publicly traded companies and some nonprofits are legally required to publish annually. Written primarily for shareholders, the report also addresses other **audiences** and stakeholders, such as employees, bankers, labor unions, the financial media, and local elected officials. An annual report usually covers the high points of the previous year's operations and finances, and forecasts the coming year's operations. It may also explain the company's current direction and highlight its strengths. If weaknesses have developed or failures have occurred, the annual report may analyze them and explain the efforts being made to overcome them.

Begin with a study of your company's annual reports of the past several years for content, **style**, and **format**. Then review and use the steps of the writing process outlined in the "Checklist of the Writing Process" on pages xxv–xxvi. Finally, collaborate closely with your company's (or outside contractor's) graphic designers and production staff. Learn their file-format requirements, schedule **photographs**, and determine milestones for producing print and digital versions of the report. See also **business plans**, **collaborative writing**, **mission statements**, **selecting the medium**, and **writing for the Web**.

Structure and Parts

Some annual reports are lavishly produced publications that present the company and its operations in glowing terms; others are spartan financial summaries that merely meet the legal requirements for annual financial

reporting. For details, visit www.sec.gov/fast-answers/answers-annrephtm
.html. Most are a combination of both. Annual reports vary greatly in
organization, but they typically include five major sections:

- Financial highlights
- A statement to the shareholders or a letter from the president
- A narrative section on the company's operations
- A financial statement
- A listing of the company's board of directors and officers

Financial Highlights.   The financial highlights section is a brief review
of the company's sales and earnings that usually precedes the statement
to the stockholders, sometimes even appearing on the inside front cover.
This section often compares sales and earnings for three years and typically includes the percentage of change from year to year.

Statement to Shareholders.   This section is a direct statement to shareholders from the company's president or the chair of the board of directors. It sets the stage for the rest of the report. This section should not
repeat the financial facts already cited in the financial highlights; instead,
it should interpret the entire year's performance, touch on plans and
future directions, and give the company's explanations for any failures.

This statement may be an in-depth review of the company's operations during the past year or a brief summary of the entire report. A
brief summary is sometimes followed by a question-and-answer section
in which the president of the company reviews the past year's operations.

Narrative Section.   The narrative section of the annual report is normally
used to present company operations and new products or developments
in a positive light. Topics for this section might include the following:

- Major profit factors in the last year's performance
- Prospects for increasing stock dividends
- Significant new products or services
- The company's performance compared with that of its competition
- Outlook for next year (for the company as a whole or by divisions)
- Major acquisitions and restructuring
- Significant organizational changes
- Research and development
- Global operations and economic climate (when appropriate)

- Service and support operations
- Social responsibilities (such as environmental responsibility and community service)

Financial Statement.   The financial statement should be uncluttered and inviting. Most annual reports include a comparison of financial results from the past three years. Most financial statements include the following topics:

- A company balance sheet
- A statement of income
- Changes in financial position
- An independent auditor's statement
- Footnotes, as necessary

Financial statement footnotes should be simple and direct, avoiding technical accounting terms; the auditor's statement should be no more than one-third of a page.

Board of Directors and Company Officers.   The final part of the annual report lists the company's board of directors and their corporate affiliations. Many annual reports also include a photograph of each director, as well as a listing of the company's officers by name and title—often with photographs that personalize what is essentially a financial report. The officers generally include the chair of the board of directors, the president, vice presidents, the secretary, the treasurer, and legal counsel.

Preparing the Report

First, interview the president of the company to determine the general direction of the report. Next, interview vice presidents or division heads to determine the proper emphasis to place on each division's performance (but stay within the general direction established by the president or chair). See **interviewing for information**.

Compose a list of primary topics, as previously described, and allot space as necessary to each division or subsidiary in order to make decisions such as these:

- Whether to show sales and earnings as a company total only or by division as well
- What should be included in charts and graphs
- How lavish or spartan the report should be in appearance and cost
- What media should be used to publish and distribute the report

Tone is critical in writing and designing an annual report. The annual report should convey the image your company has established or wants to establish.

Design and Visuals.   Typography, graphics, and design communicate a message about a company as strongly as words do. Select visual elements that enhance your company's image and accurately reflect your industry. See **layout and design** and **visuals**.

Use photographs and visuals liberally, although purposefully, in the narrative section to enhance the company's image, and complement the photographs and visuals with informative and well-written captions. Choose only those photographs and illustrations that will make the maximum contribution to the report's theme. Both photographs and their captions are critical in enlivening your annual report and putting a human face on your company. Colorful photographs that are carefully composed and show action or people enjoying themselves attract favorable interest.

Charts and **graphs** enable readers to grasp numerical material quickly and easily, provided that they are not so complex that they defeat the purpose. Subjects that most easily lend themselves to graphs and charts, usually shown in a three-year comparison arrangement, are the following:

- Assets
- Capital expenditures
- Dividends
- Earnings (by product groups or divisions)
- Industry growth
- Inventories
- Liabilities
- Net worth
- Price trends
- Reserves
- Sales (by product groups or divisions)
- Source and disposition of funds (taxes, wages, working capital)

The following information is normally printed on the inside front and back covers of the annual report: (1) notice of the annual meeting; (2) corporate address; and (3) names of transfer agents, registrar, and stock exchange. Some annual reports use the inside front cover solely for the announcement of the annual meeting.

✔ Review past annual reports for their content, style, and format.

✔ Review the annual reports of organizations similar to yours (see www
.annualreports.com).

✔ Interview senior company officials to learn which issues they wish to
highlight.

✔ Allocate topics and space to reach your company's target audiences.

✔ Adopt a writing style and a layout and design consistent with your
company's image.

✔ Consider available enhancements and applications for digital versions of
the report.

✔ Work closely with the graphic designers and your production staff to
ensure that the report is professionally designed and produced
on schedule.

antonyms

An antonym is a word with a meaning opposite that of another word
(*good/bad*, *wet/dry*, *fresh/stale*). Many pairs of words that look as if
they are antonyms, such as *limit/delimit*, are not. See also **dictionaries**,
synonyms, and **word choice**.

apostrophes

An apostrophe (') is used to show possession or to indicate the omission
of letters. Sometimes it is also used to avoid confusion with certain plurals of words, letters, and **abbreviations**.

Showing Possession

An apostrophe is used with an *s* to form the possessive case of some
nouns (the *report's* title). For further advice on using apostrophes to
show possession, see **possessive case**.

Indicating Omission

An apostrophe is used to mark the omission of letters or **numbers** in a
contraction or a date (*can't*, *I'm*, *I'll*, the class of '17).

Forming Plurals

An apostrophe can be used in forming the plurals of letters, words, or lowercase abbreviations if confusion might result from using *s* alone and thus forming a word.

▶ The search program does not find *a*'s and *i*'s.

▶ Do not replace all *of which*'s in the document.

▶ *I*'s need to be distinguished from the number 1.

▶ The prescription included several *bid*'s. [*Bid* is an abbreviation used for "twice daily medications."]

In general, however, add only *s* in roman (or regular) type when referring to words as words or capital letters. See also **italics**.

▶ Five *and*s appear in the first sentence.

▶ The applicants received *A*s and *B*s in their courses.

Do not use an apostrophe for plurals of abbreviations with all capital letters (*PDFs*) or a final capital letter (*ten PhDs*) or for plurals of numbers (*7s, the late 1990s*).

appendixes

An appendix—located at the end of a **formal report**, a **proposal**, or another long document—supplements or clarifies the information in the body of the document. Appendixes (or *appendices*) can provide information that is too detailed or lengthy for the primary **audience** of the document. For example, an appendix could contain such material as **maps**, statistical analyses, **résumés** of key personnel involved in a proposed project, or other documents needed by secondary readers.

A document may have more than one appendix, with each providing only one type of information. When you include more than one appendix, arrange them in the order they are mentioned in the body of the document. List the titles and beginning page numbers of the appendixes in the **table of contents**. Begin each appendix on a new page, and identify each with a letter, starting with the letter *A* (*Appendix A: Sample Questionnaire*). If you have only one appendix, title it simply "Appendix."

application cover letters

Job applications require both a **résumé** and a cover letter, even if it is a relatively short **e-mail** (or *e-note*) with an attached résumé. The application cover letter is essentially a **sales letter** in which you demonstrate how your skills, knowledge, and experience will benefit an employer by meeting the requirements of a position. See also **cover letters**, **letters**, and **persuasion**.

The letter must quickly capture the employer's attention, allow readers to easily skim the contents, and point to the attached or enclosed résumé. It should (1) introduce you as a candidate with the skills that can contribute to the particular organization, (2) explain what particular job interests you and why, (3) highlight for the reader specific qualifications in your résumé that match the position, and (4) provide the opportunity for an interview. See **job search** and **interviewing for a job**.

The job ad in Figure A–7 seeks someone with experience in a professional design environment for a natural history museum. Figure A–8 (page 38) shows a cover letter for a résumé that responds to the job ad in Figure A–7. (The applicant's résumé is shown in Figure R–8 on page 470.)

Position: Junior Graphic Designer
Company: Natural History Museum
Location: Los Angeles, CA 90015

Description
The Natural History Museum of Los Angeles County is an equal-opportunity employer committed to ecological biodiversity, preservation, conservation, and education. The Museum seeks a full-time Junior Graphic Designer to join an in-house Promotions team, conceptualizing and creating digital and print content for exhibits, lectures, concerts, summer festival days, and related events. This position requires a collaborative approach to design, resourcefulness in executing a wide range of projects, an artistic and critical eye, and superior organization and communication skills. Video experience a plus. This position will report to the Creative Services Manager.

Requirements
B.A. or B.F.A. in graphic design or related field
Experience in a professional design environment
Online portfolio demonstrating visual branding solutions

Expert use of Adobe Creative Suite, especially Photoshop and Illustrator
Proficiency in HTML and CSS (hand-coding a plus)
Experience with project management software (Basecamp a plus)

FIGURE A–7. Partial Job Ad (Description and Requirements)

Send	Cancel	Save Draft	Add Attachment	Signature	Options ▶

TO Judith Castro <jcastro@naturalhistoryla.org>

CC [   ] Show BCC

Names position sought → **Subject** JUNIOR GRAPHIC DESIGNER

📄 jsgoodman-gdesign-resume.pdf   Download

Dear Ms. Castro:

Highlights volunteer experience → A graphic designer at Dyer/Khan, Jodi Hammel, informed me that you are recruiting for a Junior Graphic Designer in your Marketing Department. Having participated in substantial volunteer activities at a local public museum, I would fit well in this position.

I bring strong, up-to-date academic and practical skills in multimedia tools and graphic arts production, as indicated in my enclosed résumé. Further, I have recent project management experience at Dyer/Khan, where I was responsible for the development of client brochures, newsletters, and posters. As Project Manager, I coordinated the project time lines, budgets, and production with clients, staff, and vendors.

Mentions relevant experience and specific projects → My experience in the Los Angeles area media and entertainment community should help me make use of state-of-the-art design. For example, I helped upgrade the CGI logo for Paramount Pictures, and the Director of Marketing commended my work. My work with leading motion picture, television, and music companies should help me develop exciting marketing tools that museum visitors and patrons will find attractive.

Could we schedule a meeting at your convenience? Please e-mail me at jgoodman@gmail.com, or call me any weekday morning at 412-555-1212 (cell). Thank you for your consideration.

Includes portfolio link → Sincerely,

Joshua S. Goodman

Portfolio: www.gooddesign.com

FIGURE A–8. Application Cover Letter (Graduate Applying for a Graphic Design Job)

The sample application letters shown in Figures A–9 (page 39) and A–10 (page 40) also follow the guidelines described in this entry. In each sample, the **emphasis**, **tone**, and **style** are tailored to fit the employer's need and highlight the applicant's qualifications. Note that the letter shown in Figure A–10 matches the résumé in Figure R–9 (Robert Mandillo) on pages 471–72.

| Send | ✕ Cancel | Save Draft | Add Attachment | Signature | Options ▶ |

| TO | Patrice Crandall <pcrandall@abels.com> |
| CC | | Show BCC |

Subject | Application for Summer Internship

📄 Parker_Resume.doc   Download

Names position sought

Dear Ms. Crandall:

I learned from your Web site that you are hiring undergraduates for summer internships. An internship with Abel's buyer-training program interests me because your program is one of the best in the industry.

Explains interest

My experiences at Metro University with the Alumni Relations Program and the University Center Committee demonstrate my communication and persuasive abilities as well as my understanding of compromise and negotiation. For example, in the alumni program, I persuaded both uninvolved and active alumni to become more engaged with the direction of the university. On the University Center Committee, I balanced the students' demands with the financial and structural constraints of the administration. With these skills, as outlined in the attached résumé, I can ably assist the members of your department with their summer projects.

Highlights skills, experience that benefit employer

I look forward to an interview with you at your convenience. Thank you for your consideration.

Mentions availability, provides contact information

Sincerely,

Marsha S. Parker

1251 Pine St.
Providence, RI 02901
(401) 555-9568

FIGURE A–9. Application Cover Letter Sent as an E-mail (College Student Applying for an Internship)

WRITER'S CHECKLIST   Tailoring a Cover Letter to a Job Ad

✔ Read the job ad carefully, and follow the instructions precisely.

✔ Provide context by referring to the job ad or mentioning how you learned about a possible opening.

✔ Match the tone of your letter to the language of the ad.

✔ Show how the job is appropriate for you while using vocabulary from the ad. See **word choice**.

(continued)

WRITER'S CHECKLIST   **Tailoring a Cover Letter to a Job Ad** (*continued*)

✔ Avoid copying sections of text verbatim from the job ad.

✔ Show that you meet or exceed the employer's minimum requirements.

✔ Describe how you are upgrading your skills in any areas in which you fall short.

Dear Ms. Smathers:

During the recent NOMAD convention in Washington, Karen Jarrett, Director of Operations, informed me of an opening at Aerospace Technologies for a manager of new product development. My extensive background in engineering exhibit design and management makes me an ideal candidate for this position.

I have been manager of the Exhibit Design Lab at Wright-Patterson Air Force Base for the past seven years. During that time, I received two Congressional Commendations for models of a space station laboratory and a docking/repair port. My experience in advanced exhibit design would enable me to help develop AT's wind tunnel and aerospace models. Further, I have just learned this week that my exhibit design presented at NOMAD received a "Best of Show" Award.

As described on the enclosed résumé, I not only have work-place management experience but also have recently received an M.B.A. from the University of Dayton. As a student in the M.B.A. program, I won the Luson Scholarship to complete my course work as well as the Jonas Outstanding Student Award.

I would be happy to discuss my qualifications in an interview at your convenience. Please contact me at (937) 555-1212 or at mand@juno.com. I look forward to speaking with you.

Sincerely,

Robert Mandillo

Enclosure: Résumé

Annotations (left margin):

- Names position, explains how he heard about job
- Highlights relevant experience, commendations
- Emphasizes academic background and awards
- Mentions availability, provides contact information

FIGURE A–10. Application Cover Letter (Applicant with Years of Experience)

Opening

In the opening paragraph, provide **context** by indicating how you heard about the position, and name the specific job title or area. If you have been referred to a company by an employee, a career counselor, a professor, or someone else, be sure to say so ("I understand from Mr. John Smith, Director of Operations, that your agency . . ."). Show enthusiasm by explaining why you are interested in the job, and demonstrate your initiative as well as your knowledge of the organization by relating your interest to some facet of the organization, as in Figure A–8.

Body

In the middle **paragraphs**, use specific examples to demonstrate that you are qualified for the job. Aim for **conciseness**, and limit the content by focusing on one clearly stated basic point in each topic sentence. For example, your second paragraph might focus on educational achievements, and your third paragraph might focus on work experience. Do not just tell readers that you are qualified—*show* them by including examples and details. ("Most recently, as an intern at SJX Engineering, I assisted in the infrastructure design for a multimillion-dollar seaside resort.") Highlight a notable achievement that portrays your value, and refer the reader to your enclosed résumé. Do not simply list information found in your résumé; rather, indicate how your talents can make valuable contributions to the company.

Closing

In the final paragraph, request an interview. Let the reader know how to reach you by including your phone number and professional e-mail address (see Writer's Checklist: Maintaining Professionalism on pages 168–69). End with a statement of goodwill, as shown in the examples in this entry.

Proofreading and Follow-up

Proofread your letter *carefully*. Research shows that many employers eliminate candidates from consideration when they notice even one spelling, grammatical, or mechanical error. Such errors give employers the impression that you are careless in the way you present yourself professionally. See **proofreading**.

After a reasonable period, consider following up with a reminder. ("I wrote to you a week ago about your graphic design position, and I wonder if that position is still available.") Your initiative will portray your sincere interest in the opportunity. This approach may also provoke a need for action in the reviewer — for example, the need to pass your application to the hiring authority.

appositives

An appositive is a **noun** or noun **phrase** that follows and amplifies another noun or noun phrase. It has the same grammatical function as the noun it complements.

▶ George Thomas, *the noted economist*, summarized the president's speech in a confidential memo.

▶ The noted economist *George Thomas* summarized the president's speech in a confidential memo.

For detailed information on the use of **commas** with appositives, see **restrictive and nonrestrictive elements**.

If you are in doubt about the **case** of an appositive, check it by substituting the appositive for the noun it modifies. See also **pronouns**.

▶ My boss gave the two of us, Jim and ~~I~~ *me*, the day off. [You would not say "My boss gave *I* the day off."]

articles

Articles (*a*, *an*, *the*) function as **adjectives** because they modify the items they designate by either limiting them or making them more specific. Articles may be indefinite or definite.

The indefinite articles, *a* and *an*, denote an unspecified item.

▶ *A* package was delivered yesterday. [*not* a specific package]

The choice between *a* and *an* depends on the sound rather than on the letter following the article, as described in the entry **a / an**.

The definite article, *the*, denotes a particular item.

▶ *The* package was delivered yesterday. [*one* specific package]

Do not omit all articles from your writing in an attempt to be concise. Including articles costs nothing; eliminating them makes reading more difficult. (See also **telegraphic style**.) However, do not overdo it. An article can be superfluous.

▶ I'll meet you in *a* half *an* hour. [Choose one article and eliminate the other.]

Whether to use a definite or an indefinite article is determined by what you can safely assume about your audience's knowledge. In both the following sentences, you can safely assume that the reader can clearly identify the noun. Therefore, use a definite article.

▶ Did you know that yesterday was *the* coldest day of the year so far? [The modified noun refers to *yesterday*.]

▶ *The* man who left his briefcase in the conference room was in a hurry. [The relative phrase *who left his briefcase in the conference room* restricts and therefore identifies the man.]

In the following sentence, however, you cannot assume that the reader can clearly identify the noun.

▶ *A* package is on the way. [It is impossible to identify specifically what package is meant.]

A more important question for some people is when *not* to use articles. These generalizations will help. Do not use articles with the following:
   Singular proper nouns

   ▶ Utah, Main Street, Harvard University, Mount Hood

Plural nonspecific count nouns (when making generalizations)

   ▶ Helicopters are the new choice of transportation for the rich and famous.

Singular mass nouns

   ▶ She loves coffee.

Plural count nouns used as complements

   ▶ Those women are physicians.

See also **English as a second language**.

as / because / since

As, *because*, and *since* are commonly used to mean "because." To express cause, *because* is the strongest and most specific connective for unequivocally stating a causal relationship. ("*Because* she did not have an MBA, she was not offered the job.")

   Since is a weak substitute for *because* as a connective to express cause. However, *since* is an appropriate connective when the emphasis is on circumstance, condition, or time rather than on cause and effect. ("*Since* it went public, the company has earned a profit every year.")

As is the least definite connective to indicate cause; its use for that purpose is best avoided. See also **subordination**.

Avoid colloquial, nonstandard, or wordy phrases sometimes used instead of *as*, *because*, or *since*. See also **as much as / more than**, **as such**, **as well as**, **conciseness**, and **due to / because of**.

PHRASE	REPLACE WITH
being as, being that	because, since
inasmuch as, insofar as	since, because
on account of	because
on the grounds of / that	because
due to the fact that	because, since

as much as / more than

The phrases *as much as* and *more than* are sometimes incorrectly combined, especially when separated by intervening phrases.

▶ The auditors had as much, if not more, influence in planning the

      as

  program ~~than~~ the accountants did.
       ^

as such

The phrase *as such* is seldom useful and should be omitted.

▶ Patients, ~~as such,~~ should be partners in their treatment decisions.

as well as

Do not use *as well as* with *both*. The two expressions have similar meanings; use one or the other, and adjust the verb as needed.

           and   *are*

▶ Both management ~~as well as~~ labor ~~is~~ required to negotiate.
                  ^   ^

▶ ~~Both~~ Management as well as labor is required to negotiate.

audience

Considering the needs of your audience is crucial to achieving your **purpose**. When you are writing to a specific reader, for example, you may find it useful to visualize a reader sitting across from you as you write. (See **correspondence**.) Likewise, when writing to an audience composed of relatively homogeneous readers, you might create an image of a composite reader and write for *that* reader. In such cases, using the **"you" viewpoint** and an appropriate **tone** will help you meet the needs of your readers as well as achieve an effective **business writing style**. For meeting the needs of an audience composed of listeners, see **presentations**.

Analyzing Your Audience's Needs

Determine the readers' needs relative to your purpose and goals by asking key questions during **preparation**.

- Who specifically is your reader? Do you have multiple readers? Who needs to see or use the document?

- What do your readers already know about your subject? What are your readers' attitudes about the subject? (Are they skeptical? Supportive? Anxious? Bored?)

- What particular information about your readers (experience, training, and work habits, for example) might help you write at the appropriate level of detail? (See **scope**.)

- What does the **context** or medium suggest about meeting the readers' expectations for content? (See **layout and design** and **selecting the medium**.)

- Do you need to adapt your message for international readers? If so, see **global communication**, **global graphics**, and **international correspondence**.

In the workplace, your readers are often less familiar with the subject than you are. You have to be careful, therefore, when writing on a topic that is unique to your area of specialization. Be sensitive to the needs of those whose training or experience lies in other areas; provide definitions of nonstandard terms and explanations of principles that you, as a specialist, take for granted. See also **defining terms**.

Writing for Varied and Multiple Audiences

In writing to a broad or varied audience, such as when **writing for the Web**, visualize a few readers who have different backgrounds but who share purpose or need in reading your text. For documents aimed at multiple audiences with different needs, consider segmenting the document for different groups of readers: an **executive summary** for top managers, an appendix with detailed data for technical specialists, and a body for those readers who need to make decisions based on a detailed discussion. See also **formal reports** and **proposals**.

When you have multiple audiences with various needs but cannot segment your document, first determine your primary, or most important, readers — such as those who will make decisions based on your content — and be sure to meet their needs. Then meet the needs of secondary readers, such as those who need only some of the document's contents, making sure not to sacrifice the needs of your primary readers. See also **persuasion** and "Five Steps to Successful Writing" (page xvii).

augment / supplement

Augment means to increase or magnify in size, degree, or effect. ("Our retirees can *augment* their incomes through consulting.") *Supplement* means to add something to make up for a deficiency. ("This patient should *supplement* his diet with Vitamin D3.")

average / median / mean

The *average* (or arithmetic *mean*) is determined by adding two or more quantities and dividing the sum by the number of items totaled. For example, if one report is 10 pages, another is 30 pages, and a third is 20 pages, their *average* length is 20 pages. It is incorrect to say that "each report averages 20 pages" because each report is a specific length.

▶ *The three reports average*
~~Each report averages~~ 20 pages.

The *median* is the middle number in a sequence of numbers. For example, the *median* of the series 1, 3, 4, 7, 8 is 4.

awhile / a while

The **adverb** *awhile* means "for a short time." The **preposition** *for* should not precede *awhile* because *for* is inherent in the meaning of *awhile*. The two-word noun **phrase** *a while* means "a period of time."

▶ Wait ~~for~~ *awhile* before sending the e-mail.

▶ Wait for *a while* ~~awhile~~ before sending the e-mail.

awkwardness

Any writing that strikes readers as awkward — that is, as forced or unnatural — impedes their understanding. The following checklist and the entries indicated will help you smooth out most awkward passages.

Eliminating Awkwardness

✔ Strive for **clarity** and **coherence** during **revision**.

✔ Check for **organization** to ensure that your writing develops logically.

✔ Keep **sentence construction** as direct and simple as possible.

✔ Use **subordination** appropriately, and avoid needless **repetition**.

✔ Correct any **logic errors** within your sentences.

✔ Revise for **conciseness**, and avoid **expletives** where possible.

✔ Use the active **voice** unless you have a justifiable reason to use the passive voice.

✔ Eliminate jammed or misplaced **modifiers**, and for particularly awkward constructions, apply the tactics in **garbled sentences**.

B

bad / badly

Bad is the **adjective** form that follows such linking **verbs** as *feel* and *look*. ("We don't want to look *bad* at the meeting.") *Badly* is an **adverb**. ("The shipment was *badly* damaged.") To say "I feel *badly*" would mean, literally, that your sense of touch is impaired.

balance / remainder

One meaning of *balance* is "a state of equilibrium"; another meaning is "the amount of money in a bank account after deposits and withdrawals have been credited and debited." *Remainder*, in all applications, means "what is left over."

beside / besides

Besides, meaning "in addition to" or "other than," should be carefully distinguished from *beside*, meaning "next to" or "apart from." ("*Besides* two of us from Marketing, three people from Production stood *beside* the president during the ceremony.")

between / among

Between is normally used to relate two items or persons. ("Preferred stock offers a middle ground *between* bonds and common stock.") *Among* is used to relate more than two. ("The subcontracting was distributed *among* three firms.")

between you and me

The expression *between you and I* is incorrect. Because the **pronouns** are **objects** of the **preposition** *between*, the objective **case** of the personal pronoun (*me*) must be used.

▶ Between you and ~~I~~, Joan should be promoted.
            me

bi- / semi-

When used with periods of time, *bi-* means "two" or "every two," as in *published biweekly*, meaning "once in two weeks." The prefix *semi-* means "half of" or "occurring twice within a period of time," as in *published semimonthly*, meaning "twice a month." Because these **prefixes** often cause confusion, substitute expressions like *every two months* or *twice a month* where possible. Normally *bi-* and *semi-* are joined with the following element without a space or **hyphen**.

biannual / biennial

In conventional usage, *biannual* means "twice during the year," and *biennial* means "every other year." See also **bi- / semi-**.

biased language

Biased language refers to words and expressions that offend because they make inappropriate assumptions or stereotypes about gender, ethnicity, physical or mental disability, age, or sexual orientation. Even if used unintentionally, biased language can damage your credibility.

Sexist Language

Sexist language can be an outgrowth of sexism—the arbitrary stereotyping of men and women—that can breed and reinforce inequality. To avoid sexism in your writing, treat men and women equally and use nonsexist occupational descriptions.

B

INSTEAD OF	CONSIDER
chairman, chairwoman	chair, chairperson
man-hours	staff hours, worker hours
policeman, policewoman	police officer
salesman, saleswoman	salesperson

Use parallel terms to describe men and women.

INSTEAD OF	USE
ladies and men	ladies and gentlemen, women and men
Ms. Jones and Bernard Weiss	Ms. Jones and Mr. Weiss, Mary Jones and Bernard Weiss

One common way of handling **pronoun references** that could apply equally to a man or a woman is to use the expression *his or her*. Repeated use of this phrase, however, can be awkward; to avoid overuse, try rewriting the sentence in the plural. See also **he / she**.

> ▸ ~~Every employee~~ *All employees* should submit ~~his or her~~ *their* expense ~~report~~ *reports* by Monday.

Another solution is to omit pronouns completely if they are not essential to the meaning of the sentence.

> ▸ Every employee should submit ~~his or her~~ *an* expense report by Monday.

◀ **PROFESSIONALISM NOTE** The easiest way to avoid bias is simply not to mention differences among people unless the differences are relevant to the discussion. Keep current with accepted usage and, if you are unsure of the appropriateness of an expression or the tone of a passage, have several colleagues assess the material. See also **ethics in writing**. ▸

bibliographies

A bibliography is an alphabetical list of books, articles, online sources, and other works that have been consulted in preparing a document or that are useful for reference purposes. A bibliography provides a convenient list of sources in a standardized form for readers interested in getting further information on the topic or in assessing the scope of the **research**.

A list of references or works cited refers to works actually cited in the text; a bibliography also includes works consulted for general background information. For information on using various citation styles, see **documenting sources**.

Entries in a bibliography are listed alphabetically by the author's last name. If an author is unknown, the entry is alphabetized by the first word in the title (other than *A*, *An*, or *The*). Entries also can be arranged by subject and then ordered alphabetically within those categories.

An annotated bibliography includes complete bibliographic information about a work (author, title, place of publication, publisher, and publication date) followed by a brief description or evaluation of what the work contains. The following is an annotation of a historical bibliography:

Alred, G. J., Reep, D. C., & Limaye, M. R. (1981). *Business and technical writing: An annotated bibliography of books, 1880–1980*. Metuchen, NJ: Scarecrow.

This 240-page bibliography annotates books that "deal significantly with writing or the analysis of writing, either for business or in technical and professional contexts" from 1880 through 1980. The nine-page "Introduction" surveys and assesses the collected works. Each 100- to 250-word annotation describes the purpose of the book, its scope, primary and unusual topics covered, pedagogical materials, and historical interest. Included are 27 previous bibliographies (books and articles), 847 books in the main section, and 230 items in unannotated lists ("Industry and Society Style Guides"; "Government Style Guides"; "Publishing"; "Oral Communication"; and "Style, Language, and Readability"). The book concludes with coauthor, title, and subject indexes.

blogs and forums

A *blog* (from *Web log*) is a Web-based journal in which an individual or a blogger team post entries (displayed from the most recent to the earliest posting) that document experiences, express opinions, provide information, and respond to other bloggers on subjects of mutual interest. A blog should have a well-defined focus (or subject), **audience**, and **purpose**. You will also need to establish and maintain a regular posting schedule. As you plan a blog, survey such popular blogging platforms as WordPress (www.wordpress.com) and Tumblr (www.tumblr.com) and consult with your information technology and marketing staff on how a blog might contribute to your organization.

Although blogs may allow readers to post comments, a *forum* typically fosters a wider "conversation" in which site visitors can not only respond to the posts of others but also begin new topics or discussion

B

threads. Organizations often use forums for customer or technical support; therefore, monitoring and responding to messages is crucial. If your Web site features a forum, you must promote it, contribute content, and solicit content from users; otherwise, the forum will quickly lose its usefulness and fade. See also **social media** and **writing for the Web**.

Organizational Uses

Organizations create blogs and forums to help meet such goals as attracting and retaining clients or customers, promoting goodwill, obtaining valuable feedback on their products and services, providing support to clients or customers, and developing a sense of community among their customers and employees. Blogs and forums can be both external and internal.

External sites are publicly available on the Internet both for an organization's customers or clients and for executives, spokespeople, or employees to share their views. Blogs and forums can help build loyalty for a company because customers can make a direct connection with the organization's representatives and with other customers. They can also exchange current information that may not be available in published documents or elsewhere online. *Internal sites* are usually created for an organization's employees and can be accessed only through the company's intranet. Internal blogs may serve as interactive newsletters that help build a sense of community within an organization or as a way to share "breaking news" about product development, employee benefits, or new team members.

Writing Style

Write blog or forum entries in an informal, conversational style that uses contractions, first person, and active voice. (See **style** and **clarity**.)

BLOG POSTING   Check out the latest concept for our new Toyota Camry dashboards—we've added enough space to hold your coffee and a digital device by moving the air ducts. Tell us what you think.

FORUM POSTING   I'm new to this thread, but I'm surprised no one's discussed the issue of confidentiality. My experience has been that Facebook's recent changes in privacy settings are just confusing. Have I missed something?

Keep your sentences and paragraphs concise. Use bulleted lists, italics, and other design elements, such as boldface and white space if possible. (See **layout and design** and **visuals**.) Doing so can help readers scan the postings or text to find information that is interesting or relevant to them. Keep headlines short, meaningful, and direct to catch readers' attention and increase visual appeal and readability. Where helpful, provide links to other sites and resources that participants might find useful. When blogs expand or forums become popular, you may need to organize them using *categories* (links to discussion topics) or *tags* (keywords for searching the site's postings).

❖ **ETHICS NOTE** Because organizations expect employees to assume full responsibility for the content they post on a company blog or forum, you must maintain high ethical standards. See also **ethics in writing**.

- Do not post information that is confidential, proprietary, or sensitive to your employer.

- Do not attack competitors or use abusive language toward other participants while making strong points on topics.

- Do not post content that is profane, libelous, or harassing, or that violates the privacy of others. See also **biased language**.

- Be aware that everything you post becomes permanently accessible to a wide public audience, especially for external sites.

- Obtain permission before using any material that is protected by **copyright, patents, and trademarks**, and identify sources for **quotations**. See also **plagiarism**. ❖

both . . . and

Statements using the *both . . . and* construction should always be balanced grammatically and logically. See also **parallel structure**.

▶ To succeed in management, you must be able *both* to develop
writing skills *and* ~~mastering~~ presentation skills.
                    to master

brackets

The primary use of brackets ([ ]) is to enclose a word or words inserted by the writer or editor into a quotation.

▶ The text stated, "Web sites can be categorized as either static [non-changing] or interactive [responding to user activity]."

B

Brackets are used to set off a parenthetical item within parentheses.

▶ We must credit Emanuel Foose (and his brother Emilio [1912–1982]) for founding the institute.

Brackets are also used to insert the Latin word *sic*, indicating that a writer has quoted material exactly as it appears in the original, even though it contains a misspelled or wrongly used word. See also **abbreviations** and **quotations**.

▶ The contract states, "Tinted windows will be installed to protect against son [*sic*] damage."

brainstorming

Brainstorming, a form of free association used to generate ideas about a topic, can be done individually or in groups. Brainstorming can stimulate creative thinking and reveal fresh perspectives and new connections. When brainstorming alone, jot down as many random ideas as you can think of about the topic. When working in a group, designate a person to record ideas the group suggests. Do not stop to analyze ideas or hold back, looking for only the "best" ideas; just note everything that comes to mind. After compiling a list of initial ideas, ask *what*, *when*, *who*, *where*, *how*, and *why* for each idea, then list additional details that those questions bring to mind. When you run out of ideas, analyze each one you recorded, discarding those that are redundant or not relevant. Then group the remaining items in the most logical order, based on your **purpose** and the needs of the **audience**, to create a tentative outline of the document. Although the outline will be sketchy and incomplete, it will show where further brainstorming or research is needed and provide a framework for any new details that additional research yields. (See **outlining**.)

Many writers find a technique called *clustering* (also called *mind mapping*), as shown in Figure B–1, helpful in recording and organizing ideas created during a brainstorming session. To cluster, begin on a blank page, a flip chart, or an outline tool such as a Bubbl.us mind map. Think of a key term that best characterizes your topic, and put it in a boxed or bubbled area at the center of the page. Figure B–1 shows brainstorming about the best way to communicate with customers, so the chosen topic was "Customer communication." Then think of subtopics most closely related to the main topic. In Figure B–1, the main topic ("Customer communication") led to such subtopics as "Advertising," "Internet," and "Direct mail." Place the subtopics in boxes or bubbles, connecting each to the center topic like spokes to a wheel hub. Repeat the exercise for each subtopic. In Figure B–1, for example, the subtopic

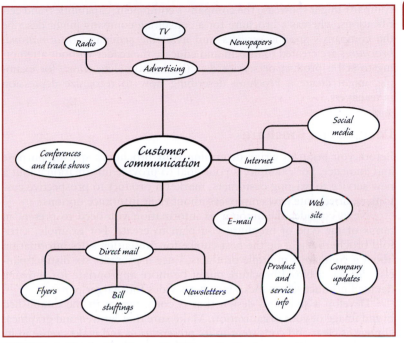

B

FIGURE B–1. Cluster Map from a Brainstorming Session

"Internet" stimulated the additional subtopics "E-mail," "Web site," and "Social media." Continue the process until you map all possible ideas.

brochures

Brochures are short publications, typically printed and folded into pamphlets or leaflets, that promote a business and its products and services to a target **audience**. The **purpose** of a brochure is to inform, persuade, or both. Compared with flyers, brochures typically allow information to be better compartmentalized and presented in a smaller space. Brochures may be distributed in paper or online, typically as PDF files. See also **selecting the medium**, **persuasion**, and **promotional writing**.

Types of Brochures

The two major types of brochures are sales brochures and informational brochures. *Sales brochures* are created specifically to sell a company's products and services. For example, a brochure for a manufacturing

B

company might showcase the company's equipment, capabilities, and certifications, whereas a brochure for a consulting company might describe the company's specific services and available seminars. *Informational brochures* are created to inform and educate the reader without attempting to sell a product or service directly. A counseling clinic, for example, might create a brochure describing how to recognize depression in teenagers.

Designing a Brochure

Before you begin to write, determine your brochure's specific purpose and audience. For example, is your goal to provide information about a new service to existing customers, market a product to prospective customers, or educate new employees about their insurance options?

Next, consider the amount of information you need to present in terms of the type of brochure you plan to create. For example, a trifold brochure might be the best choice for presenting sales information about a company's multiple products, since it provides six distinct panels, whereas a bifold brochure might be more appropriate for showing detailed product schematics, since it provides four larger panels.

Develop a style and design that is consistent with the established brand image of your organization. Make sure that written and graphical content is clear and consistent in its presentation and makes sense in its placement. For example, a brochure for a cruise line might feature photos of passengers and a short title on the front panel, a brief discussion of the line's history on the first inside panel, details on the company's ships on subsequent panels, and contact information on the back panel. See Figures B–2 and B–3, which showcase a company's capabilities through the use of **graphs**, bulleted **lists**, and images.

Cover Panel.   The main goal of the front cover panel is to gain the audience's attention and to show the purpose of the brochure clearly. It should identify the organization or product being promoted through a headline, logo, and carefully selected image. Keep the amount of text to a minimum. Reserve the back cover panel for your organization's complete contact information and any necessary legal or copyright disclaimers. If your audience needs to locate your company, include a **map**.

First Inside Panel.   The first inside panel of a brochure should again identify the organization and attract the reader with headlines and brief, readable content. This panel is typically used to tell an organization's "story," to highlight its history and accomplishments, or to describe how material will be presented in subsequent panels.

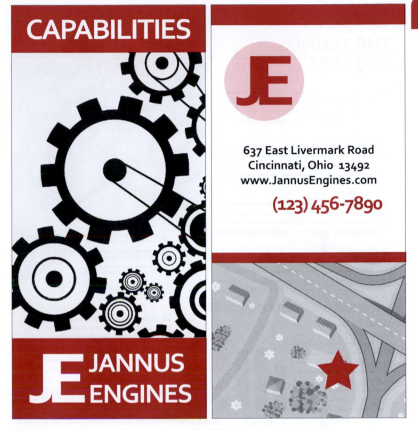

FIGURE B–2. Front and Back Panels of a Bifold Brochure

Subsequent Panels. Subsequent panels should describe the product or service from the reader's point of view, clearly stating any benefits or solutions it offers. Include relevant and accurate supporting facts, testimonials, and visuals, such as **photographs** and cutaway **drawings**. Use subheadings and bulleted **lists** to break up the text and highlight key points. In the final panel, be clear about the action you want the reader to take, such as calling to arrange a quote, placing an order using the included discount code, or following the included map to visit your showroom.

B

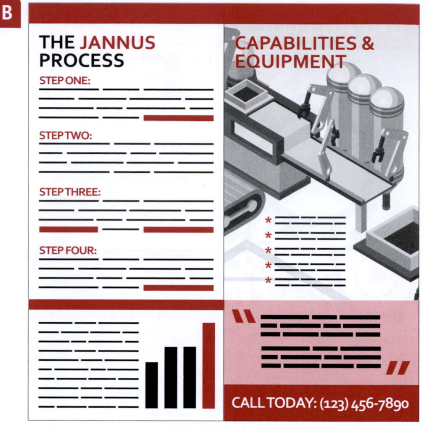

FIGURE B–3. Center Panels of a Bifold Brochure

WRITER'S CHECKLIST   **Designing a Brochure**

✔ Evaluate your content to ensure that the information you provide is consistent and logical.

✔ Stimulate your thinking by examining brochures for products or services similar to yours.

✔ Create a thumbnail sketch for each panel to help you decide on the number of panels needed, place text, and select visuals. See **layout and design**.

✔ Experiment with margins, spacing, and the amount of text on each panel. You may need to edit content to allow for adequate white space for readability and to ensure that the most important information is visually highlighted and easily found.

(continued)

WRITER'S CHECKLIST   Designing a Brochure (*continued*)

✔ Experiment with fonts and formatting, such as using a different font for short testimonials or headlines, but do not overuse unusual fonts or alternative styles.

✔ Choose colors coordinated with your brand, but consider that while color may be worth the cost for high-end products or services, economical black-and-white printing may be more appropriate for internal documents.

✔ Evaluate the selection of images: Do they accurately portray the subject? Are they high quality and properly licensed? (See **copyrights, patents, and trademarks**.) Refrain from using clip art unless it fits with your purpose.

✔ Consider ways to repurpose your brochure for digital accessibility and for use on **social media**.

bulleted lists (*see* lists)

business plans

A business plan is a **proposal** that allows potential supporters to evaluate ideas for a new business venture. Business plans are written primarily for bankers and other outside funders or consultants and sometimes for internal **audiences** (mostly senior management). Usually readers are targeted to provide funding, resources, cooperation, or, in the context of a large corporation, approval or financial support for an operational plan.

Purposes and Audience

A business plan can fulfill a single **purpose** or several purposes. The most common include the following:

- *To persuade potential investors or lenders to finance a business venture.* A comprehensive business plan allows investors to review objectively the company's assumptions, facts, and future outlook.

- *To allow reviewers (usually senior management) within a company to assess the profitability and goals of a new internal business venture.* They typically want to evaluate economic forecasts and determine future profitability and perhaps provide creative direction.

B

Before you write a business plan, identify and analyze your audience. The purposes of a business plan can differ dramatically, depending on which audience you are trying to convince. If you are addressing a banker, the central purpose of the business plan is to obtain funding for the new venture; to accomplish that, you need to demonstrate credibility by documenting a solid history of financial success. If you are addressing senior management, the central purpose is to demonstrate how the venture is likely to add value to the company. See also **persuasion**.

When writing a business plan, find out which issues are of most interest to your audience, and respond directly to those issues. If you are writing for multiple audiences with diverse interests and needs, be comprehensive in addressing all interests and needs in your plan.

Format, Length, and Sections

Because the audiences and purposes of business plans vary, the lengths and designs of the plans vary as well. Business plans can be as brief as one page, but they typically run between four and ten pages. The length also depends on the nature and complexity of the proposed business ideas.

The contents and sections will vary, but many plans (like **formal reports**) include a title page, a **table of contents**, and an **executive summary**. Most plans cover the following topic areas in subsequent sections: company description and strategy, market analysis and strategy, marketing plan, financial analysis, and supporting documents.

Company Description and Strategy

The first section of a business plan typically describes the company's functions, products, and services; its overall strategy in a vision or **mission statement**; its goals and milestones; and its management team and key members.

Business Description.   A business plan should begin with a concise but complete description of the type of organization, its products, and its services, as well as a brief mention of the company's place in the market.

- Identify the company's legal name and status.
- Explain exactly what the company does.
- Define the percentage and growth opportunity of each product or service, and describe the customer base.

- Describe current products or services and what makes them unique and competitive.
- Mention products and services in development.

Use this section to describe the company's competitive advantage and the cost versus benefits of its current and anticipated expenses.

Vision and Mission Statements.   Vision and mission statements can be the same; however, they often are written separately and serve different purposes. Vision statements broadly describe the perceived future of the company, and mission statements usually summarize the purpose of the business. Vision and mission statements may vary in length from one sentence to multiple pages. When both are included, a mission statement usually precedes a vision statement.

Goals and Milestones.   State short-term as well as long-term goals, with a timetable showing when the company expects to achieve specific milestones. Be realistic, especially when defining and setting short-term goals. Identify in specific, measurable terms what the company can reasonably achieve within a specified time frame.

Management and Key Team Members.   Identify all members of management. Describe their strengths, including any experiences or skills that particularly contribute to the business or to a specific venture.

Identify those who will work closely with management, such as accountants, lawyers, insurance agents, and partners. Briefly describe their backgrounds and qualifications. If you are proposing that new positions be added to the company, mention that in the plan and describe basic elements of a human resources policy, such as working hours, wages, vacation time, and sick leave. You can include **résumés** of candidates for the new positions in **appendixes**, along with other supporting documents.

Market Analysis and Strategy

Perhaps most important, the business plan needs to define and analyze the market and the competitive climate in which the writer proposes to launch the business venture. Once you have demonstrated a solid understanding of the market, describe the new venture or the new product or service, and propose your strategy for launching the venture and managing it over time to contribute to overall profits.

This section of the business plan also needs to identify and analyze the major competitors and describe how the company will address the competition to ensure that its products and services will make a strong entry into the marketplace. See also **research**.

B

Marketing Plan

Provide a specific plan for advertising and promoting products or services. Indicate the specific actions the company will take to achieve its sales and promotional objectives. This section is often written by a marketing director and includes discussions of promotional strategies and costs in different market channels, as well as sales projections for each market segment. See also **collaborative writing**.

Financial Analysis

In one or more subsections, present the company's financial plan and financial statements, especially if the business plan's purpose is to obtain venture capital. Provide historical information about financial status as well as projections about the company's financial growth. Identify both strengths and weaknesses, including new opportunities for growth, areas where the company can control costs, and ways of restructuring to make the company more efficient. Predict problems and describe the company's strategy to prevent or minimize their effects. These sections often benefit from strategically placed **graphs** and **tables**.

Provide complete and detailed financial statements (perhaps in an appendix). Bankers and other investors typically want to see a balance sheet, profit-and-loss statements, a three-year cash-flow projection, and source and use-of-funds statements. Until the business venture is up and running, the company might be able to provide only projections of profit-and-loss statements or balance sheets. Also describe the company's liability and property insurance. Make estimates of calculations conservative by using slightly low or low-end sales and margin figures and by slightly overstating expected costs.

Supporting Documents

In appendixes, provide résumés of key members of management and any other supporting information that demonstrates the company's potential and management's credibility. Other documents might include positive reviews of a new product, service, or venture, or positive articles about the company from industry or the popular press. Finally, provide copies of contracts with impressive clients (with the clients' permission) or information that would demonstrate relationships between the company and such clients. For further information, go to www.sba.gov and search for "business plans."

business writing style   **B**

Business writing has evolved from a formal and elaborate **style** to one that is more personal and direct. Business writing today varies from the casual style you might use in a **text message** to the formal, legalistic style found in contracts. For most **e-mails**, **letters**, and **memos**, a style between those two extremes is generally appropriate. Writing that is too formal can alienate your **audience**. But an inappropriate attempt to be informal may strike readers as insincere and unprofessional, especially clients or those you do not know well.

> *Dear   :*
> ▶ ~~Hey~~ Jane~~,~~
>
> *Your proposal arrived today, and it looks good.*
> ~~Just got your proposal. It's awesome!~~

The use of personal **pronouns** is important in **correspondence**. In fact, one way you can make your business writing natural and persuasive is through the use of the **"you" viewpoint**, which often uses the pronoun *you* to place the reader's interest foremost.

❖ **ETHICS NOTE** Be careful when you use the pronoun *we* in writing to clients and others outside your organization because you are committing your organization to what you have written. In general, when a statement is your opinion, use *I*; when it is company policy, use *we*. Do not refer to yourself in the third person by using *one* or *the writer*. It is perfectly natural and appropriate to refer to yourself as *I* and to the reader as *you*. In a **report**, however, you may be writing to more than one reader and may not necessarily want to refer to collective readers as *you*. See also **ethics in writing**, **persuasion**, and **point of view**. ❖

The best writers strive to write in a style that is so clear that their message cannot be misunderstood. In fact, you cannot be persuasive without being clear. One way to achieve **clarity**, especially during **revision**, is to eliminate overuse of the passive **voice**. Although the passive voice is sometimes necessary, often it not only makes your writing dull but also makes it ambiguous, indirect, or overly impersonal.

You can also achieve clarity with **conciseness**. Proceed cautiously here, however, because business writing should not be an endless series of short, choppy sentences that are blunt or deliver too little information to be helpful to the reader. (See also **sentence variety** and **telegraphic style**.) Appropriate and effective **word choice** is also essential to clarity. Finally, the careful use of **punctuation** can promote clarity. See also "Five Steps to Successful Writing" (page xvii).

B buzzwords

Buzzwords are popular words or phrases that, because of an intense period of overuse, tend to lose their freshness and precision. They often become popular through their association with technology, popular culture, or even sports. See also **jargon** and **word choice**.

▶ action items, face time, F2F meeting, impact [as a verb], same page, takeaway [as a noun], touch base, 24/7, win/win

Obviously, the words in this example are appropriate when used in the right **context**. See also **interface**.

We include buzzwords in our vocabulary because they *seem* to give force and vitality to our language. Actually, they often sound like an **affectation** in business writing.

C

can / may

In writing, *can* refers to capability ("I *can* have the project finished today"). *May* refers to possibility ("I *may* be in Boston on Monday") or permission ("*May* I leave early?").

cannot

Cannot is one word ("We *cannot* meet today").

capital / capitol

Capital refers either to financial assets or to the city that hosts the government of a state or a nation. *Capitol* refers to the building in which a state or national legislature meets. *Capitol* is often written with a small *c* when it refers to a state building, but it is always capitalized when it refers to the home of the U.S. Congress in Washington, D.C.

capitalization

The use of capital, or uppercase, letters is determined by custom. Capital letters are used to call attention to certain words, such as proper **nouns** and the first word of a sentence. Use capital letters carefully because they can affect a word's meaning (*march* / *March*, *china* / *China*) and because many spell checkers would fail to identify such an error.

65

C

Proper Nouns

Capitalize proper nouns that name specific persons, places, or things (Pat Wilde, Peru, Business Writing 205, Microsoft). When in doubt, consult a general or subject-area dictionary.

Common Nouns

Common nouns name general classes or categories of people, places, things, concepts, or qualities rather than specific ones and are not capitalized (person, country, business writing class, company).

First Words

The first letter of the first word in a sentence is always capitalized. ("Of the plans submitted, ours is best.") The first word after a **colon** is capitalized when the colon introduces two or more sentences (independent **clauses**) or when the colon precedes a formal statement or question.

▶ The meeting will address only one issue: What is the firm's role in environmental protection?

If a subordinate element follows the colon or if the thought is closely related, use a lowercase letter following the colon.

▶ We kept working for one reason: the approaching deadline.

The first word of a complete sentence in **quotation marks** is capitalized.

▶ Peter Drucker said, "The most important thing in communication is to hear what isn't being said."

The first word in the salutation (Dear Mr. Smith:) and in the complimentary close (Sincerely yours,) are capitalized, as are the names of the recipients. See also **letters**.

Specific Groups

Capitalize the names of ethnic groups, religions, and nationalities (Native American, Christianity, Mongolian). Do not capitalize the names of social and economic groups (middle class, unemployed).

Specific Places

Capitalize the names of all political divisions (Ward Six, Chicago, Cook County, Illinois) and geographic divisions (Europe, Asia, North America, the Middle East). Do not capitalize geographic features unless they are part of a proper name.

▶ The *mountains* in some areas, such as the *Great Smoky Mountains*, make cell-phone reception difficult.

The words *north*, *south*, *east*, and *west* are capitalized when they refer to sections of the country. They are not capitalized when they refer to directions.

▶ I may relocate further *west*, but my family will remain in the *South*.

Specific Institutions, Events, Concepts

Capitalize the names of institutions, organizations, and associations (U.S. Department of Health and Human Services). An organization usually capitalizes the names of its internal divisions and departments (Aeronautics Division, Human Resources Department). Types of organizations are not capitalized unless they are part of an official name (a business communication association, Association for Business Communication). Capitalize historical events (the Great Depression of the 1930s). Capitalize words that designate holidays, specific periods of time, months, or days of the week (Labor Day, the Renaissance, January, Monday). Do not capitalize seasons of the year (spring, summer, autumn, winter) unless they are used in a title (Winter Semester Schedule).

Titles of Works

Capitalize the initial letters of the first, last, and major words in the title of a book, an article, a play, or a film. Do not capitalize **articles**, coordinating **conjunctions**, or **prepositions** unless they begin or end the title (*The Wealth of Nations*). Capitalize prepositions within **titles** when they contain five or more letters (*Between, Within, Until, After*) unless you are following a style that recommends otherwise. The same rules apply to the subject lines of **e-mails** or **memos**. However, various citation styles may have different requirements for using capital letter in titles in references or footnotes. See **documenting sources**.

Professional and Personal Titles

Titles preceding proper names are capitalized (Ms. Berger, Senator King). Appositives following proper names are not normally capitalized (Angus King, *senator* from Maine). However, the word *president* is often capitalized when it refers to the chief executive of a national government. See **appositives**.

Job titles used with personal names are capitalized (H. S. Kim, *Division Manager*). Job titles used without personal names are not capitalized. ("The *division manager* will meet us tomorrow.") Use capital letters to designate family relationships only when they occur before a name (my uncle, Uncle Fred).

C

Abbreviations and Letters

Capitalize **abbreviations** if the words they stand for would be capitalized, such as MBA (Master of Business Administration). Capitalize letters that serve as names or indicate shapes (vitamin B, U-turn).

Miscellaneous Capitalizations

The first word of a complete sentence enclosed in **dashes**, **brackets**, or **parentheses** is not capitalized when it appears as part of another sentence.

▶ We must improve our safety record this year (accidents last year were up 10 percent).

When specifically identified by number, certain units, such as parts and chapters of books and rooms in buildings, are capitalized (Chapter 5, Ch. 5; Room 72, Rm. 72). Minor divisions within such units are not capitalized unless they begin a sentence (page 11, verse 14, seat 12).

---

case

DIRECTORY

Subjective Case 69	Appositives 70
Objective Case 69	Determining the Case of Pronouns 70
Possessive Case 70	

Grammatical case indicates the functional relationship of a **noun** or a **pronoun** to the other words in a sentence. Nouns change form only in the possessive case; pronouns may change form in the subjective, objective, or possessive case.

The case of a noun or pronoun is always determined by its function in a **phrase**, **clause**, or sentence. If it is the subject of a phrase, clause, or sentence, it is in the subjective case; if it is an **object** in a phrase, clause, or sentence, it is in the objective case; if it reflects possession or ownership and modifies a noun, it is in the possessive case. Figure C–1 is a chart of pronouns in the subjective, objective, and possessive cases. See also **sentence construction**.

The subjective case can indicate the person or thing acting ("*He* sued the vendor"), the person or thing acted on ("*He* was sued by the vendor"), or the topic of description ("*He* is the vendor"). The objective case can indicate the thing acted on ("The vendor sued *him*") or the person or thing acting but in the objective position ("The vendor was sued by *him*"). (See also **voice**.) The possessive case indicates the person or thing owning or possessing something ("It was *his* company"). See also **modifiers**.

SINGULAR	SUBJECTIVE	OBJECTIVE	POSSESSIVE
First Person	I	me	my, mine
Second Person	you	you	your, yours
Third Person	he, she, it	him, her, it	his, her, hers, its
PLURAL	SUBJECTIVE	OBJECTIVE	POSSESSIVE
First Person	we	us	our, ours
Second Person	you	you	your, yours
Third Person	they	them	their, theirs

FIGURE C–1. Pronoun-Case Chart

Subjective Case

A pronoun is in the subjective case (also called *nominative case*) when it represents the person or thing acting or is the receiver of the action even though it is in the subject position.

▶ *I* wrote a proposal.

A linking **verb** links a pronoun to its antecedent to show that they identify the same thing. Because they represent the same thing, the pronoun is in the subjective case even when it follows the verb, which makes it a subjective complement.

▶ *She* is the new manager. [subject]

▶ The new manager is *she*. [subjective complement]

The subjective case is used after the words *than* and *as* because of the understood (although unstated) portion of the clauses in which those words appear.

▶ George is as good a designer as *I* [am].

▶ Our subsidiary can do the job better than *we* [can].

Objective Case

A pronoun is in the objective case (also called the *accusative case*) when it indicates the person or thing receiving the action that is expressed by a verb in the active voice.

▶ The company promoted *me* in July.

Pronouns that follow action verbs (which excludes all forms of the verb *be*) must be in the objective case. Do not be confused by an additional name ("The company promoted John and *me* in July").

C

A pronoun is in the objective case when it is the object of a **preposition** or gerund or the subject of an infinitive.

▶ Between *you* and *me*, his facts are questionable. [objects of a preposition]

▶ Training *him* was the best thing I could have done. [object of a gerund]

▶ We asked *them* to return the deposit. [subject of an infinitive]

English does not differentiate between direct objects and indirect objects; both require the objective form of the pronoun. See also **complements**.

▶ The interviewer seemed to like *me*. [direct object]

▶ They wrote *me* a letter. [indirect object]

Possessive Case

A noun or pronoun is in the possessive case when it represents a person, place, or thing that possesses something. To make a singular noun possessive, add *'s* (the *manufacturer's* robotic inventory system). With plural nouns that end in *s*, show the possessive by placing an apostrophe after the *s* that forms the plural (a *managers'* meeting). For other guidelines, see **possessive case**.

Appositives

An **appositive** is a noun or noun phrase that follows and amplifies the meaning of another noun or noun phrase. Because it has the same grammatical function as the noun it complements, an appositive should be in the same case as the noun it complements.

▶ Two auditors, Jim Knight and *I*, were asked to review the books. [subjective case]

▶ The group leader selected two members to represent the department—Mohan Pathak and *me*. [objective case]

Determining the Case of Pronouns

One test to determine the proper case of a pronoun is to try it with a transitive verb, such as *resembled* or *hit*. If the pronoun would logically precede the verb, use the subjective case; if it would logically follow the verb, use the objective case.

▶ *She* [*He, They*] resembled her father. [subjective case]

▶ Angela resembled *him* [*her, them*]. [objective case]

In the following example, try omitting the noun to determine the case of the pronoun. The proper pronoun will sound correct.

SENTENCE	(*We / Us*) pilots fly our own airplanes.
INCORRECT	*Us* fly our own airplanes.
CORRECT	*We* fly our own airplanes.

To determine the case of a pronoun that follows *as* or *than*, mentally add the words that are omitted but understood.

▶ The other sales representative is not paid as well as *she* [is paid]. [You would not write "*Her* is paid."]

▶ His partner was better informed than *he* [was informed]. [You would not write "*Him* was informed."]

If pronouns in compound constructions cause problems, try using them singly to determine the proper case.

SENTENCE	(*We / Us*) and the clients are going to lunch.
CORRECT	*We* are going to lunch.

For advice on when to use *who* and *whom*, see **who / whom**.

cause-and-effect method of development

The cause-and-effect **method of development** is a common strategy to explain why something happened or why you think something will happen. The goal is to make as plausible as possible the relationship between a situation and either its cause or its effect. The conclusions you draw about the relationships should be based on evidence you have gathered. Like all methods, this one is often used in combination with others. If you were examining a problem with multiple causes, for example, you might combine this method of development with the **order-of-importance method of development** as you examine each cause and its effect.

Evaluating Evidence

Because not all the evidence you gather will be of equal value, keep in mind the following guidelines:

- *Your facts and arguments should be relevant to your topic.* Be careful not to draw a conclusion that your evidence does not support. For example, you may have researched some statistics showing

C

that an increasing number of Americans are licensed to fly small airplanes cannot be used as evidence for a decrease in new car sales in the United States.

- *Your evidence should be sufficient.* Not having enough evidence can lead to false conclusions.

  ▶ Driver-training classes do not help prevent auto accidents. Two people I know who completed driver-training classes were involved in accidents.

A thorough investigation of the usefulness of driver-training classes in keeping down the accident rate would require more than one or two examples. It would require a systematic comparison of the driving records for a representative sample of drivers who had completed driver training and those who had not.

- *Your evidence should be representative.* If you conduct a survey to obtain your evidence, do not solicit responses from only individuals or groups whose views are identical to yours; be sure you obtain responses from a diverse population.

- *Your evidence should be demonstrable.* Two events that occur close to each other in time or place may or may not be causally related. For example, the fact that new traffic signs were placed at an intersection and the next day an accident occurred does not prove that the signs caused the accident. You must demonstrate the relationship between the two events with pertinent facts and arguments. See **logic errors**.

Linking Causes to Effects

To show a true relationship between a cause and an effect, you must demonstrate that the existence of the one *requires* the existence of the other. It is often difficult to establish beyond any doubt that one event was the cause of another event. More often, a result will have more than one cause. As you research a subject, your task is to determine which cause or causes are most plausible.

When several probable causes are equally valid, report your findings accordingly, as in the following excerpt from an article on the use of an energy-saving device called a furnace-vent damper. The damper is a metal plate that fits inside the flue or vent pipe of a furnace to allow poisonous gases to escape up the flue. Tests run on several dampers showed a number of probable causes for their malfunctioning.

  ▶ One damper was sold without proper installation instructions, and another was wired incorrectly. Two of the units had slow-opening dampers (15 seconds) that prevented the [furnace] burner from firing. And one damper jammed when exposed to a simulated fuel temperature of more than 700 degrees.

—Don DeBat, "Save Energy but Save Your Life, Too," *Family Safety*

The investigator located more than one cause of damper malfunctions and reported on them. Without such a thorough account, recommendations to prevent malfunctions would be based on incomplete evidence.

center on

Use the phrase *center on* in writing, not *center around*. ("The experiments *center on* the new discovery.") Often, however, the idea intended by *center on* is better expressed by other words.

▶ The hearings on computer security ~~centered on~~ *dealt with* access codes.

chronological method of development

The chronological **method of development** arranges the events under discussion in sequential order, as in Figure C–2, emphasizing time as it begins with the first event and continues chronologically to the last. **Trip reports**, **instructions**, work schedules, some **minutes of meetings**, and certain **incident reports** are among the types of writing in which information is organized chronologically. Chronological order is typically used in **narration**.

In the e-mail shown in Figure C–2, a retail store manager describes the steps taken over a one-year period to reduce shoplifting at his store. After providing important background information, the writer presents the steps taken in chronological order.

cite / sight / site

Cite means "acknowledge" or "quote an authority." ("The speaker *cited* several famous economists.") *Sight* is the ability to see. ("He feared that he might lose his *sight*.") *Site* is a plot of land (a construction *site*) or the place where something is located (a storage *site*).

C

To:	Joanna Sanchez, Vice President for Marketing
From:	Larry Brown, Manager, Downtown Branch
Date:	September 16, 2018
Subject:	Reducing Shoplifting at the Downtown Store

Overview

Over the past year and based on our shared concerns, my staff and I have worked to reduce the amount of shoplifting in the downtown store. We have spent much time, effort, and money on the problem, which we hope will be alleviated during the Christmas shopping season. Let me recap the specific measures we have taken.

Task Force
In October, we formed a task force of salespeople, buyers, managers, and executive staff to recommend ways of curtailing shoplifting and methods of implementing our recommendations. We met four times during January and twice in March to reach our final recommendations.

Mark IV Surveillance System

Sequence of events organized by date

In April, we installed a Mark IV System, which uses closed-circuit TV cameras at each exit. The cameras, which are linked with our security office, are capable of taping signals from all exits simultaneously. The task force felt the Mark IV System might be useful in detecting a pattern of specific individuals entering and leaving the store. This system, which became operational on April 20, has been very helpful in reducing the number of thefts.

Employee Training
During May and June, we held employee workshops on detecting shoplifters. Security, Inc., a consulting firm, led the workshops and provided not only lectures and tips on spotting shoplifters but also demonstrations of common techniques shoplifters use to divert store personnel. All those who attended thought the workshops were quite helpful.

Other Steps Taken
Because the task force determined that certain items were particularly vulnerable to shoplifters, we decided in July to restructure some of the display areas. Our purpose was to make those areas less isolated from the view of clerks and other store personnel. The remodeling, most of which was relatively minor, was completed over the summer months.

For the fall and holiday sales, we have hired extra uniformed security guards. The guards from Security, Inc., should be able to deter first-time shoplifters, although we know that this step will not eliminate the problem altogether.

Conclusion identifies next steps, invites response

We believe the steps we have taken will substantially reduce our losses from theft. Of course, after we have reviewed the figures at the end of the year, the task force will meet again in January to assess the success of the methods we have used. If you need more details, please let me know.

FIGURE C–2. Chronological Method of Development

clarity

Clarity is essential to effective communication with your **readers**. You cannot achieve your **purpose** or a goal like **persuasion** without clarity.

A logical **method of development** and an outline will help you avoid presenting your reader with a jumble of isolated thoughts. A method of development and an outline that puts your thoughts into a logical, meaningful sequence brings **coherence** as well as **unity** to your writing. Clear **transition** contributes to clarity by providing the smooth flow that enables the reader to connect your thoughts with one another without conscious effort. See also **outlining**.

Proper **emphasis** and **subordination** are mandatory if you want to achieve clarity. If you do not use those two complementary techniques wisely, all your clauses and sentences will appear to be of equal importance; your reader will only be able to guess which are most important, which are least important, and which fall somewhere in between. The **pace** at which you present your ideas is also important to clarity; if the pace is not carefully adjusted to both the topic and the reader, your writing will appear cluttered and unclear.

Point of view establishes through whose eyes or from what vantage point the reader views the subject. A consistent point of view is essential to clarity; if you inappropriately switch from the first person to the third person in midsentence, you are certain to confuse your reader.

Precise **word choice** contributes to clarity and helps eliminate **ambiguity** and **awkwardness**. **Vague words**, **clichés**, poor use of **idioms**, and inappropriate **usage** detract from clarity. That **conciseness** is a requirement for clear writing should be evident to anyone who has ever attempted to decipher a product liability or privacy statement. For clarity, remove unnecessary words from your writing. See also **plain language**.

clauses

A clause is a group of words that contains a subject and a predicate. (See **sentence construction**.) Every sentence must contain at least one independent, that is, a clause that can stand alone as a sentence: "*The scaffolding fell* when the rope broke." A dependent clause must be attached to an independent clause: "I was at the St. Louis branch *when the decision was made*. If a dependent clause is not attached to an independent clause, it becomes a **sentence fragment**.

Dependent (or subordinate) clauses are useful in making the relationship between thoughts clearer and more succinct than if the ideas were presented in a choppy series of simple sentences or in a compound sentence. Dependent clauses are especially effective for expressing thoughts that describe or explain another statement.

C

CHOPPY	The recycling facility is located between Millville and Darrtown. Both villages use it. [The two thoughts are of approximately equal importance.]
SUBORDINATED	The recycling facility, *which is located between Millville and Darrtown*, is used by both villages. [One thought is subordinated to the other.]

Too much **subordination**, however, can be confusing and foster wordiness. See also **conciseness**.

▶ He selected instructors whose classes ~~had a slant that was~~ *were* specifically designed for ~~students who intended to go into accounting.~~ *accounting students.*

A clause can be connected to the rest of its sentence by a coordinating **conjunction**, a subordinating conjunction, a relative **pronoun**, or a conjunctive **adverb**.

▶ It was 500 miles to the facility, *so* we made arrangements to fly. [coordinating conjunction]

▶ Drivers will need to be alert *because* snow may cause hazardous conditions near the entrance to the warehouse. [subordinating conjunction]

▶ Robert M. Fano was the scientist *who* developed the earliest multiple-access computer system at MIT. [relative pronoun]

▶ We arrived in the evening; *nevertheless*, we began the tour of the facility. [conjunctive adverb]

clichés

Clichés are expressions that have been used for so long they are no longer fresh but come to mind easily because they are so familiar. Clichés are often wordy and vague, and they can be confusing, especially to speakers of **English as a second language**. A better, more direct word or phrase is given for each of the following clichés.

INSTEAD OF	USE
all over the map	scattered, unfocused
the game plan	strategy, schedule
last but not least	last, finally

Some writers use clichés in a misguided attempt to appear casual or spontaneous, just as other writers try to impress readers with **buzzwords**.

Although clichés may come to mind easily while you are **writing a draft**, eliminate them during **revision**. See also **affectation**, **conciseness**, and **international correspondence**.

C

coherence

Writing is coherent when the relationships among ideas are clear to readers. The major components of coherent writing are a logical sequence of related ideas and clear transitions between those ideas. See also **clarity** and **organization**.

Presenting ideas in a logical sequence is the most important requirement in achieving coherence. The key to achieving a logical sequence is a good outline. (See **outlining**.) An outline forces you to establish a beginning, a middle, and an end. That structure contributes greatly to coherence by enabling you to experiment with sequences and lay out the most direct route to your **purpose** without digressing.

Thoughtful **transition** is also essential; without it, your writing cannot achieve the smooth flow from sentence to sentence and **paragraph** to paragraph that results in coherence.

During **revision**, check your draft carefully for coherence. If possible, have someone else review it to see how well it expresses the relationships among ideas. See also **unity**.

collaborative writing

Collaborative writing occurs when two or more writers work together to produce a single document for which they share responsibility and decision-making authority. Collaborative writing teams are formed when (1) the size of a project or the time constraints imposed on it require a joint effort, (2) the project involves multiple areas of expertise, or (3) the project requires the melding of divergent views into a single perspective that is acceptable to the whole team or to another group. Many types of collaborations are possible, from the collaboration of a primary writer with a variety of contributors and reviewers to a highly interactive collaboration in which everyone on a team plays a relatively equal role in shaping the document.

Tasks of the Collaborative Writing Team

The collaborating team strives to achieve a compatible working relationship by dividing the work in a way that uses each writer's expertise and experience to its advantage. The team should also designate a coordinator,

C

who will guide the team members' activities, organize the project, and ensure **coherence** and consistency within the document. The coordinator's duties can be determined by mutual agreement, assigned by management, or assigned on a rotating basis if the team often works together.

Planning.   The team members collectively identify the **audience**, **purpose**, **context**, and **scope** of the project. See also **meetings** and "Five Steps to Successful Writing" (page xvii).

At this stage, the team establishes a project plan that may include guidelines for communication among team members, version control (naming, dating, and managing document drafts), review procedures, and writing **style** standards that team members are expected to follow. The plan includes a schedule with due dates for completing initial research tasks, outlines, drafts, reviews, revisions, and the final document.

◖ **PROFESSIONALISM NOTE** Deadlines must be met because team members rely on one another, and one missed deadline can delay the entire project. A missed project deadline can result in a lost opportunity or, in the case of **proposals**, disqualify an application. Individual writers must adjust their schedules and focus on their own writing process to finish drafts and meet the deadline. ◗

Research and Writing.   The team next completes initial **research** tasks, elicits comments from team members, creates a broad outline of the document (see **outlining**), and assigns writing tasks to individual team members based on their expertise. Depending on the project, each team member further researches an assigned segment of the document, expands and develops the broad outline, and produces a draft from the detailed outline. See also **writing a draft**.

Reviewing.   Keeping the audience's needs and the document's purpose in mind, each team member critically yet diplomatically reviews the other team members' drafts, from the overall **organization** to the **clarity** of each **paragraph**, and offers advice to help improve the writers' work. Team members can easily solicit feedback by sharing files and then working with track and comment features that allow reviewers to suggest changes without deleting the original text.

Revising.   In this final stage, individual writers evaluate their colleagues' reviews and accept, reject, or build on their suggestions. Then the team coordinator can consolidate all drafts into a final master copy and maintain and evaluate it for consistency, **tone**, and coherence. See also **revision**.

◖ **PROFESSIONALISM NOTE** As you collaborate, be ready to tolerate some disharmony, but temper it with mutual respect. Team members may have differing perspectives that can easily lead to conflict, ranging from minor differences to major showdowns. However, creative differences resolved respectfully can energize the team and actually strengthen a finished document by compelling writers to reexamine assumptions and issues in unanticipated ways. See **listening**. ▶

C

Using Collaborative Writing Software

Software and online systems help teams work together on a common writing task whether they are in the same office or in different countries. Online synchronous whiteboards, for example, allow teams to collaborate online and discuss and edit texts in real time. Many such technologies also make it easy to conduct live chat sessions, share documents, track changes from one version of a document to the next, alert collaborators when a document is altered, and export documents for offline editing. Word processing; Web-based file sharing; and collaborative systems like wikis, Google Docs, and Microsoft Word Online enable team members to draft, review, edit, and comment with text or voice on their collective work. Project management programs can also help organize and manage schedules as well as track versions and deadlines. See also **document management**.

WRITER'S CHECKLIST   **Writing Collaboratively**

✔ Designate one person as the team coordinator.

✔ Identify the audience, purpose, context, and scope of the project.

✔ Create a project plan, including a schedule and style or format standards.

✔ Create a working outline of the document.

✔ Assign sections or tasks to each team member.

✔ Research and write drafts of each document section.

✔ Use the agreed-upon standards for style and format.

✔ Exchange sections for team member reviews.

✔ Revise sections as needed.

✔ Meet the established deadlines for drafts, revisions, and final versions.

✔ Consider using online tools to facilitate working with team members.

---

collection letters

Collection letters serve two purposes: (1) collecting an overdue bill and (2) preserving the customer relationship. In some states, legal requirements may force you to use an attorney to write such letters. See also **correspondence** and **letters**.

C

Most companies use a series of collection letters like those shown in Figures C–3 through C–5, in which the letters become increasingly demanding and urgent. All letters should be courteous and show a genuine interest in the customer as well as concern for whatever problems may be preventing prompt payment. See also **"you" viewpoint**.

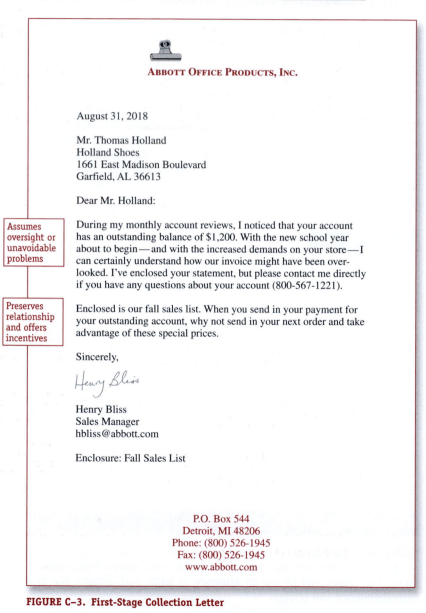

ABBOTT OFFICE PRODUCTS, INC.

August 31, 2018

Mr. Thomas Holland
Holland Shoes
1661 East Madison Boulevard
Garfield, AL 36613

Dear Mr. Holland:

Assumes oversight or unavoidable problems

During my monthly account reviews, I noticed that your account has an outstanding balance of $1,200. With the new school year about to begin—and with the increased demands on your store—I can certainly understand how our invoice might have been overlooked. I've enclosed your statement, but please contact me directly if you have any questions about your account (800-567-1221).

Preserves relationship and offers incentives

Enclosed is our fall sales list. When you send in your payment for your outstanding account, why not send in your next order and take advantage of these special prices.

Sincerely,

Henry Bliss

Henry Bliss
Sales Manager
hbliss@abbott.com

Enclosure: Fall Sales List

P.O. Box 544
Detroit, MI 48206
Phone: (800) 526-1945
Fax: (800) 526-1945
www.abbott.com

FIGURE C–3. First-Stage Collection Letter

Dear Mr. Holland:

We are concerned that we have not heard from you about your overdue account of $1,200 even though we have written three times in the past 90 days. Because you have always been one of our best customers, we have to wonder if some special circumstances have caused the delay. If so, please feel free to discuss the matter with us.

> Firmer tone asking about special difficulties

By sending us your payment today, you can preserve your excellent credit record. Because you have always paid your account promptly, we are sure that you will want to settle this balance now. If your balance is more than you can pay at present, we will be happy to work out mutually satisfactory payment arrangements.

> Benefits of responding and payment options

Please use the enclosed envelope to send in your check, or call (800) 526-1945 to discuss your account.

Sincerely,

FIGURE C–4. Second-Stage Collection Letter

Dear Mr. Holland:

Your account in the amount of $1,200 is now 180 days overdue. You have already received a generous extension of time and, in fairness to our other customers, we cannot permit a further delay in payment.

> Reflects urgency

Because you have not responded to any of our letters, we must turn your account over to our attorney for collection if we do not receive full payment within the next 10 days.

> Outlines next steps

Why not avoid this unpleasant situation by making a fund transfer or sending your check in the enclosed return envelope within 10 days, or by calling (800) 526-1945 to discuss payment.

> Maintains courtesy

Sincerely,

FIGURE C–5. Third-Stage Collection Letter

C

The first stage should include reminders stamped on the invoice ("overdue"), form letters, or brief personal notes. These early reminders should maintain a friendly **tone**, as shown in Figure C–3.

In the second stage, your tone should be firm, but it should never be rude, sarcastic, or threatening. Ask directly for payment, and inquire whether some circumstances are preventing payment. Make it easy for the customer to respond, as shown in Figure C–4.

Third-stage collection letters reflect a sense of urgency because the customer has not responded to your previous letters. Although your tone should remain courteous, make your demand for payment explicit, as shown in Figure C–5. Point out how reasonable you have been, and urge the customer to pay at once to avoid a collection service or legal action.

colons

The colon (:) is a mark of introduction that alerts readers to the close connection between the preceding statement and what follows.

Colons in Sentences

A colon links independent **clauses** to words, **phrases**, clauses, or lists that identify, rename, emphasize, amplify, explain, or illustrate the sentence that precedes the colon.

▶ Two topics will be discussed: *the new accounting system and the new bookkeeping procedures.* [phrases that identify]

▶ Only one thing will satisfy Mr. Sturgess: *our finished report.* [appositive (renaming) phrase for **emphasis**]

▶ Any organization is confronted with two separate, though related, information problems: *It must maintain an effective internal communication system and an effective external communication system.* [clause to amplify and explain]

▶ Heart patients should make key lifestyle changes: *stop smoking, exercise regularly, eat a low-fat diet, and reduce stress.* [list to identify and illustrate]

Colons with Salutations, Titles, Citations, and Numbers

A colon follows the salutation in formal **correspondence**, even when the salutation refers to a person by first name.

▶ Dear Professor Jeffers: *or* Dear Mary:

Colons separate titles from subtitles and separate references to sections of works in citations. See also **documenting sources**.

▶ "'We Regret to Inform You': Toward a New Theory of Negative Messages"

▶ *International Journal of Business Communication* 51:279–303 [volume 51, pages 279–303]

Colons separate numbers in time references and indicate numerical ratios.

▶ 9:30 a.m. [9 hours and 30 minutes]

▶ The cement is mixed with water and sand at a ratio of 5:3:1. [The colon is read as the word *to*.]

Punctuation and Capitalization with Colons

A colon always goes outside **quotation marks**.

▶ This was the real meaning of the manager's "suggestion": Cooperation within our department must improve.

As this example shows, the first word after a colon may be capitalized if the statement following the colon is a complete sentence and functions as a formal statement or question. If the element following the colon is subordinate, however, use a lowercase letter to begin that element. See also **capitalization**.

▶ We have only one way to stay within our present budget: to reduce expenditures for research and development.

Unnecessary Colons

Do not place a colon between a **verb** and its **objects**.

▶ Three fluids that clean pipettes are/ water, alcohol, and acetone.

Likewise, do not use a colon between a **preposition** and its objects.

▶ I may be transferred to/ Tucson, Boston, or Miami.

Do not insert a colon after *including*, *such as*, or *for example* to introduce a simple list.

▶ Do not use office Internet access for personal activities such as/ social networking, shopping, gaming, and accessing personal e-mail.

C

One common exception is made when a verb or preposition is followed by a stacked **list**; however, it may be possible to introduce the list with a complete sentence instead.

> ▶ *The following manufacturers* ~~Manufacturers that~~ produce computer monitors ~~include:~~ :
>
> Apple   Acer   Gateway
> HP   Philips   Samsung

comma splice

A comma splice is a grammatical error in which two independent **clauses** are joined by only a **comma**.

INCORRECT   It was 500 miles to the facility, we arranged to fly.

A comma splice can be corrected in several ways.

1. Substitute a **semicolon**, a semicolon and a conjunctive **adverb** followed by a comma, or a comma and a coordinating **conjunction**.

   - It was 500 miles to the facility; we arranged to fly. [semicolon]

   - It was 500 miles to the facility; *therefore,* we arranged to fly. [conjunctive adverb]

   - It was 500 miles to the facility, *so* we arranged to fly. [coordinating conjunction]

2. Create two sentences.

   - It was 500 miles to the facility. *We* arranged to fly.

3. Subordinate one clause to the other. (See **subordination**.)

   - *Because it was 500 miles to the facility,* we arranged to fly.

See also **sentence construction** and **sentence faults**.

commas

DIRECTORY

Like all **punctuation**, the comma (,) helps **readers** understand the writer's meaning and prevents **ambiguity**. Notice how the comma helps make the meaning clear in the second example.

AMBIGUOUS	To be successful managers with MBAs must continue their education.
CLEAR	To be successful, managers with MBAs must continue their education.

Do not follow the old myth that you should insert a comma wherever you would pause if you were speaking. Effective use of commas depends on an understanding of **sentence construction**.

Linking Independent Clauses

Use a comma before a coordinating **conjunction** (*and*, *but*, *or*, *nor*, and sometimes *so*, *yet*, and *for*) that links independent **clauses**.

▶ The new microwave disinfection system was delivered, *but* the installation will require an additional week.

However, if two independent clauses are short and closely related—and there is no danger of confusing the reader—the comma may be omitted. Both of the following examples are correct.

▶ The cable snapped and the power failed.

▶ The cable snapped, and the power failed.

Enclosing Elements

Commas are used to enclose nonessential information in nonrestrictive clauses, phrases, and parenthetical elements. See also **restrictive and nonrestrictive elements**.

▶ Our new factory, *which began operations last month*, should add 25 percent to total output. [nonrestrictive clause]

▶ The accountant, *working quickly and efficiently*, finished early. [nonrestrictive phrase]

▶ We can, *of course*, expect their lawyer to call us. [parenthetical element]

Yes and *no* are set off by commas.

▶ *Yes*, I think we can finish by the deadline.

C

A **direct address**, as well as an **interjection** (*oh, well, indeed, yes, no*), should be enclosed in commas.

▶ You will note, *Jeff*, that the budget figure matches our estimate. [direct address]

▶ We must, indeed, rethink the proposal. [interjection]

If the direct address or interjection appears at the beginning of the sentence, only one comma following the direct address or interjection is needed.

An **appositive** phrase (which reidentifies another expression in the sentence) is enclosed in commas.

▶ Our company, *NT Insurance Group*, won several awards last year.

Interrupting parenthetical and transitional words or phrases are usually set off with commas. See also **transition**.

▶ The report, *therefore*, needs to be revised.

Commas are omitted when the word or phrase does not interrupt the continuity of thought.

▶ I *therefore* recommend that we begin construction.

For other means of punctuating parenthetical elements, see **dashes** and **parentheses**.

Introducing Elements

Clauses and Phrases.   Generally, place a comma after an introductory clause or phrase, especially if it is long, to identify where the introductory element ends and the main part of the sentence begins.

▶ *Because we have not yet reached our hiring goals for the Sales Division,* we recommend the development of an aggressive recruiting program.

A long modifying phrase that precedes the main clause should always be followed by a comma.

▶ *During the first series of field-performance tests at our Colorado proving ground,* the new engine failed to meet our expectations.

When an introductory phrase is short and closely related to the main clause, the comma may be omitted.

▶ *In two seconds* a decision was reached.

A comma should always follow an absolute phrase, which modifies the whole sentence.

▶ *The presentation completed,* we returned to our offices.

Words and Quotations. Certain types of introductory words are followed by a comma. One example is a transitional word or phrase that connects the preceding clause or sentence with the thought that follows.

▶ *Furthermore*, we should include college job fairs in our recruiting plans, provided our budget is approved.

▶ *For example*, this change will make us more competitive in the global marketplace.

Use a comma to separate a direct **quotation** from its introduction.

▶ Morton and Lucia White *said*, "People live in cities but dream of the countryside."

Do not use a comma when giving an indirect quotation.

▶ Morton and Lucia White *said that* people dream of the countryside, even though they live in cities.

When an **adverb** closely modifies the **verb** or the entire sentence, it should not be followed by a comma.

▶ *Perhaps* we can still solve the high turnover problem. *Certainly* we should try. [*Perhaps* and *certainly* closely modify each statement.]

Separating Items in a Series

Although the comma before the last item in a series is sometimes omitted, it is generally clearer to include it.

▶ Random House, Bantam, Doubleday, and Dell were once separate publishing companies. [Without the final comma, "Doubleday and Dell" might refer to one company or two.]

Phrases and clauses in coordinate series are also punctuated with commas.

▶ Plants absorb noxious gases, act as receptors of dirt particles, and cleanse the air of other impurities.

When phrases or clauses in a series contain commas, use **semicolons** rather than commas to separate the items.

▶ Among those present were John Howard, President of the Howard Paper Company; Thomas Martin, CEO of AIR Recycling, Inc.; and Larry Stanley, President of Northland Papers.

When **adjectives** modifying the same noun can be reversed and make sense, or when they can be separated by *and*, they should be separated by commas.

▶ The aircraft featured a *modern, sleek, swept-wing* design.

C

When an adjective modifies a phrase, no comma is required.

▶ She investigated the *damaged inventory-control system*. [The adjective *damaged* modifies the phrase *inventory-control system*.]

Never separate a final adjective from its noun.

▶ He is a conscientious, honest, reliable/worker.

Clarifying and Contrasting

Use a comma to separate two contrasting thoughts or ideas.

▶ The project was finished on time, but not within the budget.

Use a comma after an independent clause that is only loosely related to the dependent clause that follows it or that could be misread without the comma.

▶ I should be able to finish the plan by July, even though I lost time because of illness.

Showing Omissions

A comma sometimes replaces a verb in certain elliptical constructions.

▶ Some were punctual; *others, late*. [The comma replaces *were*.]

It is better, however, to avoid such constructions in business writing.

Using with Numbers and Names

Commas are conventionally used to separate distinct items. Use commas between the elements of an address written on the same line (but not between the state and the ZIP Code).

▶ Kristen James, 4119 Mill Road, Dayton, Ohio 45401

A full date that is written in month-day-year format uses a comma preceding and following the year.

▶ November 30, 2025, is the payoff date.

Do not use commas for dates in the day-month-year format, which is used in many parts of the world and by the U.S. military.

▶ Note that 30 November 2025 is the payoff date.

Do not use commas when showing only the month and year or month and day in a **date**.

▶ The target date of May 2020 is optimistic, so I would like to meet on March 4 to discuss our options.

Use commas to separate the elements of large arabic numbers.

▶ 1,528,200 feet

In many countries, the comma is a decimal marker, with periods or spaces used for large numbers (1.528.200 meters or 1 528 200 meters). A comma may be substituted for the colon in the salutation of a personal **letter** or **e-mail**. Do not, however, use a comma in the salutation of a formal business letter or e-mail, even if you use the person's first name.

▶ Dear Marie, [personal letter or e-mail]

▶ Dear Marie: [formal business letter or e-mail]

Use commas to separate the elements of geographic names.

▶ Toronto, Ontario, Canada

Use a comma to separate names that are reversed (*Smith, Alvin*), and use commas with professional **abbreviations**.

▶ Jim Rogers Jr., M.D., chaired the conference. [*Jr.* or *Sr.* does not require a comma.]

Using with Other Punctuation

Conjunctive adverbs (*however, nevertheless, consequently, for example, on the other hand*) that join independent clauses are preceded by a **semicolon** and followed by a comma. Such adverbs function both as **modifiers** and as connectives.

▶ The idea is good; *however,* our budget is not sufficient.

As shown earlier in this entry, use semicolons rather than commas to separate items in a series when the items themselves contain commas. When a comma should follow a phrase or clause that ends with words in parentheses, the comma always appears outside the closing parenthesis.

▶ Although we left late (at 7:30 p.m.), we arrived on time.

Commas always go inside **quotation marks**.

▶ The status display indicates "*ready,*" but the unit requires an additional warm-up period.

Except with abbreviations, a comma should not be used with a **dash**, an **exclamation mark**, a **period**, or a **question mark**.

▶ "Have you finished the project?/" she asked.

Avoiding Unnecessary Commas

C

A number of common writing errors involve placing commas where they do not belong. As stated earlier, such errors often occur because writers assume that a pause in a sentence should be indicated by a comma.

Do not place a comma between a subject and a verb or between a verb and its **object**.

▶ The location of our booth at this year's conference,/ made attracting visitors difficult.

▶ She has often said,/ that one company's failure is another's opportunity.

Do not use a comma between the elements of a compound subject or a compound predicate consisting of only two elements.

▶ The director of the design department,/ and the supervisor of the quality-control section were opposed to the new schedules.

▶ The design director listed five major objections,/ and asked that the new schedule be reconsidered.

Do not include a comma after a coordinating conjunction such as *and* or *but*.

▶ The chairperson formally adjourned the meeting, but,/ the members of the committee continued to argue.

Do not place a comma before the first item or after the last item of a series.

▶ The products we discounted include,/ desks, chairs, and tables.

▶ It was a fast, simple, inexpensive,/ process.

Do not use a comma to separate a prepositional phrase from the rest of the sentence unnecessarily.

▶ We discussed the final report,/ on the new project.

compare / contrast

When you *compare* things, you point out similarities or both similarities and differences. ("We should *compare* both brands before making our choice.") When you *contrast* things, you point out only the differences. ("Their speaking styles *contrast* sharply.") In either case, you compare or contrast only things that are part of a common category.

When *compare* is used to establish a general similarity, it is followed by *to*. ("He *compared* our receiving the grant *to* winning a marathon.") When *compare* is used to indicate a close examination of similarities or differences, it is followed by *with*. ("We *compared* the features of the new copier *with* those of the current one.")

Contrast is normally followed by *with*. ("The new policy *contrasts* sharply *with* the earlier one.") When the **noun** form of *contrast* is used, one speaks of the *contrast between* two things or of one thing being *in contrast to* the other.

comparison

When you are making a comparison, be sure that both or all of the elements being compared are clearly evident to your **reader**.

▶ The Nicom 3 software is better. *than the Nicom 2 software*

The things being compared must be of the same kind.

▶ Hard-side luggage offers more protection than fabric. *luggage*

Be sure to point out the parallels or differences between the things being compared. Do not assume your reader will know what you mean.

▶ Washington is farther from Boston than *it is from* Philadelphia.

A double comparison in the same sentence requires that the first comparison be completed before the second one is stated.

▶ The discovery of electricity was one of the great ~~if not the greatest~~ scientific discoveries in history *, if not the greatest*.

Do not attempt to compare things that are not comparable.

▶ Agricultural experts note that ~~storage space is reduced by~~ *baled hay requires* 40 percent ~~compared with baled~~ *less storage space than loose* hay. [*Storage space* is not comparable to *baled hay*.]

comparison method of development

As a **method of development**, comparison points out similarities and differences between the elements of your subject. The comparison method

C

of development can help **readers** understand a difficult or unfamiliar subject by relating it to a simpler or more familiar one.

You must first determine the basis for the **comparison**. For example, if you were comparing bids from contractors for a remodeling project at your company, you would most likely compare such factors as price, previous experience, personnel qualifications, availability, and completion date. Once you have determined the basis or bases for comparison, you can determine the most effective way to structure your comparison: whole by whole or part by part.

In the *whole-by-whole method*, all the relevant characteristics of one item are examined before all the relevant characteristics of the next item. The descriptions of typical woodworking glues in Figure C–6 are organized according to the whole-by-whole method. This document would be useful for those readers who wish to learn about all types of wood glues.

If your **purpose** is to help readers consider the various characteristics of all the glues, the information might be arranged according to the *part-by-part method of comparison*, in which the relevant features

Glue type 1

Glue type 2

Glue type 3

Glue type 4

White glue is the most useful all-purpose adhesive for light construction, but it cannot be used on projects that will be exposed to moisture, high temperature, or great stress. Wood that is being joined with white glue must remain in a clamp until the glue dries, which takes about 30 minutes.

Aliphatic resin glue has a stronger and more moisture-resistant bond than white glue. It must be used at temperatures above 50 °F. The wood should be clamped for about 30 minutes. . . .

Plastic resin glue is the strongest of the common wood adhesives. It is highly moisture resistant, though not completely waterproof. Sold in powdered form, this glue must be mixed with water and used at temperatures above 70 °F. It is slow setting, and the joint should be clamped for four to six hours. . . .

Contact cement is a very strong adhesive that bonds so quickly it must be used with great care. It is ideal for mounting sheets of plastic laminate on wood. It is also useful for attaching strips of veneer to the edges of plywood. Because this adhesive bonds immediately when two pieces are pressed together, clamping is not necessary, but the parts to be joined must be carefully aligned before being placed together. Most brands are flammable, and the fumes can be harmful if inhaled. To meet current safety standards, this type of glue must be used in a well-ventilated area, away from flames or heat.

FIGURE C–6. Whole-by-Whole Method of Comparison

Woodworking adhesives are rated primarily according to their bonding strength, moisture resistance, and setting time.

Bonding strength is categorized as very strong, moderately strong, or adequate for use with little stress. Contact cement and plastic resin glue bond very strongly, while aliphatic resin glue bonds moderately strongly. White glue provides a bond least resistant to stress.

The *moisture resistance* of woodworking glues is rated as high, moderate, or low. Plastic resin glue and contact cement are highly moisture resistant, aliphatic resin glue is moderately moisture resistant, and white glue is least moisture resistant.

Setting time for the glues varies from an immediate bond to a four-to-six-hour bond. Contact cement bonds immediately and requires no clamping. Because the bond is immediate, surfaces being joined must be carefully aligned before being placed together. White glue and aliphatic resin glue set in 30 minutes; both require clamping to secure the bond. Plastic resin, the strongest wood glue, sets in four to six hours and also requires clamping.

Glue traits

Trait 1

Trait 2

Trait 3

FIGURE C–7. Part-by-Part Method of Comparison

of the items are compared one by one (as shown in Figure C–7). The part-by-part method could accommodate further comparison—such as temperature ranges, special warnings, and common use.

Comparisons can also be made effectively with the use of **tables**, as shown in Figure C–8. The advantage of a table is that it provides a quick reference, allowing readers to see and compare all the information at once. The disadvantage is that a table cannot convey as much related detailed information as a narrative description can.

	White Glue	**Aliphatic Resin Glue**	**Plastic Resin Glue**	**Contact Cement**
Bonding Strength	Low	Moderate	High	High
Moisture Resistance	Low	Moderate	High	High
Setting Time	Thirty minutes	Thirty minutes	Four to six hours	Bonds on contact
Common Uses	Light construction	General purpose	General purpose	Laminate and veneer to wood

FIGURE C–8. Comparison Using a Table to Illustrate Key Differences

complaints

C

A complaint message, sent by **e-mail** or **letter**, describes a problem that the writer requests the recipient to solve. The **tone** of the message is important: If your message is angry and belligerent, you may not be taken seriously. Likewise, immediately posting a complaint to a company's **social media** site or to a public forum might be seen as an attack rather than an honest attempt to work out a problem and reach a resolution. Assume that the recipient will be conscientious in correcting the problem. However, anticipate reader reactions or rebuttals. See **audience** and **correspondence**.

▶ I reviewed my user manual's "Safe Operating Guidelines" carefully before I installed the device. [This assures readers you followed instructions.]

Without such explanations, readers may be tempted to dismiss your complaint. Figure C–9 shows a complaint message that details a billing problem. Although the circumstances and severity of the problem may

---

↱ Send   ✕ Cancel   ▤ Save Draft   ◀|) Add Attachment   ✉ Signature   Options ▶

| **TO** | customerservice@ST3.com |
| **CC** | Show BCC |

Subject | ST3 Diagnostic Scanners

🗋 MKeller_ST3-1179R.pdf   <u>Download</u>

Background — On July 13, I ordered nine ST3 Diagnostic Scanners (order # ST3-1179R). The scanners were ordered from your customer Web site.

Problem — On August 3, I received seven HL monitors from your parts warehouse in Newark, New Jersey. I immediately returned those monitors with a note indicating that a mistake had been made. However, not only have I failed to receive the ST3 scanners that I ordered, but I have also been billed repeatedly for the seven monitors.

Supporting documents and instructions — I have attached a copy of my confirmation e-mail, the shipping form, and the most recent bill. If you cannot send me the scanners I ordered by September 15, please cancel my order.

Sincerely,

Marissa Keller

FIGURE C–9. Complaint Message (Sent as E-mail)

vary, you should generally do the following when composing an effective complaint message:

1. Identify the problem or faulty item(s), and include relevant invoice numbers, part names, and dates.
2. Explain logically, clearly, and specifically what went wrong, especially for a problem with a service. (Avoid guessing why you *think* some problem occurred.)
3. State what you expect the reader to do to solve the problem.
4. Include or attach a copy of the receipt, bill, or contract, or perhaps **photographs** of damaged parts, and keep the original(s) for your records.

Be sure to check the company's Web site for any instructions on submitting a complaint. When you cannot find specific instructions, you may address your complaint to Customer Service for large organizations. In smaller organizations, you might write to a vice president in charge of sales or service, or directly to the owner. Often, a well-written e-mail, followed if necessary by a letter sent through standard mail, will elicit the best response. If you do not receive a timely response to your complaint, try sending it to a different person in the company. See also **adjustment messages** and **refusal letters**.

complement / compliment

Complement means "anything that completes a whole" (see also **complements**). It is used as either a **noun** or a **verb**.

▶ A *complement* of four employees would bring our staff up to its normal level. [noun]

▶ The two programs *complement* one another perfectly. [verb]

Compliment means "praise." It too is used as either a noun or a verb.

▶ The manager's *compliment* boosted staff morale. [noun]

▶ The manager *complimented* the staff on its proposal. [verb]

complements

A complement is a word, **phrase**, or **clause** used in the predicate of a sentence to complete the meaning of the sentence.

▶ Pilots fly *airplanes*. [word]

- To invest is *to risk losses*. [phrase]
- John knew *that he would be late*. [clause]

Four types of complements are generally recognized: direct **object**, indirect object, objective complement, and subjective complement. See also **sentence construction**.

A *direct object* is a **noun** or noun equivalent that receives the action of a transitive **verb**; it answers the question *What?* or *Whom?* after the verb.

- I designed *a Web site*. [noun phrase]
- I like *to work*. [verbal]
- I like *it*. [pronoun]
- I like *what I saw*. [noun clause]

An *indirect object* is a noun or noun equivalent that occurs with a direct object after certain kinds of transitive verbs, such as *give*, *wish*, *cause*, and *tell*. It answers the question *To whom or what?* or *For whom or what?*

- We should buy the *office* a *scanner*. [*Scanner* is the direct object, and *office* is the indirect object.]

An *objective complement* completes the meaning of a sentence by revealing something about the object of its transitive verb. An objective complement may be either a noun or an **adjective**.

- They call him *a genius*. [noun phrase]
- We painted the building *white*. [adjective]

A *subjective complement*, which follows a linking verb rather than a transitive verb, describes the subject. A subjective complement may be either a noun or an adjective.

- His sister is *a consultant*. [noun phrase follows linking verb *is*]
- His brother is *ill*. [adjective follows linking verb *is*]

compose / constitute / comprise

Compose and *constitute* both mean "make up the whole." The parts *compose* or *constitute* the whole. ("The nine offices *compose* the division. Unethical activities *constitute* cause for dismissal.") *Comprise* means "include," "contain," or "consist of." The whole *comprises* the parts. ("The division *comprises* nine offices.")

compound words

A compound word is made from two or more words that function as a single concept. A compound may be hyphenated, written as one word, or written as separate words (*low-level, underestimate, post office*).

If you are not certain whether a compound word should use a **hyphen**, check a dictionary.

Be careful to distinguish between compound words (*greenhouse*) and words that simply appear together but do not constitute compound words (*green house*). For plurals of compound words, generally add *s* to the last letter (*bookcases* and *Web sites*). However, when the first word of the compound is more important to its meaning than the last, the first word takes the *s* (*editors in chief*). Possessives are formed by adding *'s* to the end of the compound word (the *editor in chief's* desk, the *pipeline's* diameter, the *post office's* hours). See also **possessive case**.

conciseness

Concise writing is free of unnecessary words, **phrases**, **clauses**, and sentences without sacrificing **clarity** or appropriate detail. Conciseness is not a synonym for brevity; a long **report** may be concise, while its **abstract** may be brief and concise. Conciseness is always desirable, but brevity may or may not be desirable in a given passage, depending on the writer's **purpose**. (See also **text messaging**.) Although concise sentences are not guaranteed to be effective, wordy sentences always sacrifice some of their readability and **coherence**.

Causes of Wordiness

Modifiers that repeat an idea present or implicit in the word being modified contribute to wordiness by being redundant. See also **reason is [because]**.

basic essentials	*completely* finished
final outcome	*present* status

Coordinated synonyms that merely repeat each other contribute to wordiness.

each and every	*basic and fundamental*
finally and for good	*first and foremost*

Excess qualification also contributes to wordiness.

perfectly clear	*completely* accurate

Expletives, relative **pronouns**, and relative **adjectives**, although they have legitimate purposes, often result in wordiness.

WORDY	*There are* [expletive] many Web designers *who* [relative pronoun] are planning to attend the conference, at *which* [relative adjective] time the committee should meet.
CONCISE	Because many Web designers plan to attend the conference, the committee should meet then.

Circumlocution (a long, indirect way of expressing things) is a leading cause of wordiness. See also **gobbledygook**.

WORDY	The payment to which a subcontractor is entitled should be made promptly so that in the event of a subsequent contractual dispute we, as general contractors, may not be held in default of our contract by virtue of nonpayment.
CONCISE	Pay subcontractors promptly. Then, if a contractual dispute occurs, we cannot be held in default of our contract because of nonpayment.

Balance is important. When conciseness is overdone, writing can become choppy and ambiguous. (See also **telegraphic style**.) Too much conciseness can produce a style that is not only too brief but also too blunt, especially in **correspondence**.

WRITER'S CHECKLIST   **Achieving Conciseness**

Wordiness is understandable when you are **writing a draft**, but it should not survive **revision**.

✔ Use **subordination** to achieve conciseness.

- The financial report was carefully documented, *five-page* ~~and it covered five pages.~~

✔ Avoid **affectation** by using simple words and phrases.

WORDY	It is the policy of the company to provide Internet access to enable employees to conduct the online communication necessary to discharge their responsibilities; such should not be utilized for personal communications or nonbusiness activities.
CONCISE	Employee Internet access should be used only for appropriate company business.

(continued)

WRITER'S CHECKLIST   **Achieving Conciseness** (*continued*)

✔ Eliminate redundancy.

> **WORDY**   Post-installation testing, which is offered to all our customers at no further cost to them whatsoever, is available with each Line Scan System One purchased from this company.
>
> **CONCISE**   Free post-installation testing is offered with each purchase of a Line Scan System One.

✔ Change the passive **voice** to the **active voice** and the indicative **mood** to the imperative mood whenever possible.

> **WORDY**   Bar codes are normally used when an order is intended to be displayed on a monitor, and inventory numbers are normally used when an order is to be placed with the manufacturer.
>
> **CONCISE**   Use bar codes to display the order on a monitor, and use inventory numbers to place the order with the manufacturer.

✔ Eliminate or replace wordy introductory phrases or pretentious words and phrases (*in the case of, it appears that, needless to say*).

REPLACE	WITH
in order to, with a view to	to
due to the fact that, for the reason that, owing to the fact that, the reason for	because
by means of, by using, in connection with, through the use of	by, with
at this time, at this point in time, at present, at the present	now, currently

✔ Do not overuse **intensifiers**, such as *very, more, most, best, quite, great, really,* and *especially*. Instead, provide specific and useful details.

✔ Use the search-and-replace command to locate and revise wordy expressions, including *to be*, and unnecessary helping **verbs**, such as *will*.

conclusions

The conclusion of a document ties the main ideas together and can even clinch a final significant point. This final point may, for example, make a prediction or offer a judgment, summarize key findings, or recommend a course of action. Figure C–10 is a conclusion from a proposal to reduce a company's health-care costs by having the employer

C

Conclusion and Recommendation

Summarizes key points

Enrolling employees in the deluxe program at AeroFitness would allow them to receive a one-month free trial membership. Those interested in continuing could then join the club and receive a 30 percent discount on the $1,200 annual fee and pay only half of the one-time membership fee of $500. The other half of the membership fee ($250) would be paid for by ABO. If employees leave the company, they would have the option of purchasing ABO's share of the membership to continue at AeroFitness or selling their half of the membership to another ABO employee wishing to join AeroFitness.

Points to benefits

Club membership allows employees at all five ABO warehouses to participate in the program. The more employees who participate, the greater the long-term savings in ABO's health-care costs. Overall, implementing this program will help ABO, Inc., reduce its health-care costs while building stronger employee relations by offering employees a desirable benefit. If this proposal is adopted, I have some additional thoughts about publicizing the program to encourage employee participation that I would be pleased to share.

Makes a recommendation

I recommend, therefore, that ABO, Inc., participate in the corporate membership program at AeroFitness Clubs, Inc., by subsidizing employee memberships. Offering this benefit to employees will demonstrate ABO's commitment to the importance of a healthy workforce.

FIGURE C–10. Conclusion

sponsor employee health-club memberships. Notice that it summarizes key points, points to the benefits, and makes a recommendation.

The way you conclude depends on your **purpose**, the needs of your **audience**, and the **context**. For example, a lengthy sales **proposal** might conclude persuasively with a summary of the proposal's salient points and the company's relevant strengths. The following examples are typical concluding strategies.

RECOMMENDATION

Our findings suggest that you need to alter your marketing to adjust to the changing demographics for your products. We recommend that your placement of ads include . . .

SUMMARY

As this report describes, we would attract more recent graduates with the following strategies:

1. Establish our presence on social media to reach college students before they graduate.
2. Increase our attendance at college career fairs.
3. Establish more internships and work-study programs.

JUDGMENT

Based on the scope and degree of the storm's damage, the current construction code for roofing on light industrial facilities is inadequate.

IMPLICATION

Although our estimate calls for a substantially higher budget than in the three previous years, we believe that it is reasonable given our planned expansion.

PREDICTION

Although I have exceeded my original estimate for equipment, I have reduced my labor costs; therefore, I will easily stay within the original bid.

The concluding statement may merely present ideas for consideration, call for action, or deliberately provoke thought.

IDEAS FOR CONSIDERATION

The new prices become effective the first of the year. Price adjustments are routine for the company, but some of your customers will not consider them acceptable. Please bear in mind the needs of both your customers and the company as you implement these price adjustments.

CALL FOR ACTION

Please make a payment of $250 now if you wish to keep your account active. If you have not responded to our previous letters because of some special hardship, I will be glad to work out a solution with you.

THOUGHT-PROVOKING STATEMENT

Can we continue to accept the losses incurred by inefficiency? Or should we take the necessary steps to control it now?

Be especially careful not to introduce a new topic when you conclude. A conclusion should always relate to and reinforce the ideas presented earlier in your writing. Moreover, the conclusion must be consistent with what the **introduction** promised the report would examine (its purpose) and how it would do so (its method).

For guidance about the location of the conclusions section in a report, see **formal reports**. For short closings, see **correspondence** and entries on specific types of documents throughout this book.

conjunctions

A conjunction connects words, **phrases**, or **clauses** and can also indicate the relationship between the elements it connects.

Coordinating conjunctions join two sentence elements that have identical functions. The coordinating conjunctions are *and*, *but*, *or*, *for*, *nor*, *yet*, and *so*.

▶ Nature *and* technology affect petroleum prices. [joins two **nouns**]

▶ To hear *and* to listen are two different things. [joins two phrases]

▶ I would like to include the survey, *but* that would make the report too long. [joins two clauses]

Coordinating conjunctions in the titles of books, articles, plays, and movies should not be capitalized unless they are the first or last word in the title.

▶ Our library contains *Consulting and Financial Independence* as well as *So You Want to Be a Consultant?*

Occasionally, a conjunction may begin a sentence; in fact, conjunctions can be strong transitional words and at times can provide **emphasis**. See also **transition**.

▶ I realize that the project is more difficult than expected and that you have encountered staffing problems. *But* we must meet our deadline.

Correlative conjunctions are used in pairs. The correlative conjunctions are *either . . . or*, *neither . . . nor*, *not only . . . but also*, *both . . . and*, and *whether . . . or*.

▶ The auditor will arrive on *either* Wednesday *or* Thursday.

Subordinating conjunctions connect sentence elements of different relative importance, normally independent and dependent clauses. Frequently used subordinating conjunctions are *so*, *although*, *after*, *because*, *if*, *where*, *than*, *since*, *as*, *unless*, *before*, *that*, *though*, and *when*.

▶ I left the office *after* I had finished the report.

Conjunctive adverbs function as conjunctions because they join two independent clauses. The most common conjunctive **adverbs** are *however, moreover, therefore, further, then, consequently, besides, accordingly, also,* and *thus.*

▶ The engine performed well in the laboratory; *however,* it failed under road conditions.

connotation / denotation

The *denotations* of a word are its literal meanings, as defined in a dictionary. The *connotations* of a word are its meanings and associations beyond its literal definitions. For example, the denotations of *Hollywood* are "a district of Los Angeles" and "the U.S. movie industry as a whole"; for many people, its connotations are "glamour, opulence, and superficiality."

Often words have particular connotations for **audiences** within professional groups and organizations. Choose words with both the most accurate denotations and the most appropriate connotations for the **context**. See also **defining terms** and **word choice**.

consensus

Because *consensus* means "harmony of opinion" among most of those in a group, the phrases *consensus of opinion* and *general consensus* defeat **conciseness**. The word *consensus* can be used to refer only to a group.

▶ The ~~general~~ consensus ~~of opinion~~ among investors is that the board of directors should be replaced.

context

Context is the environment or circumstances in which writers produce documents and within which readers interpret the meanings of those documents, whether they are **reports** or **correspondence**. This entry considers the significance of context for workplace writing and suggests how you can be aware of it as you write. See also **audience**.

The context for any document is determined by interrelated events or circumstances both inside and outside an organization. For example, when you write a **proposal** to fund a project within your company,

C

the economic condition of that company is part of the context that will determine how your proposal is received. If the company has recently laid off a dozen employees, its management may not be inclined to approve a proposal to expand its operations—regardless of how well the proposal is written.

When you correspond with someone, the events that prompted you to write shape the context of the message and affect what you say and how you say it. If you write to a customer in response to a complaint, for example, the **tone** and approach of your message will be determined by the context—what you find when you investigate the issue. Is your company fully or partly at fault? Has the customer incorrectly used a product? contributed to a problem? (See also **adjustment messages**.) If you write **instructions** for staff members who must use high-volume document-processing equipment, other questions will reveal the context. What are the lighting and other physical conditions near the equipment? Will these physical conditions affect the **layout and design** of the instructions? What potential safety issues might the users encounter?

Assessing Context

Each time you write, the context needs to be clearly in your mind so that your document will achieve its **purpose**. The following questions are starting points to help you become aware of the context, how it will influence your approach and your readers' interpretation of what you have written, and how it will affect the decisions you need to make during the writing process. See also "Five Steps to Successful Writing" (page xvii).

- What is your professional relationship with your readers, and how might that affect the tone, **style**, and **scope** of your writing?

- What is "the story" behind the immediate reason you are writing— that is, what series of events or perhaps previous documents led to your need to write?

- What is the preferred medium of your readers, and which medium is best suited to your purpose? See also **selecting the medium**.

- What specific factors (such as competition, finance, and regulation) are important to your organization or department?

- What is the corporate culture in which your readers work, and what are the key values found in its mission statement?

- What current events within or outside an organization or a department may influence how readers interpret your writing?

- What national cultural differences might affect your readers' expectations or interpretations of the document? See also **global communication**.

As these questions suggest, context is specific each time you write and often involves the history of a specific organization or your past dealings with individual readers.

Signaling Context

Because context is so important, remind your reader in some way of the context for your writing, as in the following opening for a cover message to a proposal. (See **cover messages**.)

> ▶ During our meeting last week on improving quality, you mentioned that we have previously required usability testing only for documents going to high-profile clients because of the costs involved. The idea occurred to me that we might try less extensive usability testing for many of our other clients. Because you asked for suggestions, I have proposed in the attached document a method of limited usability testing for a broad range of clients in order to improve overall quality while keeping costs at a minimum.

Of course, as described in **introductions**, providing context for a reader may require only a brief background statement or short reminders.

> ▶ Several weeks ago, a financial adviser noticed a recurring problem in the software developed by CGF Systems. Specifically, error messages repeatedly appeared when, in fact, no specific trouble . . .

> ▶ Jane, as I promised in my e-mail yesterday, I've attached the personnel budget estimates for the next fiscal year.

As the last example suggests, provide context for attachments to **e-mail**.

continual / continuous

Continual implies "happening over and over" or "frequently repeated." ("Writing well requires *continual* practice.") *Continuous* implies "occurring without interruption" or "unbroken." ("The *continuous* roar of the machinery was deafening.")

contractions

A contraction is a shortened spelling of a word or phrase, with an **apostrophe** substituting for the missing letter or letters (*cannot / can't*; *have not / haven't*; *it is / it's*). Contractions are often used in speech and informal writing; they are generally not appropriate in **reports**, **proposals**, and formal **correspondence**. See also **business writing style**.

C

copyrights, patents, and trademarks

This entry offers advice for writers both in the classroom and in the workplace related to copyrights, patents, and trademarks. See also **plagiarism** and **visuals**.

Copyrights

Copyright establishes legal protection for original works of authorship, including literary, dramatic, musical, artistic, and other intellectual works in printed or electronic form; it gives the copyright owner exclusive rights to reproduce, distribute, perform, or display a work. Copyright protects all original works of authorship from the moment of their creation, regardless of whether they are published or contain a notice of copyright (©).

❖ **ETHICS NOTE** If you plan to reproduce copyrighted material in your own publication or on your Web site, you must obtain permission from the copyright holder unless one of the following exceptions applies. To do otherwise is a violation of U.S. law. ❖

Permissions.   To seek permission to reproduce copyrighted material, you must contact the copyright holder. In some cases, it is the author; in other cases, it is the publisher of the work. For Web sites, read the site's "terms-of-use" information (if available), and **e-mail** your request to the appropriate party. State specifically which portion of the work you wish to reproduce and how you plan to use it. The copyright holder has the right to charge a fee and specify conditions and limits of use.

Exceptions.   Some material—including text, **visuals**, and digital forms— may be reproduced without permission. The rules governing copyright can be complex, so it is prudent to carefully check the copyright status of anything you plan to reproduce.

- *Fair use.* A small amount of material from a copyrighted source may be used for educational purposes (such as classroom hand-outs), commentary, criticism, news reporting, and scholarly reports without permission or payment as long as the use satisfies the "fair-use" criteria, as described at the U.S. Copyright Office Web site, www.copyright.gov. Whether a particular use qualifies as fair use depends on all the circumstances.

- *Company boilerplate.* In the workplace, employees often borrow material freely from in-house manuals and reports, as well as other company documents, to save time and ensure consistency. Using such "boilerplate," or "repurposed," material is not a copyright violation because the company is considered the author of works prepared by its employees on the job. See also **repurposing**.

- *Public domain material.* Works created by or for the U.S. government and not classified or otherwise protected are in the public domain—that is, they are not copyrighted. The same is true for older written works when their copyright has lapsed or never existed. Be aware that some otherwise public domain works may include "value-added" features—such as introductions, visuals, and indexes—that may be copyrighted separately from the original work and thus may require permission.

- *Copyleft Web material.* Some public access Web sites, such as Wikipedia, follow the "copyleft" principle and grant permission to freely copy, distribute, or modify material so long as the modified material is also made freely available on the same basis.*

❖ **ETHICS NOTE** The Internet has changed the face of copyright, creating an illusion of universal access to online material, when in fact permission is often required to alter or use it in any way. Alternative forms of permissions—like those offered by Creative Commons—allow users to freely incorporate specific content into their documents and to license their own original content. Still, even when you use material that may be reproduced or published without permission, you must give appropriate credit to the source from which the material was taken, as described in **documenting sources** and **plagiarism**. ❖

Patents

The United States Patent and Trademark Office (USPTO) defines a patent as an intellectual property right granted by the U.S. government to an inventor for a limited time in exchange for public disclosure of the invention when the patent is granted. U.S. patents differ from copyright in that they protect inventions rather than written, musical, and artistic works.

The USPTO grants three types of patents.

- *Design patents* cover the invention of new designs for manufactured items (for example, a design for a mobile phone, desk chair, or car hood) and are valid for fourteen years.

- *Plant patents* cover inventions for new plant varieties (for example, an ornamental shrub or a disease-resistant orange tree) and are valid for twenty years.

---

*"Copyleft" is a play on the word *copyright* and is the effort to free materials from many of the restrictions of copyright. See http://en.wikipedia.org/wiki/Copyleft.

C

- *Utility patents* cover inventions of machinery, manufacturing processes, or new materials (for example, a personal three-dimensional printer, composite material for a car bumper, or a technique to mine the seabed for minerals) and are valid for twenty years.

To obtain information about international patents, links to patent offices around the world, and tutorials on patent laws in different countries and regions, visit the global online patent resource the Lens at www .lens.org.

Trademarks

A trademark is a word, phrase, graphic symbol, logo, or some other device that identifies and distinguishes the goods of one merchant or manufacturer from those of others. The two primary marks are trademarks and service marks.

- *Trademarks* identify physical commodities (automobiles, computers, shoes) distributed through interstate commerce.

- *Service marks* identify services (the preparation and sale of food, the provision of transportation or lodging, the sale of life or health insurance).

The term *trademark* is often used to refer to both trademarks and service marks.*

Trademarks for goods and services registered with the USPTO include the ® symbol or the phrase "Reg. U.S. Pat. & TM off." The phrase "Patent Pending" on a manufactured item means that the inventor has

FIGURE C–11. Sample Trademarks

*The USPTO registers other less frequently used types of marks that have different registration requirements than trademarks and service marks: certification marks, collective marks, collective trademarks, and collective service marks. These are described at www.uspto.gov.

applied for a patent on the item. Before trademarks are registered with the USPTO, service providers commonly use the superscript symbol ^{SM}. Trademark names must be capitalized. When citing a trademark, include the superscript trademark symbol ® if it's used in the trademark name.

To obtain additional information about patents and trademarks, go to the FAQ page of the U.S. Patent and Trademark Office Web site at www.uspto.gov/learning-and-resources/general-faqs.

---

correspondence

DIRECTORY

Correspondence in the workplace—whether through **e-mail**, **letters**, **memos**, or another medium—requires many of the steps described in "Five Steps to Successful Writing" (page xvii). As you prepare even a simple e-mail, for example, you might study previous messages (**research**) and then list or arrange the points you wish to cover (**organization**) in an order that is logical for your readers. See also **selecting the medium**.

Corresponding with others in the workplace also requires that you focus on both establishing and maintaining a positive working relationship with your readers and conveying a professional image of yourself and your organization. See also **audience**.

Audience and Writing Style

Effective correspondence uses an appropriate conversational style. To achieve that style, imagine your reader sitting across from you and write to the reader as if you were talking face to face. Take into account your reader's needs and feelings. Ask yourself, "How might I feel if I received this letter or e-mail?" and then tailor your message accordingly. Remember, an impersonal and unfriendly message to a customer or client can tarnish the image of you and your business, but a thoughtful and sincere one can enhance it.

Whether you use a formal or an informal writing style depends entirely on your reader and your **purpose**. You might use an informal (or casual) style, for example, with a colleague you know well and a formal (or restrained) style with a client you have not met.

C

CASUAL	It worked! The new process is better than we had dreamed.
RESTRAINED	You will be pleased to know that the new process is more effective than we expected.

You will probably find yourself using the restrained style more frequently than the casual style. Remember that an overdone attempt to sound casual or friendly can sound insincere. However, do not adopt so formal a style that your writing reads like a legal contract. **Affectation** not only will irritate and baffle readers but also can waste time and produce costly errors.

AFFECTED	Per yesterday's discussion, we no longer possess an original copy of the brochure requested. Please be advised that a PDF copy is attached herewith to this e-mail.
IMPROVED	We are out of printed copies of the brochure we discussed yesterday, so I am attaching a PDF copy to this e-mail.

The improved version is not only clearer and less stuffy but also more concise. See also **business writing style** and **conciseness**.

Openings and Closings

The opening of any correspondence should identify the subject and often the main point of the message.

▶ Attached is the final installation report, which I hope you can review by Monday, December 14. You will notice that the report includes . . .

When your reader is not familiar with the subject or background of a problem, you may provide an introductory paragraph before stating the main point of the message. Doing so is especially important in correspondence that will serve as a record of crucial information. Generally, long or complex subjects benefit most from more thorough **introductions**. However, even when you are writing a short message about a familiar subject, remind readers of the **context**. In the following example, words that provide context are shown in *italics*.

▶ *As Maria recommended*, I reviewed the office reorganization plan. I like most of the features; however, the location of the receptionist and assistant . . .

Do not state the main point first when (1) readers are likely to be highly skeptical or (2) key readers, such as managers or clients, may disagree with your position. In those cases, a more persuasive tactic is to state the problem or issue first, then present the specific points supporting your final recommendation, as is discussed under the heading "indirect pattern" (page 114). See also **persuasion**.

Your closing can accomplish many important tasks, such as building positive relationships with readers, encouraging colleagues and employees, letting recipients know what you will do or what you expect of them, and stating any assignment deadlines.

► I will discuss the problem with the marketing consultant and let you know by Wednesday (August 5) what we are able to change.

Routine statements are sometimes unavoidable. ("If you have further questions, please let me know.") However, try to make your closing work for you by providing specific prompts to which the reader can respond. See also **conclusions**.

► Thanks again for the report, and let me know if you want me to send you a copy of the test results.

Goodwill and the "You" Viewpoint

Write concisely, but do not be so blunt that you risk losing the reader's goodwill. Responding to a vague written request with "Your request was unclear" or "I don't understand" could offend your reader. Instead, establish goodwill to encourage your reader to provide the information you need.

► I will be glad to help, but I need additional information to locate the report you requested. Specifically, can you give me the report's title, release date, or number?

Although this version is a bit longer, it is more tactful and will elicit a helpful response. See also **telegraphic style**.

You can also build goodwill by emphasizing the reader's needs or benefits. Suppose you received a refund request from a customer who forgot to include the receipt with the request. In a response to that customer, you might write the following:

WEAK   We must receive the sales receipt before we can process a refund. [The writer's needs are emphasized: "*We* must."]

If you consider how to keep the customer's goodwill, you could word the request this way:

IMPROVED   Please send the sales receipt so that we can process your refund. [Although polite, the sentence still focuses on the writer's needs: "so that *we* can process."]

You can put the reader's needs and interests foremost by writing from the reader's perspective. Often, doing so means using the words *you* and *your* rather than *we*, *our*, *I*, and *mine*—a technique called the **"you" viewpoint**. Consider the following revision:

EFFECTIVE	So that you can receive your refund promptly, please mail or fax the sales receipt. [The reader's needs are emphasized with *you* and *your*.]

This revision stresses the reader's benefit and interest. By emphasizing the reader's needs, the writer will be more likely to accomplish the purpose: to get the reader to act. See also **positive writing**.

If overdone, however, goodwill and the "you" viewpoint can produce writing that is fawning and insincere. Messages that are full of excessive praise and inflated language may be ignored—or even resented—by the reader.

EXCESSIVE PRAISE	You are just the kind of astute client that deserves the finest service that we can offer—and you deserve our best deal. Understanding how carefully you make decisions, I know you'll think about the advantages of using our consulting service.
REASONABLE	From our earlier correspondence, I understand your need for reliable service. We strive to give all our priority clients our full attention, and after you have reviewed our proposal, I am confident you will appreciate our "five-star" consulting option.

WRITER'S CHECKLIST   **Using Tone to Build Goodwill**

Use the following guidelines to achieve a **tone** that builds goodwill with your recipients.

✔ Be respectful, not demanding.

DEMANDING	Submit your answer in one week.
RESPECTFUL	I would appreciate your answer within one week.

✔ Be modest, not arrogant.

ARROGANT	My attached report is thorough, and I'm sure that you won't be able to continue without it.
MODEST	The attached report contains details of the refinancing options that I hope you will find useful.

✔ Be polite, not sarcastic.

SARCASTIC	I just now received the shipment we ordered six months ago. I'm sending it back—we can't use it now. Thanks a lot!
POLITE	I am returning the shipment we ordered on March 12. Unfortunately, it arrived too late for us to be able to use it.

(continued)

WRITER'S CHECKLIST   **Using Tone to Build Goodwill** (*continued*)

✔   Be positive and tactful, not negative and condescending.

NEGATIVE   Your complaint about our prices is way off target. Our prices are definitely not any higher than those of our competitors.

TACTFUL   Thank you for your suggestion concerning our prices. We believe, however, that our prices are comparable to those of our competitors.

Direct and Indirect Patterns

Direct Pattern.   The direct pattern is effective in workplace correspondence because readers appreciate messages that get to the main point quickly. The direct pattern shown in the following list also accomplishes the goals described on pages 110–11.

1. Main point of message
2. Explanation of facts or details
3. Goodwill closing

The direct pattern is especially appropriate for presenting good news, as shown in Figure C–12. This message presents the good news in the opening (the main point), follows with an explanation of the facts, and closes by looking toward the future (goodwill). The direct pattern may

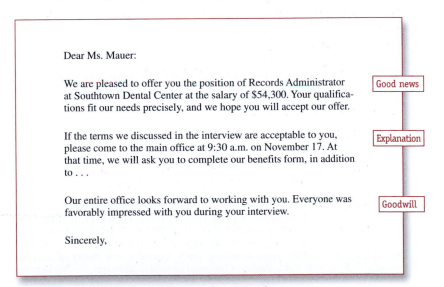

Dear Ms. Mauer:

We are pleased to offer you the position of Records Administrator at Southtown Dental Center at the salary of $54,300. Your qualifications fit our needs precisely, and we hope you will accept our offer.   **Good news**

If the terms we discussed in the interview are acceptable to you, please come to the main office at 9:30 a.m. on November 17. At that time, we will ask you to complete our benefits form, in addition to . . .   **Explanation**

Our entire office looks forward to working with you. Everyone was favorably impressed with you during your interview.   **Goodwill**

Sincerely,

FIGURE C–12. A Direct-Pattern Message (Good News)

C

also be appropriate for negative messages in situations where little is at stake for the writer or reader and the reasons for the negative message are relatively unimportant.

▶ Dear Mr. Coleman:

   We do not have the part you requested currently in stock, but we hope to have it within the next month. Our supplier, who has been reliable in the past, assures us that the manufacturer that produces those parts will be able . . . [Continues with details and goodwill closing.]

Indirect Pattern.   The indirect pattern delays stating the main point and may be effective when you need to present especially sensitive or negative messages. Research has shown that people form their impressions and attitudes very early when reading correspondence. For this reason, presenting bad news, refusals, or sensitive messages *indirectly* is often more effective than presenting negative information directly, especially if the stakes are high.* See also **refusal letters**.

   As with any type of writing, imagine how your audience will react to your message. Consider the thoughtlessness in the job rejection that follows:

▶ Dear Ms. Mauer:

   Your application for the position of Records Administrator at Southtown Dental Center has been rejected. We found someone more qualified than you.

   Sincerely,

Although the message is concise and uses the pronouns *you* and *your*, the writer has not considered how the recipient will feel as she reads the message. The message is, in short, rude. The pattern of this message is (1) bad news, (2) curt explanation, (3) close.

   The indirect pattern for such bad-news correspondence allows the explanation or details to lead logically and tactfully to the negative message, as in the following pattern:

1. Context of message
2. Explanation or details
3. Bad news or negative message
4. Goodwill closing

The opening (traditionally called a "buffer") should provide a context for the subject and establish a professional tone. However, it must not

*Alred, G. J. (1993). "We regret to inform you": Toward a new theory of negative messages. In B. R. Sims (Ed.), *Studies in technical communication* (pp. 17–36). Urbana, IL: U of North Texas & NCTE.

mislead the reader to believe that good news may follow, and it must not contain irrelevant information.*

The body should provide an explanation by reviewing the details or facts that led to the negative decision or refusal. Give the negative message simply, based on the facts; do not belabor the bad news or provide an inappropriate apology. Neither the details nor an overdone apology can turn bad news into something positive. Your goal should be to establish for the reader that the writer or organization has been *reasonable* given the circumstances. To accomplish this goal, you need to organize the explanation carefully and logically.

The closing should establish or reestablish a positive relationship through goodwill or helpful information. Consider, for example, the revised bad-news message, shown in Figure C–13. This message carries the same disappointing news as the message in the preceding example, but the writer of this message begins by not only introducing the subject but also thanking the reader for her time and effort. Then the writer explains why Ms. Mauer was not accepted for the job and offers her encouragement by looking toward a potential future opportunity. Bad news is never pleasant; however, information that either puts the bad news in perspective or makes the bad news reasonable maintains respect between the writer and the reader. The goodwill closing reestablishes an amicable professional relationship.

The indirect pattern can also be used in relatively short e-mail messages and memos. Consider the unintended secondary message a manager conveys in the following notice:

WEAK   It has been decided that the office will be open the day after Thanksgiving.

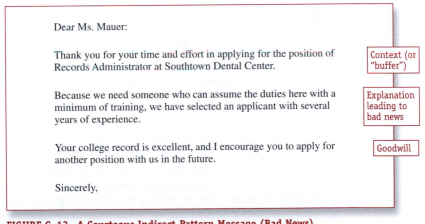

Dear Ms. Mauer:

Thank you for your time and effort in applying for the position of Records Administrator at Southtown Dental Center. — Context (or "buffer")

Because we need someone who can assume the duties here with a minimum of training, we have selected an applicant with several years of experience. — Explanation leading to bad news

Your college record is excellent, and I encourage you to apply for another position with us in the future. — Goodwill

Sincerely,

FIGURE C–13. A Courteous Indirect-Pattern Message (Bad News)

*Locker, K. O. (1999). Factors in reader responses to negative letters: Experimental evidence for changing what we teach. *Journal of Business and Technical Communication, 13*(1), 29.

"It has been decided" not only sounds impersonal but also communicates an authoritarian, management-versus-employee tone. The passive voice also suggests that the decision maker does not want to say "I have decided" and thus accept responsibility for the decision. One solution is to remove the first part of the sentence.

IMPROVED　　The office will be open the day after Thanksgiving.

The best solution, however, would be to suggest that there is a good reason for the decision and that employees are privy to (if not a part of) the decision-making process.

EFFECTIVE　　Because we must meet the December 15 deadline for submitting the Bradley Foundation proposal, the office will be open the day after Thanksgiving.

By describing the context of the bad news first (the need to meet the deadline), the writer focuses on the reasoning behind the decision to work. Employees may not necessarily like the message, but they will at least understand that the decision is not arbitrary and is tied to an important deadline.

Clarity and Emphasis

A clear message is one that is adequately developed and emphasizes your main points. The following example illustrates how adequate development is crucial to the **clarity** of your message.

VAGUE　　　Be more careful on the loading dock.

DEVELOPED　To prevent accidents on the loading dock, follow these procedures:
　　　　　　　1. Check to make sure . . .
　　　　　　　2. Load only items that are rated . . .
　　　　　　　3. Replace any defective parts . . .

Although the first version is concise, it is not as clear and specific as the "developed" revision. Do not assume your readers will know what you mean: vague messages are easily misinterpreted.

Lists.　Vertically stacked words, phrases, and other items distinguished with numbers or bullets can effectively highlight such information as steps in sequence, materials or parts needed, key or concluding points, and recommendations. As described in **lists**, provide context and be careful not to overuse lists. A message that consists almost entirely of lists is difficult to understand because it forces readers to connect separate and disjointed items. Further, lists lose their impact when they are overused.

Headings.　**Headings** are particularly useful because they call attention to main topics, divide material into manageable segments, and signal a

C

shift in subject. Readers can scan the headings and read only the section or sections appropriate to their needs.

Subject Lines. Subject lines for e-mails, memos, and some letters announce the topic and focus of the correspondence. Because they also aid filing and later retrieval, they should be specific and accurate.

VAGUE	Subject: Tuition Reimbursement
VAGUE	Subject: Time-Management Seminar
SPECIFIC	Subject: Tuition Reimbursement for Time-Management Seminar

Capitalize all major words in a subject line. Lowercase articles, prepositions, and conjunctions with fewer than five letters unless they are the first or last words. Remember that the subject line should not substitute for an opening that provides context for the message. See also **titles**.

WRITER'S CHECKLIST   **Correspondence and Accuracy**

✔ Begin by establishing your purpose, analyzing your reader's needs, determining your **scope**, and considering the context.

✔ Prepare an outline, even if it is only a list of points to be covered in the order you want to cover them. (See **outlining**.)

✔ Write the first draft. (See **writing a draft**.)

✔ Allow for a cooling-off period prior to **revision** or seek a colleague's advice, especially for correspondence that addresses a problem.

✔ Revise the draft, checking for key problems in clarity and **coherence**.

✔ Use the appropriate or standard format for letters, memos, and so forth.

✔ Check for accuracy: make sure that all facts, figures, and dates are correct.

✔ Use effective **proofreading** techniques to check your **punctuation**, **grammar**, **spelling**, and appropriate **usage**.

✔ Consider who should receive a copy of the message and in what order the names or e-mail addresses should be listed (alphabetize if rank does not apply).

✔ Remember that when you send a message or sign a letter, you are accepting responsibility for it.

---

cover messages (or transmittals)

A cover **e-mail**, **memo**, or **letter** accompanies a document (such as a **proposal**), a digitial file, or other material. It identifies an item that is being sent, the person to whom it is being sent, the reason that it is being sent, and any content that should be highlighted for **readers**. (See **purpose**.)

C

| → Send | ✕ Cancel | 📄 Save Draft | 📎 Add Attachment | ✉ Signature | Options ▶ |

TO	AHammersmith@IDC.com
CC		Show BCC
Subject	Annual Energy Estimate Report
📄 AnnualEnergyEstimate.sc.pdf	**Download**

Dear Mr. Hammersmith:

Provides context

Attached is the report estimating our energy needs for the year as requested by John Brenan, Vice President, on September 5.

Describes attachment

The report is a result of several meetings with the manager of plant operations and her staff and an extensive survey of all our employees. The survey was delayed by the transfer of key staff in Building A. However, the report will provide the information you need in order to furnish us with a cost estimate for the installation of your Mark II Energy Saving System.

Closes with thanks and offer

We would like to thank Diana Biel of ESI for her assistance in preparing the survey. If you need any more information, please let me know.

Best wishes,

Sophia Crane

FIGURE C–14. Cover Message

A cover message (or transmittal) provides a permanent record for both the writer and the reader. For cover messages accompanying **résumés**, see **application cover letters**.

The cover message shown in Figure C–14 is concise, but it also includes such details as how the information for the **report** was gathered.

credible / creditable

Something is *credible* if it is believable. ("The statistics in this report are *credible*.") Something is *creditable* if it is worthy of praise or credit. ("The accountant did a *creditable* job.")

critique

A *critique* is a written or an oral evaluation of something. Avoid using *critique* as a **verb** meaning "criticize."

▶ Please ~~critique~~ his job description.
    prepare a   *of*

D

dangling modifiers

Phrases that do not clearly and logically refer to the correct **noun** or **pronoun** are called *dangling modifiers*. Dangling modifiers usually appear at the beginning of a sentence as an introductory **phrase**.

DANGLING   *While eating lunch*, the computer malfunctioned. [*Who was eating lunch?*]

CORRECT   While *I* was eating lunch, the computer malfunctioned.

Dangling modifiers can appear at the end of the sentence as well.

DANGLING   The program gains efficiency *by eliminating the superfluous coding*. [*Who* eliminates the superfluous coding?]

CORRECT   The program gains efficiency *when you* eliminate the superfluous coding.

To correct a dangling modifier, add the appropriate subject to either the dangling modifier or the main **clause**.

DANGLING   After finishing the research, the proposal was easy to write. [The appropriate subject is *I*, but it is not stated in either the dangling phrase or the main clause.]

CORRECT   After *I* finished the research, the proposal was easy to write. [The pronoun *I* is now the subject of an introductory clause.]

CORRECT   After finishing the research, *I* found the proposal easy to write. [The pronoun *I* is now the subject of the main clause.]

For a discussion of misplaced modifiers, see **modifiers**.

D

dashes

The em dash (—), usually called just the "dash," can perform all the punctuation duties of linking, separating, and enclosing. The dash is indicated by two consecutive **hyphens** that may auto-correct to a dash, depending on the program settings.*

Use the dash cautiously to indicate more **emphasis**, informality, or abruptness than the other punctuation marks would show. A dash can emphasize a sharp turn in thought.

▶ The project will end May 13—unless we receive additional funding.

A dash can indicate an emphatic pause.

▶ The project will begin—after we are under contract.

Sometimes, to emphasize contrast, a dash is used with *but*.

▶ We completed the survey quickly—*but* the results were not accurate.

A dash can be used before a final summarizing statement or before repetition that has the effect of an afterthought.

▶ It was hot near the heat-treating ovens—steaming hot.

Such a statement may also complete the meaning of the **clause** preceding the dash.

▶ We try to write as we speak—or so we believe.

Dashes set off parenthetical elements more sharply and emphatically than **commas** do. Unlike dashes, **parentheses** tend to deemphasize what they enclose. Compare the following sentences:

▶ Only one person—the president—can authorize such activity.

▶ Only one person, the president, can authorize such activity.

▶ Only one person (the president) can authorize such activity.

Dashes can be used to set off parenthetical elements that contain commas. The first word after a dash is capitalized only if it is a proper **noun**.

▶ Three of the applicants—John Evans, Rosalita Fontiana, and Kyong-Shik Choi—seem well qualified for the job.

*In publishing and HTML coding, the term *em dash* and other terms or codes are often used for dashes, hyphens, and related special characters. For detailed discussions, see *The Chicago Manual of Style*, Seventeenth Edition (sections 6.75–6.94), or a reputable HTML guide, such as the *Web Style Guide*, Fourth Edition (Yale University Press, 2016).

The dash can also indicate the omission of letters. ("Mr. A—admitted his error.")

Another type of dash is the en dash (–), which is used between letters and numbers to indicate *to* or *through* (*pages 84–92, the years 2015–2018, the letters A–Z, the Detroit–Toledo Expressway*).

D

data

In formal and scholarly writing, *data* is generally used as a plural, with *datum* as the singular form. In much informal writing, however, *data* is considered a collective singular **noun**. Base your **usage** on whether your readers are likely to consider the data as a single collection or as a group of individual facts. Whatever you use, be sure that your **pronouns** and **verbs** agree in number with the selected usage. See also **agreement**.

▶ These *data are* persuasive. *They indicate* a need for additional research questions. [formal]

▶ The attached *data is* confidential. *It is* the result of a survey of employee records. [less formal]

dates

In the United States, full dates are generally written in the month-day-year format, with a comma preceding and following the year.

▶ November 30, 2025, is the payoff date.

Do not use **commas** in the day-month-year format, which is used in many parts of the world and by the U.S. military.

▶ Note that 30 November 2025 is the payoff date.

No commas are used when showing only the month-year or month-day in a date.

▶ The target date of May 2020 is optimistic, so I would like to meet on March 4 to discuss our options.

When writing days of the month without the year, use the cardinal number ("March 4") rather than the ordinal number ("March 4th"). Of course, in speech or **presentations**, use the ordinal number ("March fourth").

Avoid the strictly numerical form for dates (11/6/18) because the date is not always immediately clear, especially in **international correspondence**. In many countries, 11/6/18 means June 11, 2018, rather than

D

November 6, 2018. Writing out the name of the month makes the entire date immediately clear to all readers.

Centuries often cause confusion with **numbers** because their spelled-out forms, which are not capitalized, do not correspond to their numeral designations. The twentieth century, for example, is the 1900s: 1900–1999.

When the century is used as a **noun**, do not use a **hyphen** between the number and the word *century*.

▶ During the twenty-first century, technology transformed business practices.

When the centuries are written as **adjectives**, however, use hyphens.

▶ Twenty-first-century technology relies on innovation.

de facto / de jure

De facto means that something exists or is a fact and therefore is accepted for practical purposes. *De jure* means that something legally exists.

▶ The law states that no signs should be erected along Highway 127. Storeowners have disregarded that law, and many signs exist along Highway 127. The presence of the signs along Highway 127 is *de facto* but not *de jure*—their presence is "a fact," but it is not "lawful."

Limit the use of Latin and legal terms because they can easily become an **affectation**.

defective / deficient

If something is *defective*, it is faulty. ("The wiring was *defective*.") If something is *deficient*, it is lacking or is incomplete in an essential component. ("The firm was *deficient* in meeting its legal obligations.")

defining terms

Defining key terms and concepts is often essential for **clarity**. Terms can be defined either formally or informally, depending on your **purpose**, your **audience**, and the **context**.

A *formal definition* is a form of classification. You define a term by placing it in a category and then identifying the features that distinguish it from other members of the same category.

TERM	CATEGORY	DISTINGUISHING FEATURES
An *auction* is	a public sale	in which property passes to the highest bidder through successively increased offers.

An *informal definition* explains a term by giving a more familiar word or phrase as a **synonym**.

▶ Businesses can have *symbiotic*, or *mutually beneficial*, relationships with their competitors and partners.

State definitions positively; focus on what the term *is* rather than what it is not.

NEGATIVE   In a legal transaction, *real property* is not personal property.

POSITIVE   *Real property* is legal terminology for the right or interest a person has in land and the permanent structures on that land.

For a discussion of when negative definitions are appropriate, see **definition method of development**.

Avoid circular definitions, which merely restate the term to be defined.

CIRCULAR   *Spontaneous combustion* is fire that begins spontaneously.

REVISED   *Spontaneous combustion* is the self-ignition of a flammable material through a chemical reaction.

In addition, avoid "is when" and "is where" definitions. Such definitions fail to include the category and are too indirect.

a binding agreement between two or more parties.

▶ A *contract* is ~~when two or more parties agree to something.~~

definite / definitive

Definite and *definitive* both apply to what is precisely defined, but *definitive* more often refers to what is complete and authoritative. ("Once we receive a *definite* proposal, our attorney can provide a *definitive* legal opinion.")

definition method of development

Definition is often essential to **clarity** and accuracy. Although **defining terms** may be sufficient, sometimes definitions need to be expanded through (1) extended definition, (2) definition by analogy, (3) definition by cause, (4) definition by components, (5) definition by exploration of origin, and (6) negative definition. See also **methods of development**.

Extended Definition

When you need more than a simple definition to explain an idea, use an extended definition, which explores a number of qualities of the item being defined. How an extended definition is developed depends on your **audience** and on the complexity of the subject. Readers familiar with a topic might be able to handle a long, fairly complex definition, whereas readers less familiar with a topic might require simpler language and more basic information.

The easiest way to give an extended definition is with specific examples. Examples give readers easy-to-picture details that help them see and thus understand the term being defined.

> ▶ Form, which is the shape of landscape features, can best be represented both by small-scale features, such as *trees* and *shrubs*, and by large-scale elements, such as *mountains* and *mountain ranges*.

Definition by Analogy

An analogy can help a nonspecialist understand an unfamiliar term by showing its similarities with a more familiar term. In the following description of "management by objective," notice how the writer develops an analogy to make a point.

> ▶ Management by objective has been quite popular, but the key to its success is carefully selecting objectives. Think, for example, of a golfer who wishes to improve by hitting the ball farther. Every decision the golfer makes is governed by that goal—hitting the ball as far as possible. The golfer is thus managing the game by objective. However, the golfer is shortsighted because golf is as much a game of accuracy as it is of hitting balls for distance. In fact, some of the decisions the golfer makes to hit the ball farther might well be counterproductive to achieving the larger goal of obtaining the lowest possible score. Likewise, when a company decides to use a management-by-objective strategy, it must be certain that the objective is appropriate for achieving the desired results.

Definition by Cause

Some terms are best defined by an explanation of their causes, as the following explanation of the term *stagflation* illustrates.

▶ Traditional economic theory says that a decline in business activity and employment causes the rate of inflation to decrease. However, in the 1970s, because of massive increases in energy prices, the economy stagnated while higher energy prices worked their way into the cost of virtually everything, and the currency inflated. To describe that condition, economist Paul Samuelson coined the term *stagflation*.

Definition by Components

Sometimes a formal definition of a concept can be made simpler by breaking the concept into its component parts. In the following example, the formal definition of *fire* is given in the first paragraph, and the component parts are given in the second.

FORMAL DEFINITION	Fire is the visible heat energy released from the rapid oxidation of a fuel. A substance is "on fire" when the release of heat energy from the oxidation process reaches visible light levels.
COMPONENT PARTS	The classic fire triangle illustrates the elements necessary to create fire: *oxygen*, *heat*, and *burnable material* (*fuel*). Air provides sufficient oxygen for combustion; the intensity of the heat needed to start a fire depends on the characteristics of the burnable material. A burnable substance is one that will sustain combustion after an initial application of heat to start the combustion.

Definition by Exploration of Origin

Under certain circumstances, the meaning of a term can be clarified and made easier to remember by an exploration of its origin. Medical terms, because of their sometimes unfamiliar Greek and Latin roots, especially benefit from an explanation of this type. Tracing the derivation of a word can also be useful when you want to explain why a word has favorable or unfavorable associations, particularly if your goal is to influence your reader's attitude toward an idea or activity. See also **persuasion**.

▶ Efforts to influence legislation generally fall under the head of *lobbying*, a term that once referred to people who prowled the lobbies of houses of government, buttonholing lawmakers and trying to get them to take certain positions. Lobbying today is all of this, and much more, too. It is a respected—and necessary—activity. It tells the legislator which way the winds of public opinion are blowing, and it helps inform [legislators] of the implications of certain bills, debates, and resolutions [that they must face].

—Bill Vogt, *How to Build a Better Outdoors*

D Negative Definition

In some cases, it is useful to point out what something is *not* in order to clarify what it is. A negative definition is effective only when the reader is familiar with the item with which the defined item is being contrasted. In a crane operator's manual, for instance, a negative definition is used to show that, for safety reasons, a hydraulic crane cannot be operated in the same manner as a lattice boom crane.

▶ A hydraulic crane is *not* like a lattice boom crane [a friction machine] in one very important way. In most cases, the safe lifting capacity of a lattice boom crane is based on the *weight needed to tip the machine*. Therefore, operators of friction machines sometimes depend on signs that the machine might tip to warn them of impending danger. This practice is very dangerous with a hydraulic crane.

—*Operator's Manual* (Model W-180), Harnischfeger Corporation

description

The key to effective description is the accurate presentation of details, as in Figures D–1 and D–2. In Figure D–1, notice that the simple description contained in the purchase order includes five specific details (in addition to the part number), structured logically.

Shopping Cart				
				Continue shopping Print shopping cart

Part No.	Description	Quantity	Item Price	Total
IW 8421	Infectious-waste bags, 12″ × 14″, heavy-gauge polyethylene, red double closures with self-sealing adhesive strips	5 boxes containing 200 bags per box	$32.98	$164.90
			Subtotal	$164.90
			Shipping charges	$7.99
			Total	$172.89
				Submit order

FIGURE D–1. Simple Description

Protect Windows and Doors

Protecting windows and doors is one of the most effective actions you can take to reduce your risk of wind damage. High winds and windborne debris can easily break unprotected windows and cause doors to fail. Once wind enters a building, the likelihood of severe structural damage increases, and the contents of the building will be exposed to the elements. The most reliable method of protecting windows and doors is installing permanent storm shutters. Alternatives include using temporary plywood covers, replacing existing glass with impact-resistant glass, and covering existing glass with a protective film.

Permanent storm shutters are usually made of aluminum or steel and are attached to a building in such a way that they can be closed quickly before a storm arrives. One type is the "rolldown" shutter (as shown above), which is contained in a housing mounted above the window and lowered when necessary. Manually and motor-operated models are available.

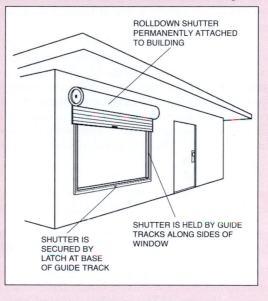

ROLLDOWN SHUTTER PERMANENTLY ATTACHED TO BUILDING

SHUTTER IS HELD BY GUIDE TRACKS ALONG SIDES OF WINDOW

SHUTTER IS SECURED BY LATCH AT BASE OF GUIDE TRACK

FIGURE D–2. Illustrated Description
SOURCE: Federal Emergency Management Agency, www.fema.gov.

Complex descriptions, of course, involve more details. In describing a mechanical device, for example, describe the whole device and its function before giving a detailed description of how each part works. The description should conclude with an explanation of how each part contributes to the functioning of the whole.

In descriptions intended for an **audience** unfamiliar with the topic, details are crucial. Details help readers visualize the specifics of the new image, object, or idea that the writer wants to convey. In the following description of a company's headquarters, notice the detailed discussion of colors, shapes, and features. The writer assumes that the reader knows such terms as *colonial design* and *haiku fountain*.

▶ Their company's headquarters, which reminded me of a rural college campus, are located north of the city in a 90-acre lush, green wooded area. The complex consists of five three-story build-ings of redbrick colonial design. The buildings are spaced about 50 feet apart and are built in a U-shape surrounding a reflection pool that frames a striking haiku fountain.

You can also use analogy, as described in **figures of speech**, to explain unfamiliar concepts in terms of familiar ones, such as "U-shape" in the previous example.

Visuals can be powerful aids in descriptive writing, especially when they show features too intricate to explain completely in words. The example in Figure D–2 on page 127 illustrates a storm-shutter installation that small businesses can use to protect windows from windborne-debris damage. Note that the description concentrates on the types of shutters available and their function. The illustration, with call-outs highlight-ing important features, largely eliminates the need for extensive written details to describe their relationship to one another and their function.

design (*see* layout and design)

differ from / differ with

Differ from suggests that two things are not alike. ("Our earlier pro-posal *differs from* the current one.") *Differ with* indicates disagreement between persons. ("The architect *differed with* the contractor on the proposed site.")

different from / different than

In formal writing, the preposition *from* is used with *different*. ("The product I received is *different from* the one I ordered.") *Different than* is used when it is followed by a clause. ("The actual cost was *different than* we estimated in our proposal.")

direct address

Direct address refers to a sentence or phrase in which the person being spoken or written to is explicitly named. It is often used in **presentations** and in **e-mail** messages. Notice that the person's name in a direct address is set off by **commas**: ("*Jane*, call me when you arrive.")

discreet / discrete

Discreet means "having or showing prudent or careful behavior." ("Because the matter was personal, he asked Bob to be *discreet*.") *Discrete* means something is "separate, distinct, or individual." ("Plans for the corporate headquarters include five *discrete* buildings.")

D

disinterested / uninterested

Disinterested means "impartial, objective, unbiased."

▶ Like good judges, researchers should be passionately interested in the problems they tackle but completely *disinterested* when they seek to solve those problems.

Uninterested means simply "not interested."

▶ Despite Asha's enthusiasm, her manager remained *uninterested* in the project.

division-and-classification method of development

An effective **method of development** for a complex subject is either to divide it into manageable parts and then discuss each part separately (division) or to classify (or group) individual parts into appropriate categories and then discuss each category separately (classification). See also **instructions** and **process explanation**.

Division

You might use division to describe a physical object, such as the parts of a copy machine; to examine an organization, such as a company; or to explain the components of a system, such as the Internet. The emphasis in division as a method of development is on breaking down a complex whole into a number of like units—it is easier to consider smaller units and to examine the relationship of each to the other than to attempt to discuss the whole. The basis for division depends, of course, on your subject and your **purpose**.

If you were a financial planner describing the types of mutual funds available to your investors, you could divide the variety available into three broad categories: money-market funds, bond funds, and stock funds. Such division would be accurate, but it would be only a first-level grouping of a complex whole. The three broad categories could, in turn, be subdivided into additional groups based on investment strategy, as follows:

MONEY-MARKET FUNDS
- Taxable money market
- Tax-exempt money market

BOND FUNDS
- Taxable bonds
- Tax-exempt bonds
- Balanced (mix of stocks and bonds)

STOCK FUNDS
- Balanced
- Equity income
- Domestic growth
- Growth and income
- International growth
- Small capitalization
- Aggressive growth
- Specialized

Specialized stock funds could be further subdivided as follows:

SPECIALIZED STOCK FUNDS
- Communications
- Energy
- Environmental services
- Financial services
- Gold
- Health services
- Technology
- Utilities
- Worldwide capital goods

Classification

The process of classification is the grouping of a number of units (such as people, objects, or ideas) into related categories. Consider the following list:

triangular file	steel tape ruler	needle-nose pliers
vise	pipe wrench	keyhole saw
mallet	tin snips	C-clamps
rasp	hacksaw	plane
glass cutter	ball-peen hammer	steel square
spring clamp	claw hammer	utility knife
crescent wrench	folding extension ruler	slip-joint pliers
crosscut saw	tack hammer	utility scissors

To group the items in the list, you would first determine what they have in common. The most obvious characteristic they share is that they all belong in a carpenter's tool chest. With that starting point, you can begin to group the tools into related categories. Pipe wrenches belong with slip-joint pliers because both tools grip objects. The rasp and the plane belong with the triangular file because all three tools smooth rough surfaces. By applying this kind of thinking to all the items in the list, you can group (classify) the tools according to function (Figure D–3).

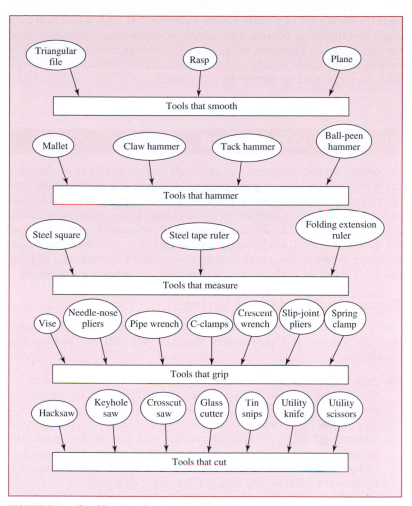

FIGURE D–3. Classification (Tools Placed into Categories)

To classify a subject, you must first sort the individual items into the largest number of comparable groups. For explaining the functions of carpentry tools, the classifications (or groups) in Figure D–3 (smoothing, hammering, measuring, gripping, and cutting) are excellent. For recommending which tools a new homeowner should buy first, however, those classifications are not helpful—each group contains tools that a new homeowner might want to purchase right away.

Once you have established the basis for the classification, apply it consistently, putting each item in only one category. For example, it might seem logical to classify needle-nose pliers as both a tool that cuts and a tool that grips because most needle-nose pliers have a small section for cutting wires. However, the primary function of needle-nose pliers is to grip. So listing them only under "tools that grip" would be consistent with the basis used for listing the other tools.

D

document management

Document management refers to processes and programs that allow for the organized storage and quick retrieval of digital documents. These procedures allow organizations to track a document's changes and contributors, and provide tools designed to quickly locate a single document within a larger archive. Unlike content-management systems designed to allow for the easy creation, modification, and display of data within a final document or Web site, document-management systems are designed to keep track of the full life cycle of a single document. See **content management**.

Document-Management Systems

Various technologies exist to help organizations and individuals manage their documents, and each system provides different but overlapping capabilities:

- *Search tools.* Many document-management programs, including those found on most personal computers, allow a document to be quickly located through a keyword search. These tools often rely on metadata to help locate the correct document quickly. "Metadata" refers to extra information that a writer includes with a document, such as a short description of the document, a series of keywords, the document's collaborators, or information on the document's purpose and relationship to a larger project.

- *Workflow and version management.* Document-management programs can simplify the workflow necessary to move a draft to publication by tracking a document as it is edited and passed from employee to employee. In doing so, these systems automatically record changes to the document as progressing "versions," complete with data on who made changes, when changes were made, and who is next responsible for working on the document. Some systems allow writers to temporarily check out, or lock, a document in order to prevent others from working with that document at the same time. Other systems automatically restrict access to specific documents or to all documents at specific points in the composing or revision process.

- *Document capture and linking.* Document-management systems can also house large collections of documents and related items, and allow documents (such as those related to a single project) to be easily linked together and categorized. For example, product photographs, competitor sales sheets, topical e-mails, and scanned magazine or journal articles can be stored with the document generated from that information.

Regardless of the tools or programs available within your organization, consistency and ease of use are key to successful document management. Take the time to carefully learn and follow your organization's best practices. See also **adapting to new technologies**.

If your organization does not have a dedicated process or program in place, consider implementing your own document-management practices. For example, consistency in a file's name and placement within a folder hierarchy or document group allows members of an organization to quickly locate the latest version of a given document. When setting your document's filename and location, consider where it will appear in an existing list of documents. Construct filenames from left to right, beginning with the most general category and ending with the most specific detail. For example, the introduction to the second version of an annual report could be named "AnnualReport-Introduction-2019-V2.pdf." Since most systems automatically store creation and revision dates, a filename with substantial details allows for a specific document to be found quickly through an electronic search or by scanning a directory either alphabetically or chronologically.

documenting sources

DIRECTORY

Documenting sources achieves three important purposes:

- It allows readers to locate and consult the sources used and to find further information on the subject.

- It enables writers to support their assertions and arguments in such documents as **proposals**, **reports**, and trade journal articles.

- It helps writers give proper credit to others and thus avoid **plagiarism** by identifying the sources of facts, ideas, **visuals**, **quotations**, and paraphrases. See also **paraphrasing**.

D

APA

This entry shows citation models and sample pages for three principal documentation systems: American Psychological Association (APA), Chicago Manual of Style (CMS), and Modern Language Association (MLA). The following examples compare these three styles for citing a book by one author: *Work Smarter with LinkedIn* by Alexandra Samuel, which was published in 2017 by Harvard Business Review in Boston, Massachusetts.

- The APA system of citation is often used in the social sciences. It is referred to as an author-date method of documentation because parenthetical in-text citations and a reference list (at the end of the paper) in APA style emphasize the author(s) and date of publication so that the currency of the research is clear.

APA IN-TEXT CITATION   (Author's surname, date)

PARENTHETICAL CITATION   (Samuel, 2017)

                                                    Author's name (date)

SENTENCE WITH SIGNAL PHRASE   Alexandra Samuel (2017) explains

                                                    that . . .

APA REFERENCES ENTRY

Author. (Publication date).   Title (italics)   Publisher

Samuel, A. (2017). *Work smarter with LinkedIn*. Harvard Business Review.

- The *Chicago Manual of Style* (*CMS*) is widely used in publishing and various academic specialties. It presents two systems of documentation: the notes and bibliography system and the author-date system. The author-date system uses in-text citations similar to those in MLA style (see page 135) and bibliography entries similar to those in APA style (except that the publication date is not given in parentheses). This text shows the notes and bibliography system, which uses the more traditional footnotes (at the bottom of the page) or endnotes (at the end of the document) and a bibliography.

   The *Chicago Manual of Style* (*CMS*) offers two options:

1. A full bibliography with shortened footnotes (or endnotes)
2. A selected bibliography (most important works cited) with footnotes providing full bibliographic information for all sources at first mention and shortened footnotes thereafter

CMS IN-TEXT CITATION

Samuel explains that . . .[1]

CMS FOOTNOTES — FULL BIBLIOGRAPHIC INFORMATION

Footnote   Author's name
number   (first name first)   Title (italics)   City

   1. Alexandra Samuel, *Work Smarter with LinkedIn* (Boston:
     Harvard Business Review, 2017), 12–13.

         Publisher   Publication   Pages cited
                      date

CMS FOOTNOTES — SHORTENED

Footnote   Author's   Title
number   surname   (shortened, italics)

   1. Samuel, *Work Smarter*, 12–13.

                  Pages cited

CMS BIBLIOGRAPHY ENTRY

  Author's name
  (surname first)   Title (italics)   City   Publisher

Samuel, Alexandra. *Work Smarter with LinkedIn*. Boston: Harvard
    Business Review, 2017.

               Publication date

- The MLA system is used in literature and the humanities. MLA
  style uses parenthetical in-text citations and a list of works cited
  and places greater importance on the pages on which cited information can be found than on the publication date.

MLA IN-TEXT CITATION

                    (Author Pages cited)

PARENTHETICAL CITATION   (Samuel 12–13)
                       Author's name

SENTENCE WITH SIGNAL PHRASE Alexandra Samuel explains that . . .
                    (pp. 12–13).———— Pages cited

MLA WORKS-CITED ENTRY

Author's surname, first name   Title (italics)   Publisher

Samuel, Alexandra. *Work Smarter with LinkedIn*. Harvard Business Review,
    2017.

        ———— Publication date

D

APA

These systems are described in full detail in the following style manuals:

> *Publication Manual of the American Psychological Association.*
> 6th ed., American Psychological Association, 2010. See also
> www.apastyle.org.
>
> *The Chicago Manual of Style.* 17th ed., University of Chicago Press, 2010.
> See also www.chicagomanualofstyle.org.
>
> *MLA Handbook.* 8th ed., Modern Language Association, 2016. See also
> www.mla.org/style.

See also **bibliographies** and **research**.

APA Documentation

APA In-Text Citations.　Generally, cite the author or authors in a signal phrase (the authors' names plus an appropriate verb in the past tense—*reported*—or present perfect tense—*has argued*), with the publication date in parentheses following the name(s). If you do not cite the author(s) in a signal phrase, include a parenthetical citation including the author's (or authors') surname(s) followed by the publication date. Include a page reference for all quotations.

SIGNAL PHRASE	Slade (2012) has claimed that "we look to machines to perform human functions: They provide communications, calculations, care, and company" (p. 9).
PARENTHETICAL CITATION	Technology that once remedied loneliness may now lead to feelings of seclusion and sadness (Slade, 2012).

When APA parenthetical citations are needed midsentence, place them after the closing quotation marks and continue with the sentence.

▶ In short, these "prosthetic substitutes" (Slade, 2012, p. 13) replace the flesh-and-blood friends in our lives.

If the APA parenthetical citation follows a block quotation, place it after the final punctuation mark.

▶ . . . a close collaboration with the marketing staff and the development group is essential. (Thompson, 2010)

When a work has two authors, cite both names joined by the word "and" in a signal phrase or an ampersand (&) in a parenthetical citation:

▶ Barlett and Steele (2012) argued that . . .

▶ (Barlett & Steele, 2012)

For citations of works with three or more authors, include only the last name of the first author followed by "et al." (not italicized and with a period after "al.") in all in-text citations, except when this might cause confusion (as when you cite multiple works by the first named author and different co-authors). When two or more works by different authors are cited in the same parentheses, list the citations alphabetically and use semicolons to separate them: (Bartlett & Steele, 2012; Dauch, 2012).

APA Documentation Models. In reference lists, APA requires that the first word of book and article titles and subtitles be capitalized and all other words—except proper nouns (*Einstein*) and proper adjectives (*Cartesian, French*)—be lowercased. In titles of periodicals, capitalize all major words.

For online versions of books and articles, include retrieval information at the end of the citation. If a DOI (digital object identifier, a permanent code) is available, include that; if not, include the URL. (No periods follow DOIs or URLs.) If no date is available, use "(n.d.)." Include a retrieval date only if the content (like a Twitter profile) is intended to be changed regularly.

BOOKS (PRINT AND ELECTRONIC)

Single Author

Wheeler, A. (2012). *Designing brand identity: An essential guide for the whole branding team.* John Wiley & Sons.

Kranich, N. (2004). *The information commons.* Brennan Center for Justice. http://brennancenter.org/publication/information-commons

Multiple Authors

Kaye, B., & Giulioni, J. W. (2012). *Help them grow or watch them go: Career conversations employees want.* Berrett-Koehler Publishers.

Corporate Author

Standard and Poor's. (2012). *Standard and Poor's 500 guide.* The McGraw-Hill Companies.

Edition Other Than First

Mongan, J., Giguere, E., & Kindler, N. (2013). *Programming interviews exposed: Secrets to landing your next job* (3rd ed.). Wiley Publishing.

Multivolume Work

Kozlowski, S. W. J. (Ed.). (2012). *The Oxford handbook of organizational psychology* (Vols. 1–2). Oxford University Press.

D

APA

Work in an Edited Collection

Snider, L. (2013). The technological advantages of stock market traders. In S. Will, S. Handelman, & D. C. Brotherton (Eds.), *How they got away with it: White collar criminals and the financial meltdown* (pp. 151–170). Columbia University Press.

Encyclopedia or Dictionary Entry

Satterwhite, M. (2014). Decision making. In *Encyclopedia of business and finance* (3rd ed., Vol. 1, pp. 202–203). Macmillan Reference. http://go.galegroup.com/ps/i.do?p=GVRL&v=2.1&it=r&id=GALE%7CCX3727500091&asid=9ca00312919e3480a72e988bf3652b9b

ARTICLES IN PERIODICALS (PRINT AND ELECTRONIC)
Magazine Article

Paul, I. (2012, September). Spotify takes on Pandora. *Macworld, 29*(9), 71.

Vlahos, J. (2019, March). Alexa, I want answers. *Wired,* 58–65. https://www.wired.com/story/amazon-alexa-search-for-the-one-perfect-answer/

Journal Article

Moriarty, J. (2010). Participation in the workplace: Are employees special? *Journal of Business Ethics, 92*(3), 373–384.

Boiral, O., Henri, J.-F., & Talbot, D. (2012). Modeling the impacts of corporate commitment on climate change. *Business Strategy and the Environment, 21*(8), 495–516. https://doi.org/10.1002/bse.723

Newspaper Article

Jones, R. (2012, December 4). Nations meet to discuss web rules. *Wall Street Journal*, B7.

Metz, Cade. (2017, August 16). Microsoft teaches autonomous gliders to make decisions on the fly. *The New York Times*. https://nyti.ms/2v0DSJc

Article with an Unknown Author

What sold, for how much, and why? (2009, Fall). *Modern, 1*(2), 22.

OTHER ELECTRONIC AND MULTIMEDIA SOURCES
Web Sites and Web Pages

Cite an entire Web site only if you borrow ideas or information from its homepage.

U.S. debt clock. Retrieved October 21, 2019, from https://www.usdebtclock.org/

Albright, A. (2019, July 25). *The global education challenge: Scaling up to tackle the learning crisis*. The Brookings Institution. https://www.brookings.edu/wp-content/uploads/2019/07/Brookings_Blum_2019_education.pdf

BBC News. (2019, October 31). *Goats help save Ronald Reagan Presidential Library*. https://bbc.com/news/world-us-canada-50248549

Messages and Posts

If an online message or post is not accessible to all readers, cite it in the text of your paper only. For any messages or posts that are accessible to your readers, use the author's real name, if given, followed by the pseudonym or screen name in brackets, exactly as in the source. If you know only the screen name, begin with that name without brackets. If the posting is undated, use "n.d." in parentheses. If untitled, include up to the first twenty words of the post or caption, or use a description of the post in square brackets. Include any emojis, hashtags, and links from the post if possible (each counts as one word), and keep unconventional spelling or capitalization as is. If you cannot use an actual emoji (☺), then include its name in square brackets ("[kissing face emoji]") instead. Describe images, or recordings, and the type of post in brackets following the title. Include an access date only if the post is not archived or if the content is likely to change.

ScienceModerator. (2018, November 16). *Science discussion: We are researchers working with some of the largest and most innovative companies using DNA to help people* [Online forum post]. Reddit. https://www.reddit.com/r/science/comments/9xlnm2/science_discussion_we_are_researchers_working/

Georgia Aquarium. (2019, October 10). *Meet the bigfin reef squid* [Video]. Facebook. https://www.facebook.com/GeorgiaAquarium/videos/2471961729567512/

Smithsonian [@smithsonian]. (n.d.). *#Apollo50* [Highlight]. Instagram. Retrieved October 15, 2019, from https://www.instagram.com/stories/highlights/17902787752343364/

Tweet

Schiller, Caitlin [@caitlinschiller]. (2019, September 26). *Season 6 of Simplify is here! Today we launch with the one and only @susancain, author of* Quiet [Thumbnail with link attached] [Tweet]. Twitter. http://twitter.com/caitlinschiller/status/1177214094191026176

Blog Post

Fister, B. (2019, February 14). Information literacy's third wave. *Library Babel Fish*. https://www.insidehighered.com/blogs/library-babel-fish/information-literacy%E2%80%99s-third-wave

Film

Peele, J. (Director). (2017). *Get out* [Film]. Universal Pictures.

D

APA

Radio, Television, or Podcast Program or Episode

Johnson, B. (Host). (2017, August 14). *Weaponized audio technology* [Radio program]. In *Marketplace tech*. Retrieved from https://www.marketplace.org/shows/marketplace-tech/08142017-mtech

Koppel, T. (Host). (2009, February 28). The fast lane (Season 1, Episode 6) [TV series episode]. In T. Bettag (Executive Producer), *Koppel: People's republic of capitalism*. Discovery Channel.

Abumrad, J., & Krulwich, R. (Hosts). (2002–present). *Radiolab* [Audio podcast]. WNYC Studios. https://www.wnycstudios.org/podcasts/radiolab/podcasts

Longoria, J. (Host & Producer). (2019, April 19). Americanish [Audio podcast episode]. In J. Abumrad & R. Krulwich (Hosts), *Radiolab*. WNYC Studios. https://www.wnycstudios.org/podcasts/radiolab/articles/americanish

Interview

Parrado, N. (2011, March 27). *Nando Parrado, plane crash survivor* [Interview with C. Gracie; audio file]. The Interview Archive; BBC World Service. https://www.bbc.co.uk/programmes/p00fhjnb

Brochure or Factsheet

National Council of State Boards of Nursing. (2018). *A nurse manager's guide to substance use disorder in nursing* [Brochure].

World Health Organization. (2019, July 15). *Immunization coverage* [Fact sheet]. https://www.who.int/news-room/fact-sheets/detail/immunization-coverage

Government Document

National Park Service. (2019, April 11). *Travel where women made history: Ordinary and extraordinary places of American women*. U.S. Department of the Interior. https://www.nps.gov/subjects/travelwomenshistory/index.htm

Report

Berchick, E. R., Barnett, J. C., & Upton, R. D. (2019, September 10). *Health insurance coverage in the United States: 2018* (Report No. P60-267). U.S. Census Bureau. https://www.census.gov/library/publications/2019/demo/p60-267.html

Ford Foundation International Fellowships Program. (2019). *Leveraging higher education to promote social justice: Evidence from the IFP alumni tracking study*. https://p.widencdn.net/kei61u/IFP-Alumni-Tracking-Study-Report-5

APA Sample Pages

14

This report examines the nature and disposition of the 3,458 ethics cases handled companywide by CGF's ethics officers and managers during 2014. The purpose of such reports is to provide the Ethics and Business Conduct Committee with the information necessary for assessing the effectiveness of the first year of CGF's Ethics Program (Davis et al., 2016). According to Matthias Jonas (2015), recommendations are given for consideration "in planning for the second year of the Ethics Program" (p. 152).

The Office of Ethics and Business Conduct was created to administer the Ethics Program. The director of the Office of Ethics and Business Conduct, along with seven ethics officers throughout CGF, was given the responsibility for the following objectives, as described by Rossouw (1997):

> Communicate the values, standards, and goals of CGF's Program to employees. Provide companywide channels for employee education and guidance in resolving ethics concerns. Implement companywide programs in ethics awareness and recognition. Employee accessibility to ethics information and guidance is the immediate goal of the Office of Business Conduct in its first year. (p. 1543)

The purpose of the Ethics Program, established by the Committee, is to "promote ethical business conduct through open communication and compliance with company ethics standards" (Jonas, 2017, p. 89). To accomplish this purpose, any ethics policy must ensure confidentiality and anonymity for employees who raise genuine ethics concerns. The procedure developed at CGF guarantees that employees can . . .

Page number in upper right corner

One-inch margins, text double-spaced

Long quotes (40+ words) indented half an inch, no quotation marks

In-text citation for quotations includes page number

FIGURE D–4. APA Sample Page (from a Report)

D

APA

21

References

Davis, W. C., Marks, R., & Tegge, D. (2016). *Working in the system: Five new management principles.* St. Martin's Press.

Jonas, M. (2015). The Internet and ethical communication: Toward a new paradigm. *Journal of Ethics and Communication, 32*(2), 147–177.

Jonas, M. (2017). Ethics in organizational communication: A review of the literature. *Journal of Ethics and Communication, 40*(3), 79–99. https://doi.org/ 10.9798/0838-2180025856

National Science Foundation. (2017, January 6). *Conflicts of interest and standards of ethical conduct.* https://www. nsf.gov/pubs/manuals/manual15.pdf

Rossouw, G. J. (1997). Business ethics in South Africa. *Journal of Business Ethics, 16*(3), 1539–1547. https://doi .org/10.1023/A:1005858930223

Schipper, F. (2017). Transparency and integrity: Contrary concepts? In K. Homann, P. Koslowski, & C. Luetge (Eds.), *Globalisation and business ethics* (pp. 101–118). Ashgate Publishing. http://www. tandfebooks.com

Soloman, P. (Host). (2012, August 16). Money and Ethics. [TV series episode]. In L. Winslow (Executive producer), *NewsHour.* Newshour Productions; PBS. http://video. unctv.org/video/2268858765/

FIGURE D–5. APA Sample List of References

CMS Documentation

CMS Footnotes and Endnotes. CMS footnote and endnote citations use superscript numerals in the text with corresponding numbered footnotes (at the bottom of the page where referenced) or endnotes (on a separate page at the end of the paper). The *CMS* recommends footnotes for the reader's ease. However, if you have numerous long footnotes that are difficult to fit on their respective pages, consider using endnotes.

Place superscript numbers at the end of the summary, paraphrase, quotation, or sentence, after the punctuation marks. Indent the first line of the footnote or endnote entry half an inch. Use the number (followed by a period) corresponding to the number in the text, but do not make it superscript. Include the author's name (first name first); the title of the source (in quotation marks for shorter works, such as article titles, and in italics for longer works, such as books); the title (in italics) of the longer work in which the source appeared (if any); the city of publication and publisher (separated by a colon) and the year of publication, enclosed in parentheses; page number(s) of the passage cited; and the URL (if the cited work is digital), all separated by commas.

▶ Holder's memo was nonetheless written in the wake of a year of fairly vigorous prosecutions of companies that had committed crimes like theft, fraud, and market manipulation.[4]

▶ 4. Matt Taibbi, *The Divide: American Injustice in the Age of the Wealth Gap* (New York: Spiegel & Grau, 2014), 47.

If the bibliography contains all the works cited in the notes, or if the work has been cited in full previously, you may abbreviate the note to eliminate duplication of information. Use the author's last name, a shortened version of the title (the first few important words in the same order as the title), and the page number(s) of the material cited.

▶ 4. Taibbi, *Divide*, 47.

The *CMS* recommends that references to online sources, in addition to the usual content, also provide a URL, preferably a URL that includes a digital object identifier (DOI, a permanent code) or another permalink. If a direct link will not be accessible to your readers, include the name of the database through which you accessed the source. For online books, you may include the URL, the name of the database, or the format (such as *Kindle*), whichever is most likely to help readers locate and assess the source. If the source is unpaginated or if it repaginates in response to changes in the screen or font size, include the section heading, chapter number (for example, *chap. 5*), paragraph number (for example, *para. 6, par. 6,* or *¶6*) if available, or even a descriptive phrase, so readers can more readily locate the section you refer to. If you cite an online source with no publication or "last update" date, include an access date in its place, immediately before the URL.

CMS *Documentation Models*

BOOKS (PRINTED AND ELECTRONIC)

Single Author

    1. Nassim Nicholas Taleb, *Antifragile: Things That Gain from Disorder* (New York: Random House, 2012), 29.

Taleb, Nassim Nicholas. *Antifragile: Things That Gain from Disorder.* New York: Random House, 2012.

    2. Willard Eugene Hotchkiss, *Higher Education and Business Standards* (Boston: Houghton-Mifflin, 1918), chap. 2, http://gutenberg.org/ebooks/29674.

Hotchkiss, Willard Eugene. *Higher Education and Business Standards.* Boston: Houghton-Mifflin, 1918, http://gutenberg.org/ebooks/29674.

    3. Peter W. Cardon, *Business Communication: Developing Leaders for a Networked World* (New York: McGraw-Hill, 2014), Kindle.

Cardon, Peter W. *Business Communication: Developing Leaders for a Networked World.* New York: McGraw-Hill, 2014. Kindle.

Two or Three Authors

    4. Beverly Kaye and Julie Winkle Guilioni, *Help Them Grow or Watch Them Go: Career Conversations Employees Want* (San Francisco: Berrett-Koehler, 2012), 120.

Kaye, Beverly, and Julie Winkle Guilioni. *Help Them Grow or Watch Them Go: Career Conversations Employees Want.* San Francisco: Berrett-Koehler, 2012.

Four or More Authors

    5. Bruce Jefferson et al., *Urban Water Recycling: Techniques and Applications* (Burlington, MA: Butterworth-Heinemann, 2013), 277.

Jefferson, Bruce, Paul Jeffrey, Claire Diaper, and James Crook. *Urban Water Recycling: Techniques and Applications.* Burlington, MA: Butterworth-Heinemann, 2013.

Multiple Books by Same Author

    6. Suze Orman, *Suze Orman's 2009 Action Plan: Keeping Your Money Safe and Sound* (New York: Spiegel & Grau, 2009), 54.

7. Suze Orman, *The Money Class: How to Stand in Your Truth and Create the Future You Deserve* (New York: Spiegel & Grau, 2012), 212.

In the bibliography, list the works alphabetically by title.

Orman, Suze. *The Money Class: How to Stand in Your Truth and Create the Future You Deserve*. New York: Spiegel & Grau, 2012.

———. *Suze Orman's 2009 Action Plan: Keeping Your Money Safe and Sound*. New York: Spiegel & Grau, 2009.

Corporate Author

8. J. K. Lasser Institute, *J. K. Lasser's Your Income Tax 2010: For Preparing Your 2009 Tax Return* (New York: Wiley, 2009), 65.

J. K. Lasser Institute. *J. K. Lasser's Your Income Tax 2010: For Preparing Your 2009 Tax Return*. New York: Wiley, 2009.

Edition Other Than First

9. James M. Kouzes and Barry Z. Posner, *The Leadership Challenge: How to Make Extraordinary Things Happen in Organizations*, 5th ed. (New York: Jossey-Bass, 2012), 17.

Kouzes, James M., and Barry Z. Posner. *The Leadership Challenge: How to Make Extraordinary Things Happen in Organizations*. 5th ed. New York: Jossey-Bass, 2012.

Multivolume Work

10. Standard and Poor's, *Standard and Poor's Register of Corporations, Directors, and Executives* (New York: Standard and Poor's, 2010), 2:128.

Standard and Poor's. *Standard and Poor's Register of Corporations, Directors, and Executives*. 2 vols. New York: Standard and Poor's, 2010.

Work in an Edited Collection

11. Laureen Snider, "The Technological Advantages of Stock Market Traders," in *How They Got Away with It: White Collar Criminals and the Financial Meltdown*, ed. Susan Will, Stephen Handelman, and David C. Brotherton (New York: Columbia University Press, 2013), 155.

Snider, Laureen. "The Technological Advantages of Stock Market Traders." In *How They Got Away with It: White Collar Criminals and the Financial Meltdown*, edited by Susan Will, Stephen Handelman, and David C. Brotherton, 151–70. New York: Columbia University Press, 2013.

D

CMS

D

CMS

Encyclopedia or Dictionary Entry

12. *World Book Encyclopedia*, 2007 ed., s.v. "particle detector."

13. Wikipedia, s.v. "Labor Theory of Value," last modified September 19, 2017, 21:08, https://en.wikipedia.org/wiki/Labor_theory_of_value.

Well-known reference books, such as encyclopedias and dictionaries, are not included in the bibliography. The titles of reference Web sites with no print counterpart, like Wikipedia, are generally not italicized. For Web sites that do not indicate when they were published or most recently updated, include an access date. For sites that are updated frequently (again, like Wikipedia), include the date the entry was last modified along with a time stamp.

ARTICLES IN PERIODICALS (PRINT AND ELECTRONIC)

Magazine Article

14. Nathan Heller, "Mark as Read: What Do We Learn When Our Private E-mail Becomes Public," *New Yorker*, July 24, 2017, 28–31.

Heller, Nathan. "Mark as Read: What Do We Learn When Our Private E-mail Becomes Public." *New Yorker*, July 24, 2017, 28–31.

15. Mariette DiChristina, "Designing the City of Tomorrow Today," *Scientific American*, July 2017, 4, http://www.scientificamerican.com/article/designing-the-city-of-tomorrow-today/.

DiChristina, Mariette. "Designing the City of Tomorrow Today." *Scientific American*, July 2017, 4. http://www.scientificamerican.com/article/designing-the-city-of-tomorrow-today/.

Journal Article

16. Jeffrey Moriarty, "Participation in the Workplace: Are Employees Special?" *Journal of Business Ethics* 92, no. 3 (2010): 373.

Moriarty, Jeffrey. "Participation in the Workplace: Are Employees Special?" *Journal of Business Ethics* 92, no. 3 (2010): 373–84.

17. Honor J. Passow and Christian H. Passow, "What Competencies Should Undergraduate Engineering Programs Emphasize? A Systematic Review," *Journal of Engineering Education* 106, no. 3 (2017): 475–526, Academic Search Complete.

Passow, Honor J., and Christian H. Passow. "What Competencies Should Undergraduate Engineering Programs Emphasize? A Systematic Review." *Journal of Engineering Education* 106, no. 3 (2017): 475–526. Academic Search Complete.

18. Oliver Boiral, Jean-François Henri, and David Talbot, "Modeling the Impacts of Corporate Commitment on Climate Change," *Business Strategy and the Environment* 21, no. 8 (2012): 497, https://doi.org/10.1002/bse.723.

Boiral, Oliver, Jean-François Henri, and David Talbot. "Modeling the Impacts of Corporate Commitment on Climate Change." *Business Strategy and the Environment* 21, no. 8 (2012): 495–516. https://doi.org/10.1002/bse.723.

D

CMS

Newspaper Article

19. Rory Jones, "Nations Meet to Discuss Web Rules," *Wall Street Journal*, December 4, 2012, sec. B.

20. Cade Metz, "Chips Off the Old Block: Computers Are Taking Design Cues from Human Brains," *New York Times*, September 18, 2017, https://nyti.ms/2y5xcLS.

The *CMS* notes that newspaper articles are typically cited in the text or notes, not in the bibliography. If a bibliography entry were needed, however, it would look like this:

Metz, Cade. "Chips Off the Old Block: Computers Are Taking Design Cues from Human Brains." *New York Times*, September 18, 2017. https://nyti.ms/2y5xcLS.

Article with an Unknown Author

21. "What Sold, for How Much, and Why?" *Modern*, Fall 2009, 22.

"What Sold, for How Much, and Why?" *Modern*, Fall 2009, 22.

OTHER ELECTRONIC SOURCES AND MULTIMEDIA SOURCES

Unlike online magazines and journals, less formally published online sources, such as Web content (including Web sites and Web pages, blogs, and social media), are typically cited only in the text or notes. If a bibliography entry is needed, begin with the author or site sponsor. (In a note, the site sponsor follows the title of the Web site; in a bibliography entry, if needed, the site sponsor appears in the author position.) Include as much information as you would for any other source, but be aware that full bibliographic information may not be available. If readers will not recognize the source type, include the relevant label (*Web site, blog*) in parentheses following the title. Titles of Web sites are not italicized. If a site is frequently updated (as with a blog or a wiki), include a time stamp along with the date last modified. If a blog is part of another publication, include that title as well. If you cite comments on a blog post, include the date the comment was posted following the name of the commenter. If an author publishes under a pseudonym but you know the writer's actual name, you may include it following the pseudonym in square brackets ([ ]).

Entire Web Site

22. Association for Business Communication (Web site), accessed September 19, 2014, http://www.businesscommunication.org.

Web sites are typically sited only in the notes. However, if a bibliography entry is needed, it would look like this:

Association for Business Communication (Web site). Accessed September 19, 2014. http://www.businesscommunication.org.

Short Work from a Web Site, with an Author

23. Michael Calore, "Personalize Your Map with a Custom Map Marker," Webmonkey, October 7, 2010, http://www.webmonkey.com/2010/10/personalize-your-map-with-a-custom-map-marker.

Calore, Michael. "Personalize Your Map with a Custom Map Marker." Webmonkey, October 7, 2010. http://www.webmonkey.com/2010/10/personalize-your-map-with-a-custom-map-marker.

Short Work from a Web Site, with a Corporate or an Organizational Author

24. "Global Diversity and Inclusion," Microsoft, last modified 2017, https://www.microsoft.com/en-us/diversity.

Microsoft. "Global Diversity and Inclusion." Last modified 2017. https://www.microsoft.com/en-us/diversity.

Short Work from a Web Site, with an Unknown Author

25. "Women-Owned Business," U.S. Small Business Administration, last modified July 20, 2009, http://www.sba.gov/business-guide/grow/women-owned-businesses-programs.

U.S. Small Business Administration. "Women-Owned Business." Last modified July 20, 2009. http://www.sba.gov/business-guide/grow/women-owned-businesses-programs.

Article Posted on a Wiki

26. "Labor Theory of Value," Wikipedia, Wikimedia Foundation, last modified September 19, 2017, 21:08, http://en.wikipedia.org/wiki/labor_theory_of_value.

E-mail Message and Other Personal Communications

27. Ari Kalil, "Customer Satisfaction Survey," e-mail message to author, January 12, 2014.

E-mail messages and other personal communications, such as letters and text messages, are usually cited in the text but are omitted from bibliographies.

Online Posting (Lists, Forums, Discussion Boards)

28. Senior scholar, "Re: Surviving the Job Search," Chronicle Forums, *Chronicle of Higher Education*, March 15, 2009, http://www.chronicle.com/forums/index.php/topic,40486.msg1221730.html#msg1221730.

Blog Posts and Comments on Blog Posts

29. Barbara Brynko, "Weathering Turbulent Times," *Infotoday Blog*, November 30, 2009, http://www.infotodayblog.com/2009/11/30/weathering-turbulent-times.

Brynko, Barbara. "Weathering Turbulent Times." *Infotoday Blog*, November 30, 2009. http://www.infotodayblog.com/2009/11/30/weathering-turbulent-times.

30. OllyPye [Lynne Forbes], December 12, 2015, comment on Graham Readfern, "Paris Agreement a Victory for Climate Change and Ultimate Defeat for Fossil Fuels," *Planet Oz* (blog), *Guardian*, http://www.theguardian.com/environment/planet-oz/2015/dec/12/paris-agreement-a-victory-for-climate-science-and-ultimate-defeat-for-fossil-fuels#comments-64993862.

OllyPye [Lynne Forbes]. December 12, 2015. Comment on Graham Readfern, "Paris Agreement a Victory for Climate Change and the Ultimate Defeat for Fossil Fuels." *Planet Oz* (blog). *Guardian*. http://www.theguardian.com/environment/planet-oz/2015/dec/12/paris-agreement-a-victory-for-climate-science-and-ultimate-defeat-for-fossil-fuels#comments-64993862.

Film or Video

31. Ken Chiu, "Trends in Mobile Gaming," China 2.0 Conference, Stanford Program on Regions of Innovations and Entrepreneurship, September 28, 2012, Stanford CA, video, 01:53, http://www.youtube.com/watch?v=zPD1ZyrilNw.

Chiu, Ken. "Trends in Mobile Gaming." China 2.0 Conference, September 28, 2012. Stanford Program on Regions of Innovations and Entrepreneurship, Stanford, CA. Video, 01:53. http://www.youtube.com/watch?v=zPD1ZyrilNw.

Radio or Television Program, or Podcast

32. "Dobbs Law," *Lou Dobbs Tonight*, CNN, May 14, 2013.

"Dobbs Law." *Lou Dobbs Tonight*. CNN. May 14, 2013.

D

CMS

33. Felix Salmon, Anna Szymanski, and Jordan Weissman, "The Bad Eggs Edition," episode 167, July 29, 2017, on *Slate Money*, produced by Daniel Schroeder, podcast audio, 1:14:19, http://www.slate.com/articles/podcasts/slate_money/2017/07/anthony_scaramucci_productivity_and_hampton_creek_s_eggless_mayo_on_slate.html.

Salmon, Felix, Anna Szymanski, and Jordan Weissman. "The Bad Eggs Edition." Episode 167. Produced by Daniel Schroeder. *Slate Money*, July 29, 2017. Podcast audio, 1:14:19. http://www.slate.com/articles/podcasts/slate_money/2017/07/anthony_scaramucci_productivity_and_hampton_creek_s_eggless_mayo_on_slate.html.

OTHER SOURCES

Visual from a Secondary Source

The *CMS* classifies visuals as tables and illustrations (such as paintings, photographs, drawings, maps, and charts). If a table or an illustration is under copyright, follow the citation requirements of the copyright owner. If a table or an illustration is not under copyright, include a source note following the caption or directly under the illustration. Include the artist or author (if known), the title of the work, publication details including the copyright date, and any original figure or table number.

Source: Reproduced by permission of the publisher from Neil Lindeman, "Subjectivized Knowledge and Grassroots Advocacy: An Analysis of an Environmental Controversy in Northern California," *Journal of Business and Technical Communication* 27, no. 1 (2014): 77, table 1, © 2014 by SAGE Publications.

Source: "Global Warming Effects" [map], *National Geographic*, n.d., accessed October 2, 2014, http://green.nationalgeographic.com/environment/global-warming/gw-impacts-interactive.html.

If the illustration is cited in the bibliography, then you may abbreviate the credit line in the source note.

Source: Table from Lindeman (2014).

Lindeman, Neil. "Subjectivized Knowledge and Grassroots Advocacy: An Analysis of an Environmental Controversy in Northern California." *Journal of Business and Technical Communication* 27, no. 1 (2014): 77, table 1.

Published Interview

34. Robert Barro, "Interview with Robert Barro," interview by Conor Clarke, *Atlantic*, February 5, 2009, https://www.theatlantic.com/politics/archive/2009/02/an-interview-with-robert-barro/370/.

Barro, Robert. "Interview with Robert Barro." By Conor Clarke. *Atlantic*, February 5, 2009. https://www.theatlantic.com/politics/archive/2009/02/an-interview-with-robert-barro/370/.

Personal Communications

35. Mahmood Sariolghalam, interview by the author, January 29, 2010.

36. Monica Pascatore, text message to the author, April 10, 2017.

Personal communications are generally not included in bibliographies.

Brochure or Pamphlet

37. Library of Congress, *Copyright Basics*, U.S. Copyright Office, 2012, 4, https://www.copyright.gov/circs/circ01.pdf.

Library of Congress. *Copyright Basics*. U.S. Copyright Office, 2012. https://www.copyright.gov/circs/circ01.pdf.

Government Document

38. "Highlights of Women's Earnings in 2015," *BLS Reports*, no. 1064, U.S. Department of Labor, Bureau of Labor Statistics, November 2016, https://www.bls.gov/opub/reports/womens-earnings/2015/pdf/home.pdf.

U.S. Department of Labor, Bureau of Labor Statistics. "Highlights of Women's Earnings in 2015." *BLS Reports*, no. 1064. November 2016. https://www.bls.gov/opub/reports/womens-earnings/2015/pdf/home.pdf.

Report

39. *World Development Report: Governance and the Law*, World Bank, 2017, https://openknowledge.worldbank.org/handle/10986/25880.

World Bank. *World Development Report: Governance and the Law*. 2017. https://openknowledge.worldbank.org/handle/10986/25880.

CMS *Sample Pages*

Litzinger 14

This report examines the nature and disposition of the 3,458 ethics cases handled companywide by CGF's ethics officers and managers during 2014. The purpose of such reports is to provide the Ethics and Business Conduct Committee with the information necessary for assessing the effectiveness of the first year of CGF's Ethics Program.[1] According to Matthias Jonas, recommendations are given for consideration "in planning for the second year of the Ethics Program."[2]

The Office of Ethics and Business Conduct was created to administer the Ethics Program. The director of the Office of Ethics and Business Conduct was given the responsibility for the following objectives, as described by Rossouw:

> Communicate the values, standards, and goals of CGF's Program to employees. Provide companywide channels for employee education and guidance in resolving ethics concerns. Implement companywide programs in ethics awareness and recognition. Employee accessibility to ethics information and guidance is the immediate goal of the Office of Business Conduct in its first year.[3]

The purpose of the Ethics Program, according to Treviño, Weaver, and Reynolds, is to "promote ethical business conduct through open communication and compliance with company ethics standards."[4] To

1. W. C. Davis, Roland Marks, and Diane Tegge, *Working in the System: Five New Management Principles* (New York: St. Martin's, 2016), 142.
2. Matthias Jonas, "The Internet and Ethical Communication: Toward a New Paradigm," *Journal of Ethics and Communication* 32, no. 3 (2015): 152.
3. George J. Rossouw, "Business Ethics in South Africa," *Journal of Business Ethics* 16, no. 3 (2001): 1543, https://doi.org/10.1023/A:1005858930223.
4. Treviño, Linda K., Gary R. Weaver, and Scott J. Reynolds, "Behavioral Ethics in Organizations: A Review," *Journal of Management* 32, no. 6 (2006): 951–90, https://doi.org/10.1177/0149206306294258.

FIGURE D–6. *CMS* Sample Page (from a Report)

Bibliography

Davis, W. C., Roland Marks, and Diane Tegge. *Working in the System: Five New Management Principles.* New York: St. Martin's, 2016.

International Business Ethics Institute, 2017. http://berkleycenter.georgetown.edu/organizations/international-business-ethics-institute.

Jonas, Matthias. "Ethics in Organizational Communication: A Review of the Literature." *Journal of Ethics and Communication* 40, no. 3 (2017): 79–99. https://doi.org/10.9798/0838-2180025856.

——. "The Internet and Ethical Communication: Toward a New Paradigm." *Journal of Ethics and Communication* 32, no. 3 (2015): 147–77. https://doi.org/10.9798/0822-2133028965.

National Science Foundation. *Conflicts of Interest and Standards of Ethical Conduct.* NSE Manual No. 15, January 6, 2017. https://www.nsf.gov/pubs/manuals/manual15.pdf.

Rossouw, George J. "Business Ethics in South Africa." *Journal of Business Ethics* 16, no. 3 (2001): 1539–47, https://doi.org/10.1023/A:1005858930223.

Schipper, Fritz. "Transparency and Integrity: Contrary Concepts?" In *Globalisation and Business Ethics*, edited by Karl Homann, Peter Koslowski, and Christoph Luetge, 101–18. Burlington, VT: Ashgate, 2017. http://www.tandfebooks.com/action/showBook?doi=10.4324/9781315585048.

Soloman, Paul. "Money and Ethics." *NewsHour*, August 16, 2012. Video, 12:30. http://video.unctv.org/video/2268858765/.

List alphabetized by authors' last names and double-spaced

Hanging-indent style used for entries

Heading centered.

D

CMS

FIGURE D–7. *CMS* **Sample Bibliography**

MLA Documentation

MLA In-Text Citations.   The MLA parenthetical citation within the text of a paper gives a brief citation listing the author and relevant page number(s), separated only by a space.

▶ Achieving results is one thing while maintaining results is another because "like marathon runners, companies hit a performance wall" (Studer 3).

When no author is named, provide a shortened title of the work (the first noun and any modifiers) in parentheses.

▶ As Studer writes, the poor performance of a few employees will ulti-mately affect the performance—and the morale—of all employees (8).

If the author is cited in the text, include only the page number(s) in paren-theses. If no page reference is available, as with a work from a Web site, use a paragraph or section number if provided; do not create your own.

▶ In 1810, Peter Durand invented the can, which was later used to provide soldiers and explorers with canned rations and ultimately "saved legions from sure starvation" ("Forgotten Inventors").

If the parenthetical citation refers to a long, indented quotation (more than four lines when run in), set the quotation as a block indented half an inch, and place the parenthetical citation outside the punctuation of the last sentence.

▶ Frank Sprague, a naval officer and inventor, devised a new electric motor that transformed American subway systems:

> [His engine] produced no sparks. It could operate at a constant speed for long stretches, whether it was pulling 20 pounds, 200 pounds, or more. When Sprague's idol and mentor Thomas Edison visited the exhibition and saw Sprague's motor, he had one thing to say: "His is the only true motor." ("Forgotten Hero")

If you are using more than one work by the same author, give a short-ened version of the title in the parenthetical citation unless you name the title in the text (a "signal phrase"). A citation for Quint Studer's book *Results That Last: Hardwiring Behaviors That Will Take Your Company to the Top* would appear as (Studer, *Results* 93).

MLA Documentation Models.   The *MLA Handbook*, Eighth Edition, encourages writers to think of citations as being made up of three core elements—the author, the title of the source, and the "container" in which the source appears. The container might be a magazine, a newspa-per, a journal, or an anthology. (Note: If the source is a book, the source is self-contained, and the publication information follows the title.) Follow each of these main sections with a period. Other information that you should include about the container includes the following:

- names of the editors
- version or edition number
- number (volume and issue for a journal, volume number for a multivolume work)
- name of the publisher (omit business words or abbreviations, such as *Company* or *Inc.*)
- publication date
- location information (page numbers, URL, or DOI)

Follow each bit of information about the container with a comma, except the last. End the citation with a period.

If a source appears in multiple containers, add information about the second following that of the first. For example, if you access an article in a journal via a database, the journal is container 1, and the database is container 2; if you download a selection from a book from an online database, the book is container 1, and the database is container 2.

In the case of books, which are self-contained, follow the title of the source with a period, then add the publication information. MLA style no longer requires that you include the city of publication.

BOOKS (PRINT AND ELECTRONIC)

Single Author

Wheeler, Alina. *Designing Brand Identity: An Essential Guide for the Whole Branding Team.* John Wiley and Sons, 2012.

Dolbear, A. E. *The Machinery of the Universe: Mechanical Conceptions of Physical Phenomena.* E. and J. B. Young, 1897. *Project Gutenberg,* www.gutenberg.org/ebooks/29444.

Multiple Authors

Kaye, Beverly, and Julie Winkle Giulioni. *Help Them Grow or Watch Them Go: Career Conversations Employees Want.* Berrett, 2012.

Corporate Author

Standard and Poor's. *Standard and Poor's 500 Guide.* McGraw-Hill Education, 2013.

Edition Other Than First

Mongan, John, Eric Giguere, and Noah Kindler. *Programming Interviews Exposed: Secrets to Landing Your Next Job.* 3rd ed., John Wiley and Sons, 2013.

Multivolume Work

Kozlowski, Steve W. J., editor. *The Oxford Handbook of Organizational Psychology*. Oxford UP, 2012. 2 vols.

D. E. Knuth. *The Art of Computer Programming*. vol. 4, Addison-Wesley, 2009.

Work in an Edited Collection

Snider, Laureen. "The Technological Advantages of Stock Market Traders." *How They Got Away with It: White Collar Criminals and the Financial Meltdown,* edited by Susan Will, Stephen Handelman, and David C. Brotherton, Columbia UP, 2013, pp. 151–70.

Encyclopedia or Dictionary Entry

"Agent Technology." *Wiley Encyclopedia of Computer Science and Engineering*, edited by B. W. Wah, John Wiley and Sons, 2009.

Brunblecombe, P. "Air Pollution Episodes." *Encyclopedia of Environmental Health*, edited by Jerome O. Nriagu, vol. 1, Elsevier, 2011, pp. 39–45. *Gale Virtual Reference Library*, go.galegroup.com/ps/retrieve .do?resultlisttype=9780444522726&prodid=gvrl&Isetoc=true& docid=gale|cx1503700016.

ARTICLES IN PERIODICALS (PRINT AND ELECTRONIC)

Magazine Article

Heller, Nathan. "Mark as Read: What Do We Learn When Our Private E-mail Becomes Public." *The New Yorker*, 24 July 2017, pp. 28–31.

DiChristina, Mariette. "Designing the City of Tomorrow Today." *Scientific American*, July 2017, p. 4, www.scientificamerican.com/article/ designing-the-city-of-tomorrow-today/.

Journal Article

Moriarty, Jeffrey. "Participation in the Workplace: Are Employees Special?" *Journal of Business Ethics*, vol. 92, no. 3, 2010, pp. 373–84.

Passow, Honor J., and Christian H. Passow. "What Competencies Should Undergraduate Engineering Programs Emphasize? A Systematic Review." *Journal of Engineering Education*, vol. 106, no. 3, July 2017, pp. 475–526. *Academic Search Complete*, doi:10.1002/jee.20171.ONLINE.

Shrestha, Maria E. I., et al. "Urban Energy Scenario: The Case of the Kathmandu Valley." *Journal of Engineering and Technological Sciences*, vol. 49, no. 2, 2017, pp. 210–24, journals.itb.ac.id/index .php/jets/article/view/5073/2810.

Newspaper Article

Jones, Rory. "Nations Meet to Discuss Web Rules." *The Wall Street Journal,* 4 Dec. 2012, p. B7.

Metz, Cade. "Chips Off the Old Block: Computers Are Taking Design Cues from Human Brains." *The New York Times*, 18 Sept. 2017, nyti.ms/2y5xcLS.

Article with an Unknown Author

"What Sold, for How Much, and Why?" *Modern*, vol. 1, no. 2, 2009, p. 22.

OTHER ELECTRONIC AND MULTIMEDIA SOURCES

Entire Web Site

Society for Technical Communication. 2017, www.stc.org.

Short Work from a Web Site, with an Author

Marshall, Rosalie. "IBM Bolsters Green Sensor Portfolio." *Business-Green*, 18 Aug. 2009, www.businessgreen.com/bg/news/1802285/ibm-bolsters-green-sensor-portfolio.

Short Work from a Web Site, with an Unknown Author

"Women-Owned Businesses." *U.S. Small Business Administration*, 20 July 2009, www.sba.gov/business-guide/grow/women-owned-businesses-programs.

Article Posted on a Wiki

"Labor Theory of Value." *Wikipedia*, 2 Sept. 2017, en.wikipedia.org/wiki/Labor_theory_of_value.

Online Posting and Comments (Lists, Forums, Discussion Boards, Blogs)

trabb. "Surviving the Job Search." *Chronicle Forums*, 15 Mar. 2009, *Chronicle of Higher Education*, www.chronicle.com/forums/index.php/topic,40486.0.html.

scamster. "Re Surviving the Job Search," by trabb. *Chronicle Forums*, 17 Aug. 2017, *Chronicle of Higher Education*, www.chronicle.com/forums/index.php/topic,40486.1230.html.

E-mail Message

Kalil, Ari. "Customer Satisfaction Survey." Received by Gerald Alred, 12 Jan. 2018.

Map or Chart

"Australia." *Perry-Castañeda Library Map Collection*, U of Texas, 1999, www.lib.utexas.edu/maps/australia/australia_pol99.jpg.

Film or Video

Chiu, Ken. "Trends in Mobile Gaming." Stanford U, 15 Nov. 2012, www.youtube.com/watch?v=zPD1ZyrilNw.

Radio or Television Program

"Obama's Failures Have Made Millennials Give Up Hope." *The Rush
Limbaugh Show*, hosted by Rush Limbaugh, Premiere Radio
Networks, 14 Apr. 2014, www.rushlimbaugh.com/daily/2014/04/14/
obama_s_failures_have_made_millennials_gi[ve_up_hope.

"Hacks or Malfunction, US Election Infrastructure Still Vulnerable." *The
Rachel Maddow Show*, hosted by Rachel Maddow, MSNBC, 1 Sept.
2017, www.msnbc.com/rachel-maddow-show.

Podcast

McDougall, Christopher. "How Did Endurance Help Early Humans Survive?"
TED Radio Hour, National Public Radio, 20 Nov. 2015, www.npr.org/
2015/11/20/455904655/how-did-endurance-help-early-humans-
survive.

Broadcast Interview

Russell, David O. Interview by Terry Gross. *Fresh Air*, WNYC, 20 Feb. 2014.

Personal Interview

Andersen, Elizabeth. Personal interview, 29 Nov. 2014.

Brochure or Pamphlet

Historic Preservation Tax Incentives. United States, Department of the
Interior, National Park Service, 2016, www.nps.gov/tps/tax
-incentives.htm.

Government Document

Highlights of Women's Earnings in 2015. Bureau of Labor Statistics, U.S.
Department of Labor, Nov. 2016, www.bls.gov/opub/reports/womens
-earnings/2015/home.htm.

Report

World Development Report: Governance and the Law. World Bank, 2017,
hdl.handle.net/10986/25880.

MLA Sample Pages

Litzinger 14

Author's last name and page number

D

MLA

One-inch margins. Text double-spaced

This report examines the nature and disposition of the 3,458 ethics cases handled companywide by CGF's ethics officers and managers during 2014. The purpose of such reports is to provide the Ethics and Business Conduct Committee with the information necessary for assessing the effectiveness of the first year of CGF's Ethics Program (Davis et al. 142). According to Matthias Jonas, recommendations are given for consideration "in planning for the second year of the Ethics Program" ("Internet" 152).

In-text citations give author name and page number. Brief title used when no author named

The Office of Ethics and Business Conduct was created to administer the Ethics Program. The director of the Office of Ethics and Business Conduct, along with seven ethics officers throughout CGF, was given the responsibility for the following objectives, as described by Rossouw:

Long quote indented one inch, double-spaced, without quotation marks

> Communicate the values, standards, and goals of CGF's Program to employees. Provide companywide channels for employee education and guidance in resolving ethics concerns. Implement companywide programs in ethics awareness and recognition. Employee accessibility to ethics information and guidance is the immediate goal of the Office of Business Conduct in its first year. (1543)

The purpose of the Ethics Program, according to Jonas, is to "promote ethical business conduct through open communication and compliance with company ethics standards" ("Ethics" 89). To accomplish this purpose, any ethics policy must ensure con-

FIGURE D–8. MLA Sample Page (from a Report)

D

MLA

Litzinger 15

Works Cited

Conflicts of Interest and Standards of Ethical Conduct. U.S. National

Science Foundation, NSF Manual No. 15, 6 Jan. 2017,

www.nsf.gov/pubs/manuals/manual15.pdf.

Davis, W. C., et al. *Working in the System: Five New Management*

Principles. St. Martin's Press, 2016.

International Business Ethics Institute. 2017, berkleycenter.georgetown

.edu/organizations/international-business-ethics-institute.

Jonas, Matthias. "Ethics in Organizational Communication:

A Review of the Literature." *Journal of Ethics and*

Communication, vol. 40, no. 3, 2017, pp. 79–99,

doi:10.9798/0838-2180025856.

Jonas, Matthias. "The Internet and Ethical Communication: Toward

a New Paradigm." *Journal of Ethics and Communication,*

vol. 32, no. 1, 2015, pp. 147–77.

Rossouw, George J. "Business Ethics in South Africa." *Journal of*

Business Ethics, vol. 16, no. 14, Oct. 1997, pp. 1539–47,

doi:10.1023/A:1005858930223.

Sariolghalam, Mahmood. Personal interview, 29 Jan. 2017.

Schipper, Fritz. "Transparency and Integrity: Contrary

Concepts?" *Globalisation and Business Ethics*, edited

by Karl Homann et al., Ashgate Press, 2017, pp. 101–18,

doi:10.4324/9781315585048.

Soloman, Paul. "Money and Ethics." *NewsHour*, PBS, 16 Aug. 2012.

UNCTV.org, video.unctv.org/video/2268858765/.

Heading
centered

Alphabet-
ized by
authors'
last names
or title and
double-
spaced

Hanging-
indent style
used for
entries

FIGURE D–9. MLA Sample List of Works Cited

double negatives

A double negative is the use of an additional negative word to reinforce an expression that is already negative. In writing and speech, avoid such constructions.

UNCLEAR We don't have none. [This sentence literally means that we have some.]

CLEAR We have none.

Barely, *hardly*, and *scarcely* cause problems when writers do not recognize that the words are already negative.

> The corporate policy ~~doesn't~~ hardly covers the problem.

Not unfriendly, *not without*, and similar constructions are not double negatives because in such constructions two negatives are meant to suggest the gray area between negative and positive meanings. Be careful how you use such constructions; they can be confusing to the reader and should be used only if they serve a purpose.

> He is *not unfriendly*. [He is neither hostile nor friendly.]

> It is *not without* regret that I offer my resignation. [I have mixed feelings rather than only regret.]

The correlative **conjunctions** *neither* and *nor* may appear together in a clause without creating a double negative, so long as the writer does not attempt to use the word *not* in the same clause.

> It was ~~not,~~ *neither,* as a matter of fact, ~~neither~~ his duty nor his desire to dismiss the employee.

> It was not, as a matter of fact, ~~neither~~ *either* his duty ~~nor~~ *or* his desire to dismiss the employee.

Negative forms are full of traps that often entice writers into **logic errors**, as illustrated in the following example:

ILLOGICAL The book reveals *nothing* that has *not* already been published in some form, but some of it is, I believe, relatively unknown.

In this sentence, "some of it" can logically refer only to "*nothing* that has *not* already been published." The sentence can be corrected by stating the idea in more **positive writing**.

D

LOGICAL   Everything in the book has been published in some form, but some of it is, I believe, relatively unknown.

drawings

A drawing can depict an object's appearance and illustrate the steps in procedures or **instructions**. It can emphasize the significant parts or functions of a device or product, omit what is not significant, and focus on details or relationships that a **photograph** cannot reveal. Think about your need for drawings during your **preparation** and **research**. Include the drawings in your outline, indicating approximately where each should be placed ("drawing of . . ." enclosed in **brackets**). For advice on integrating drawings into your text, see **outlining** and **visuals**.

Consider your medium, as well as your **purpose** and **audience**, when choosing the type of drawing to include. For example, publishing to an online digital format (such as a Web page) could allow you to include a line drawing that can be enlarged, automatically breaking into labeled cutaway parts. See also **infographics** and **selecting the medium**.

The types of drawings discussed in this entry are conventional line drawings, exploded-view drawings, cutaway drawings, and clip-art images.

A conventional line drawing is appropriate if your audience needs an overview of a series of steps or an understanding of an object's appearance or construction, as in Figure D–10.

PULL

the pin: Some extinguishers require releasing a lock latch, pressing a puncture lever, or taking another first step.

FIGURE D–10. Conventional Line Drawing

An exploded-view drawing, like that in Figure D–11, can be useful when you need to show the proper sequence in which parts fit together or to show the details of individual parts. Figure D–11 shows owners of a Xerox WorkCentre copier how to safely unpack the machine and its key parts.

Installation

As you unpack the WorkCentre, familiarize yourself with its contents. After the WorkCentre is installed, and the Ready Indicator is lit, the WorkCentre is ready to make copies.

IMPORTANT: Save the carton and packing materials. They should be used to repack the WorkCentre if it has to be shipped for servicing or in case you move.

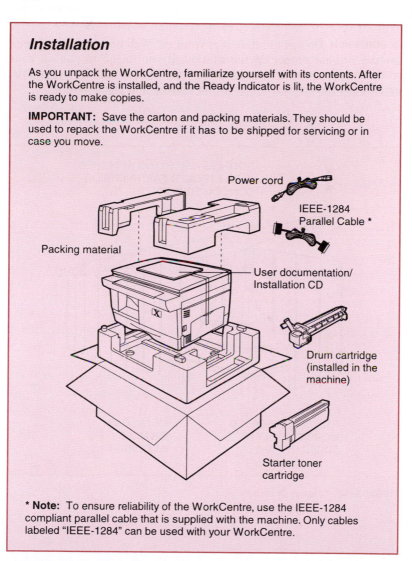

Power cord

IEEE-1284 Parallel Cable *

Packing material

User documentation/ Installation CD

Drum cartridge (installed in the machine)

Starter toner cartridge

* Note: To ensure reliability of the WorkCentre, use the IEEE-1284 compliant parallel cable that is supplied with the machine. Only cables labeled "IEEE-1284" can be used with your WorkCentre.

FIGURE D–11. Exploded-View Drawing
SOURCE: Xerox Corporation.

D

A cutaway drawing, like the one in Figure D–12, can be useful when you need to show the internal parts of a device or structure and illustrate their relationship to the whole.

If you need only general-interest images to illustrate **newsletters** and **brochures** or to create **presentation** slides, consider using free noncopyrighted clip-art drawings from online specialty sources. You may also consider purchasing images from online stock-image companies.

❖ **ETHICS NOTE** Do not use drawings from the Web or other copyrighted sources without proper documentation; if you intend to publish your work, seek permission from the copyright holder. See also **copyrights**, **patents and trademarks**, **documenting sources**, and **plagiarism**. ❖

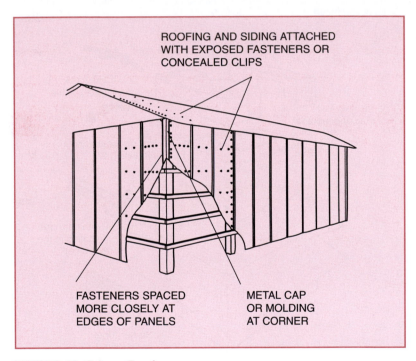

FIGURE D–12. Cutaway Drawing

| WRITER'S CHECKLIST | Creating and Using Drawings |

✔ Seek the help of graphics specialists for drawings that require a high degree of accuracy and precision.

✔ Show equipment and other objects from the point of view of the person who will use them.

✔ When illustrating a subsystem, show its relationship to the larger system of which it is a part.

✔ Draw the parts of an object in proportion to one another, and identify any parts that are enlarged or reduced.

✔ When a sequence of drawings is used to illustrate a process, arrange them from left to right or from top to bottom on the page.

✔ Label parts in the drawing so that the text references to them are clear and consistent.

✔ Depending on the complexity of what is shown, label the parts themselves, as in Figure D–11, or use a key, as in Figure G–11 on page 244.

due to / because of

Due to (meaning "caused by") is acceptable following a linking **verb**.

▶ His absence was *due to* a work-related injury.

Due to is not acceptable, however, when it is used with a nonlinking verb to replace *because of*.

▶ He left work ~~due to~~ illness.
  because of

E

each

When *each* is used as a subject, it takes a singular **verb** or **pronoun**. ("*Each* of the reports *is* to be submitted ten weeks after *it* is assigned.") When *each* refers to a plural subject, it takes a plural verb or pronoun. ("The reports *each have* company logos on *their* title pages.")

economic / economical

Economic refers to the production, development, and management of material wealth. ("Tax rates have an *economic* impact on communities.") *Economical* simply means "not wasteful or extravagant." ("Employees should be as *economical* as possible in their equipment purchases.")

editing (*see* revision *and* proofreading)

e.g. / i.e.

The abbreviation *e.g.* stands for the Latin *exempli gratia*, meaning "for example"; *i.e.* stands for the Latin *id est*, meaning "that is." Because the English expressions (*for example* and *that is*) are clear to all **readers**, avoid the Latin *e.g.* and *i.e.* **abbreviations** except to save space in notes and **visuals**. If you must use *i.e.* or *e.g.*, do not italicize either of them. If *i.e.* or *e.g.* connects two independent clauses, a **semicolon** should precede the abbreviation, and a **comma** should follow it.

▶ The conference reflected international viewpoints; e.g., speakers included Germans, Italians, Japanese, Chinese, and Americans.

If *i.e.* or *e.g.* connects a **noun** and an **appositive**, a comma should precede it and follow it.

▶ The conference included speakers from five countries, i.e., Germany, Italy, Japan, China, and the United States.

ellipses

E

An ellipsis is the omission of words from quoted material; it is indicated by three spaced **periods** called *ellipsis points* (. . .). When you use ellipsis points, omit original punctuation marks unless they are necessary for **clarity** or the omitted material comes at the end of a quoted sentence.

ORIGINAL TEXT	"Promotional material sometimes carries a fee, particularly in high-volume distribution to schools, although prices for these publications are much lower than the development costs when all factors are considered."
WITH OMISSION AND ELLIPSIS POINTS	"Promotional material sometimes carries a fee . . . although prices for these publications are much lower than the development costs. . . ."

Notice in the preceding example that the final period is retained and what remains of the quotation is grammatically complete. When the omitted part of the quotation is preceded by a period, retain the period and add the three ellipsis points after it, as in the following example.

ORIGINAL TEXT	"Of the 172 major ethics cases reported, 57 percent were found to involve unsubstantiated concerns. Misinformation was the cause of unfounded concerns of misconduct in 72 cases. Forty-four cases, or 26 percent of the total cases reported, involved incidents partly substantiated by ethics officers as serious misconduct."
WITH OMISSION AND ELLIPSIS POINTS	"Of the 172 major ethics cases reported, 57 percent were found to involve unsubstantiated concerns. . . . Forty-four cases, or 26 percent of the total cases reported, involved incidents partly substantiated by ethics officers as serious misconduct."

Do not use ellipsis points when the beginning of a quoted sentence is omitted. Notice in the following example that the comma is dropped to prevent a grammatical error. See also **quotations**.

▶ The ethics report states that "26 percent of the total cases reported involved incidents partly substantiated by ethics officers as serious misconduct."

e-mail

E

E-mail (or *email*) functions in the workplace as a primary medium to exchange information and share electronic files with colleagues, clients, and customers. E-mail messages range from short, informal notes to longer, more formal communications. For general writing strategy and appropriate professional style, see **correspondence**. See also **letters**, **memos**, and **selecting the medium**.

Review and Confidentiality

Avoid the temptation to send the first draft of a message without rereading it for clarity and appropriateness. As with all correspondence, your message should include all crucial details and be free of grammatical and factual errors, ambiguities, and unintended implications. See **proofreading** and **spelling**.

Keep in mind that e-mails are easily forwarded and are never truly deleted. Most companies back up and save all their e-mail messages and are legally entitled to monitor e-mail use. Companies can be compelled, depending on circumstances, to provide e-mail and digital messaging logs in response to legal requests. Consider the content of all your messages in the light of these possibilities, and carefully review your message before you click "Send."

◀ **PROFESSIONALISM NOTE** Be especially careful when sending messages to superiors in your organization or to people outside the organization. Spending extra time reviewing your e-mail can save you the embarrassment caused by a carelessly written message. One helpful strategy is to write the draft and revise your e-mail before filling in the "To" line with the address of your recipient. ▶

WRITER'S CHECKLIST   **Maintaining Professionalism**

✔ Review your organization's policy regarding the appropriate use of e-mail.

✔ Do not forward jokes or *spam*, discuss office gossip, or use **biased language**.

(continued)

✔ Do not send *flames* (e-mails that contain abusive, obscene, or derogatory language) to attack someone. See also **blogs and forums**.

✔ Avoid *abbreviations* (*BTW* for *by the way*, for example), emoticons, and emojis used in personal e-mail, discussion forums, **text messaging**, and **instant messaging and live chat**.

✔ Use typographical features (like bold or colors) carefully to provide **emphasis**. Do not write in all lowercase letters or in ALL UPPERCASE LETTERS.

✔ Base your personal e-mail username on your personal name (smith123@domain.com). Avoid clever names (sushilover@domain.com), since you may need to use your account for professional or **job search** purposes.

✔ Write a cover message when including attachments ("Attached is a copy of . . ."), and double-check that it is indeed attached. See **cover letters**.

✔ Always sign the e-mail and use a signature block (see Figure E–1 on page 170); doing so is both polite and a way to avoid possible confusion.

✔ Send a "courtesy response" informing the sender when you need additional time to reply or when you need to confirm that you have received a message or an attachment.

✔ When absent, use "out of office" autoresponder messages that state the dates you will be unavailable or an alternative way to reach you and who to contact in your absence. Add a reminder to your calendar to remove the message the day you return.

Writing and Design

Make the main point early and use short paragraphs to avoid dense blocks of text. For longer and more detailed messages, provide a brief paragraph overview at the beginning. Adapt forwarded messages by revising the subject line to reflect the current content and cut irrelevant previous text or highlight key text, based on your **purpose** and **context**.

Provide a specific subject line, as described on page 117, after composing the message so that your topic is precise and clear to the reader. An empty subject line is unprofessional and may be interpreted as spam and thus routed to junk mail.

Adapt your salutation and complimentary closing to your **audience** and the context.

• When e-mail functions as a traditional business letter, consider the standard salutation (*Dear Ms. Tucker:* or *Dear Docuform Customer:*) and closing (*Sincerely,* or *Best wishes,*).

- When you send e-mail to individuals or small groups inside an organization, you may wish to adopt a more personal greeting (*Dear Andy,* or *Dear Project Colleagues,*) and closing (*Regards*, or *Good luck*).

- When e-mail functions as a personal note to a friend or close colleague, you can use an informal greeting (*Hi, Mike,* or *Hello, Jenny*) or only a first name and a closing (*Take care,* or *Best,*).

Be aware that in some cultures, professionals do not refer to recipients or colleagues by their first names. See **international correspondence**.

Many companies and professionals include signature blocks (also called *signatures*) at the bottom of their messages. Signatures, which are set to appear at the end of every e-mail, supply information traditionally provided on company letterhead. Many organizations provide graphic signature forms or formatting standards. If yours does not, consider the following guidelines for formatting text-based signatures:

- Keep line length to sixty characters or fewer to avoid unpredictable line wraps.

- Test your signature block in plain-text e-mail systems to verify your format.

- Avoid using quotations, aphorisms, proverbs, or other sayings from popular culture, religion, or poetry in professional signatures.

The pattern shown in Figure E–1 is typical.

➦ Send ✕ Cancel ▤ Save Draft ✚ Add Attachment ✉ Signature Options ▶

TO	
Subject	

Daniel J. Vasquez, Benefits Manager ← Name and Title
Human Resources Department ← Department or Division
Fencon Insurance Corporation ← Company Name
P.O. Box 5413 Salinas, CA 93962 ← Mailing Address
Tel: 888-719-6620 Fax: 888-719-5500 ← Phone and Fax
www.fencon.com/benefits ← Web Address

FIGURE E–1. E-mail Signature Block

WRITER'S CHECKLIST   **Managing Your E-mail and Reducing Overload**

E

✔ Avoid becoming involved in an e-mail exchange if a phone call or meeting would be more efficient.

✔ Consider whether an e-mail message could prompt an unnecessary response from the recipient, and make clear to the recipient whether you expect a response.

✔ Send a copy ("cc:") of an e-mail only when the person copied needs or wants the information, and don't expect a response.

✔ Review all messages on a subject before responding to avoid dealing with issues that are no longer relevant.

✔ Set priorities for reading e-mail by skimming sender names and subject lines as well as where you appear (in the "to" or "cc:" line).

✔ Check the e-mail address before sending an e-mail to make sure it is correct.

✔ Determine the best way to organize e-mails in your system: using flags to highlight topics, search commands to find topics, or folders to group e-mails. You may want to save important e-mails as PDFs in an appropriate folder.

✔ Check your in-box regularly, and try to either clear it or categorize it and file new messages by the end of each day.

❖ **ETHICS NOTE** The blind-copy (*bcc:*) function allows writers to send copies of a message to someone without the primary receiver's knowledge. Use the bcc: notation with great care. Sending sensitive or confidential information to a third party as a blind copy without the original recipient's knowledge is unethical when used to play office politics. The blind-copy function is both ethical and useful, however, when used to protect the privacy of the e-mail addresses of a large group of recipients. Keep in mind that such addresses might be visible to your supervisors or your company's IT team. ❖

◀ **PROFESSIONALISM NOTE** Double-check your "To" box addressees carefully before hitting the "Send" button. The auto-fill feature in e-mail programs automatically fills in the names of recipients and other information in your "To" box based on the first few letters you type. Although it is a convenient feature, be aware that your e-mail can easily wind up in the wrong in-box when the names of people in your address book are similar (Donna/Donnie) or when two people share the same last name. The result can lead to embarrassing misunderstandings or to confidential information being sent to the wrong people. ▶

emphasis

Emphasis in writing means highlighting the facts and ideas you consider important and subordinating those of secondary importance. You can achieve emphasis with any of these techniques: position, climactic order, sentence length, sentence type, active **voice**, **repetition**, **intensifiers**, direct statements, long **dashes**, and typographical devices.

E

Achieving Emphasis

Position.   Place the idea in a conspicuous position. The first and last words of a sentence, **paragraph**, or document stand out.

▶   Moon craters are important to understanding the earth's history because they reflect geological history.

The term *moon craters* is emphasized because it appears at the beginning of the sentence, and *geological history* is emphasized because it appears at the end of the sentence. See also **subordination**.

Climactic Order.   List the ideas or facts within a sentence in sequence from least to most important, as in the following example. See also **lists**.

▶   Discontinuation of the HGX212 line of circuit boards would cause some technicians to be relocated to other cities, some to be reclassified to a lower grade, and some to lose their jobs.

Sentence Length.   Vary sentence length strategically. A short sentence that follows a long sentence or a series of long sentences stands out in the reader's mind, as in the short sentence that ends the following paragraph ("We must cut costs."). See **sentence construction**.

▶   We have already reviewed the problem the accounting department has experienced during the past year. We could continue to examine the causes of our problems and point an accusing finger at all the culprits beyond our control, but in the end it all leads to one simple conclusion. We must cut costs.

Sentence Type.   Vary sentences by the strategic use of a compound sentence, a complex sentence, or a simple sentence. See **sentence variety**.

▶   The report submitted by the committee was carefully illustrated, and it covered five pages of single-spaced copy. [This compound sentence carries no special emphasis; it contains two coordinate independent clauses.]

► The committee's report, which was carefully illustrated, covered five pages of single-spaced copy. [This complex sentence emphasizes the size of the report.]

► The carefully illustrated report submitted by the committee covered five pages of single-spaced copy. [This simple sentence emphasizes that the report was carefully illustrated.]

E

Active Voice. Use the active voice to emphasize the performer of an action: Make the performer the subject of the **verb**.

► Our department designed the new system. [This sentence emphasizes *our department*, which is the performer and the subject of the verb, *designed*.]

Repetition. Repeat key terms, as in the use of the word *remains* and the phrase *come and go* in the following sentence.

► Similarly, atoms *come and go* in a molecule, but the molecule *remains*; molecules *come and go* in a cell, but the cell *remains*; cells *come and go* in a body, but the body *remains*; persons *come and go* in an organization, but the organization *remains*.
　　　　　　　　　　　　　—Kenneth Boulding, *Beyond Economics*

Intensifiers. Although you can use intensifiers (*most*, *much*, *very*) for emphasis, this technique is so easily abused that it should be used with caution.

► The final proposal is *much* more persuasive than the first one. [The intensifier *much* emphasizes the contrast.]

Direct Statements. Use direct statements, such as "most important," "foremost," or someone's name in a **direct address**.

► Most important, keep in mind that everything you do affects the company's bottom line.

► John, I believe we should rethink our plans.

Long Dashes. Use a dash to call attention to a particular word or statement.

► The job will be done—after we are under contract.

Typographical Devices. Use *italics*, **bold type**, underlining, color, and CAPITAL LETTERS—but use them sparingly because overuse can create visual clutter and cause readers to ignore truly important information. See also **capitalization**, **italics**, and **layout and design**.

English as a second language

E

Learning to write well in a second language takes a great deal of effort and practice. The most effective way to improve your command of written English is to read widely beyond the reports and professional articles your job requires, such as magazines, newspapers, articles, novels, biographies, and any other writing that interests you. In addition, listen carefully to native speakers on television, on the radio, on podcasts, and in person. Do not hesitate to consult a native speaker of English—especially for important writing tasks, such as **e-mails**, **memos**, and **reports**. Focus on those particular areas of English that give you trouble. This entry covers several areas often confusing to nonnative speakers and writers of English. See also **global communication**.

Count and Mass Nouns

Count nouns refer to things that can be counted (*tables, pencils, projects, employees*). *Mass nouns* (also called *noncount nouns*) identify things that cannot be counted (*electricity, air, loyalty, information*). This distinction can be confusing with words like *electricity* and *water*. Although we can count kilowatt-hours of electricity and bottles of water, counting becomes inappropriate when we use the words *electricity* and *water* in a general sense, as in "*Water* is an essential resource." Following is a list of typical mass **nouns**.

advice	equipment	news	technology
biology	furniture	oil	transportation
business	honesty	precision	waste
education	money	research	work

The distinction between something that can and something that cannot be counted determines the form of the noun to use (singular or plural), the kind of **article** that precedes it (*a, an, the,* or no article), and the kind of limiting **adjective** it requires (such as *fewer* or *less* and *much* or *many*). (See also **fewer / less**.) Notice that count and mass nouns are always common nouns; they are not proper nouns, such as the names of people.

Articles and Modifiers

Every singular count noun must be preceded by an article (*a*, *an*, or *the*), a demonstrative adjective (*this*, *that*, *these*, or *those*), a possessive adjective (*my*, *your*, *her*, *his*, *its*, *our*, *their*, or *whose*), or some expression of quantity (*one*, *two*, *several*, *many*, *a few*, *a lot of*, *some*, *no*). The article, adjective, or expression of quantity appears either directly in front of the noun or in front of the whole noun phrase.

- ▶ Beth read *a* report last week. [article]
- ▶ *Those* reports Beth read were long. [demonstrative adjective]
- ▶ *Their* report was long. [possessive adjective]
- ▶ *Some* reports Beth read were long. [indefinite adjective]

The articles *a* and *an* are used with count nouns that refer to one item of the whole class of like items.

- ▶ Matthew has *a* pen. [Matthew could have any pen.]

The article *the* is used with nouns that refer to a specific item that both the reader and the writer can identify.

- ▶ Matthew has *the* pen. [Matthew has a specific pen that is known to both the reader and the writer.]

When making generalizations with count nouns, writers can either use *a* or *an* with a singular count noun or use no article with a plural count noun. Consider the following generalization using an article.

- ▶ *An* egg is a good source of protein. [any egg, all eggs, eggs in general]

However, the following generalization uses a plural count noun with no article.

- ▶ *Eggs* are a good source of protein. [any egg, all eggs, eggs in general]

When you are making a generalization with a mass noun, do not use an article in front of the mass noun.

- ▶ *Sugar* is bad for your teeth.

Gerunds and Infinitives

Nonnative writers of English are often puzzled about whether to use a gerund or an infinitive as a direct object of a **verb** (see **verbals**) because no structural rule exists for distinguishing which form to use. Any particular verb may take an infinitive as its object, others may take a gerund, and still others take either an infinitive or a gerund. At times, even the base form of the verb is used.

▶ He enjoys *working*. [gerund as a complement]

▶ She promised *to fulfill* her part of the contract. [infinitive as a complement]

▶ The president had the manager *assign* her staff to another project. [basic verb form as a complement]

To make such distinctions accurately, rely on what you hear native speakers use or what you read. You might also consult a reference book for ESL students.

Adjective Clauses

Because of the variety of ways adjective clauses are constructed in different languages, they can be particularly troublesome. The following guidelines will help you form adjective clauses correctly.

Place an adjective clause directly after the noun it modifies.

▶ The tall woman is a vice president of the company ~~who is standing across the room.~~ *who is standing across the room*

The adjective clause *who is standing across the room* modifies *woman*, not *company*, and thus should come directly after *woman*.

Avoid using a relative pronoun with another pronoun in an adjective clause.

▶ The man who ~~he~~ sits at that desk is my boss.

Present Perfect Verb Tense

In general, use the present perfect **tense** to refer to events completed in the past that have some implication for the present.

PRESENT PERFECT   She *has performed* the experiment three times. [She might perform it again.]

When a specific time is mentioned, however, use the simple past tense.

SIMPLE PAST   I *wrote* the letter yesterday morning. [The action, *wrote*, does not affect the present.]

Use the present perfect with a *since* or *for* phrase to describe actions that began in the past and continue in the present.

- This company *has been* in business *for* fifteen years.
- This company *has been* in business *since* 2000.

Present Progressive Verb Tense

The present progressive tense is especially difficult for those whose native language does not use this tense. The present progressive tense is used to describe some action or condition that is ongoing (or in progress) in the present and may continue into the future.

PRESENT
PROGRESSIVE   I *am searching* for an error in the document. [The search is occurring now and may continue.]

In contrast, the simple present tense more often relates to routine actions.

SIMPLE PRESENT   I *search* for errors in my documents. [I regularly search for errors, but I am not necessarily searching now.]

English, varieties of

Written English includes two broad categories: standard and nonstandard. Standard English is used in business, industry, government, education, and all professions. It has rigorous and precise criteria for capitalization, punctuation, spelling, and usage. Nonstandard English does not conform to such criteria; it is often regional in origin, or it reflects the special usages of a particular ethnic or social group. As a result, although nonstandard English may be vigorous and colorful, its usefulness as a means of communication is limited to certain contexts and to people already familiar and comfortable with it in those contexts. It rarely appears in printed material except for special effect. Nonstandard English is characterized by inexact or inconsistent **capitalization**, **punctuation**, **spelling**, diction, and **usage** choices.

Colloquial English

Colloquial English is spoken English or writing that uses words and expressions common to casual conversation. ("We need to get him up to speed.") Colloquial English is appropriate in some kinds of writing (personal letters, notes, some **e-mail**) but not in most workplace writing.

Dialectal English

Dialectal English is a social or regional variety of the language that is comprehensible to people of that social group or region but may be incomprehensible to outsiders. Dialect, which is usually nonstandard

English, involves distinct **word choice**, grammatical forms, and pronunciations. For example, residents of southern Louisiana who descended from French colonists speak a dialect often referred to as Cajun.

Localisms

A localism is a regional wording or phrasing. For example, a large sandwich on a long split roll is known in various regions of the United States as a *sub*, *hero*, *hoagie*, *grinder*, *poor boy*, or *torpedo*. Localisms should normally be avoided in workplace writing, unless the writer is confident that all readers will be familiar with a term.

Slang

Slang is an informal vocabulary composed of **figures of speech** and colorful words used in humorous or extravagant ways. There is no objective test for slang, and many standard words are given slang applications. For instance, slang may be a familiar word used in a new way (*chill* meaning "relax") or a completely new word (*selfie* meaning "an informal photograph taken of oneself").

Most slang is short lived and has meaning only for a narrow **audience**. Sometimes, however, slang becomes standard because the word fills a legitimate need. *Skyscraper* and *date* (as in "go on a date"), for example, were once considered slang expressions. Nevertheless, although slang may be valid in informal and personal writing or fiction, it should generally be avoided in workplace writing. See also **jargon** and **business writing style**.

equal / unique / perfect

Logically, *equal* (meaning "having the same quantity or value as another"), *unique* (meaning "one of a kind"), and *perfect* (meaning "a state of highest excellence") are words with absolute meanings and therefore should not be compared. However, colloquial usage of *more* and *most* as **modifiers** of *equal*, *unique*, and *perfect* is so common that an absolute prohibition on such use is impossible.

▶ Our system is more unique [*or* more perfect] than theirs.

Some writers try to overcome the problem by using *more nearly* (*more nearly equal*, *more nearly unique*, *more nearly perfect*). When clarity and preciseness are critical, the use of comparative degrees with *equal*, *unique*, and *perfect* can be vague. It is best to avoid using comparative degrees with absolute terms. See also **comparison**.

VAGUE	Ours is a *more equal* percentage split than theirs.
PRECISE	Our percentage split is 51–49; theirs is 54–46.

etc.

Etc. is an abbreviation for the Latin *et cetera*, meaning "and others" or "and so on." Therefore, do not use the redundant phrase *and etc.* Likewise, do not use *etc.* at the end of a series introduced by the phrases *such as* and *for example* — those phrases already indicate unnamed items of the same category. Use *etc.* with a logical progression (*1, 2, 3, etc.*) and when at least two items are named. Do not italicize *etc.*

▶ The sorting machine processes coins (pennies, nickels, etc.) and then packages them for redistribution.

Otherwise, avoid *etc.* because the reader may not be able to infer what other items a list might include.

VAGUE	He will bring notepads, paper clips, etc., to the trade show.
CLEAR	He will bring notepads, paper clips, and other office supplies to the trade show.

ethics in writing

Ethics refers to the choices we make that affect others for good or ill. Ethical issues are inherent in writing and speaking because what we write and say can influence others. Further, how we express ideas affects our audience's perceptions of us and our organization's ethical stance. See also **audience**.

❖ **ETHICS NOTE** No book can describe how to act ethically in every situation, but this entry describes some typical ethical lapses to watch for during **revision**.* In other entries throughout this book, ethical issues are highlighted using the symbols surrounding this paragraph. ❖

Avoid language that attempts to evade responsibility. Some writers use the passive **voice** because they hope to avoid responsibility or to obscure an issue: "It has been decided" (*Who* has decided?) or "Several mistakes were made" (*Who* made them?).

*Information from Sims, B. R. (1993). Linking ethics and language in the technical communications classroom. *Technical communication quarterly* 2(3): 285–99.

E

Avoid deceptive language. Do not use words with more than one meaning to circumvent the truth. Consider the company document that stated, "A nominal charge will be assessed for using our facilities." When clients objected that the charge was actually very high, the writer pointed out that the word *nominal* means "the named amount" in addition to "very small." In that situation, clients had a strong case in charging that the company was attempting to be deceptive. The use of various **abstract words**, technical and legal **jargon**, and **euphemisms** is unethical when those words and phrases are used to mislead readers or to hide a serious or dangerous situation, even though technical or legal experts could interpret those words and terms as accurate. See also **word choice**.

Do not deemphasize or suppress important information. Not including information that a reader would want to have, such as potential safety hazards or hidden costs for which a customer might be responsible, is unethical and possibly illegal. Likewise, do not hide information in dense paragraphs of **gobbledygook** with small type and little white space, as is common in credit-card contracts. Use such **layout and design** features as legible type sizes, bulleted or numbered **lists**, and footnotes to highlight information that is important to readers.

Do not mislead with partial or self-serving information. For example, avoid the temptation to highlight a feature or service that readers would find attractive but that is available only with certain product models or at extra cost. (See also **logic errors** and **positive writing**.) Readers could justifiably object that you have given them a false impression to sell them a product or service, especially if you also deemphasize the extra cost or other special conditions.

In general, treat others—individuals, companies, groups—with fairness and with respect. Avoid language that is biased, racist, or sexist or that perpetuates stereotypes. See also **biased language**.

Finally, be aware that both **plagiarism** and violations of **copyright** not only are unethical but also can have serious professional and legal consequences for you in the classroom and on the job.

WRITER'S CHECKLIST   **Writing Ethically**

Ask yourself the following questions:

✔ *Am I willing to take responsibility, publicly and privately, for what I have written?* Make sure you can stand behind what you have written.

✔ *Is the document or message honest and truthful?* Scrutinize findings and conclusions carefully. Make sure that the data support them.

✔ *Am I acting in my employer's, my client's, the public's, or my own best long-term interest?* Have an impartial and appropriate outsider review and comment on what you have written.

(continued)

| **WRITER'S CHECKLIST** | **Writing Ethically** (*continued*) |

✔ *Does the document or message violate anyone's rights?* If information is confidential and you have serious concerns, consider a review by the company's legal staff or an attorney.

✔ *Am I ethically consistent in my writing?* Consistently apply the principles outlined here and those you have assimilated throughout your life.

✔ *How will your reader interpret your message?* If you were the intended reader, consider whether the message is acceptable and respectful.

If the answers to these questions do not come easily, consider asking a trusted colleague to review and comment on what you have written.

euphemisms

A euphemism is an inoffensive substitute for a word or phrase that could be distasteful, offensive, or too blunt: *passed away* for *died*; *previously owned* or *preowned* for *used*; *lay off* or *downsize* for *fire* or *terminate* employees. Used judiciously, euphemisms can help you avoid embarrassing or offending someone.

❖ **ETHICS NOTE** Euphemisms can also hide the facts of a situation (*incident* or *event* for *accident*) or be a form of **affectation** if used carelessly. Avoid them especially in **international correspondence** and other forms of **global communication** where their meanings could be not only confusing but also misleading. See also **ethics in writing**. ❖

everybody / everyone

Both *everybody* and *everyone* are usually considered singular and take singular **verbs** and **pronouns**.

▶ *Everyone* here *leaves* at 4:30 p.m.

▶ *Everybody* at the meeting presented *his or her* individual assessment.

However, their meaning can be obviously plural.

▶ *Everyone* thought the plan should be rejected, and I really couldn't blame *them*.

Although normally written as one word, they can be written as two words if you wish to emphasize each individual in a group. ("*Every one* of the team members contributed to this discovery.") See also **agreement**.

E   everyday / every day

Everyday (one word) is an **adjective** that means "commonplace," "normal," or "ordinary." *Every day* (two words) means "each day."

▶ We now purchase *everyday* office supplies from MCL Products.

▶ I need to travel to the construction site *every day* this week.

exclamation marks

The exclamation mark (!) indicates strong feeling, urgency, elation, or surprise ("Hurry!" "Great!" "Wow!"). (See also **interjections**.) However, it cannot make an argument more convincing, lend force to a weak statement, or call attention to an intended irony.

An exclamation mark can be used after a whole sentence or an element of a sentence.

▶ This meeting—please note it well!—concerns our budget deficit.

When used with **quotation marks**, the exclamation mark goes outside unless what is quoted is an exclamation.

▶ The paramedic shouted, "Don't touch the victim!" The bystander then, according to a witness, "jumped like a kangaroo"!

In **instructions**, the exclamation mark is often used in cautions and warnings ("Danger!" "Stop!") or enclosed within a triangle ⚠. See also **emphasis**.

executive summaries

An executive summary consolidates the principal points of a **formal report** or another long document. Executive summaries differ from **abstracts** in that **readers** scan abstracts to decide whether to read the work in full. An executive summary may be the only section of a longer work read by many readers, so it must accurately and concisely represent the original document. It should restate the document's **purpose**, **scope**, methods, findings, **conclusions**, and recommendations, as well as summarize how results were obtained or the reasons for the recommendations. Executive summaries tend to be about 10 percent of the length and generally follow the same sequence of the documents they summarize.

Write the executive summary so that it can be read independently of the report or proposal it summarizes. Executive summaries may occasionally include a figure, table, or footnote—if that information is essential to the summary. However, do not refer by number to figures, tables, or references contained elsewhere in the document. See the sample executive summary in Figure F–6 (pages 207–8).

WRITER'S CHECKLIST   **Writing Executive Summaries**

✔ Write the executive summary after you have completed the original document.

✔ Avoid or define terminology that may not be familiar to your intended **audience**.

✔ Spell out all uncommon symbols and **abbreviations**.

✔ Make the summary concise, but do not omit transitional words and phrases (*however, moreover, therefore, for example, next*).

✔ Include only information discussed in the original document.

✔ Place the executive summary at the beginning of the body of the report, as described in **formal reports**.

---

expletives

An expletive is a word that fills the position of another word, phrase, or clause. *It* and *there* are common expletives.

▶ *It* is certain that he will be promoted.

In the example, the expletive *it* occupies the position of subject in place of the real subject, *that he will be promoted.* Expletives are sometimes necessary to avoid **awkwardness**, but they are commonly overused, and most sentences can be better stated without them.

  Many   *were*
▶ ~~There were many~~ files lost when we converted to the new server.

In addition to its grammatical use, the word *expletive* means a profane exclamation or oath.

E

explicit / implicit

An *explicit* statement is one expressed directly, with precision and clarity.

▶ He gave us *explicit* directions to the Wausau facility.

An *implicit* meaning is one that is not directly expressed.

▶ Although the CEO did not mention the lawsuit directly, the company's commitment to ethical practices was *implicit* in her speech.

exposition

Exposition, or *expository writing*, refers to writing intended primarily to inform **readers** by presenting facts and ideas in direct and concise language; it usually relies less on colorful or figurative language than writing meant to be expressive or persuasive. It is aimed at readers' understanding rather than at their imagination or emotions. For this reason, exposition is widely used in **reports**, **memos**, and other types of technical and workplace writing. Expository writing aims to provide accurate, complete information and to analyze it for readers. As with all workplace writing, include only enough information to meet your readers' needs and your **purpose**. See also **audience** and **business writing style**.

F

fact

Expressions containing the word *fact* ("due to the *fact* that," "except for the *fact* that," "as a matter of *fact*," or "because of the *fact* that") are often wordy substitutes for more accurate terms. See **conciseness** and **logic errors**.

> *Because*
> ► ~~Due to the fact that~~ the sales force has had a high turnover rate, ˄sales have declined.

Do not use the word *fact* to refer to matters of judgment or opinion.

> *In my opinion,*
> ► ~~It is a fact that~~ sales are poor in the Midwest because of insuffi-˄cient market research.

The word *fact* is, of course, valid when facts are what is meant.

> ► Our study uncovered numerous facts to support your conclusion.

FAQs (Frequently Asked Questions)

An FAQ is a **list** of questions, paired with their answers, that readers will likely ask about products, services, or other information presented on a Web site or in customer-oriented documents. By presenting commonly sought information in one place, FAQs save readers from searching through an entire Web site or document to find what they need.

A well-planned FAQ list can help create a positive impression with customers or clients because the writer acknowledges that the reader's time is valuable. An FAQ list also helps a company spend less time responding to questions. However, an FAQ list is not a substitute for solving problems with a product or service.

❖ **ETHICS NOTE** If customers are experiencing numerous problems because of a product design or programming flaw, you need to work with your company's product developers to correct the problem rather than attempting to avoid the issue by burying it within an FAQ. ❖

185

F

Questions to Include

Develop the list of questions and their answers by brainstorming with colleagues who are regularly in contact with customers. If customers frequently ask about company stock information and request **annual reports**, for example, your FAQ list could include the question "How do I obtain a copy of your latest annual report?" This question can be followed with a brief answer that includes the Web address from which the annual report can be downloaded or the name, phone number, and e-mail address of the person who distributes the annual reports. See also **writing for the Web**.

Organization

Organize the list so that readers can find the information they need quickly and easily. List your questions in decreasing **order of importance** for your readers so that they can obtain the most important information first. If you have a number of questions that are related to a specific topic, such as investor relations, product returns, or completing forms, group them into categories and identify each category with a heading, such as "Investor Relations," "Shipping," and "Forms." You may also want to create a **table of contents** at the top of the FAQ page so that readers can quickly find the topics relevant to their interests.

Study other FAQ lists for products or services similar to yours. Analyze them for their approach and organization: Can you find answers quickly, or do you need to scroll through many pages to find them? Are the questions plus answers separated into logical categories or listed in random order? Is it easy to differentiate a question from its answer? Do the answers provide too little or too much information? Does the FAQ list offer specialized search tools to help readers find information for longer FAQs?

Placement

The location of your FAQ list should enable readers to find answers quickly. On Web sites, an FAQ page is usually linked from the homepage. In small printed documents, such as **brochures**, FAQs are usually highlighted and placed after the body of the document.

WRITER'S CHECKLIST **Developing FAQs**

✔ *Focus on your reader.* Write your questions and answers from a **"you" viewpoint** and with a positive, conversational **tone**.

✔ *Separate long FAQ lists into groups.* Group related questions under topic **headings**. For long online FAQ lists, consider listing only questions and include links to separate pages, each containing an individual question and answer.

(continued)

✔ *Distinguish questions from answers.* Use boldface for questions and use white space to separate questions from answers. Be sparing in your use of multiple colors, **italics**, or other formatting styles that can make the list difficult to read.

✔ *Keep questions and answers concise.* If a question has a long answer, add a link to a separate Web page or refer to an appropriate page number in a printed document.

✔ *Keep the list updated.* Review and update FAQs at least monthly — or more frequently if your content changes often.

✔ *Give readers the opportunity to respond.* Provide an e-mail link for existing and potential customers to submit questions they would like to see added to the FAQ list.

✔ *Consider available tools for automating the process.* Many content-management systems, for example, have built-in FAQ-writing software.

feasibility reports

When organizations consider a new project — developing a new product or service, purchasing equipment, or moving operations — they first try to determine the project's chances for success. A feasibility report presents evidence about the practicality of a proposed project based on specific criteria, as in Figure F–1. It answers such questions as the following: Is new construction or development necessary? Is sufficient staff available? What are the costs? Is funding available? What are the legal or regulatory ramifications? Based on the findings of this analysis, the report offers logical conclusions and recommends whether the project should be carried out. When feasibility reports stress specific steps that should be taken as a result of a study of a problem or an issue, they are often referred to as *recommendation reports*. In the condensed feasibility report shown in Figure F–1, a consultant conducts a study to determine how to upgrade a company's computer system and Internet capability.

Before beginning to write a feasibility report, analyze the needs of the **audience** as well as the **context** and **purpose** of the study. Then write a purpose statement, such as "The purpose of this study is to determine the feasibility of expanding our Pacific Rim operations," to guide you or a collaborative team. See also **brainstorming** and **collaborative writing**.

Report Sections

Every feasibility report should contain an **introduction**, a body, a **conclusion**, and a recommendation. See also **proposals** and **formal reports**.

Introduction.   The introduction states the purpose of the report, describes the circumstances that led to the report, and includes any

F

Introduction

The purpose of this report is to determine which of two proposed options would best enable Darnell Business Forms Corporation to upgrade its file servers and its Internet capacity to meet its increasing data and communication needs. . . .

Purpose of report

Background.   In October 2014, the Information Development Group put the MACRON System into operation. Since then, the volume of processing transactions has increased fivefold (from 1,000 to 5,000 updates per day). This increase has severely impaired system response time; in fact, average response time has increased from 10 seconds to 120 seconds. Further, our new Web-based client-services system has increased exponentially the demand for processing speed and access capacity.

Reasons for report

Scope.   We have investigated two alternative solutions to provide increased processing capacity: (1) purchase of an additional Aurora processor to supplement the one in operation and (2) purchase of an Icardo 60 with expandable peripherals to replace the Aurora processor currently in operation. The two alternatives are evaluated here, according to both cost and expanded capacity for future operations.

Alternatives presented

Additional Aurora Processor

Purchasing a second Aurora processor would require increased annual maintenance costs, salary for a second computer specialist, increased energy costs, and a one-time construction cost for necessary remodeling and installing Internet connections.

Detailed cost analysis

Annual maintenance costs	$35,000
Annual costs for computer specialist	75,000
Annual increased energy costs	7,500
Total annual operating costs	$117,500
Construction cost (one-time)	50,000
Total first-year costs	$167,500

The installation and operation of another Aurora processor are expected to produce savings in system reliability and readiness.

FIGURE F–1. Feasibility Report (*continued*)

System Reliability.   An additional Aurora would reduce current downtime periods from four to two per week. Downtime recovery averages 30 minutes and affects 40 users. Assuming that 50 percent of users require system access at a given time, we determined that the following reliability savings would result:

2 downtimes × 0.5 hours × 40 users × 50% × $50/hour overtime × 52 weeks = $52,000 annual savings.

[The feasibility report would also discuss the second option— purchase of the Icardo 60 and its long-term savings.]

Conclusion
A comparison of costs for both systems indicates that the Icardo 60 would cost $2,200 more in first-year costs.

	Aurora	Icardo 60
Net additional operating costs	$56,300	$84,000
One-time construction costs	50,000	24,500
First-year total	$106,300	$108,500

Installation of an additional Aurora processor would permit the present information-processing systems to operate relatively smoothly and efficiently. It would not, however, provide the expanded processing capacity that the Icardo 60 processor would for implementing new subsystems required to increase processing speed and Internet access.

Recommendation
The Icardo 60 processor should be purchased because of the long-term savings and because its additional capacity and flexibility will allow for greater expansion in the future.

3

FIGURE F–1. Feasibility Report (*continued*)

pertinent background information. It may also discuss the **scope** of the report, any procedures or methods used in the analysis of alternatives, and any limitations of the study.

Body.   The body of the report presents a detailed review of the alternatives for achieving the goals of the project. Examine each option according to specific criteria—such as cost and financing, availability of staff, and other relevant requirements—identifying the subsections with **headings** to guide readers.

Conclusion.   The conclusion interprets the available options and leads to one option as the best, or most feasible.

Recommendation.   The recommendation section clearly presents the writer's (or team's) opinion on which alternative best meets the criteria as summarized in the conclusion.

F

few / a few

In certain contexts, *few* carries more negative overtones than does the phrase *a few*.

NEGATIVE   The report offers *few* helpful ideas.
POSITIVE   The report offers *a few* helpful ideas.

fewer / less

Fewer refers to items that can be counted (count **nouns**). ("*Fewer* employees retired than we expected.") *Less* refers to mass quantities or amounts (mass nouns). ("We had *less* rain this year than forecasts predicted.") See also **English as a second language**.

figuratively / literally

Literally means "actually" and is often confused with *figuratively*, which means "metaphorically." To say that someone "*literally* turned green with envy" would mean that the person actually changed color.

▶ In the winner's circle the jockey was, *figuratively* speaking, ten feet tall.

▶ When he said, "Let's bury our competitors," he did not mean it *literally*.

Avoid the use of *literally* to reinforce the importance of something.

▶ She was ~~literally~~ the best of the applicants.

figures of speech

A figure of speech is an imaginative expression that often compares two things that are basically not alike but have at least one thing in common. For example, if a device is cone shaped and has an opening at the narrow end, you might say that it looks like a volcano.

Figures of speech can clarify the unfamiliar by relating a new concept to one with which readers are familiar. In that respect, they help establish understanding between the specialist and the nonspecialist. (See **audience**.) Figures of speech can help translate the abstract into the concrete; in the process of doing so, they can also make writing more colorful and graphic. (See also **abstract / concrete words**.) A figure of speech must make sense, however, to achieve the desired effect.

F

ILLOGICAL   Without the fuel of tax incentives, our economic engine would operate less efficiently. [An engine would not operate at all without fuel.]

Figures of speech must also be consistent to be effective.

▶ We must get our sales program *back on course*, and we are

steer the effort.
counting on you to ~~carry the ball.~~
                    ^

A figure of speech should not overshadow the point the writer is trying to make. It is better to use no figure of speech at all than to use a trite one. A surprise that comes "like a bolt out of the blue" seems stale and not much of a surprise. See also **clichés** and **idioms**.

Types of Figures of Speech

Analogies are comparisons that show the ways in which two objects or concepts are similar and are often used to make one of them easier to understand. The following example explains a computer search technique by comparing it to the use of keywords in a dictionary.

▶ *Indexed sequential processing* on a computer works the same way as searching for a word in a dictionary. You might scan the keywords located at the top of each dictionary page that identify the first and last words on each page until you find the keywords that encompass the word you seek. Indexed sequential processing works the same way with computer files.

Hyperboles are gross exaggerations used to achieve an effect or **emphasis**.

▶ We were dead after working all night on the grant proposal.

Litotes are understatements, for emphasis or effect, achieved by denying the opposite of the point you are making.

▶ Over 1,600 pages is no small size for a book.

Metaphors are figures of speech that point out similarities between two things by treating them as though they were the same thing.

▶ The astronaut's *umbilical cord* carries life-sustaining oxygen for spacewalking.

Metonyms are figures of speech that use one aspect of a thing to represent it, such as *the blue* for the sky and *wheels* for a car.

▶ The economist predicted a decrease in *hard-hat* jobs.

Personification is a figure of speech that attributes human characteristics to nonhuman things or abstract ideas. We might refer, for example, to the *birth* of a planet or apply emotions to machines.

▶ She said that she was frustrated with the *stubborn* security system.

Similes are direct comparisons of two essentially unlike things, linking them with the word *like* or *as*.

▶ Reconstructing the plane's fuselage following the accident was *like piecing together a jigsaw puzzle.*

Avoid figures of speech in **global communication** and **international correspondence** because people in other cultures may translate figures of speech literally and be confused by their meanings.

fine

When used in expressions such as "I feel *fine*" or "a *fine* day," *fine* is colloquial and, like the word *nice*, is often too vague for business writing. Use the word *fine* to mean "refined," "delicate," or "pure."

▶ A *fine* film of oil covered the surface of the water.

▶ *Fine* crystal is made in Austria.

▶ The court made a *fine* distinction between the two statutes.

first / firstly

First and *firstly* are both adverbs. Avoid *firstly* in favor of *first*, which sounds less stiff than *firstly*. See also **numbers**.

flowcharts

A flowchart is a diagram using symbols, words, or pictures to show the stages of a process in sequence from beginning to end. A flowchart provides an overview of a process and allows the **reader** to identify its essential steps quickly and easily. Flowcharts can take several forms. The steps might be represented by labeled blocks, as shown in Figure F–2; pictorial symbols, as shown in Figure F–3; or ISO (International Organization for Standardization) symbols, as shown in Figure F–4. Useful tools for constructing flowcharts include Microsoft PowerPoint, Visio, SmartDraw, and Lucidchart.

For advice on integrating flowcharts into your text, see **visuals**. See also **global graphics** and **infographics**.

F

WRITER'S CHECKLIST   **Creating Flowcharts**

✔ Label each step in the process or identify each step with labeled blocks, pictorial representations, or standardized symbols.

✔ Follow the standard flow directions: left to right and top to bottom. Indicate any nonstandard flow directions with arrows.

✔ Include a key (or callouts) to define symbols your **audience** may not understand.

✔ Use standardized symbols for flowcharts that document computer programs and other information-processing procedures, as detailed in *Information Processing — Documentation Symbols and Conventions for Data, Program and System Flowcharts, Program Network Charts, and System Resources Charts*, ISO 5807: 1985. (Publication available at www.iso.org.)

FIGURE F–2. Flowchart Using Labeled Blocks

F

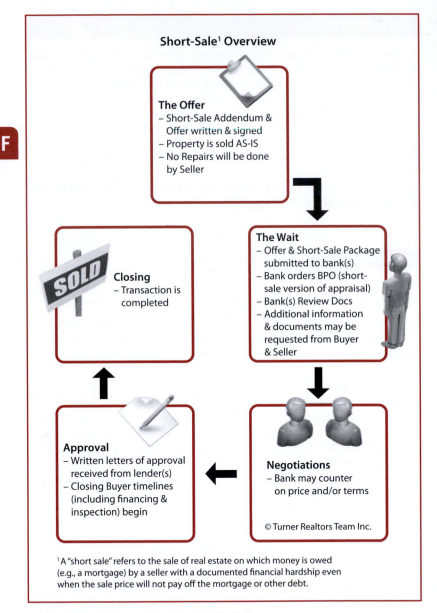

Short-Sale[1] Overview

The Offer
– Short-Sale Addendum &
  Offer written & signed
– Property is sold AS-IS
– No Repairs will be done
  by Seller

The Wait
– Offer & Short-Sale Package
  submitted to bank(s)
– Bank orders BPO (short-
  sale version of appraisal)
– Bank(s) Review Docs
– Additional information
  & documents may be
  requested from Buyer
  & Seller

Closing
– Transaction is
  completed

Approval
– Written letters of approval
  received from lender(s)
– Closing Buyer timelines
  (including financing &
  inspection) begin

Negotiations
– Bank may counter
  on price and/or terms

© Turner Realtors Team Inc.

[1] A "short sale" refers to the sale of real estate on which money is owed
(e.g., a mortgage) by a seller with a documented financial hardship even
when the sale price will not pay off the mortgage or other debt.

FIGURE F–3. Flowchart Using Pictorial Symbols
SOURCE: http://portlandrealestateblog.com/short-sales/.

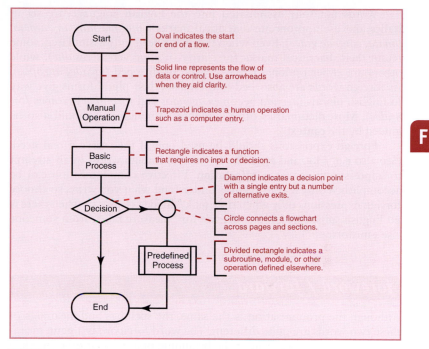

FIGURE F–4. Common ISO Flowchart Symbols (with Annotations)

footnotes (*see* documenting sources)

forceful / forcible

Although *forceful* and *forcible* are both **adjectives** meaning "character-ized by or full of force," *forceful* is usually limited to persuasive ability and *forcible* to physical force.

▶ John made a *forceful* presentation at the committee meeting.

▶ Firefighters must often make *forcible* entries into buildings.

foreign words in English

The English language has a long history of borrowing words from other languages. Most borrowing occurred so long ago that we seldom recognize the borrowed terms (also called *loan words*) as being of foreign origin (*kindergarten* from German, *animal* from Latin, *church* from Greek).

Words not fully assimilated into the English language are set in **italics** and use appropriate diacritical marks (*sine qua non*, *in camera*, *piñata*, *coup de grâce*). Even when they have been fully assimilated, some retain their diacritical marks for clarity (*résumé* versus *resume*), while others are either optional (*café* or *cafe*) or dropped (*facade*, *apropos*). As foreign words are absorbed into English, their plural forms give way to English plurals (*agenda* becomes *agendas* and *formulae* becomes *formulas*). Most dictionaries offer guidance, although you should also be guided by the **context**.

Foreign expressions should be used only if they serve a real need. (See also **e.g. / i.e.** and **etc.**) The overuse of foreign words in an attempt to impress your reader is **affectation**. Effective communication can be accomplished only if your readers understand what you write, so choose foreign expressions only when they make an idea clearer or when there is no English substitute (*schadenfreude* for "pleasure taken from someone else's misfortune").

foreword / forward

Although the pronunciation is the same, the spellings and meanings of these two words are quite different. The word *foreword* is a **noun** meaning "introductory statement at the beginning of a book or other work."

▶ The director wrote a *foreword* for the report.

The word *forward* is an **adjective** or **adverb** meaning "at or toward the front."

▶ Sliding the throttle to the *forward* position [adjective] will cause the boat to move *forward*. [adverb]

form letters

A form letter or message is a type of **correspondence** (including **letters** and **e-mail**) in which the identical (or near identical) message is sent to more than one person; only the name and address of the recipient differ. The recipients' names, addresses, and other information may be stored and merged with the text of the message.

When to Use Form Letters

Form letters and e-mails are ideal for simultaneously reaching hundreds or thousands of customers, clients, or employees with announcements and other information. In fact, **sales letters** are usually mass-produced. Form letters and e-mails are also useful for situations that occur regularly, such as responses to inquiries, standard orders, acknowledgments of orders, and early-stage **collection letters**. (See also **acknowledgments** and **inquiries and responses**.) Of course, if a particular situation calls for an individual response (such as an **adjustment message** in response to a complaint), a form letter is not the best choice. Most people resent obviously impersonal treatment when they believe they deserve individual attention.

◀ **PROFESSIONALISM NOTE** For routine circumstances, few readers object to an obvious form letter or message, especially if the information is clear and the **tone** is positive. For example, a computer company may send purchasers a brief form letter or e-mail to let them know their orders have been shipped and when to expect delivery. ▶

Writing Form Letters

By using the principles of correspondence and the **"you" viewpoint**, you can produce a form letter or e-mail tailored to your potential **audience** and to your **purpose**. Even though your readers know they are reading a form letter or message, you should personalize the message to fit the recipients' situation as much as possible.

PERSONAL   If you have a question about your MAX-PC and cannot find the answer in the User's Guide, visit our Web site or get 24-hour personal assistance at our customer help number. [This sentence seems aimed more at the individual reader.]

Be careful about using first names to personalize messages—the name that appears in a database might be different from the name familiar to the recipient's friends (William/Bill or Kimberly/Kim). Further, many cultures avoid first names when addressing all but those closest to them. (See also **international correspondence**.)

Form letters and e-mails that do not need to be personalized often use a "headline lead" to replace the standard salutation, as shown in Figure F–5. By "talking" directly to the reader, you can make form letters and messages less stiff and impersonal. Some form letters can be personalized by adding a typed or handwritten postscript.

Repurposing Form Letters

Paragraphs from previously used form letters and messages can be combined with newly written paragraphs that are tailored to fit a specific **context**. Repurposed paragraphs are ideal for use in recurring

F

> **Here's your copy of the *User's Guide***
>
> for your X-WRITER system. This publication is designed to
> acquaint you with the hardware and WORDWRITE software. . . .

FIGURE F–5. Headline Lead

circumstances that require more personal and varied responses than form
letters or e-mails provide. (See **repurposing**.) They are useful, for example, when you wish either to adapt parts of the correspondence for particular readers or to construct sets of messages from standardized parts,
as in **application cover letters**, **reference letters**, **refusal letters**, and some
memos. Be sure to provide adequate **transition** and proofread carefully.

formal reports

Formal reports are usually written accounts of major projects that
require substantial **research**, and they often involve more than one
writer. See also **collaborative writing**.

Most formal reports are divided into three primary parts—front
matter, body, and back matter—each of which contains a number of
elements. The number and arrangement of the elements vary depending
on the subject, the length of the report, and the kinds of material covered. Many organizations have a preferred style for formal reports and
furnish guidelines for report writers. If you are not required to follow a
specific style, use the **format** recommended in this entry. The following
list includes most of the elements a formal report might contain, in the
order they typically appear. (The items shown with page numbers appear
in the sample formal report on pages 203–19.) Often, a **cover message**
or **memo** precedes the front matter and identifies the report by title, the
person or persons to whom it is sent, the reason it was written, the **scope**,
and any information that the **audience** considers important, as shown
on page 203.

FRONT MATTER
Title Page (204)
Abstract (205)
Table of Contents (206)
List of Figures
List of Tables

Foreword
Preface
List of Abbreviations and Symbols

BODY
Executive Summary (207)
Introduction (209)
Text (including headings) (212)
Conclusions (217)
Recommendations (217)
Explanatory Notes
References (or Works Cited) (219)

BACK MATTER
Appendixes
Bibliography
Glossary
Index

Front Matter

The front matter serves several functions: It explains the writer's **purpose**, describes the scope and type of information in the report, and lists where specific information is covered in the report. Not all formal reports include every element of front matter described here. A title page and table of contents are usually mandatory. But the scope of the report and its **context**, as well as the intended audience, determine whether the other elements are included.

Title Page.   Although the formats of title pages may vary, they often include the following:

- *The full title of the report.* The title describes the topic, scope, and purpose of the report, as discussed in **titles**.

- *The name of the writer(s), principal investigator(s), or compiler(s).* Sometimes contributors identify themselves by their job title or role on the project (*Olivia Jones, Principal Investigator*).

- *The date(s) of the report.* For one-time reports, use the date the report is distributed. For reports issued periodically (monthly, quarterly, or yearly), the subtitle shows the period that the report covers, and the distribution date is shown elsewhere on the title page, as shown in Figure F–6 on page 203.

- *The name of the organization for which the writer(s) works.*

- *The name of the organization to which the report is being submitted.* Include this information if the report is written for a customer or client.

F

Front-matter pages are numbered with roman numerals. The title page should not be numbered, as in the example on page 204, but it is considered page i for subsequent pagination. The back of the title page, which is left blank and unnumbered, is considered page ii, so the abstract falls on page iii. The body of the report begins with arabic number 1, and a new chapter or large section typically begins on a new right-hand (odd-numbered) page. Reports with printing on only one side of each sheet can be numbered consecutively regardless of where new sections begin. Center page numbers at the bottom of each page throughout the report.

Abstract. An **abstract**, which normally follows the title page, high-lights the major points of the report, as shown on page 205, enabling readers to decide whether to read the report.

Table of Contents. A **table of contents** lists all the major sections or **headings** of the report in their order of appearance, as shown on page 206, along with their page numbers. If the report is distributed electron-ically, link headings in the table of contents (as well as figure numbers and titles in a list of figures, and table numbers and titles in a list of tables) to the relevant sections of the report.

List of Figures. All **visuals** contained in the report—**drawings, photographs, maps,** charts, and **graphs**—are labeled as figures. When a report contains more than five figures, list them, along with their page numbers, in a separate section, beginning on a new page immediately following the table of contents. Number figures consecutively with arabic numbers.

List of Tables. When a report contains more than five **tables,** list them, along with their titles and page numbers, in a separate section immedi-ately following the list of figures (if there is one). Number tables consec-utively with arabic numbers.

Foreword. A foreword is an optional introductory statement about a formal report or publication that is written by someone other than the author(s). The foreword author is usually an authority in the field or an executive of the organization sponsoring the report. The foreword author's name and affiliation appear at the end of the foreword, along with the date it was written. The foreword provides background information about the publication's significance, and places it in the context of other works in the field. The foreword precedes the preface when a work has both.

Preface. The preface, another type of optional introductory statement, is written by the author(s) of the formal report. It may announce the work's purpose, scope, and context (including any special circumstances leading to the work). A preface may also specify the audience for a work, those who helped in its preparation, and permissions obtained for the use of copyrighted works. See also **copyrights, patents, and trademarks**.

List of Abbreviations and Symbols.   When a report uses numerous **abbreviations** and symbols that readers may not be able to interpret, the front matter may include a section listing symbols and abbreviations with their meanings.

Body

The body is the section of the report that provides context for the report, describes in detail the methods and procedures used to generate the report, demonstrates how results were obtained, describes the results, draws conclusions, and, if appropriate, makes recommendations.

Executive Summary.   The body of the report begins with the **executive summary**, which provides a more complete overview of the report than the abstract does. See an example on pages 207–8, and review the **abstract** entry cross-referenced earlier.

Introduction.   The **introduction** gives readers any general information — such as the report's purpose, scope, and context — necessary to understand the detailed information in the report (see pages 209–11).

Text.   The text of the body presents, as appropriate, the details of how the topic was investigated, how a problem was solved, what alternatives were explored, and how the best choice among them was selected. This information is enhanced by the use of visuals, tables, **headings**, and references that both clarify the text and persuade the reader. See also **persuasion**.

Conclusions.   The **conclusions** section pulls together the results of the research and interprets the findings of the report, as shown on page 217.

Recommendations.   Recommendations, which are sometimes combined with conclusions, state what course of action should be taken based on the earlier arguments and conclusions of the study, as shown on pages 217–18.

Explanatory Notes.   Occasionally, reports contain notes that amplify terms or points that might interrupt the text of the report. Such notes may be included as footnotes, or they may appear in a "Notes" section at the end of the report.

References (or Works Cited). A list of references or works cited appears in a separate section if the report refers to or quotes directly from research sources. If your employer has a preferred reference style, follow it; otherwise, use one of the guidelines provided in the entry **documenting sources**. For a relatively short report, place a reference or works-cited section at the end of the body of the report, as shown on page 219. For a report with a number of sections or chapters, place a reference or works-cited section at the end of each major section or chapter. In either case, begin the reference or works-cited section on a new page. If a particular reference appears in more than one section or chapter, repeat it in full in each appropriate reference section.

❖ **ETHICS NOTE** Always identify the sources of any facts, ideas, **quotations**, and paraphrases you include in a report. Even if unintentional, **plagiarism** is unethical and may result in formal academic misconduct charges in a college course. On the job, it can result in legal action or even dismissal. Repurposed in-house material ("boilerplate") may not require a citation—see **repurposing**. ❖

Back Matter

The back matter of a formal report contains supplementary material, such as where to find additional information about the topic (bibliography), and expands on certain subjects (appendixes). Other back-matter elements define special terms (glossary) and provide information on how to easily locate information in the report (index). For very large formal reports, back-matter sections may be individually numbered or labeled (Appendix A, Appendix B).

Appendixes. An **appendix** clarifies or supplements the report with information that is too detailed or lengthy for the primary audience but is relevant to secondary audiences.

Bibliography. A **bibliography** lists alphabetically all the sources that were consulted to prepare the report—not just those cited in the report—and suggests additional resources that readers might want to consult.

Glossary. A **glossary** is an alphabetical list of specialized terms used in the report and their definitions.

Index. An index is an alphabetical list of all the major topics and subtopics discussed in the report. It cites the page numbers where discussion of each topic can be found, allowing readers to find information on topics quickly and easily. The index is always the final section of a report. Most word-processing programs can save you time by creating an index automatically based on keywords that you mark while composing the report. See also **indexing**.

Sample Formal Report

Figure F–6 shows the typical sections of a formal report. Keep in mind that the number and arrangement of the elements vary depending on the context, especially the requirements of an organization or a client.

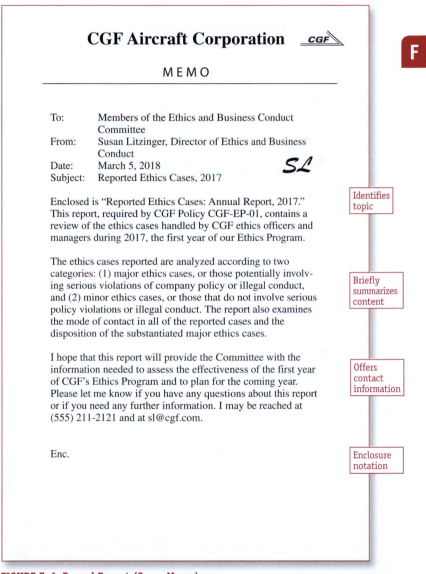

CGF Aircraft Corporation   *CGF*

MEMO

To: Members of the Ethics and Business Conduct Committee
From: Susan Litzinger, Director of Ethics and Business Conduct
Date: March 5, 2018
Subject: Reported Ethics Cases, 2017

Enclosed is "Reported Ethics Cases: Annual Report, 2017." This report, required by CGF Policy CGF-EP-01, contains a review of the ethics cases handled by CGF ethics officers and managers during 2017, the first year of our Ethics Program.

Identifies topic

The ethics cases reported are analyzed according to two categories: (1) major ethics cases, or those potentially involving serious violations of company policy or illegal conduct, and (2) minor ethics cases, or those that do not involve serious policy violations or illegal conduct. The report also examines the mode of contact in all of the reported cases and the disposition of the substantiated major ethics cases.

Briefly summarizes content

I hope that this report will provide the Committee with the information needed to assess the effectiveness of the first year of CGF's Ethics Program and to plan for the coming year. Please let me know if you have any questions about this report or if you need any further information. I may be reached at (555) 211-2121 and at sl@cgf.com.

Offers contact information

Enc.

Enclosure notation

FIGURE F–6. Formal Report (Cover Memo)

F

Full title

REPORTED ETHICS CASES
Annual Report, 2017

Author's name and job title

Prepared by Susan Litzinger
Director of Ethics and Business Conduct

Report Distributed March 5, 2018

Company name

Prepared for
The Ethics and Business Conduct Committee
CGF Aircraft Corporation

No page number

FIGURE F–6. Formal Report (*continued*) (Title Page)

Reported Ethics Cases—2017

ABSTRACT

This report examines the nature and disposition of 3,458 ethics cases handled companywide by CGF Aircraft Corporation's ethics officers and managers during 2017. The purpose of this annual report is to provide the Ethics and Business Conduct Committee with the information necessary for assessing the effectiveness of the Ethics Program's first year of operation. Records maintained by ethics officers and managers of all contacts were compiled and categorized into two main types: (1) major ethics cases, or cases involving serious violations of company policies or illegal conduct, and (2) minor ethics cases, or cases not involving serious policy violations or illegal conduct. This report provides examples of the types of cases handled in each category and analyzes the disposition of 30 substantiated major ethics cases. Recommendations for planning for the second year of the Ethics Program are (1) continuing the channels of communication now available in the Ethics Program, (2) increasing financial and technical support for the Ethics Hotline, (3) disseminating the annual ethics report in some form to employees to ensure employee awareness of the company's commitment to uphold its Ethics Policies and Procedures, and (4) implementing some measure of recognition for ethical behavior to promote and reward ethical conduct.

Summarizes purpose

Methods and scope

Conclusions and recommendations

Lowercase roman numerals used on front-matter pages

iii

FIGURE F–6. Formal Report (*continued*) (Abstract)

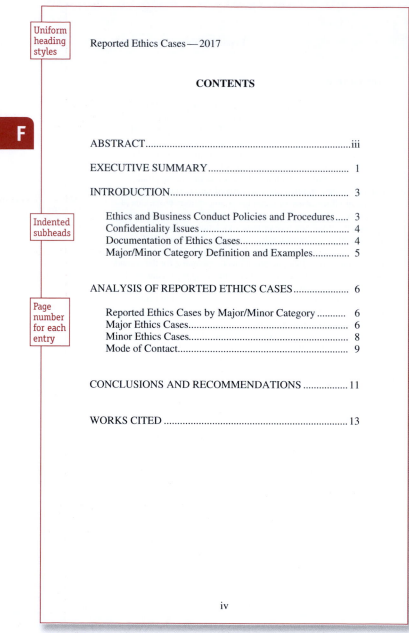

Uniform heading styles

Reported Ethics Cases — 2017

CONTENTS

iv

FIGURE F–6. Formal Report (*continued*) **(Table of Contents)**

F

Reported Ethics Cases—2017

EXECUTIVE SUMMARY

This report examines the nature and disposition of the 3,458 ethics cases handled by the CGF Aircraft Corporation's ethics officers and managers during 2017. The purpose of this report is to provide CGF's Ethics and Business Conduct Committee with the information necessary for assessing the effectiveness of the first year of the company's Ethics Program.

States purpose

Effective January 1, 2017, the Ethics and Business Conduct Committee (the Committee) implemented a policy and procedures for the administration of CGF's new Ethics Program. The purpose of the Ethics Program, established by the Committee, is to "promote ethical business conduct through open communication and compliance with company ethics standards." The Office of Ethics and Business Conduct was created to administer the Ethics Program. The director of the Office of Ethics and Business Conduct, along with seven ethics officers throughout the corporation, was given the responsibility for the following objectives:

Provides background information

- Communicate the values and standards for CGF's Ethics Program to employees.

- Inform employees about company policies regarding ethical business conduct.

- Establish companywide channels for employees to obtain information and guidance in resolving ethics concerns.

- Implement companywide ethics-awareness and education programs.

Employee accessibility to ethics information and guidance was available through managers, ethics officers, and an ethics hotline.

Major ethics cases were defined as those situations potentially involving serious violations of company policies or illegal conduct. Examples of major ethics cases included cover-up of defective workmanship or use of defective parts in products; discrimination in hiring and promotion; involvement in monetary or other kickbacks; sexual harassment; disclosure of proprietary or company information; theft; and use of corporate Internet resources for inappropriate purposes, such as conducting personal business, gambling, or access to pornography.

Describes scope

1

FIGURE F–6. Formal Report (*continued*) (Executive Summary)

F

Reported Ethics Cases — 2017

Minor ethics cases were defined as including all reported concerns not classified as major ethics cases. Minor ethics cases were classified as informational queries from employees, situations involving coworkers, and situations involving management.

Summarizes conclusions

The effectiveness of CGF's Ethics Program during the first year of implementation is most evidenced by (1) the active participation of employees in the program and the 3,458 contacts employees made regarding ethics concerns through the various channels available to them and (2) the action taken in the cases reported by employees, particularly the disposition of the 30 substantiated major ethics cases. Disseminating information about the disposition of ethics cases, particularly information about the severe disciplinary actions taken in major ethics violations, sends a message to employees that unethical or illegal conduct will not be tolerated.

Includes recommendations

Based on these conclusions, recommendations for planning the second year of the Ethics Program are (1) continuing the channels of communication now available in the Ethics Program, (2) increasing financial and technical support for the Ethics Hotline, the most highly used mode of contact in the ethics cases reported in 2017, (3) disseminating this report in some form to employees to ensure their awareness of CGF's commitment to uphold its Ethics Policies and Procedures, and (4) implementing some measure of recognition for ethical behavior, such as an "Ethics Employee of the Month" award to promote and reward ethical conduct.

Executive summary is about 10 percent of report length

2

FIGURE F–6. Formal Report (*continued*) (Executive Summary)

Reported Ethics Cases—2017

INTRODUCTION

This report examines the nature and disposition of the 3,458 ethics cases handled companywide by CGF's ethics officers and managers during 2017. The purpose of this report is to provide the Ethics and Business Conduct Committee with the information necessary for assessing the effectiveness of the first year of CGF's Ethics Program. Recommendations are given for the Committee's consideration in planning for the second year of the Ethics Program.

Opening states purpose

Ethics and Business Conduct Policies and Procedures

Effective January 1, 2017, the Ethics and Business Conduct Committee (the Committee) implemented Policy CGF-EP-01 and Procedure CGF-EP-02 for the administration of CGF's new Ethics Program. The purpose of the Ethics Program, established by the Committee, is to "promote ethical business conduct through open communication and compliance with company ethics standards" (CGF, "Ethics and Conduct").

Subheads signal shifts in topic

The Office of Ethics and Business Conduct was created to administer the Ethics Program. The director of the Office of Ethics and Business Conduct, along with seven ethics officers throughout CGF, was given the responsibility for the following objectives:

- Communicate the values, standards, and goals of CGF's Ethics Program to employees.
- Inform employees about company ethics policies.
- Provide companywide channels for employee education and guidance in resolving ethics concerns.
- Implement companywide programs in ethics awareness, education, and recognition.
- Ensure confidentiality in all ethics matters.

List identifies key points

Employee accessibility to ethics information and guidance became the immediate and key goal of the Office of Ethics and Business Conduct in its first year of operation. The following channels for contact were set in motion during 2017:

3

FIGURE F–6. Formal Report (*continued*) (Introduction)

F

F

Reported Ethics Cases—2017

- Managers throughout CGF received intensive ethics training; in all ethics situations, employees were encouraged to go to their managers as the first point of contact.

- Ethics officers were available directly to employees through face-to-face or telephone contact, to managers, to callers using the Ethics Hotline, and by e-mail.

- The Ethics Hotline was available to all employees, 24 hours a day, seven days a week, to anonymously report ethics concerns.

Confidentiality Issues
CGF's Ethics Policy ensures confidentiality and anonymity for employees who raise genuine ethics concerns. Procedure CGF-EP-02 guarantees appropriate discipline, up to and including dismissal, for retaliation or retribution against any employee who properly reports any genuine ethics concern.

Documentation of Ethics Cases
The following requirements were established by the director of the Office of Ethics and Business Conduct as uniform guidelines for the documentation by managers and ethics officers of all reported ethics cases:

- Name, position, and department of individual initiating contact, if available

- Date and time of contact

Includes detailed methods

- Name, position, and department of contact person

- Category of ethics case

- Mode of contact

- Resolution

Managers and ethics officers entered the required information in each reported ethics case into an ACCESS database file, enabling efficient retrieval and analysis of the data.

FIGURE F–6. Formal Report (*continued*) (Introduction)

F

Reported Ethics Cases—2017

Major/Minor Category Definition and Examples
Major ethics cases were defined as those situations potentially
involving serious violations of company policies or illegal
conduct. Procedure CGF-EP-02 requires notification of the
Internal Audit and the Law departments in serious ethics cases.
The staffs of the Internal Audit and the Law departments
assume primary responsibility for managing major ethics cases
and for working with the employees, ethics officers, and
managers involved in each case.

Examples of situations categorized as major ethics cases:

- Cover-up of defective workmanship or use of defective
  parts in products

- Discrimination in hiring and promotion

- Involvement in monetary or other kickbacks from
  customers for preferred orders

- Sexual harassment

- Disclosure of proprietary customer or company
  information

- Theft

- Use of corporate Internet resources for inappropriate
  purposes, such as conducting private business, gambling,
  or gaining access to pornography

Organized by
decreasing
order of
importance

Minor ethics cases were defined as including all reported
concerns not classified as major ethics cases. Minor ethics
cases were classified as follows:

- Informational queries from employees

- Situations involving coworkers

- Situations involving management

5

FIGURE F–6. Formal Report (*continued*) (Introduction)

F

Reported Ethics Cases—2017

ANALYSIS OF REPORTED ETHICS CASES

Reported Ethics Cases, by Major/Minor Category
CGF ethics officers and managers companywide handled a total of 3,458 ethics situations during 2017. Of these cases, only 172, or 5 percent, involved reported concerns of a serious enough nature to be classified as major ethics cases (see Fig. 1). Major ethics cases were defined as those situations potentially involving serious violations of company policy or illegal conduct.

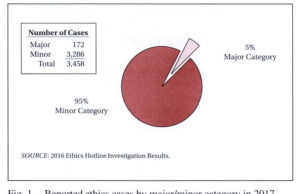

Number of Cases	
Major	172
Minor	3,286
Total	3,458

5%
Major Category

95%
Minor Category

SOURCE: 2016 Ethics Hotline Investigation Results.

> Text introduces figure

> Number and title identify figure

Fig. 1.   Reported ethics cases by major/minor category in 2017.

Major Ethics Cases
Of the 172 major ethics cases reported during 2017, 57 percent, upon investigation, were found to involve unsubstantiated concerns. Incomplete information or misinformation most frequently was discovered to be the cause of the unfounded concerns of misconduct in 98 cases. Forty-four cases, or 26 percent of the total cases reported, involved incidents partly substantiated by ethics officers as serious misconduct;

6

FIGURE F–6. Formal Report (*continued*) (Body Text)

F

Reported Ethics Cases—2017

however, these cases were discovered to also involve inaccurate information or unfounded issues of misconduct.

Only 17 percent of the total number of major ethics cases, or 30 cases, were substantiated as major ethics situations involving serious ethical misconduct or illegal conduct (2016 Ethics Hotline) (see Fig. 2).

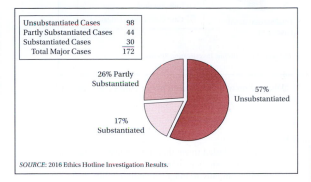

Unsubstantiated Cases	98
Partly Substantiated Cases	44
Substantiated Cases	30
Total Major Cases	172

26% Partly Substantiated

57% Unsubstantiated

17% Substantiated

SOURCE: 2016 Ethics Hotline Investigation Results.

Identifies source of information

Fig. 2.   Major ethics cases in 2017.

Of the 30 substantiated major ethics cases, seven remain under investigation at this time, and two cases are currently in litigation. Disposition of the remainder of the 30 substantiated reported ethics cases included severe disciplinary action in five cases: the dismissal of two employees and the demotion of three employees. Seven employees were given written warnings, and nine employees received verbal warnings (see Fig. 3).

FIGURE F–6. Formal Report (*continued*) (Body Text)

Reported Ethics Cases—2017

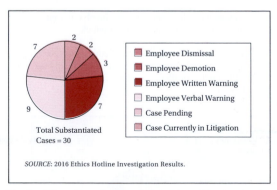

SOURCE: 2016 Ethics Hotline Investigation Results.

Fig. 3.   Disposition of substantiated major ethics cases in 2017.

Minor Ethics Cases

Minor ethics cases included those that did not involve serious violations of company policy or illegal conduct. During 2017, ethics officers and company managers handled 3,286 such cases. Minor ethics cases were further classified as follows:

Presents findings in detail

• Informational queries from employees

• Situations involving coworkers

• Situations involving management

As might be expected during the initial year of the Ethics Program implementation, the majority of contacts made by employees were informational, involving questions about the new policies and procedures. These informational contacts comprised 65 percent of all contacts of a minor nature and numbered 2,148. Employees made 989 contacts regarding ethics concerns involving coworkers and 149 contacts regarding ethics concerns involving management (see Fig. 4).

8

FIGURE F–6. Formal Report (*continued*) **(Body Text)**

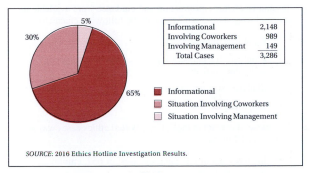

Reported Ethics Cases — 2017

Informational	2,148
Involving Coworkers	989
Involving Management	149
Total Cases	3,286

- Informational
- Situation Involving Coworkers
- Situation Involving Management

SOURCE: 2016 Ethics Hotline Investigation Results.

Fig. 4.   Minor ethics cases in 2017.

Mode of Contact

The effectiveness of the Ethics Program rested on the dissemination of information to employees and the provision of accessible channels through which employees could gain information, report concerns, and obtain guidance. Employees were encouraged to first go to their managers with any ethical concerns, because those managers would have the most direct knowledge of the immediate circumstances and individuals involved.

Other channels were put into operation, however, for any instance in which an employee did not feel able to go to his or her manager. The ethics officers companywide were available to employees through telephone conversations, face-to-face meetings, and e-mail contact. Ethics officers also served as contact points for managers in need of support and assistance in handling the ethics concerns reported to them by their subordinates.

The Ethics Hotline became operational in mid-January 2017 and offered employees assurance of anonymity and confidentiality. The Ethics Hotline was accessible to all employees on a 24-hour, 7-day basis. Ethics officers companywide took responsibility on a rotational basis for handling calls reported through the hotline.

Assesses findings

9

FIGURE F–6. Formal Report (*continued*) (Body Text)

F

Reported Ethics Cases — 2017

In summary, ethics information and guidance were available to all employees during 2017 through the following channels:

- Employee to manager
- Employee telephone, face-to-face, and e-mail contact with ethics officer
- Manager to ethics officer
- Employee Hotline

The mode of contact in the 3,458 reported ethics cases was as follows (see Fig. 5):

- In 19 percent of the reported cases, or 657, employees went to managers with concerns.
- In 9 percent of the reported cases, or 311, employees contacted an ethics officer.
- In 5 percent of the reported cases, or 173, managers sought assistance from ethics officers.
- In 67 percent of the reported cases, or 2,317, contacts were made through the Ethics Hotline.

> Bulleted lists help organize and summarize information

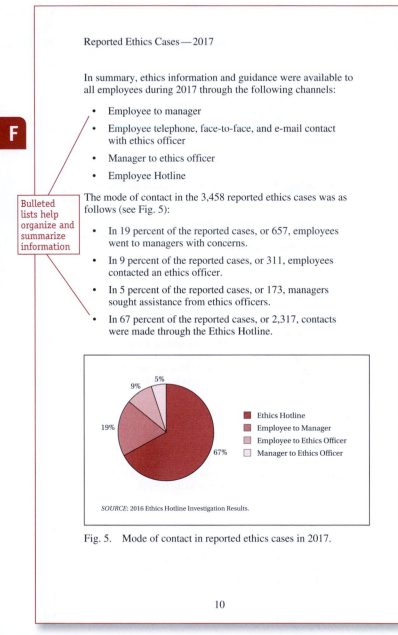

SOURCE: 2016 Ethics Hotline Investigation Results.

Fig. 5.   Mode of contact in reported ethics cases in 2017.

10

FIGURE F–6. Formal Report (*continued*) (Body Text)

Reported Ethics Cases — 2017

CONCLUSIONS AND RECOMMENDATIONS

The effectiveness of CGF's Ethics Program during the first year of implementation is most evidenced by (1) the active participation of employees in the program and the 3,458 contacts employees made regarding ethics concerns through the various channels available to them, and (2) the action taken in the cases reported by employees, particularly the disposition of the 30 substantiated major ethics cases.

Pulls together findings

One of the 12 steps to building a successful Ethics Program identified by Frank Navran in *Workforce* magazine is an ethics communication strategy. Navran explains that such a strategy is crucial in ensuring

Uses sources for support

> that employees have the information they need in a timely and usable fashion and that the organization is encouraging employee communication regarding the values, standards and the conduct of the organization and its members. (119)

The 3,458 contacts by employees during 2017 attest to the accessibility and effectiveness of the communication channels that exist in CGF's Ethics Program.

An equally important step in building a successful ethics program is listed by Navran as "Measurements and Rewards," which he explains as follows:

> In most organizations, employees know what's important by virtue of what the organization measures and rewards. If ethical conduct is assessed and rewarded, and if unethical conduct is identified and dissuaded, employees will believe that the organization's principals mean it when they say the values and code of ethics are important. (121)

Long quotation in MLA style

Disseminating information about the disposition of ethics cases, particularly information about the severe disciplinary actions taken in major ethics violations, sends a message to employees that unethical or illegal conduct will not be tolerated. Making public such actions taken in cases of ethical misconduct provides "a golden opportunity to make other employees aware that the behavior is unacceptable and why" (Ferrell et al.).

Interprets findings

11

FIGURE F–6. Formal Report (*continued*) (Conclusions and Recommendations)

Reported Ethics Cases—2017

With these two points in mind, I offer the following recommendations for consideration for plans for the Ethics Program's second year:

F

- Maintain the channels of communication now available in the Ethics Program

- Increase financial and technical support for the Ethics Hotline, the most highly used mode of contact in the reported ethics cases in 2017

- Disseminate this report in some form to employees to ensure employees' awareness of CGF's commitment to uphold its Ethics Policy and Procedures

- Implement some measure of recognition for ethical behavior, such as an "Ethics Employee of the Month," to promote and reward ethical conduct

To ensure that employees see the value of their continued participation in the Ethics Program, feedback is essential. The information in this annual review, in some form, should be provided to employees. Knowing that the concerns they reported were taken seriously and resulted in appropriate action by Ethics Program administrators would reinforce employee involvement in the program.

Although the negative consequences of ethical misconduct contained in this report send a powerful message, a means of communicating the *positive* rewards of ethical conduct at CGF should be implemented. Various options for recognition of employees exemplifying ethical conduct should be considered and approved. See "Create and Evaluate a Code of Conduct."

Continuation of the Ethics Program's successful 2017 operations, with the implementation of the above recommendations, should ensure the continued pursuit of the Ethics Program's purpose: "to promote a positive work environment that encourages open communication regarding ethics and compliance issues and concerns."

FIGURE F–6. Formal Report (*continued*) (Conclusions and Recommendations)

Reported Ethics Cases—2017

WORKS CITED

"Create and Evaluate a Code of Conduct." *Business Ethics Forum*, Management Logs, 12 Sept. 2009, http://businessethics-forum.blogspot.com/.

"Ethics and Conduct at CGF Aircraft Corporation." CGF Aircraft Corporation, 1 Jan. 2015, www.cgf.com/ethicsandconduct2015.

Ferrell, O. C., et al. *Business Ethics: Ethical Decision Making and Cases*. 9th ed., Houghton Mifflin, 2013.

Navran, Frank. "12 Steps to Building a Best-Practices Ethics Program." *Workforce,* vol. 76, no. 9, 1997, pp. 117–22, www.workforce.com/1997/09/01/12-steps-to-building-a-best-practices-ethics-program/.

"2016 Ethics Hotline Investigation Results." CGF Aircraft Corporation, 15 Jan. 2017, www.cgf.com/ethicshotlineinvestigation2016.

F

This report uses MLA style

13

FIGURE F–6. Formal Report (*continued*) (Works Cited)

format

Format refers to both the organization of information in a document and the physical arrangement of information on the page.

In one sense, format refers to the conventions that govern the scope and placement of information in such job-related writing as **formal reports**, **proposals**, and various types of **correspondence**. For example, in formal reports, the **table of contents** precedes the preface but follows the title page and the **abstract**. Likewise, although variations exist, parts of **letters**—such as inside address, salutation, and complimentary closing—are arranged in standard patterns. See also **e-mail** and **memos**.

Format also refers to the general physical appearance of a finished document. You can use styles and templates in word-processing programs to automate the design of headings, paragraphs, lists, and visuals. (Using styles and templates also helps make word-processing documents accessible to screen readers.) See also **layout and design** and **writing for the Web**.

former / latter

Former refers to the first and *latter* refers to the last of two items in a sentence or paragraph. Because these terms make the reader look to previous material to identify the reference, they complicate reading and are best avoided.

forms

Forms are used widely to gather data and information from respondents in a standardized design. Figure F–7 shows an example of a typical form used for a medical claim. See also **questionnaires**.

An effective form makes it easy for one person to supply information and for another person to retrieve, record, and interpret that information. Ideally, a form should be self-explanatory to someone seeing it for the first time. When preparing a form, determine the kind of information you are seeking, and arrange the requests for information or questions in a logical order. To ensure the usability of the form, test it with people from your target **audience** or others before distributing the final version.

❖ **ETHICS NOTE** Information gathered on forms can be sensitive, personal, or subject to confidentiality laws, so make sure to request information in a way that is not invasive or illegal. Unless otherwise indicated on

104-M S A
**Section 125 Flexible Spending Account
(FSA) Claim Form**

Form title

Employee Name: _____

Social Security Number: _____-___-_____

Name of Employer: _____

Employee Signature: _____

Writing
lines

F

COMPLETE SECTION BELOW FOR MEDICAL, DENTAL, OR VISION
REIMBURSEMENT

Instructions

CLAIM TYPE I: MEDICAL CARE ACCOUNT

Amount of Expense Incurred: $_____

Dates of Services: from _____ to _____

COMPLETE SECTION BELOW FOR REIMBURSEMENT OF CHILD CARE
OR ADULT DEPENDENT CARE

Instructions

CLAIM TYPE II: DEPENDENT-CARE ACCOUNT

Amount of Expense Incurred: $_____

Name of Dependent-Care Provider: _____

Provider Social Security or Federal ID Number: _____-___-_____

EMAIL, FAX, OR MAIL FORM WITH COPIES OF DOCUMENTATION TO
THE ADDRESS BELOW.

Specialized Benefit Services, Inc.
P.O. Box 498
Framingham, MA 01702
Fax: (508) 877-1182
fsa@sbcclaims.com

Mailing and
contact
information

For additional claim forms or to submit claims online, go to:
www.sbsclaims.com

FIGURE F–7. Form (for a Medical Claim)

the form, the person filling out the form should have the expectation of confidentiality. If you are concerned about issues of confidentiality or legality, check your organization's policy; in a classroom seek your instructor's advice. ❖

Choosing Paper or Digital

You can develop forms as printed documents or interactive digital versions. Printed forms can help individuals in some manufacturing and service industries. Printed forms can also be useful at conferences or other in-person events. Digital forms, however, are especially well suited for conference or seminar registrations, job applications, and various order forms. Digital forms not only standardize respondents' interfaces but also link to databases that tabulate and interpret data. A digital form can be encrypted for security and programmed to ensure that all necessary fields are completed correctly before the form can be successfully submitted. See also **writing for the Web**.

Designing a Form

At the top of the form, clearly indicate preliminary information, such as the name of your organization, the title of your form, and any reference number. Place instructions at the beginning of the form or at the beginning of each section of the form and use **headings** or other design elements, such as the boldface type and shaded text boxes in Figure F–7. Place instructions for submitting printed forms or distributing the copies of multiple-copy forms at the bottom of each page. For printed forms, allow space for elements such as signatures and dates.

You can design digital forms specific to your needs with form-design software, word-processing software, or markup languages (such as HTML or PHP/MySQL). At the end of digital forms, include a "submit" button to record the data, to open a new page, or to send a confirming e-mail reporting successful completion. See also **layout and design**.

Entry Lines and Fields.   A print form can be designed so that the person filling it out provides information on a writing line, in a writing block, or in square boxes. A *writing line* is simply a rule with a caption, such as the line for "Employee Name" shown in Figure F–7. A *writing block* is essentially the same as a writing line, except that each entry is enclosed in a ruled block, making it unlikely for the respondent to associate a caption with the wrong line.

When it is possible to anticipate all likely responses, you can make the form easy to fill out by writing the question on the form, supplying a labeled box for each anticipated answer, and asking the respondent to check the appropriate boxes. Such a design also makes it easy to tabulate the data.

For digital forms, these functions are accomplished with form fields such as text boxes, option (or *radio*) buttons, drop-down menus, lists, and check boxes, which can be aligned using table cells or grouping. Each form field should have a label prompting users to type information or to select from a list of options. Labels for text boxes, drop-down menus, and lists should be positioned to the left; labels for radio buttons and check boxes should be positioned to the right. Be sure also to indicate required form fields.

Sequencing Entries.   The main portion of the form includes the entries that are required to obtain the necessary data. Arrange entries in an order that will be the most logical to the person filling out the form.

- Open with questions that are easy for respondents to complete or answer.

- Sequence entries to fit the subject matter. A form requesting travel reimbursement would logically be organized chronologically from the beginning to the end of the appropriate period.

- If the response to one item is based on the response to another item, be sure the items appear in the correct order.

- Group requests for related information together whenever possible.

Writing Questions

Forms should ask questions in ways that are best suited to the types of data you hope to collect. The two main types are open-ended questions and closed-ended questions.

- *Open-ended questions* allow respondents to answer questions in their own words. Such questions are most appropriate if you wish to elicit responses you may not have anticipated (as in a complaint form) or if there are too many possible answers to use a multiple-choice format. However, the responses to open-ended questions can be difficult to tabulate and analyze.

- *Closed-ended questions* provide a list of options from which the respondent can select, limiting the range of possible responses. When you want to make sure you receive a standardized, easy-to-tabulate response, use any of the types of closed-ended questions that follow:
  - *Multiple choice*: Choose one (or sometimes more than one) response from a preset list of options.
  - *Ranked choice*: Rank items according to preference, such as selecting vacation days or choosing job assignments.

- *Forced choice*: Choose between two preset options, such as yes/no or male/female.
- *Likert choice*: Choose among a range of options on a numerically defined scale, such as 1 = very unsatisfied, 3 = neither satisfied nor unsatisfied, or 5 = very satisfied.

Be sure your questions are both simple and specific, and provide enough space for an adequate response.

F

▶ Would your department order another X2L Copier? Yes ☐ No ☐

Questions are often worded as captions. Keep captions brief and to the point; avoid wordy repetition by combining related information under an explanatory heading.

WORDY   What make of car (or vehicle) do you drive? _____

What year was it manufactured? _____

What model is it? _____

What is the body style? _____

CONCISE   Vehicle Information

Make _____   Year _____

Model _____   Body Style _____

Make captions (*Make*, *Model*, *Year*, *Body Style*) as specific as possible. If a requested date is other than the date on which the form is being filled out, the caption should read, for example, "Effective date" or "Date issued," rather than simply "Date." As in all writing, put yourself in your reader's place and imagine what sort of requests would be clear.

For detailed and up-to-date information on designing paper and digital forms, see www.stcsig.org/usability/topics/forms.html.

forums (*see* blogs and forums)

fragments (*see* sentence fragments)

functional shift

Many words shift easily from one **part of speech** to another, depending on how they are used. When they do, the process is called a *functional shift*, or a shift in function.

▶ It takes ten minutes to *walk* from the sales office to the accounting department. However, the long *walk* reduces efficiency. [*Walk* shifts from **verb** to **noun**.]

▶ I talk to Jim in the Chicago office on the *phone* every day. He was concerned about the office *phone* expenses. He will *phone* the home office from London. [*Phone* shifts from noun to **adjective** to verb.]

▶ *After* we discuss the project, we will begin work. *After* lengthy discussions, we began work. The partners worked well together forever *after*. [*After* shifts from **conjunction** to **preposition** to **adverb**.]

Jargon is often the result of functional shifts. In hospitals, for example, an *attending physician* is often referred to simply as the "attending" (a shift from an adjective to a noun). Likewise, in nuclear plant construction, a *reactor containment building* is called a "containment" (a shift from an adjective to a noun). Do not shift the function of a word indiscriminately merely to shorten a phrase or an expression. See also **affectation**, **audience**, and **conciseness**.

F

G

garbled sentences

A garbled sentence is one that is so tangled with structural and grammatical problems that it cannot be repaired. Garbled sentences often result from an attempt to squeeze too many ideas into one sentence.

► My job objectives are accomplished by my having a diversified background which enables me to operate effectively and efficiently, consisting of a degree in computer science, along with twelve years of experience, including three years in Staff Engineering-Packaging sets a foundation for a strong background in areas of analyzing problems and assessing economical and reasonable solutions.

Do not try to patch such a sentence; rather, analyze the ideas it contains, list them in a logical sequence, and then construct one or more entirely new sentences. The preceding example contains the following five ideas:

- My job requires that I analyze problems to find economical and workable solutions.
- My diversified background helps me accomplish my job.
- I have a computer science degree.
- I have twelve years of job experience.
- Three of these years have been in Staff Engineering-Packaging.

Using those five ideas—together with **parallel structure**, **sentence variety**, **subordination**, and **transition**—the writer might have described the job as follows:

► My job requires that I analyze problems to find economical and workable solutions. Both my education and experience help me achieve this goal. Specifically, I have a computer-science degree and twelve years of job experience, three of which have been in the Staff Engineering-Packaging Department.

See also **clarity**, **mixed constructions**, and **sentence construction**.

gender

In English grammar, *gender* refers to the classification of **nouns** and **pronouns** as masculine, feminine, and neuter. The gender of most words can be identified only by the choice of the appropriate pronoun (*he, she, it*). Only these pronouns and a select few nouns (*man/woman, buck/doe*) or noun forms (*heir/heiress*) reflect gender. Many such nouns have been replaced by single terms that apply to both sexes. See also **agreement** and **he / she**.

Writers must make sure that nouns and pronouns within a grammatical construction agree in gender. A pronoun, for example, must agree with its noun antecedent in gender. We refer to a woman as *she* or *her*, not as *it*; to a man as *he* or *him*, not as *it*; to a building as *it*, not as *he* or *she*.

Nonnative speakers of English may be confused if their native language assigns gender because the English language has so few gender distinctions. Be sure to follow the guidelines for nonsexist writing under **biased language**.

G

general and specific methods of development

General and specific **methods of development** organize information either from general points to specific details (Figure G–1) or from specific details to a general conclusion (Figure G–2). As with all methods of development, most writers blend and use combinations of methods.

General to Specific

The general-to-specific method of development is especially useful for teaching **readers** about something with which they are not familiar because you can begin with generally known information and progress to new and increasingly specific details. This method can also be used to support a general statement with facts or examples that validate the statement. For example, if you begin your writing with the general statement "Companies that diversify are more successful than those that do not," you could follow that statement with examples and statistics that prove to the reader that companies that diversify are, in fact, more successful than companies that do not.

A memo or short report organized entirely in a general-to-specific sequence discusses only one point. All other information in the document supports the general statement, as illustrated in Figure G–1 (on page 228) from a memo about locating additional computer-chip suppliers.

Subject: Expanding Our Supplier Base for Computer Chips

General statement
Based on the information presented at the supply meeting on April 13, we recommend that the company initiate relationships with computer-chip manufacturers. Several events make such an action necessary.

Supporting information
Our current supplier, Datacom, is experiencing growing pains and is having difficulty shipping the product on time. Specifically, we can expect a reduction of between 800 and 1,000 units per month for the remainder of this fiscal year. The number of units should stabilize at 15,000 units per month thereafter.

Specific details
Domestic demand for our computers continues to grow. Demand during the current fiscal year is up 500,000 units over the last fiscal year. Our sales projections for the next five years show that demand should peak next year at about 830,000 units given the consumer demand, which will increase exponentially.

Finally, our expansion into the Czech Republic and Kazakhstan markets will require additional shipments of at least 175,000 units per quarter for the remainder of this fiscal year. Sales Department projections put global computer sales at double that rate, or 350,000 units per fiscal year, for the next five years.

FIGURE G–1. General-to-Specific Method of Development

Specific to General

Specific-to-general development is especially useful when you wish to persuade skeptical readers of a general principle with an accumulation of specific details and evidence that reach a logical **conclusion**. It carefully builds its case, often with examples and analogies in addition to facts or statistics, and it does not actually make its point until the end. (See also **order-of-importance method of development**.) Figure G–2 is an example of the specific-to-general method of development.

global communication

The continual expansion of the global marketplace and the growing need for many businesses to participate globally means that the ability to communicate with international audiences from varied backgrounds is essential. See **audience**.

Recently, a government agency studied the use of passenger-side air bags in 4,500 accidents involving nearly 7,200 front-seat passengers of the vehicles involved. Nearly all the accidents occurred on routes that had a speed limit of at least 40 mph. Only 20 percent of the adult front-seat passengers were riding in vehicles equipped with passenger-side air bags. Those riding in vehicles not equipped with passenger-side air bags were more than twice as likely to be killed as passengers riding in vehicles with such air bags.

    A conservative estimate is that 40 percent of the adult front-seat passenger-vehicle deaths could be prevented if all vehicles came equipped with passenger-side air bags. Children, however, should always ride in the backseat because other studies have indicated that a child can be killed by the deployment of an air bag. For adult front-seat passengers in an accident, chances of survival are far greater if the vehicle is equipped with a passenger-side air bag.

> Specific details

> General conclusion

G

FIGURE G–2. Specific-to-General Method of Development

Many entries in this book, such as **meetings** and **résumés**, are based on dominant cultural patterns in the United States. The treatment of such topics might be very different in other cultures, where leadership styles, persuasive strategies, and even legal constraints differ.

As illustrated in the entry for **international correspondence**, organizational patterns, forms of courtesy, and ideas about efficiency can vary significantly from culture to culture. What might be seen as direct and efficient in the United States could be considered blunt and even impolite in other cultures. The explanations for these differing ways of viewing communication are complex. Researchers often measure cultural differences through such concepts as the importance of honor or saving face, perceptions of time, and preferences for avoiding uncertainty. Because cultures evolve and global communication affects cultural patterns, you must be able to adapt to cultural variations. Figure G–3 (on page 230) shows an ineffective global business communication, whereas Figure G–4 (on page 231) demonstrates an effective global business communication. The checklist that follows offers useful approaches that can help you adapt. See also **global graphics**.

G

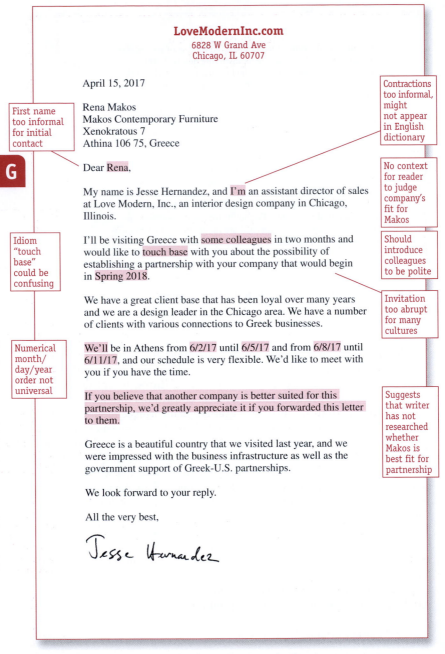

LoveModernInc.com
6828 W Grand Ave
Chicago, IL 60707

April 15, 2017

Rena Makos
Makos Contemporary Furniture
Xenokratous 7
Athina 106 75, Greece

Dear Rena,

My name is Jesse Hernandez, and I'm an assistant director of sales at Love Modern, Inc., an interior design company in Chicago, Illinois.

I'll be visiting Greece with some colleagues in two months and would like to touch base with you about the possibility of establishing a partnership with your company that would begin in Spring 2018.

We have a great client base that has been loyal over many years and we are a design leader in the Chicago area. We have a number of clients with various connections to Greek businesses.

We'll be in Athens from 6/2/17 until 6/5/17 and from 6/8/17 until 6/11/17, and our schedule is very flexible. We'd like to meet with you if you have the time.

If you believe that another company is better suited for this partnership, we'd greatly appreciate it if you forwarded this letter to them.

Greece is a beautiful country that we visited last year, and we were impressed with the business infrastructure as well as the government support of Greek-U.S. partnerships.

We look forward to your reply.

All the very best,

Jesse Hernandez

Annotations:

First name too informal for initial contact

Contractions too informal, might not appear in English dictionary

No context for reader to judge company's fit for Makos

Idiom "touch base" could be confusing

Should introduce colleagues to be polite

Invitation too abrupt for many cultures

Numerical month/day/year order not universal

Suggests that writer has not researched whether Makos is best fit for partnership

FIGURE G–3. Ineffective Global Business Communication

LoveModernInc.com
6828 W Grand Ave
Chicago, IL 60707

April 15, 2017

Rena Makos
Makos Contemporary Furniture
Xenokratous 7
Athina 106 75, Greece

Dear Ms. Makos:

Uses formal salutation

I am writing to inquire about the possibility of a partnership between your company and Love Modern, Inc., an interior design company in Chicago, Illinois. Our director of sales, Kristina Roberts, saw your Modern Club chair at last year's Atlanta International Gifts & Home Furnishings Market and was impressed by its design and quality. We are interested in carrying products from your furniture line in our stores for the Spring 2018 season with the option of continuing that line in future seasons.

Provides context and uses appropriate tone

Our company offers an established customer base and a record of previous successes in partnerships such as the one we propose. Love Modern annually ranks in the top ten for furniture sales in the state of Illinois, and we are known for providing excellent customer service and high-quality modern furniture. We are known for introducing new furniture designers, including rising international designers, to the Chicago metropolitan area. Your company has become highly regarded across Athens for innovative updates to classic designs, a quality that our customers appreciate. We believe that a partnership between our companies could benefit both equally.

Provides background and strong evidence of success

Ms. Roberts and I will be in Athens June 2–5, 2017, and again June 8–11, 2017. If you are available to meet during our visits, please let me know, and I will arrange details for our meeting. During this meeting, we would begin negotiations for the details of this partnership. I expect that it will take no more than two hours. If you are not available to meet in person on the dates listed above, I would be pleased to set up alternative meeting times using Skype. If you would like to see a list of successful partnerships and industry rankings, go to LoveModernInc.com/mediafacts.php.

Uses clear date format and includes useful details

We at Love Modern are excited by the possibilities of working with Makos Contemporary Furniture. We look forward to your reply.

Offers polite closing and shows enthusiasm for partnership

Sincerely,

Jesse Hernandez

Includes full contact information below signature line

Assistant Director of Sales
1 (555) 555-5555
jhernandez@LoveModernInc.com

FIGURE G–4. Effective Global Business Communication

WRITER'S CHECKLIST   **Communicating Globally**

✔ Discuss the differing cultures within your company or region to reinforce the idea that people can interpret verbal and nonverbal communications differently.

✔ Invite global and intercultural communication experts to speak at your workplace. Companies in your area may have employees who could be resources for cultural discussions.

✔ Understand that the key to effective communication with global audiences is recognizing that cultural differences, despite the challenges they may present, offer opportunities for growth for both you and your organization.

✔ Consult with someone from your intended audience's culture. Many phrases, gestures, and visual elements are so subtle that only someone from that culture can explain the effect they may have on others from that culture. See also **global graphics**.

✔ Intercultural Press is a source for "intercultural, multicultural and cross-cultural studies and informative country guides to help you do business and form strong relationships in foreign countries." See www .hodder.co.uk/Nicholas%20Brealey/Nicholas%20Brealey.page. Geert Hofstede, a leading researcher in national and organizational culture, also offers cultural comparison tools and other resources on his Web site. See geert-hofstede.com/.

---

global graphics

In a global business and technology environment, **graphs** and other **visuals** require the same careful attention given to other aspects of **global communication**. The complex cultural connotations of visuals challenge writers to think beyond their own experience when they are aiming for audiences outside their own culture.

Symbols, images, and even colors are not free from cultural associations — they depend on **context**, and context is culturally determined. For instance, in North America, a red cross is commonly used as a symbol for first aid or a hospital. In Muslim countries, however, a cross (red or otherwise) represents Christianity, whereas a crescent (usually green) signifies first aid or a hospital. A manual for use in Honduras could indicate "caution" by using a picture of a person touching a finger below the eye. In France, however, that gesture means "You can't fool me."

Figure G–5 shows two different graphics depicting weight lifters. The drawing on the left may be appropriate for U.S. audiences and

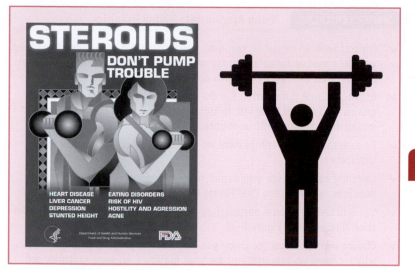

G

FIGURE G–5. Graphics for U.S. (left) and Global (right) Audiences

others. However, that graphic would be highly inappropriate in many cultures, where the image of a partially clothed man and woman in close proximity would be contrary to deeply held cultural beliefs and even laws about the public depiction of men and women. The drawing at the right in Figure G–5, however, depicts a weight lifter with a neutral icon that avoids the connotations associated with more realistic images of people.

These examples suggest why the International Organization for Standardization (ISO) established agreed-upon symbols, such as those shown in Figure G–6, for public signs, guidebooks, and manuals.*

FIGURE G–6. International Organization for Standardization (ISO) Symbols

*Learn more through the useful illustrations in "The International Language of ISO Graphical Symbols" at www.iso.org/publication/PUB100243.html.

WRITER'S CHECKLIST   Using Appropriate Global Graphics

✔ Consult with an expert or test your use of graphics with individuals from your intended audience's country who understand the effect that visuals may have on that **audience**. See also **presentations**.

✔ Organize visual information for the intended audience. Some culture groups read visuals from left to right in clockwise rotation; others read visuals from right to left in counterclockwise rotation.

✔ Be sure that your graphics have no unintended political or religious implications.

✔ Carefully consider how you depict people in visuals — body exposure, positions, and clothing (see Figure G–5).

✔ Use outlines or neutral abstractions to represent human beings. Consider stick figures, as in Figure G–6.

✔ Choose neutral colors (or those you know are appropriate) or gray scale, which carries no connotation, for your graphics. In some cultures, red symbolizes good fortune or joy; in others, red indicates danger.

✔ Check your use of punctuation marks, which are as language specific as symbols. For example, in North America, the question mark generally represents the need for information or help. In many countries, that symbol has no meaning at all.

✔ Create simple visuals with universal shapes, as illustrated in Figure G–6.

✔ Explain the meaning of icons or symbols that cannot be changed, such as a company logo.

glossaries

A glossary is an alphabetical list of definitions of specialized terms used in a **formal report**, a manual, or another long document. You may want to include a glossary if some readers in your **audience** are not familiar with specialized or technical terms you use.

Keep glossary entries concise, and be sure they are written in language that all the readers of your document can understand.

▶ *Amortize*: To write off an expenditure by prorating it over a specific period of time.

Arrange the terms alphabetically, with each entry beginning on a new line. The definitions then follow the terms, dictionary style. In a formal report, the glossary begins on a new page and appears after the appendix(es) and bibliography.

Including a glossary does not relieve you of the responsibility of **defining terms** that your reader will not know when those terms are first mentioned in the text.

gobbledygook

Gobbledygook is writing that suffers from an overdose of traits guaranteed to make it stuffy, pretentious, and wordy. Such traits include the overuse of big and mostly abstract words, **affectation** (especially long variants), **buzzwords**, **clichés**, **euphemisms**, inappropriate **jargon**, stacked **modifiers**, and **vague words**. (See also **abstract / concrete words**.) Gobbledygook is writing that attempts to sound official (officialese), legal (legalese), or scientific. Consider the following statement from an auto-repair release form.

G

LEGALESE   I hereby authorize the above repair work to be done along with the necessary material and hereby grant you and/or your employees permission to operate the car or truck herein described on streets, highways, or elsewhere for the purpose of testing and/or inspection. An express mechanic's lien is hereby acknowledged on above car or truck to secure the amount of repairs thereto.

DIRECT   You have my permission to do the repair work listed on this work order and to use the necessary material. You may drive my vehicle to test its performance. I understand that you will keep my vehicle until I have paid for all repairs.

See also **clarity**, **conciseness**, **plain language**, and **word choice**.

good / well

Good is an **adjective**, and *well* is an **adverb**.

ADJECTIVE   Janet presented a *good* plan.

ADVERB   She presented the plan *well*.

Well can also be used as an adjective to describe health (a *well* child, *wellness* programs). See also **bad / badly**.

grammar

Grammar is the systematic description of the way words work together to form a coherent language. In that sense, it is an explanation of the structure of a language. However, grammar is popularly taken to mean the set of rules that governs how a language ought to be spoken and written. In that sense, it refers to the **usage** conventions of a language.

Those two meanings of grammar are easily confused. To clarify the distinction, consider the expression *ain't*. Unless used intentionally to add colloquial flavor, *ain't* is unacceptable because its use is considered nonstandard. Yet taken strictly as a **part of speech**, the term functions perfectly well as a verb. Whether it appears in a declarative sentence ("I ain't going") or an interrogative sentence ("Ain't I going?"), it conforms to the normal pattern for all verbs in the English language. Although readers may not approve of its use, they cannot argue that it is ungrammatical in such sentences.

To achieve **clarity**, you need to know grammar both as a description of the way words work together and as the conventions of usage. Knowing the conventions of usage helps you select the appropriate over the inappropriate word or expression. (See also **word choice**.) A knowledge of grammar helps you diagnose and correct problems arising from how words and phrases function in relation to one another. Understanding **dangling modifiers**, for example, helps you avoid or correct a construction that obscures the intended meaning. For a complete list of grammar entries, see the Contents by Topic on the inside front cover.

grant proposals

Grant proposals are written to nonprofit and government organizations to request the approval of and funding for projects that solve a problem or fulfill a need. A scientist, for example, may write a grant proposal to the National Institutes of Health requesting a specific sum of money to study a new cancer therapy, or the executive director of Habitat for Humanity may write a grant proposal to a local government requesting funding to purchase supplies to construct new housing for disadvantaged families in the area.

The advice in the entry **proposals** for assessing audience and purpose, writing persuasively, maintaining **ethics in writing**, and managing a project within a tight deadline applies as well to writing grant proposals. This entry focuses on the particular needs of grant-proposal writers.

Granting organizations typically post opportunities, along with detailed application guidelines, on their Web sites and specify their requirements for the format and content of proposals. Most federal, state, and large nonprofit government grants are now submitted electronically, and various sections may have imposed word, character, or content limits that are enforced electronically. When preparing a proposal document, always organize its elements in the exact order described or required in the request for proposals (RFP) or in the grant maker's guidelines. Although application guidelines and processes may differ from one organization to another, grant proposals generally require the following sections at a minimum:

- Cover message
- Title page
- Application form
- Introduction (summary)
- Literature review (if needed)
- Project narrative
  - *Project description*
  - *Project outcomes*
  - *Budget narrative*
  - *Task schedule*
- Organization description
- Conclusion
- Attachments

G

Cover Message

Usually one page long, the **cover message** (or letter) should identify who you are and your professional affiliation. It should specify the grant that you are applying for, summarize the proposed project, and include the amount of funding you are requesting.

Title Page

On a single page, show the **title** of the project, the names of project staff and their affiliations, the date submitted, and the name of the recipient's organization. This page serves as the cover of the grant proposal.

Application Form

Especially in online grant applications, an application form may replace the cover message or letter and title page. This form may be one or more pages and may require you to check boxes, fill in blanks, or insert brief descriptions or other information into text boxes or blank spaces. A word or character limit (typically 250–400 words) may be imposed or enforced. An official signature (or its electronic equivalent) is often required. This form may request detailed information about the applicant organization, such as the staff's or board of directors' demographic composition or the organization's human resources policies.

Introduction

The **introduction** or summary is your proposal at a glance—it briefly describes (within a given limit) the problem to be solved and projects the expected outcomes of your grant proposal. If substantial **research** is involved, you may also describe your proposed research methods (interviews, questionnaires, videos, observations, and so on) in a separate paragraph. See also **abstracts**.

Literature Review

The literature review lists the relevant research sources you consulted in preparing your proposal. Also called a *References* or *Works Cited* section, it allows reviewers of your proposal to assess your familiarity with current research in the field. Is your research up to date? Thorough? Pertinent? Be selective: Include only relevant journal articles, books, interviews, broadcasts, **blogs and forums**, and other sources. In nonresearch proposals (those not based on secondary or formal research), a limited number of citations are frequently included within the project narrative or as footnotes or endnotes.

Project Narrative

The heart of the proposal, the project narrative describes in detail the scope of the work, expected outcomes, a list of tasks, a project activity schedule from start to finish, and estimated costs. Be specific and thorough.

Project Description.   The project description includes an overview of the project and details of how the research project or program will be conducted (its methodology). In nonresearch proposals, include a succinct *statement of need*—also called a *case statement*—which presents the facts and evidence that support the need for the project. The information presented can come from authorities in the field as well as from your organization's own experience or research. A logical and persuasive statement of need demonstrates that your company or nonprofit organization sufficiently understands the situation and is therefore capable of addressing it satisfactorily. Clearly indicate why or how your solution improves on existing or previous ones, and cite evidence to support this. Emphasize the benefits of the proposed activities for the grant maker's intended constituency or target population, and explain why your solution to the problem or plan to fulfill the need should be approved. Most RFPs and grant-maker guidelines provide a list of specific questions for applicants to answer or required topics that must be persuasively addressed in this section.

Project Outcomes.   Having described the preparations and justification for the program, the grant writer must describe the outcomes or deliverables of the proposal—what the funding organization can expect as a result of the time, labor, and financial support it has invested in the program. Outcomes are stated as quantifiable objectives—improvements in reading scores, volume of carbon emission reductions, aerobic fitness measures, and so on. Grant proposals, especially those solicited by government agencies, must also provide detailed plans for collecting, analyzing, and interpreting data to evaluate the success or failure of the research or program in achieving the stated outcomes.

Budget Narrative. Next, include a budget-narrative section that provides a detailed listing of costs for personnel, equipment, building renovations, and other grant-related expenses. This information must be clear, accurate, and arranged in an easily understood format for those evaluating the data (usually in a **table**). Many granting organizations, including government agencies, require that specified budget forms be used. If your proposal is approved, you are being entrusted with funds belonging to someone else, and you are accountable for them. Your cost estimates may also be subject to changes over which you have no control, such as price increases for equipment, software, or consulting assistance. The project may also require ongoing funding following completion of the grant's tasks. Either provide an estimate of such costs, or note that they will appear in a Future Funding or Sustainability section.

Task Schedule. Next, prepare a schedule of tasks that need to be performed in order to implement the program or complete the project. Arrange them as bulleted points in sequence from first to last, with due dates for each, or present them in a table or perhaps in a Gantt chart, as described in **graphs**.

Organization Description

The organization description may follow the Introduction or it may be placed just prior to the Conclusion, depending on RFP requirements or the granting organization's guidelines. Describe the applicant organization briefly in terms of mission, history, qualifications, and credibility (significant, related accomplishments), taking care to include all information requested in the RFP or grant guidelines. Granting organizations consider not only the merits of the proposed program or research but also your organization's standing in the community and similar advantages.

Conclusion

This brief wrap-up section emphasizes the benefits or advantages of your project. This section affords you one more opportunity to give the funding organization a reason why your proposal merits its support. Emphasize the benefits of the research, program, or other activities for the grant maker's intended constituency or target population. Finally, express your appreciation for the opportunity to submit the proposal, and close with a statement of your willingness to provide further information.

G

Attachments

Funding organizations request supporting information, such as nonprofit-status documentation, copies of legal documents (for example, articles of incorporation or bylaws), or lists of information that you may need to design and compose yourself. Provide a comprehensive list of attachments, and clearly label each item to guide the grant reviewer in evaluating the proposal package. See also **appendixes**.

G

WRITER'S CHECKLIST   **Writing Grant Proposals**

✔ Analyze the granting organization's RFP or guidelines carefully to best formulate your request to match its funding interests and priorities.

✔ Review the descriptions of proposal contexts, strategies, and types in the **proposals** entry.

✔ Respond to every question or address every topic requested.

✔ Strive for **conciseness** in the narrative without sacrificing **clarity** — make every word count.

✔ Emphasize the benefits of your proposal to the granting organization and its constituents.

✔ Follow all instructions meticulously, because failure to include requested information or to observe format requirements may be grounds for rejection or lack of review.

✔ Review the final grant proposal carefully. Because many online submission systems do not have a spell-check function, draft sections in a word-processing program, then paste them into the electronic form.

---

graphs

A graph presents numerical or quantitative data in visual form and offers several advantages over presenting data within the text or in **tables**. Trends, movements, distributions, comparisons, and cycles are more readily apparent in graphs than they are in tables. However, although graphs present data in a more comprehensible form than tables do, they are often less precise. For that reason, some **audiences** may need graphs to be accompanied by tables that give exact data. The types of graphs described in this entry include line graphs, bar graphs, pie graphs, and picture graphs. For advice on integrating graphs within text, see **visuals**; for information about using presentation graphics, see **presentations**. For combining graphs with other elements, see **infographics**.

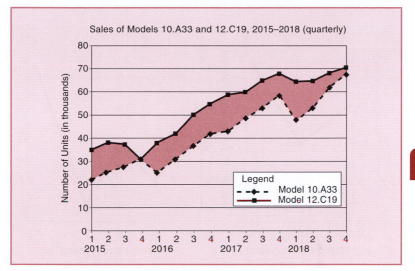

FIGURE G–7. Double-Line Graph (with Shading)

Line Graphs

A line graph shows the relationship between two variables or sets of numbers by plotting points in relation to two axes drawn at right angles (Figure G–7). The vertical axis usually represents amounts, and the horizontal axis usually represents increments of time. Line graphs that portray more than one set of variables (double-line graphs) allow for comparisons between two sets of data for the same period of time. You can emphasize the difference between the two lines by shading the space between them, as shown in Figure G–7.

❖ **ETHICS NOTE** Be especially careful to proportion the vertical and horizontal scales so that they present the data precisely and free of visual distortion. To do otherwise is not only inaccurate but potentially unethical. (See **ethics in writing**.) In Figure G–8 (on page 242), the graph at the left gives the appearance of a slight decline followed by a steady increase in investment returns because the scale is compressed, with some years selectively omitted. The graph at the right represents the trend more accurately because the years are evenly distributed without omissions. ❖

Bar Graphs

Bar graphs consist of horizontal or vertical bars of equal width, scaled in length to represent some quantity. They are commonly used to show (1) quantities of the same item at different times, (2) quantities of

G

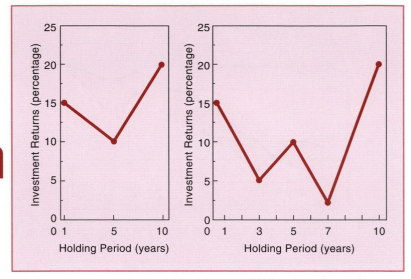

FIGURE G–8. Distorted (left) and Distortion-Free (right) Expressions of Data

different items at the same time, and (3) quantities of the different parts of an item that make up a whole (in which case, the segments of the bar graph must total 100 percent). The horizontal bar graph in Figure G–9 shows the quantities of different items for the same period of time.

Bar graphs can also show the different portions of an item that make up the whole, as shown in Figure G–10. Such a bar graph is divided

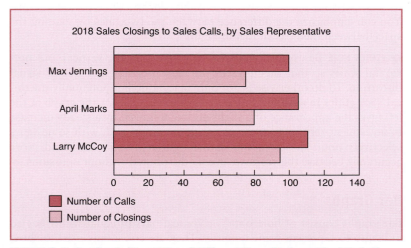

FIGURE G–9. Bar Graph (Quantities of Different Items During a Fixed Period)

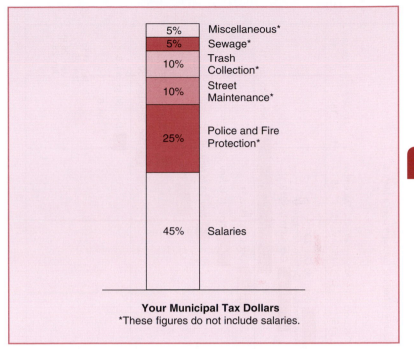

5%	Miscellaneous*
5%	Sewage*
10%	Trash Collection*
10%	Street Maintenance*
25%	Police and Fire Protection*
45%	Salaries

Your Municipal Tax Dollars
*These figures do not include salaries.

G

FIGURE G–10. Bar (Column) Graph (Showing the Parts That Make Up the Whole)

according to the appropriate proportions of the subcomponents of the item. This type of graph, also called a *column graph* when constructed vertically, can indicate multiple items. Where such items represent parts of a whole, as in Figure G–10, the segments in the bar graph must total 100 percent. Note that in addition to labels, each subdivision of a bar graph must be marked clearly by color, shading, or crosshatching, with a key or labels that identify the subdivisions represented. Be aware that three-dimensional graphs can make sections seem larger than the amounts they represent.

A Gantt chart is a type of horizontal bar graph designed to plan and track the status of projects from beginning to end. As shown in Figure G–11 (on page 244), the horizontal axis represents the length of a project divided into time increments—days, weeks, or months. The timeline usually runs across the top of the chart. The vertical axis represents the individual tasks that make up the project and can include a second column listing the staff responsible for each task. The horizontal bars in the body of the chart identify each task and show its beginning and end dates. Gantt charts are often prepared with spreadsheet or project-management software. See also **collaborative writing**.

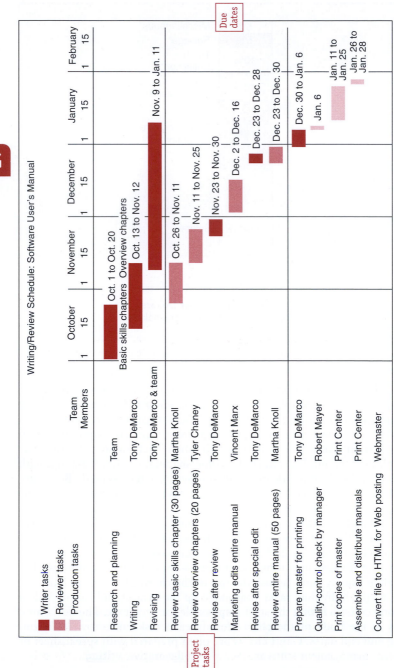

G

Writing/Review Schedule: Software User's Manual

Due dates

Project tasks

	Team Members				
Research and planning	Team	Oct. 1 to Oct. 20			
Writing	Tony DeMarco	Oct. 13 to Nov. 12			
Revising	Tony DeMarco & team		Nov. 9 to Jan. 11		
Review basic skills chapter (30 pages)	Martha Knoll	Oct. 26 to Nov. 11			
Review overview chapters (20 pages)	Tyler Chaney	Nov. 11 to Nov. 25			
Revise after review	Tony DeMarco	Nov. 23 to Nov. 30			
Marketing edits entire manual	Vincent Marx	Dec. 2 to Dec. 16			
Revise after special edit	Tony DeMarco	Dec. 23 to Dec. 28			
Review entire manual (50 pages)	Martha Knoll	Dec. 23 to Dec. 30			
Prepare master for printing	Tony DeMarco	Dec. 30 to Jan. 6			
Quality-control check by manager	Robert Mayer	Jan. 6			
Print copies of master	Print Center	Jan. 11 to Jan. 25			
Assemble and distribute manuals	Print Center	Jan. 26 to Jan. 28			
Convert file to HTML for Web posting	Webmaster				

Writer tasks
Reviewer tasks
Production tasks

Basic skills chapters   Overview chapters

FIGURE G–11. Gantt Chart Showing Project Schedule

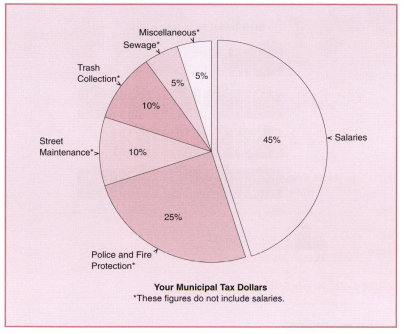

FIGURE G–12. Pie Graph (Showing Percentages of the Whole)

Pie Graphs

A pie graph presents data as wedge-shaped sections of a circle. The circle equals 100 percent, or the whole, of some quantity, and the wedges represent how the whole is divided. Many times, the data shown in a bar graph could also be depicted in a pie graph. For example, Figure G–10 shows percentages of a whole in bar-graph form. Figure G–12 shows the same data converted into a pie graph, dividing "Your Municipal Tax Dollars" into wedge-shaped sections that represent percentages, with salaries emphasized. Pie graphs provide a quicker way of presenting information than can be shown in a table, yet a more detailed breakdown of the same information often accompanies a pie graph.

Picture Graphs

Picture graphs are modified bar graphs that use pictorial symbols of the item portrayed. Each symbol corresponds to a specified quantity of the item, as shown in Figure G–13 (on page 246). Note that for precision and clarity, the picture graph includes the total quantity following the symbols.

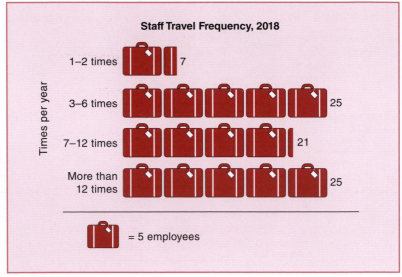

FIGURE G–13. Picture Graph

WRITER'S CHECKLIST	Creating Graphs

FOR ALL GRAPHS

✔ Give your graph a descriptive title that is accurate and concise.

✔ Use, as needed, a key or legend that lists and defines symbols (see Figure G–7).

✔ Include a source line under the graph at the lower left when the data come from another source.

✔ Place explanatory footnotes directly below the figure caption or label (see Figures G–10 and G–12).

FOR LINE GRAPHS

✔ Indicate the zero point of the graph (the point where the two axes intersect).

✔ Insert a break in the scale if the range of data shown makes it inconvenient to begin at zero.

✔ Divide the vertical axis into equal portions, from the least amount (or zero) at the bottom to the greatest amount at the top.

✔ Divide the horizontal axis into equal units from left to right, and label the units to show what they represent.

(continued)

✔ Make all lettering read horizontally if possible, although the caption or label for the vertical axis is usually positioned vertically (see Figure G–7).

FOR BAR GRAPHS

✔ Differentiate among the types of data each bar or part of a bar represents by color, shading, or crosshatching.

✔ Avoid three-dimensional graphs when they make bars seem larger than the amounts they represent.

FOR PIE GRAPHS

✔ Make sure that the complete circle is equivalent to 100 percent.

✔ Sequence the wedges clockwise from largest to smallest, beginning at the 12 o'clock position, whenever possible.

✔ Limit the number of items in the pie graph to avoid clutter and to ensure that the wedges are thick enough to be clear. (Some software allows users to open and examine wedges in greater detail.)

✔ Give each wedge a distinctive color, pattern, shade, or texture.

✔ Label each wedge with its percentage value, and keep all callouts (labels that identify the wedges) horizontal.

✔ Detach a wedge, as shown in Figure G–12, if you wish to draw attention to a particular segment of the pie graph.

FOR PICTURE GRAPHS

✔ Use picture graphs to add interest to **presentations** and documents (such as **newsletters**) that are aimed at wide audiences.

✔ Choose symbols that are easily recognizable. See also **global graphics**.

✔ Let each symbol represent the same number of units.

✔ Indicate larger quantities by using more symbols instead of larger symbols, because relative sizes are difficult to judge accurately.

✔ Indicate the total quantity following the symbols, as shown in Figure G–13.

✔ Indicate the zero point of the graph when appropriate.

G

H

he / she

The use of either *he* or *she* to refer to both sexes excludes half of the population. (See also **biased language**.) To avoid this problem, you could use the phrases *he or she* and *his or her*. ("Whoever is appointed will find *his or her* task difficult.") However, *he or she* and *his or her* are clumsy when used repeatedly, as are *he/she* and similar constructions. One solution is to reword the sentence to use a plural **pronoun**; if you do, change the **nouns** or other pronouns to match the plural form.

►   *Administrators*   *their jobs*   *they understand*
    ~~The administrator~~ cannot do ~~his or her job~~ until ~~he or she under-~~
    ~~stands~~ the organization's culture.

In other cases, you may be able to avoid using a pronoun altogether.

►   *an*
    Everyone must submit ~~his or her~~ expense report by Monday.

Of course, a pronoun cannot always be omitted without changing the meaning of a sentence. Another solution is to omit troublesome pronouns by using the imperative **mood**.

►   *Submit all*   *s*
    ~~Everyone must submit his or her~~ expense report~~s~~ by Monday.

headers and footers

A *header* in a **formal report** or other document appears at the top of each page, and a *footer* appears at the bottom of each page. The header and footer shown in Figure H–1 are typical. The header or footer should include at least the page number but may also include the document title, the topic (or subtopic) of a section, the date of the document, the names of the author or recipients, and other identifying information to help **readers** keep track of where they are in the document. Keep your headers and footers concise, because too much information in them can create visual clutter. For examples of headers used in correspondence, see **letters** and **memos**. See also **layout and design** and **writing for the Web**.

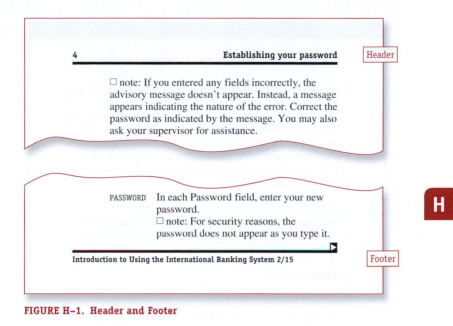

FIGURE H–1. Header and Footer

headings

Headings (also called *heads*) are titles or subtitles that highlight main topics and signal topic changes within the body of a document, whether an **e-mail**, a **memo**, a **report**, or a Web page. (See also **writing for the Web**.) Headings help **readers** find information and divide the material into comprehensible segments. Some documents, such as **formal reports** and **proposals**, may need several levels of headings (as shown in Figure H–2 (on page 250)) to indicate major divisions, subdivisions, and even smaller units. If possible, avoid using more than four levels of headings. See also **layout and design**.

Headings typically represent the major topics of a document. In a short document, you can use the major divisions of your outline as headings; in a longer document, you may need to use both major and minor divisions.

General Heading Style

No one format for headings is correct. Often an organization settles on a standard format, which everyone in that organization follows. Sometimes a client for whom a report or proposal is being prepared requires a particular format. In the absence of specific guidelines, follow the system illustrated in Figure H–2.

H

First-level head → **DISTRIBUTION CENTER LOCATION REPORT**

The committee initially considered 30 possible locations for the proposed new distribution center. Of these, 20 were eliminated almost immediately for unfavorable zoning regulations, inadequate transportation infrastructure, etc. Of the remaining 10 locations, the committee selected for intensive study the 3 that seemed most promising: Chicago, Minneapolis, and Salt Lake City. We have now visited these 3 cities, and our observations and recommendations follow.

Second-level head → **CHICAGO**

Of the three cities, Chicago presently seems to the committee to offer the greatest advantages, although we wish to examine these more carefully before making a final recommendation.

Third-level head → **Selected Location**

Though not at the geographic center of the United States, Chicago is the demographic center to more than three-quarters of the U.S. population. It is within easy reach of our corporate headquarters in New York. And it is close to several of our most important suppliers of components and raw materials—those, for example, in Columbus, Detroit, and St. Louis. Several factors were considered essential to the location, although some may not have had as great an impact on the selection....

Fourth-level head → *Air Transportation.*　Chicago has two major airports (O'Hare and Midway) and a number of suburban airports. Both domestic and international air-cargo service are available....

Sea Transportation.　Except during the winter months when the Great Lakes are frozen, Chicago is an international seaport....

Rail Transportation.　Chicago is served by the following major railroads....

FIGURE H–2. Headings Used in a Document

Decimal Numbering System

The decimal numbering system uses a combination of numbers and decimal points to differentiate among levels of headings. Some documents, such as **policies and procedures**, benefit from the decimal numbering system for ease of cross-referencing sections. For an example of the decimal numbering system of headings, see **outlining**.

WRITER'S CHECKLIST   **Using Headings**

✔ Use headings to signal a new topic. Use a lower-level heading to indicate a new subtopic within the larger topic.

✔ Make headings concise but specific enough to be informative, as in Figure H–2.

✔ Avoid too many or too few headings or levels of headings; too many clutter a document, and too few fail to provide recognizable structure.

✔ Ensure that headings at the same level are of relatively equal importance and have **parallel structure**.

✔ Subdivide sections only as needed; when you do, try to subdivide them into at least two lower-level headings.

✔ Do not allow a heading to substitute for discussion; the text should read as if the heading were not there.

✔ Do not leave a heading as the final line of a page. If two lines of text cannot fit below a heading, start the section at the top of the next page.

H

hyphens

The hyphen (-) is used primarily for linking and separating words and parts of words. The hyphen often improves **clarity** (as in *re-sign* and *resign*). The hyphen is sometimes confused with the **dash** (—), which has many other functions.

Hyphens with Compound Words

Some **compound words** are formed with hyphens (*able-bodied, over-the-counter*). Hyphens are also used with multiword **numbers** from twenty-one through ninety-nine and fractions when they are written out (*three-quarters*). Most current dictionaries indicate whether compound words are hyphenated, written as one word, or written as separate words.

Hyphens with Modifiers

Two- and three-word **modifiers** that express a single thought are hyphenated when they precede a **noun**.

▶ It was a *well-written* report.

However, a modifying phrase is not hyphenated when it follows the noun it modifies.

▶ The report was *well written*.

If each of the words can modify the noun without the aid of the other modifying word or words, do not use a hyphen (a *new laser* printer). If the first word is an **adverb** ending in -*ly*, do not use a hyphen (a *privately held* company). A hyphen is always used as part of a letter or number modifier (*A-frame house*, *22-inch monitor*).

In a series of unit modifiers that all have the same term following the hyphen, the term following the hyphen need not be repeated throughout the series; for greater smoothness and brevity, use the term only at the end of the series.

▶ The third-, fourth-, and fifth-floor laboratories were inspected.

Hyphens with Prefixes and Suffixes

A hyphen is used with a **prefix** when the root word is a proper noun (*pre-Columbian*, *anti-American*, *post-Newtonian*). A hyphen may be used when the prefix ends and the root word begins with the same vowel (*re-enter*, *anti-inflammatory*). A hyphen is used when *ex-* means "former" (*ex-dean*, *ex-CEO*) and may be used to emphasize a prefix. ("He is *anti-change*.") The **suffix** -*elect* is hyphenated (*president-elect*).

Hyphens and Clarity

The presence or absence of a hyphen can alter the meaning of a sentence.

AMBIGUOUS   We need a biological waste management system.

That sentence could mean one of two things: (1) We need a system to manage "biological waste" or (2) We need a "biological" system to manage waste.

CLEAR   We need a *biological-waste* management system. [1]

CLEAR   We need a biological *waste-management* system. [2]

To avoid confusion, some words and modifiers should always be hyphenated. *Re-cover* does not mean the same thing as *recover*, for example; the same is true of *un-ionized* and *unionized*.

Other Uses of the Hyphen

Hyphens are used between letters to show how a word is spelled.

▶ In his e-mail, he misspelled *believed* as b-e-l-e-i-v-e-d.

The en dash (see **dashes**) is preferred in ranges (*pages 44–46, letters A–L*), but hyphens are used when the en dash is not available as a special character.

Hyphens are commonly used in telephone numbers (*800-555-1212*), Web addresses (*computer-parts.com*), filenames (*report-15.doc*), and similar number/symbol combinations. See also **dates**.

Hyphens are also used to divide words at the end of a line, especially for full-justified margins within small columns. The following are standard guidelines for using hyphens to divide words at the end of lines.

- Do not divide one-syllable words.

- Divide words at syllable breaks, which you can determine with a dictionary.

- Do not divide a word if only one letter would remain at the end of a line or if fewer than three letters would start a new line.

- Do not divide a word at the end of a page; carry the word over to the next page.

- If a word already has a hyphen in its spelling, divide the word at the existing hyphen.

- Do not use a hyphen to break a URL or an e-mail address at the end of a line.

I

idioms

An idiom is a group of words that has a special meaning apart from its literal meaning. Someone "*runs* for political office" in the United States, for example, while a candidate "*stands* for office" in the United Kingdom. Because such expressions are specific to a culture, nonnative speakers must memorize them.

Idioms are often constructed with **prepositions** that follow **adjectives** (*similar to*), **nouns** (*need for*), and **verbs** (*approve of*). Some idioms can change meaning slightly with the preposition used, as in *agree to* ("consent") and *agree with* ("in accord"). The following are typical idioms that give nonnative speakers trouble.

call off [cancel]	hand in [submit]
call on [visit a client]	hand out [distribute]
drop in on [visit unexpectedly]	look up [research a subject]
find out [discover information]	run into [meet by chance]
get through with [finish]	run out of [deplete supply]
give up [quit]	watch out for [be careful]

Idioms often provide helpful shortcuts. In fact, they can make writing more natural and lively. Avoid them, however, if your writing is to be translated into another language or read in other English-speaking countries. Because no language system can fully explain such usages, a reader must check dictionaries or usage guides to interpret the meaning of idioms. See also **English as a second language**, **global communication**, and **international correspondence**.

illustrations (*see* visuals)

imply / infer

If you *imply* something, you hint at or suggest it. ("Her e-mail *implied* that the project would be delayed.") If you *infer* something, you reach a conclusion based on evidence or interpretation. ("The manager *inferred* from the e-mail that the project would be delayed.")

in / into

In means "inside of"; *into* implies movement from the outside to the inside. ("We were *in* a meeting when the intern brought copies of the contract *into* the conference room.")

in order to

Most often, *in order to* is a meaningless filler phrase that is dropped into a sentence without thought. See also **conciseness**.

>   *To*
> ▶ ~~In order to~~ access the Web site, enter the user name and password.

However, the phrase *in order to* is sometimes essential to the meaning of a sentence.

> ▶ The committee will need to leave by 3 p.m. in order to make the 5 p.m. flight.

In order to also helps control the **pace** of a sentence, even when it is not essential to the meaning of the sentence.

> ▶ The committee must know the estimated costs *in order to* evaluate the feasibility of the project.

in terms of

When used to indicate a shift from one kind of language or terminology to another, the phrase *in terms of* can be useful.

> ▶ *In terms of* gross sales, the year has been relatively successful; however, *in terms of* net income, it has been discouraging.

When simply dropped into a sentence because it easily comes to mind, *in terms of* is meaningless **affectation**. See also **conciseness**.

> ▶ She was thinking ~~in terms~~ of subcontracting much of the work.

incident / incidence

Incident refers to a particular occurrence or event. ("The *incident* went unreported.") *Incidence* refers to the rate of occurrence of something. ("We found a high *incidence* of type 2 diabetes.")

incident reports

The incident report is used to analyze such events as accidents, failures, or health emergencies. For example, the report shown in Figure I–1 describes an accident involving personal injury. The report assesses the causes of the problem and suggests changes necessary to prevent its recurrence. Because it is usually an internal document, an incident report normally appears as a **memo** or on a standard incident report form.

In the subject line, state the precise problem you are reporting. Then, in the body of the report, provide a detailed, precise description of the event. What happened? Where and when did the problem occur? Was anybody hurt? Was there any property damage? Was there a work stoppage?

In your **conclusion**, state what has been or will be done to correct the conditions that led to the event. That may include, for example, recommendations for training in safety practices, using improved equipment, and wearing protective clothing. See also **reports**.

❖ **ETHICS NOTE** Because insurance claims, workers' compensation awards, and even lawsuits may hinge on the information contained in an incident report, be sure to include precise times, dates, locations, treatment of injuries, names of any witnesses, and any other crucial information. (Notice the careful use of language and factual detail in Figure I–1.) Be thorough and accurate in your analysis of the problem, and support any judgments or conclusions with facts. Be objective: Always use a neutral **tone**, and avoid assigning blame. If you speculate about the cause of the problem, make it clear to your **readers** that you are speculating. See also **ethics in writing**. ❖

indexing

An index is an alphabetical list of all the major topics and subtopics in a written work. It cites the pages where each topic can be found and allows **readers** to find particular topics quickly and easily, as shown in Figure I–2 (page 258). The index comes at the very end of the work. Do not attempt to compile an index until pages are finalized, because terminology and page numbers will not be accurate before then.

The key to compiling a useful index is selectivity. Instead of listing every possible reference to a topic, select references to passages where the topic is fully discussed or significantly mentioned. For index entries like those in Figure I–2, choose key terms that best represent a topic. Key terms are those words or phrases that a reader would most likely look for in an index. For example, the key terms in a reference to the development of legislation about environmental impact statements would probably be *legislation* and *environmental impact statement*, not *development*. In

Consolidated Energy, Inc.

To: Marvin Lundquist, Vice President
           Administrative Services

From: Kalo Katarlan, Safety Officer
           Field Service Operations

Date: August 20, 2018

Subject: Field Service Employee Accident on August 6, 2018

The following is an initial report of an accident that occurred on Monday,
August 6, 2018, involving John Markley, and that resulted in two days of
lost time.

Accident Summary

John Markley stopped by a rewiring job on German Road. Chico Ruiz
was working there, stringing new wire, and John was checking with
Chico about the materials he wanted for framing a pole. Some tree
trimming had been done in the area, and John offered to help remove
some of the debris by loading it into the pickup truck he was driving.
While John was loading branches into the bed of the truck, a piece
broke off in his right hand and struck his right eye.

Accident Details

1. John's right eye was struck by a piece of tree branch. John had just
   undergone laser surgery on his right eye on Friday, July 27, to
   reattach his retina.
2. John immediately covered his right eye with his hand, and Chico
   Ruiz gave him a paper towel with ice to cover his eye and help ease
   the pain.

7. On Thursday, August 9, John returned to his eye surgeon. Although
   bruised, his eye was not damaged, and the surgically reattached
   retina was still in place.

Recommendations

To prevent a recurrence of such an accident, the Safety Department will
require the following actions in the future:

- When working around and moving debris such as tree limbs or
  branches, all service crew employees must wear safety eyewear with
  side shields.
- All service crew employees must always consider the possibility of
  shock for an injured employee. If crew members cannot leave the job
  site to care for the injured employee, someone on the crew must
  call 911 and alert the Service Center. The Service Center phone
  number is printed in each service crew member's handbook.

I

Headings
define
content

FIGURE I–1. Incident Report

monitoring programs, 27–44 ——————————— Main entry
  aquatic, 42
  ecological, 40 ——————————————— Subentries
  meteorological, 37
    operational, 39
    preoperational, 37 ——————————— Sub-subentries
  radiological, 30
  terrestrial, 41, 43–44 ————————————— Subentries
  thermal, 27

FIGURE I–2. Index Entry (with Main Entry, Subentries, and Sub-subentries)

selecting index terms, use chapter or section titles only if they include such key terms. For index entries on **tables** and **visuals,** use the words from their titles that will function as key terms a reader might seek.

Most word-processing programs include tools that provide a quick and efficient way to create an alphabetical subject index of your document. The index generated by your word-processing software will still need careful review, but using the software to create the first draft can save time. If you need to index a highly complex document, you may want to consider specialized indexing software, designed for use by professional indexers and publishers.

indiscreet / indiscrete

Indiscreet means "lacking in prudence or sound judgment." ("His public discussion of the proposed merger was *indiscreet.*") *Indiscrete* means "not divided or divisible into parts." ("The separate departments, once combined, become *indiscrete.*") See also **discreet / discrete**.

infographics

Infographics are visual forms of communication that make complex information understandable by combining text, numbers, icons, **graphs**, **flowcharts**, **drawings**, and other **visuals** into a unified whole, as shown in Figure I–3. They are often used to educate wide audiences and can be especially useful for **instructions** and **presentations**. Infographics might be used to show an overview of a process (how to take out a personal loan), a natural phenomenon (the evolution of an animal species), an accident (the anatomy of a train wreck), or a project plan (public transportation options in a city and projected passenger use). Each of these subjects might prove difficult to illustrate concisely with text or with images alone. See also **tables**.

FIGURE I–3. Infographic

SOURCE: Department of Energy, https://www.energy.gov/eere/bioenergy/bioenergizeme-infographic-challenge-travel-future-bioenergy

Infographics can be static, noninteractive visuals intended for public display, print publication, or high-resolution online download. They can also take digital, interactive forms, including such tools as mouseover pop-ups that reveal additional details or animated elements that showcase multiple cause-and-effect scenarios.

They are frequently created by graphic designers who collaborate with subject-area experts on the content. However, professionals without a formal design background can also create infographics for the workplace using a range of free online tools. Search for "tools for creating infographics," or visit such sites as piktochart.com, infogr.am, and creately.com. See *Writer's Checklist: Creating Infographics* (on page 260).

Note the infographic in Figure I–3 depicting how bioenergy fuels transportation. It combines explanatory text, typographic devices, images, and data, all organized into a unified overview of this growing trend. It also cites the source information for the infographic. This process could have been described in a text-dense article, but the impact and explanatory power of the graphic are striking.

WRITER'S CHECKLIST   **Creating Infographics**

✔ Use images appropriate to the topic, **purpose**, and **audience**.

✔ Select images (illustrations and icons), where possible, that are self-explanatory.

✔ Arrange text and images in the appropriate sequence to illustrate a process.

✔ Do not use dated or obsolete images or icons.

✔ Use culturally neutral images for international audiences (see **global graphics**).

✔ Use design elements — logo, typeface, colors — consistent with your organization's branding practices.

✔ Ensure that all types of data, graphics, and illustrations are uniform in color and design (see **layout and design**).

✔ Check the text for **conciseness**, **clarity**, and accuracy.

✔ Cite your sources of information appropriately (see **plagiarism**).

---

inquiries and responses

The purpose of writing inquiry messages is to obtain responses to requests or to specific questions, as in Figure I–4, which shows a college student's request for information from an official at a power company. Inquiries may benefit either the reader (as in requests for information about a product that a company sells) or the writer (as in the student's inquiry in Figure I–4). Inquiries that primarily benefit the writer require the use of **persuasion** and special consideration of the needs of the **audience**. See also **correspondence**.

Respond to an inquiry by answering promptly, and be sure to answer every inquiry or question asked, as shown in Figure I–5 (on page 262). How long and how detailed your response should be depends on the nature of the question and the information the writer provides. If you have received an inquiry that you feel you cannot answer, find out who can and forward the inquiry to that person. The person who replies to a forwarded inquiry should state in the first paragraph of the response who has forwarded the original inquiry, as shown in Figure I–5.

➦ Send ✕ Cancel ▤ Save Draft ⊶ Add Attachment ⊃ Signature	Options ▶

TO SMetcalf@MillerAssociates.com

CC _____ Show BCC

Subject Info Request: Heating Systems

Dear Ms. Metcalf:

As an architecture student at the University of Dayton, I am working with a team of students to design an energy-efficient house for a class project. We need information on heating systems based on the specifications of our design. To meet our deadline, we would appreciate any information you could provide by November 17.

> Background and reason for request

The house we are designing contains 2,000 square feet of living space (17,600 cubic feet) and meets all the requirements in your brochure "Insulating for Efficiency." We need the following information, based on the southern Ohio climate:

> Necessary details

- The proper-size heat pump for our design.
- The wattage of the supplemental electrical heating units required.
- The estimated power consumption and rates for those units for one year.

> Questions for recipient

We will be happy to send you our preliminary design report. If you have questions or suggestions, contact me at kparsons@fly.ud.edu or call 513-229-4598.

> Contact information and thanks

Thank you for your help.

Kenneth Parsons

FIGURE I–4. Inquiry

WRITER'S CHECKLIST   **Writing Inquiries and Responding**

✔ Make your questions specific, clear, and concise to receive a prompt, helpful reply.

✔ Phrase your request so that the reader will know immediately the type of information you are seeking, why you need it, and how you will use it.

✔ Present questions in a numbered or bulleted **list**, if possible, to make it easy for your reader to respond.

✔ Keep the number of questions to a minimum to improve your chances of receiving a prompt response.

(continued)

➡ Send ✕ Cancel ▤ Save Draft ⏚ Add Attachment ✏ Signature	Options ▶
TO	kparsons@fly.ud.edu
CC	SMetcalf@MillerAssociates.com	Show BCC
Subject	RE: Info Request: Heating Systems

Dear Mr. Parsons:

Context of inquiry Susan Metcalf forwarded to me your October 13 inquiry about the house that your architecture team is designing. I can estimate the heating requirements of a typical home of 17,600 cubic feet as follows:

- For such a home, we would generally recommend a heat pump capable of delivering 40,000 Btus, such as our model AL-42 (17 kilowatts).
- With the AL-42's efficiency, you don't need supplemental heating units.
- Depending on usage, the AL-42 unit averages between 1,000 and 1,500 kilowatt-hours from December through March. To determine the current rate for such usage, check with Dayton Power and Light Company.

Specific responses

Offer of further help, closing I can give you an answer that would apply specifically to your house based on its particular design (such as number of stories, windows, and entrances). If you send me more details, I will be happy to provide more precise figures for your interesting project.

Regards,

Ian Mori

FIGURE I–5. Response to an Inquiry

WRITER'S CHECKLIST **Writing Inquiries and Responding** (*continued*)

✔ Offer some incentive for the reader to respond, if possible, such as sharing the results of your research. See **"you" viewpoint**.

✔ Promise to keep responses confidential, when appropriate.

✔ Provide a date by which you need a response.

✔ Close by thanking the reader for taking the time to respond, and provide your contact information, as shown in Figure I–4.

✔ Respond to an inquiry promptly if you have the information and authority.

✔ Check organizational policy and special issues related to your response.

✔ Notify the writer if you need to forward the inquiry to someone else for response.

inside / inside of

In the phrase *inside of*, the word *of* is redundant and should be omitted.

▶ The switch is just inside ~~of~~ the door.

Using *inside of* to mean "in less time than" is colloquial and should be avoided in writing.

▶ They were finished ~~inside of~~ an hour.
  in less than

instant messaging and live chat

Instant messaging and live chat are communications media that allow both real-time text communications and the transfer of text or other files, such as an image or a document. (See also **text messaging**.) Instant messaging and live chat are especially useful to those who are working in an environment that demands near-instant, brief written exchanges between two or more participants. See also **e-mail** and **selecting the medium**.

When writing instant messages or chat, keep your responses simple and to the point, covering only one subject in each message to prevent confusion and inappropriate responses. Because screen space is often limited and speed is essential, many who communicate this way use abbreviations and shortened spellings ("u" for "you"). Be sure that your reader will understand such abbreviations; when in doubt, avoid them.

❖ **ETHICS NOTE** Be sure to follow your employer's policies, such as those concerning confidentiality. If no specific policy exists, check with your management before using these media. ❖

WRITER'S CHECKLIST | Privacy and Security with Instant Messaging and Chat

✔ Set up distinct business and professional contact lists (or accounts) to avoid inadvertently sending a personal message to a business associate.

✔ Learn the options (such as away messages) and security limitations, and set the preferences that best suit your use of the system.

✔ Save significant exchanges (or logs) for future reference.

✔ Be aware that instant messages and chats can be saved by your recipients and may be archived by your employer. (See the Professionalism Note on page 168.)

✔ Do not use professional IM or chat for office gossip or inappropriate exchanges.

instructions

Business writers often prepare many kinds of instructions for coworkers. (See also **policies and procedures**.) Instructions that are clear and easy to follow can build goodwill because they help **readers** complete tasks efficiently and prevent miscommunication. To write effective instructions, you must thoroughly understand the process or system you are describing. Keep in mind that the most effective instructions often combine written elements and visual elements that reinforce each other. See also **process explanation**.

Writing Instructions

Consider the level of knowledge of primary and secondary readers in your **audience**. If all your readers have good backgrounds in the topic, you can use fairly specialized terms. If that is not the case, use **plain language** or include a **glossary** of specialized terms that you cannot avoid. See also **repurposing**.

Clear and easy-to-follow instructions are written as commands in the imperative **mood**, active **voice**, and (whenever possible) present **tense**.

▶ *Sign the* ~~The~~ insurance request ~~will be signed by the employee.~~

Although **conciseness** is important in instructions, **clarity** is essential. You can make sentences shorter by leaving out some **articles** (*a*, *an*, *the*), some **pronouns** (*you*, *this*, *these*), and some **verbs**, but such sentences may result in **telegraphic style** and be harder for the reader to understand. For example, the first version of the following instruction for submitting a medical claim is confusing.

CONFUSING   Submit negotiated claim to HR with statement from attending.

CLEAR   Submit the negotiated claim to the Human Resources Office with the statement of the attending physician who prescribed the treatment.

One good way to make instructions easy to follow is to divide them into short, simple steps in their proper sequence. Steps can be organized with words (*first*, *next*, *finally*) that indicate time or sequence.

▶ *First*, determine the problem the customer is having with the computer. *Next*, observe the system in operation. *At that time*, question the customer until you are sure that the problem has been explained completely. *Then* analyze the problem and make any necessary adjustments.

You can also use numbers, as in the following:

▶ 1. Open the top cover and remove the toner cartridge.
2. Use the green handle to lift the paper access plate.
3. Slowly and carefully pull the jammed paper out of the printer.

Consider using the numbered- or bulleted-list feature of your word-processing software to create sequenced steps. See **lists**.

Plan ahead for your reader. If the instructions in step 2 will affect a process in step 9, say so in step 2. Sometimes your instructions have to make clear that two operations must be performed simultaneously. Either state that fact in an **introduction** to the specific instructions, or include both operations in one step.

CONFUSING   1. Hold down the CONTROL key.
2. Press the RETURN key before releasing the CONTROL key.

CLEAR   1. While holding down the CONTROL key, press the RETURN key.

Alert your readers to any potentially hazardous actions before they reach the applicable step.

If your instructions involve many steps, break them into stages, each with a separate heading so that each stage begins again with step 1. Using **headings** as dividers is especially important if your reader is likely to be performing the operation as he or she reads the instructions.

Illustrating Instructions

Illustrations should be developed together with the text, especially for complex instructions. Using **drawings**, **flowcharts**, **infographics**, **maps**, **photographs**, and other **visuals** fosters clarity by enabling your readers to identify relationships more easily than they would from long explanations.

Consider the **layout and design** of your instructions to most effectively integrate visuals. Highlight important visuals and text by making them stand out from the surrounding text. Consider using boxes and boldface or distinctive headings. Experiment with font style, size, and color to determine which devices are most effective.

The instructions in Figure I–6 (page 266) guide the reader through the steps of streaking a saucer-sized disk of material (called *agar*) used to grow bacteria colonies. The purpose is to thin out the original specimen (the *inoculum*) so that the bacteria will grow in small, isolated colonies. This section could be part of other, larger instructional documents for which streaking is only one step among others.

I

STREAKING AN AGAR PLATE

Distribute the inoculum over the surface of the agar in the following manner:

1. Beginning at one edge of the saucer, thin the inoculum by streaking back and forth over the same area several times, sweeping across the agar surface until approximately one-quarter of the surface has been covered. *Sterilize the loop in an open flame.*
2. Streak at right angles to the originally inoculated area, carrying the inoculum out from the streaked areas onto the sterile surface with only the first stroke of the wire. Cover half of the remaining sterile agar surface. *Sterilize the loop.*
3. Repeat as described in Step 2, covering the remaining sterile agar surface.

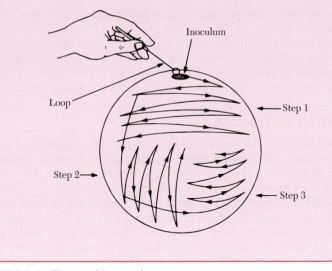

FIGURE I–6. Illustrated Instructions

Finally, to test the accuracy and clarity of your instructions, ask someone who is not familiar with the task to follow your directions. A first-time user can spot missing steps or point out passages that should be worded more clearly.

WRITER'S CHECKLIST   Writing Instructions

✔ Use the imperative mood and the active voice.

✔ Use short sentences and simple present tense as much as possible.

✔ Avoid **jargon** that your readers might not know, including undefined **abbreviations**.

✔ Do not use elegant variation (two different words for the same thing). See also **affectation**.

✔ Eliminate any **ambiguity**.

✔ Use effective visuals and highlighting devices.

✔ Test your instructions by having someone follow them while you observe.

✔ Provide a warning before any potentially hazardous steps.

I

insure / ensure / assure

Insure, *ensure*, and *assure* all mean "make secure or certain." *Assure* refers to people, and it alone has the connotation of setting a person's mind at rest. ("I *assure* you that the equipment will be available.") *Ensure* and *insure* mean "make secure from harm." Only *insure* is widely used in the sense of guaranteeing the value of life or property.

▶ We need all the data to *ensure* the success of the project.

▶ We should *insure* the contents of the warehouse.

intensifiers

Intensifiers are **adverbs** that emphasize degree, such as *very*, *quite*, *rather*, *such*, and *too*. Although intensifiers serve a legitimate and necessary function, unnecessary intensifiers can weaken your writing. Eliminate those that do not make an obvious contribution, or replace them with specific details. See also **conciseness**, **emphasis**.

▶ The team learned the ~~very~~ good news that it had been awarded a ~~rather substantial monetary~~ *$10,000* prize for its design.

Some words (such as *perfect*, *impossible*, and *final*) do not logically permit intensification because, by definition, they do not allow degrees of comparison. Although **usage** often ignores that logical restriction, avoid such comparisons in business writing. See also **adjectives**, **conciseness**, and **equal / unique / perfect**.

interface

An *interface* is a surface that provides a common boundary between two bodies or areas. The bodies or areas may be conceptual or physical ("the *interface* of a computer and an external storage device"). Do not use *interface* as a substitute for the verbs *cooperate*, *interact*, or even *work with*. See also **affectation** and **buzzwords**.

I

interjections

An interjection is a word or phrase standing alone or inserted into a sentence to exclaim or to command attention. Grammatically, it has no connection to the sentence. An interjection can be strong (*Hey! Ouch! Wow!*) or mild (*oh, well, indeed*). A strong interjection is followed by an **exclamation mark**.

▶ *Wow!* Profits more than doubled last quarter.

A weak interjection is followed by a **comma**.

▶ *Well,* we need to rethink the proposal.

An interjection inserted into a sentence usually requires a comma before it and after it.

▶ We must, *indeed,* rethink the proposal.

Because they get their main expressive force from sound, interjections are more common in speech than in writing. Use them sparingly.

international correspondence

Business **correspondence** varies among national cultures. Organizational patterns, persuasive strategies, forms of courtesy, levels of comfort with uncertainty, and ideas about efficiency differ from country to country. For example, in the United States, direct, concise correspondence usually demonstrates courtesy by not wasting the reader's time. In many other countries, however, such directness and brevity may suggest to readers that the writer is dismissive or lacking in manners. (See **audience** and **tone**.) Similarly, a U.S. writer might consider one brief **letter** or **e-mail** sufficient to communicate a request, while a writer in another country might expect an exchange of three or four e-mails to pave the way for action.

Cultural Differences in Correspondence

When you read correspondence from businesspeople in other cultures or countries, be alert to variations in such features as customary expressions, openings, and closings. For example, business writers in some cultures traditionally use indirect openings that may express good wishes about the recipient's family or compliment the reader's success or prosperity. Consider deeper issues as well, such as how writers from other cultures express bad news. Some cultures traditionally express negative messages, such as **refusals**, indirectly to avoid embarrassing the recipient. Such differences in correspondence are often based on cultural perceptions of time, face-saving, and other traditions. The features and communication styles of specific national cultures are complex; the entries **global communication** and **global graphics** provide information and resources for cross-cultural study.

Cross-Cultural Examples

Figures I–7 and I–8 (on pages 270–72) show a draft and a final version of a letter written by an American businessperson to a Japanese businessperson. The opening and closing of the draft in Figure I–7 do not include enough of the politeness strategies that are important in Japanese culture, and the informal salutation inappropriately uses the recipient's first name (*Dear Ichiro:*). This draft also contains **idioms** and **figures of speech** (*looking forward, company family*), **jargon** (*transport*), **contractions** (*I'm, don't*), informal language (*just e-mail or fax, Cheers*), and humor and allusion (*"ptomaine palace" across from our main offices*).

Compare that letter to the one in Figure I–8, which is written in language that is courteous, literal, and specific. This revised letter begins with concern about the recipient's family and prosperity because that opening honors traditional Japanese patterns in business correspondence. The letter is free of slang, idioms, and jargon. The sentences are shorter than in the draft; in addition, the writer uses bulleted lists to break up the paragraphs, avoids contractions, spells out months, and uses twenty-four-hour–clock time.

When writing for international readers, rethink the ingrained habits that define how you express yourself, learn as much as you can about the cultural expectations of others, and focus on politeness strategies that demonstrate your respect for readers. Doing so will help you achieve **clarity** and mutual understanding with international readers.

I

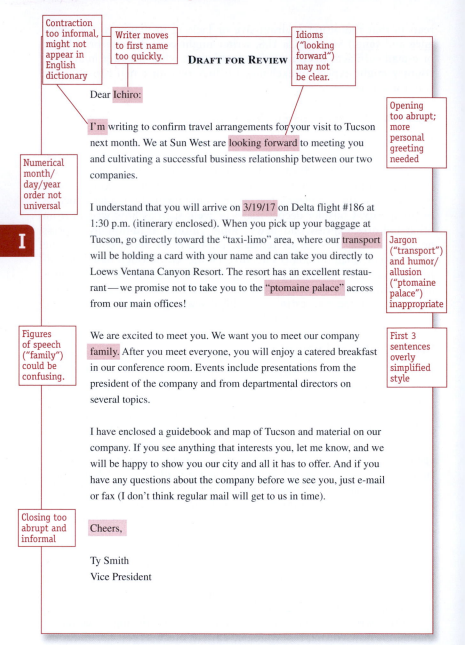

Contraction too informal, might not appear in English dictionary

Writer moves to first name too quickly.

DRAFT FOR REVIEW

Idioms ("looking forward") may not be clear.

Opening too abrupt; more personal greeting needed

Numerical month/day/year order not universal

Jargon ("transport") and humor/allusion ("ptomaine palace") inappropriate

Figures of speech ("family") could be confusing.

First 3 sentences overly simplified style

Closing too abrupt and informal

Dear Ichiro:

I'm writing to confirm travel arrangements for your visit to Tucson next month. We at Sun West are looking forward to meeting you and cultivating a successful business relationship between our two companies.

I understand that you will arrive on 3/19/17 on Delta flight #186 at 1:30 p.m. (itinerary enclosed). When you pick up your baggage at Tucson, go directly toward the "taxi-limo" area, where our transport will be holding a card with your name and can take you directly to Loews Ventana Canyon Resort. The resort has an excellent restaurant—we promise not to take you to the "ptomaine palace" across from our main offices!

We are excited to meet you. We want you to meet our company family. After you meet everyone, you will enjoy a catered breakfast in our conference room. Events include presentations from the president of the company and from departmental directors on several topics.

I have enclosed a guidebook and map of Tucson and material on our company. If you see anything that interests you, let me know, and we will be happy to show you our city and all it has to offer. And if you have any questions about the company before we see you, just e-mail or fax (I don't think regular mail will get to us in time).

Cheers,

Ty Smith
Vice President

FIGURE I–7. Inappropriate International Correspondence (Draft Marked for Revision)

Sun West Corporation, Inc.

2565 North Armadillo
Tucson, AZ 85719
Phone: (602) 555-6677
Fax: (602) 555-6678   sunwest.com

March 5, 2018

Ichiro Katsumi
Investment Director
Toshiba Investment Company
1-29-10 Ichiban-cho
Tokyo 105, Japan

Dear Mr. Katsumi:

I hope that you and your family are well and prospering in the new year. We at Sun West Corporation are very pleased that you will be coming to visit us in Tucson this month. It will be a pleasure to meet you, and we are gratified and honored that you are interested in investing in our company.

> Less abrupt and informal

So that we can ensure that your stay will be pleasurable, we have taken care of all of your travel arrangements. You will

- Depart Narita–New Tokyo International Airport on Delta Airlines flight #75 at 1700 on March 19, 2018.
- Arrive at Los Angeles International Airport at 1050 local time and depart for Tucson on Delta flight #186 at 1205.
- Arrive at Tucson International Airport at 1330 local time on March 19.
- Depart Tucson International Airport on Delta flight #123 at 1845 on March 26.
- Arrive in Salt Lake City, Utah, at 1040 and depart on Delta flight #34 at 1115.
- Arrive in Portland, Oregon, at 1210 local time and depart on Delta flight #254 at 1305.
- Arrive in Tokyo at 1505 local time on March 27.

> Helpful details, formatted for quick reference

If you need additional information about your travel plans or information on Sun West Corporation, please call, fax, or e-mail me directly at tsmith@sunwest.com. That way, we will receive your message in time to make the appropriate changes or additions.

FIGURE I–8. Appropriate International Correspondence

Mr. Ichiro Katsumi   2   March 5, 2018

After you arrive in Tucson, a chauffeur from Skyline Limousines will be waiting for you at Gate 12. He or she will be carrying a card with your name, will help you collect your luggage from the baggage claim area, and will then drive you to the Loews Ventana Canyon Resort. This resort is one of the most prestigious in Tucson, with spectacular desert views, high-quality amenities, and one of the best golf courses in the city. The next day, the chauffeur will be back at the Ventana at 0900 to drive you to Sun West Corporation.

Standard business writing with context for events

We at Sun West Corporation are excited to meet you and introduce you to all the staff members of our hardworking and growing company. After you meet everyone, you will enjoy a catered breakfast in our conference room. At that time, you will receive a schedule of events planned for the remainder of your trip. Events include presentations from the president of the company and from departmental directors on

- The history of Sun West Corporation
- The uniqueness of our products and current success in the marketplace
- Demographic information and the benefits of being located in Tucson
- The potential for considerable profits for both our companies with your company's investment

We encourage you to read through the enclosed guidebook and map of Tucson. In addition to events planned at Sun West Corporation, you will find many natural wonders and historical sites to see in Tucson and in Arizona in general. If you see any particular event or place that you would like to visit, please let us know. We will be happy to show you our city and all it has to offer.

Respectful standard closing

Again, we are honored that you will be visiting us, and we look forward to a successful business relationship between our two companies.

Sincerely,

Ty Smith

Ty Smith
Vice President

Enclosures (2)

FIGURE I–8. Appropriate International Correspondence (*continued*)

WRITER'S CHECKLIST   **Writing International Correspondence**

✔ Observe the guidelines for courtesy, such as those in the *Writer's Checklist: Using Tone to Build Goodwill* on page 112.

✔ Write clear and complete sentences: Unusual word order or rambling sentences will frustrate and confuse readers. See **garbled sentences**.

✔ Avoid an overly simplified style that may offend or any **affectation** that may confuse the reader. See also **English as a second language**.

✔ Avoid humor, irony, and sarcasm; they are easily misunderstood outside their cultural **context**.

✔ Do not use idioms, jargon, slang expressions, unusual **figures of speech**, or **allusions** to events or attitudes particular to life in the United States. See **clarity** and **style**.

✔ Consider whether necessary technical terminology can be found in abbreviated English-language dictionaries; if it cannot, carefully define such terminology.

✔ Do not use contractions or **abbreviations** that may not be clear to international readers.

✔ Avoid inappropriate informality, such as using first names too quickly.

✔ Write out **dates**, whether in the month-day-year style (*June 11, 2018*, not *6/11/18*) used in the United States or the day-month-year style (*11 June 2018*, not *11/6/18*) used in many other parts of the world.

✔ Specify time zones or refer to international standards, such as Greenwich Mean Time (GMT) or Universal Time Coordinated (UTC).

✔ Use international measurement standards, such as the metric system (*18 °C, 14 cm, 45 kg*), where possible.

✔ Consult local laws concerning e-mail to ensure that you are in compliance with those regulations, particularly marketing messages. For example, some countries require businesses to have an individual's express consent before sending that person any e-mail messages.

✔ Ask someone from your intended audience's culture or with appropriate expertise to review your draft before you complete your final **proofreading**.

I

interviewing for information

Interviewing others who have knowledge of your subject is often an essential method of **research** in business writing.

Determining the Proper Person to Interview

Many times, your subject or **purpose** logically points to the proper person to interview for information. For example, if you were writing a feasibility report about marketing consumer products in India, you would want to interview someone with extensive experience in that area. The following sources can help you determine the appropriate person to interview: (1) workplace colleagues or faculty in appropriate academic departments, (2) local chapters of professional societies, (3) "Contact" and "About" sections on organizational Web sites, and (4) targeted Internet searches.

Preparing for the Interview

Before the interview, learn as much as possible about the person you are going to interview and the organization for which he or she works.

◀ **PROFESSIONALISM NOTE** When you contact the prospective interviewee, explain who you are, why you would like an interview, the subject and purpose of the interview, the best setting or medium for the interview (in person, phone, videoconference, e-mail), and approximately how much time it will take. You should also ask permission if you plan to record the interview, and let your interviewee know that you will allow him or her to review your draft. ▶

After you have made the appointment, prepare a list of questions to ask your interviewee. Avoid vague, general questions. A question such as "Do you think the Web would be helpful for you?" is too general to elicit useful information. It is better to ask specific but open-ended questions, such as the following: "Many physicians in your specialty are using the Web to answer routine patient questions. How might providing such information on your Web site affect your relationship with your patients?"

Conducting the Interview

Arrive promptly or connect on time if videoconferencing, and be prepared to guide the discussion. During the interview, take only memory-jogging notes that will help you recall the conversation later; do not ask your interviewee to slow down so that you can take detailed notes. As the interview is reaching a close, take a few moments to skim your notes and ask the interviewee to clarify anything that is ambiguous.

◀ **PROFESSIONALISM NOTE** If you plan to conduct an interview using videoconferencing, find an environment that is quiet and allows you to focus on the interview. Be mindful of your surroundings, personal appearance, and the appearance of your videoconferencing platform because all will be conveyed to the person you are interviewing. Make sure that you can take notes in a way that allows you to maintain your focus on your subject, as described in **listening**. Finally, ensure that you are using high-quality, reliable software and connections. ▶

Expanding Your Notes Soon After the Interview

Immediately after leaving the interview, use your memory-jogging notes to help you mentally review the interview and expand those notes. Do not postpone this step; otherwise, you risk forgetting important points. See also **note-taking**.

Interviewing by Phone or E-mail

When an interviewee is not available for a face-to-face meeting or videoconference, consider a phone interview. Most of the principles for conducting face-to-face interviews apply to phone interviews; be aware, however, that phone calls do not offer the important nonverbal cues of face-to-face or video meetings. Consider using a high-quality headset or speakerphone to make note taking easier.

Another alternative is to consider an **e-mail** interview, in which you exchange a number of back-and-forth messages. Such an interview, however, lacks the spontaneity and the immediacy of an in-person, a video, or a phone conversation. Before you send any questions, make sure that your contact is willing to participate and respond to follow-up clarifications. As a courtesy, give the respondent a general idea of the number of questions you plan to ask and the level of detail you expect. When you send the questions, ask for a reasonable deadline from the interviewee ("Would you be able to send your response by . . . ?").

I

WRITER'S CHECKLIST   **Interviewing Successfully**

✔ Be pleasant but purposeful. You are there to get information, so don't be timid about asking leading questions on the subject.

✔ Use the list of questions you have prepared, starting with the less complex topics to get the conversation started and moving toward the more challenging ones.

✔ Let your interviewee do most of the talking. Remember that the interviewee is the expert.

✔ Be objective. Do not offer your opinions on the subject. You are there to get information, not to debate.

✔ Ask additional questions as they arise.

✔ Do not get sidetracked. If the interviewee strays too far from the subject, ask a specific question to direct the conversation back on track.

(continued)

✔ If you use audio or video recording, do not let it lure you into relaxing so that you neglect to ask crucial questions.

✔ After thanking the interviewee, ask permission to contact him or her again to clarify a point or two as you complete your interview notes.

✔ A day or two after the interview, send a thank-you note to the interviewee.

interviewing for a job

I

Job interviews can take place in person, by phone, or by Skype or a similar program and may last thirty minutes to several hours. Sometimes an initial job interview is followed by a series of additional interviews. Often just one or two people conduct the interview, but on occasion a group or panel of four or more attend. Because it is impossible to know exactly what to expect, it is important to be well prepared. See also **job search**.

Before the Interview

Before the interview, learn everything you can about the organization, drawing on both internal, company-produced materials—including Web sites, annual reports, and corporate advertisements—and external sources—such as newspaper articles about an organization and industry reports ranking a company alongside its competitors. Ask yourself questions such as the following:

- What kind of organization (profit, nonprofit, government) is it?

- What are the mission, goals, and objectives of the organization?

- What types of services or products does the company provide?

- What is the organization's history, and what sort of reputation has it built over time?

- Does the company operate locally, regionally, or internationally?

- Is the company privately owned or employee owned?

- How many employees are there?

- Is the company a subsidiary of a larger operation?

- How long has the company been in business?

- How does the company differentiate itself from its competitors?
  - How does it advertise its mission, expectations, and benefits to potential employees?
  - What strategies does it employ to market its products and services to clients or consumers?
- Where and how will I fit in? Does there appear to be opportunity for advancement?

You can obtain information from current employees, the company's Web site, press releases, prospectuses, annual reports, business articles about the company, and local news sources. The company's Web site in particular may help you learn about the company's size, sales volume, product line, credit rating, branch locations, subsidiary companies, new products and services, expansion plans, and similar information. Careful Internet **research** can provide important background information, but do not hesitate to seek help from a librarian for sources accessible through a library, such as Dun & Bradsteet's *Million Dollar Directory*, Standard & Poor's *Register of Corporations, Directors and Executives*, and *Thomas' Register*.

Try to anticipate the questions an interviewer might ask, and think through your answers in advance. Be sure you understand a question before answering it, and avoid responding too quickly with a rehearsed reply. The most appealing tone to adopt for interviews is conversational, which will allow you to come across as natural and relaxed as opposed to overly rehearsed. The following are traditional questions you might be asked during an interview:

- What are your short-term and long-term occupational goals?
- Where do you see yourself five years from now?
- What are your major strengths and weaknesses?
- Do you work better with others or alone?
- What academic or career accomplishment are you particularly proud of? Describe it.
- Why are you leaving your current job?
- May we contact your previous employer?
- Why do you want to work for this organization?
- What will you bring to the organization?
- What salary and benefits do you expect? (see page 280 for salary negotiations)
- What is an example of a mistake from which you learned something valuable?
- What is your greatest accomplishment? Why?

Some employers, however, rather than ask straightforward questions, use behavioral interviews that focus on asking the candidate to provide examples or respond to hypothetical situations. Interviewers who use behavior-based questions are looking for specific examples from your experience. Prepare for the behavioral interview by recollecting challenging situations or problems that you successfully resolved. Examples of behavior-based questions include the following:

- Tell me about a time when you experienced conflict while on a team.

- If I were your boss and you disagreed with a decision I made, what would you do?

- How have you used your leadership skills to bring about change?

- Tell me about a time when you failed and what you learned from the experience.

Other kinds of interviews are also becoming more common. For example, airline companies have routinely interviewed multiple applicants for onboard positions simultaneously in group settings. Surrounded by job applicants, individuals are positioned to respond to a crisis with a passenger (played by an actor) or a technical failure. As they respond, individuals or groups with the authority to make hiring decisions evaluate applicants' decision-making choices and group dynamics. It is important in such settings to consider which outcomes are most in line with the organization's goals and values.

Organizations are sometimes willing to share information about their interviewing approach when scheduling applicants. Feel free to inquire about the type of interview process you might expect beforehand, and ask whether it would be appropriate to bring particular materials with you to the interview (see the following section, "During the Interview") or whether you might be better prepared in other ways. Maintain a confident and enthusiastic tone when asking questions about what to expect during the interview, since the goal should be to communicate your desire to make a professional impression on the interviewer and other members of the organization.

◀ **PROFESSIONALISM NOTE** Plan to arrive ten to fifteen minutes early to the interview; never be late. Always bring extra copies of your résumé, a note pad, samples of your work or portfolio (if applicable), and a list of references with contact information. Turn off any electronic devices prior to your arrival. If you are asked to complete an application form, read it carefully before you write and proofread it when you are finished. The form provides a written record for company files and indicates to the company how well you follow directions and complete a task. ▶

During the Interview

The interview enables a potential employer to learn about you, and it allows you to learn how you might fit into that organization. The interview actually begins when you arrive. What you wear and how you act make a first impression. In general, dress professionally and in a manner that is appropriate for working in the particular organization and in the position for which you are applying. Usually, it is wise to dress simply and conservatively, avoid extremes in fragrance and cosmetics, and be well groomed. Also, be polite to other employees you meet. Think of the interview from start to finish as your first day on the job. First impressions matter. The development of a professional identity begins early—if not when you enter college, then by the time you start taking courses in your major area of study—and continues to take shape as you start your career.

◖ **PROFESSIONALISM NOTE** Be aware that visible tattoos and body piercings are not acceptable in many white-collar and service-industry positions. Employers are within their legal rights to maintain such a policy if they believe your appearance might negatively affect the image of the organization. Act prudently if you suspect tattoos and piercings are not acceptable—cover tattoos and remove piercings. ◗

Behavior.   After introductions, thank the interviewer for his or her time, express your pleasure at meeting him or her, and remain standing until you are offered a seat. Sit up straight (good posture suggests self-assurance), maintain eye contact with the interviewer, and try to appear relaxed and confident. During the interview, use nervous energy to your advantage by channeling it into the alertness that you will need to listen and respond effectively. Do not attempt to take extensive notes. You can jot down a few facts, but keep your focus on the interviewer. Do not use an electronic device (laptop or tablet) unless you need to showcase a portfolio. See also **listening**.

Responses.   When you answer questions, stay on topic. Respond directly to the question, and then provide concrete evidence to support your answer. For example, if you reveal to the interviewer that you do not have formal leadership experience, refer to a specific officer position that you were elected to in an organization, or describe your responsibilities as a trainer for other employees at your part-time job during college. Avoid simple yes or no answers—they usually do not allow the interviewer to learn enough about you. Some interviewers allow a silence to fall just to see how you will react. The burden of conducting the interview is the interviewer's, not yours—and he or she may interpret your rush to fill a void in the conversation as a sign of insecurity. If such a silence makes you uncomfortable, be ready to ask an intelligent question about the company, drawing on the research you have done about the organization and the particular position to which you are applying.

If the interviewer overlooks important points, bring them up. Let the interviewer mention salary first. Doing so yourself may indicate that you are more interested in the money than in the work. Make sure, however, that you are aware of prevailing salaries and benefits in your field and geographic region.

Interviewers look for a degree of self-confidence and an applicant's understanding of the field, as well as genuine interest in the field, the company, and the job. Ask questions to communicate your interest in the job and the company. Interviewers respond favorably to applicants who can communicate and present themselves well.

❖ **ETHICS NOTE** Questions that seem personal, appear to breach legal ethics, or otherwise make you uncomfortable not only can be hard to answer but also can quickly erode the confidence you worked so hard to build during your preparation. Remaining composed and remembering that the employer's objective is simply to determine whether you are the best candidate for the position will help you respond appropriately to difficult questions. Be brief, concise, and truthful in your answers. Common questions that may broach sensitive subjects may include the following:

- Have you ever experienced a layoff or been terminated?
- Why did you stay with previous employers on average for just a year?
- Why do you have such a large gap of employment between these dates? ❖

Salary.   Salary negotiations can take place at the end of a job interview, after a formal job offer, or over the course of several conversations. Prepare by determining salary ranges in your field by checking Web sites, such as salary.com, payscale.com, and glassdoor.com. If you are on campus, check with your career-development office, which can advise you on local salary ranges.

Remember that you are negotiating a package and not just a starting salary. Some employers have excellent benefits packages that can balance a lower base salary, as the following possibilities suggest:

- Tuition reimbursement for continued education
- Payment of relocation costs
- Paid personal leave or paid vacations
- Overtime potential and compensation
- Flexible hours and work-from-home options
- Health, dental, optical, and disability coverage
- Retirement and pension plans
- Profit sharing: investment or stock options
- Bonuses or cost-of-living adjustments
- Commuting or parking-cost reimbursement
- Family leave or elder-care benefits

If you do not wish to provide a specific salary requirement during a job interview, you can respond with a salary range that you know would be reasonable for someone at your level in your line of work in that region of the country. For example, you could say, "I would hope for a salary somewhere between $35,000 and $45,000, but of course this is negotiable." The salary range you provide should be in line with the industry average (see **job search**). Throughout this process, focus on what is most important to you (not others) and on what you would find acceptable.

If you decide to request a salary on the higher end of the average range in the particular industry to which you are applying, be prepared to offer specific, concrete evidence of experiences and skills you have developed that warrant a higher salary. Once you have gained some work experience in the industry, you will be in a better position to make such a request. In the meantime, though, you may refer to projects you have completed in college courses, computer software programs with which you have gained expertise, or internships in the field.

Conclusion.   At the conclusion of the interview, thank the interviewer for his or her time. Be sure to make note of each interviewer's name, or request business cards if convenient. Reiterate your interest in the position, and try to get an idea of when the company expects to make a final decision. Reaffirm friendly contact with a firm handshake.

After the Interview

After you leave the interview, jot down the pertinent information you obtained, as it may be helpful in comparing job offers. As soon as possible following a job interview, send the interviewer(s) a thank-you note or e-mail. Many interviewers and other employees you have met will appreciate a handwritten note that mentions a personal detail about your time at the organization, for example, thanking an individual who recommended a particularly good restaurant for lunch. Such messages also often include the following:

- Your thanks for the interview and to individuals or groups that gave you special help or attention during the interview

- The name of the specific job for which you interviewed

- Your impression of the opportunity

- Your confidence that you can perform the job well

- An offer to provide further information or to answer further questions

Figure I–9 (on page 282) shows a typical example of follow-up correspondence.

If you are offered a job you want, accept the offer verbally and write a brief letter of acceptance as soon as possible — certainly within a week. If you do not want the job, write a refusal letter or e-mail, as described in **acceptances / refusals**.

222 Morewood Avenue
Pittsburgh, PA 15212
June 2, 2018

Ms. Emily Harrison, Director
Marketing Division
Harper Communications
1201 S. Figueroa Street
Los Angeles, CA 90015

Dear Ms. Harrison:

> **Thanks interviewer and names job**

Thank you for the recent opportunity to interview for the entry-level position in the Marketing Division at Harper Communications. I appreciated learning more about the exciting directions being undertaken at your organization and being introduced to some of the projects I would be involved in if selected for the position.

> **Emphasizes specific trait that excites her about the company**

During my visit, I was especially interested in the innovative branding campaign underway for one of Harper Communications' beverage industry clients. The energy I experienced when speaking with Mr. Joseph Turner, director of marketing, and Ms. Helen Markett, one of Harper Communications' senior marketing professionals, showed me the kind of environment I hope to join as I pursue my career in the field.

> **Offers further information**

I look forward to continuing our conversation about what lies ahead at Harper Communications and how I might contribute to these goals. If I can address any further questions you might have or provide additional evidence of my work, please contact me. Thank you again for your consideration.

Sincerely,

Kathleen Adwell

Kathleen Adwell

FIGURE I–9. Follow-up Correspondence

In some instances, you may be interested in accepting a position but are more enthusiastic about a competing organization with which you have interviewed but that has not yet made you an offer. If you face this situation, it is appropriate to notify the interviewer with whom you spoke at the competing organization to let him or her know that you have been offered a position elsewhere but are still interested in pursuing a position with his or her organization.

introductions

Every document must have either an opening or an introduction. Usually an opening simply focuses the reader's attention on your topic and then proceeds to the body of your document. A full-scale introduction, discussed later in this entry, sets the stage by providing information necessary to understand the discussion that follows in the body. In general, **correspondence** and routine **reports** need only an opening; **formal reports**, major **proposals**, and other complex documents need a full-scale introduction. For a discussion of comparable sections for Web sites, see **writing for the Web**. See also **conclusions**.

Routine Openings

When your **audience** is familiar with your topic or if what you are writing is brief or routine, then a simple opening will provide adequate **context**, as shown in the following examples.

LETTER
Dear Mr. Ignatowski:
You will be happy to know that we corrected the error in your bank balance. The new balance shows . . .

E-MAIL
Jane, as I promised in my e-mail yesterday, I've attached the human resources budget estimates for fiscal year 2018.

MEMO
To date, 18 of the 20 specimens your department submitted for analysis have been examined. Our preliminary analysis indicates . . .

Opening Strategies

Opening strategies are aimed at focusing readers' attention and motivating them to read the entire document.

Objective.   You might open with a statement of a project's objective so that readers have a basis for judging the results.

▶ The primary goal of this project was to develop new techniques to solve the problem of waste disposal. Our first step was to investigate . . .

Problem Statement.   To give readers the perspective of your report, briefly describe the problem that led to the study or project being reported.

▶ Several weeks ago a manager noticed a recurring problem in the software developed by Datacom Systems. Specifically, error messages repeatedly appeared when, in fact, no specific trouble . . . After an extensive investigation, we found that Datacom Systems . . .

For proposals or formal reports, of course, problem statements may be more elaborate and part of the full-scale introduction, which is discussed later in this entry.

Scope.   You may present the **scope** of your document in your opening. By providing the parameters of your material, the limitations of the subject, or the amount of detail to be presented, your readers can determine whether they want or need to read your document.

▶ This pamphlet provides a review of the requirements for obtaining a private pilot's license. It is not intended as a textbook to prepare you for the examination itself; rather, it outlines the steps you need to take and the costs involved.

Background.   The background or history of a subject may provide interest, perspective, or insight into a subject. Consider the following example from a newsletter describing the process of oil drilling:

▶ From the bamboo poles the Chinese used when the pyramids were young to today's giant rigs drilling in deep water, there has been considerable progress in the search for oil. But whether in ancient China or a modern city, underwater or on a mountaintop, the objective of drilling has always been the same—to manufacture a hole in the ground, inch by inch.

Summary.   You can provide a summary opening by describing in abbreviated form the results, conclusions, or recommendations of your article or report. Be concise: Do not begin a summary by writing "This report summarizes . . . "

CHANGE   This report summarizes the advantages offered by the photon as a means of examining the structural features of the atom.

TO   As a means of examining the structure of the atom, the photon offers several advantages.

Interesting Detail.   Often an interesting detail will attract the readers' attention and pique their curiosity. Readers of an **annual report** for a manufacturer of telescopes and scientific instruments, for example, may be persuaded to invest if they believe that the company is developing innovative, cutting-edge products.

▶ The rings of Saturn have puzzled astronomers ever since they were discovered by Galileo in 1610 using the first telescope. Recently, even more rings have been discovered.

Our company's Scientific Instrument Division designs and manufactures research-quality, computer-controlled telescopes that promise to solve the puzzles of Saturn's rings by enabling scientists to use multicolor differential photometry to determine the rings' origins and compositions.

Definition.   Although a definition can be useful as an opening, do not define something with which your audience is familiar or provide a definition that is obviously a contrived opening (such as "Webster defines *technology* as . . ."). A definition should be used as an opening only if it offers insight into what follows.

▶ *Risk* is often a loosely defined term. In this report, risk refers to a qualitative combination of the probability of an event and the severity of the consequences of that event. In fact, . . .

Anecdote.   An anecdote can be used to attract and build interest in a subject that may otherwise be mundane; however, this strategy is best suited to longer documents and **presentations**.

▶ In his poem "The Calf Path" (1895), Sam Walter Foss tells of a wandering, wobbly calf trying to find its way home at night through the lonesome woods. It made a crooked path, which was taken up the next day by a lone dog. Then "a bellwether sheep pursued the trail over vale and steep, drawing behind him the flock, too, as all good bellwethers do." This forest path became a country lane that bent and turned and turned again. The lane became a village street, and at last the main street of a flourishing city. The poet ends by saying, "A hundred thousand men were led by a calf near three centuries dead."

Many companies today follow a "calf path" because they react to events rather than planning.

Quotation.   You can use a quotation to stimulate interest in your subject. To be effective, however, the quotation must be pertinent—not any loosely related quotation you find.

▶ Richard Smith, founder of PCS Corporation, recently said, "I believe that managers need to be more 'people smart' than ever before. The management style of today involves much more than just managing the operations of a department—it requires understanding the personalities that comprise a corporation." His statement represents a growing feeling among corporate leaders that . . .

Forecast.   Sometimes you can use a forecast of a new development or trend to gain the audience's attention and interest.

▶ In the not-too-distant future, we may be able to use a handheld medical diagnostic device similar to those in science fiction to assess the physical condition of accident victims. This project and others are now being developed at Seldi Group, Inc.

Persuasive Hook.   Although all opening strategies contain persuasive elements, the hook uses **persuasion** most overtly. A Web site touting the newest innovation in tax-preparation software might address readers as follows:

▶ Welcome to the newest way to do your taxes! TaxPro EZ ends the headache of last-minute tax preparation with its unique TaxPro app.

Full-Scale Introductions

The purpose of a full-scale introduction is to give readers enough general information about the subject to enable them to understand the details in the body of the document. (See Figure F–6, pages 203–19.) An introduction should accomplish any or all of the following:

- *State the subject.* Give background information, such as definition, history, or theory, to provide context for your readers.

- *State the purpose.* Make your readers aware of why the document exists and whether the material provides a new perspective or clarifies an existing perspective.

- *State the scope.* Tell readers the amount of detail you plan to cover.

- *Preview the development of the subject.* Especially in a longer document, outline how you plan to develop the subject. Providing such information allows readers to anticipate how the subject will be presented and helps them evaluate your conclusions or recommendations.

Consider writing an opening or introduction last. Many writers find that only after they have drafted the body of the document do they have a full enough perspective on the subject to introduce it adequately.

investigative reports

An investigative **report** offers a precise analysis of a workplace problem or issue in response to a need for information. The investigative report shown in Figure I–10 (on page 288), for example, evaluates whether a company should adopt a program called Basic English to prepare documentation for and to train non–English-speaking readers.

Open an investigative report with a statement of its primary and any secondary **purposes**, then define the **scope** of your investigation. If the report includes a survey of opinions, for example, indicate the number of people surveyed and other identifying information, such as income categories and occupations. (See also **questionnaires**.) Include any information that is pertinent in defining the depth of the investigation. Then report your findings and discuss their significance with your **conclusions**.

Sometimes the person requesting the investigative report may need to make recommendations based on your findings. In that case, the report may be referred to as a *recommendation report*. See also **feasibility reports** and **incident reports**.

I

italics

Italics is a style of type used to denote **emphasis** and to distinguish book titles, foreign expressions, and certain other elements. You may need to italicize words that require special emphasis in a sentence. ("Contrary to projections, sales have *not* improved.") Do not overuse italics for emphasis, however. ("*This* will hurt *you* more than *me*.")

Foreign Words and Phrases

Foreign words and phrases are italicized: *bonjour*, *guten tag*, the sign said "*Se habla español*." Foreign words that have been fully assimilated into English need not be italicized: cliché, etiquette, vis-à-vis, de facto, résumé. When in doubt about whether to italicize a word, consult a current dictionary.

Titles

Italicize the titles of separately published documents (print or electronic), such as books, Web and blog sites, periodicals, newspapers, pamphlets, brochures, and legal cases.

▶ *Turning Workplace Conflicts into Collaboration* [book] was reviewed in the *New York Times* [newspaper].

Memo

To: Noreen Rinaldo, Training Manager
From: Charles Lapinski, Senior Instructor
Date: February 6, 2018
Subject: Adler's Basic English Program

Context and primary purpose

As requested, I have investigated Adler Medical Instruments' (AMI's) Basic English Program to determine whether we might adopt a similar program.

Defines subject

AMI's program teaches medical technologists outside the United States who do not speak or read English to understand procedures written in a special 800-word vocabulary called *Basic English*. This program eliminates the need for AMI to translate its documentation into a number of different languages. The Basic English Program does not attempt to teach the medical technologists to be fluent in English but, rather, to recognize the 800 basic words that appear in Adler's documentation.

Course Analysis

Describes subject and depth of investigation

The course teaches technologists a basic medical vocabulary in English; it does not provide training in medical terminology. Students must already know, in their own language, the meaning of medical vocabulary (e.g., the meaning of the word *hemostat*). Students must also have basic knowledge of their specialty, must be able to identify a part in an illustrated parts book, must have used AMI products for at least one year, and must be able to read and write in their own language.

Students receive an instruction manual, an illustrated book of equipment with parts and their English names, and pocket references containing the 800 words of the Basic English vocabulary plus the English names of parts. Students can write the corresponding word in their language beside the English word and then use the pocket reference as a bilingual dictionary. The course consists of 30 two-hour lessons, each lesson introducing approximately 27 words. No effort is made to teach pronunciation; the course teaches only recognition of the 800 words.

Course Success

Provides details of report

The 800-word vocabulary enables the writers of documentation to provide medical technologists with any information that might be required because the subject areas are strictly limited to usage, troubleshooting, safety, and operation of AMI medical equipment. All nonessential words (*apple*, *father*, *mountain*, and so on) are eliminated, as are most synonyms (for example, *under* appears, but *beneath* does not).

Conclusions and Recommendations

Provides analysis and recommendations

AMI's program appears to be quite successful, and a similar approach could also be appropriate for us. I see two possible ways in which we could use some or all of the elements of AMI's program: (1) in the preparation of our student manuals or (2) as AMI uses the program.

I think it would be unnecessary to use the Basic English methods in the preparation of manuals for all of our students. Most of our students are English speakers to whom an unrestricted vocabulary presents no problem.

As for our initiating a program similar to AMI's, we could create our own version of the Basic English vocabulary and write our instructional materials in it. Because our product lines are much broader than AMI's, however, we would need to create illustrated parts books for each of the different product lines.

FIGURE I–10. Investigative Report

▶ *CNN Money* [Web site] reports that "written communication skills remain a top priority for U.S. businesses."

Abbreviations of such titles are italicized if their spelled-out forms would be italicized.

▶ The *NYT* is one of the nation's oldest newspapers.

Italicize the titles of CDs, DVDs, movies, plays, long poems, paintings, sculptures, and long musical works.

DVD	*Computer Security Tutorial*
PLAY	Arthur Miller's *Death of a Salesman*
LONG POEM	T. S. Eliot's *The Wasteland*
MUSICAL WORK	Gershwin's *Porgy and Bess*

Use **quotation marks** for parts of publications, such as chapters of books and sections within larger works.

▶ *Small Business Trends* (smallbiztrends.com) [blog] posted "Microbusiness Economic Trends: Into the Future." [article]

Proper Names

The names of ships, trains, and aircraft (but not the companies or governments that own them) are italicized: U.S. aircraft carrier *Independence*, Amtrak's passenger train *Coast Starlight*. Craft that are known by model or serial designations are not italicized: DC-7, Boeing 747.

Words, Letters, and Figures

Words, letters, and figures discussed as such are italicized.

▶ The word *inflammable* is often misinterpreted.

▶ The *S* and *6* keys on my keyboard do not function.

Subheads

Subheads in a report are sometimes italicized.

▶ *Training Managers.* We are leading the way in developing first-line managers who not only are professionally competent but . . .

Exceptions

Some titles are not set off by italics, quotation marks, or underlining, although they are capitalized.

▶ Professional Writing [college course title], the Constitution, the Bible, Lincoln's Gettysburg Address, the Lands' End Catalog.

Keep in mind your **context**, especially as you prepare material for screen display, as in **writing for the Web**. See also **headings** and **layout and design**.

its / it's

Its is a possessive **pronoun** and does not use an **apostrophe**. *It's* is a **contraction** of *it is*.

▶ *It's* important that the sales department meet ~~its'~~ *its* quota.

See also **expletives** and **possessive case**.

I

J

jargon

Jargon is a specialized slang that is unique to an occupational or a professional group. For example, human resource personnel use the term *headhunter* to describe specialists who recruit professional and executive personnel. Jargon is at first understood only by insiders; over time, it may become known more widely and become a **buzzword**. If all your readers are members of a particular occupational group, jargon may provide an efficient means of communicating. However, if you have any doubt that your entire **audience** is part of such a group, avoid using jargon. See also **affectation**, **functional shift**, **gobbledygook**, and **plain language**.

J

job descriptions

Most companies use formal job descriptions to specify the duties of and requirements for many of the positions in the organization.* Job descriptions fulfill several important functions: They provide information on which equitable salary scales can be based, they help management determine whether all functions within a company are adequately supported, and they let both prospective and current employees know exactly what is expected of them. Together, all the job descriptions in a company present a picture of the organization's structure. The job description shown in Figure J–1 (on page 292) is typical. It never mentions the person holding the job described; instead, it focuses on the job and the qualifications required to fill the position.

Although job-description formats vary from organization to organization, they commonly contain the following sections:

- The *accountability* section identifies, by title only, the person to whom the employee reports.

- The *scope of responsibilities* section provides an overview of the primary and secondary functions of the job and states, if applicable, who reports to the employee.

---

*Job descriptions are sometimes called *position descriptions*, a term also used for formal announcements of openings for professional or administrative positions.

PUBLICATIONS MANAGER
GCW Systems

Accountability

Reports directly to the Vice President, Advertising and Public Relations.

Scope of Responsibilities

The Publications Manager plans, coordinates, and supervises the design and development of sales brochures, advertisements, Web sites, and customer manuals required to support the sale, installation, and maintenance of company products and services. The manager is responsible for the administration of the Publications Department. The supervisor of customer publications, the supervisor of internal publications, and the division Webmaster report to the Publications Manager.

Specific Duties

- Directs an organization currently comprising 20 people, including supervisors, writers, designers, and production staff
- Screens, selects, and hires qualified applicants for the department
- Prepares a formal orientation program to familiarize trainees with the production of printed materials
- Evaluates the performance of and determines the salary adjustments for all department employees
- Plans documentation to support new and existing products
- Subcontracts publications and acts as a purchasing agent when needed
- Offers editorial advice to supervisors
- Develops and manages an annual budget for the Publications Department
- Recommends new and appropriate uses for the department within the company

Requirements

- B.A. in professional writing or equivalent
- Minimum of three years' professional writing experience and a general knowledge of design and current production software
- Minimum of two years' management experience and a knowledge of the general principles of management
- Strong interpersonal skills

FIGURE J–1. Job Description

- The *specific duties* section gives a detailed account of the particular duties of the job as concisely as possible.

- The *requirements* section lists the required or preferred education, training, experience, and licensing for the job.

WRITER'S CHECKLIST | **Writing Job Descriptions**

✔ Before attempting to write your job description, list all the different tasks you do in a week or a month. Otherwise, you will almost certainly leave out some of your duties.

✔ Focus on content. Remember that you are describing your job, not yourself.

✔ List your duties in the decreasing order of importance. Knowing how your various duties rank in importance makes it easier to set valid job qualifications.

✔ Begin each statement of a duty with a **verb**, and be specific. Write "Orient new staff members to the department" rather than "New staff orientation."

✔ Review existing job descriptions that are considered well written.

job search

J

Individuals seek jobs for a number of reasons, including to

- Gain experience in a particular field.

- Develop contacts with professionals, and strengthen networking skills.

- Build concrete evidence of skills and knowledge for inclusion in a professional portfolio.

- Diversify skills and knowledge to help set a job seeker apart from the competition.

- Explore another career option prior to a career shift or an opportunity that complements current employment (for instance, a freelance career that can be developed on the side).

- Participate in activities that support personal values and character traits.

Whether you are applying for your first job or want to change careers entirely, begin by assessing your knowledge, skills, interests, and abilities through brainstorming. Next, consider your career goals and values.* For instance, do you prefer working independently or collaboratively?

*A good source for stimulating your thinking is the most recent edition of *What Color Is Your Parachute? A Practical Manual for Job-Hunters & Career-Changers* by Richard N. Bolles, published by Ten Speed Press. Also, it is a good idea to head to your university's career services office to ask for current information about industries in which you have interest as well as any positions that have been listed with the office. While you are there, you might inquire about the possibility of signing up to take a personality test, like the Myers-Briggs Type Indicator, or a career aptitude test; both can provide clues to the types of work and work environments in which you might be most successful.

Do you enjoy public settings? Do you like meeting people? How important are career stability and location? What would you most like to be doing in the immediate future? In two years? In five years? Be honest: What kinds of tasks and responsibilities, big and small, would you like to occupy your days?

Once you have narrowed your goals and identified a professional area that is right for you, consider the following sources to locate the job and work environment you are seeking. It is important to consult both internal sources (documents and other kinds of evidence produced by the organization to which you are applying) and external sources (perspectives on the organization written by an outside party). Some examples of sources from each perspective follow:

Internal Sources:

- Informational interviews with organizational insiders
- Published job ads announcing current position openings
- Organizational Web sites
- Annual reports
- Corporate ads speaking to the identity and reputation of an organization
- Employees currently working for an organization

External Sources:

- Newspaper articles about an organization
- Industry reports that speak to the successes and failures of several organizations, including the one to which you are applying
- Unpaid reviews of an organization's products and services
- Forecasts by investment and workforce experts

Organization is key to a successful job search. Keep files, preferably electronic and hard copy, for potential jobs, and include in each file copies of job ads, **application letters**, **résumés**, follow-up correspondence, and contact information. Consider logging your job-search activity on a spreadsheet or any other accessible format so that you can always easily determine who you have contacted and why. Whatever system you use, keeping track of names and what you have sent to potential employers is crucial.

In an era when multiple communications are sent daily through e-mail, texting, and a variety of social-media outlets, it is crucial to record the names and positions of individuals from an organization with whom you have corresponded in any form. Set up file folders for e-mail exchanges. For example, keep all messages you exchange with an organization's human resources director and any other individuals from the organization in one place for easy reference.

◀ **PROFESSIONALISM NOTE** *Personal branding* is a concept introduced by business guru Tom Peters that has increasingly gained in popularity. Businesses work to establish a positive image and a reputation for high-quality products and the successful execution of services. Personal branding is the idea of marketing a positive image or reputation of yourself. For example, if you are a consultant who sells products or services, your consistently professional and successful execution of services will be remembered as a core part of your brand. By learning how to influence other people's perceptions of your brand, you will gain an immediate advantage over the competition. See "Seven Things You Can Do to Build an Awesome Personal Brand" by Shama Hyder at www.forbes.com.

Many components of the job search discussed in this entry can help you establish a strong personal brand. As you evaluate the opportunities of networking, social media, and internships, for example, keep in mind the core message you would like to send about yourself. Every interaction provides opportunities to enhance your visibility through a full suite of job-search materials. These materials may include a video résumé, business cards, a narrative biography, LinkedIn and other **social media** profiles, a personal Web site, a portfolio, reference letters, and testimonials. As you prepare these materials, project a consistent and unified branding message across all media outlets.

To achieve consistency of your brand and to enter a job or career that is personally and professionally satisfying, you must be honest with yourself about what you bring to the workplace and how you self-identify. Avoid trying to maintain a personal brand that sounds like a good fit for a particular organization but that does not genuinely reflect your values, interests, and goals.

Along with "personal branding," consider the way in which you "package" yourself for the job search. Qualified applicants for a position will likely possess many of the same credentials (for instance, an undergraduate degree in a relevant discipline or a required license for entering a particular field) and similar experiences (for example, an internship during college). It is important to consider, then, what unique traits or experiences set you apart from your competitors. These can include anything from a meaningful mission trip in which you participated to a passion you have for painting to a significant feature of your upbringing. By combining your unique feature with qualifications that employers expect to see in applicants' materials, you can set yourself apart. For example, each of the following statements reflects effective applicant packaging:

- In addition to bringing knowledge of current marketing theory and practice to this position, my experiences of watching my parents grow their dry cleaning business in our small town taught me much about the importance of building relationships in the community.

- My grades in my civil engineering courses and the leadership roles I played in group projects reveal my commitment to the field. It was my summer work for Habitat for Humanity, though, that taught me the importance of using my training to serve the community.

Networking and Informational Interviews

Career-development experts agree that many open positions are filled through networking. Networking involves communicating with people who can provide useful advice or who may know of potential jobs in your interest areas. Your network may include people already working in your chosen field, contacts in professional organizations, professors, family members, or friends. Discussion groups and networking sites, such as LinkedIn, can be helpful in this process. In general, you should always be networking, even when you do not need assistance. Even a simple gesture, such as providing a reference for a recently unemployed colleague, can go a long way toward expanding your network.

Informational interviews are appointments you schedule with working professionals who can give you "insider" views of an occupation or industry. These brief meetings (usually 20 to 30 minutes) also offer you the chance to learn about employment trends as well as leads for employment opportunities. Because you ask the questions, these interviews allow you to participate in an interview situation that is less stressful than the job interview itself. To make the most of informational interviews, prepare carefully and review both **interviewing for information** and **interviewing for a job**.

Campus Career Services

A visit to a college career-development center is another good way to begin your job search. Government, business, and industry recruiters often visit campus career offices to interview prospective employees; recruiters also keep career counselors aware of their companies' current employment needs and provide them with job descriptions. Career counselors not only help you select a career but also put you in touch with the best and most current resources—identifying where to begin your search and saving you time. Career-development centers often hold workshops on résumé preparation and offer other job-finding resources on their Web sites.

Strategic Web Searches

In addition to professional and social-networking sites, you can use the Web in several ways to enhance your job search.

- Consult sites that give advice about careers, job seeking, and résumé preparation like www.careerbuilder.com.

- Learn about businesses and organizations that may hire employees in your field by visiting their Web sites. Such company sites often describe the company's culture, list job openings, provide instructions for applicants, and offer an overview of employee benefits.

- You can learn about jobs in your field and post your résumé for prospective employers at privately owned or government-sponsored online employment databases. For instance, among the many resources found at CareerOneStop (www.careeronestop.org), a job seeker can research salary ranges for a particular region or career field. This tool is particularly valuable when you are moving to a new location, considering a career transition, or determining a valid salary and benefits range for negotiating compensation packages.

Social Media

Social-media sites, such as LinkedIn, allow you to connect with people of like-minded interests both on an individual level and in a broad forum. Social media provides the opportunity to develop a positive image of your work through comments, personal and professional profiles, résumés, associations to which you belong, and your connections. These components of your social-media presence can help enhance your reputation and personal brand.

◀ **PROFESSIONALISM NOTE** Surveys show that employers and employment recruiters peruse social media and search engines before recruiting candidates, so carefully consider the material that you post online when using such media as LinkedIn, Facebook, and Twitter. Keep in mind that many software packages allow prospective employers to compile an overview of a job seeker's online presence. Share online only what you would comfortably share with your boss, and regularly check the privacy settings on any sites that you use. It is important to remain consistent to your personal brand in any communications you share online, which is all the more reason to articulate a brand that is genuine. ▶

Job Advertisements

Many employers advertise job openings on their Web sites, job boards, social-media sites, and newspapers. Because job listings can differ, search in both the printed and Web editions of local and big-city newspapers under *employment* or *job market*. Use the search options they provide or the general strategies for database searches discussed in the entry **research**.

A human-relations specialist interested in training, for example, might find the specialty listed under "Human Resources" or "Consulting Services." Depending on a company's or government agency's needs, the listing could be even more specific, such as "Software Education Specialist" or "Learning and Development Coordinator."

Set up job alerts on job-aggregator sites, such as indeed.com and simplyhired.com, and scour job boards, company Web sites, and newspaper listings for jobs that meet your criteria and send you e-mail notifications. As you read the ads, take notes on salary ranges, job locations, job duties and responsibilities, and even the terminology used in the ads to describe the work.

Not all organizations publish job ads. Rather, they rely on current employees to spread news of any hiring needs to contacts in their personal and professional networks. It is appropriate to send a "prospecting" application letter and résumé to an organization to let the human resources director or other appropriate representative know that you are interested in working with the organization and in what capacities.

Remember, too, that job ads are often wish lists—descriptions of *ideal* candidates for a position. Not everyone who applies will meet all the requirements listed, nor may the individual who is ultimately selected for the position. Pay attention to the language used in an ad to determine which qualifications are "required" as opposed to "desired" or "preferred."

Trade and Professional Journal Listings

Many industry associations publish periodicals of interest to people working in the industry. Such periodicals often contain job listings. To learn about the trade or professional associations for your occupation, consult online resources offered by your library or campus career office. Also, head to the central office for your major to see what kinds of resources are available for students pursuing careers in related fields. Often, those who are on the forefront of the discipline will be in the loop regarding which industries and organizations are seeking employees, are in the process of expanding, or are interested in taking on students for internships or co-ops.

Employment Agencies (Private, Temporary, Government)

Private employment agencies are organizations that are in business to help people find jobs. Be sure you understand who is paying the agency's fee. Often the employer pays the agency's fee; however, if you have to pay, make sure you know exactly how much. As with any written agreement, read the fine print carefully.

A staffing agency or temporary placement agency could match you with an appropriate temporary or permanent job in your field. Temporary work for an organization for which you might want to work permanently is an excellent way to build your network while continuing your job search. Choose an employment or a temporary-placement agency carefully. Some are well established and reputable; others are not. Check with your local Better Business Bureau and your college career office before you sign any agreements.

Recruitment firms (sometimes called *headhunters*) are hired by organizations to fill general needs or specific positions. Especially if you have experience in a field, it is a good idea to make connections with recruiters on networking sites like LinkedIn. You can also search online for recruiters who specialize in your career field, and send your résumé to them through their Web-site form or by e-mail. Even if there is no suitable job opportunity, a résumé submitted to a recruitment firm could turn up in a future database search.

Local, state, and federal government agencies also offer many free or low-cost employment services. Locate local government agencies in Web or telephone directories under the name of your city, county, or state. For information on occupational trends, see the Occupational Outlook Handbook at www.bls.gov/oco. For information on jobs with the federal government, see the U.S. Office of Personnel Management at www.opm.gov or USAJOBS, the federal government's official jobs site, at www.usajobs.gov. For information on salary negotiations, see page 280.

J

Internships and Co-ops

As you evaluate job options, consider taking an internship or a co-op. Internships typically last from six weeks to an entire semester (if not longer), whereas co-ops (or cooperatives) are often taken on by a student while in school, with the understanding that the position may become full time once the student completes his or her education. An internship or a co-op provides you with the chance to gain experience in a field through a variety of career opportunities. It enables you to

- Try a position without making a permanent commitment.
- Explore a field to clarify your career goals.
- Develop skills and gain experience in a new field or industry.
- Evaluate a prospective employer or firm.
- Acquire a mentor in the workplace.
- Establish networking contacts and professional references.
- Position yourself for a future job offer with the employer.

Ask if the internship is paid or unpaid during your interview. If it is not paid, find out how the internship will benefit you based on recent legal criteria for unpaid internships. (See "Fact Sheet #71: Internship Programs Under The Fair Labor Standards Act" on the U.S. Department of Labor's Web site, www.dol.gov.) For-profit employers are required to pay interns at least the minimum wage unless the internship experience is designed for the benefit of the intern, such as training that would be given in an educational environment. When this condition is met, the employer is not required to pay the intern for the internship.

To locate internship opportunities, begin with your campus career-development office. Such offices usually post internship opportunities on their Web site, but you can also make appointments with counselors or take advantage of walk-in hours. Finally, try www.internships.com, a site that lists internships by type of employer, location, means of compensation (paid or unpaid), and whether the work is full or part time.

Service Internship and "Gap Year" Opportunities

Not all internships involve working for an organization that is in your chosen field. Increasingly, students are choosing to spend a period of time following graduation working in a position sponsored by organizations like Teach for America.

One option that many college graduates consider before pursuing full-time employment in a field that dovetails with their major and career goals is to apply for a position with AmeriCorps or the Peace Corps. These governmental organizations seek volunteers for a limited amount of time (usually between one and two years) to help improve the lives of individuals in the United States and abroad.

AmeriCorps offers opportunities for Americans who are interested in contributing their talents to "nonprofits, schools, public agencies, and community and faith-based groups across the country" (www.nationalservice .gov/programs/americorps). A specific example of an AmeriCorps program is City Year, which requires selected applicants to work for one year in an urban school that lacks sufficient resources.

Working for the Peace Corps can take volunteers to all corners of the world, on such missions as rebuilding structures damaged by tsunamis in places like Thailand or helping farmers in developing countries like Nepal attempt new techniques in agriculture.

There are advantages to spending a gap year (or more) in these kinds of positions. In addition to learning new skills, interacting with people from different locales and backgrounds, and having the opportunity in some cases to acquire another language, governmental programs like these will often assist in the repayment of student loans.

Direct Inquiries

If you would like to work for a particular firm, peruse the organization's Web site to see if any openings for individuals with your qualifications are advertised. You may also e-mail or call the human resources director or the head of a particular division to which you are interested in applying. Remember that all correspondence, even a simple phone call, should be professional, because every interaction with an organization reflects your identity. Such contacts work best if you have networked, as described earlier in this entry.

A related strategy is to prepare a prospecting letter—a highly targeted letter that outlines why your skills and credentials would be valuable to the employer. Before writing the letter, research the employer to find out about any upcoming plans, goals, and even obstacles to its success. Your prospecting letter can show that you understand the challenges the employer is facing and you want to be part of the solution. Describe what you expect to accomplish, both short term and long term, if given the opportunity.

Other Application Genres

Other kinds of documents, print and digital, are used for pursuing positions in the contemporary workplace.

- Application forms: Some organizations ask applicants to complete online or print application forms, providing information about work history in an accessible and standard format. When completing these forms, be sure to answer all questions, targeting the word count specified in the instructions. If a specific word count is not provided, gauge the preferred length for responses according to the amount of space provided.

- LinkedIn profile: LinkedIn is an online site for managing professional profiles and networking with individuals in related fields. Many employers will check LinkedIn profiles as a first step in the screening process. Check your LinkedIn profile frequently to see what comments have been added by those who visit your page and to ensure that all information is updated.

- Digital (and print) portfolios: Throughout college, it is important to keep a careful record of your accomplishments, whether academic achievements (for example, being named to the dean's list or earning awards for work in a particular class) or participation in campus organizations and clubs. A digital or print (usually bound) portfolio will offer evidence of the knowledge, skills, and personal traits that you claim to possess when applying for a position. In addition to a résumé and a reflective statement, which will unify the other materials in your portfolio, include samples of your work in classes and jobs, images of events or programs in which you participated, letters of reference, and any other evaluations of your work.

- Video résumés: Applicants are increasingly producing more sophisticated multimedia résumés in addition to traditional print versions. Like digital portfolios, video résumés provide extras—for example, short taped statements by the applicant to further demonstrate an item listed on the résumé or a link to supporting images.

❖ **ETHICS NOTE** Providing false information on your job application can result in a dismissal and will reflect poorly on your character. Be honest and keep in mind that if you are wrong for a position and lie to obtain it, the employer can just as easily discover this after you are hired. ❖

J

WRITER'S CHECKLIST   **Completing Job Applications: Print and Online**

✔ Read the entire application, and keep your résumé at hand before you begin.

✔ Copy and paste responses to online applications, as appropriate, from your current résumé.

✔ Provide all requested information, and complete irrelevant entries with *N/A* (for "not applicable").

✔ List a specific job title for the "Position Seeking" entry—entries "any" or "open" receive less consideration.

✔ List salary requirements as "negotiable," or give a range commensurate with the industry and region.

✔ Use positive phrases if asked why you left a previous employer: "relocation," "seeking new challenge," "career advancement," or possibly "will discuss at interview."

✔ List references (with their permission) who can speak to your professionalism, character, or work ethic.

✔ Attach a brief cover letter and résumé with your completed job application, if possible.

✔ Proofread for accuracy and consistency: Review the instructions, and check all entries or fields, dates, position titles, links, grammar, and spelling.

✔ Make sure you date, sign (if print), and submit or post the application by the deadline.

✔ Save for your records a copy or screen capture of your completed application.

❖ **ETHICS NOTE** When faced with questions that are sensitive, you must carefully consider your response. If the question does not seem to raise a problem, you can choose to answer it. If you feel the question is inappropriate, you can respond with *N/A* or another response (such as a line through the blank); this will indicate that you have read the content.

Understanding that many employers conduct background checks on candidates to protect their interests will help you determine the validity of a question. For example, a banking institution might be concerned about a candidate's credit history, current debts, or bankruptcy status, or a government organization might be concerned about citizenship or ties to foreign countries. ❖

J

K

kind of / sort of

The phrases *kind of* and *sort of* should be used only to refer to a class or type of things.

► We require a special *kind of* training to ensure employee safety.

Do not use *kind of* or *sort of* to mean "rather," "somewhat," or "somehow." That usage can lead to vagueness; it is better to be specific.

VAGUE   It was *kind of* a bad year for the company.

SPECIFIC   The company's profits fell 10 percent last year.

know-how

The informal term *know-how*, meaning "special competence or knowledge," should be avoided in formal writing **style**.

► The applicant has impressive marketing ~~know-how~~. *skill.*

L

lay / lie

Lay is a transitive **verb**—a verb that requires a direct object to complete its meaning—that means "place" or "put."

▶ We will *lay* the foundation one section at a time.

The past-tense form of *lay* is *laid*.

▶ We *laid* the first section of the foundation last month.

The perfect-tense form of *lay* is also *laid*.

▶ Since June, we *have laid* all but two sections of the foundation.

Lay is frequently confused with *lie*, which is an intransitive verb—a verb that does not require an object to complete its meaning—that means "recline" or "remain."

▶ People in shock should *lie* down with their legs slightly elevated.

The past-tense form of *lie* is *lay* (not *lied*). This form causes the confusion between *lie* and *lay*.

▶ The injured employee *lay* still for approximately five minutes.

The perfect-tense form of *lie* is *lain*.

▶ The injured employee *had lain* still for five minutes before the EMTs arrived.

layout and design

DIRECTORY

Thoughtful layout and design can make even the most complex information accessible and give readers a favorable impression of the writer and the organization. To accomplish those goals, a design should help readers find information easily; offer a simple and uncluttered presentation; and highlight structure, hierarchy, and order. The design must also fit the **purpose** of the document and its **context**. For example, clients paying a high price for consulting services might expect a more sophisticated, polished design, while employees aware of pressing deadlines and budgets are likely to accept—or even expect—a standard, functional design for internal documents.

L

Design Principles

Readers are quick to make inferences based on the pattern, form, and organization of document elements. When creating documents and **visuals**, use those instincts to your advantage by keeping in mind three major principles of design: grouping, contrast, and repetition.

Grouping.　　Grouping highlights relationships among items on a page or screen, which helps readers grasp how information is organized and what is important. Grouping can occur in three different ways.

- *Proximity*: Items that are close together seem like part of a group, while items that are far apart seem dissimilar. Related items (for example, a heading and the paragraph that follows it) should be closer together than less closely related items (a heading and the paragraph above the heading).

- *Similarity*: Items that share qualities (such as size, shape, or color) are viewed as similar and tend to be associated as part of a group.

- *Alignment*: Items that are aligned tend to be seen as part of a group. If the items in a bulleted list are aligned with one another and indented from the rest of the text, for example, readers immediately recognize them as related.

Contrast. Contrast sets items apart and helps readers quickly grasp which items are different from one another. For example, to emphasize one data bar in a graph, you might give it a different color or pattern from the other bars. To give readers an easy way to navigate a long document, you might contrast the headings from the body text by making them larger or a different color from the surrounding text.

Repetition. Repetition communicates consistency and predictability through repeated patterns of design elements whether on a page, screen, table, or visual. Inconsistencies in these patterns are confusing and distracting. If like items on a page (headings, footers, bulleted lists) vary slightly from one another in their design, readers will not know whether the items are supposed to be part of a related group. Consistency ensures that the patterns in a document or visual are clear and unambiguous. Repetition thus allows the users of a document to focus on the things the writer wishes to emphasize.

Typography

Typography refers to the style and arrangement of type on a page. A complete set of all the letters, numbers, and symbols available in one typeface (or style) is called a *font*. The letters in a typeface have a number of distinctive characteristics, as shown in Figure L–1.

L

Typeface and Type Size. For most on-the-job writing, select a typeface primarily for its legibility. Avoid typefaces that make text difficult to read or that may distract readers. Instead, choose popular typefaces with which readers are familiar, such as Times New Roman or Arial.

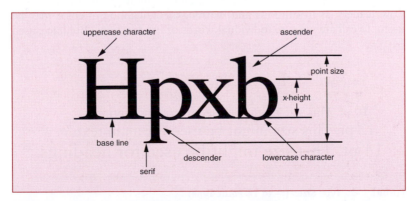

FIGURE L–1. Primary Components of Letter Characters

Avoid using more than two typefaces in the text of a document. For documents like **brochures** and **newsletters**, however, you may wish to use distinctively different typefaces for contrast among various elements, such as headlines, **headings**, inset **quotations**, and sidebars. Experiment before making final decisions, keeping in mind your **audience**.

One way typefaces are characterized is by the presence or absence of serifs. Serif typefaces have projections, as shown in Figure L–1; sans serif styles do not. (*Sans* is French for "without.") The text of this book is set in Sabon, a serif typeface. Although sans serif type has a clean and uncluttered look, serif type is easier to read in print, especially in the smaller sizes. Sans serif, however, works well for headings (like the entry titles in this book) and for Web sites and documents read on-screen.

Ideal font sizes for the main text of paper documents range from 10 to 12 points.* However, for some elements or documents, you may wish to select typeface sizes that are smaller (as in footnotes) or larger (as in headlines for brochures). See Figure L–2 for a comparison of type sizes in a serif typeface.

Your readers and the distance from which they will read a document should help determine type size. For example, **instructions** that will rest on a table at which the reader stands require a larger typeface than a document that will be read up close. For **presentations** and **writing for the Web**, preview your document to see the effectiveness of your choice of point sizes and typefaces.

L

Type Style and Emphasis. One method of achieving emphasis through typography is to use uppercase letters. HOWEVER, LONG STRETCHES OF ALL UPPERCASE LETTERS ARE DIFFICULT TO READ. (See also **e-mail**.) Use all uppercase letters only in short spans, such as in headings. Likewise, use **italics** sparingly, because *continuous italic type reduces legibility and thus slows readers*. Of course, italics are useful if your aim is to slow readers, as in cautions and warnings. Highlighting in color may be useful to call attention to individual words or brief sections. **Boldface**, used

---

6 pt. This size might be used for dating a source.

8 pt. This size might be used for footnotes.

10 pt. This size might be used for figure captions.

12 pt. This size might be used for main text.

14 pt. This size might be used for headings.

FIGURE L–2. Type Sizes (6- to 14-Point Type)

*A point is a unit of type size equal to 0.01384 inch, or approximately 1/72 of an inch.

in moderation, may be the best cuing device because it is visually different yet retains the customary shape of letters and numbers.

Page-Design Elements

Thoughtfully used design elements can provide not only emphasis but also visual logic within a document by highlighting organization. The following typical elements can make your document accessible and effective: justification, headings, headers and footers, lists, columns, white space, and color. Some of these elements are illustrated in the **formal report** on pages 198–219.

Justification.   Left-justified (ragged-right) margins are generally easier to read than full-justified margins, especially for text using wide margins on 8½ × 11" pages. Left justification is also better if full justification causes your word-processing or desktop-publishing software to insert irregular spaces between words, producing unwanted white space or unevenness in blocks of text. Full-justified text is more appropriate for publications aimed at a broad audience that expects a more formal, polished appearance. Full justification is also useful with narrow, multiple-column formats because the spaces between the columns (called *alleys*) need the definition that full justification provides. The body text of this book is full justified.

L

Headings.   Headings reveal the organization of a document and help readers decide which sections they need to read. Provide typographic contrast between headings and the body text with either a different typeface or a different style (**bold**, *italic*, CAPS, and so on). Headings are often effective in boldface sans serif typeface that contrasts with a body text in a serif typeface.

Headers and Footers.   A header in a report, a letter, or another document appears at the top of each page (as in this book), and a footer appears at the bottom of each page. Document pages may have headers or footers (or both) that include such elements as the topic or subtopic of a section, the date the document was written, the page number, and the document name. Keep your headers and footers concise, because too much information in them can create visual clutter. However, a multipage document should, at a minimum, include the page number in a header or footer. For headers used in letters and memos, see **correspondence**.

Lists.   Vertically stacked words, phrases, and other items with numbers or bullets can effectively highlight such information as steps in sequence, materials or parts needed, key or concluding points, and recommendations. For further detail, see **lists**.

Columns.   Consider how columns may improve the readability of your document. A single-column format works well with larger typefaces, double-spacing, and left-justified margins. For smaller typefaces and single-spaced lines, the two-column structure keeps text columns narrow enough so that readers need not scan back and forth across the width of the entire page for every line. Columns of different size can separate main text from secondary material. Avoid a single word or line carried over to the top of the next column or page; likewise, avoid opening a paragraph or stranding a word at the end of a column or page.

White Space.   The area on a page or screen that is free of text or design elements is called white space. It is an important element of design because it visually frames text and other elements, and breaks pages into manageable chunks. For example, white space between paragraphs or sections can serve as a visual cue to signal the ending or beginning of a topic or section.

Color.   Color and screening (shaded areas on a page) can distinguish one part of a document from another or unify a series of documents. They can set off sections within a document, highlight examples, or emphasize warnings. In **tables**, screening can highlight column titles or sets of data to which you want to draw the reader's attention.

Visuals

Readers notice visuals before they notice text, and they notice larger visuals before they notice smaller ones. Thus, the size of an illustration suggests its relative importance. For newsletter articles and publications aimed at wide audiences, consider especially the proportion of the visual to the text. Magazine designers have traditionally used the three-fifths rule: Page layout is more dramatic and appealing when the major element (**photograph**, **drawing**, or other visual) occupies three-fifths rather than one-half of the available space.

Visuals can be gathered in one place (for example, at the end of a report), but placing them in the text closer to their accompanying explanations makes them more effective. Illustrations in the text also provide visual relief. For advice on the placement of visuals, see the *Writer's Checklist: Creating and Integrating Visuals* on pages 542–43.

Icons.   Icons are simplified pictorial or symbolic representations that are used online as links to programs (as in apps), commands, or files. In a printed document, icons can indicate a recurring feature or quality, such as a special cross-reference. Icons must be simple and easily recognized without accompanying text. For example, on the Web, national flags might symbolize different language versions of a document. For advice on using icons that are culturally appropriate, see **global graphics**.

Captions.   Captions are titles that highlight or describe visuals. Captions often appear below figures and above tables; they may be aligned with the visual to the left, or they may be centered.

Rules.   Rules are vertical or horizontal lines used to enclose material in a box or to divide one area of the page from another. For example, rules and boxes set off visuals from surrounding explanations or highlight warning statements from the steps in instructions.

Page Layout and Thumbnails

Page layout involves combining typography, design elements, and visuals on a page to make a coherent whole. The flexibility of your design is affected by your design software, your method of printing the document, your budget, and whether your employer or client requires you to use a template.

Before you spend time positioning actual text and visuals on a page, especially for visually complex documents such as brochures, you may want to create a thumbnail sketch, in which blocks of simulated text and visuals indicate the placement of elements. You can go further by roughly assembling all the thumbnail pages to show the size, shape, form, and general style of a large document. Such a mock-up, called a *dummy*, allows you to see how a finished printed document will look.

L

lend / loan

Both *lend* and *loan* can be used as **verbs**, but *lend* is more common. ("The bank can *lend* [or *loan*] them the money.") Unlike *lend*, *loan* can be a **noun**. ("The bank approved our *loan*.")

letters

Business letters—normally written for those outside an organization—are often the most appropriate choice for formal communications with professional associates or customers. Letters may be especially effective for those people who receive a high volume of **e-mail** and other electronic messages. Letters printed on organizational letterhead communicate formality, respect, and authority. See **correspondence** for advice on writing strategy and style. See also **selecting the medium**.

Although templates are available to format business letters, they may not provide the appropriate dimensions and elements you need. The following sections offer specific advice on formatting and related etiquette for business letters.*

Letter Format

If your employer requires a particular letter format, use it. Otherwise, follow the design guidelines shown in Figure L–3, which illustrates the popular *full-block style*. In this format, the entire letter is aligned at the left margin. To achieve a professional appearance, center the letter on the page vertically and horizontally. Regardless of the default margin provided by a template, it is more important to establish a picture frame of blank space surrounding the text of the letter. When you use organizational stationery with letterhead at the top of the page, consider the bottom of the letterhead as the top edge of the paper. The right margin should be approximately as wide as the left margin. To give a fuller appearance to short letters, increase both margins to about an inch and a half. Use your full-page or print-preview feature to check for proportion.

Heading

Unless you are using letterhead stationery, place your full return address and the date in the heading. Because your name appears at the end of the letter, it need not be included in the heading. Spell out words such as *street*, *avenue*, *first*, and *west* rather than abbreviating them. You may either spell out the name of the state in full or use the standard postal service abbreviation. The date usually goes directly beneath the last line of the return address. Do not abbreviate the name of the month. Begin the heading about two inches from the top of the page. If you are using letterhead that gives the company address, enter only the date, about three lines below the last line of the letterhead.

Inside Address

The inside address includes the recipient's full name, title, and address. Place the inside address two to six lines below the date, depending on the length of the letter. The inside address should be aligned with the left margin, and the left margin should be at least one inch wide.

Salutation

Place the salutation, or *greeting*, two lines below the inside address, and align it with the left margin. In most business letters, the salutation

---

*For additional details on letter formats and design, you may wish to consult a guide such as Sabin, W. A. (2010). *The Gregg reference manual* (11th ed.). New York, NY: McGraw-Hill.

Letterhead

520 Niagara Street
Braintree, MA 02184

Phone: (781) 787-1175
Fax: (781) 787-1213
EvansTE.com

EVANS
and Associates

Transportation Engineers

Date

May 15, 2018

Mr. George W. Nagel
Director of Operations
Boston Transit Authority
57 West City Avenue
Boston, MA 02210

Inside address

Salutation

Dear Mr. Nagel:

Enclosed is our final report evaluating the safety measures for
the Boston Intercity Transit System.

We believe that the report covers the issues you raised in our last
meeting and that you will be pleased with the results. However, if
you have any further questions, we would be happy to meet with
you again at your convenience.

Body

We would also like to express our appreciation to Mr. L. K.
Sullivan of your committee for his generous help during our
trips to Boston.

Complimentary closing

Sincerely,

Carolyn Brown

Signature

Writer's signature block

Carolyn Brown, Ph.D.
Director of Research
cbrown@EvansTE.com

CB/ls
Enclosure: Final Safety Report
cc: ITS Safety Committee Members

End notations

FIGURE L–3. Full-Block-Style Letter (with Letterhead)

contains the recipient's personal title (*Mr.*, *Ms.*, *Dr.*) and last name, followed by a colon. If you are on a first-name basis with the recipient, use only the first name in the salutation.

Address women as *Ms.* unless they have expressed a preference for *Miss* or *Mrs.* However, professional titles (*Professor*, *Senator*, *Major*) take precedence over *Ms.* and similar courtesy titles.

When a person's first name could refer to either a woman or a man, one solution is to use both the first and last names in the salutation (*Dear Pat Smith*:).

For multiple recipients, the following salutations are appropriate:

▶ Dear Professor Allen and Dr. Rivera: [two recipients]

▶ Dear Ms. Becham, Ms. Moore, and Mr. Stein: [three recipients]

▶ Dear Colleagues: [*Members*, or other suitable collective term]

Subject Line

An optional element in a letter is a subject line, which should follow the salutation. Insert one blank line above and one blank line below the subject line. The subject line in a letter functions as it does for e-mail and other correspondence: as an aid in focusing the topic and filing the letter. (For more information, see the subsection on creating subject lines on page 117.)

Subject lines are especially useful if you are writing to a large company and do not know the name or title of the recipient. In such cases, you may address a letter to an appropriate department or identify the subject in a subject line and use no salutation.

▶ National Medical Supply Group
501 West National Avenue
Minneapolis, MN 55407

Attention: Customer Service Department

Subject: Defective Cardio-100 Stethoscopes

I am returning six stethoscopes with damaged diaphragms that . . .

In other circumstances in which you do not know the recipient's name, use a title appropriate to the **context** of the letter, such as *Dear Customer* or *Dear IT Professional*.

Body

The body of the letter should begin two lines below the salutation (or any element that precedes the body, such as a subject or an attention line). Single-space within and double-space between paragraphs, as shown in Figure L–3. To provide a fuller appearance to a very short letter, you can increase the side margins or increase the font size. You can also insert extra space above the inside address, the writer's signature block, and the initials of the person typing the letter—but do not exceed twice the recommended space for each of these elements.

Complimentary Closing

Type the complimentary closing two spaces below the body. Use a standard expression, such as *Sincerely*, *Sincerely yours*, or *Yours truly*. (If the recipient is a friend as well as a business associate, you can use a less formal closing, such as *Best wishes* or *Best regards* or simply *Best*.) Capitalize only the initial letter of the first word, and follow the expression with a comma.

Writer's Signature Block

Type your full name four lines below and aligned with the complimentary closing. On the next line, include your business title, if appropriate. The following lines may contain your individual contact information, such as a telephone number or an e-mail address, if not included in the letterhead or the body of your letter. Sign the letter in the space between the complimentary closing and your name.

End Notations

Business letters sometimes require additional information that is placed at the left margin, two spaces below the typed name and title of the writer in a long letter, four spaces below in a short letter.

Reference initials show the letter writer's initials in capital letters, followed by a slash mark (or colon), and then the initials of the person typing the letter in lowercase letters, as shown in Figure L–3. When the writer is also the person typing the letter, no initials are needed.

Enclosure notations indicate that the writer is sending material (such as an invoice or an article) along with the letter. Note that you should mention the enclosure in the body of the letter. Enclosure notations may take several forms:

- ▶ Enclosure: Final Safety Report
- ▶ Enclosures (2)
- ▶ Enc. *or* Encs.

Copy notation ("cc:") tells the reader that a copy of the letter is being sent to the named recipient(s) (see Figure L–3). Use a blind-copy notation ("bcc:") when you do not want the addressee to know that a copy is being sent to someone else. A blind-copy notation appears only

L

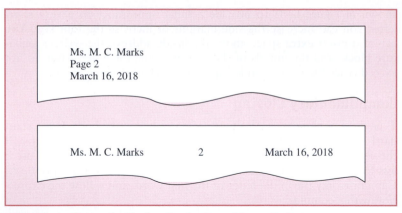

FIGURE L–4. Alternative Headers for the Second Page of a Letter

on the copy, not on the original ("bcc: Dr. Brenda Shelton"). See the Ethics Note in **e-mail** on page 171.

Continuing Pages

If a letter requires a second page (or, in rare cases, more), always carry at least two lines of the body text over to that page. Use plain (nonletterhead) paper of quality equivalent to that of the letterhead stationery for the second page. It should have a header with the recipient's name, the page number, and the date. Place the header text in the upper left-hand corner or across the page, as shown in Figure L–4.

like / as

To avoid confusion between *like* and *as*, remember that *like* is a **preposition** and *as* (or *as if*) is a **conjunction**. Use *like* with a **noun** or **pronoun** that is not followed by a **verb**.

▶ The supervisor still behaves *like* a novice.

Use *as* before **clauses**, which contain verbs.

▶ He responded *as* we hoped he would.

▶ The presentation seemed *as if* it would never end.

Like and *as* are used in **comparisons**: *Like* is used in constructions that omit the verb, and *as* is used when the verb is retained.

▶ He adapted to the new system *like* a duck to water.

▶ He adapted to the new system *as* a duck adapts to water.

listening

Effective listening enables the listener to understand the directions of an instructor, the message in a speaker's **presentation**, the goals of a manager, and the needs and wants of customers. Above all, it lays the foundation for productive communication.

Fallacies About Listening

Most people assume that because they can hear, they know how to listen. In fact, *hearing* is passive, whereas *listening* is active. Hearing voices in a crowd or a ringing telephone requires no analysis and no active involvement—we have no choice but to hear such sounds. Listening, however, requires actively focusing on a speaker, interpreting the message, and assessing its worth. Listening also requires that you consider the **context** of messages and the differences in meaning that may be the result of differences in the speaker's and the listener's occupation, education, culture, sex, race, or other factors. See also **biased language**, **connotation / denotation**, **English as a second language**, and **global communication**.

Active Listening

To become an active listener, you need to take the following steps:

Step 1: Make a Conscious Decision. The first step to active listening is simply making up your mind to listen. Active listening requires a conscious effort. This well-known precept offers good advice: "Seek first to understand and *then* to be understood."*

Step 2: Define Your Purpose. Knowing why you are listening can go a long way toward managing the most common listening problems: letting your attention drift, formulating your response while the speaker is still talking, and interrupting the speaker. To help you define your purpose for listening, ask yourself these questions:

- What kind of information do I hope to get from this exchange, and how will I use it?

- What kind of message do I want to send while I am listening? (Do I want to portray understanding, determination, flexibility, competence, or patience?)

- What factors—boredom, daydreaming, anger, impatience—might interfere with listening during the interaction? How can I keep these factors from placing a barrier between the speaker and me?

*Covey, S. R. (2004). *The seven habits of highly effective people: Powerful lessons in personal change* (15th ed.). New York, NY: Free Press.

Step 3: Take Specific Actions.   Becoming an active listener requires a willingness to become a responder rather than a reactor. A *reactor* simply says the first thing that comes to mind or draws a conclusion without checking to make sure that he or she accurately understands the message. In contrast, a *responder* waits to be certain that he or she understands the speaker's intended message before responding. Take the following actions to help you become a responder and not a reactor.

- Make a conscious effort to be impartial when evaluating a message. For example, do not dismiss a message because you dislike the speaker or are distracted by the speaker's appearance, mannerisms, or accent.

- Slow down the communication by asking for more information or by **paraphrasing** the message received before you offer your thoughts. Paraphrasing lets the speaker know you are listening, gives the speaker an opportunity to clear up any misunderstanding, and keeps you focused.

- Listen with empathy by putting yourself in the speaker's position. When people feel they are being listened to empathetically, they tend to respond with appreciation and cooperation, thereby improving the communication.

- Take notes, when possible, to help you stay focused on what a speaker is saying. **Note-taking** not only communicates your attentiveness to the speaker but also reinforces the message and helps you remember it.

Step 4: Adapt to the Situation.   The requirements of active listening differ from one situation to another. For example, when you are listening to a lecture, you may be listening only for specific information. However, if you are working on a team project that depends on everyone's contribution, you need to listen at the highest level so that you can gather information as well as pick up on nuances the other speakers may be communicating. See also **collaborative writing**.

lists

Vertically stacked lists of words, **phrases**, and other items are often highlighted with bullets, numbers, or letters to set them apart from surrounding text. Lists can save readers time by allowing them to see at a glance specific items or key points. They also help readers by breaking up complex statements and by focusing on such information as steps in sequence, materials or parts needed, questions or concluding points, and recommendations, as shown in Figures L–5 and I–1 (page 257).

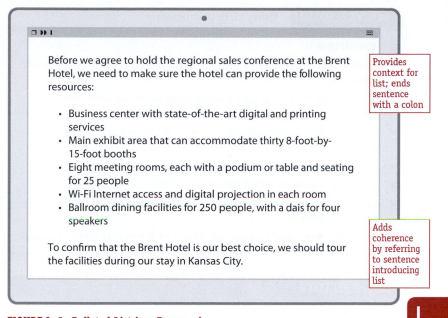

Before we agree to hold the regional sales conference at the Brent Hotel, we need to make sure the hotel can provide the following resources:

- Business center with state-of-the-art digital and printing services
- Main exhibit area that can accommodate thirty 8-foot-by-15-foot booths
- Eight meeting rooms, each with a podium or table and seating for 25 people
- Wi-Fi Internet access and digital projection in each room
- Ballroom dining facilities for 250 people, with a dais for four speakers

To confirm that the Brent Hotel is our best choice, we should tour the facilities during our stay in Kansas City.

Provides context for list; ends sentence with a colon

Adds coherence by referring to sentence introducing list

FIGURE L–5. Bulleted List in a Paragraph

L

As Figure L–5 also shows, you should provide **context** for a list with an introductory sentence followed by a **colon** (or no punctuation for an incomplete sentence). Ensure **coherence** by following the list with some reference to the list or the statement that introduced it.

WRITER'S CHECKLIST **Using Lists**

Follow your organization's practices, or use these guidelines for consistency and formatting.

CONSISTENCY

✔ Do not overuse lists or create extended lists in documents or in **presentation** slides.

✔ List only comparable items, such as tasks or equipment, that are balanced in importance (as in Figure L–5).

✔ Begin each listed item in the same way — whether with **nouns**, **verbs**, or other **parts of speech** — and maintain **parallel structure** throughout.

✔ List bulleted items in a logical order, keeping your **audience** and **purpose** in mind. See also **methods of development** and **persuasion**.

(continued)

FORMATTING

✔ Capitalize the first word in each listed item, unless doing so is visually awkward.

✔ Use **periods** or other ending **punctuation** when the listed items are complete sentences.

✔ Avoid **commas** or **semicolons** following items, and do not use the **conjunction** *and* before the last item in a list.

✔ Use numbers to indicate sequence or rank.

✔ Follow each number with a period.

✔ Use bullets (round, square, arrow) when you do not wish to indicate rank or sequence.

✔ When lists need subdivisions, use letters with numbers (see **outlining**).

logic errors

Logic is the study of the principles of reasoning. In most writing, especially in writing intended to persuade an **audience**, logic is essential to demonstrating that your conclusions are valid. This entry describes typical errors in logic that can undermine the point you are trying to communicate and your credibility. See also **persuasion**.

❖ **ETHICS NOTE** Many logic errors occur unintentionally. However, when they are used intentionally to mislead **readers**, that practice is unethical. See also **ethics in writing**. ❖

Lack of Reason

When a statement is contrary to the reader's common sense, that statement is not reasonable. If, for example, you stated, "New York City is a small town," your reader might immediately question your statement. However, if you stated, "Although New York City's population is over eight million, it is composed of neighborhoods that function as small towns," your reader could probably accept the statement as reasonable.

Sweeping Generalizations

Sweeping generalizations are statements that are too broad or all-inclusive to be supportable. They are statements that disregard exceptions: A flat statement such as "Management is never concerned about employees" ignores evidence that many managers are in fact concerned for their employees. Such generalizations weaken your credibility.

Non Sequiturs

A non sequitur is a statement that does not logically follow a previous statement.

▶ I cleared off my desk, and the report is due today.

The missing link in these statements is that the writer cleared his or her desk to make space for materials to help finish the report that is due today. Avoid non sequiturs by making sure you explicitly state the logical connections of ideas and facts in your writing.

False Cause

A false cause (also called *post hoc, ergo propter hoc*) refers to the logical fallacy that because one event followed another event, the first somehow caused the second.

▶ I didn't bring my umbrella today. No wonder it is now raining.

▶ Because we now have our board meetings at the Education Center, our management turnover rate has declined.

Such errors in reasoning can happen when the writer hastily concludes that two events are related without examining whether a causal connection between them actually exists.

Biased or Suppressed Evidence

A conclusion reached as a result of biased or suppressed evidence — self-serving data, questionable sources, purposely omitted or incomplete facts — is both illogical and unethical. Suppose you are preparing a report on the acceptance of a new policy among employees. If you distribute **questionnaires** only to those who think the policy is effective, the resulting evidence will be biased. Intentionally ignoring relevant data that might not support your position not only produces inaccurate results but is unethical.

Fact Versus Opinion

Distinguish between fact and opinion. Facts include verifiable data or statements; opinions are personal conclusions that may or may not be based on facts. For example, it is verifiable that distilled water boils at 100 °C; that it tastes better or worse than tap water is an opinion. Distinguish facts from opinions so that readers can draw their own conclusions.

Loaded Arguments

When you include an opinion in a statement and then reach conclusions that are based on that statement, you are loading the argument. Consider the following opening for a memo:

▶ I have several suggestions to improve the poorly written policy manual. First, we should change . . .

Unless everyone agrees that the manual is poorly written, readers may reject a writer's entire message because they disagree with this loaded premise. Conclusions reached with loaded statements are weak and can produce negative reactions in readers who detect the loading.

loose / lose

Loose is an **adjective** meaning "not fastened" or "unrestrained." ("He discovered a *loose* wire.") *Lose* is a **verb** meaning "be deprived of" or "fail to win." ("I hope we do not *lose* the contract.")

L

M

malapropisms

A malapropism is a word that sounds similar to the one intended but is ludicrously wrong in the **context**.

INCORRECT   Our employees are less *sedimentary* now that we have a fitness center.

CORRECT   Our employees are less *sedentary* now that we have a fitness center.

Intentional malapropisms are sometimes used in humorous writing; unintentional malapropisms can confuse readers and embarrass a writer. See also **figures of speech**.

maps

Maps are often used to show specific geographic areas and features (such as roads, mountains, and rivers). They can also illustrate geographic distributions of populations, climate patterns, corporate branch office locations, and so forth. The map in Figure M–1 (page 324), from an environmental assessment, shows the overlapping geographic areas served by three electric utilities in Missouri, Iowa, and Illinois. Note that the map contains a figure number and title, scale of distances, key (or legend), compass, and distinctive highlighting for emphasis. Maps are often used in **reports**, **proposals**, **brochures**, environmental impact statements, and other documents in which readers need to know the location or geographic orientation of natural and human-constructed features. For maps and cartographic resources, see www.lib.utexas.edu/maps.

WRITER'S CHECKLIST   **Creating and Using Maps**

✔ Follow the guidelines discussed in **visuals** for placement of maps.

✔ Label each map clearly, and assign each map a figure number if it is one of a number of illustrations.

(continued)

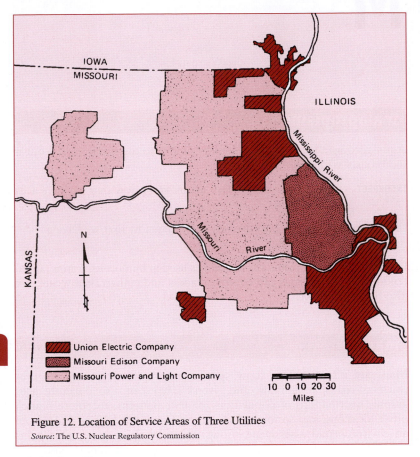

Figure 12. Location of Service Areas of Three Utilities

Source: The U.S. Nuclear Regulatory Commission

FIGURE M–1. Map

WRITER'S CHECKLIST   **Creating and Using Maps** (*continued*)

✔ Clearly identify all significant boundaries while eliminating those unnecessary for your purposes.

✔ Eliminate unnecessary information that may clutter a map. For example, if the purpose of the map is to show population centers, do not include mountain elevations, rivers, or other physical features.

✔ Include a scale of miles/kilometers or feet/meters to give your readers an indication of the map's proportions.

✔ Indicate which direction is north with an arrow or a compass symbol.

(*continued*)

WRITER'S CHECKLIST   **Creating and Using Maps** (*continued*)

✔ Emphasize key features by using color, shading, dots, crosshatching, or other appropriate symbols.

✔ Include a key, or legend, that explains what the different colors, shadings, or symbols represent.

✔ Consider **copyright** and potential **plagiarism** when incorporating maps found online into your documents.

maybe / may be

Maybe (one word) is an **adverb** meaning "perhaps." ("*Maybe* the legal staff can resolve this issue.") *May be* (two words) is a **verb** phrase. ("It *may be* necessary to hire a specialist.")

media / medium

Media is the plural of *medium* and requires a plural **verb**.

▶ Many communication *media are* available today.

▶ The Internet *is* a multifaceted *medium*.

M

meetings

Meetings enable people to share information and collaborate more productively than exchanges of multiple messages or conversations allow. Like a **presentation**, a successful meeting requires planning and preparation. See also **selecting the medium**.

Planning a Meeting

Begin by determining the focus of the meeting, deciding who should attend, and choosing the best time and place to hold it. Prepare an agenda for the meeting, and determine who should take the minutes.

Determine the Purpose of the Meeting.   The first step in planning a meeting is to focus on the desired outcome by asking questions to help you determine the meeting's **purpose**: What should participants know, believe, or be able to do as a result of attending the meeting? Once you've narrowed your focus, write a purpose statement for the meeting that answers the questions *what* and *why*.

▶ The purpose of this meeting is to gather ideas from the sales force [*what*] in order to create a successful sales campaign for our new Model PN-4 tablet computer [*why*].

Decide Who Should Attend.   Determine first the key people who need to attend the meeting. If a meeting must be held without some key participants, ask for their contributions prior to the meeting or invite them to participate by speakerphone, videoconference, or other remote methods.

Choose the Meeting Time.   Schedule a meeting for a time when all or most key people can attend. Consider other factors, such as time of day and length of the meeting, that can influence its outcome:

- Monday morning is often a time people use to prepare for the coming week's work.

- Friday afternoon is often when people focus on completing the current week's tasks.

- Long meetings may need to include breaks to allow participants to respond to messages and take restroom breaks.

- Meetings held during the last fifteen minutes of the day will be quick, but few people will remember what happened.

- Remote participants may need consideration for their time zones.

Choose the Meeting Location.   Having a meeting at your own location can give you an advantage: You feel more comfortable than your guests, who are new to the surroundings. Holding the meeting on someone else's premises, however, can signal cooperation. For balance, especially when people are meeting for the first time or are discussing sensitive issues, meet at a neutral site, where no one gains an advantage and attendees may feel freer to participate.

Establish the Agenda.   A tool for focusing the group, the agenda is an outline of what the meeting will address, as shown in Figure M–2. Always prepare an agenda, even if it is only an informal list of main topics. Ideally, the agenda should be distributed to attendees a day or two before the meeting. For a longer meeting in which participants are required to make a presentation, try to distribute the agenda a week or more in advance.

   The agenda should list the attendees, the meeting time and place, and the topics you plan to discuss. If the meeting includes presentations, list the time allotted for each speaker. Finally, indicate an approximate length for the meeting so that participants can plan the rest of their day.

Sales Meeting Agenda

Purpose:	To get input for a sales campaign for the PN-4 Tablet Computer
Date:	Wednesday, May 9, 2018
Place:	Conference Room E
Time:	9:30 a.m.–11:00 a.m.
Attendees:	Advertising Manager, Sales Manager and Reps, Customer Service Manager

Topic	Presenter	Time
PN-4 Tablet	Bob Arbuckle	9:30–9:45
The Campaign	Maria Lopez	9:45–10:00
The Sales Strategy	Mary Winifred	10:00–10:15
Discussion	Led by Dave Grimes	10:15–11:00

FIGURE M–2. Meeting Agenda

If the agenda is distributed in advance of the meeting, it should be accompanied by a memo or an e-mail informing people of the following:

- The purpose of the meeting
- The date and place of the meeting
- The meeting start and stop times
- The names of the people invited
- Instructions on how to prepare for the meeting

Figure M–3 (page 328) shows a cover message to accompany an agenda.

Assign the Minute-Taking. Delegate the minute-taking to someone other than the leader. The minute-taker should record major decisions and assigned tasks. To avoid misunderstandings, clarify that the minute-taker needs to record each assignment, the person responsible for it, and its due date. If the minute-taker will need to follow any legal or organizational rules for recording the minutes, establish that in advance of the meeting. The minute-taker is responsible for distributing the minutes to everyone, including appropriate nonattendees. For a standing committee, it is best to rotate the responsibility of taking minutes. See also **minutes of meetings** and **note-taking**.

| ➤ Send | ✕ Cancel | 📄 Save Draft | 📎 Add Attachment | 📧 Signature | Options ▶ |

TO	Advertising Manager, Sales Manager, Sales Representatives, Customer Service Manager
CC		Show BCC
Subject	Planning Meeting for PN-4 Tablet

📄 Sales Meeting Agenda.doc (29 KB) Download

Purpose of the Meeting
The purpose of this meeting is to get your ideas for the upcoming introduction and sales campaign for our new PN-4 tablet.

Date, Time, and Location
Date: May 9, 2018
Time: 9:30 a.m.–11:00 a.m.
Place: Conference Room E (go to the ground floor, take a right off the elevator, third door on the left)

Attendees
The groups addressed above.

Meeting Preparation
Everyone should be prepared to offer suggestions on the following items:

- Sales features of the new PN-4 tablet
- Techniques for selling the PN-4 tablet
- Customer profile of potential buyers
- FAQs — questions customers may ask
- Anticipated support services (instructions, ancillaries)

Agenda
Please see the attached document.

FIGURE M–3. E-mail Announcing a Meeting with an Attached Agenda

Conducting the Meeting

Assign someone to write on a board or project an image of information that needs to be viewed by everyone present.

During the meeting, keep to your agenda; however, create a productive environment by allowing room for differing views and fostering an environment in which participants listen respectfully to one another.

- Consider the feelings, thoughts, ideas, and needs of others — do not let your own agenda blind you to other points of view.

- Help other participants feel valued and respected by **listening** to them and responding to what they say.

- Respond positively to the comments of others whenever possible.

- Consider communication styles and approaches that are different from your own, particularly those from other cultures. See also **global communication**.

Deal with Conflict.   Despite your best efforts, conflict is inevitable. However, conflict is potentially valuable; when managed positively, it can stimulate creative thinking by challenging complacency and showing ways to achieve goals more efficiently or economically. See **collaborative writing**.

Members of any group are likely to vary in their personalities and attitudes, and you may encounter people who approach meetings differently. Consider the following tactics for the interruptive, negative, rambling, overly quiet, and territorial personality types.

- The *interruptive person* rarely lets anyone finish a sentence and may intimidate the group's quieter members. Tell that person in a firm but nonhostile tone to let the others finish in the interest of getting everyone's input. By addressing the issue directly, you signal to the group the importance of putting common goals first.

- The *negative person* has difficulty accepting change and often considers a new idea or project from a negative point of view. Such negativity, if left unchecked, can demoralize the group and suppress enthusiasm for new ideas. If the negative person brings up a valid point, however, ask for the group's suggestions to remedy the issue being raised. If the negative person's reactions are not valid or are outside the agenda, state the necessity of staying focused on the agenda and perhaps recommend a separate meeting to address those other issues.

- The *rambling person* cannot collect his or her thoughts quickly enough to verbalize them succinctly. Restate or clarify this person's ideas. Try to strike a balance between providing your own interpretation and drawing out the person's intended meaning.

- The *overly quiet person* may be timid or may just be deep in thought. Ask for this person's ideas, being careful not to embarrass the person. In some cases, you can have a quiet person jot down his or her ideas and give them to you later.

- The *territorial person* fiercely defends his or her group against real or perceived threats and may refuse to cooperate with members of other departments, companies, and so on. Point out that although such concerns may be valid, everyone is working toward the same overall goal, and that goal should take precedence.

M

◖ **PROFESSIONALISM NOTE** Many businesses discourage or do not allow smartphones and digital devices in meetings. If your organization allows such devices, meeting attendees should keep them on silent or on vibrator mode and out of sight so that they do not interrupt the meeting. If you are expecting a crucial call, inform the meeting chair and leave the room to respond. The best practice is to have a colleague or your assistant take the call or bring a note to you in the meeting when the call comes in. ◗

Close the Meeting.   Just before closing the meeting, review all decisions and assignments. Paraphrase each to help the group focus on what individual participants have agreed to do and to ensure that the minutes will be complete and accurate. Now is the time to raise questions and to clarify any misunderstandings. Set a date by which everyone at the meeting can expect to receive copies of the minutes. Finally, thank everyone for participating, and close the meeting on a positive note.

WRITER'S CHECKLIST   **Planning and Conducting Meetings**

✔ Develop a purpose statement for the meeting to focus your planning.

✔ Invite only those essential to fulfilling the purpose of the meeting.

✔ Select a time and place convenient to all those attending.

✔ Create an agenda, and distribute it at least a day or two before the meeting.

✔ Assign someone to take meeting minutes.

✔ Ensure that the minutes record key decisions; assignments; due dates; and the date, time, and location of any follow-up meeting.

✔ Follow the agenda to keep everyone focused.

✔ Respect the views of others and how they are expressed.

✔ Use the strategies in this entry for handling conflict and attendees whose style of expression may make it difficult to get everyone's best thinking.

✔ Close the meeting by reviewing key decisions and assignments.

---

memos

Memos use a standard format (*To:*, *From:*, *Date:*, *Subject:*). Even for organizations in which **e-mail** messages are used for routine communication and other internal documents, a printed or an attached memo with organizational letterhead can communicate with formality and authority. In addition, a memo can offer the full range of word-processing features for short **reports** and **proposals**. Paper memos are also useful in manu-facturing and service industries, as well as in other businesses where employees do not have easy access to e-mail. For a discussion of writing strategies for memos, see **correspondence**. See also **selecting the medium**.

Memo Format

The memo shown in Figure M–4 (page 332) illustrates a typical memo format. As this example illustrates, the use of **headings** and **lists** foster clarity by providing **emphasis** and highlighting organization. See also **letters**. For a discussion of subject lines, see page 117.

◀ **PROFESSIONALISM NOTE** As with e-mail, be alert to the practices of address-ing and distributing memos in your organization. Consider who should receive or needs to be copied on a memo and in what order—senior managers, for example, take precedence over junior managers. If rank does not apply, alphabetizing recipients by last name is safe. ▶

Some organizations ask writers to initial or sign formal memos that are printed (*hard copy*) to verify that the writer accepts responsibility for a memo's content.

methods of development

M

A logical method of development satisfies the readers' need for shape and structure in a document, whether it is an **e-mail**, a **report**, or a Web page. It helps you as a writer move smoothly and logically from the **introduction** to a **conclusion**. Choose the method or combination of methods that best suits your subject, **audience**, and **purpose**. Following are the most common methods.

- **Cause-and-effect method of development** begins with either the cause or the effect of an event. This approach can be used to develop a report that offers a solution to a problem, beginning with the problem and moving on to the solution, or vice versa.

- **Chronological method of development** emphasizes the time element of a sequence, as in an **incident report** that traces events as they occurred in time.

- **Comparison method of development** is useful when writing about a new topic that is in many ways similar to another topic that is more familiar to your readers.

- **Definition method of development** extends definitions with details, examples, comparisons, or other explanatory devices. See also **defining terms**.

Professional Publishing Services

MEMORANDUM

TO: Barbara Smith, Publications Manager

FROM: Hannah Kaufman, Vice President *HK* — Handwritten initials may be used with printed formal memos.

DATE: April 13, 2018

SUBJECT: Schedule for ACM Electronics Brochures

ACM Electronics has asked us to prepare a comprehensive set of brochures for its Milwaukee office by August 10, 2018. We have worked with similar firms in the past, so this job should be relatively easy to prepare. I estimate that the job will take nearly two months. Ted Harris has requested time and cost estimates for the project. Fred Moore in production will prepare the cost estimates, and I would like you to prepare a tentative schedule for the project.

Additional Personnel
In preparing the schedule, check the status of the following:
- Production schedule for all staff writers
- Availability of freelance writers
- Availability of dependable graphic designers

Ordinarily, we would not need to depend on outside personnel; however, because our bid for the *Wall Street Journal* special project is still under consideration, we could be short of staff in June and July. Further, we have to consider vacations that have already been approved.

Time Estimates
Please give me time estimates by April 20. A successful job done on time will give us a good chance to obtain the contract to do ACM Electronics' annual report for its stockholders' meeting this fall.

I am mailing separately several brochures that may be helpful.

cc: Ted Harris, President — Copy notation may be placed at top with memo heading.
       Fred Moore, Production Editor

FIGURE M–4. Typical Memo Format (Printed or Attached to E-mail)

- **Division-and-classification method of development** either separates a whole into component parts and discusses each part separately (*division*) or groups parts into categories that clarify the relationship of the parts (*classification*).

- **General and specific methods of development** proceed either from general information to specific details or from specific information to a general conclusion.

- **Order-of-importance method of development** presents information in either decreasing order of importance, as in a **proposal** that begins with the most important point, or increasing order of importance, as in a **presentation** that ends with the most important point.

- **Sequential method of development** emphasizes the order of elements in a process and is particularly useful when writing step-by-step **instructions**.

- **Spatial method of development** describes the physical appearance of an object or area from top to bottom, inside to outside, front to back, and so on.

Rarely does a writer rely on only one of these methods. Documents often blend methods of development. For example, in a report that describes the organization of a company, you might use elements from three methods of development. You could divide the larger topic (the company) into operations (division and classification), arrange the operations according to what you see as their impact within the company (order of importance), and present their manufacturing operations in the order they occur (sequential). When **outlining** a document, you may base your major division on one primary method of development appropriate to your purpose and then subordinate other methods to it.

minutes of meetings

Organizations and committees refer to official records of their **meetings** as *minutes*. Because minutes are often used to record decisions and to settle disputes, they must be accurate, complete, and clear. When approved, minutes of meetings are official and can be used as evidence in legal proceedings. A section from the minutes of a meeting is shown in Figure M–5 (page 334).

Keep your minutes brief and to the point. Except for recording formally presented motions, which must be transcribed word for word, summarize what occurs and paraphrase discussions. To keep the minutes concise, follow a set format, and use **headings** for each major point discussed. See also **note-taking**.

M

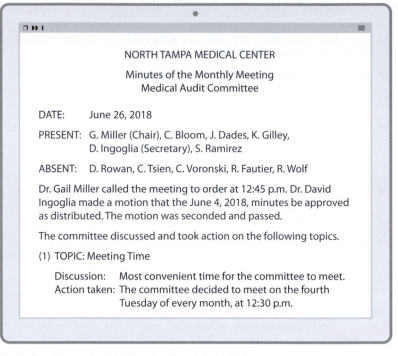

FIGURE M–5. Minutes of a Meeting (Partial Section)

Avoid abstractions and generalities; always be specific. Refer to everyone in the same way—a lack of consistency in titles or names may suggest deference to one person at the expense of another. Avoid **adjectives** and **adverbs** that suggest good or bad qualities, as in "Mr. Sturgess's *capable* assistant read the *comprehensive* report to the subcommittee." Minutes should be objective and impartial.

If a member of the committee is to follow up on something and report back to the committee at its next meeting, clearly state the person's name and the responsibility he or she has accepted.

WRITER'S CHECKLIST   **Items to Include in Minutes of Meetings**

✔ The name of the group or committee holding the meeting
✔ The topic of the meeting
✔ The kind of meeting (a regular meeting or a special meeting called to discuss a specific subject or problem)

(continued)

✔ The number of members present and, for committees or boards of ten or fewer members, the names of those present and absent

✔ The place, time, and date of the meeting

✔ A statement that the chair and the secretary were present or the names of any substitutes

✔ A statement that the minutes of the previous meeting were approved or revised

✔ A list of any reports that were read and approved

✔ All the main motions that were made, with statements as to whether they were carried, defeated, or tabled (vote postponed), and the names of those who made and seconded the motions (motions that were withdrawn are not mentioned)

✔ A full description of resolutions that were adopted and a simple statement of any that were rejected

✔ A record of all ballots, indicating the number of votes cast for and against resolutions

✔ The time the meeting was adjourned (officially ended) and the place, time, and date of the next meeting

✔ The recording secretary's signature and typed name and, if desired, the signature of the chairperson

M

mission statements

A mission statement articulates an organization's unique reason for being and attempts to motivate its stakeholders (employees, customers, and stockholders) to pursue common goals. (See **audience**.) A good mission statement can achieve a focused allocation of organizational resources by answering questions such as the following: Why do we exist? What is our business? What are we trying to accomplish? A good mission statement can foster the success of an organization.

Mission statements can be distributed in an organization's **annual report**, framed for display, or repurposed for the Web and **social media** applications. (See also **repurposing**.) Figure M–6 (page 336) shows a typical mission statement.

Writing a Mission Statement

Most mission statements have certain elements in common, such as a statement of purpose; a description of the organization's line of business; and an acknowledgment of the organization's stakeholders, including

BARTLETT BANKARD MISSION STATEMENT

Core goal

The strategic mission of Bartlett Bankard Corporation is to build high-performance, full-service community banks where people matter.

How goal will be achieved

We offer and deliver competitive product lines that meet targeted customer needs and expectations while maintaining asset quality, capital strength, and earnings performance. We provide those products only when we are able to deliver them with the service and quality our customers deserve. For the Corporation to continue to fulfill these goals, we must be able to guarantee that the four cornerstones of our success — our customers, our employees, our communities, and our shareholders — are always firmly in place.

We must respond to:

Our customers: They are our business. We will provide them with the products they want and need.

Our employees: They are The Bank. Our customers know them as The Bank. We will provide them with the training, the working environment, and the recognition that encourage and promote growth.

Commitment to stakeholders

Our communities: Their success is our success. As a corporation and personally as individuals, we will meet the financial and public service needs of our communities.

Our shareholders: They are the owners of the Corporation, and as our shareholders, they are entitled to a fair return on their investment.

FIGURE M–6. Mission Statement

customers, employees, and stockholders. Following is a list of various goals that mission statements may be aimed to achieve:

- Reflect an organization's purpose, function, and primary reason for existing
- Guide the development and execution of organizational strategies

- Offer benchmarks toward which long-range goals can be targeted and against which progress can be measured

- Build and communicate company values over periods of time, thus providing an organization and its employees with a sense of identity

- Distinguish an organization from others of the same type, and identify the scope of the organization's operations in product and market terms

Before beginning to write a mission statement, get approval of your general approach from top management. Then determine who will write the draft. In a small organization, the top person normally writes it. In a large organization, it is often written by a committee made up of representatives from key stakeholder groups.

Gather as much information as possible about your organization and its goals by interviewing top management and researching annual reports and other company documents. If you have a committee to assist you, use **brainstorming** to answer the following questions, which will help you understand the **context** of the mission statement:

- Why was our organization established?

- Who are our customers and clients? What needs do we meet?

- What image do we want our products and services to project?

- What message do we want to send the community, customers, stockholders, and employees about the organization?

- Where do we see our organization in five or ten years?

- What does our organizational culture need to be to get us there?

Next, create an outline (see **outlining**) and then write a draft (see **writing a draft**). As you write, try to find words and phrases that capture the essence of the organization's purpose and goals. Avoid **jargon**, **buzzwords**, platitudes, meaningless superlatives, overuse of the word *quality*, and other language that can move readers to cynicism. A mission to "Be the best computer manufacturer in the world" sounds good, but "To develop products that adapt to the ever-changing needs of our customers" is a good deal more definable, measurable, and actionable—and it is motivational.

When you are satisfied with your draft, circulate it to selected reviewers (involving as many employees, customers, and stockholders as possible, to give everyone a sense of ownership). Then revise the draft based on the feedback you receive.

Format and Length

The format and length may vary, from a pithy one-sentence statement—such as a pet-food company's concise "To enhance the well-being of

M

dogs and cats"—to a longer document that includes the company's vision, values, philosophy, objectives, and strategies. Avoid a lengthy mission statement because readers will more readily remember a shorter statement and incorporate its values into their daily business activities and planning. You can find mission statements at organizational Web sites as well as at general sites, such as www.missionstatements.com. See also **business plans**.

mixed constructions

A mixed construction is a sentence in which the elements do not sensibly fit together. The problem may be a **grammar** error, a **logic error**, or both.

> ▶ Because the copier wouldn't start ~~explains why~~ we called a technician.

The original sentence mixes a subordinate **clause** (*because the copier wouldn't start*) with a **verb** (*explains*) that attempts to incorrectly use the subordinate clause as its subject. The revision correctly uses the **pronoun** *we* as the subject of the main clause. See also **sentence construction**.

M

modifiers

Modifiers are words, phrases, or clauses that expand, limit, or make more specific the meaning of other elements in a sentence. Although we can create sentences without modifiers, we often need the detail and clarification they provide.

WITHOUT MODIFIERS   Production decreased.

WITH MODIFIERS   *Glucose* production decreased *rapidly*.

Most modifiers function as **adjectives** or **adverbs**. Adjectives describe qualities or impose boundaries on the words they modify.

> ▶ *noisy* machinery, *ten* files, *this* printer, *a* workstation

An adverb modifies an adjective, another adverb, a **verb**, or an entire **clause**.

> ▶ Under test conditions, the brake pad showed *much* less wear than it did under actual conditions. [The adverb *much* modifies the adjective *less*.]

> ▶ The redesigned brake pad lasted *much* longer. [The adverb *much* modifies another adverb *longer*.]

▶ The wrecking ball hit the wall of the building *hard*. [The adverb *hard* modifies the verb *hit*.]

▶ *Surprisingly*, the motor failed even after passing all those durability and performance tests. [The adverb *surprisingly* modifies an entire clause.]

Adverbs are **intensifiers** when they increase the impact of adjectives (*very* fine, *too* high) or adverbs (*very* slowly, *rather* quickly). Be cautious using intensifiers; their overuse can lead to vagueness and a resulting lack of precision.

Stacked (Jammed) Modifiers

Stacked (or *jammed*) modifiers are strings of modifiers preceding **nouns** that make writing unclear or difficult to read.

▶ Your *staffing-level authorization reassessment* plan should result in a major improvement.

The noun *plan* is preceded by three long modifiers, a string that forces the reader to slow down to interpret its meaning. Stacked modifiers often result from the overuse of **buzzwords** or **jargon**. See how breaking up the stacked modifiers makes the example easier to read.

▶ Your plan for reassessing the staffing-level authorizations should result in a major improvement.

Misplaced Modifiers

A modifier is misplaced when it applies to the wrong word or phrase. A misplaced modifier can cause **ambiguity**.

▶ We *almost* lost all the files. [The files were *almost* lost but were not.]

▶ We lost *almost* all the files. [Most of the files were in fact lost.]

Note the two meanings possible when the phrase is shifted in the following sentences:

▶ The equipment *without the accessories* sold the best. [Different types of equipment were available, some with and some without accessories.]

▶ The equipment sold the best *without the accessories*. [One type of equipment was available, and the accessories were optional.]

To avoid ambiguity, place clauses as close as possible to the words they modify.

M

REMOTE	We sent the brochure to several local firms *that had four-color art.*
CLOSE	We sent the brochure *that had four-color art* to several local firms.

Squinting Modifiers

A squinting modifier is one that can be interpreted as modifying either of two sentence elements simultaneously, thereby confusing readers about which is intended.

▶ We agreed *on the next day* to make the adjustments. [Did they agree *to make the adjustments* on the next day? Or on the next day, did they agree *to make the adjustments*?]

A squinting modifier can sometimes be corrected simply by changing its position, but often it is better to rewrite the sentence.

▶ We agreed that *on the next day* we would make the adjustments. [The adjustments were to be made *on the next day*.]

▶ *On the next day*, we agreed that we would make the adjustments. [The agreement was made *on the next day*.]

See also **dangling modifiers**.

mood

The grammatical term *mood* refers to the **verb** functions that indicate whether the verb is intended to make a statement, ask a question, give a command, or express a hypothetical possibility.

The *indicative mood* states a fact, gives an opinion, or asks a question.

▶ The setting *is* correct. / *Is* the setting correct?

The *imperative mood* expresses a command, suggestion, request, or plea. In the imperative mood, the implied subject *you* is not expressed. ("*Install* the system today.")

The *subjunctive mood* expresses something that is contrary to fact or that is conditional, hypothetical, or purely imaginative; it can also express a wish, a doubt, or a possibility. In the subjunctive mood, *were* is used instead of *was* in clauses that speculate about the present or future, and the base form (*be*) is used following certain verbs, such as *propose*, *request*, or *insist*. See also progressive **tense**.

▶ If we *were* to close the sale today, we would meet our monthly goal.

▶ The senior partner insisted that she [I, you, we, they] *be* the project leader.

The most common use of the subjunctive mood is to express that the writer considers a condition to be contrary to fact. If the condition is not considered to be contrary to fact, use the indicative mood.

SUBJUNCTIVE   If I *were* president of the firm, I would change several hiring policies.

INDICATIVE   Although I *am* president of the firm, I don't control every aspect of its policies.

Ms. / Miss / Mrs.

Ms. is used in business and public life to address or refer to a woman. Some women may indicate a preference for *Ms.*, *Miss*, or *Mrs.*, which you should honor. If a woman has an academic or a professional title, use the appropriate form of address (*Doctor*, *Professor*, *Captain*) instead of *Ms.*, *Miss*, or *Mrs.* See also **biased language**.

M

mutual / common

Common is used when two or more persons (or things) share something or possess it jointly.

▶ We have a *common* desire to make the program succeed.

▶ Our departments have *common* office space.

Mutual may also mean "shared" (*mutual* friend, of *mutual* benefit), but it usually implies something given and received reciprocally and is used with reference to only two persons or parties.

▶ Evans respects Roth, and from my observations, the respect is *mutual*. [Roth also respects Evans.]

N

narration

Narration is a writing that describes a series of events in a prescribed (often chronological) sequence. Much narrative writing explains how something happened: a laboratory procedure, a site visit, an accident, a decision reached at an important meeting. See also **chronological method of development**, **trip reports**, and **incident reports**.

Effective narration rests on two key writing techniques: a careful, accurate sequencing of events and a consistent **point of view** on the part of the narrator. Narrative sequence and essential shifts in the sequence are signaled in three ways: chronology (clock and calendar time), transitional words pertaining to time (*before*, *after*, *next*, *first*, *while*, *then*), and verb tenses that indicate whether something has happened (past **tense**) or is under way (present tense). The point of view indicates the writer's relation to the information being narrated as reflected in the use of **person**. Narration usually expresses a first- or third-person point of view. First-person narration indicates that the writer is a participant, and third-person narration indicates that the writer is writing about what happened to someone or something else.

The narrative shown in Figure N–1 tells the story of a train accident at the Chicago Loop in detail so that any lessons learned could be used to improve safety. Although narration often exists in combination with other forms of discourse (**description**, **exposition**, **persuasion**), avoid interrupting a narrative with lengthy explanations or analyses. Explain only what a reader would need to follow the events. See **audience**.

nature

Nature, when used to mean "kind" or "sort," is vague. Avoid this usage in your writing. Say exactly what you mean.

► The ~~nature of~~ *exclusionary clause in* the contract caused the problem.

The Accident

On the morning of the accident, two night-shift signal maintainers were repairing a switch at tower 18. Between 4:00 and 4:30 a.m., two day-shift maintainers joined them.[1] As the two crews conferred about the progress of the repair, Green Line train run 1 approached the tower. A trainee was operating the train, and a train operator/line instructor[2] was observing. Both crew members on the train later stated that they had not heard the control center's radioed advisory that workers were on the track structure at tower 18. The line instructor said that as the train approached the tower with a *proceed* (green) signal, he observed wayside maintenance personnel from about 150 feet away and told the trainee to stop the train, which he did. One of the maintainers gave the train a hand signal to proceed, and the train continued on its way. Shortly after the train left, the night-shift maintainers also left.

> Context, conditions leading to accident

The day-shift maintainers continued to work. Just before the accident, they removed a defective part and started to install a replacement. According to both men, they were squatting over the switch machine. One was facing the center of the track and attaching wires, while the other was facing the Loop with his back to the normal direction of train movements. He was shining a flashlight on the work area.

> Sequence of events prior to accident

The accident train approached the tower on the *proceed* signal. One maintainer later said that he remembered being hit by the train, while the other said that he was hit by "something." A train operator/line instructor was operating the train, and a trainee was observing. Both later said that they had not seen any wayside workers. They said that they had heard noise that the student described as a "thump" in the vicinity of the accident and caught a "glimpse" of something.

> Description of accident

Both maintainers later stated that they had not seen or heard the train as it approached. After being struck, one of the maintainers fell from the structure. The other fell to the deck of the platform on the outside of the structure. He used his radio to tell the control center that he and another maintainer had been "hit by the train." Emergency medical personnel were dispatched to the scene, and an ambulance took both men to a local hospital.

In the meantime, the accident train continued past the tower and stopped at the next station, Clark and Lake, where the crew members inspected the train from the platform and found no damage. They continued on their way until they heard the radio report that workers had been struck by a train. They stopped their train at the next station and reported to a supervisor.

According to the operator of the accident train, nothing had distracted her from her duties, and she had been facing forward and watching the track before the train arrived at tower 18. The trainee supported her account. Both crew members said that they had not heard the control center's radioed advisory that workers were on the track structure at tower 18.

> Third-person account of events

---

[1] All times referred to in this report are central standard time.
[2] Line instructors are working train operators who provide on-the-job training to operator trainees.

FIGURE N–1. Narration from an Accident Report
SOURCE: National Transportation Safety Board, "Railroad Accident Brief: Chicago Transit Authority, DCA-02-FR-005, Chicago, Illinois, February 26, 2002." www.ntsb.gov /investigations/AccidentReports/Reports/RAB0304.pdf

needless to say

The phrase *needless to say* sometimes occurs in speech and writing. Eliminate the phrase, or replace it with a more descriptive **word choice**.

▶ ~~Needless to say,~~ *Service logs indicate that* staff reductions have decreased customer loyalty.

newsletter articles

If your organization publishes a **newsletter**, you may be asked to contribute an article on a subject in your area of expertise. In fact, an article is a good way to promote your work or your department.

Before you begin to write, consider the traditional questions of journalism (*Who* did it? *What* was done? *Where* was it done? *When* was it done? *Why* was it done?) and then add *how*, which may be of as much interest to your colleagues as any of the five *w*'s. Next, determine whether the company or management has an official policy toward or attitude about your subject. If it does, adhere to it as you prepare your article. See also **audience** and **context**.

Review several fairly recent issues of the newsletter, and study the **style** and **tone** of the writing and the approach used for various kinds of subjects. Then ask yourself the following question about your subject: What is its significance to the organization and to my coworkers? The answer to that question should help you establish the style, tone, and approach for your article and also heavily influence your conclusion.

Research for a newsletter article frequently consists of **interviewing for information**. Interview key personnel concerned with your subject. Get all available information and all points of view. Be sure to give maximum credit to the maximum number of people by quoting statements from those involved in projects and naming those who have developed initiatives. See also **quotations**.

Figure N–2 shows an article written for *Connection*, a newsletter produced by Ken Cook Company and distributed to current and prospective clients. This article describes how the company employed a third-party expert to perform an audit of the company's Quality Management System (designed to comply with ISO 9001:2000 standards). Notice the inset quotation (sometimes called a *pull quote*), which draws **readers** to the article and gives them a sense of the article's content. By describing this process, the article aims to demonstrate Ken Cook Company's "commitment to quality."

What Does ISO 9001:2000 Mean to the Supply Chain?

You may have noticed that some companies promote their goods and services as ISO 9001:2000 certified. But what does that mean to the supply chain? If you're responsible for making the purchasing decisions at your company, you're looking for a supplier that provides consistent, conforming, quality products and/or services.

According to the International Organization for Standardization (ISO) website, "The objective of ISO 9001:2000 is to provide a set of requirements that, if they are effectively implemented, will provide you with confidence that your supplier can consistently provide goods and services that meet your needs and expectations and comply with applicable regulations."

ISO 9001:2000 is a recognized international standard that sets the criteria for an organization's Quality Management System (QMS). Those companies that are ISO certified have a QMS meeting the requirements of ISO 9001:2000, the only standard in the ISO 9000 family that can be used for the purpose of conformity assessment.

To provide its clients with the highest level of confidence in its products and services, and to meet all stated requirements and applicable regulatory requirements, Ken Cook Co. pursues continuous improvement and the highest level of a Quality Management System in order to comply with ISO 9001:2000.

In 2003, Ken Cook Co. sought out an accredited, impartial third-party certification body to perform an audit of its QMS. Ken Cook Co. chose an accredited organization in order to verify the certifying body's independence and competence to carry out the certification process.

The certification body selected was accredited by ANAB (formerly ANSI-RAB), the accreditation body of the American National Standards Institute (ANSI) and the American Society for Quality (ASQ). As a result, Ken Cook Co.'s QMS was assessed and certified as meeting the requirements of ISO 9001:2000.

> ❝ **Ken Cook Co.'s internal audit process documentation indicates excellent methodology for system monitoring. This is a best practice system.** ❞
>
> *- Wayne Uttke, lead auditor, Verisys Registrars*

As a purchaser, this information should provide you with confidence in Ken Cook Co.'s ability to provide consistent, conforming goods and services. ISO 9001:2000 requires Ken Cook Co. to monitor the levels of satisfaction of its customers and to provide feedback in order to improve the effectiveness of its QMS.

Ken Cook Co. has maintained ISO certification since 2003 and successfully renewed certification in July 2006. The

certifying body deemed several internal activities as best practices—including management planning and review and Ken Cook Co.'s internal auditing system.

Regarding the internal auditing system, Wayne Uttke, lead auditor for Verisys Registrars, noted, "Ken Cook Co.'s internal audit process documentation indicates excellent methodology for system monitoring. This is a best practice system."

Ken Cook Co. is pleased to have incorporated these, and other high standards into every aspect of its day-to-day business. Robert T. Haukohl, Executive Vice President overseeing production operations, confirmed, "ISO 9001:2000 is now working seamlessly within Ken Cook Co. and has been fully integrated into our business model. This is exactly what we have been striving for and takes us to a new level of quality management."

ISO 9001:2000 is a useful basis for organizations to be able to demonstrate that they are managing their business to achieve consistent quality goods and services. As a supply chain tool, this ISO standard can provide you with the confidence that your supplier understands what you expect from them and the peace of mind that its Quality Management System has been recognized as superior. Ken Cook Co. is your partner in product documentation and demonstrates its commitment to quality through successful attainment of ISO 9001:2000 and continuous improvement.

World Class Owner's Manuals at IBEX *(continued from page 2)*

At the trade show, Ken Cook Co. is offering a coupon that entitles the bearer one free evaluation of their current boat owner's manual, a $250 value. The evaluation will report on compliance with the ABYC T-24 elements, ISO/DIS 10240 elements and a CE certification checklist.

Come to IBEX 2006 for the Ken Cook Co. presentation of "World Class Owner Manuals" Workshop. The workshop is free to attendees at IBEX 2006, but seating is limited—so come early! Renowned professionals in the boatbuilding industry will discuss how you can advance your business, gain a

clear understanding of the evolving government and industry regulations worldwide and hear about new processes being used in boatbuilding today. While you're there, also visit Ken Cook Co. at Booth 1118.

6   www.kencook.com   October/November 2006

N

Ken Cook/De Santis Collection

FIGURE N–2. Newsletter Article

WRITER'S CHECKLIST   **Writing Newsletter Articles**

✔ Write an intriguing **title** to catch the audience's attention; **rhetorical questions** often work well.

✔ Include as many eye-catching **photographs** or **visuals** as appropriate to entice your audience to read the lead **paragraph** of your **introduction**. See also **layout and design**.

(continued)

✔ Fashion a lead (or *lede*), or first paragraph, that will encourage further reading. The first paragraph generally makes the **transition** from the title to the body of the article.

✔ Offer a well-developed presentation of your subject to hold readers' interest to the end of the article.

✔ Write a **conclusion** that emphasizes the significance of your subject to your audience and stresses the points you want your readers to retain. See **emphasis**.

✔ Follow the steps listed in the "Checklist of the Writing Process" on pages xxv–xxvi as you prepare your newsletter article.

newsletters

Newsletters are designed to inform and to create and sustain interest and membership in an organization. They can also be used to sell products and services. We show an example of a newsletter in the entry **newsletter articles** (page 344). The Web site for the American Marketing Association also provides a number of sample e-newsletters (www.ama .org/publications/eNewsletters/Pages/default.aspx). See also **blogs and forums**.

Types of Newsletters

Organizational newsletters, like the one shown in Figure N–2 (page 345), are sent to employees, clients, or members of an association to keep them informed about issues regarding their company or group, such as the development of new products or policies or the accomplishments of individuals or teams. Stories in organizational newsletters can both enhance the group's image and foster pride among employees of the organization's products or services. For example, Figure N–2 shows how important quality management is to Ken Cook Company.

Subscription newsletters are designed to attract and build a readership interested in buying specific products or services or in learning more about a specific subject. Subscribers are buying information, and they expect value for their money. For example, a person with experience in the stock market could create a financial newsletter and charge subscribers a monthly fee for the investing advice in that newsletter; a person who collects movie memorabilia could create an online newsletter that includes stories about ways to find and sell rare movie posters.

Developing Newsletters

Before you begin to develop a newsletter, decide on its **purpose** and the specific **audience** you will target; then make sure the newsletter's appearance and content reflect the shared interests and values of the readership. Newsletters often involve **collaborative writing** in which different individuals work on design, content, and project management. See also **persuasion** and **promotional writing**. If you are asked to contribute an article to a newsletter, see **newsletter articles**.

You will need to develop a contact list of your readers and decide on the most strategic way to get the newsletter to these readers: postal mail, interoffice mail, e-mail, or Web or blog posting. Consider using a list-hosting service.*

◖ **PROFESSIONALISM NOTE** Update your subscriber lists regularly to be sure you are contacting only those who wish to continue receiving your newsletter. You risk damaging your reputation and that of your company if you badger former customers or current clients with unwanted mail or e-mail. Include an opt-out waiver with each newsletter sent, giving subscribers the opportunity to remove themselves from your mailing list. If sending a newsletter electronically, be sure to include opt-out instructions to ensure compliance with such laws as the CAN-SPAM Act of 2003. ◗

Your **research** should include a review of trade journals, industry blogs, business and technology magazines, Web news sites, and other sources to find specific angles for the articles that will appeal to your select audience. Attempt to provide content that your readers will not find elsewhere—for example, by interviewing and profiling customers, association members, or employees. Check your facts meticulously—newsletter readers are generally specialists in their fields. Because newsletters are often distributed to branches and clients abroad, see **global communication** and **global graphics**. See also **interviewing for information**.

As shown in Figure N–2, a newsletter's format should be simple and consistent yet visually appealing to your readership. Use the active **voice** and a conversational **tone**. Use **headings** and bullets to break up the text, and make the newsletter easy to read. Keep your sentences simple and your paragraphs short. See **conciseness** and **layout and design**.

Using desktop-publishing or Web-development software, create newspaper columns and one or two **visuals** per page that complement the text. On the front page, identify the organization and include the date, volume and issue numbers, and a contents box. For Web newsletters, follow the principles of good Web design. See also **photographs** and **writing for the Web**.

---

*E-mail list-hosting services have their own servers and provide commercial delivery of premium e-mail that often contains graphic and other digital forms used for advertising.

N

nominalizations

A nominalization is a **noun** form of a **verb** that is often combined with vague and general (or "weak") verbs, like *make*, *do*, *give*, *perform*, and *provide*. Avoid nominalizations when you can use specific verbs that communicate the same idea more directly and concisely.

▶ The staff should ~~perform an evaluation of~~ *evaluate* the new software.

If you use nominalizations solely to make your writing sound more formal, the result will be **affectation**. See also **business writing style**, **conciseness**, **plain language**, and **voice**.

none

None can be either a singular or a plural **pronoun**, depending on the context. See also **agreement**.

▶ *None* of the material *has* been ordered. [Always use a singular **verb** with a singular **noun**—in this case, "material."]

▶ *None* of the clients *has* been called yet. [Use a singular verb even with a plural noun (*clients*) if the intended emphasis is on the idea of *not one*.]

▶ *None* of the clients *have* been called yet. [Use a plural verb if you intend *none* to refer to all clients.]

For **emphasis**, substitute *no one* or *not one* for *none* and use a singular verb.

▶ We paid the retail price for three of the machines, ~~none~~ *not one* of which was worth the money.

nor / or

Nor always follows *neither* in sentences with continuing negation. ("They will *neither* support *nor* approve the plan.") Likewise, *or* follows *either* in sentences. ("The firm will accept *either* a short-term *or* a long-term loan.")

Two or more singular subjects joined by *or* or *nor* usually take a singular **verb**. However, when one subject is singular and one is plural, the verb agrees with the subject nearer to it. See also **conjunctions** and **parallel structure**.

SINGULAR   Neither the *architect* nor the *client was* happy with the design.

PLURAL   Neither the *architect* nor the *clients were* happy with the design.

SINGULAR   Neither the *architects* nor the *client was* happy with the design.

note-taking

The purpose of note-taking is to summarize and record information you extract during **research**. The challenge in taking notes is to condense someone else's thoughts into your own words without distorting the original thinking. As you extract information, let your knowledge of the **audience** and the **purpose** of your writing guide you. For taking notes at a meeting, see **minutes of meetings**.

❖ **ETHICS NOTE** Resist copying your source word for word as you take notes; instead, paraphrase the author's idea or concept. If you only change a few words from a source and incorporate that text into your document without giving credit to your source, you will be guilty of **plagiarism**. See also **paraphrasing**. ❖

If an expert source states something that is especially precise, striking, or noteworthy or that reinforces your point, you can justifiably quote the source directly and incorporate it into your document. If you use a direct quotation, enclose the material in **quotation marks** in your notes. In your finished writing, document the source of your quotation. You will rarely need to quote anything longer than a paragraph. See also **documenting sources** and **quotations**.

When taking notes on abstract ideas, as opposed to factual data, do not sacrifice **clarity** for brevity—notes expressing concepts can lose their meaning if they are too brief. The test is whether you can understand the note a week later and recall the significant ideas of the passage.

N

WRITER'S CHECKLIST   **Taking Notes**

✔ Ask yourself the following questions: What information do I need to fulfill my purpose? What are the needs of my audience?

✔ Record only the most important ideas and concepts. Be sure to record all vital names, dates, and definitions.

✔ When in doubt about whether to take a note, consider the difficulty of finding the source again should you want it later.

✔ Use direct or indirect quotations when sources state something that is precise, striking, or noteworthy, or that succinctly reinforces a point you are making.

✔ Photocopy, scan, or download pages, and highlight passages that you intend to quote.

✔ Give proper credit. Record the author; title; publisher; place; page number; URL; and date of publication, posting, or retrieval. (On subsequent notes from the same source, include only the author and page number or URL.)

(continued)

WRITER'S CHECKLIST **Taking Notes** (*continued*)

✔ Record notes in a way that you find efficient and useful for **outlining**, whether using the latest note-taking software or traditional index cards.

✔ Check your notes for accuracy against the original material before moving on to another source.

Nouns

DIRECTORY

A noun is a **part of speech** that names a person, a place, a thing, a concept, an action, or a quality.

Types of Nouns

The two basic types of nouns are proper nouns and common nouns. *Proper nouns*, which are capitalized, name specific people, places, and things (*H. G. Wells, Boston, United Nations, Nobel Prize*). See also **capitalization**.

Common nouns, which are not capitalized unless they begin sentences or appear in **titles**, name general classes or categories of persons, places, things, concepts, actions, and qualities (*writer, city, organization, award*). Common nouns include concrete nouns, abstract nouns, collective nouns, count nouns, and mass nouns.

Concrete nouns are common nouns used to identify those things that can be discerned by the five senses (*paper, keyboard, glue, nail, grease*).

Abstract nouns are common nouns that name ideas, qualities, or concepts that cannot be discerned by the five senses (*loyalty, pride, valor, peace, devotion*).

Collective nouns are common nouns that indicate a group or collection. They are plural in meaning but singular in form (*audience, jury, staff, committee*). (See "Collective Nouns" on page 351 for advice on using singular or plural forms with collective nouns.)

Count nouns are concrete nouns that identify things that can be separated into countable units (*desks, envelopes, printers, pencils, books*).

Mass nouns are concrete nouns that identify things that cannot be separated into countable units (*water, air, electricity, oil, cement*). See also **English as a second language**.

Noun Functions

Nouns function as subjects of **verbs**, direct and indirect objects of verbs, objects of **prepositions**, subjective and objective **complements**, or **appositives**.

▶ The *metal* failed during the test. [subject]

▶ The bricklayer cemented the *blocks* efficiently. [direct object of a verb]

▶ The state presented our *department* a safety award. [indirect object]

▶ The event occurred within the *year*. [object of a preposition]

▶ A dynamo is a *generator*. [subjective complement]

▶ The regional manager was appointed *chairperson*. [objective complement]

▶ Philip Garcia, the *treasurer*, gave his report last. [appositive]

Words normally used as nouns can also be used as **adjectives** and **adverbs**.

▶ It is *company* policy. [adjective]

▶ He went *home*. [adverb]

Collective Nouns

When a collective noun refers to a group as a whole, it takes a singular verb and pronoun.

▶ The staff *was* divided on the issue and could not reach *its* decision until May 15.

When a collective noun refers to individuals within a group, it takes a plural verb and pronoun.

▶ The staff *have returned* to *their* offices after the conference.

A better way to emphasize the individuals on the staff would be to use the phrase *the staff members*.

▶ The staff members *have returned* to *their* offices after the conference.

Treat organization names and titles as singular.

▶ LRM Associates *has* grown 30 percent in the last three years; *it* will move to a new facility in January.

N

Plural Nouns

Most nouns form the plural by adding -s (*desk/desks, pen/pens*). Nouns ending in *ch, s, sh, x,* and *z* form the plural by adding -es.

▶ *search/searches, glass/glasses, wish/wishes, six/sixes, buzz/buzzes*

Nouns that end in a consonant plus *y* form the plural by changing the *y* to *ies* (*delivery/deliveries*). Some nouns ending in *o* add -es to form the plural, but others add only -s (*tomato/tomatoes, dynamo/dynamos*). Some nouns ending in *f* or *fe* add -s to form the plural; others change the *f* or *fe* to *ves*.

▶ cliff/cliffs, cafe/cafes, hoof/hooves, knife/knives

Some nouns require an internal change to form the plural.

▶ woman/women, man/men, mouse/mice, goose/geese

Some nouns do not change in the plural form.

▶ many *fish*, several *deer*, fifty *sheep*

Some nouns remain in the plural form whether singular or plural.

▶ headquarters, means, series, crossroads

Hyphenated and open compound nouns form the plural in the main word.

▶ sons-in-law, high schools, editors in chief

Compound nouns written as one word add -s to the end (two *tablespoonfuls*).

If you are unsure of the proper usage, check a dictionary. See **possessive case** for a discussion of how nouns form possessives.

number (grammar)

Number is the grammatical property of **nouns, pronouns,** and **verbs** that signifies whether one thing (*singular*) or more than one thing (*plural*) is being referred to. (See also **agreement.**) Nouns normally form the plural by simply adding -s or -es to their singular forms.

▶ *Partners* in successful *businesses* are not always personal friends.

Some nouns require an internal change to form the plural.

▶ woman/women, man/men, goose/geese, mouse/mice

All pronouns except *you* change internally to form the plural.

▶ I/we, he/they, she/they, it/they

By adding *-s* or *-es*, most verbs show the singular of the third **person**, present **tense**, indicative **mood**.

▶ he *stands*, she *works*, it *goes*

The verb *be* normally changes form to indicate the plural.

SINGULAR   I *am* ready to begin work.

PLURAL   We *are* ready to begin work.

---

numbers

The standards for using numbers vary; however, unless you are following an organizational or a professional style manual, observe the following guidelines.

Numerals or Words

Write numbers from zero through nine as words, and write numbers ten and above as numerals.

▶ I rehearsed my presentation *three* times.

▶ The association added *152* new members.

Spell out numbers that begin a sentence, however, even if they would otherwise be written as numerals.

▶ *One hundred and fifty-two* new members joined the association.

If spelling out such a number seems awkward, rewrite the sentence so that the number does not appear at the beginning ("We added *152* new members.").

Spell out approximate and round numbers.

▶ We've had *more than a thousand* requests this month.

In most writing, spell out ordinal numbers under nine (*first* through *ninth*) and use numerals over nine (*10th*, *11th*, and so on) or when

N

they modify a century (*the twenty-first century*). However, avoid ordinal numbers in **dates** (use *March 30* or *30 March*, not *March 30th*). In mathematical copy or in copy with lots of numbers, it may be less awkward to use numerals consistently, except at the beginning of a sentence.

Plurals

Indicate the plural of numerals by adding *-s* (*7s, the late 1990s*). Form the plural of a written number (like any noun) by adding *-s* or *-es* or by dropping the *y* and adding *-ies* (*elevens, sixes, twenties*). See also **apostrophes**.

Measurements

Express units of measurement as numerals (*3 miles, 45 cubic feet, 9 meters*). When numbers run together in the same phrase, write one as a numeral and the other as a word.

> ▸ The order was for ~~12 6-foot tables.~~ *12 six-foot tables.*

Generally give percentages as numerals and write out the word *percent*. ("Approximately *85 percent* of the land has been sold.") However, in a **table**, use a numeral followed by the percent symbol (*85%*).

Fractions

Express fractions as numerals when they are written with whole numbers (*27½ inches, 4¼ miles*). Spell out fractions when they are expressed without a whole number (*one-fourth, seven-eighths*). Always write decimal numbers as numerals (*5.21 meters*).

Money

In general, use numerals to express exact or approximate amounts of money.

> ▸ We need to charge *$28.95* per unit.

> ▸ The new system costs *$60,000*.

Use words to express indefinite amounts of money.

> ▸ The printing system may cost *several thousand dollars*.

Use numerals and words for rounded amounts of money over one million dollars.

> ▸ The contract is worth *$6.8 million*.

Use numerals for more complex or exact amounts.

▶ The corporation paid *$2,452,500* in taxes last year.

For amounts under a dollar, use numerals and the word *cents* ("The pens cost *75 cents* each") unless other numerals that require dollar signs appear in the same sentence.

▶ The business-card holders cost *$10.49* each, the pens cost *$.75* each, and the pencil cup holders cost *$6.49* each.

Time

Divide hours and minutes with **colons** when *a.m.* or *p.m.* follows (*7:30 a.m., 11:30 p.m.*). Do not use colons with the 24-hour system (*0730, 2330*). Spelled-out time is not followed by *a.m.* or *p.m.* (*seven o'clock in the evening*).

Dates

In the United States, dates are usually written in a month-day-year sequence (*August 11, 2018*). Never use the strictly numerical form for dates (*8/11/18*) because the date is not immediately clear, especially in **international correspondence**.

Addresses

N

Spell out numbered streets from one through ten unless space is at a premium (*East Tenth Street*). Write building numbers as numerals. The only exception is the building number *one* (*One East Monument Street*). Write highway numbers as numerals (*U.S. 40, Ohio 271, I-94*).

Documents

Page numbers are written as numerals in manuscripts (*page 37*). Chapter and volume numbers may appear as numerals or words (*Chapter 2* or *Chapter Two, Volume 1* or *Volume One*), but be consistent. Express figure and table numbers as numerals (*Figure 4, Table 3*).

Do not follow a word representing a number with a numeral in parentheses that represents the same number. Doing so is redundant.

▶ Send five (5) copies of the report.

O

objects

Objects are **nouns** or noun equivalents: **pronouns**, **verbals**, and noun **phrases** or **clauses**. The three kinds of objects are direct objects, indirect objects, and objects of **prepositions**. See also **complements**.

A *direct object* answers the question *what?* or *whom?* about a **verb** and its **subject**.

▶ We sent a *full report*. [We sent *what?*]

▶ Michelle e-mailed the *client*. [Michelle e-mailed *whom?*]

An *indirect object* is a noun or noun equivalent that occurs with a direct object after certain kinds of transitive verbs, such as *give*, *wish*, *cause*, and *tell*. The indirect object answers the question *to whom or what?* or *for whom or what?* The indirect object always precedes the direct object.

▶ We sent the *general manager* a full report. [*Report* is the direct object; the indirect object, *general manager*, answers the question, "We sent a full report *to whom?*"]

The *object of a preposition* is a noun or pronoun that is introduced by a preposition, forming a prepositional phrase.

▶ At the *meeting*, the district managers approved the contract. [*Meeting* is the object, and *at the meeting* is the prepositional phrase.]

OK / okay

The expression *okay* (also spelled *OK*) is common in informal writing, but it should be avoided in most business writing.

▶ Mr. Sturgess ~~gave his okay to~~ the project. [*approved* written above]

on / onto / upon

On is normally used as a **preposition** meaning "attached to" or "located at." ("Install the shelf *on* the north wall.") *On* also stresses a position of rest. ("The victim lay *on* the stretcher.") *Onto* implies movement to a position on or movement up and on. ("The commuters surged *onto* the platform.") *Upon* is a formal word for *on*, whose use is unnecessary in most contexts. *Upon* is the correct choice, however, when referring to when something happened or needs to happen. ("The report is due *upon* completion of the project.")

one

When used as an indefinite **pronoun**, *one* may help you avoid repeating a **noun**. ("We need a new plan, not an old *one*.") *One* is often redundant in phrases in which it restates the noun, and it may take the proper emphasis away from the **adjective**.

▶ The training program was not ~~a unique one.~~ *unique.*

One can also be used in place of a noun or personal pronoun in a statement. ("*One* cannot ignore *one's* physical condition.") Using *one* in that way is formal and impersonal; in any but the most formal writing, you should address your reader directly and personally as *you*. ("*You* cannot ignore *your* physical condition.") See also **point of view**.

0

one of those . . . who

A dependent **clause** beginning with *who* or *that* and preceded by *one of those* takes a plural **verb**. See also **agreement**.

▶ She is *one of those* managers *who are* concerned about their writing.

In this example, *who* refers to a plural antecedent (*managers*) and thus takes a plural verb (*are*).

If the phrase *one of those* is preceded by *the only*, however, the verb should be singular.

▶ She is *the only one of those* managers *who is* concerned about her writing. [The verb is singular because its subject, *who*, refers to a singular antecedent, *one*. If the sentence were reversed, it would read, "Of those managers, she is *the only one who is* concerned about her writing."]

online professional profile

Online professional profiles—such as those on LinkedIn, AngelList, and Academia.edu, and in Figure O–1—can help you in your job search as well as in your efforts to network with colleagues, clients, and customers. Online profiles can often be posted on community sites for professional associations, like IEEE's Collabratec. They typically include information on education, skills and abilities, work history, certifications, recommendations, awards and honors, and interests. Accessed through Web browsers or mobile devices, these sites include tools to communicate and network with colleagues and friends, including the ability to recommend one another for particular skills or knowledge and to connect with others through status updates (see also **social media**) and private messaging. In addition, some sites, like LinkedIn, have profiles for companies, nonprofit organizations, and other groups.

As a job seeker, you can use your online professional profile to share your qualifications and interests with potential employers and colleagues. Employment agencies and human resources staff often search these profile sites to find possible candidates for job openings. You can also ask friends and colleagues to review your online profile to see if it matches any job openings or needs in their workplaces.

Personally, you can use your online profile to network with others in the same career or field as you. These personal connections can help you solve problems, share industry news, and collaborate on projects. Although these are personal uses, be sure to stick with professional information in your updates and on your online profile. Post more personal information on other sites, such as Facebook, rather than on professional networking sites.

Choosing the Appropriate Site

When choosing a site, consider the information it allows you to share and the fields and careers of those already on the site. Consider, too, your **audience** and **purpose** for the profile: Do you want to connect with potential employers? Are you hoping to network with others in the field? Do you plan to build a portfolio where you can archive your work? Your answers to questions like these will help you decide which site is best for you. For example, an engineering or accounting student looking for a job after graduation would probably choose LinkedIn, where she can post information about her education and skills using keywords that will attract and interest potential employers. An undergraduate student interested in entering graduate school might build a profile on Academia.edu, which will allow her to post papers she has written and her curriculum vitae (CV) along with basic personal

Joshua S. Goodman
Creative Graphic Designer
RCS School of Design
Pittsburgh, Pennsylvania

My specialty is working with marketing to provide clients with the first-rate digital, print, and Web skills they need at a lightening pace.

I bring strong, up-to-date academic and practical skills in multimedia tools and graphic arts production. For example, at Dyer/Khan, I developed client brochures, newsletters, and posters, and I coordinated project time lines, budgets, and production with clients, staff, and vendors.

My experience with leading motion picture, television, and music companies strengthened my knowledge of state-of-the-art design.

Web site: https://www.gooddesign.com/

Experience

Assistant Designer, Dyer/Khan (Summers 2015, 2016)

Assistant Designer in a versatile design studio. Responsible for design, layout, comps, mechanicals, and project management. Clients included Paramount Pictures, Mattel Electronics, and Motown Records

Photo Editor, Paramount Pictures Corporation (Summer 2014)

Photo Editor for merchandising department. Established art files for movie and television properties. Edited images used in merchandising. Maintained archive and database.

Production Assistant, Grafis (Summer 2013)

Production Assistant at fast-paced design firm. Assisted with comps, mechanicals, and miscellaneous studio work. Clients included ABC-TV, A&M Records, and Ortho Products Division

Education

RCS School of Design
BFA, Graphic Design
2013–2017

Activities: Member, Pittsburgh Graphic Design Society

Courses: Graphic Design, Corporate Identity, Industrial Design, Graphic Imaging Processes, Color Theory, Computer Graphics, Typography, Serigraphy, Photography, Video Production

Skills

- Adobe Creative Cloud and Creative Suite
- JavaScript
- QuarkXPress
- MapEdit (Image Mapping)
- Macromedia Dreamweaver
- Adobe Flash Professional
- Microsoft Access/Excel
- XML/HTML
- iGrafx
- CorelDRAW

Strong description of skills, experience

Link to supporting materials to illustrate capabilities

Details of work experience matches other job-search documents

Duties and accomplishments described

Courses and memberships listed

Skills listed using industry-specific terms

FIGURE O-1. Online Profile

information. A student interested in cutting-edge technology or product development might create a profile on AngelList, which is a network for startups.

Writing Style and Tips

The writing style for your online profile is similar to the style for your résumé and other job-search documents. Focus on composing a professional and honest statement of your education, experience, and other details. In addition, pay close attention to the **context**, **purpose**, and **audience** of your message, ensuring that your message is clear, precise, and free of grammatical errors. See **proofreading**.

The information that you publish on your online profile is immediately available to the public and can have long-lasting effects. Do not post anything on your profile that you would not want to follow you throughout your career. You can, of course, update your profile as necessary, but once information has been published, it can be archived or printed so that readers can still access what you have written. If the site that you choose allows you to create a personalized link to your profile, use the name that you go by professionally.

Personal Information and Overview. As on a résumé, include some personally identifying information, such as your name and location, but omit specifics, such as street address, phone number, or e-mail address. Include a strong description of your skills and experience in the opening summary. Beyond the basic identifying information at the top of your profile, these opening descriptions are critical to making a good first impression. Most profiles allow you to add links to your Web site or to upload examples of your work. Add supporting materials that illustrate your skills and capabilities.

In particular, pay attention to sections such as the summary on LinkedIn or the biography on Academia.edu, which allow you to include descriptive details of your qualifications, interests, personal brand, and career goals. Leaving these sections blank or writing only a sentence or brief phrase reduces the power of your profile. Use the full space to tell readers why they should connect with you.

These sites include a place for a profile photo. Look at the profiles of others in your field to determine whether self-portraits are typically used in your industry. If you decide to include a photograph, choose a professional and current image. (Remember that photographs may not be appropriate in all professions.) You should be shown wearing the clothes that you might wear to an interview or when on the job. Ensure that there are no distractions or unnecessary objects in the background of the image. Finally, choose an image that is specifically for your professional profile. This is not the place to use an image from which you have cut out family members or friends.

O

Experience, Education, and Skills.   Outline your experience, just as you would on your résumé. Be sure that the details on your profile (such as the dates of employment) are consistent with your résumé and other job-search documents but not necessarily identical. Concentrate on representing your personal brand (see **job search**, page 295) with the information that you share.

In addition to listing the details of your experience, provide a description of your duties and accomplishments. These specifics will help potential employers and colleagues visualize your experience. Take advantage of the description area in the education section by listing specific courses or accomplishments (such as scholarships or the dean's list). List your skills, using industry-specific terms, tools, or software. For example, rather than stating "image editing" as a skill, state exactly what software you are proficient with. If you have industry certifications, list that information as well.

only

The word *only* should be placed immediately before the word or phrase it modifies. See also **modifiers**.

▶ We ~~only~~ lack *only* financial backing.

Be careful with the placement of *only* because it can change the meaning of a sentence.

▶ *Only* he said that he was tired. [He alone said that he was tired.]

▶ He *only* said that he was tired. [He actually was not tired, although he said he was.]

▶ He said *only* that he was tired. [He said nothing except that he was tired.]

▶ He said that he was *only* tired. [He said that he was nothing except tired.]

order-of-importance method of development

The order-of-importance **method of development** is a particularly effective and common organizing strategy. This method can use one of two ordering strategies—decreasing order (Figure O–2), which is often best for written documents, and increasing order, which is especially effective for oral **presentations**.

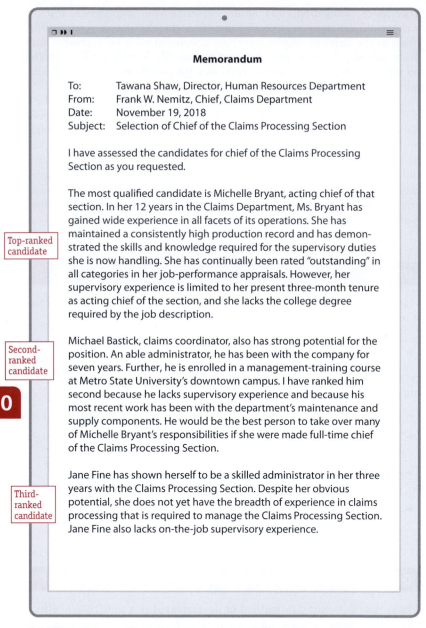

Memorandum

To: Tawana Shaw, Director, Human Resources Department
From: Frank W. Nemitz, Chief, Claims Department
Date: November 19, 2018
Subject: Selection of Chief of the Claims Processing Section

I have assessed the candidates for chief of the Claims Processing Section as you requested.

[Top-ranked candidate] The most qualified candidate is Michelle Bryant, acting chief of that section. In her 12 years in the Claims Department, Ms. Bryant has gained wide experience in all facets of its operations. She has maintained a consistently high production record and has demonstrated the skills and knowledge required for the supervisory duties she is now handling. She has continually been rated "outstanding" in all categories in her job-performance appraisals. However, her supervisory experience is limited to her present three-month tenure as acting chief of the section, and she lacks the college degree required by the job description.

[Second-ranked candidate] Michael Bastick, claims coordinator, also has strong potential for the position. An able administrator, he has been with the company for seven years. Further, he is enrolled in a management-training course at Metro State University's downtown campus. I have ranked him second because he lacks supervisory experience and because his most recent work has been with the department's maintenance and supply components. He would be the best person to take over many of Michelle Bryant's responsibilities if she were made full-time chief of the Claims Processing Section.

[Third-ranked candidate] Jane Fine has shown herself to be a skilled administrator in her three years with the Claims Processing Section. Despite her obvious potential, she does not yet have the breadth of experience in claims processing that is required to manage the Claims Processing Section. Jane Fine also lacks on-the-job supervisory experience.

FIGURE O–2. Decreasing Order-of-Importance Method of Development

Decreasing Order

Decreasing order begins with the most important fact or point, then moves to the next most important, and so on, ending with the least important. This order is especially appropriate for a **memo** or other **correspondence** addressed to a busy decision maker (see Figure O–2), who may be able to reach a decision after considering only the most important points. If you're addressing a **report** to various **readers**, some of whom may be interested in only the major points and others who may need all the information, decreasing order may be ideal for your **purpose**.

The advantages of decreasing order are that it (1) gets the reader's attention immediately by presenting the most important point first, (2) makes a strong initial impression, and (3) ensures that even the most hurried reader will not miss the most important point.

Increasing Order

Increasing order begins from the least important point or fact, then progresses to the next more important, and builds finally to the most important or strongest point.

In workplace contexts, increasing order of importance can be effective in writing but is more often used in oral presentations in which (1) you want to save your strongest points until the end or (2) you need to build the ideas point by point to an important **conclusion**.

Many oral presentations benefit especially from increasing order because it leaves the **audience** with the strongest points freshest in their minds. For example, consider an oral presentation to an audience of managers in which you must present the benefits of a new quality management system. You might begin with a benefit that is valid but of the least value to the organization generally and build to the benefit that is most valuable to all operations within the organization. The disadvantage of increasing order, especially for written documents, is that it begins weakly, and the reader may become impatient or distracted before reaching your main point.

O

organization

Organization is essential to the success of a **formal report**, a Web page, or an effective **presentation**. Good organization is achieved by **outlining** and by using a logical and appropriate **method of development** that suits your subject, your **audience**, and your **purpose**.

During the organization stage of the writing process, consider a **layout and design** that will highlight structure, hierarchy, and order, and determine the **format** appropriate to your subject and purpose. If you intend to

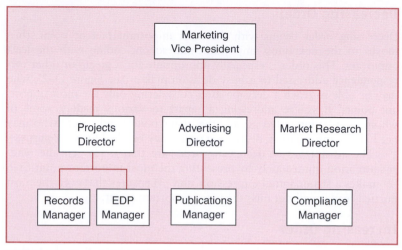

FIGURE O–3. Organizational Chart

include **visuals** with your writing, consider them as you create your outline, especially if they need to be prepared by someone else while you are writing and revising the draft. See also "Five Steps to Successful Writing" (page xvii).

O

organizational charts

An organizational chart shows how the various divisions or units of an organization are related to one another. This type of **visual** is useful when you want to give **readers** an overview of an organization or to display the lines of authority within it, as in Figure O–3.

The title of each organizational component (office, section, division) is placed in a separate box. The boxes are then linked to a central authority. If readers need the information, include the name of the person and position title in each box.

outlining

An outline is the skeleton of the document you are going to write; at the least, it should list the main topics and subtopics of your subject in a logical **method of development**.

Advantages of Outlining

An outline provides structure to your writing by ensuring that it has a beginning (**introduction**), a middle (main body), and an end (**conclusion**). Using an outline offers many other benefits:

- Larger and more complex subjects are easier to handle because an outline breaks them into manageable parts.

- Like a road map, an outline indicates a starting point and keeps you moving logically so that you do not lose your way before you arrive at your conclusion.

- Parts of an outline are easily moved around so that you can choose the most effective arrangement of your ideas. (The outline feature in your word-processing program is useful for checking the organization of a document before revising.)

- Creating a good outline frees you from concerns of **organization** while you are **writing a draft**.

- An outline enables you to provide **coherence** and **transition** so that one part flows smoothly into the next without omitting important details.

- **Logic errors** are much easier to detect and correct in an outline than in a draft.

- An outline helps with **collaborative writing** because it enables a team to refine a project's **scope**, divide responsibilities, and maintain focus.

O

Types of Outlines

Two types of outlines are most common: short topic outlines and lengthy sentence outlines. A *topic outline* consists of short phrases arranged to reflect your primary method of development. A topic outline is especially useful for short documents, such as **e-mails**, **letters**, or **memos**. See also **correspondence**.

For a large writing project, create a topic outline first, and then use it as a basis for creating a sentence outline. A *sentence outline* uses a complete sentence for each idea that may become the topic sentence for a paragraph. If most of your notes can be shaped into topic sentences for paragraphs in your rough draft, you can be relatively sure that your document will be well organized. See also **note-taking** and **research**.

Creating an Outline

For large and complex subjects with many pieces of information, the first step is to group your research notes into related categories. Sort your notes by major and minor division headings. For example, the major divisions for this discussion of outlining could be as follows:

   I. Advantages of outlining
  II. Types of outlines
 III. Creating an outline

The second step is to establish your minor divisions within each major division. Using a method of development, create your minor points and arrange them under their major division, then label them with capital letters.

  II. Types of outlines
     A. Topic outlines
     B. Sentence outlines] **Division and Classification**
 III. Creating an outline
     A. Establish major and minor divisions.
     B. Sort notes by major and minor divisions.] **Sequential**
     C. Complete the sentence outline.

You will sometimes need more than two levels of headings. If your subject is complicated, you may need three or four levels of headings to better organize all your ideas in proper relationship to one another. In that event, use the following numbering scheme:

  I. First-level heading
    A. Second-level heading
      1. Third-level heading
        a. Fourth-level heading

The third step is to mark each of your notes with the appropriate roman numeral and capital letter. Arrange the notes logically within each minor heading, and mark each with the appropriate sequential arabic number. As you do, make sure your organization is logical and your headings have **parallel structure**. For example, all the second-level headings under "III. Creating an outline" are complete sentences in the active **voice**.

Treat **visuals** as an integral part of your outline, and plan approximately where each should appear. Either include a rough sketch of the visual, or write "illustration of . . ." at each location. As with other information in an outline, freely move, delete, or add visuals as needed.

Another outlining format is the decimal numbering system, as shown in the following example:

  1. FIRST-LEVEL HEADING
    1.1 Second-level heading
    1.2 Second-level heading
      1.2.1 Third-level heading
      1.2.2 Third-level heading
        1.2.2.1 Fourth-level heading
        1.2.2.2 Fourth-level heading
    1.3 Second-level heading
  2. FIRST-LEVEL HEADING

O

This system should not go beyond the fourth level because the numbers get too cumbersome beyond that point. In many documents, such as **policies and procedures**, the decimal numbering system is carried over from the outline to the final version of the document for ease of cross-referencing sections.

Create your draft by converting your notes into complete sentences and **paragraphs**. If you have a sentence outline, the most difficult part of the writing job is over. However, remember that any outline is flexible; it may need to change as you write the draft, but it should always be your point of departure and return.

outside [of]

In the phrase *outside of*, the word *of* is redundant.

▶ Place the equipment outside ~~of~~ the meeting room.

Do not use *outside of* to mean "aside from" or "except for."

Except for
▶ ~~Outside of~~ his frequent absences, Jim has a good work record.

over [with]

In the expression *over with*, the word *with* is redundant; such words as *completed* or *finished* often better express the thought.

0

▶ The conference room will be available when the managers' meeting is over ~~with.~~

▶ The conference room will be available when the managers' meeting is
finished.
~~over with.~~

P

pace

Pace is the speed at which you present ideas to the reader. Your goal should be to achieve a pace that fits your **audience**, **purpose**, and **context**. The more knowledgeable the reader is about the subject, the faster your pace can be. Be careful, though, not to lose control of the pace. In the following example, the first version piles facts on top of each other at a rapid pace. The second version presents the same facts at a controlled pace in two more easily assimilated sentences. In addition, the second version achieves a different and more desirable **emphasis**.

RAPID	The corporate records database (CRD) contains each employee's full name, mailing address, social security number, and current job classification and is intended to help individual departments and offices process records for every one of the 21,000 employees worldwide.
CONTROLLED	The corporate records database (CRD) contains identifying information for every one of the 21,000 employees worldwide. The CRD enables individual departments and offices to process employee records, and it contains each employee's full name, mailing address, social security number, and current job classification.

paragraphs

A paragraph performs three functions: It (1) develops the unit of thought stated in the topic sentence; (2) provides a logical break in the material; and (3) creates a visual break on the page, which signals a new topic.

Topic Sentence

A topic sentence states the paragraph's main idea; the rest of the paragraph supports and develops that statement with related details. The topic sentence, which is often the first sentence, tells the reader what the paragraph is about.

> ▶ *The cost of training new employees is high.* In addition to the cost of classroom facilities and instructors, an organization must pay employees their regular salary while they sit in the classroom. For the companies to break even on this investment in their professional employees, those employees must stay in the job for which they have been trained for at least one year.

The topic sentence is usually most effective early in the paragraph, but a paragraph can lead to the topic sentence, which is sometimes done to achieve **emphasis**.

> ▶ Energy does far more than simply make our daily lives more comfortable and convenient. Suppose someone wanted to stop—and reverse—the economic progress of this nation. What would be the surest and quickest way to do it? Simply block the nation's ability to produce energy! The nation would face a devastating economic crisis. *Our economy, in short, is energy based.*

On rare occasions, the topic sentence may logically fall in the middle of a paragraph.

> ▶ It is time to insist that science does not progress by carefully designed steps called "experiments," each of which has a well-defined beginning and end. *Science is a continuous and often a disorderly and accidental process.* We shall not do the young psychologist any favor if we agree to reconstruct our practices to fit the pattern demanded by current scientific methodology.
> —B. F. Skinner, "A Case History in Scientific Method"

Paragraph Length

A paragraph should be just long enough to deal adequately with the subject of its topic sentence. A new paragraph should begin whenever the subject changes significantly. A series of short, undeveloped paragraphs can indicate poor **organization** by breaking a single idea into several pieces. A series of long paragraphs, however, can fail to provide the reader with manageable subdivisions of thought. Paragraph length should aid the reader's understanding of ideas.

Occasionally, a one-sentence paragraph is acceptable if it is used as a **transition** between longer paragraphs or as a one-sentence **introduction** or **conclusion** in **correspondence**.

Writing Paragraphs

Careful paragraphing reflects the writer's logical organization and helps the reader follow the writer's thoughts. A good working outline makes it easy to group ideas into appropriate paragraphs. (See also **outlining**.) The following partial topic outline plots the course of the subsequent paragraphs:

TOPIC OUTLINE (PARTIAL)

I.   Advantages of Chicago as location for new facility
    A. Transport infrastructure
        1. Rail
        2. Air
        3. Truck
        4. Sea (except in winter)
    B. Labor supply
        1. Engineering and scientific personnel
            a. Similar companies in area
            b. Major universities
        2. Technical and manufacturing personnel
            a. Community college programs
            b. Custom programs

RESULTING PARAGRAPHS

Probably the greatest advantage of Chicago as a location for our new facility is its excellent transport facilities. The city is served by three major railroads. Both domestic and international air-cargo service are available at O'Hare International Airport; Midway Airport's convenient location adds flexibility for domestic air-cargo service. Chicago is a major hub of the trucking industry, and most of the nation's large freight carriers have terminals there. Finally, except in the winter months, when the Great Lakes are frozen, Chicago is a seaport, accessible through the St. Lawrence Seaway.

Chicago's second advantage is its abundant labor force. An ample supply of engineering and scientific staff is assured not only by the presence of many companies engaged in activities similar to ours but also by the presence of several major universities in the metropolitan area. Similarly, technicians and manufacturing personnel are in abundant supply. The colleges in the Chicago City College system, as well as half a dozen other two-year colleges in the outlying areas, produce graduates with associate's degrees in a wide variety of technical specialties appropriate to our needs. Moreover, three of the outlying colleges have expressed an interest in developing off-campus courses attuned specifically to our requirements.

Paragraph Unity and Coherence

A good paragraph has **unity** and **coherence** as well as adequate development. *Unity* is singleness of purpose, based on a topic sentence that states the core idea of the paragraph. When every sentence in the paragraph develops the core idea, the paragraph has unity. *Coherence* is holding to one point of view, one attitude, one tense; it is the joining of sentences into a logical pattern. Transitional words tie ideas together and lead to coherence, as shown by the boldfaced italicized words in the following paragraph.

TOPIC SENTENCE *Over the past several months, I have heard complaints about the Merit Award Program. Specifically,* many employees feel that this program should be linked to annual *salary increases.* They believe that *salary increases* would provide a much better incentive than the current $500 to $700 cash awards for exceptional service. *In addition,* these *employees believe* that their supervisors consider the cash awards a satisfactory alternative to salary increases. Although I don't think this practice is widespread, the fact that the *employees believe* that it is justifies a reevaluation of the Merit Award Program.

Simple enumeration (*first, second, then, next,* and so on) also provides effective transition within paragraphs. Notice how the boldfaced italicized words and phrases give coherence to the following paragraph.

▶ Most adjustable office chairs have nylon tubes that hold metal spindle rods. To keep the chair operational, lubricate the spindle rods occasionally. *First,* loosen the set screw in the adjustable bell. *Then,* lift the chair from the base. *Next,* apply the lubricant to the spindle rod and the nylon washer. *When you have finished,* replace the chair and tighten the set screw.

parallel structure

Parallel structure requires that sentence elements that are alike in function be alike in grammatical form as well. This structure achieves an economy of words, clarifies meaning, expresses the equality of the ideas, and achieves **emphasis**. Parallel structure assists **readers** because it allows them to anticipate the meaning of a sentence element on the basis of its construction.

Parallel structure can be achieved with words, **phrases**, or **clauses**.

▶ If you want to benefit from the jobs training program, you must be *punctual, courteous,* and *conscientious.* [parallel words]

P

▶ If you want to benefit from the jobs training program, you must recognize the importance *of punctuality*, *of courtesy*, and *of conscientiousness*. [parallel phrases]

▶ If you want to benefit from the jobs training program, *you must arrive punctually*, *you must behave courteously*, and *you must study conscientiously*. [parallel clauses]

Correlative **conjunctions** (*either . . . or*, *neither . . . nor*, *not only . . . but also*) should always join elements that use parallel structure. Both parts of the pairs should be followed immediately by the same grammatical form: two similar words, two similar phrases, or two similar clauses.

▶ Viruses carry either *DNA* or *RNA*, never both. [parallel words]

▶ Clearly, neither *serological tests* nor *virus isolation studies* alone would have been adequate. [parallel phrases]

▶ Either *we must increase our production efficiency* or *we must decrease our production goals*. [parallel clauses]

To make a parallel construction clear and effective, it is often best to repeat an **article**, a **pronoun**, a helping **verb**, a **preposition**, a subordinating conjunction, or the mark of an infinitive (*to*).

▶ The association has *a* mission statement and *a* code of ethics. [article]

▶ The software is popular *because* it is compatible across platforms and *because* it is easily customized. [subordinating conjunction]

Parallel structure is especially important in creating **lists**, outlines, **tables of contents**, and **headings** because it lets readers know the relative value of each item. See also **outlining**.

Faulty Parallelism

Faulty parallelism results when joined elements are intended to serve equal grammatical functions but do not have equal grammatical form.

Faulty parallelism sometimes occurs because a writer tries to compare items that are not comparable.

NOT PARALLEL   The company offers special college training to help hourly employees move into professional careers, like engineering management, software development, service technicians, and sales trainees. [Notice faulty comparison of occupations—*engineering management* and *software development*—to people—*service technicians* and *sales trainees*.]

To avoid faulty parallelism, make certain that each element in a series is similar in form and structure to all others in the same series.

PARALLEL   The company offers special college training to help hourly employees move into professional careers, like *engineering management*, *software development*, *technical services*, and *sales*.

paraphrasing

Paraphrasing is restating or rewriting the essential ideas of another writer in your own words. The following example is an original passage and a paraphrased version that accurately restates the essential information in a form appropriate for a **report**.

ORIGINAL   Generally, the goals of workplace professionals demand that they think in specific, practical, and immediately applicable ways; those of us in the academy must think in terms that are more abstract, conceptual, and long-term. It is understandable, then, that works that might be highly valued by either practitioners or academics can seem entirely irrelevant to the other.
            —Gerald J. Alred, "Bridging Cultures: The Academy and the Workplace," *Journal of Business Communication*

PARAPHRASE   Practitioners who value specific, practical goals and academics who need to think in abstract, long-term ways understandably value different works (Alred, 2006).

❖ **ETHICS NOTE** Because paraphrasing does not quote a source word for word, quotation marks are not used. However, paraphrased material should be credited because the *ideas* are taken from someone else. See also **note-taking**, **plagiarism**, and **quotations**. ❖

parentheses

Parentheses are used to enclose explanatory or digressive words, phrases, or sentences. Material in parentheses often clarifies or defines the preceding text without altering its meaning.

▶   She severely bruised her tibia (or shinbone) in the accident.

Parenthetical information may not be essential to a sentence (in fact, parentheses deemphasize the enclosed material), but it may be helpful to some readers.

Parenthetical material does not affect the punctuation of a sentence, and any punctuation (such as a **comma** or **period**) should appear following the closing parenthesis.

▶ She could not fully extend her knee because of a torn meniscus (or cartilage), and she suffered pain from a severely bruised tibia (or shinbone).

When a complete sentence within parentheses stands independently, the ending punctuation is placed inside the final parenthesis.

▶ The project director listed the problems her staff faced. (This was the third time she had complained to the board.)

For some constructions, however, you should consider using **subordination** rather than parentheses.

▶ The early tests showed little damage ~~(the attending physician was~~ *, which pleased the attending physician,* ~~pleased),~~ but later scans revealed abdominal trauma.

Parentheses are also used to enclose numerals or letters that indicate sequence.

▶ The following sections deal with (1) preparation, (2) research, (3) organization, (4) writing, and (5) revision.

Do not follow spelled-out **numbers** with numerals in parentheses representing the same numbers.

▶ Send five ~~(5)~~ copies of the report.

Use **brackets** to set off a parenthetical item that is already within parentheses.

▶ We should be sure to give Emanuel Foose (and his brother Emilio [1912–1982]) credit for his part in founding the institute.

See also **documenting sources** and **quotations**.

parts of speech

The term *parts of speech* describes the class of words to which a particular word belongs, according to its function in a sentence.

PART OF SPEECH	FUNCTION
noun, **pronoun**	naming / referring
verb	acting / asserting
adjective, **adverb**	describing / modifying
conjunction, **preposition**	joining / linking
interjection	exclaiming

Many words can function as more than one part of speech. See also **functional shift**.

party

In legal language, *party* refers to an individual, a group, or an organization. ("The injured *party* sued my client.") The term *party* is inappropriate in all but legal writing; when you are referring to a person, use the word *person*.

> ▶ The ~~party~~ *person* whose file you requested is here now.

Party is appropriate when it refers to a group. ("Jim arranged a tour of the facility for the members of our *party*.")

per

When *per* is used to mean "for each," "by means of," "through," or "on account of," it is appropriate (*per* gallon, *per* capita, *per* diem). When used to mean "according to" (*per* your request, *per* your order), the expression is **jargon** and should be avoided.

> ▶ As ~~per our discussion,~~ *we discussed,* I will send revised instructions.

percent / percentage

The word *percent* is normally used instead of the symbol % ("only 15 *percent*"), except in **tables**, where space is at a premium. *Percentage*, which is never used with **numbers**, indicates a general size ("only a small *percentage*").

P

periods

A period is a mark of **punctuation** that usually indicates the end of a declarative or an imperative sentence. Periods are also used to end questions that are actually polite requests, or instructions to which an affirmative response is assumed. ("Will you call me as soon as he arrives.") See also **sentence construction**. Periods, or dots, when used to indicate omissions are called **ellipses**, and rows of dots that link topics with page numbers are called *leaders* in **tables of contents**.

Periods in Quotations

Use a **comma**, not a period, after a declarative sentence that is quoted in the context of another sentence.

▶ "There is every chance of success," she stated.

A period is placed inside **quotation marks**. See also **quotations**.

▶ He stated clearly, "My vote is yes."

Periods with Parentheses

Place a period outside the final parenthesis when a parenthetical element ends a sentence.

▶ The institute was founded by Harry Denman (1902–1972).

Place a period inside the final parenthesis when a complete sentence stands independently within **parentheses**.

▶ The project director listed the problems her staff faced. (This was the third time she had complained to the board.)

Other Uses of Periods

Use periods following the numerals in a numbered **list** and following the complete sentences in a list.

▶ 1. Enter your name and PIN.
2. Enter your address with ZIP Code.
3. Enter your home telephone number.

P

Use periods after initials in names (*Wilma T. Grant, J. P. Morgan*). Use periods as decimal points with **numbers** (*27.3 degrees Celsius, $540.26, 6.9 percent*). Use periods to indicate certain **abbreviations** (*Ms., Dr., Inc.*). When a sentence ends with an abbreviation that ends with a period, do not add another period. ("Please meet me at 3:30 p.m.")

Period Faults

When a period is inserted prematurely, the result is a **sentence fragment**.

FRAGMENT   After a long day at the office, during which we finished the quarterly report. We left hurriedly for home.

SENTENCE   After a long day at the office, during which we finished the quarterly report, we left hurriedly for home.

When two independent clauses are joined without any punctuation, the result is a *fused*, or *run-on*, *sentence*. Adding a period between the clauses is one way to correct a run-on sentence.

RUN-ON   Bill was late for ten days in a row Ms. Sturgess had to dismiss him.

CORRECT   Bill was late for ten days in a row. Ms. Sturgess had to dismiss him.

Other options are to add a comma and a coordinating **conjunction** (*and*, *but*, *for*, *or*, *nor*, *so*, or *yet*) between the clauses, to add a **semicolon**, or to add a semicolon with a conjunctive **adverb**—such as *therefore* or *however*—followed by a comma.

person

Person refers to the form of a personal **pronoun** that indicates whether the pronoun represents the speaker, the person spoken to, or the person or thing spoken about. A pronoun representing the speaker is in the *first* person. ("*I* could not find the answer in the manual.") A pronoun that represents the person or people spoken to is in the *second* person. ("*You* will be a good manager.") A pronoun that represents the person or people spoken about is in the *third* person. ("*They* received the news quietly.") The following list shows first-, second-, and third-person pronouns. See also **case**, **number**, and **one**.

PERSON	SINGULAR	PLURAL
First	I, me, my, mine	we, us, our, ours
Second	you, your, yours	you, your, yours
Third	he, him, his, she, her, hers, it, its	they, them, their, theirs

personal / personnel

Personal is an **adjective** meaning "of or pertaining to an individual person" (*a personal problem*). *Personnel* is a **noun** meaning "a group of people engaged in a common job" (*military personnel*). Be careful not to use *personnel* when the word you need is *persons*, *people*, or a more descriptive word.

▶ The remaining ~~personnel~~ *employees* will be moved next Thursday.

P

persons / people

The word *persons* is used to refer to a specific category or number of people, often in legal or official contexts. ("Admittance is limited to *persons* 18 and over.") In all other contexts, use *people*. ("We need more qualified *people* to fill the vacant positions.")

persuasion

Persuasive writing attempts to convince an **audience** to adopt the writer's point of view or take a particular action. Workplace writing often uses persuasion to reinforce ideas that readers already have, to convince readers to change their current ideas, or to lobby for a particular suggestion or policy (as in Figure P–1). You may find yourself advocating for safer working conditions, justifying the expense of a new program, or writing a **proposal** for a large purchase. See also **context** and **purpose**. In persuasive writing, you must support your appeal with logic and a sound presentation of facts, statistics, and examples. See also **logic errors**. A writer also gains credibility, and thus persuasiveness, through the readers' impressions of the document's appearance. For this reason, consider carefully a document's **layout and design**.

❖ **ETHICS NOTE** Never make false claims. You should also acknowledge any real or potentially conflicting opinions; doing so allows you to anticipate and overcome objections and builds your credibility. See also **ethics in writing** and **promotional writing**. ❖

The **memo** shown in Figure P–1 was written to persuade the marketing staff to participate actively in a change to a new server. Notice that not everything in this memo is presented in a positive light. Change brings disruption and challenges—and the writer acknowledges that fact.

A persuasive technique that places the focus on your reader's interest and perspective is discussed in the entry **"you" viewpoint**. See also **correspondence**.

photographs

Photographs are effective in catching the readers' attention and adding personal relevance to **brochures**, **newsletters**, **annual reports**, **presentations**, and other **promotional writing**. Photographs are also an effective way to illustrate products in print and online catalogs. They are often used for instructions to show the appearance of an object, although they cannot depict the internal workings of a mechanism or

Interoffice Memo

TO: Marketing Staff
FROM: Harold Kawenski, MIS Administrator
DATE: April 23, 2018
SUBJECT: Changeover to the NRT/R4 System

As you all know, the merger with Datacom has resulted in dramatic growth in our workload—a 30 percent increase in our customer support services. To manage this expansion, we will soon install the NRT/R4 server and QCS Enterprise software with Web-based applications. You can contribute to making a smooth transition to the QCS system.

QCS Challenges
The changeover to the QCS system, understandably, will cause some disruption at first. We will need to (1) transfer many of our legacy programs and software applications to the new system and (2) learn to navigate in the R4 and QCS environments. Once we have made these adjustments, however, I am convinced we will welcome the changes.

QCS Benefits
The QCS system will provide smooth access to up-to-date marketing and product information when we need it. This system will speed processing dramatically and give us access to all relevant company-wide databases. Because we anticipate that our workload will increase another 20 percent in the next several months, a timely conversion to the QCS system will be invaluable.

Training and Support
To cope with the changes, we will offer training sessions next week on our intranet. I have attached a schedule and sign-up form with specific class times. We will also provide a technical-support hotline at extension 4040, which will be available during business hours; e-mail support at qcs-support@conco.com; and online help documentation.

Response Date
Please return your form and e-mail me by Monday, April 30, with suggestions or questions about the impact of the changeover on your department. I look forward to working with you to make this system a success.

Attachments: Training Schedule and Sign-Up Form

> Headings indicate paragraph topics.

P

FIGURE P–1. Persuasive Memo

below-the-surface details of objects or structures. Such details are better represented in **drawings**. See also **readers**.

Figure P–2 shows a photograph from an interactive Web presentation for buyers of corporate aircraft. This photograph is one in a series that simulates a pilot's "walk-around"—a procedure in which pilots visually examine an aircraft in a 360-degree safety inspection prior to takeoff. In this photo, the stair steps are lowered to show the relative size of the aircraft.

For **reports**, treat photographs as you do other **visuals**, giving them figure numbers, callouts (labels) to identify key features, and captions, if needed. Position the figure number and caption so that readers can view them and the photograph from the same orientation.

❖ **ETHICS NOTE** Be careful to avoid **plagiarism** by appropriately **documenting sources** for photographs and by obtaining permission from the **copyright** holder if you plan to publish photographs that you do not take yourself. For such photos, you should provide a source line, as shown in Figure P–2. For stock images obtained through services like Getty Images (www.gettyimages.com), you will need to obtain a license

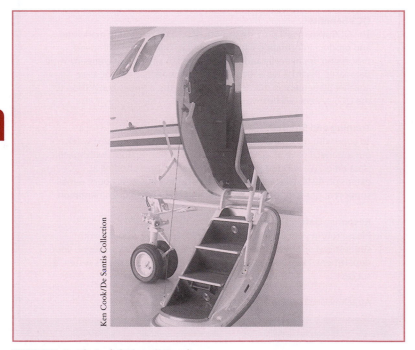

Ken Cook/De Santis Collection

FIGURE P–2. Photo (of Aircraft Door)

and pay a fee, depending on the final use. If you do take your own photographs, be sure to get the full name, contact information, and permission of any persons featured before publishing. ❖

---

phrases

DIRECTORY

A phrase is a meaningful group of words that does not make a complete statement because it lacks both a subject and a predicate, as opposed to **clauses**. Phrases, which are based on **nouns**, nonfinite **verb** forms, or verb combinations, provide context within a clause or sentence in which they appear. See also **sentence construction**.

▶ She reassured her staff *by her calm confidence.* [phrase]

A phrase may function as an **adjective**, an **adverb**, a noun, or a verb.

▶ The subjects *on the agenda* were all discussed. [adjective]

▶ We discussed the project *with great enthusiasm.* [adverb]

▶ *Working hard* is her way of life. [noun]

▶ The human resources director *should have been notified.* [verb]

Even though phrases function as adjectives, adverbs, nouns, or verbs, they are normally named for the kind of word around which they are constructed—**preposition**, participle, infinitive, gerund, verb, or noun. A phrase that begins with a preposition is a *prepositional phrase*, a phrase that begins with a participle is a *participial phrase*, and so on. For typical verb phrases and prepositional phrases that can cause difficulty for speakers of **English as a second language**, see **idioms**.

Prepositional Phrases

A preposition is a word that shows relationship and combines with a noun or **pronoun** (its **object**) to form a modifying phrase. A prepositional phrase, then, consists of a preposition plus its object and the object's modifiers.

▶ *After the meeting*, the district managers adjourned *to the cafeteria.*

P

Prepositional phrases, because they normally modify nouns or verbs, usually function as adjectives or adverbs. A prepositional phrase may function as an adverb of motion ("Turn the dial four degrees *to the left*") or an adverb of manner ("Answer customers' questions *in a courteous fashion*"). A prepositional phrase may also function as an adverb of place and may appear in different places in the sentence.

▶ *In home and office computer systems*, security is essential.

▶ Security is essential *in home and office computer systems*.

Prepositional phrases may function as adjectives; when they do, they follow the nouns they modify.

▶ Food waste *with a high protein content* can be processed into animal food.

Be careful when you use prepositional phrases, because separating a prepositional phrase from the noun it modifies can cause **ambiguity**.

AMBIGUOUS   *The woman* standing by the security guard *in the gray suit* is our division manager.

CLEAR   *The woman in the gray suit* who is standing by the security guard is our division manager.

Watch as well for the overuse of prepositional phrases where **modifiers** would be more economical.

OVERUSED   The man *with gray hair in the blue suit with pinstripes* is the former president *of the company*.

ECONOMICAL   The *gray-haired* man in the *blue pin-striped* suit is the former *company* president.

Participial Phrases

A participle is any form of a verb that is used as an adjective. A participial phrase consists of a participle plus its object and its modifiers.

▶ The division *having the largest sales increase* will win the award.

The relationship between a participial phrase and the rest of the sentence must be clear. For that reason, every sentence containing a participial phrase must have a noun or pronoun that the participial phrase modifies; if it does not, the result is a dangling participial phrase.

Dangling Participial Phrases.   A dangling participial phrase occurs when the noun or pronoun that the participial phrase is meant to modify is not stated but only implied. See also **dangling modifiers**.

DANGLING	*Being unhappy with the job*, his efficiency suffered. [His efficiency was not unhappy with the job; what the participial phrase really modifies— *he*—is not stated but merely implied.]
CORRECT	*Being unhappy with the job*, he grew less efficient. [In this version, what the participial phrase modifies— *he*—is explicitly stated.]

Misplaced Participial Phrases. A participial phrase is misplaced when it is too far from the noun or pronoun it is meant to modify and so appears to modify something else.

MISPLACED	We saw a large warehouse *driving down the highway*.
CORRECT	*Driving down the highway*, we saw a large warehouse.

Infinitive Phrases

An infinitive is the basic form of a verb (*go*, *run*, *talk*), without the restrictions imposed by **person** and **number**. An infinitive is generally preceded by the word *to* (which is usually a preposition but in this use is called the *sign*, or *mark*, of the infinitive). An infinitive phrase consists of the word *to* plus an infinitive and any objects or modifiers.

▶ *To improve as a writer*, you must be willing *to accept criticism*.

Do not confuse a prepositional phrase beginning with *to* with an infinitive phrase. In an infinitive phrase, *to* is followed by a verb; in a prepositional phrase, *to* is followed by a noun or pronoun.

PREPOSITIONAL PHRASE	We went *to the building site*.
INFINITIVE PHRASE	Our firm tries *to provide a comprehensive training program*.

The implied subject of an introductory infinitive phrase should be the same as the subject of the sentence. If it is not, the phrase is a dangling modifier. In the following example, the implied subject of the infinitive is *you* or *one*, not *practice*.

▶ To learn a new language, ~~practice is needed.~~ *you must practice.*

Gerund Phrases

A gerund is a **verbal** ending in *-ing* that is used as a noun. A gerund phrase consists of a gerund plus any objects or modifiers and always functions as a noun.

| SUBJECT | *Preparing an annual report* is a difficult task. |
| DIRECT OBJECT | She liked *chairing the committee*. |

Verb Phrases

A verb phrase consists of a main verb and its helping verb.

▶ He *is* [helping verb] *working* [main verb] hard this summer.

Words can appear between the helping verb and the main verb of a verb phrase. ("He *is* always *working*.") The main verb is always the last verb in a verb phrase.

Questions often begin with a verb phrase. ("*Will* he *audit* their account?") The adverb *not* may be appended to a helping verb in a verb phrase. ("He *did not work* today.")

Noun Phrases

A noun phrase consists of a noun and its modifiers. ("Have *the two new employees* fill out *these forms*.")

plagiarism

Plagiarism is the use of someone else's unique ideas without acknowledgment or the use of someone else's exact words without **quotation marks** and appropriate credit. Plagiarism is considered to be the theft of someone else's creative and intellectual property and can result in legal action, academic sanctions, and serious professional consequences. See also **copyright**, **ethics in writing**, and **research**.

Citing Sources

Quoting a passage—including cutting and pasting a passage from an Internet source into your work—is permissible only if you enclose the passage in quotation marks and properly cite the source. For detailed guidance on quoting correctly, see **quotations**. If you intend to publish, reproduce, or distribute material that includes quotations from published works, including Web sites, you may need to obtain written permission from the copyright holders of those works.

Even Web sites that grant permission to copy, distribute, or modify material under the "copyleft" principle, such as Wikipedia, nonetheless caution that you must give appropriate credit to the source from which material is taken (see http://en.wikipedia.org/wiki/Wikipedia:Citing_Wikipedia).

Paraphrasing the words and ideas of another *also requires that you cite your source*, even though you do not enclose paraphrased ideas or materials in quotation marks. (See also **documenting sources**.) Paraphrasing a passage without citing the source is permissible only when the information paraphrased is common knowledge.

Common Knowledge

Common knowledge generally refers to information that is widely known and readily available in handbooks, manuals, atlases, and other references. For example, the "law of supply and demand" is common knowledge and is found in nearly every economics textbook.

Common knowledge also refers to information within a specific field that is generally known and understood by most others in that field — even though it is not widely known by those outside the field.

An indication that something is common knowledge is its appearance in multiple sources without citation. However, when in doubt, cite the source.

❖ **ETHICS NOTE** In the workplace, employees often borrow material freely from in-house manuals, reports, and other company documents. Using or **repurposing** such material is neither plagiarism nor a violation of copyright. For information on the use of public domain and government material, see **copyright**. ❖

plain language

Plain language is writing that is logically organized and understandable on the first reading. Such writing avoids unnecessary **jargon**, **affectation**, and technical terminology. Even with the best of intentions, however, you cannot always avoid using specialized terms and concepts. Therefore, assess your **audience** carefully to ensure that your language connects with their level of knowledge. Replace jargon and complex legal wording with familiar words or terms when possible.

COMPLEX	The systems integration specialist must be able to visually perceive the entire directional response module.
PLAIN LANGUAGE	The operator must be able to see the entire control panel.

If you are a health-care provider, for example, use the appropriate plain-language equivalent for medical terminology with patients in conversations and written guidelines: *bleeding* instead of *hemorrhaging*, *heart attack* instead of *myocardial infarction*, *stitches* instead of *sutures*. If a plain-language alternative does not exist, define or explain a technical term on its first use and use **visuals** where necessary.

WRITER'S CHECKLIST   **Using Plain Language**

✔ Identify your average reader's level of technical knowledge.

✔ Avoid unnecessary jargon and legal language.

✔ Avoid confusing terms and constructions.

- Define necessary **abbreviations** and acronyms.
- Use the same words consistently for the same things.
- Do not give an obscure meaning to a word.

✔ Use the active **voice** for directness and for identifying the doer of an action.

✔ Use the second **person** (*you/yours*) or imperative **mood** to write directly to the reader.

✔ Write coherent sentences.

- Aim for one message in each sentence.
- Break up complex information into smaller, easier-to-understand units.
- Use **positive writing** and the present **tense** as much as possible.

✔ Select word placement carefully.

- Keep subjects and **objects** close to their **verbs**.
- Put *only, always,* and other conditional words next to the words they modify.

Plain-language principles are especially useful when writing **international correspondence**. For format and visual elements that promote **clarity**, see **layout and design** and **lists**. See also **English as a second language**. For information on plain-language laws and practices, see www .plainlanguage.gov/site/about.cfm and plainlanguagenetwork.org.

point of view

Point of view is the writer's relation to the information presented, as reflected in the use of grammatical **person**. The writer usually expresses the point of view in first-, second-, or third-person personal **pronouns**.

Use of first person indicates that the writer is a participant or an observer. Use of second or third person indicates that the writer is giving directions, **instructions**, or advice or is writing about other people or something impersonal.

FIRST PERSON	*I* scrolled down to find the settings option.
SECOND PERSON	*You* need to scroll down to find the settings option. [*You* is explicitly stated.] Scroll down to find the settings option. [*You* is understood in such an instruction.]
THIRD PERSON	*He* scrolled down to find the settings option.

Consider the following sentence, revised from an impersonal to a more personal point of view. Although the essential meaning of the sentence does not change, the revision indicates that people are involved in the communication.

▶ ~~It is regrettable~~ *I regret* that the equipment shipped on

Friday ~~is unacceptable.~~ *we cannot accept*

Some people think they should avoid the pronoun *I* in business writing, but doing so often leads to awkward sentences, with people referring to themselves in the third person as *one* or as *the writer* instead of as *I*.

▶ ~~The writer believes~~ *I believe* that this project will be completed by July.

However, do not use the personal point of view when an impersonal point of view would be more appropriate or more effective because you need to emphasize the subject matter over the writer or the reader. In the following example, it does not help to personalize the situation; in fact, the impersonal version may be more tactful.

PERSONAL	I received objections to my proposal from several of your managers.
IMPERSONAL	Several managers have raised objections to the proposal.

Whether you adopt a personal or an impersonal point of view depends on the **purpose** and the **audience** of the document. For example, in an informal **e-mail** to an associate, you would most likely adopt a personal point of view. However, in a **report** to a large group or in **global communications**, you would probably emphasize the subject and avoid sounding impolite by using an impersonal point of view. (In some cultures, stating an opinion in writing may be considered impolite or unnecessary.) See also **plain language**.

P

❖ **ETHICS NOTE** Avoiding the first person may convey the impression that the writer is evading responsibility. (See **voice**.) When using the first person, think carefully about whether to use the singular *I* or the plural *we*. In company **correspondence**, using the pronoun *we* may be interpreted as reflecting company policy, whereas *I* clearly reflects personal opinion. Which pronoun to use should be decided according to whether you are speaking for yourself (*I*) or for the company (*we*).

▶ *I* understand your frustration with the price increase, but *we* must now add the import tax to the sales price. ❖

policies and procedures

A *policy* states an organization's position on a subject; a *procedure* may describe the steps or provide **instructions** for carrying out the policy. Policies and procedures are often written at the same time, usually by top or middle managers. Policies and procedures are subjected to a careful review process, often by legal staff. Writing these documents requires careful planning as well as precise language and **word choice** so that the policies and procedures are clear and understandable. See also **plain language**.

Policies

A statement of policy may be preceded by an explanation of the policy's purpose or rationale. Specific details then follow in numbered sections, as in the following company policy regarding tuition refunds.

1. TUITION REIMBURSEMENT POLICY
   1.1 The Tuition Reimbursement Plan is available only to full-time staff.
   1.2 To receive a reimbursement, an individual must be employed by the company at the time of enrollment and at the time of completion of the course. Should an individual's employment be terminated because of a reduction of staff, fees will be refunded for approved courses upon their satisfactory completion.
   1.3 Satisfactory completion means that the employee has completed the course work and has achieved a grade at least one level above passing. If a course is not satisfactorily completed, reimbursement may be deferred if the employee, upon completion of the degree, attains a cumulative grade average of at least C (B for most graduate-degree programs).

Policies may be kept in loose-leaf binders or posted on an organization's internal Web site so that they can be easily referred to and updated.

P

Procedures

Procedures provide a step-by-step explanation of how to carry out a policy. They often provide instructions not only for employees but also for managers, who must ensure that the company's policy is properly implemented.

To prepare for writing procedures, keep track of who must do what. An easy and effective way is to create a chart, as shown in Figure P–3. Draw a vertical line down a page. Label the left column "Actor" and the right column "Directions." Under "Actor," list who must perform the action in each step; under "Directions," describe each step of the procedure fully and in the correct sequence. In effect, the list serves as an outline for the procedure you will write. The draft created from the chart in Figure P–3 might look like this:

1. PROCEDURES
   1.1 Tuition Reimbursement Approval
      1.1.1 An employee who meets school requirements and is interested in receiving tuition reimbursement should gain the approval of his or her manager and submit the request to the Human Resources (HR) Department. HR may ask the manager to justify, in writing, the benefits of the academic work, if the reason is not obvious.
      1.1.2 After reaching an agreement, the employee should complete Sections I and II of Form F-6970. After HR has obtained two levels of management approval—from the employee's supervisor and the

Actor	Directions
Employee	Determines his or her eligibility for academic work, gains manager's approval, and submits request to human resources (HR)
Human Resources Department	Reviews request and, if reason is not obvious, asks manager to justify, in writing, the benefits of approving the academic work
Employee	Completes Sections I and II of Form F-6970
Human Resources Department	Sends form to employee's supervisor and department head for approval
Employee	Submits proof of course enrollment and fee payment to HR for reimbursement

FIGURE P–3. Procedures Chart

head of the department—it approves the employee's
enrollment in the course or degree program.

1.1.3 The employee who has been granted approval
must submit to HR proof of enrollment and
payment of appropriate fees to receive tuition
reimbursement.

positive writing

Presenting positive information as though it were negative is confusing
to **readers**.

NEGATIVE   If the error does *not* involve data transmission, the backup
function will *not* be used.

In this sentence, the reader must reverse two negatives to understand
the exception that is being stated. (See also **double negatives**.) The following sentence presents the exception in a positive and straightforward manner. See also **plain language**.

POSITIVE   The backup function is used only when the error involves
data transmission.

❖ **ETHICS NOTE** Negative facts or conclusions, however, should be stated
negatively; stating a negative fact or conclusion positively is deceptive
because it can mislead the reader.

DECEPTIVE   In the first quarter of this year, employee exposure to
airborne lead averaged within 10 percent of acceptable
state health standards.

ACCURATE   In the first quarter of this year, employee exposure to
airborne lead averaged 10 percent below acceptable
state health standards.

See also **ethics in writing**. ❖

Even if what you are saying is negative, do not state it more negatively than necessary.

NEGATIVE   We are withholding your shipment because we have not
received your payment.

POSITIVE   We will forward your shipment as soon as we receive your
payment.

See also **correspondence** and **"you" viewpoint**.

possessive case

A **noun** or **pronoun** is in the possessive case when it represents a person, place, or thing that possesses something. Possession is generally expressed with an **apostrophe** and an *s* ("the *report's* title"), with a prepositional **phrase** using *of* ("the title *of the report*"), or with the possessive form of a pronoun ("*our* report").

Practices vary for some possessive forms, but the following guidelines are widely used. Above all, be consistent.

Singular Nouns

Most singular nouns show the possessive case with *'s*.

- the *hospital's* medical staff   the *witness's* testimony
  an *employee's* paycheck   the *bus's* schedule

When pronunciation with *'s* is difficult or when a multisyllable noun ends in a *z* sound, you may use only an apostrophe.

- *New Orleans'* convention hotels

Plural Nouns

Plural nouns that end in *-s* or *-es* show the possessive case with only an apostrophe.

- the *managers'* reports   the *companies'* joint project
  the *employees'* paychecks   the *witnesses'* testimony

Plural nouns that do not end in *-s* show the possessive with *'s*.

- *children's* clothing, *women's* resources, *men's* shoes

Apostrophes are not always used in official names ("*Consumers* Union") or for words that may appear to be possessive nouns but function as **adjectives** ("a *computer peripherals* supplier").

Compound Nouns

Compound nouns form the possessive with *'s* following the final letter.

- the *attorney general's* decision, the *editor-in-chief's* desk, the *pipeline's* diameter

Plurals of some compound expressions are often best expressed with a prepositional phrase ("presentations *of the editors in chief*").

P

Coordinate Nouns

Coordinate nouns show joint possession with *'s* following the last noun.

► *Fischer and Goulet's* partnership was the foundation of their business.

Coordinate nouns show individual possession with *'s* following each noun.

► The difference between *Barker's* and *Washburne's* test results was not statistically significant.

Possessive Pronouns

The possessive pronouns (*its, whose, his, her, our, your, my, their*) do not require apostrophes. ("Even good systems have *their* flaws.") Only the possessive form of a pronoun should be used with a gerund (a noun formed from an *-ing* **verb**).

► The safety officer insisted on *our* wearing protective clothing. [*Wearing* is the gerund.]

Possessive pronouns are also used to replace nouns. ("The responsibility was *theirs*.") See also **its / it's**.

Indefinite Pronouns

Some indefinite pronouns (*all, any, each, few, most, none, some*) form the possessive case with the **preposition** *of*.

► We tested both packages and found bacteria on the surface *of each*.

Other indefinite pronouns (*everyone, someone, anyone, no one*) use *'s*.

► *Everyone's* contribution is welcome.

P

prefixes

A prefix is a letter or group of letters placed in front of a root word that changes the meaning of the root word. When a prefix ends with a vowel and the root word begins with a vowel, the prefix is often separated from the root word with a **hyphen** (*co-opt, anti-inflammatory*). Some words with the double vowel are written without a hyphen (*cooperate*) and others with or without a hyphen (*re-elect* or *reelect*).

Prefixes, such as *neo-* (derived from a Greek word meaning "new"), are often hyphenated when used with a proper **noun** (*neo-Keynesian*).

Such prefixes are not normally hyphenated when used with common nouns, unless the base word begins with the same vowel (*neonatal, neo-orthodoxy*).

A hyphen may be necessary to clarify the meaning of a prefix; for example, *reform* means "correct" or "improve," and *re-form* means "change the shape of." When in doubt, check a current dictionary.

preparation

The preparation stage of the writing process is essential. By determining the needs of your **audience**, your **purpose**, the **context**, and the **scope** of coverage, you will come to understand what information you need to gather during **research**. See also **collaborative writing** and "Five Steps to Successful Writing" (pages xvii–xxiii).

WRITER'S CHECKLIST   Preparing to Write

✔ Determine who your readers are, and learn certain key facts about them — their knowledge, attitudes, expectations, and needs relative to your subject.

✔ Determine the document's primary purpose: What exactly do you want your readers to know, believe, or do when they have finished reading your document?

✔ Consider the context of your message and how it should affect your writing.

✔ Establish the scope of your document — the type and amount of detail you must include — not only by understanding your readers' needs and purpose but also by considering any external constraints, such as word limits for trade journal articles or how you might need to compress text, as in **writing for the Web**.

✔ Select the medium appropriate to your readers and purpose. See also **selecting the medium**.

P

prepositions

A preposition is a word that links a **noun** or **pronoun** to another sentence element by expressing such relationships as direction (*to, into, across, toward*), location (*at, in, on, under, over, beside, among, by, between, through*), time (*before, after, during, until, since*), or position (*for*, *against*, *with*). Together, the preposition, its **object** (the noun or pronoun), and the object's **modifiers** form a prepositional **phrase**, which acts as a modifier.

▶ Answer help-line questions *in a courteous manner*. [The prepositional phrase *in a courteous manner* modifies the **verb** *answer*.]

The object of a preposition (the word or phrase following the preposition) is always in the objective **case**. When the object is a compound expression, both nouns and pronouns should be in the objective case. For example, the phrase "between you and *me*" is frequently and incorrectly written as "between you and *I*." *Me* is the objective form of the pronoun, and *I* is the subjective form.

Many words that function as prepositions also function as **adverbs**. If the word takes an object and functions as a connective, it is a preposition; if it has no object and functions as a modifier, it is an adverb.

PREPOSITIONS   The thermostat is *behind* the column *in* the conference room.

ADVERBS   The customer lagged *behind*; then he came *in* and sat down.

Certain verbs, adverbs, and adjectives are normally used with certain prepositions (interested *in*, aware *of*, equated *with*, adhere *to*, capable *of*, object *to*, infer *from*). See also **idioms**.

Prepositions at the End of a Sentence

A preposition at the end of a sentence can be an indication that the sentence is awkwardly constructed.

▶ ~~The~~ branch office ~~is where she was at.~~

She was at the .

However, if a preposition falls naturally at the end of a sentence, leave it there. ("I don't remember which file name I saved it *under*.")

Prepositions in Titles

Capitalize prepositions in **titles** when they are the first or last words, or when they contain five or more letters (unless you are following a style that recommends otherwise). See also **capitalization**.

▶ The newspaper column "In My Opinion" included a review of the article "New Concerns About Distance Education." [*In* and *About* are prepositions.]

Preposition Errors

Do not use redundant prepositions, such as "off *of*," "in back *of*," "inside *of*," and "at *about*."

| EXACT | The client will arrive at ~~about~~ four o'clock. |
| APPROXIMATE | The client will arrive ~~at~~ about four o'clock. |

Avoid unnecessarily adding the preposition *up* to verbs.

► Call ~~up and~~ ^to^ see if he is in his office.

Do not omit necessary prepositions.

► He was oblivious ^to^ and not distracted by the view from his office window.

See also **conciseness** and **English as a second language**.

---

presentations

P

To prepare an effective presentation, determine your **purpose** and analyze your **audience**. Then **research** your subject and logically organize the information that supports your point of view or proposal. Presentations differ from written documents because your spoken delivery requires as much attention as your content, and your **organization** and **visuals** must be adapted to the audience that will view your presentation.

Determining Your Purpose

Determine your primary purpose by asking the following question: What do I want the audience to know, believe, or do when I have finished the presentation? Based on the answer to that question, write a purpose statement that answers the *what?* and *why?* questions.

► The purpose of my presentation is to convince my company's senior management of the need to hire a full-time social-media marketing coordinator [*what*] so that they will be persuaded to allocate additional funds in the budget for this position in the next fiscal year [*why*].

Analyzing Your Audience

Once you have determined the desired end result of the presentation, ask yourself these questions about your audience so that you can tailor your presentation to their needs.

- What is their level of experience or knowledge about your topic?
- What are their educational levels, ages, and other demographics?
- What is their attitude toward your topic and—based on that attitude—what are their possible concerns, fears, or objections?
- Are there subgroups in the audience with different concerns or needs?
- What questions might audience members ask about this topic?

Gathering Information

Once you have focused the presentation, you need to find the facts and arguments that support your point of view or the action you propose. As you gather information, keep in mind that you should give the audience only what will accomplish your goals; too much detail will overwhelm them, and too little will not adequately inform your listeners or support your recommendations.

Structuring the Presentation

Focus on your audience as listeners. Listeners are freshest at the outset and refocus their attention near the end. Take advantage of that pattern. Give your audience a brief overview of your presentation at the beginning, use the body to develop your ideas, and end with a summary of what you covered and, if appropriate, a call to action. See also **listening** and **methods of development**.

The Introduction.　　Include in the **introduction** an opening that focuses your audience's attention, as in the following examples:

▶ [*Definition of a problem*] "You have to write an important report, and you'd like to incorporate lengthy handwritten notes from several meetings. But handwriting all those pages seems an incredible waste of time! Have I got a solution for you."

▶ [*An attention-getting statement*] "As many as 70 million Americans have high blood pressure."

▶ [*A rhetorical question*] "Would you be interested in a full-size computer keyboard that's waterproof, noiseless, and rolls up like a rubber mat?"

▶ [*A personal experience*] "On a recent business trip, my rental car's navigation system had me on the wrong highway—and thirty miles in the wrong direction! After I managed to head in the right direction, I realized: we need a mobile alert app."

▶ [*An appropriate quotation*] "According to researchers at the Massachusetts Institute of Technology, 'Garlic and its cousin, the onion, confer major health benefits—including fighting cancer, infections, and heart disease.'"

Following your opening, use the introduction to provide an overview of the presentation. An overview can include general or background information that will be needed to understand the detailed information that follows, or it can preview how you have organized the material.

▶ This presentation analyzes three high-volume, networked on-demand printers for us to consider purchasing. Based on a comparison of all three, I will recommend the one I believe best meets our needs. To do so, I'll discuss the following five points:

1. Why we need a networked high-volume printer [*the problem*]
2. The basics of networked on-demand technology [*general information*]
3. The criteria I used to compare the three printer models [*comparison*]
4. The printer models I compared and why [*possible solutions*]
5. The printer I propose we buy [*proposed solution*]

The Body.   If your goal is to persuade, present the evidence that will convince the audience to accept your conclusions and act on them. (See **persuasion**.) If you are discussing a problem, demonstrate that it exists and offer a solution or range of possible solutions. For example, if your introduction stated that the problem for a company is low profits, high costs, or outdated technology, you could use the following approach:

1. Prove your point.
   • Strategically organize the facts and data you need.
   • Present the information using easy-to-understand visuals.
2. Offer solutions.
   • Increase profits by lowering production costs.
   • Cut overhead to reduce costs, or abolish specific programs or product lines.
   • Replace outdated technology, or upgrade existing technology.

P

3. Anticipate questions ("How much will it cost?") and objections ("We're too busy now—when would we have time to learn the new software?"), and incorporate the answers into your presentation.

Transitions.   Planned **transitions** should appear between the introduction and the body, between major points in the body, and between the body and the closing. Transitions are simply a sentence or two to let the audience know that you are moving from one topic to the next. They also prevent a choppy presentation and provide the audience with assurance that you know where you are going and how to get there.

▶ Before getting into the specifics of each printer I compared, I'd like to present the benefits of networked on-demand printers in general. That information will provide you with the background you'll need to compare the differences among the printers and their capabilities, which I discuss in this presentation.

It is also a good idea to pause for a moment after you have delivered a transition between topics to let your listeners shift gears with you. Remember, they do not know your plan.

The Closing.   Your closing is what your audience is most likely to remember, so use that time to be strong and persuasive. If your purpose is to motivate the listeners to take action, ask them to do what you want them to do. If it is to open your listeners' minds, conclude by stating why your position is viable. Consider the following typical closing.

▶ Based on all the data, I believe that the Worthington TechLine 5510 Production Printer best suits our needs. It produces 40 pages per minute *more* than its closest competitor and provides modular systems that can be upgraded to support new applications. The Worthington is also compatible with our current network, and staff training at our site is included with our purchase. Although the initial cost is higher than that for the other two models, the additional capabilities, compatibility with most standard environments, lower maintenance costs, and strong customer-support services make it a better value.

   I recommend we allocate the funds necessary for this printer by the fifteenth of this month to be well prepared for the production of next quarter's customer publications.

This closing brings the presentation full circle and asks the audience to fulfill the purpose of the presentation—exactly what a **conclusion** should do.

Using Visuals

Well-planned visuals can add interest, focus, and emphasis to your presentation. Charts, graphs, and illustrations can greatly increase audience understanding and retention of information, especially for complex issues and technical information that could otherwise be misunderstood or overlooked.

❖ **ETHICS NOTE** Be sure to provide credit for any visual taken from a print or an online source. You can include a citation either on an individual visual (such as a slide) or in a list of references or works cited that you distribute to your audience. For information on citing visuals, see **documenting sources**. ❖

You can create and present the visual components of your presentation by using a variety of media—flip charts, whiteboards or chalkboards, or presentation software. See also **layout and design**.

◀ **PROFESSIONALISM NOTE** If your presentation contains a lot of details or complex drawings, prepare handouts for your audience, on which they can jot down notes for future reference. ▶

Flip Charts.   Flip charts, usually on easels, are ideal for use with smaller groups in a conference room or classroom and work well for **brainstorming** with your audience.

Whiteboards or Chalkboards.   The whiteboards or chalkboards common to classrooms are convenient for creating sketches and for jotting down notes during your presentation.

Presentation Software.   Presentation software, such as Microsoft PowerPoint, Prezi, and open-source products, helps you integrate text, audio, images, links, and video content into your presentation. These programs and others that offer various collaborative and file-sharing capabilities constantly evolve and require that you keep current with the latest versions and enhancements. (See **adapting to new technologies**.) Avoid using too many enhancements, which may distract your audience from your message. Figure P–4 (page 400) shows well-balanced slides for a presentation based on the sample formal report in Figure F–6.

◀ **PROFESSIONALISM NOTE** Be sure to prepare for potential technical difficulties. Should you encounter a technical snag during the presentation, stay calm and give yourself time to solve the problem. If you cannot solve the problem, move on without the technology. As a precaution, always carry a printout of your slides and copies for your audience, and save a backup copy of your digital presentation file. ▶

P

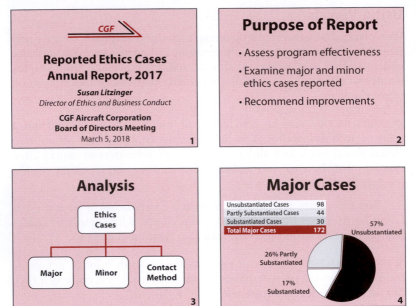

FIGURE P–4. Presentation Slides

WRITER'S CHECKLIST   Using Visuals in a Presentation

✔ Limit each visual to a number of words that can be quickly read by your audience.

✔ Use a font size readable to audience members at the back of the room.

✔ Limit the number of items in **lists** to no more than five or six per visual, and use numbers if sequence is important and bullets if not.

✔ Create lists with **parallel structure** and balanced content.

(continued)

| WRITER'S CHECKLIST | **Using Visuals in a Presentation** (*continued*) |

✔ Make your visuals consistent in font style, size, and spacing.

✔ Consider the contrast between your content and the background to ensure that text and images are clear to those in the audience.

✔ Use only one or two illustrations per visual (or slide) to avoid clutter.

✔ Use graphs, charts, and **infographics** to show data trends.

✔ Avoid overloading your presentation with so many visuals that you distract or tax the audience's concentration: One visual for every two minutes is a common guideline.

✔ Avoid using sound or visual effects in presentation software that distract from the content or may seem unprofessional.

✔ Do not read the text on your visual word for word. Your audience can read the visuals; they look to you to develop the key points.

✔ Match your delivery of the content to your visuals. Do not put one visual on the screen and talk about the previous visual or the next one.

Delivering a Presentation

Once you have outlined and drafted your presentation and prepared your visuals, you are ready to practice your presentation and delivery techniques. See also **outlining**.

Practice.   Familiarize yourself with the sequence of the material— major topics, notes, and visuals—in your outline. Once you feel comfortable with the content, you are ready to practice the presentation (in front of others if possible).

P

PRACTICE ON YOUR FEET AND OUT LOUD.   Try to practice on-site to get the feel of the room: the lighting, the equipment, the seating, the location of outlets and switches, and so forth. Practice out loud to gauge the length of your presentation, to uncover problems (such as awkward transitions), and to eliminate verbal tics (for example, "um," "you know," and "like").

PRACTICE WITH YOUR VISUALS AND TEXT.   Integrate your visuals into your practice sessions to help your presentation go more smoothly. Operate the equipment (computer or presentation system) until you are comfortable with it.

Delivery Techniques That Work.   Your delivery is both aural and visual. In addition to your words and message, your nonverbal communication affects your audience. Be animated—your words have impact and staying power when they are delivered with physical and vocal animation. If you want listeners to share your point of view, show enthusiasm for your topic. The most common delivery techniques include making eye contact; using movement and gestures; and varying voice inflection, projection, and pace.

EYE CONTACT.   The best way to establish rapport with your audience is through eye contact. In a large audience, directly address those who seem most responsive to you in different parts of the room. Doing so also gives you important visual cues about how your message is being received. Do the listeners seem engaged? Based on your observations, you may need to adjust your pace.

MOVEMENT.   Animate the presentation with physical movement. Take a step or two to one side after you have been talking for a minute or so. That type of movement is most effective at transitional points in your presentation, such as between major topics or after pauses or emphases. Too much movement, however, can be distracting, so try not to pace.

Another way to integrate movement into your presentation is to walk to the screen and point to the visual as you discuss it. Touch the screen with the pointer and then turn back to the audience before beginning to speak (remember the three *t*'s: touch, turn, and talk).

GESTURES.   Gestures both animate your presentation and help communicate your message. Most people gesture naturally when they talk; nervousness, however, can inhibit gesturing during a presentation. Keep one hand free, and use that hand to gesture.

VOICE.   Your voice can be an effective tool in communicating your sincerity, enthusiasm, and command of your topic. *Vocal inflection* is the rise and fall of your voice at different times, such as the way your voice naturally rises at the end of a question ("You want it *when?*"). Conversational delivery and eye contact promote the feeling among audience members that you are addressing them directly. Use vocal inflection to highlight differences between key and subordinate points.

PROJECTION.   Most presenters think they are speaking louder than they are. Remember that your presentation will be ineffective for anyone in the audience who cannot hear you. Correct projection problems by practicing out loud with someone listening from the back of the room.

PACE.   Be aware of the speed at which you deliver your presentation. If you speak too fast, your words will run together, making it difficult for your audience to follow. If you speak too slowly, your listeners will become impatient and distracted.

Presentation Anxiety.   Everyone experiences nervousness before a presentation. Instead of letting fear inhibit you, channel your nervous energy into a helpful stimulant. The best way to master anxiety is to know your topic thoroughly—knowing what you are going to say and how you are going to say it will help you gain confidence and reduce anxiety as you become immersed in your subject.

Preparing for and Delivering a Presentation

✔ Prepare a set of notes that will trigger your memory during the presentation.

✔ Make as much eye contact as possible with your audience to establish rapport and maximize opportunities for audience feedback.

✔ Animate your delivery by integrating movement, gestures, and vocal inflection into your presentation. However, keep your movements and speech patterns natural.

✔ Speak loudly and slowly enough to be heard and understood.

✔ Review *Writer's Checklist: Using Visuals in a Presentation* (pages 400–401) as well as this entry's advice on presentation delivery.

For tips on communicating with cross-cultural audiences, see **global communication**, **global graphics**, and **international correspondence**.

press releases

The purpose of a press release (or *news release*) is both to inform the public about the company and its products and services, and to enhance the organization's brand identity. Large corporations and institutions usually have their own public relations staff or use outside agencies. However, if you work for a small company without public relations resources, you may be called on to write a press release.

The press release should be clear, concise, and written with particular attention to the five *w*'s: *who*, *what*, *where*, *when*, and *why*. Begin the first paragraph with the place and date of the announcement, as shown in Figure P–5 (on page 404). Put all critical information in the first paragraph, then use the decreasing **order-of-importance method of development** to organize the following paragraphs. Use the final paragraph to provide a brief overview of the organization as well as its products, services, and locations. Make sure your facts are accurate, and be careful to define any unfamiliar terms.

News releases are usually distributed through online outlets as well as by local newspapers and television and radio stations. Organizations also post versions of releases on their own Web sites or **social media** sites, and distribute them to trade and professional associations. See also **blogs and forums** and **newsletter articles**.

News Release
_____

BENTLEY PLASTICS
3535 Michigan Avenue ■ Chicago, IL 60653

Contact: Marjorie Kohls
E-mail: mkohls@bentley.com
Phone: (312) 712-1946
Fax: (312) 712-1950

FOR IMMEDIATE RELEASE

Mark Williams Joins Bentley Plastics as Vice President

Chicago, Illinois, May 22, 2018: Marketing expert and author Mark Williams has been appointed Vice President of Marketing at Bentley Plastics, a manufacturer of polymer tubing and coils. He will direct the Illinois and Indiana district sales offices and coordinate overseas distribution through the company's Singapore office. Williams will travel extensively throughout Southeast Asia while developing marketing channels for Bentley.

    Formerly, Williams was director of services with International Marketing Associates, a consulting group in New York. While at IMA, he developed a computer-based marketing center that linked textile firms in the United States, Finland, and Great Britain. A graduate of the Columbia University Graduate School of Business, Williams is the author of *Marketing Dynamics*, a book used in marketing classrooms at major universities.

    Bentley Plastics, founded in 1978 and headquartered in Chicago, is one of the world's largest producers of plastic tubing. With plants in Skokie, Illinois, and Gary, Indiana, Bentley Plastics is able to produce more than 80 million linear feet of tubing per year.

# # #

Main message

Company background

FIGURE P–5. Press Release

WRITER'S CHECKLIST   **Preparing Press Releases**
_____

✔ Use company stationery with a minimum of one-inch margins.
✔ Use boldface type for the headlines and double-space paragraphs for easy reading and copying.

(continued)

✔ Consider including a professional photograph of a new hire (head shot) or product.

✔ Use "*-more-*" centered at the bottom of the page when you need to indicate that another page follows.

✔ Allow one blank line, then center "# # #" or "*-30-*" or "*-End-*" to indicate where the press release ends.

✔ Send the release to a specific person, such as a business or technology editor or blogger.

principal / principle

Principal, meaning "an amount of money on which interest is earned or paid" or "a chief official in a school or court proceeding," is sometimes confused with *principle*, which means "a basic truth or belief."

▶ The bank will pay 3.5 percent on the *principal*.

▶ He sent an e-mail to the *principal* of the high school.

▶ She objected to the idea on *principle*.

Principal is also an adjective, meaning "main" or "primary." ("My *principal* objection is that it will be too expensive.")

process explanation

A process explanation may describe the steps in a process, an operation, or a procedure, such as the steps necessary to start a small business. The **introduction** often presents a brief overview of the process or lets **readers** know why it is important for them to become familiar with the process you are explaining. Be sure to define terms that readers might not understand and provide **visuals** to clarify the process. See also **defining terms** and **instructions**.

In describing a process, use transitional words and phrases to create unity within **paragraphs**, and select **headings** to provide a **transition** from one step to the next. The example of a "Tuition Reimbursement Approval" on page 389 describes a step-by-step process.

progress and activity reports

Progress reports provide details on the tasks completed for major work-place projects, whereas *activity reports* focus on the ongoing work of individual employees. Both are sometimes called *status reports*. Although many organizations use standardized templates and others use Web-based report forms, the content and structure shown in Figures P–6 and P–7 are typical. See also **reports**.

Progress Reports

A progress report provides information to decision-makers about the status of a project—whether it is on schedule and within budget. Progress reports are often submitted by a contracting company to a client company, as shown in Figure P–6. They are used mainly for projects that involve many steps and are issued at regular intervals to describe what has been done and what remains to be done. Progress reports help projects run smoothly by helping managers assign work, adjust schedules, allocate budgets, and order supplies and equipment. All progress reports for a particular project should have the same **format**.

The **introduction** to the first progress report should identify the project, methods used, necessary materials, expenditures, and completion date. Subsequent reports summarize the progress achieved since the preceding report and list the steps that remain to be taken. The body of the progress report should describe the project's status, including such details as schedules and costs, a statement of the work completed, and perhaps an estimate of future progress. The report ends with **conclusions** and recommendations about changes in the schedule, materials, techniques, and other information important to the project.

Activity Reports

Within an organization, employees often submit activity reports to managers on the status of ongoing projects. Managers may combine the activity reports of several individuals or teams into larger activity reports and, in turn, submit those larger reports to their own managers. The activity report shown in Figure P–7 (page 408) was submitted by a manager (Wayne Tribinski) who supervises 11 employees; the reader of the report (Kathryn Hunter) is Tribinski's manager.

Because the activity report is issued periodically (usually monthly) and contains material familiar to its **readers**, it normally needs no introduction or conclusion, although it may need a brief opening to provide **context**. Although the format varies from company to company, these sections are typical: Current Projects, Current Problems, Plans for the Next Period, and Current Staffing Level (for managers).

Hobard Construction Company

9032 Salem Avenue
Lubbock, TX 79409

www.hobardcc.com
(808) 769-0832
Fax: (808) 769-5327

August 14, 2018

Walter M. Wazuski
County Administrator
109 Grand Avenue
Manchester, NH 03103

Report recipient

Dear Mr. Wazuski:

Subject: Progress Report 8 for July 31, 2018

Period covered and status

The renovation of the County Courthouse is progressing on schedule and within budget. Although the cost of certain materials is higher than our original bid indicated, we expect to complete the project without exceeding the estimated costs because the speed with which the project is being completed will reduce overall labor expenses.

Costs

Materials used to date have cost $178,600, and labor costs have been $293,000 (including some subcontracted plumbing). Our estimate for the remainder of the materials is $159,000; remaining labor costs should not exceed $400,000.

Work Completed

As of July 31, we finished the installation of the circuit-breaker panels and meters, the level-one service outlets, and all the subfloor wiring. The upgrading of the courtroom, the upgrading of the records-storage room, and the replacement of the air-conditioning units are in the preliminary stages.

Work Scheduled

We have scheduled the upgrading of the courtroom to take place from August 28 to October 9, the upgrading of the records-storage room from October 15 to November 16, and the replacement of the air-conditioning units from November 23 to December 17. We see no difficulty in having the job finished by the scheduled date of December 21.

Sincerely yours,

Tran Nuguélen

Tran Nuguélen
ntran@hobardcc.com

P

FIGURE P–6. Progress Report (Using Letter Format)

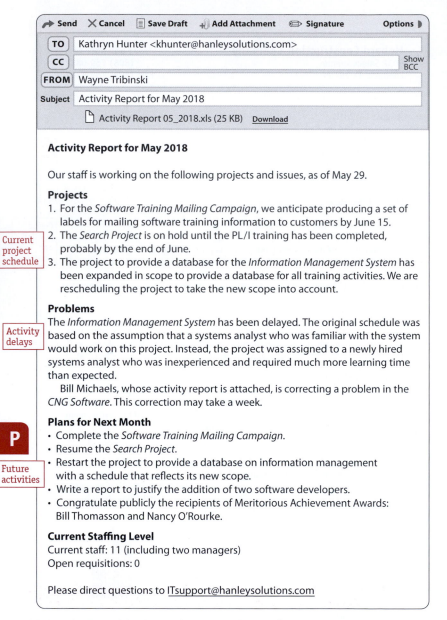

➤ Send ✕ Cancel 📄 Save Draft 📎 Add Attachment ✉ Signature	Options ▶

TO Kathryn Hunter <khunter@hanleysolutions.com>

CC _____ Show BCC

FROM Wayne Tribinski

Subject Activity Report for May 2018

📄 Activity Report 05_2018.xls (25 KB) <u>Download</u>

Activity Report for May 2018

Our staff is working on the following projects and issues, as of May 29.

Projects

1. For the *Software Training Mailing Campaign*, we anticipate producing a set of labels for mailing software training information to customers by June 15.

Current project schedule →

2. The *Search Project* is on hold until the PL/I training has been completed, probably by the end of June.
3. The project to provide a database for the *Information Management System* has been expanded in scope to provide a database for all training activities. We are rescheduling the project to take the new scope into account.

Problems

Activity delays →

The *Information Management System* has been delayed. The original schedule was based on the assumption that a systems analyst who was familiar with the system would work on this project. Instead, the project was assigned to a newly hired systems analyst who was inexperienced and required much more learning time than expected.

Bill Michaels, whose activity report is attached, is correcting a problem in the *CNG Software*. This correction may take a week.

Plans for Next Month

- Complete the *Software Training Mailing Campaign*.
- Resume the *Search Project*.

Future activities →

- Restart the project to provide a database on information management with a schedule that reflects its new scope.
- Write a report to justify the addition of two software developers.
- Congratulate publicly the recipients of Meritorious Achievement Awards: Bill Thomasson and Nancy O'Rourke.

Current Staffing Level

Current staff: 11 (including two managers)
Open requisitions: 0

Please direct questions to ITsupport@hanleysolutions.com

FIGURE P–7. Activity Report (Using E-mail Format)

P

promotional writing

Promotional writing is vital to the success of any company or organization; high-quality, state-of-the-art products or services are of little value if customers and clients do not know they exist. Although you may not be a marketing or public relations specialist, you may be asked to prepare promotional (or marketing) materials, especially if you work for a small organization or are self-employed. Even at a large company, you may contribute to Web sites, **brochures**, **newsletters**, **press releases**, **sales letters**, **blogs and forums**, or **social media** feeds. See also **collaborative writing** and **writing for the Web**.

Many other documents described in this book often include the additional or secondary purpose of promoting an organization. For example, **adjustment letters**, which are usually concerned with resolving a specific problem, offer opportunities to promote your organization.

WRITER'S CHECKLIST   Promotional Writing

✔ Analyze the needs, interests, concerns, makeup, and activities of your **audience**.

✔ Conduct adequate **research** to understand your audience, especially by talking to those with firsthand knowledge of the product or service. (See **interviewing for information**.)

✔ Use the principles of **persuasion** to gain attention, build interest, reduce resistance, and motivate readers to act.

✔ Optimize your keywords, phrases, and search tags to reach the greatest number of interested readers.

✔ Make information visually appealing through strong **organization**, **layout and design**, and **visuals** that are well integrated with the text.

✔ Write with **clarity**, **coherence**, and **conciseness** to help your readers understand the message and to achieve your **purpose**.

❖ **ETHICS NOTE** Because readers are persuaded only if they believe the source is credible, do not overstate claims and avoid possible **logic errors**. See also **ethics in writing**. ❖

pronoun reference

A **pronoun** should refer clearly to a specific antecedent. Avoid vague and uncertain references.

▶ We got the account ~~as a result of our proposal. It was a big one.~~ *, which was a big one,*

For **coherence**, place pronouns as close as possible to their antecedents—distance increases the likelihood of **ambiguity**.

▶ The office building next to City Hall *, praised for its architectural design, is* ~~is praised for its architectural design.~~

A general (or broad) reference or one that has no real antecedent is a problem that often occurs when the word *this* is used by itself.

▶ He deals with personnel problems in his work. This *experience* helps him in his personal life.

Another common problem is a hidden reference, which has only an implied antecedent.

▶ A high-lipid, low-carbohydrate diet is "ketogenic" because it favors ~~their~~ *the* formation *of ketone bodies*.

Do not repeat an antecedent in parentheses following the pronoun. If you feel you must identify the pronoun's antecedent in that way, rewrite the sentence.

AWKWARD   The senior partner first met Bob Evans when he (Evans) was a trainee.

IMPROVED   Bob Evans was a trainee when the senior partner first met him.

IMPROVED   When the senior partner first met Bob Evans, Bob was a trainee.

For advice on avoiding pronoun-reference problems with gender, see **biased language**.

pronouns

DIRECTORY

Case 412	Number 413
Gender 413	Person 414

A pronoun is a word that is used as a substitute for a **noun** (the noun for which a pronoun substitutes is called the *antecedent*). Using pronouns in place of nouns relieves the monotony of repeating the same noun over and over. See also **pronoun reference**.

Personal pronouns refer to the person or people speaking (*I, me, my, mine; we, us, our, ours*); the person or people spoken to (*you, your, yours*); or the person, people, or thing(s) spoken of (*he, him, his; she, her, hers; it, its; they, them, their, theirs*). See also **person** and **point of view**.

▶ If *their* figures are correct, *ours* must be in error.

Demonstrative pronouns (*this, these, that, those*) indicate or point out the thing being referred to.

▶ *This* is my desk. *These* are my coworkers. *That* will be a difficult job. *Those* are incorrect figures.

Relative pronouns (*who, whom, which, that*) perform a dual function: (1) They take the place of nouns, and (2) they connect and establish the relationship between a dependent **clause** and its main clause.

▶ The department manager decided *who* would be hired.

Interrogative pronouns (*who, whom, what, which*) are used to ask questions.

▶ *What* is the trouble?

Indefinite pronouns specify a class or group of persons or things rather than a particular person or thing (*all, another, any, anyone, anything, both, each, either, everybody, few, many, most, much, neither, nobody, none, several, some, such*).

▶ Not *everyone* liked the new procedures; *some* even refused to follow them.

A *reflexive pronoun*, which always ends with the suffix *-self* or *-selves*, indicates that the subject of the sentence acts upon itself. See also **sentence construction**.

▶ The electrician accidentally shocked *herself*.

The reflexive pronouns are *myself, yourself, himself, herself, itself, oneself, ourselves, yourselves,* and *themselves*. *Myself* is not a substitute for *I* or *me* as a personal pronoun.

▶ Victor and ~~myself~~ *I* completed the report on time.

▶ The assignment was given to Ingrid and ~~myself~~ *me.*

Intensive pronouns are identical in form to the reflexive pronouns, but they perform a different function: Intensive pronouns emphasize their antecedents.

▶ I *myself* asked the same question.

P

Reciprocal pronouns (*one another*, *each other*) indicate the relationship of one item to another. *Each other* is commonly used when referring to two persons or things, and *one another* when referring to more than two.

▶ Lashell and Kara work well with *each other*.

▶ The crew members work well with *one another*.

Case

Pronouns have forms to show the subjective, objective, and possessive cases.

SINGULAR	SUBJECTIVE	OBJECTIVE	POSSESSIVE
First person	I	me	my, mine
Second person	you	you	your, yours
Third person	he, she, it	him, her, it	his, her, hers, its

PLURAL	SUBJECTIVE	OBJECTIVE	POSSESSIVE
First person	we	us	our, ours
Second person	you	you	your, yours
Third person	they	them	their, theirs

A pronoun that functions as the subject of a clause or sentence is in the subjective **case** (*I*, *we*, *he*, *she*, *it*, *you*, *they*, *who*). The subjective case is also used when the pronoun follows a linking **verb**.

▶ *She* is my boss.

▶ My boss is *she*.

P

A pronoun that functions as the object of a verb or **preposition** is in the objective case (*me*, *us*, *him*, *her*, *it*, *you*, *them*, *whom*).

▶ Ms. Davis hired Tom and *me*. [object of verb]

▶ Between *you* and *me*, she's wrong. [object of preposition]

A pronoun that expresses ownership is in the **possessive case** (*my*, *mine*, *our*, *ours*, *his*, *her*, *hers*, *its*, *your*, *yours*, *their*, *theirs*, *whose*).

▶ He took *his* notes with him on the business trip.

▶ We took *our* notes with us on the business trip.

A pronoun **appositive** takes the case of its antecedent.

▶ Two systems analysts, Joe and *I*, were selected to represent the company. [*Joe and I* is in apposition to the subject, *two systems analysts*, and must therefore be in the subjective case.]

▶ The manager selected two representatives—Joe and *me*. [*Joe and me* is in apposition to *two representatives*, which is the object of the verb, *selected*, and therefore must be in the objective case.]

If you have difficulty determining the case of a compound pronoun, try using the pronoun singly.

▶ In his letter, Eldon mentioned *him* and *me*.
In his letter, Eldon mentioned *him*.
In his letter, Eldon mentioned *me*.

▶ *They* and *we* must discuss the terms of the merger.
They must discuss the terms of the merger.
We must discuss the terms of the merger.

When a pronoun modifies a noun, try it without the noun to determine its case.

▶ [*We / Us*] pilots fly our own planes.
We fly our own planes. [You would not write, "*Us* fly our own planes."]

▶ He addressed his remarks directly to [*we / us*] technicians.
He addressed his remarks directly to *us*. [You would not write, "He addressed his remarks directly to *we*."]

Gender

A pronoun must agree in gender with its antecedent. A problem sometimes occurs because the masculine pronoun has traditionally been used to refer to both sexes. To avoid the sexual bias implied in such usage, use *he or she* or the plural form of the pronoun, *they*.

All   *they choose.*
▶ ~~Each~~ may stay or go as ~~he chooses.~~

As in this example, when the singular pronoun (*he*) changes to the plural (*they*), the singular indefinite pronoun (*each*) must also change to its plural form (*all*). See also **agreement** and **biased language**.

Number

Number is a frequent problem with a few indefinite pronouns (*each*, *either*, *neither*, and those ending with *-body* or *-one*, such as *anybody*, *anyone*, *everybody*, *everyone*, *nobody*, *no one*, *somebody*, and *someone*) that are normally singular and thus require singular verbs and corresponding singular pronouns.

▶ As *each member arrives* for the meeting, please hand *him or her* a copy of the confidential report. *Everyone* must return the copy before *he or she* leaves. *Everybody* on the committee *understands* that *neither* of our major competitors *is* aware of the new process we have developed.

Person

Third-person personal pronouns usually have antecedents.

▶ Gina presented the report to the members of the board of directors. *She* [Gina] first summarized *it* [the report] for *them* [the directors] and then asked for questions.

First- and second-person personal pronouns do not normally require antecedents.

▶ *I* like my job.

▶ *You* were on vacation at the time.

▶ *We* all worked hard on the project.

proofreading

Proofreading is essential whether you are writing a brief e-mail or a high-stakes résumé. Grammar checkers and spell checkers are important aids to proofreading, but they can make writers overconfident. If a typographical error results in a legitimate English word (for example, *coarse* instead of *course*), the spell checker will not flag the misspelling. You may find some of the tactics discussed in **revision** useful when proofreading; in fact, you may find passages during proofreading that will require further revision.

◀ **PROFESSIONALISM NOTE** Proofreading not only demonstrates that you respect readers (who can be distracted, irritated, or misled by errors in writing) but also reflects that you are professional in the way you approach your work. ▶

Whether the material you proofread is your own writing or that of someone else, proofread in several stages. Although you need to tailor the stages to the specific document and to your own problem areas, the following *Writer's Checklist* should provide a useful starting point.

Traditional handwritten proofreaders' marks are illustrated in the *Chicago Manual of Style*, 17th edition, Figures 2.6 and 2.7.

FIRST-STAGE REVIEW

✔ Appropriate **format**, as for **reports** or **correspondence**

✔ Consistent style, including **headings**, terminology, spacing, and fonts

✔ Correct numbering of figures and **tables**

SECOND-STAGE REVIEW

✔ Specific **grammar** and **usage** problems

✔ Appropriate **punctuation**

✔ Correct and consistent **abbreviations** and **capitalization**

✔ Correct **spelling** (including names and places)

✔ Accurate Web, **e-mail**, or other addresses

✔ Accurate data in tables, figures, and **lists**

✔ Cut-and-paste errors; for example, a result of moved or deleted text and **numbers**

FINAL-STAGE REVIEW

✔ Review of your overall goals: **audience** needs and **purpose**

✔ Appearance of the document (see **layout and design**)

✔ Review by a trusted colleague, especially for crucial documents (see **collaborative writing**)

proposals

P

DIRECTORY

A proposal is a document written to persuade readers that what is proposed will benefit them by solving a problem or fulfilling a need. When you write a proposal, therefore, you must convince readers that they need what you are proposing, that it is practical and appropriate, and that you are the right person or organization to provide the proposed product or service. See also **persuasion** and **"you" viewpoint**.

Proposal Strategies

For any proposal, support your assertions with relevant facts, statistics, and examples. Your supporting evidence must lead logically to your proposed plan of action or solution. Cite relevant sources that provide strong credibility to your argument. Do not wander from your main point or make false claims. See **ethics in writing**.

Audience and Purpose.   Proposals often require more than one level of approval, so take into account all the readers in your **audience** and their levels of technical knowledge. For example, if your primary reader is an expert on your subject but an executive who must approve the proposal is not, provide an **executive summary** written in nontechnical language. You might also include a **glossary** of terms used in the body of the proposal or an **appendix** that explains highly detailed information in nontechnical language. If your primary reader is not an expert, write the proposal with the nonexpert in mind but include an appendix that contains the technical details.

Writing a persuasive proposal can be simplified by composing a concise statement of **purpose**—the exact problem or opportunity that your proposal is designed to address. Composing a purpose statement first will also help you and any collaborators understand the direction, **scope**, and goals of your proposal.

Project Management.   Proposal writers are often faced with writing high-quality, persuasive proposals under tight organizational deadlines. Dividing the task into manageable parts is the key to accomplishing your goals, especially when proposals involve substantial **collaborative writing**. For example, you might set deadlines for completing various proposal sections or stages of the writing process. Proposal-management software allows businesses to automate the more routine tasks while easily tracking multiple versions.

Proposal Context and Types

Understanding the **context** of the proposal will help you determine the most appropriate writing strategy. In general, to persuade those within your organization to make a change or an improvement or perhaps to fund a project, you would write an *internal proposal*. To persuade those outside your company to agree to a plan or take a course of action, you would write an *external proposal*.

✔ Analyze your audience carefully to determine how to best meet your readers' needs or requirements.

✔ Write a concise purpose statement at the outset to clarify your proposal's goals.

✔ Divide the writing task into manageable segments, and develop a time line for completing tasks.

✔ Review the descriptions of proposal contexts, structure, and types in this entry.

✔ Focus on the proposal's benefits to readers, and anticipate their questions or objections.

✔ Incorporate evidence to support the claims of your proposal.

✔ Select an appropriate, visually appealing format (unless one is defined by the request for proposals). See **layout and design**.

✔ Use a confident, positive **tone** throughout the proposal.

Internal Proposals

The purpose of an internal proposal is to suggest a change or an improvement within the writer's organization. It is addressed to a superior who has the authority to accept or reject the proposal. Internal proposals are typically reviewed by one or more departments for cost, practicality, and potential benefits, so take account of all relevant audience members. Two common types of internal proposals—informal and formal—are often distinguished from each other by the frequency with which they are written and by the degree of change they propose.

Informal Internal Proposals.   Informal internal proposals are the most common type of proposal and typically include small spending requests, requests for permission to hire new employees or increase salaries, and requests to attend conferences or purchase new equipment. In writing informal or routine proposals, highlight any key benefits to be realized.

Formal Internal Proposals.   Formal internal proposals usually involve requests to commit large sums of money or to recommend large-scale reorganizations. They are usually organized into sections that describe a problem, propose a solution, and offer to implement the suggested recommendation. The body, in turn, is further divided into sections to reflect the subject matter. The proposal may begin with a section describing the background or history of an issue and go on to discuss options for addressing the issue in separate sections.

P

The *introduction* of your internal proposal should establish that a problem exists and needs a solution. If the audience is not convinced that there is a problem, your proposal will not succeed. After you identify the problem, summarize your solution and indicate its benefits and estimated total cost. Notice how the **introduction** in Figure P–8 states the problem directly and then summarizes the proposed solution.

The *body* of your internal proposal should offer a practical solution to the problem and provide the details necessary to inform and persuade your readers. In the body, describe the problem for which you are offering a solution; the methodology of your proposed solution; details about equipment, materials, and staff; cost breakdowns; and a comprehensive schedule. Figure P–8 provides a section from the body of an internal proposal.

The *conclusion* of your internal proposal should tie everything together, restate your recommendation, and close with a spirit of cooperation (offering to set up a meeting, supply additional information, or provide any other assistance that might be needed). Keep your conclusion brief, as in Figure P–8. See **conclusions**.

If your proposal cites information that you obtained through **research**, such as published reports, government statistics, or interviews, follow the conclusion with a list of works cited that provides complete publication information for each source.

External Proposals

External proposals are prepared for clients and customers outside your company. They are either submitted in response to a request for goods and services from another organization (a solicited proposal) or sent to an organization without a prior request (an unsolicited proposal). The **grant proposal** (pages 236–40) is a type of external proposal. Such proposals are usually submitted to nonprofit or government organizations to request funding.

Solicited Proposals.   These proposals seek the most qualified company to help an organization reach its goals by issuing a request for proposals (RFP) or an invitation for bids (IFB) to companies that compete for the work.

An RFP often defines a need or problem and allows those who respond to propose possible solutions. The procuring organization generally distributes an RFP to several predetermined vendors. The RFP usually outlines the specific requirements for the ideal solution. For example, if an organization needs a new accounting system, it may require the proposed system to create customized reports. The RFP also may define specific formatting requirements, such as page length, font type and size,

ABO, Inc.
Interoffice Memo

To: Joan Marlow, Director, Human Resources Division

From: Leslie Galusha, Chief   *ᵡG*
            Employee Benefits Department

Date: June 15, 2018

Subject: Proposal to Reduce Employee Health-Care Costs

Health-care and workers' compensation insurance costs at ABO, Inc., have risen 100 percent over the last six years. In 2012, costs were $5,675 per employee per year; in 2018, they have reached $11,560 per employee per year. This doubling of costs mirrors a national trend, with health-care costs anticipated to continue to rise at the same rate for the next ten years. Controlling these escalating expenses will be essential. They are reducing ABO's profit margin because the company currently pays 70 percent of the costs for employee coverage. | Statement of problem

Healthy employees bring direct financial benefits to companies in the form of lower employee insurance costs, lower absenteeism rates, and reduced turnover. Regular physical exercise promotes fit, healthy people by reducing the risk of coronary heart disease, diabetes, osteoporosis, hypertension, and stress-related problems. I propose that to promote regular, vigorous physical exercise for our employees, ABO implement a health-care program that focuses on employee fitness. . . . | Summary of solution

Problem of Health-Care Costs
The U.S. Department of Health and Human Services (HHS) recently estimated that health-care costs in the United States will triple by the year 2025. Corporate expenses for health care are rising at such a fast rate that, if unchecked, in seven years they will significantly erode corporate profits.

According to HHS, people who do not participate in a regular and vigorous exercise program incur double the health-care costs and are hospitalized 30 percent more days than people who exercise regularly. Nonexercisers are also 41 percent more likely to submit medical claims over $10,000 at some point during their careers than are those who exercise regularly.

These figures are further supported by data from independent studies. A model created by the National Institutes of Health (NIH) . . . | Details and evidence of problem

FIGURE P–8. Special-Purpose Internal Proposal (Introduction and Body)

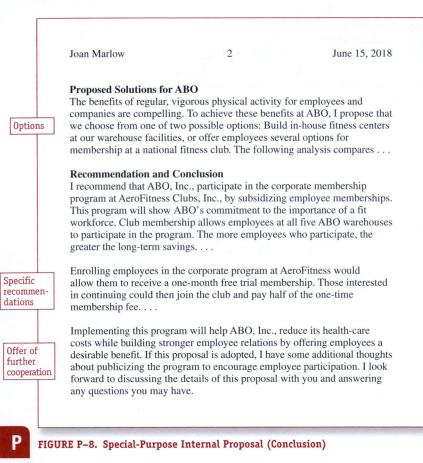

Joan Marlow   2   June 15, 2018

Proposed Solutions for ABO
The benefits of regular, vigorous physical activity for employees and
companies are compelling. To achieve these benefits at ABO, I propose that
Options — we choose from one of two possible options: Build in-house fitness centers
at our warehouse facilities, or offer employees several options for
membership at a national fitness club. The following analysis compares . . .

Recommendation and Conclusion
I recommend that ABO, Inc., participate in the corporate membership
program at AeroFitness Clubs, Inc., by subsidizing employee memberships.
This program will show ABO's commitment to the importance of a fit
workforce. Club membership allows employees at all five ABO warehouses
to participate in the program. The more employees who participate, the
greater the long-term savings. . . .

Specific recommendations — Enrolling employees in the corporate program at AeroFitness would
allow them to receive a one-month free trial membership. Those interested
in continuing could then join the club and pay half of the one-time
membership fee. . . .

Offer of further cooperation — Implementing this program will help ABO, Inc., reduce its health-care
costs while building stronger employee relations by offering employees a
desirable benefit. If this proposal is adopted, I have some additional thoughts
about publicizing the program to encourage employee participation. I look
forward to discussing the details of this proposal with you and answering
any questions you may have.

P

FIGURE P–8. Special-Purpose Internal Proposal (Conclusion)

headings, and sections. Some large organizations require that proposals
be submitted entirely online with specific requirements. When responding to RFPs, follow their requirements exactly—proposals that do not
are usually considered "noncompliant" and immediately rejected.

In contrast to an RFP, an IFB is commonly issued by federal, state,
and local government agencies to solicit bids on clearly defined products
or services. An IFB is restrictive, binding the bidder to produce an item
or a service that meets the exact requirements of the organization issuing
the IFB. The goods or services are defined in the IFB by references to
performance standards stated in technical specifications. Bidders must
be prepared to prove that their product will meet all requirements of
the specifications. The procuring organization generally publishes its IFB
online, either on its own Web site or on others, such as Federal Business

Opportunities at www.fbo.gov. Like RFPs, IFBs usually define specific format requirements; proposals that do not follow the required format can be rejected without review.

Unsolicited Proposals.   Unsolicited proposals are those submitted to a company without a prior request. Companies often operate for years with a problem they have never recognized (unnecessarily high maintenance costs, for example, or poor inventory-control methods). Many unsolicited proposals are preceded by a letter of inquiry that specifies the problem or unmet need to determine potential interest. A positive response would prompt a detailed study of the prospective client's needs. A formal proposal would then be prepared based on the results of the study.

Sales Proposals.   The sales proposal is a company's offer to provide specific goods or services to a potential buyer within a specified period of time and for a specified price. The primary purpose of a sales proposal is to demonstrate that the prospective customer's purchase of the seller's products or services will solve a problem, improve operations, or offer other benefits.

Sales proposals can be a page or two written by one person; many pages written collaboratively by several people; or hundreds of pages written by a proposal-writing team. Many sales proposals note that the offer is valid for a limited period (often 90 days). See also **collaborative writing**.

❖ **ETHICS NOTE** Once submitted, a sales proposal is a legally binding document that promises to offer goods or services within a specified time and for a specified price. ❖

Simple sales proposals typically follow the introduction-body-conclusion pattern. Long sales proposals must accommodate a greater variety of information and are organized to include some or all of the following sections specified in the RFP:

- Cover message
- Title page
- Executive or project summary
- General description of products
- Detailed solution or rationale
- Cost analysis
- Delivery schedule or work plan
- Site-preparation description
- Training requirements
- Statement of responsibilities
- Description of vendor
- Organizational sales pitch
- Conclusion
- Appendixes

COVER MESSAGE.   A long sales proposal begins with a **cover message** expressing appreciation for the opportunity to submit the proposal and offering thanks for any assistance received. The letter should acknowledge any previous positive association with the customer. Then it should summarize the recommendations offered in the proposal and express confidence that they will satisfy the customer's needs. Cover messages often list the documents attached or enclosed to help readers keep the associated documents together.

TITLE PAGE.   The title page contains the title of the proposal, the date of submission, the company to which it is being submitted, your company's name, and any symbol or logo that identifies your company.

EXECUTIVE SUMMARY.   An **executive summary**—sometimes called a *project summary*—follows the title page. Intended for the decision-maker who will ultimately accept or reject the proposal, it should summarize in nontechnical language how you plan to approach the work.

DESCRIPTION.   If your proposal offers products as well as services, it should include a general description of the products. In many cases, product descriptions will already exist as company boilerplate; be sure to check your company's files before drafting a description from scratch.

❖ **ETHICS NOTE**   Using "boilerplate" is neither **plagiarism** nor a violation of **copyright**. See also **repurposing**. ❖

RATIONALE.   Following the executive summary and general description of products, explain exactly how you plan to do what you are proposing. This section, called the *detailed solution* or *rationale*, will be read by specialists who can understand and evaluate your plan. It usually begins with a statement of the customer's problem, follows with a statement of the solution, and concludes with a statement of the benefits to the customer. In some proposals, the headings "Problem" and "Solution" are used for this section.

COST ANALYSIS.   A cost analysis itemizes the estimated cost of all the products and services that you are offering.

DELIVERY SCHEDULE.   The delivery schedule—also called a *work plan*—is a commitment to meet a specific timetable for providing agreed-upon products and services.

SITE PREPARATION.   If your recommendations include modifying your customer's physical facilities by moving walls, adding increased electrical capacity, and the like, include a site-preparation description that details the modifications required. In some proposals, the headings "Facilities" and "Equipment" are used for this section.

TRAINING. If the products and services proposed require training the customer's employees, specify the required training and its cost.

RESPONSIBILITIES. To prevent misunderstandings about what your and the customer's responsibilities will be, draw up a statement of responsibilities that explains in detail the tasks that are solely your responsibility and those that are solely the customer's responsibility.

VENDOR DESCRIPTION. The description-of-vendor section gives a profile of your company, its history, and its present position in the industry. The description-of-vendor section typically includes a list of people or subcontractors and the duties they will perform. The **résumés** of key personnel may also be placed here or in an appendix.

SALES PITCH. An organizational sales pitch usually follows the description-of-vendor section and is designed to sell the company and its general capability in the field. The sales pitch promotes the company and concludes the proposal on an upbeat note.

CONCLUSION. Some long sales proposals include a **conclusion** section that summarizes the proposal's salient points, stresses your company's strengths, and includes information about whom the potential client can contact for further information. It may also end with a request for the date the work will begin should the proposal be accepted.

APPENDIXES. Some proposals include **appendixes** made up of statistical analyses, maps, charts, tables, and résumés of the principal staff assigned to the project. Appendixes to proposals should contain only supplemental information.

Figure P–9 (on pages 424–33) shows sections from a major sales proposal.

P

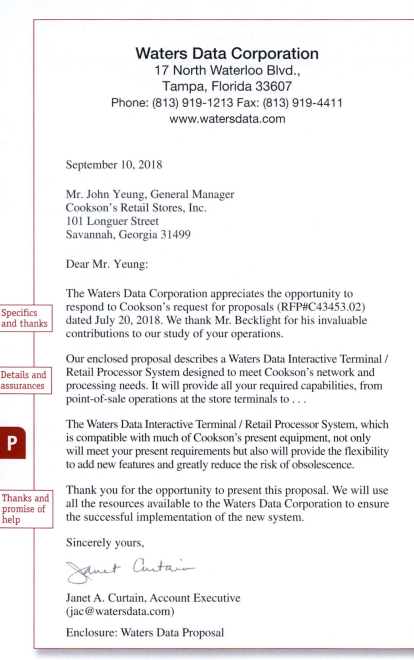

Waters Data Corporation

17 North Waterloo Blvd.,
Tampa, Florida 33607
Phone: (813) 919-1213 Fax: (813) 919-4411
www.watersdata.com

September 10, 2018

Mr. John Yeung, General Manager
Cookson's Retail Stores, Inc.
101 Longuer Street
Savannah, Georgia 31499

Dear Mr. Yeung:

Specifics and thanks

The Waters Data Corporation appreciates the opportunity to respond to Cookson's request for proposals (RFP#C43453.02) dated July 20, 2018. We thank Mr. Becklight for his invaluable contributions to our study of your operations.

Details and assurances

Our enclosed proposal describes a Waters Data Interactive Terminal / Retail Processor System designed to meet Cookson's network and processing needs. It will provide all your required capabilities, from point-of-sale operations at the store terminals to . . .

The Waters Data Interactive Terminal / Retail Processor System, which is compatible with much of Cookson's present equipment, not only will meet your present requirements but also will provide the flexibility to add new features and greatly reduce the risk of obsolescence.

Thanks and promise of help

Thank you for the opportunity to present this proposal. We will use all the resources available to the Waters Data Corporation to ensure the successful implementation of the new system.

Sincerely yours,

Janet Curtain

Janet A. Curtain, Account Executive
(jac@watersdata.com)

Enclosure: Waters Data Proposal

Figure P–9. Sales Proposal (Cover Message)

The Waters Data Proposal   September 10, 2018

EXECUTIVE SUMMARY

The Waters Data 319 Interactive Terminal / 615 Retail Processor System will provide your management with the tools necessary to manage people and equipment more profitably with procedures that will yield more cost-effective business controls for Cookson's.

Proposed system overview

The equipment and applications proposed for Cookson's were selected through the combined effort of Waters and Cookson's Management Information Systems Director, Mr. Becklight. The architecture of the system will respond to your current requirements and allow for future expansion.

The features and hardware in the system were determined from data acquired through the comprehensive survey we conducted at your stores in July of this year. The total of 71 Interactive Terminals proposed to service your four store locations is based on the number of terminals currently in use and on the average number of transactions processed during normal and peak periods. The planned remodeling of all four stores was also considered, and the suggested terminal placement has been incorporated into the working floor plan. The proposed equipment configuration and software applications have been simulated to determine system performance based on the volumes and anticipated growth rates of the Cookson's stores.

Scope summary

The information from the survey was also used in the cost justification, which was checked and verified by your controller, Mr. Deitering. The cost-effectiveness of the Waters Data Interactive Terminal / Retail Processor System is apparent. Expected savings, such as the projected 46 percent reduction in sales audit expenses, are realistic projections based on Waters Data's experience with other installations of this type.

P

Expected savings highlighted

Waters Data has a proven track record of success in the manufacture, installation, and servicing of retail business information systems stretching over decades. The system we propose will extend and strengthen our successful and long-term partnership with Cookson's.

– 1 –

FIGURE P–9. Sales Proposal (*continued*) **(Executive Summary)**

The Waters Data Proposal   September 10, 2018

GENERAL SYSTEM DESCRIPTION

The point-of-sale system that Waters Data is proposing for Cookson's includes two primary Waters products: the 319 Interactive Terminal and the 615 Retail Processor.

Waters Data 319 Interactive Terminal

The primary component in the proposed retail system is the Interactive Terminal. It contains a full microprocessor, which gives it the flexibility that Cookson's has been seeking.

Details of system and functions

The 319 Interactive Terminal provides freedom in sequencing a transaction. Users are not limited to a preset list of available steps or transactions. The terminal program can be adapted to provide unique transaction sets, each designed with a logical sequence of entry and processing to accomplish required tasks. In addition to sales transactions recorded on the selling floor, specialized transactions such as theater-ticket sales and payments can be designed for customer-service areas.

The 319 Interactive Terminal also functions as a credit authorization device, either by using its own floor limits or by transmitting a credit inquiry to the 615 Retail Processor for authorization.

Data-collection formats have been simplified so that transaction editing and formatting are much more easily accomplished. The IS manager has already been provided with documentation on these formats and has outlined all data-processing efforts that will be necessary to transmit the data to your current systems. These projections have been considered in the cost justification.

Waters Data 615 Retail Processor

The 615 Retail Processor is a minicomputer system designed to support the Waters family of retail terminals. The . . .

[*The proposal next describes the 615 Retail Processor before moving on to the detailed-solution section.*]

P

FIGURE P–9. Sales Proposal (*continued*) (General Description of Products)

PAYROLL APPLICATION

Current Procedure

Your current system of reporting time requires each hourly employee to sign a time sheet; the time sheet is reviewed by the department manager and sent to the Payroll Department on Friday evening. Because the week ends on Saturday, the employee must show the scheduled hours for Saturday and not the actual hours; therefore, the department manager must adjust the reported hours on the time sheet for employees who do not report on the scheduled Saturday or who do not work the number of hours scheduled.

The Payroll Department employs a supervisor and three full-time clerks. To meet deadlines caused by an unbalanced workflow, an additional part-time clerk is used for 20 to 30 hours per week. The average wage for this clerk is $13.00 per hour.

Advantage of Waters's System

The 319 Interactive Terminal can be programmed for entry of payroll data for each employee on Monday morning by department managers, with the data reflecting actual hours worked. This system would eliminate the need for manual batching, controlling, and data input. The Payroll Department estimates conservatively that this work consumes 40 hours per week.

Hours per week	40
Average wage (part-time clerk)	× 13.00
Weekly payroll cost	$520.00
Annual savings	$27,040

Elimination of the manual tasks of tabulating, batching, and controlling can save 0.25 hourly unit. Improved workflow resulting from timely data in the system without data-input processing will allow more efficient use of clerical hours. This would reduce payroll by the 0.50 hourly unit currently required to meet weekly check disbursement.

Eliminate manual tasks	0.25
Improve workflow	0.75
40-hour unit reduction	1.00

Hours per week	40
Average wage (full-time clerk)	15.00
Savings per week	$600.00
Annual savings	$31,200

TOTAL SAVINGS: $58,240

– 5 –

FIGURE P–9. Sales Proposal (*continued*) (Detailed Solution)

COST ANALYSIS

This section of our proposal provides detailed cost information for the Waters Data 319 Interactive Terminal and 615 Retail Processor. It then multiplies these major elements by the quantities required at each of your four locations.

319 Interactive Terminal

Equipment	Price	Maint. (1 yr.)
Terminal	$2,895	$167
Journal Printer	425	38
Receipt Printer	425	38
Forms Printer	525	38
Software	220	—
TOTALS	$4,490	$281

[*The cost section goes on to describe other costs to install the system before summarizing the costs.*]

The following table summarizes all costs.

Location	Hardware	Maint. (1 yr.)	Software
Store No. 1	$72,190	$4,975	$3,520
Store No. 2	89,190	6,099	4,400
Store No. 3	76,380	5,256	3,740
Store No. 4	80,650	5,537	3,960
Data Center	63,360	6,679	12,480
Subtotals	$381,770	$28,546	$28,100

TOTAL $438,416

System and maintenance costs

P

DELIVERY SCHEDULE

Waters normally delivers 319 Interactive Terminals and 615 Retail Processors within 30 days of the date of the contract. Upon Cookson's acceptance of this proposal, Waters will submit a specific time line for the completion of the installation.

All the software recommended in this proposal is available for immediate delivery. We do not anticipate any difficulty in meeting your tentative delivery schedule.

FIGURE P–9. Sales Proposal (*continued*) (Cost Analysis and Delivery Schedule)

SITE PREPARATION

Waters will work closely with Cookson's to ensure that each site is properly prepared prior to system installation. Cookson's is responsible for all building alterations and electrical facility changes, including the purchase and installation of communications cables, connecting blocks, and receptacles.

> System requirements and work responsibilities

Wiring
For the purpose of future site considerations, Waters's in-house wiring specifications for the system call for two twisted-pair wires and twenty-two shielded gauges. The length of communications cables must not exceed 2,500 feet.

As a guide for the power supply, we suggest that Cookson's consider the following:

1. The branch circuit (limited to 20 amps) should service no equipment other than 319 Interactive Terminals.
2. Each 20-amp branch circuit should support a maximum of three Interactive Terminals.
3. Each branch circuit must have three equal-size conductors—one hot leg, one neutral, and one insulated isolated ground.
4. Hubbell IG 5362 duplex outlets or the equivalent should be used to supply power to each terminal.
5. Server-room wiring will have to be upgraded to support the 615 Retail Processor.

You will receive a copy of Waters Data's installation and wiring procedures manual, which lists the physical dimensions, service clearance, and weight of the system components in addition to the power, logic, communications-cable, and environmental requirements.

P

FIGURE P–9. Sales Proposal (*continued*) (Site Preparation)

TRAINING

To ensure a successful installation, Waters offers the following training course for your operators.

Interactive Terminal / Retail Processor Operations
Course number: 8256
Length: three days
Tuition: $500

This course provides the student with the skills, knowledge, and practice required to operate an Interactive Terminal / Retail Processor System. Online, clustered, and stand-alone environments are covered.

We recommend that students have a department-store background and that they have some knowledge of the system configuration.

Employee training and costs

P

FIGURE P–9. Sales Proposal (*continued*) (Training)

RESPONSIBILITIES

On the basis of its years of experience in installing information-processing systems, Waters believes that a successful installation requires a clear understanding of certain responsibilities.

Waters Data's Responsibilities

Generally, Waters will provide its users with needed assistance during the installation so that live processing can begin as soon after installation as is practical. The following items describe our specific responsibilities:

- Provide operations documentation for each application that you acquire from Waters.
- Provide forms and other supplies as ordered.
- Provide specifications and technical guidance for proper site planning and installation.
- Provide adviser assistance in the conversion from your present system to the new system.

Cookson's Responsibilities

Cookson's will be responsible for the suggested improvements described earlier, as well as the following:

- Identify an installation coordinator and system operator.
- Provide supervisors and clerical personnel to perform conversion to the system.
- Establish reasonable time schedules for implementation.
- Ensure that the physical site requirements are met.
- Provide personnel to be trained as operators and ensure that other employees are trained as necessary.
- Implement and operate the system.

> Division of tasks between customer and vendor

P

– 11 –

FIGURE P–9. Sales Proposal (*continued*) (Statement of Responsibilities)

DESCRIPTION OF VENDOR

The Waters Data Corporation develops, manufactures, markets, installs, and services total business information-processing systems for selected markets. These markets are primarily in the retail, financial, commercial, industrial, health-care, education, and government sectors.

The Waters total-system concept encompasses one of the broadest hardware and software product lines in the industry. Waters computers range from small business systems to powerful general-purpose processors. Waters computers are supported by a complete spectrum of terminals, peripherals, and data-communication networks, as well as an extensive library of software products. Supplemental services and products include data centers, field service, systems engineering, and educational centers.

The Waters Data Corporation was founded in 1934 and currently has approximately 26,500 employees. The Waters headquarters is located at 17 North Waterloo Boulevard, Tampa, Florida, with district offices throughout the United States and Canada.

Vendor history and commitments

WHY WATERS?

Strong Commitment to the Retail Industry
Waters's commitment to the retail industry is stronger than ever. We are continually striving to provide leadership in the design and implementation of new retail systems and applications that will ensure our users of a logical growth pattern.

Dynamic Research and Development
Waters has spent increasingly large sums on research and development to ensure the availability of products and systems for the future. In 2017, our research-and-development expenditure for advanced systems design and technological innovations reached the $70-million level.

Leading Point-of-Sale Vendor
Waters is a leading point-of-sale vendor, having installed more than 150,000 units. The knowledge and experience that Waters has gained over the years from these installations ensure well-coordinated and effective systems implementations.

FIGURE P–9. Sales Proposal (*continued*) (Vendor Description and Organizational Sales Pitch)

The Waters Data Proposal   September 10, 2018

CONCLUSION

Waters Data welcomes the opportunity to submit this proposal to Cookson's. The Waters Data Corporation is confident that we have offered the right solution at a competitive price. Based on our hands-on analysis, our proposal takes into account your current and projected workloads and your plans to expand your facilities and operations. Our proposal will also enable Cookson's to minimize future employee costs and to enhance its accounting features.

> Final summary of system advantages

Waters has a proven track record of success in the manufacture, installation, and servicing of retail business information systems stretching over many decades. We also have a demonstrated record of success in our past business associations with Cookson's. We believe that the system we propose will extend and strengthen this partnership.

> Restatement of vendor experience and reputation

Should you require additional information about this proposal, please contact Janet A. Curtain, who will meet with you or arrange for Waters's technical staff to meet with you or send you the necessary materials.

> Offer to assist

We look forward to your decision and to continued success in our working relationship with Cookson's.

P

FIGURE P–9. Sales Proposal (Conclusion)

pseudo- / quasi-

As a **prefix**, *pseudo-*, meaning "false or counterfeit," is joined to the root word without a **hyphen** unless the root word begins with a capital letter (*pseudo*science, *pseudo*-Keynesian). *Pseudo-* is sometimes confused with *quasi-*, meaning "somewhat" or "partial." Unlike *semi-*, *quasi-* means "resembling something" rather than "half." *Quasi-* is usually hyphenated in combinations (*quasi*-marketing initiatives).

punctuation

Punctuation helps **readers** understand the meaning and relationships of words, phrases, clauses, and sentences. Marks of punctuation link, separate, enclose, indicate omissions, terminate, and classify. Most punctuation marks can perform more than one function. See also **sentence construction**.

The use of punctuation is determined by grammatical conventions and the writer's intention. Understanding punctuation is essential for writers because it enables them to communicate with **clarity** and precision. See also **grammar**.

Detailed information on each mark of punctuation is given in its own entry. The following are the 13 marks of punctuation.

apostrophe	'	**parentheses**	( )
brackets	[ ]	**period**	.
colon	:	**question mark**	?
comma	,	**quotation marks**	" "
dash	—	**semicolon**	;
exclamation mark	!	**slash**	/
hyphen	-		

See also **abbreviations**, **capitalization**, **contractions**, **dates**, **ellipses**, **italics**, and **numbers**.

P

purpose

The primary purpose, or objective, of a writing task is the answer to the following question: What do you want your **readers** to know, believe, or do once they have read your document? Be careful not to state a purpose too broadly. A statement of purpose such as "to explain continuing-education standards" is too general to be helpful during the writing process. In contrast, "to explain to members of the American Association of Critical-Care Nurses (AACN) how to determine if a continuing-education course meets AACN professional standards" is a specific purpose that will help you focus on the needs of your **audience** and what your document should accomplish. See also **context**.

The writer's primary purpose is often more complex than simply "to explain" something, as shown in the previous paragraph. Ask yourself not only *why* you are writing the document but also *what* you want your reader to believe or do after reading it. Suppose a writer for a **newsletter** has been assigned to write an article about cardiopulmonary resuscitation (CPR). In answer to the question *what?* the writer could state the purpose as "to emphasize the importance of CPR." To the question *why?* the writer might respond, "to encourage employees to sign up for evening CPR classes." Putting the answers to the two questions together, the writer's purpose might be stated as, "To write a document that will emphasize the importance of CPR and encourage employees to sign up for evening CPR classes." The primary purpose of this document is to persuade the readers of the importance of CPR, and the secondary goal is to motivate them to register for a class. Secondary goals often involve such abstract notions as to motivate, reassure, or inspire. See also **persuasion**.

If you answer the questions *what?* and *why?* and put the answers into writing as a stated purpose that includes both primary and secondary goals, you will simplify your writing task and more likely achieve your purpose. For a **collaborative writing** project, it is especially important to collectively write a statement of your purpose to ensure that the document achieves its goals. Do not lose sight of that purpose as you become engrossed in the other steps of the writing process. See also "Five Steps to Successful Writing" (pages xvii–xxiii).

P

Q

question marks

The question mark (?) most often ends a sentence that is a direct question or request.

- ▶ Where did you put the tax report? [direct question]
- ▶ Will you e-mail me if your shipment does not arrive by June 10? [request]

Use a question mark to end a statement that has an interrogative meaning—a statement that is declarative in form but asks a question.

- ▶ The tax report is finished? [question in declarative form]

Question marks may follow a series of separate items within an interrogative sentence.

- ▶ Do you remember the date of the contract? Its terms? Whether you signed it?

Use a question mark to end an interrogative clause within a declarative sentence.

- ▶ It was not until July (or was it August?) that we submitted the report.

Retain the question mark in a title that is being cited, even though the sentence in which it appears has not ended.

- ▶ *Can Investments Be Protected?* is the title of her book.

Never use a question mark to end a sentence that is an indirect question.

- ▶ He asked me where I put the tax report.

When a question is a polite request or an instruction to which an affirmative response is assumed, a question mark is not necessary.

- ▶ Will you call me as soon as he arrives. [polite request]

When used with __quotations__, the placement of the question mark is important. When the writer is asking a question, the question mark belongs outside the __quotation marks__.

▶ Did she actually say, "I don't think the project should continue"?

If the quotation itself is a question, the question mark goes inside the quotation marks.

▶ She asked, "Do we have enough funding?"

If both cases apply—the writer is asking a question and the quotation itself is a question—use a single question mark inside the quotation marks.

▶ Did she ask, "Do we have enough funding?"

questionnaires

A questionnaire is a __research__ tool consisting of a series of questions on a particular topic sent to a targeted group of individuals in an easy-to-tabulate form. It may be distributed on paper, as an __e-mail__ attachment, or as an online digital form. As you prepare a questionnaire, keep in mind your __purpose__ and your intended __audience__. See also __interviewing for information__.

Questionnaires have several advantages over the personal interview as well as several disadvantages.

ADVANTAGES
- A questionnaire allows you to gather information from more people than you could by conducting personal interviews.

- A questionnaire enables you to obtain responses from people who are difficult to reach or who are in various geographic locations.

- A questionnaire gives respondents more time to think through their answers than a personal interview would.

- A questionnaire may yield more objective data than an interview because an interviewer's tone of voice, facial expressions, or mere presence might influence an answer.

- The cost of distributing and tabulating a questionnaire is lower than the cost of conducting numerous personal interviews.

DISADVANTAGES
- Results may be slanted in favor of those people who have strong opinions on a subject because they are more likely to respond to a questionnaire than are those with only moderate views.

Q

- A questionnaire does not allow specific follow-up questions to answers.

- Distributing questionnaires and receiving responses may take longer than conducting personal interviews.

A sample cover e-mail message with a link to an online questionnaire is shown in Figure Q–1. The e-mail message and questionnaire were sent to employees in a large organization who had participated in a six-month pilot program of flexible working hours.

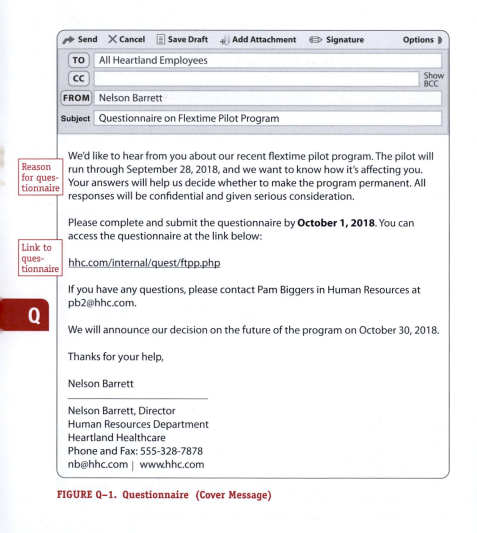

FIGURE Q–1. Questionnaire (Cover Message)

Questionnaire

+

Heartland Healthcare Flexible Working Hours Program
Questionnaire

1. **What kind of position do you occupy?**
   - ○ Supervisory   ○ Nonsupervisory

2. **Indicate to the nearest quarter of an hour when you begin work under flextime.**
   - ○ 7:00 a.m.
   - ○ 7:15 a.m.
   - ○ 7:30 a.m.
   - ○ 7:45 a.m.
   - ○ 8:00 a.m.
   - ○ 8:15 a.m.
   - ○ 8:30 a.m.
   - ○ 8:45 a.m.
   - ○ 9:00 a.m.
   - ○ Other (specify) [   ]

   Radio buttons for forced choice

3. **Where do you live?**
   - ○ Talbot County
   - ○ Montgomery County
   - ○ Greene County
   - ○ Other (specify) [   ]

4. **How do you usually travel to work?**
   - ☐ Drive alone
   - ☐ Bus
   - ☐ Train
   - ☐ Bicycle
   - ☐ Walk
   - ☐ Carpool
   - ☐ Motorcycle
   - ☐ Other (specify) [   ]

   Check box for more than one choice

5. **How has flextime affected your commuting time?**
   - ○ Increase: Approximate number of minutes [   ]
   - ○ Decrease: Approximate number of minutes [   ]
   - ○ No change

6. **If you drive alone or in a carpool, has flextime increased or decreased the amount of time it takes you to find a parking space?**
   - ○ Increased   ○ Decreased   ○ No change

7. **How has flextime affected your productivity?**
   - a. Quality of work
     - ○ Increased   ○ Decreased   ○ No change
   - b. Accuracy of work
     - ○ Increased   ○ Decreased   ○ No change
   - c. Quiet time for uninterrupted work
     - ○ Increased   ○ Decreased   ○ No change

8. **Have you had difficulty contacting coworkers who are on different schedules from yours?**
   - ○ Yes   ○ No

Q

FIGURE Q–1. Questionnaire (*continued*)

Questionnaire   +

9. Have you had trouble scheduling meetings within flexible starting and quitting times?
    ○ Yes   ○ No

10. Has flextime affected the way you feel about your job?
    ○ Yes   ○ No

    If yes, please answer (a) or (b):
    a. Feel better about job
        ○ Slightly   ○ Considerably

    b. Feel worse about job
        ○ Slightly   ○ Considerably

11. How important is it for you to have flexibility in your working hours?
    ○ Very   ○ Somewhat   ○ Not at all

12. Has flextime allowed you more time to be with your family?
    ○ Yes   ○ No   ○ N/A

13. If you are responsible for the care of a young child or children, has flextime made it easier or more difficult for you to arrange babysitting or day-care services?
    ○ Easier   ○ More difficult   ○ No change   ○ N/A

14. Do you recommend that the flextime program be made permanent?
    ○ Yes   ○ No

15. Please describe below any changes you recommend for the program.

Open response to elicit additional comments

Q

Back   Submit

Thank you for your assistance.

FIGURE Q–1. Questionnaire

Selecting the Recipients

Selecting the proper recipients for your questionnaire is crucial if you are to gather representative and usable data. Depending on the topic, you may need to include people from different geographic areas, occupations, genders, and educational backgrounds. Only by using a representative sample of your target population can you make a generalized statement based on your findings from the sample. (The best sources of information on sampling techniques are market-research and statistics texts.)

Preparing the Questions

Keep the questionnaire as brief as possible to maximize the return rate. Ask questions that are easy to understand; confusing questions will yield confusing results. Ideally, recipients should be able to answer most questions with a "yes" or "no" or by selecting one choice from among several options. Such answers are easy to tabulate and require minimum effort on the part of the respondent, thus increasing your chances of obtaining a response. For help with designing online surveys as well as collecting and analyzing the results, visit such sites as surveymonkey .com and surveygizmo.com. See also **forms**.

❖ **ETHICS NOTE** Questions should be neutral; they should not be worded in such a way as to lead respondents to give a particular answer, which can result in inaccurate or skewed data.

LEADING   Would you prefer the freedom of a four-day workweek?

NEUTRAL   Would you choose to work a four-day workweek, ten hours a day, with every Friday off? ❖

Q

WRITER'S CHECKLIST   **Designing a Questionnaire**

✔ Prepare a **cover message** or an introductory statement explaining who you are, the questionnaire's purpose, the response deadline, and how or where to send the completed questionnaire.

✔ Frame most questions in ways that are easy to tabulate; keep open-response questions to a minimum.

✔ Review the software settings for electronic forms so the survey meets your needs, such as limiting response length and ensuring anonymity.

✔ Select the appropriate response type: check box (allowing one or more choices), forced choice with radio buttons (allowing one choice from options provided), single response (such as "yes/no").

(continued)

✔ Include a section on the questionnaire for additional comments where the recipient may clarify his or her overall attitude toward the subject.

✔ Include questions about the respondent's demographics (such as age, gender, education, occupation) only if such information is essential.

✔ State whether the information provided as well as the recipient's identity will be kept confidential.

✔ Include your contact information (mailing address, phone number, and e-mail address) and be sure to thank respondents for participating.

✔ Consider offering a copy of the results or a customer discount for those who answer the questionnaire by the deadline.

quid pro quo

Quid pro quo is Latin for "one thing for another" or "this for that" in a relationship between two groups or individuals. The term may be appropriate in business and legal contexts if you are sure your **readers** understand its meaning. ("Before approving the plan, we insisted on a fair *quid pro quo*.") See also **foreign words in English**.

quotation marks

Quotation marks (" ") are used to enclose a direct quotation of spoken or written words. Quotation marks have other special uses, but they should not be used for **emphasis**.

Q

Direct Quotations

Enclose in quotation marks anything that is quoted word for word (a direct quotation) from speech or written material.

▶ The contract was explicit: "Monthly deliverables for the duration of this contract are due by close of business on the last workday of each month."

Do not enclose indirect quotations—usually introduced by the word *that*—in quotation marks. Indirect quotations are paraphrases of a writer's or speaker's words or ideas. See also **paraphrasing**.

▶ The contract stated that deliverables are due the last workday of each month.

❖ **ETHICS NOTE** When you use quotation marks to indicate that you are quoting word for word, do not make any changes or omissions inside the quoted material unless you clearly indicate what you have done. For further information on incorporating quoted material and inserting comments, see **plagiarism** and **quotations**. ❖

Use single quotation marks (' ') to enclose a quotation that appears within a quotation.

▶ John said, "Jane told me that she was going to 'stay with the project if it takes all year.'"

Words and Phrases

Use quotation marks to set off a special word or term if you need to point out that the term is being used for a unique or special purpose (that is, in the sense of the term *so-called*).

▶ A remarkable chain of events caused the sinking of the "unsink-able" *Titanic* on its maiden voyage.

Slang, colloquial expressions, and attempts at humor, although infrequent in workplace writing, should seldom be set off by quotation marks.

▶ Our first six months amounted to a ~~"shakedown cruise."~~ *shakedown cruise.*

Titles of Works

Use quotation marks to enclose **titles** of reports, short stories, articles, essays, single episodes of radio and television programs, and short musical works (including songs). However, do not use quotation marks for titles of books and periodicals, which should appear in **italics**.

▶ "Effects of Government Regulations on Motorcycle Safety" [report] cited "No-Fault Insurance and Motorcycles" [article], published in *American Motorcyclist* [periodical].

Use quotation marks for parts of publications, such as chapters of books and sections within larger works.

▶ "Microbusiness Economic Trends: Into the Future" [article] appeared in *Small Business Trends* (smallbiztrends.com) [blog].

Some titles are not set off by quotation marks, italics, or underlining, although they are capitalized.

▶ Professional Writing [college course title], the Constitution, the Bible, Lincoln's Gettysburg Address, the Lands' End Catalog

Q

Punctuation

Commas and **periods** always go inside closing quotation marks.

▶ "Reading *Computer World* gives me the insider's view," he says, adding, "It's like a conversation with the top experts."

Semicolons and **colons** always go outside closing quotation marks.

▶ He said, "I will pay the full amount"; this statement surprised us.

All other punctuation follows the logic of the context: If the punctuation is part of the material quoted, it goes inside the quotation marks; if the punctuation is not part of the material quoted, it goes outside the quotation marks.

quotations

Using direct and indirect quotations is an effective way to support a point and strengthen the credibility of your writing. But do not rely too heavily on the use of quotations, and avoid quoting anything that is longer than one paragraph.

❖ **ETHICS NOTE** When you use a quotation (or an idea of another writer), cite your source properly. If you do not, you will be guilty of **plagiarism**. See also **note-taking** and **research**. ❖

Direct Quotations

A direct quotation is a word-for-word copy of the text of an original source. Choose direct quotations (which can be of a word, a phrase, a sentence, or even a paragraph) carefully, and use them sparingly. Enclose direct quotations in **quotation marks**, and separate them from the rest of the sentence by a **comma** or **colon**. Use the initial capital letter of a quotation if the quoted material originally began with a capital letter.

▶ The economist stated, "Regulation cannot supply the dynamic stimulus that in other industries is supplied by competition."

When dividing a quotation, set off the material that interrupts the quotation with commas, and use quotation marks around each part of the quotation.

▶ "Regulation," the economist said in a recent interview, "cannot supply the dynamic stimulus that in other industries is supplied by competition."

Indirect Quotations

An indirect quotation is a paraphrased version of an original text. It is usually introduced by the word *that* and is not set off from the rest of the sentence by punctuation marks. See also **paraphrasing**.

▶ In a recent interview, he said *that* regulation does not stimulate the industry as well as competition does.

Deletions or Omissions

Deletions or omissions from quoted material are indicated by three ellipsis points (. . .) within a sentence and a period plus three ellipsis points (. . . .) at the end of a sentence. See **ellipses**.

▶ "If monopolies could be made to respond . . . we would be able to enjoy the benefits of . . . large-scale efficiency. . . ."

When a quoted passage begins in the middle of a sentence rather than at the beginning, ellipsis points are not necessary; the fact that the first letter of the quoted material is not capitalized tells the reader that the quotation begins in midsentence.

▶ Rivero goes on to conclude that "coordination may lessen competition within a region."

In omitting material, be careful not to change the author's original meaning, which would be unethical as well as inaccurate.

Inserting Material into Quotations

When it is necessary to insert a clarifying comment within quoted material, use **brackets**.

▶ "The industry is an integrated system that serves an extensive [geographic] area, with divisions existing as islands within the larger system's sphere of influence."

When quoted material contains an obvious error or might be questioned in some other way, insert the expression *sic* (Latin for "thus") in italic type and enclose it in brackets ([*sic*]) following the questionable material to indicate that the writer has quoted the material exactly as it appeared in the original.

▶ The contract states, "Tinted windows will be installed to protect against son [*sic*] damage."

Q

Incorporating Quotations into Text

Quote word for word only when a source with particular expertise states something that is especially precise, striking, or noteworthy, or that may reinforce a point you are making. Quotations must also logically, grammatically, and syntactically match the rest of the sentence and surrounding text. Notice in Figure Q–2 that the quotation blends with the content of the surrounding text, which uses **transition** to introduce and comment on the quotation.

Depending on the citation system, the style of incorporating quotations varies. For examples of two different styles, see **documenting sources**. Figure Q–2 shows APA style for a long quotation (forty or more words).

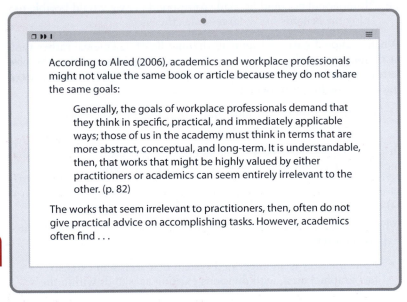

According to Alred (2006), academics and workplace professionals might not value the same book or article because they do not share the same goals:

> Generally, the goals of workplace professionals demand that they think in specific, practical, and immediately applicable ways; those of us in the academy must think in terms that are more abstract, conceptual, and long-term. It is understandable, then, that works that might be highly valued by either practitioners or academics can seem entirely irrelevant to the other. (p. 82)

The works that seem irrelevant to practitioners, then, often do not give practical advice on accomplishing tasks. However, academics often find . . .

FIGURE Q–2. Long Quotation (APA Style)

Q

R

raise / rise

Both *raise* and *rise* mean "move to a higher position." However, *raise* is a transitive **verb** and always takes an **object** ("*raise* crops"), whereas *rise* is an intransitive verb and never takes an object ("heat *rises*").

readers

The first rule of effective writing is to *help your readers*. If you overlook this commitment, your writing will not achieve its **purpose**, either for you or for your business or organization. For meeting the needs of both individual and multiple readers, see **audience**.

really

Really is an **adverb** meaning "actually" or "in fact." Although both *really* and *actually* are often used as **intensifiers** for **emphasis** or sarcasm in speech, avoid such use in formal and professional writing.

▶ Did he ~~really~~ finish the report on time?

reason is [because]

Replace the redundant phrase *the reason is because* with *the reason is that* or simply *because*. See also **conciseness**.

reference letters

Writing a reference (or recommendation) letter can range from completing an online form to composing a detailed description (see Figure R–1, page 448) of professional accomplishments and personal characteristics

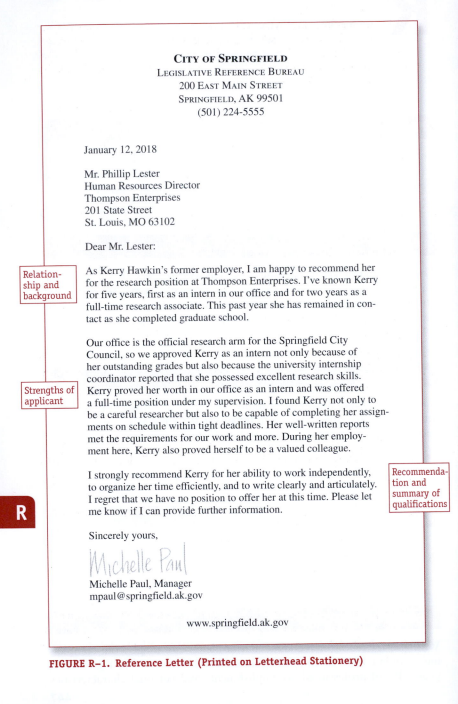

Relationship and background

Strengths of applicant

Recommendation and summary of qualifications

R

CITY OF SPRINGFIELD
LEGISLATIVE REFERENCE BUREAU
200 EAST MAIN STREET
SPRINGFIELD, AK 99501
(501) 224-5555

January 12, 2018

Mr. Phillip Lester
Human Resources Director
Thompson Enterprises
201 State Street
St. Louis, MO 63102

Dear Mr. Lester:

As Kerry Hawkin's former employer, I am happy to recommend her for the research position at Thompson Enterprises. I've known Kerry for five years, first as an intern in our office and for two years as a full-time research associate. This past year she has remained in contact as she completed graduate school.

Our office is the official research arm for the Springfield City Council, so we approved Kerry as an intern not only because of her outstanding grades but also because the university internship coordinator reported that she possessed excellent research skills. Kerry proved her worth in our office as an intern and was offered a full-time position under my supervision. I found Kerry not only to be a careful researcher but also to be capable of completing her assignments on schedule within tight deadlines. Her well-written reports met the requirements for our work and more. During her employment here, Kerry also proved herself to be a valued colleague.

I strongly recommend Kerry for her ability to work independently, to organize her time efficiently, and to write clearly and articulately. I regret that we have no position to offer her at this time. Please let me know if I can provide further information.

Sincerely yours,

Michelle Paul

Michelle Paul, Manager
mpaul@springfield.ak.gov

www.springfield.ak.gov

FIGURE R–1. Reference Letter (Printed on Letterhead Stationery)

for someone seeking employment. In Figure R–1, a former employer has written a letter for someone seeking an advanced position as a researcher.

To write an effective letter of recommendation, you must be familiar enough with the applicant's abilities and performance to offer an evaluation. Keep in mind the following:

- Identify yourself by name, title or position, employer, and contact information.

- Explain the circumstances and how long you have known the applicant, as in Figure R–1.

- Respond directly to the inquiry, carefully addressing the specific questions asked.

- Describe specifically the applicant's skills, abilities, knowledge, and character, guided by the person's **résumé** when possible.

- Communicate truthfully and without embellishment.

Mention, providing as much evidence as possible, one or two outstanding characteristics of the applicant. Organize the details in your letter using the decreasing **order-of-importance method of development**. Conclude with a brief summary of the applicant's qualifications and a clear statement of recommendation. See also **correspondence**.

❖ **ETHICS NOTE** When you are asked to serve as a reference or to supply a letter of reference, be aware that applicants have a legal right to examine what you have written about them unless they sign a waiver. ❖

refusal letters

A refusal delivers a negative message (or bad news) in the form of a **letter**, a **memo**, or an **e-mail**. The ideal refusal says no in such a way that you not only avoid antagonizing your reader but also maintain goodwill. See also **audience** and **"you" viewpoint**.

The refusal in Figure R–2 (page 450) declines an invitation to speak at a meeting, and the stakes for the writer are relatively low; however, the writer wishes to acknowledge the honor of being asked.

When the stakes are high, you must convince your reader that the bad news is *based on reasons that are logical or at least understandable* (see also **correspondence**). Stating a negative message in your opening may cause readers to react too quickly and dismiss your explanation. The pattern shown in Figure R–3 (page 451) is an effective way to handle this problem.

R

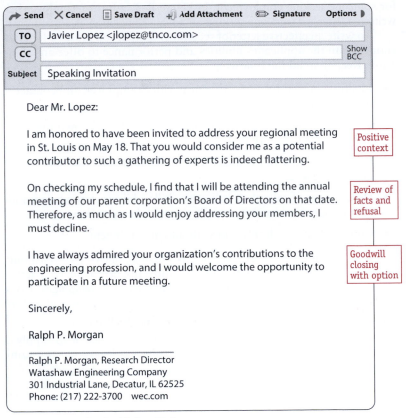

Dear Mr. Lopez:

I am honored to have been invited to address your regional meeting in St. Louis on May 18. That you would consider me as a potential contributor to such a gathering of experts is indeed flattering. — Positive context

On checking my schedule, I find that I will be attending the annual meeting of our parent corporation's Board of Directors on that date. Therefore, as much as I would enjoy addressing your members, I must decline. — Review of facts and refusal

I have always admired your organization's contributions to the engineering profession, and I would welcome the opportunity to participate in a future meeting. — Goodwill closing with option

Sincerely,

Ralph P. Morgan

Ralph P. Morgan, Research Director
Watashaw Engineering Company
301 Industrial Lane, Decatur, IL 62525
Phone: (217) 222-3700   wec.com

FIGURE R–2. Refusal with Low Stakes

R

1. *Context.* In the opening, introduce the subject, but do not provide irrelevant information or mislead the reader that good news may follow.
2. *Explanation.* Review the facts or details that lead logically to the bad news, trying to see things from your reader's point of view.
3. *Bad news.* State your refusal or negative message, based on the facts, concisely and without apology.
4. *Goodwill.* In the closing, establish or reestablish a positive relationship by providing an alternative if possible, assure the reader of your high opinion of his or her product or service, offer a friendly remark, or simply wish the reader success.

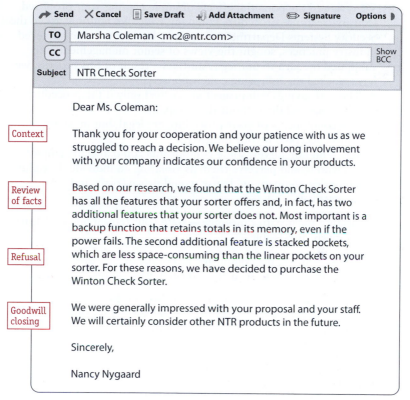

| Send | ✕ Cancel | 🗐 Save Draft | 📎 Add Attachment | ✍ Signature | Options ▶ |

TO	Marsha Coleman <mc2@ntr.com>
CC		Show BCC
Subject	NTR Check Sorter

Dear Ms. Coleman:

Context
Thank you for your cooperation and your patience with us as we struggled to reach a decision. We believe our long involvement with your company indicates our confidence in your products.

Review of facts
Based on our research, we found that the Winton Check Sorter has all the features that your sorter offers and, in fact, has two additional features that your sorter does not. Most important is a backup function that retains totals in its memory, even if the power fails. The second additional feature is stacked pockets,

Refusal
which are less space-consuming than the linear pockets on your sorter. For these reasons, we have decided to purchase the Winton Check Sorter.

Goodwill closing
We were generally impressed with your proposal and your staff. We will certainly consider other NTR products in the future.

Sincerely,

Nancy Nygaard

FIGURE R–3. Refusal with High Stakes

Your opening should provide an appropriate **context** and establish a professional **tone** by, for example, expressing appreciation for a reader's time, effort, or interest.

▶ The Screening Procedures Committee appreciates the time and effort you spent on your proposal for a new security-clearance procedure.

Next, review the circumstances of the situation sympathetically by placing yourself in the reader's position. Clearly detail the reasons you cannot do what the reader wants—even though you have not yet said you cannot do it. A good explanation should ideally detail the reasons for your refusal so thoroughly that the reader will accept the negative message as a logical conclusion, as shown in the following example.

R

▶ We reviewed the potential effects of implementing your proposed security-clearance procedure company-wide. We not only asked the Security Systems Department to review the data but also surveyed industry practices, sought the views of senior management, and submitted the idea to our legal staff. As a result of this process, we have reached the following conclusions:

- The cost savings you project are correct only if the procedure were required throughout the company.
- The components of your procedure are legal, but most are not widely accepted by our industry.
- Based on our survey, some components could alienate employees who would perceive them as violating an individual's rights.
- Enforcing company-wide use would prove costly and impractical.

Do not belabor the negative message—state your refusal quickly, clearly, and as positively as possible.

▶ For those reasons, the committee recommends that divisions continue their current security-screening procedures.

Close your message in a way that reestablishes goodwill—do not repeat the bad news. (Avoid writing "Again, we are sorry we cannot use your idea.") Ideally, provide an alternative, as in the following:

▶ Because some components of your procedure may apply in certain circumstances, we would like to feature your ideas in the next issue of *The Guardian*. I have asked the editor to contact you next week. On behalf of the committee, thank you for the thoughtful proposal.

For responding to a complaint, see **adjustment messages**. For refusing a job offer, see **acceptances / refusals**.

R

regarding / with regard to

In regards to and *with regards to* are incorrect **idioms** for *in regard to* and *with regard to*. Both *as regards* and *regarding* are acceptable variants.

▶ In ~~regards~~ to your last question, I think a meeting is a good idea.
    regard

▶ ~~With regards to~~ your last question, I think a meeting is a good idea.
    Regarding

regardless

Always use *regardless* instead of the nonstandard *irregardless*, which expresses a **double negative**. The prefix *ir-* renders the base word negative, but *regardless*—meaning "unmindful"—is already negative.

repetition

The deliberate use of repetition to build a sustained effect or to emphasize a feeling or an idea can be a powerful device. See also **emphasis**.

▶ Similarly, atoms *come and go* in a molecule, but the molecule *remains*; molecules *come and go* in a cell, but the cell *remains*; cells *come and go* in a body, but the body *remains*; persons *come and go* in an organization, but the organization *remains*.
—Kenneth Boulding, *Beyond Economics*

Repetition of keywords from a previous sentence or paragraph can also be used effectively to achieve **transition**.

▶ For many years, *oil* has been a major industrial energy source. However, *oil* supplies are limited, and other sources of energy must be developed.

Be consistent in the word or phrase you use to refer to something. In business writing, it is generally better to repeat a word or use a clear **pronoun reference** (so readers know that you mean the same thing) than to use **synonyms** to avoid repetition. See also **affectation**.

SYNONYMS	Several recent *analyses* support our conclusion. These *studies* cast doubt on the feasibility of long-range forecasting. The *reports*, however, are strictly theoretical.
CONSISTENT TERMS	Several recent *studies* support our conclusion. These *studies* cast doubt on the feasibility of long-range forecasting. *They* are, however, strictly theoretical.

Purposeless repetition, however, makes a sentence awkward and hides its key ideas. See also **conciseness**.

▶ She said that the physician ~~said that he~~ was canceling the tests.

R

reports

A report is an organized presentation of factual information, often aimed at multiple **audiences**, that may present the results of an investigation, a trip, or a research project. For any report, assessing the readers' needs is essential. Following is a list of report entries in this book:

annual reports 31		**investigative reports** 287	
feasibility reports 187		**progress and activity reports** 406	
formal reports 198		**trip reports** 529	
incident reports 256			

Formal reports often present the results of long-term projects or those that involve multiple participants. (See also **collaborative writing**.) Formal reports generally follow a precise format and include such elements as **abstracts** and **executive summaries**. Such projects may be done either for your own organization or as a contractual requirement for another organization. See also **proposals**.

Informal and short reports normally run from a few paragraphs to a few pages and ordinarily include only an **introduction**, a body, a **conclusion**, and (if necessary) recommendations. Because of their brevity, informal reports are customarily written as **correspondence**, including **e-mails**, **letters**, and **memos**.

The introduction of any report announces the subject of the report, states its **purpose**, and gives any essential background information. The body presents a clearly organized account of the report's subject—the results of a test, the status of a project, and other details readers may need. The amount of detail to include depends on your reader's knowledge, your **scope**, and the complexity of the subject.

The conclusion summarizes your findings and interprets their significance. In some reports, a final, separate section gives recommendations; in others, the conclusions and the recommendations are combined into one section. This final section suggests a course of action based on the data you have presented. See also **persuasion**.

R

repurposing

Repurposing is the copying or converting of existing content, such as written text and **visuals**, from one document or medium into another for a different **purpose**.* For example, if you are preparing a promotional

---

*The reuse of standard texts or content in technical publications is often referred to as "single-source publishing" or simply "single sourcing." Traditionally, such reuse of standard texts has been referred to as "boilerplate."

brochure, you may be able to reuse material from a product **description** that is currently published on your organization's Web site. The brochure might then be printed or placed on the Web site for downloading. See also **selecting the medium**.

In the workplace, this process saves time because content that often requires substantial effort to develop need not be re-created for each new application. The process of repurposing may be as simple as copying and pasting content from one document into another or as complex as automatically formatting and updating multiple documents, such as brochures and Web sites, through a content-management system. See also **form letters**.

Content can be repurposed exactly as it is written only if it fits the **scope**, **audience**, and purpose of the new document. If the content alters these areas, you must adapt that content to fit its new **context**, as described in the following sections.

Repurpose for the Context

Staying focused on the purpose of your new document is critical, especially when repurposing content between different media. If you are writing a sales **proposal**, for example, and you only need to describe the specifications for a product, it may be useful to repurpose the specification list from your organization's Web site. However, the purpose of the Web-site content may be *to inform* customers about your products, whereas the purpose of a proposal is *to persuade* customers to buy your products. To effectively use the repurposed content in your proposal, you may need to adapt the **tense**, **voice**, **tone**, **grammar**, and **point of view** to make the repurposed content more persuasive and fit within the context of a sales proposal.

Repurpose for the Medium

The best **style** and **format** of content written for a specific medium, such as a brochure or fact sheet, may not work as effectively when repurposed for a different medium, such as a Web site. Solid blocks of text may be easy to read in a brochure, but Web readers often need blocks of text to be separated into bulleted **lists** or short paragraphs because readers process information differently when reading on a screen. Adapt the **layout and design** of the repurposed content to accommodate your readers' needs for the medium. See **writing for the Web**.

❖ **ETHICS NOTE** In the workplace, repurposing content within an organization does not violate **copyright** because an organization owns the information it creates and can share it across the company. Likewise, a writer in an organization may use and repurpose material in the public

R

domain and, with proper attribution, content that is licensed under Creative Commons (see creativecommons.org/about).

In the classroom, of course, the use of content or someone else's unique ideas without acknowledgment or the use of someone else's exact words without **quotation marks** and appropriate credit is **plagiarism**. ❖

---

research

Research is the process of investigation—the discovery of information. To be focused, research must be preceded by **preparation**, especially consideration of your **audience**, **purpose**, and **scope**. Effective **note-taking** is essential for a coherent **organization** that strategically integrates your ideas, supporting facts, and any well-selected **quotations** into an effective draft and final document. See also **documenting sources**, **outlining**, and "Five Steps to Successful Writing" (pages xvii–xxiii).

In an academic setting, your preparatory resources include having conversations with your instructors, fellow students, and reference librarians, as well as reading a Wikipedia entry or another general reference source entry on your topic and conducting searches on the Internet. On the job, your main resources are your own knowledge and experience and that of your colleagues. In business, the most important sources of information may also include market research, **questionnaires** and surveys, focus groups, shareholder meetings, and the like. In this setting, begin by **brainstorming** with colleagues about what sources will be most useful to your topic and how you can find them.

Primary Research

Primary research is the gathering of raw data from such sources as firsthand experience, interviews, direct observation, surveys and questionnaires, focus groups, and **meetings**. In fact, direct observation and interaction are often the only ways to obtain certain kinds of information on such topics as human behavior and the functioning of organizations, as in ethnographic research. You can also conduct primary online research by participating in discussion groups and online forums and by e-mailing requests for information to specific audiences. When conducting primary research, focus on keeping accurate, complete records that indicate date, time of day, observation duration, and so on, saving interpretations for a later time. See also **blogs and forums**, **interviewing for information**, and **listening**.

❖ **ETHICS NOTE** If you conduct research that involves observation or a questionnaire at your university or college, ask your instructor whether your methods or questions are appropriate, whether you need to file an application with your school's Institutional Review Board (IRB), and the best way to obtain permission from your study subjects. ❖

Secondary Research

Secondary research is the gathering of information that has been previously analyzed, assessed, evaluated, compiled, or otherwise organized into accessible form. Sources include books, articles, online sources, audio and video recordings, podcasts, **correspondence**, **minutes of meetings**, **brochures**, and various **reports**. The following two sections—Library Research Strategies and Web Research Strategies—provide methods for finding secondary sources.

Recent periodicals and newspapers—as well as academic (.edu in the U.S.), government (.gov), and frequently updated corporate (.com) Web sites—can be good sources of current information and include the latest published interviews, articles, papers, and conference proceedings.

Wikipedia may also be a useful source for your initial research, but be sure to check the references and confirm when the document was last updated. Be aware, however, that some instructors may not accept Wikipedia as an appropriate source for a college research project because it is collaboratively written and the qualifications of the writers are unclear. See *Writer's Checklist: Evaluating Print and Online Sources* (page 462).

When a resource seems useful, read it carefully and take notes that include additional questions about your topic. Some of your questions may eventually be answered in other sources; those that remain unanswered can guide you to further research, both primary and secondary. See **paraphrasing** and **plagiarism**.

Library Research Strategies

The library provides organized paths into scholarship and specialized resources—such as subscription-only databases, indexes, catalogs, and directories—that are not accessible through standard Web searches. The first step in using library resources, either in an academic institution or in a workplace, is to develop a search strategy appropriate to the information needed for your topic. Begin by asking a reference librarian for help (in person or by phone, live chat, or e-mail) to find the best print or online resources for your topic. In addition, use your library's homepage for access to its catalogs and various databases.

Your search strategy depends on the kind of information you are seeking. For example, if you need the latest data offered by government research, check the Web, as described later in this entry. If you need a current scholarly article on a topic, search an online database (such as EBSCOhost's Academic Search Premier) subscribed to by your library. For historical background, your best resources are books, journals, and primary documents (such as a labor contract).

Online Catalogs (Locating Library Holdings). An online catalog allows you to search a library's licensed holdings, indicates an item's location and availability, and may allow you to arrange an interlibrary loan.

You can search a library's online catalog by author, title, keyword, or subject. The most common ways of searching for a specific topic are by subject or keyword. If your search turns up too many results, you can usually narrow it by using the "limit search" or "advanced search" option.

Online Databases and Indexes (Locating Articles). Most libraries subscribe to online databases, sometimes called *periodical indexes*, which are available only through a login to the library's Web site:

- *EBSCOhost's Academic Search Premier*: a large multidisciplinary database, providing full text for nearly 4,500 periodicals, including more than 7,400 abstracted and indexed peer-reviewed journals

- *Gale's Expanded Academic ASAP*: a large database covering general-interest and scholarly journals plus business, law, and health-care publications (many in full text)

- *ERIC (Educational Resources Information Center)*: a U.S. Department of Education database providing access to journals and reports in education

- *JSTOR*: a full-text, archival collection of journals in the humanities, social sciences, and sciences

- *LexisNexis Academic*: a collection of databases that is particularly strong for news, business, legal, and corporate and financial information (most articles in full text), as well as congressional, statistical, and government resources

Databases offer various ways to save your results. You may be able to save your searches and note-taking within the database itself by creating a personal account, by sending selected references and full-text articles

R

to an e-mail account, or by exporting them to citation-management software, such as RefWorks, Evernote, or Zotero. These programs allow you to build your own database of references from multiple sources, sort them into folders, and generate **bibliographies** in the format of your choice. Database search tools will vary from library to library, so contact a reference librarian at your school for guidance.

These databases are excellent resources for articles published within the last 10 to 20 years. Many include descriptive abstracts and full texts of articles. To find older articles, you may need to consult a print index, such as the *Readers' Guide to Periodical Literature* and the *New York Times Article Archive*, both of which have been digitized and may be available in some libraries.

Reference Works.   In addition to articles, books, and online sources, you may want to consult reference works such as encyclopedias, dictionaries, and manuals for a brief overview of your subject. Ask your reference librarian to recommend works and bibliographies that are most relevant to your topic. Many are available online and can be accessed through your library's homepage.

ENCYCLOPEDIAS.   Encyclopedias are comprehensive collections of articles arranged alphabetically. General encyclopedias, such as the *Encyclopaedia Britannica*, cover a wide range of subjects, while subject-specific encyclopedias—such as *The Encyclopedia of Careers and Vocational Guidance*, 17th ed. (Chicago, IL: Ferguson, 2017)—focus on specialized areas of study. The free online encyclopedia Wikipedia is a useful starting point for your research, but keep in mind that users continually update entries (with varying degrees of expert oversight).

DICTIONARIES.   Specialized dictionaries define terms used in a particular field, such as computer science, architecture, or consumer affairs, and they offer detailed definitions of field-specific terms, usually written in straightforward language.

HANDBOOKS AND MANUALS.   Handbooks and manuals are typically one-volume compilations of frequently used information in a particular field. They offer brief definitions of terms or concepts, standards for presenting information, procedures for documenting sources, and **visuals** to illustrate principles.

BIBLIOGRAPHIES.   Bibliographies list books, periodicals, and other research materials published in areas such as business, medicine, the humanities, and the social sciences.

R

OTHER LIBRARY RESOURCES. Many libraries offer special kinds of research information. For example, a library may provide subject guides that aggregate resources in topic areas popular with students. Some libraries may provide access to data that can be downloaded into statistical packages, such as SPSS (Statistical Package for the Social Sciences), for manipulation. Others offer GIS (geographic information systems) software that links data to spatial information, allowing the researcher to create detailed maps that show such factors as income, ethnicity, or purchasing habits.

Web Research Strategies

The Web varies widely in its completeness and accuracy, so you need to evaluate Internet sources critically by following the advice in *Writer's Checklist: Evaluating Print and Online Sources* (page 462).

Search Engines. Search engines use words or combinations of words that you specify to locate the documents or files that contain one or more of those words in their titles, descriptions, or text. Common search engines beyond Google include DuckDuckGo, Bing, and Yahoo! Some search engines have specialized interfaces for searching academic texts (scholar.google.com).

As comprehensive as search engines and directories may seem, none are complete or objective. Some, for example, may not index PDF files or Usenet newsgroups, and many cannot index databases and other non–HTML-based content. Search engines rank the sites they believe will be relevant to your search based on a number of criteria. Although they vary in what and how they search, you can navigate them all with strategies described in the following *Writer's Checklist*.

WRITER'S CHECKLIST   **Using Search Engines and Keywords**

✔ Check any search tips available in the engine you use, and consider any additional search phrases the search engine may suggest.

✔ Enter precise keywords and phrases that are specific to your topic, such as *nuclear power* rather than just the term *nuclear*, which would also list *nuclear family, nuclear medicine,* and other unrelated topics.

✔ Try several search engines to get more varied and relevant results.

✔ Consider using a metasearch engine, such as Dogpile (www.dogpile.com), which displays results from multiple search engines.

✔ Refine and narrow your terms as you evaluate the results of each search.

Web Subject Directories.   A subject directory organizes information by broad subject categories (business, entertainment, health, sports) and related subtopics (marketing, finance, investing). A subject-directory search eventually produces a list of specific sites that contain information about the topics you request. Directories like these can help you conduct selective, scholarly research on the Web:

IPL2	www.ipl.org
The WWW Virtual Library	www.vlib.org

Some directories and sites are devoted to specific subject areas, such as the following resources for researching a business topic:

CIO's Resource Centers	www.cio.com (use search function)
globalEDGE	http://globaledge.msu.edu
Inc.com Articles by Topic	www.inc.com (use search function)
LSU Libraries Federal Agency Directory	www.lib.lsu.edu/gov/index.html
FedStats	www.usa.gov/statistics

Evaluating Sources

The easiest way to ensure that information is valid is to obtain it from a reputable source. For online sources, be especially concerned about the validity of the information provided. Because anyone can publish on the Web, it is sometimes difficult to determine authorship of a document, and frequently a person's qualifications for speaking on a topic are absent or questionable. The online versions of established, reputable journals in medicine, management, engineering, computer software, and the like merit the same level of trust as the printed versions. The following domain abbreviations may help you determine an Internet site sponsor:

.aero	aerospace industry	.info	general use
.biz	business	.mil	U.S. military
.com	commercial	.name	individual
.coop	business cooperative	.net	network
.edu	educational institution	.org	general organization
.gov	U.S. government	.pro	professionals

But note that only a few (such as .edu and .gov) restrict who can register a Web site with a given domain, and a student may be just as likely as an expert to have a .edu domain.

   As you move away from established, reputable sites, be especially wary of wikis and unmoderated Web sites, where the author or source cannot be determined. Wikis, collectively generated Web sites such as Wikipedia, often make no guarantee of the validity of information on their sites.

R

WRITER'S CHECKLIST　Evaluating Print and Online Sources

Keep in mind the following four criteria when evaluating sources: authority, accuracy, bias, and currency.

FOR ALL SOURCES

✔ Is the resource up to date and relevant to your topic? Is it readily available?

✔ Who is the intended audience? Is it the mainstream public? A small group of professionals?

✔ Who is the author? Is the author an authority on the subject?

✔ Does the author provide enough supporting evidence and document sources so that you can verify the information's accuracy?

✔ Is the information presented in an objective, unbiased way? Are any biases made clear? Are opinions clearly labeled? Are viewpoints balanced, or are opposing opinions acknowledged?

✔ Are the language, tone, and style appropriate and cogent?

FOR A BOOK

✔ Does the preface or introduction indicate the author's or book's purpose?

✔ Does the table of contents relate to your topic? Does the index contain terms related to your topic?

✔ Are the chapters useful? Skim through one chapter that seems related to your topic — notice especially the introduction, headings, and closing.

FOR AN ARTICLE

✔ Is the publisher of the magazine or other periodical well known?

✔ What is the article's purpose? For an academic article, read the abstract; for a newspaper article, read the headline and opening sentences.

✔ Does the article contain informative diagrams or other visuals that indicate its scope?

FOR A WEB SITE

✔ Does a reputable individual, group, or organization sponsor or maintain the site?

✔ Are the purpose and scope of the site clearly stated? Check the "Mission Statement" or "About Us" pages. Does the site carry any disclaimers?

✔ Is the site updated and current? Are the links functional and up to date?

✔ Is the documentation authoritative and credible? Check the links to other sources, and cross-check facts at other reputable Web sites.

✔ Is the site well designed? Is the material well written and error-free?

resignation letters

Resignation messages, as shown in Figures R–4 and R–5 (on pages 464 and 465), should be as positive as possible, regardless of the reason you are leaving a job. As in refusals (see **acceptances / refusals**), a resignation offers the opportunity to establish a record of positive performance that can benefit your career in the long term.

You usually write a resignation **letter** (**memo** or **e-mail**) to your supervisor or to an appropriate person in the Human Resources Department. Use the following guidelines:

- Start on a positive note, regardless of the circumstances under which you are leaving.

- Consider pointing out how you have benefited from working for the company or say something complimentary about the company.

- Comment on something positive about the people with whom you have been associated.

- Explain why you are leaving in an objective, factual tone.

- Avoid angry recriminations, because your resignation will remain on file with the company and could haunt you in the future should you need references.

Your message should give enough notice to allow your employer time to find a replacement. It might be no more than two weeks, or it might be enough time to enable you to train your replacement. Some organizations may ask for a notice equivalent to the number of weeks of vacation you receive. Check the policy of your employer before you begin your letter.

The sample resignation letter in Figure R–4 is from an employee who is leaving to take a job offering greater opportunities. The memo of resignation in Figure R–5 is written by an employee who is leaving because her position has been reclassified and her supervisor has not supported her advancement, but no personal conflict is mentioned. Notice that it opens and closes positively and that the reason for the resignation is stated without apparent anger or bitterness. For strategies concerning negative messages, see **correspondence**.

R

respective / respectively

Respective is an **adjective** that means "pertaining to two or more things regarded individually." ("The committee members returned to their

227 Kenwood Drive
Austin, TX 78719
January 5, 2018

Home address

R. W. Johnson, Director of Purchasing
Barnside Appliances
1914 East 6th Street
Austin, TX 78702

Dear Mr. Johnson:

Positive opening

My three years at Barnside Appliances have been an invaluable period of learning and professional development. I arrived as a novice, and I believe that today I am a professional—primarily as a result of the personal attention and tutoring I have received from my superiors and the fine example set by both my superiors and my peers.

Reason for leaving

However, the time has come for me to move on to a company that can give me an opportunity to continue my professional development. Therefore, I have accepted a position with General Electric, where I am scheduled to begin on February 10. Thus, my last day at Barnside will be January 3. I will be happy to train my replacement during the next two weeks.

Positive closing

Many thanks for the experience I have gained, and best wishes for the future.

Sincerely,

J. L. Washburne

J. L. Washburne

FIGURE R–4. Resignation Letter (to Accept a Better Position)

respective offices.") *Respectively* is the adverb form of *respective*, meaning "singly, in the order designated."

▶ The first, second, and third prizes in the sales contest were awarded to Maria Juarez, Dan Wesp, and Simone Luce, *respectively*.

Respective and *respectively* are unnecessary if the meaning of individuality is clear.

▶ ~~The~~ committee *Each* ~~members~~ *member* prepared ~~their respective reports~~ *a report.*

MEMORANDUM

To: T. W. Haney, Vice President, Administration

From: L. R. Rupp   *LRR*

Date: February 13, 2018

Subject: Resignation from Winterhaven, effective March 2, 2018

> **Positive opening**

My five-year stay with the Winterhaven Company has been a pleasant experience, and I believe that it has been mutually beneficial.

> **Reason for leaving**

Because of the recent restructuring of my job, I have accepted a position with another company that will offer me greater advancement opportunities. I am, therefore, submitting my resignation, effective March 2.

> **Positive closing**

I have enjoyed working with my coworkers at Winterhaven and wish the company success in the future.

FIGURE R–5. Resignation Memo (Under Negative Conditions)

restrictive and nonrestrictive elements

Modifying **phrases** and **clauses** may be either restrictive or nonrestrictive. A *nonrestrictive phrase or clause* provides additional information about what it modifies, but it does not restrict the meaning of what it modifies. A nonrestrictive phrase or clause can be removed without changing the essential meaning of the sentence. It is a parenthetical element that is set off by **commas** to show its loose relationship with the rest of the sentence.

R

NONRESTRICTIVE   The annual report, *which was distributed yesterday*, shows that sales increased 20 percent last year.

A *restrictive phrase or clause* limits, or restricts, the meaning of what it modifies. If it were removed, the essential meaning of the sentence would change. Because a restrictive phrase or clause is essential to the meaning of the sentence, it is never set off by commas.

RESTRICTIVE   All employees *wishing to donate blood* may take Thursday afternoon off.

Writers need to distinguish between nonrestrictive and restrictive elements. The same sentence can take on two entirely different meanings depending on whether a modifying element is set off by commas (because it is nonrestrictive) or is not (because it is restrictive). A slip by the writer can not only mislead **readers** but also embarrass the writer.

MISLEADING   He gave a poor performance evaluation to the staff members who protested to the Human Resources Department. [This suggests he gave the poor evaluation because the staff members had protested.]

ACCURATE   He gave a poor performance evaluation to the staff members, who protested to the Human Resources Department. [This suggests that the staff members protested because of the poor evaluation.]

Use *which* to introduce nonrestrictive clauses and *that* to introduce restrictive clauses.

NONRESTRICTIVE   After John left the restaurant, *which* is one of the finest in New York, he came directly to my office.

RESTRICTIVE   Companies *that* diversify usually succeed.

résumés

DIRECTORY

R

A résumé* is a key component of an effective **job search** and the foundation for your **application cover letter**. Prospective employers use the information in the résumé and application cover letter to screen applicants and select candidates for job interviews. During a job interview, the content of your résumé and application cover letter can provide the interviewer with a guideline for developing specific questions. See also **interviewing for a job**.

Because résumés affect a potential employer's first impression, make sure that yours is well organized, carefully designed, consistently

---

*A detailed résumé for someone in an academic or a scientific area is often called a *curriculum vitae* (also *vita* or *c.v.*). It may include education, publications, projects, grants, and awards, as well as a full work history. Outside the United States, the term *curriculum vitae* is often used to mean *résumé*.

formatted, easy to read, and free of errors. Most important, target your résumé to the specific job so that the employer can easily see that you are a perfect fit. Organize the résumé in a way that highlights your strengths and fits your goals, as suggested by the examples shown in this entry. Your résumé should be concise, but its length should depend on the credentials, skills, and abilities that are a compelling match to the particular position. **Proofreading** is essential: Verify the accuracy of the information, and have someone else review it.

❖ **ETHICS NOTE** Be truthful. Many employers use outside agencies to check references and stated experience, rejecting applicants with résumés that are even slightly inaccurate or embellished. If you are hired based on false information, you may later be dismissed or even face a lawsuit for the deception. See also **ethics in writing**. ❖

Sample Résumés

The sample résumés in this entry provide starting points that you can use to tailor your résumé to your own job search. Before you design and write your résumé, look at as many samples as possible, and then organize and format your own to best highlight your strengths, present your professional goals, and make the most persuasive case to your target employers. See also **persuasion**.

- Figure R–6 (page 468) presents a conventional student résumé in which the student is seeking an entry-level position.

- Figure R–7 (page 469) shows a résumé with a variation in the design and placement of conventional headings to highlight professional credentials.

- Figure R–8 (page 470) presents a résumé for a recent graduate in a format that is appropriately unconventional for the purpose of demonstrating the student's skill in graphic design. This résumé includes a tagline, a brief description of the target job, and one or two impressive qualifications to grab the potential employer's attention. It matches the application cover letter in Figure A–8.

- Figure R–9 (pages 471–72) depicts a résumé that incorporates a qualifications summary, or profile, and focuses on the applicant's management experience. This résumé matches the application letter in Figure A–10.

- Figure R–10 (page 473) reflects the résumé of a candidate seeking to switch career fields. It uses a job title and immediately states a goal, followed by credentials.

- Figure R–11 (pages 474–76) illustrates how an applicant can organize a résumé by combining functional and chronological elements.

R

CAROL ANN WALKER

CAMPUS ADDRESS
148 University Drive
Bloomington, Indiana 47405
(812) 652-4781
caw2@iu.edu

HOME (after June 2018)
Laurel, Pennsylvania 17322
(717) 399-2712
LinkedIn.com/in/cawalker
caw@yahoo.com

EDUCATION

Bachelor of Science in Business Administration, expected June 2018
Indiana University

Emphasis: Finance   Minor: Professional Writing
GPA: 3.88 / 4.0
Senior Honor Society

FINANCIAL EXPERIENCE

FIRST BANK, INC., Bloomington, Indiana, 2017
Research Assistant, Summer and Fall Quarters
 Developed long-range planning models for the manager of corporate planning.

MARTIN FINANCIAL RESEARCH SERVICES, Bloomington, Indiana, 2016
Financial Audit Intern
 Created a design concept for in-house financial audits and provided research assistance to staff.
Associate Editor, *Martin Client Newsletter*, 2015–2016
 Wrote articles on financial planning with statistical models; developed article ideas from survey of business periodicals; edited submissions.

COMPUTER SKILLS

Software: Microsoft Word, Excel, QuickBooks, PowerPoint, InDesign, WordPress
Languages: JavaScript, CSS

VOLUNTEER ACTIVITY

Student Affiliate NAPFA (2016–2018): Weekend program to assist low-income elderly with managing their financial obligations.

R

FIGURE R–6. Student Résumé (for an Entry-Level Position)

CHRIS RENAULT, RN, ACLS, BSN

LinkedIn.com/in/chrisrenaultrn
Phoenix, AZ 85003 • (602) 555-5555 • chrisrenault@somedomain.com

**Reliable, compassionate, and competent RN seeking
medical-surgical position**

*Dedicated Registered Nurse routinely praised for strengths in patient relations; clinical
knowledge; collaboration with interdisciplinary health-care teams; chart accuracy; and
ability to treat assorted illnesses, injuries, and medical emergencies.*

Education & Nursing Credentials

UNIVERSITY OF PHOENIX— Phoenix, AZ

Bachelor of Science in Nursing (BSN), 2018 — Graduated summa cum laude (GPA: 3.9)	**Associate Degree in Nursing (AN)**, 2015 — Graduated cum laude (GPA: 3.5)

LICENSURE & CERTIFICATIONS

RN License (AZ), 4/2016 • **ACLS**, 1/2017 • **IV Practice**, 8/2017 • **CPR**, 8/2017

AFFILIATIONS

ANA (Arizona Nurses Association) • **ANA** (American Nursing Association)

Professional Experience–Clinical Rotations

- Earned excellent marks on evaluations throughout clinical rotations in diverse practice areas. Participated in activities — including patient assessment, treatment, medication disbursement, and surgical preparation — as a member of the health-care team.

- Preceptor Comments: *"Chris has an excellent ability to interact with patients and their families, showing a high degree of empathy, medical knowledge, and concern for quality and continuity of patient care."*

ROTATIONS SUMMARY

Surgery/Internal Medicine	ABC Hospital: Core Telemetry/Medical-Surgical
Emergency Medicine	ABC Hospital: Emergency Department
Cardiology	GHI Medical Center: Cardiac Telemetry
Oncology	ABC Hospital: Oncology Department
Long-Term Care	XYZ Skilled-Care Unit
Orthopedics	ABC Hospital: Orthopedic Center
Pediatrics	DEF Hospital: Pediatrics Unit
Rehabilitative Medicine	ABC Hospital: Health Rehabilitation Center

R

Volunteerism

Active Volunteer, American Cancer Society, Scottsdale, AZ Chapter,
2015 to present
Participant, Making Strides Against Breast Cancer walks, 2017, 2018

FIGURE R–7. Résumé (Highlighting Professional Credentials)

CREATIVE GRAPHIC DESIGNER

Joshua S. Goodman
LinkedIn.com/in
   /joshuasgoodman
412-555-1212
jgoodman@gmail.com
www.gooddesign.com

Merging Digital, Print, and Web skills with Marketing, Museum, and Client Experience for Success in Fast-Paced Settings

PROFESSIONAL EXPERIENCE

Assistant Designer • Dyer/Khan, Los Angeles, California
Summer 2016, Summer 2017
Assistant Designer in a versatile design studio. Responsible for design, layout, comps, mechanicals, and project management.
Clients: Paramount Pictures, Mattel Electronics, and Motown Records.

Photo Editor • Paramount Pictures Corporation, Los Angeles, California
Summer 2015
Photo Editor for merchandising department. Established art files for movie and television properties. Edited images used in merchandising. Maintained archive and database.

Production Assistant • Grafis, Los Angeles, California
Summer 2014
Production Assistant at fast-paced design firm. Assisted with comps, mechanicals, and miscellaneous studio work.
Clients: ABC-TV, A&M Records, and Ortho Products Division.

EDUCATION

RCS School of Design, Pittsburgh, Pennsylvania
BFA in Graphic Design —
May 2018
Graphic Design
Corporate Identity
Industrial Design
Graphic Imaging Processes
Color Theory
Computer Graphics
Typography
Serigraphy
Photography
Video Production

SKILLS

Adobe Creative Cloud and Creative Suite (esp. Photoshop, Illustrator, and InDesign), JavaScript, QuarkXPress, MapEdit (Image Mapping), Micromedia Dreamweaver, Adobe Flash Professional, Microsoft Access/Excel, XML, HTML, iGrafx, CorelDRAW

ACTIVITIES

Museum Docent and Design Assistant, Lee Collection
Member, Pittsburgh Graphic Design Society

R

FIGURE R–8. Recent Graduate Résumé (for Graphic Design Job)

ROBERT MANDILLO
Dayton, OH 45424 • 937.555.1212 • mand@juno.com
LinkedIn.com/in/robertmandillomba
Design Portfolio: www.robertmandillomba.com

QUALIFICATIONS SUMMARY

Quality-driven mechanical engineering manager whose tenure with
Exhibit Design Lab has been distinguished by exemplary-rated
performance and proven results. Developer of next-generation
exhibit design solutions that have led to increased leads and sales.
Qualifications reinforced by strong aptitudes in reliability engineering,
system troubleshooting, and Lean Six Sigma principles.

EXPERIENCE

MANAGER, EXHIBIT DESIGN LAB   May 2011–Present
Wright-Patterson Air Force Base, Dayton, OH

- Manage production of 1,200+ exhibit designs throughout tenure,
  supervising a team of 11 technicians in support of engineering
  exhibit design and production.

- Coordinate all phases of exhibit installations from initial concept and
  development of technical drawings to construction, installation, and
  fabrication of models.

- Ensure the attainment of manufacturing goals and compliance with
  safety standards.

- Negotiate with vendors and procure materials and supplies for
  exhibit design support.

SUPERVISOR, GRAPHICS ILLUSTRATORS   June 2008–April 2011
Henderson Advertising Agency, Cincinnati, OH

- Led team to create original design themes, layouts, and graphics for
  marketing materials, television commercials, videos, and Web sites.

- Recruited, trained, and supervised a team of five illustrators and four
  drafting mechanics.

- Established strong vendor-partner relationships, competitive rates, and
  detailed schedules that elevated quality and increased turnaround time.

R

FIGURE R–9. Résumé (Applicant with Management Experience) (*continued*)

ROBERT MANDILLO
Résumé • Page 2

Dayton, OH 45424 • 937.555.1212 • mand@juno.com
LinkedIn.com/in/robertmandillomba
Design Portfolio: www.robertmandillomba.com

EDUCATION

MASTER OF BUSINESS ADMINISTRATION (MBA), 2017
University of Dayton (Dayton, OH)

BACHELOR OF SCIENCE IN MECHANICAL ENGINEERING (BSME), 2008
Edison State College (Wooster, OH)

AFFILIATIONS

American Society of Mechanical Engineers (ASME)
National Society of Professional Engineers (NSPE)

SKILLS

Rapid Prototyping • SolidWorks • Product Development •
Machining • Product Design • CAD Manufacturing • Engineering •
Simulations • Plastics • Sheet Metal • LabVIEW Procurement &
Supply-Chain Management • Pressure Vessel Internals • R&D

FIGURE R–9. Résumé (Applicant with Management Experience) (*continued*)

Analyzing Your Background

In preparing to write your résumé, determine what kind of job you are seeking. Rarely can you construct a one-size-fits-all résumé: Potential employers will all look for something different, and you will gain increasingly diverse experiences as you progress in your career. You may benefit from preparing a few résumés with different emphases, and you may need to create a unique résumé for a single position, using the language of a particular job description as your guide. Review your credentials and consider the following as you gather information:

- Schools you attended, degrees you hold, your major field of study, academic honors you were awarded, your grade point average, selected academic projects that reflect your best work, continuing education, conferences or seminars you have attended

LINDA H. GRANGER

lhg.granger@gmail.com
(571) 577-8869 / (571) 656-3324

Sun Valley Heights, VA 20109
LinkedIn.com/in/lhgranger

INFORMATION TECHNOLOGY / SECURITY SPECIALIST

Seeking to build an exciting career in law enforcement with a focus on the application of Information Technology (IT) / Information Security (INFOSEC).

- Application Design / System Analysis
- Testing / Implementation / Integration
- Program / Project Development
- Business Policies / Procedures
- Customer / Client Service
- Dynamic Team Building / Leadership

EDUCATION

BACHELOR OF SCIENCE – INFORMATION TECHNOLOGY
Sun Valley University, VA, May 2017

INTERNSHIP / PROFESSIONAL EXPERIENCE

Federal Law Enforcement Training Center (FLETC), Arlington, VA   *June–Sept. 2017*
Volunteer — Computer, Financial, Intelligence Division

- Accepted into highly selective, competitive FLETC College Intern Summer Program
- Analyzed, evaluated, and assessed performance and operating methodology of forensic software
- Assisted law-enforcement staff and instructors with office support in efforts to advance the mission of the FLETC
- Participated in and observed basic-training classes and activities designed to develop and promote the growth of future law-enforcement candidates

Board of Education, Forrest Hills, VA   *Sept. 2015–June 2017*
Instructor / Substitute Teacher

- Provided an educational foundation designed to enable K–12 students to develop confidence, self-direction, and a lifelong interest in learning
- Fostered the development of communication, citizenship, and personal growth

AWARD / RECOGNITION

SUPERB ADMINISTRATIVE SUPPORT – FORENSIC DATA HUB
Federal Law Enforcement Training Center

R

FIGURE R–10. Résumé (Experienced Applicant Seeking Career Change)

CAROL ANN WALKER

Sometown, PA 00000 • (555) 555-5555
caw@somedomain.com • LinkedIn.com/in/carolannwalker
Twitter Handle: @carolannwalker

Award-Winning Financial Analyst

- Senior financial analyst offering proven success enhancing P&L scenarios by millions of dollars.
- Excellent analytical capabilities, with an expert foundation in statistics, financial modeling, and complex financial/business/variance analysis.
- Backed by solid credentials, industry honors, and a history of delivering goal-surpassing results.

Financial Analyst of the Year, 2017

Recipient of national award from the CFA Institute

Areas of Expertise

- Financial Analysis & Planning
- Forecasting & Trend Projection
- Trend/Variance Analysis
- Comparative Analysis
- Asset-Capacity Planning
- Economic Profit/EVA
- Business Valuation/Due Diligence
- SEC & Financial Reporting
- Risk Assessment
- Auditing/Accounting

Professional Experience

KERFHEIMER CORPORATION, Sometown, PA   2008 to Present

Senior Financial Analyst, 12/2011 to Present
Financial Analyst, 11/2008 to 12/2011

Promoted to lead team of 15 analysts in the management of financial/SEC reporting and analysis for publicly traded, $2.3 billion company and its four subsidiary entities. Develop financial/statistical models used to project and maximize corporate financial performance; provide adhoc financial analysis; and support nationwide sales team by providing financial metrics, trends, and forecasts

Key Accomplishments

- Developed long-range funding requirements crucial to firm's subsequent capture of $52 million in government and military contracts.
- Secured more than $100 million through private and government research grants.

R

FIGURE R–11. Advanced Résumé (Combining Functional and Chronological Elements) (*continued*)

———————— CAROL ANN WALKER ————————

Résumé • Page Two

Sometown, PA 00000 • (555) 555-5555
caw@somedomain.com • LinkedIn.com/in/carolannwalker
Twitter Handle: @carolannwalker

Professional Experience (*continued*)

- Facilitated a 15 percent decrease in company's long-term debt during several major building expansions by developing computer models for capital acquisition.
- Designed model that saved 65 percent in proposal-preparation time. Cited by executive VP of sales for efforts that shortened the sales cycle, which helped displace the competition.
- Partnered with department managers to provide budget planning and profitability/cost-per-unit (CPU) analysis, including income, balance sheet, and cash-flow statements.
- Jointly led large-scale systems conversion to Hyperion, including personal upload of database in Essbase. Completed initiative on time and with no interruptions to business operations.

FIRST BANK, INC., Sometown, PA   2003 to 2008

Planning Analyst, 9/2003 to 11/2008
Compiled and distributed weekly, monthly, quarterly, and annual closings/financial reports. Prepared depreciation forecasts, actual-vs.-projected financial statements, key-matrix reports, tax-reporting packages, auditor packages, and balance-sheet reviews.

Key Accomplishments

- Devised strategies to secure $6.2 million credit line at 2 percent below market rate.
- Positioned bank for continued growth by conducting business-unit analysis and cost/benefit studies to determine optimal investment strategies.
- Analyzed financial performance for consistency to plans and forecasts, investigated trends and variances, and alerted senior management to areas requiring action.
- Prepared and presented financial analysis on impacts of foreign currencies, inflationary factors, product-mix changes, merger and acquisition (M&A) activity, and capacity/fixed-cost structures.
- Achieved an average 14 percent return on all investments. Applied critical thinking and sound financial and strategic analysis in all funding options research.

R

FIGURE R–11. Advanced Résumé (Combining Functional and Chronological Elements) (*continued*)

CAROL ANN WALKER

Résumé • Page Three

Sometown, PA 00000 • (555) 555-5555
caw@somedomain.com • LinkedIn.com/in/carolannwalker
Twitter Handle: @carolannwalker

Education

THE WHARTON SCHOOL of the UNIVERSITY OF PENNSYLVANIA, Philadelphia, PA

Ph.D. in Finance, 5/2016

UNIVERSITY OF WISCONSIN, Milwaukee, WI

M.S. in Business Administration ("Executive Curriculum"), 5/2003

INDIANA UNIVERSITY, Bloomington, IN

B.S. in Business Administration, Emphasis in Finance, 5/2000

Affiliations

- CFA Institute, Member, 2003 to Present
- Association for Corporate Financial Planning (ACFP), Senior Member, 2005 to Present

Portfolio of Financial Plans Available on Request

FIGURE R–11. Advanced Résumé (Combining Functional and Chronological Elements)

R

- Jobs you have held, your principal and secondary duties in each job, when and how long you held each job, promotions you received, skills you developed in your jobs that a potential employer may value and seek in the ideal candidate, projects or accomplishments that reflect important contributions

- Other experiences and skills you have developed that would be of value for the job you seek: extracurricular activities that have contributed to your learning experience, leadership assignments you have accepted, interpersonal and communication skills you have developed (speeches, presentations, classes given), collaborative work you have performed, publications you have contributed to, computer skills you have acquired or specialized programs in which you are proficient, languages you speak, notable awards or other types of recognition

Use this information to brainstorm further details and personal attributes. Then, based on all the details, decide which to include in your résumé and how you can most effectively present your qualifications.

Returning Job Seekers

If you are returning to the workplace after an absence, most career experts say that it is important to acknowledge the gap in your career. If you are reentering the workforce because you have devoted a full-time period to care for children or dependent adults, do not undervalue such work. Although unpaid, this experience often develops important time-management, problem-solving, organizational, and interpersonal skills. Although gaps in employment can be explained in the application cover letter, the following examples illustrate how you might reflect such experiences in a résumé. These samples would be especially appropriate for an applicant seeking employment in a field related to child or health care.

► **Primary Child-Care Provider, 2015–2017** Provided full-time care to three preschool children at home. Facilitated early learning activities; taught basic academic skills, nutrition, arts, and swimming. Organized schedules and events, managed the household, and served as Neighborhood-Watch Captain.

► **Home Caregiver, 2015–2017** Provided 60 hours per week in-home care for Alzheimer's patient. Coordinated health-care and medical appointments, developed and supervised exercise programs, completed and processed complex medical forms, administered medications, organized and maintained budgets, and managed home environment.

If you have performed volunteer work during such a period, list that experience. Volunteer work often results in the same experience as does full-time, paid work, a fact that your résumé should reflect, as in the following example:

► **School Association Coordinator, 2015–2017** Managed special activities of the high school Parent-Teacher Association. Planned and coordinated meetings, scheduled events, and supervised fund-drive operations. Raised $70,000 toward refurbishing the school auditorium.

R

Organizing Your Résumé (Sections)

The following résumé sections and section headings are typical and, depending on the subject matter, may use alternative terminology, as shown in the following list. The sections you choose and the order in which you list them should depend on your experience, your goals, the employer's needs, and any standard practices in your profession.

- Heading (name and contact information)
- Job Objective vs. Headline
- Qualifications Summary (Professional Profile, Key Attributes)
- Education (Academic Background, Certifications)
- Employment Experience (Career History, Career Chronology)
- Related Knowledge, Skills, and Abilities (Professional Affiliations, Volunteer Work, Networking Assets)
- Honors and Activities (Awards, Recognition, Notable Contributions, Volunteer Work, Publications, Affiliations)
- References and Portfolios

There really is no right or wrong way to organize your résumé, and any number of organizational patterns can be effective. For example, whether you place "education" before "employment experience" depends on the job you are seeking. Organize your information in the sequence that emphasizes the credentials that will strengthen your résumé. A recent graduate without much work experience should list education first. A candidate with many years of job experience, including jobs directly related to the target position, may decide to list employment experience first. When you list information in the education and employment sections, use a reverse chronological order: most recent employer or credential first, the next most recent experience second, and so on.

R

Heading.   At the top of your résumé, include your name, the best number where you can be reached, professional **e-mail** address, and links to social-media sites where you have a professional presence. Make sure that your name stands out on the page. If you are in transition, list the city, state, and ZIP codes of your residence(s), along with relevant telephone numbers and e-mail addresses underneath your name (see Figure R-6, page 468). You can omit your street address for privacy reasons.

Job Objective vs. Headline.   Hiring managers spend mere seconds for the initial résumé review, so your career goal should be immediately evident. Job objectives and résumé headlines (or *taglines*) both introduce the material and help the reader quickly understand your reason for seeking a certain position. An objective is a narrative statement about the type of job that interests you, and it can include your career level and credentials. A headline is similar to a newspaper headline and is meant to quickly grab the employer's attention. A headline contains a brief description of your job target and one or two of your strongest qualifications. A headline can provide visual impact, especially if it appears as a banner near the top of your résumé (see Figure R–8, page 470). The following examples illustrate the difference between objectives and headlines.

SAMPLE OBJECTIVE STATEMENTS

▶ A computer-science position aimed at solving online security vulnerabilities.

▶ A position involving meeting the concerns of women, such as family planning, career counseling, or crisis management.

▶ A programming internship requiring software-development and debugging skills.

SAMPLE JOB TITLE AND HEADLINE COMBINATIONS

▶ FINANCIAL SERVICES / BANKING PROFESSIONAL
Ensuring the Financial Success of Customers, Clients, and Communities

▶ MECHANICAL ENGINEER
Developing Innovative, Efficient, Environmentally Friendly Energy Solutions

▶ FIREFIGHTER / EMT
Prevention, Mitigation, Response or Protecting Life, Property, and the Environment

◀ **PROFESSIONALISM NOTE** If you include an objective on your résumé, avoid using clichés, such as "seeking a challenging opportunity with potential for advancement" and other overused statements. ▶

Qualifications Summary. Include a brief summary of your qualifications to persuade hiring managers to select you for an interview. Sometimes called a *professional profile*, *summary statement*, or *career summary*, a qualifications summary can include skills, expertise, experience, or personal qualities that make you especially well suited to the position. You may give this section a unique heading or simply use a job title, as shown in Figures R–10 (page 473) and R–11 (pages 474–76).

Education. List the school(s) you have attended, the degree(s) you received and the dates you received them, your major field(s) of study, and any academic honors you have earned. Most career-development

R

professionals recommend that you include your grade point average (GPA) only if it is 3.0 or higher. Omit your GPA if you earned your degree long ago and are focusing on experience rather than education. List individual courses if they are unusually impressive, if they provide the opportunity to include keywords, if they are relevant to your career goals, or if your résumé is otherwise sparse (see Figure R–8). Consider including any special skills developed or projects completed in your course work. Mention high school only if you do not possess higher education or if you want to call attention to special high school achievements, awards, projects, programs, internships, or study abroad.

Employment Experience. Organize your employment experience in reverse chronological order, starting with your most recent job and working backward under a single heading. You can also organize your experience functionally, by clustering similar types of jobs into several sections with specific section headings, such as "Management," "Leadership," "Administration," or "Logistics."

Depending on the situation, one type of arrangement might be more persuasive than the other. For example, if you are applying for an accounting job but have no employment experience in accounting, simply list past and present jobs in reverse chronological order (most recent to least recent). If you are applying for a supervisory position and have had three supervisory jobs in addition to two nonsupervisory positions, you could create a section heading called "Supervisory Experience" and list the three supervisory jobs, followed by another section labeled "General Experience" to include the nonsupervisory jobs.

In general, consider the following guidelines when working on the "Experience" section of your résumé:

- Include jobs or internships when they relate directly to the position you are seeking. Including such experiences can make a résumé more persuasive if they have helped you develop relevant skills.

- Include extracurricular experiences, such as taking on a leadership position in a college organization or directing a community-service project, if they demonstrate the skills valued by a potential employer.

- List military service as a job, even though the occupational specialties may not be directly applicable to the positions for which you are applying. Give the dates served, the duty specialty, and the rank at discharge. Discuss military duties if they relate to the job you are seeking, and translate military terminology to be easily understood by hiring managers.

- For each job or experience, list both the job title and the employer name. Throughout each section, consistently begin with either the job or the company name, depending on which will likely be more impressive to potential employers.

- Under each job or experience, provide a concise description of your accomplishments. By listing your accomplishments and quantifying them with numbers, percentages, or monetary value, you will let the employer know what separates you from the competition. That said, do not omit job duties entirely; employers still want to see the scope of your responsibilities. A good strategy for organizing both duties and responsibilities is to create a brief paragraph outlining your responsibilities, followed by a bulleted list of your strongest accomplishments in the position.

- Focus as much as possible on your achievements in your work history. ("Increased employee retention rate by 16 percent by developing a training program.") Employers will picture themselves as benefiting from the same types of accomplishments.

- Use action verbs ("managed," "supervised," "developed," "achieved," "analyzed"). Be consistent when using past or present tense. Even though the résumé is about you, do not use "I" (for example, instead of "I was promoted to Section Leader," use "Promoted to Section Leader").

Related Knowledge, Skills, and Abilities.   Employers are interested in hiring applicants with a variety of skills or the ability to learn new ones quickly. Depending on the position, you might list such items as fluency in foreign languages, writing and editing abilities, specialized technical knowledge, or computer skills (including knowledge of specific languages, software, and hardware).

Honors and Activities.   List any honors and unique activities near the end of your résumé unless they are exceptionally notable or would be more persuasive for a particular objective. Include items such as student or community activities, professional or club memberships, awards received, and published works. Do not duplicate information given in other categories, and include only information that supports your employment objective. Use a heading for this section that fits its contents, such as "Activities," "Honors," "Professional Affiliations," "Memberships," or "Publications."

References and Portfolios.   Avoid specifying on your résumé that references are available unless that is standard practice in your profession or your résumé is sparse. Employers assume that a well-prepared job seeker will provide a list of professional references. Create a separate list of references in the same format design and layout as your résumé, and be ready to provide this page to prospective employers during the interview. Always seek permission from anyone you list.

A portfolio is a collection of samples in a binder or on a Web site of your most impressive work and accomplishments. The portfolio can include successful documents you have produced, letters of praise from

R

employers, copies of awards and certificates, and samples of your work. You can include the phrase "Portfolio available on request" in your résumé. If portfolios are standard in your profession, you might even include a small section that outlines the contents of your portfolio.

◀ **PROFESSIONALISM NOTE** Avoid listing your desired salary on the résumé. You could price yourself out of a job you want if the salary you list is higher than a potential employer is willing to pay, or you might not get the best possible offer if you list a low one. ▶

Digital Formats and Media

Once you have developed a strong résumé, consider adapting it for multiple media and digital formats.

E-mail–Attached Résumés.   An employer may request that you submit a résumé attached to an e-mail. If a file-format preference is not specified, send the résumé in Adobe PDF or MS Word format. Then attach the file, and treat the e-mail-message body as your cover letter.

Applicant Tracking System Résumés.   When you submit your résumé via e-mail or to an employer's Web site, it may be added to an electronic applicant tracking system (ATS). These systems parse, store, manage, and rank résumés based on criteria specified by the hiring manager. Although these systems vary, some guidelines are universal:

- Avoid fancy graphics and icons, because they will not be readable.

- Choose common titles for headers, such as "Professional Experience" and "Education."

- Incorporate keywords that are relevant to your career field in descriptions, but avoid a separate "Keyword" section that wastes valuable space.

- Use a consistent format in the placement of employer names and job titles.

In general, when developing your résumé for an ATS, try thinking like a computer, and focus on logic and consistency.

Plain-Text Résumés.   Some employers request ASCII or plain-text résumés via e-mail or their Web site, enabling the file to be easily added to résumé databases. ASCII résumés allow employers to read the file no matter what type of software they are using. You can copy and paste a plain-text résumé directly into the body of an e-mail message. To create an ASCII résumé, look for an option to "Save as" plain text in your word-processing program. After you save as a text file with a .txt extension, reopen the file in a text editor (such as Notepad for PCs or

TextWrangler for Macs) and clean up the file as needed. For more, visit resumepower.com/ascii-resumes.html.

Scannable Résumés.   A scannable-résumé format is a paper document that you mail to the employer. After it is received, the document will be scanned into an automated program and then downloaded into the company's searchable database. For such résumés, avoid decorative fonts, underlining, shading, letters that touch each other, or other features that will not scan easily. Before sending, scan the résumé yourself to make sure that it is legible.

Web-Posted Résumés.   You can use a personal Web site to post your résumé and display other items that portray your value as a candidate, such as awards and samples of your work. You can list a link to your Web site in your candidate documents and correspondence with prospective employers. For such Web sites, keep the following in mind:

- Follow the general advice for **writing for the Web**, and view your résumé and materials on several browsers.

- Consider building a multipage site for displaying a work portfolio, publications, reference letters, and other related materials.

- Provide just below your name a series of internal page links to such important categories as "experience" and "education."

- Do not include your phone number or home address on the Web site—include an e-mail "contact link" that prospective employers and recruiters can use to reach you.

- Do not advertise that you are actively seeking a job if you are currently employed; if your employer learns about your search, your job could be in jeopardy.

- Post copies of your résumé in various file formats so that employers can select the best format for their needs.

If you do not have your own Web site, you can upload your files to an online cloud storage service, such as Dropbox (www.dropbox.com), and send employers the link to your folder.

◀ **PROFESSIONALISM NOTE** When applying for a position within the U.S. government, America's largest employer, make sure your résumé's content and style are suitable for a federal application. Protocol for your federal résumé varies depending on the specific agency you are targeting, but your résumé must address how your qualifications match the requirements outlined in the vacancy announcement. Kathyrn Troutman provides excellent resources for preparing federal résumés (visit www.resume-place.com/fedresblog/federal-resume-writing). See also **job search**. ▶

revision

When you revise your draft, read and evaluate it primarily from the point of view of your **audience**. In fact, revising requires a different frame of mind than **writing a draft**. To achieve that frame of mind, experienced writers have developed the following tactics:

- Allow a "cooling period" between writing the draft and revising in order to evaluate the draft objectively.

- Read your draft aloud—often, hearing the text will enable you to spot problems that need improvement.

- Revise in passes by reading through your draft several times, each time searching for and correcting a different set of problems.

When you can no longer spot improvements, you may wish to give the draft to a colleague for review—especially for projects that are crucial for you or your organization as well as for collaborative projects, as described in **collaborative writing**.

WRITER'S CHECKLIST   **Revising Your Draft**

✔ *Completeness.* Does the document achieve its primary **purpose**? Will it fulfill the readers' needs? Your writing should give readers exactly what they need but not overwhelm them.

✔ *Appropriate introduction and conclusion.* Check to see that your **introduction** frames the rest of the document and that your **conclusion** ties the main ideas together. Both should account for revisions to the content of the document.

✔ *Accuracy.* Look for any factual inaccuracies in your draft.

✔ *Unity and coherence.* Check to see that sentences and ideas are closely tied together (**coherence**) and contribute directly to the main idea expressed in the topic sentence of each **paragraph** (**unity**). Provide **transitions** where they are missing, and strengthen those that are weak.

✔ *Consistency.* Make sure that **layout and design** and **visuals** are consistent. Refer to the same items with the same terms throughout.

✔ *Conciseness.* Prune unnecessary words, phrases, sentences, and even paragraphs. Use the search-and-replace command to find and revise wordy phrases and unnecessary helping **verbs**. See **conciseness**.

✔ *Awkwardness.* Look for **awkwardness** in **sentence construction**—especially any **garbled sentences**.

(continued)

Revising Your Draft (*continued*)

✔ *Ethical writing.* Check for **ethics in writing**, and eliminate **biased language**.

✔ *Active voice.* Use the active **voice** unless the passive voice is more appropriate.

✔ *Word choice.* Check **word choice**, and eliminate **affectation**, **clichés**, **vague words**, and unnecessary **intensifiers**. Check for unclear **pronoun references**.

✔ *Jargon.* If you are unsure that all your readers will understand any **jargon** or special terms you have used, eliminate or define those words or terms.

✔ *Grammar.* Check for grammatical errors. Treat **grammar** checker recommendations as suggestions only.

✔ *Typographical errors.* Check your final draft for typographical errors both with your spell checker and with thorough **proofreading**.

rhetorical questions

A rhetorical question does not require a specific answer because it is intended to make an **audience** think about the subject from a different perspective. The answer to a rhetorical question such as "Is space exploration worth the cost?" may not be a simple yes or no; it might be a detailed explanation of the pros and cons of space exploration.

Rhetorical questions can serve as effective **titles** or openings. The writer or speaker may answer such questions in a **presentation, newsletter article,** or blog. (See **blogs and forums**.) However, rhetorical questions should be used judiciously in other, more formal documents. A rhetorical question, for example, would not be appropriate for the title of a **report** or an **e-mail** addressed to a manager who needs to quickly understand the subject and purpose of the document or message.

R

run-on sentences

A run-on sentence, sometimes called a *fused sentence*, is two or more sentences without punctuation to separate them. The term is also sometimes applied to a pair of independent **clauses** separated by only a **comma**, although this variation is usually called a **comma splice**. See also **sentence construction** and **sentence faults**.

S

sales letters

A sales letter—print or digital **correspondence** that promotes a product, service, or business—requires both a thorough knowledge of the product or service and an understanding of the potential customer's needs.

An effective sales letter (1) catches readers' attention, (2) engages their interest, (3) convinces them that your product or service will fulfill a need or desire, and (4) confidently asks them to take the course of action you suggest. See also **persuasion**, **promotional writing**, and **tone**.

Your first task in writing a sales letter is to determine to whom your message should be sent. One good source is a list of your customers or clients. Other sources are lists of people who may be interested in similar products or services. Companies that specialize in marketing compile lists from professional associations, trade shows, and the like. Because outside lists may be expensive, select them with care.

Sales letters sent by e-mail are often more economical than print options, especially for large groups of potential and existing customers. If you choose e-mail as a medium, however, consider laws related to e-mail marketing, such as the CAN-SPAM act (www.ftc.gov/tips-advice /business-center/guidance/can-spam-act-compliance-guide-business). Consider as well that e-mail offers the ability to include multimedia (such as video and purchase links), but it also requires that content be kept targeted and short. See also **selecting the medium**.

Once you determine who is to receive your sales letter, learn as much as you can about your readers so that you can effectively tell them how your product or service will satisfy their needs. Knowledge of your **audience**—their gender, age, vocation, geographic location, educational level, financial status, and interests—will help determine your approach.

Analyze your product or service carefully to determine your strongest psychological sales points. Psychological selling involves stressing a product's benefits, which may be intangible, rather than its physical features. Select the most important psychological selling point about your product or service, and build your sales message around it. Show how your product or service will make your readers' jobs easier, increase their status, make their personal lives more pleasant, and so on. Then describe the physical features of your product in terms of their benefit to your readers. Use photos and Web links to help your readers imagine themselves using and enjoying your product or service. See also **"you" viewpoint**.

❖ **ETHICS NOTE** Be certain that any claim you make in a sales message is valid. To claim that a product is safe guarantees its absolute safety; therefore, say that the product is safe "provided that normal safety precautions are taken." Further, although you can highlight differences, do not exaggerate or speak negatively about a competitor. For further ethical and legal guidelines, visit the Data & Marketing Association Web site at thedma.org. See also **ethics in writing**. ❖

WRITER'S CHECKLIST   **Writing Sales Letters**

✔ Attract your readers' attention and pique their interest in the opening — for example, by describing a product's feature that would appeal strongly to their needs. See also **introductions**.

✔ Convince readers that your product or service is everything you say it is through case histories, free-trial use, money-back guarantee, or testimonials and endorsements. (For advice, see www.ftc.gov.)

✔ Suggest ways readers can make immediate use of the product or service. Include a brochure or a Web link with photos or videos.

✔ Minimize the negative effect price can have on readers.
  • Mention the price along with a reminder of the benefits of the product.
  • State the price in terms of units rather than sets ($20 per item, not $600 per set).
  • Identify the daily, monthly, or even yearly cost based on the estimated life of the product.
  • Suggest a series of payments rather than one total payment.
  • Compare the cost of your product with that of something readers accept readily. ("This entire package costs no more than a dinner and a concert.")

✔ Make it easy and worthwhile for customers to respond: Include instructions for ordering online or by phone, information about free delivery, or special discount codes.

✔ Include links to **social media**, and invite readers to become part of the conversation and community surrounding the product, service, or brand.

S

---

scope

Scope is the depth and breadth of detail you include in a document as defined by your audience's needs, your **purpose**, and the **context**. (See also **audience**.) For example, if you write a **trip report** about a routine visit to a company facility, your readers may need to know only the basic details and any unusual findings. However, if you prepare a trip report about a visit to a division that has experienced problems and your purpose is to suggest ways to solve those problems, your report will contain many more details, observations, and even recommendations.

You should determine the scope of a document during the **preparation** stage of the writing process, even though you may refine it later. Defining your scope will expedite your **research** and can help determine team members' responsibilities in **collaborative writing**.

Your scope will also be affected by the type of document you are writing, as well as the medium you select for your message. For example, funding organizations often prescribe the general content and length for **proposals**, and some organizations set length limits on other documents. See **selecting the medium** and "Five Steps to Successful Writing" (page xvii).

selecting the medium

Selecting the most appropriate medium (or *channel*) for communicating in the workplace depends on a wide range of factors related to your **audience**, **purpose**, and **context**. Those factors include the following:

- The audience's preferences and expectations
- The organization's practices and policies
- How widely information needs to be distributed
- The urgency of the communication
- The sensitivity or confidentiality required
- Your own most effective communication style

As this list suggests, choosing the best medium may involve personal considerations as well as the essential functions of the medium. If you need to collaborate with someone to solve a problem, for example, you may find e-mail exchanges less effective than a phone call or face-to-face meeting. If you need precise wording or a record of a complex or sensitive message, however, a written medium is often essential.

Many of the following media and forms of communication overlap and evolve as technology develops. Understanding their basic functions will help you select the most appropriate medium for your needs. See Figure S–1 for a table summarizing the media discussed in this entry. See also **adapting to new technologies**.

Medium	Use
E-mail	Primary informal or formal medium for communicating and file sharing with colleagues, clients, and customers
Memos	Internal correspondence for announcements, instructions, and reports within an organization in which employees lack ready access to e-mail
Letters	Letterhead correspondence for formal communications with professional associates outside an organization
Text and Instant Messages	*Text messages* for exchanges between people on the move or in nontraditional workspaces; *instant messages* for real-time exchanges among coworkers, customers, and suppliers
Phone Calls and Voice Mail	*Phone calls* for substantial interaction on complex or sensitive issues; *voice-mail messages* for clear and brief notes
Faxes	Faxed documents, often with handwritten additions, for viewing in their original form
Meetings and Conference Calls	*Individual and group meetings* for establishing rapport, solving problems, and reaching decisions; *conference calls* for saving travel costs
Web Conferences and Videoconferences	*Web conferences* for multiple participants through their computers, often using Web video applications; formal *videoconferences* with high-end equipment for participants at multiple locations using shared visuals or demonstrations
Web Networking and Promotion	*Intranet sites* for file and idea sharing within organizations; *public Web sites* for providing product and client access; *social-media sites* for enhancing individual and organization brand identity

FIGURE S–1. Choosing the Appropriate Medium

E-mail

E-mail functions as a primary medium to communicate and share files with colleagues, clients, and customers. Although e-mail may function as informal notes, e-mail messages should follow the writing strategy and style described in **correspondence**. All e-mail requires special review because recipients can easily forward messages and attachments and because e-mail messages are subject to legal disclosure.

Memos

Memos are appropriate for internal communication among members of the same organization, especially those who do not have ready access to e-mail (for example, employees in manufacturing or service industries). They use a standard header and are sent on paper or as attachments to e-mails. Memos can instruct employees, announce policies, report results, disseminate information, and delegate responsibilities.

Letters

Business **letters** with handwritten signatures are often appropriate for formal communications with professional associates or customers outside an organization. Letters on organizational letterhead communicate formality, respect, and authority. Letters are used with job applications, for recommendations, and in other official and social contexts.

Text and Instant Messages

Text messaging, or *texting*, is the exchange of brief written messages between mobile phones. Text messaging is effective for simple messages communicated between people on the move or in nontraditional work spaces.

Instant messaging (IM) on a computer or handheld device is an efficient way to communicate brief written exchanges in real time with coworkers, suppliers, and customers. Instant messaging requires that recipients are ready and available to participate in an immediate exchange of messages.

Phone Calls and Voice Messages

Phone calls are best used for exchanges that require substantial interaction and the ability of participants to interpret each other's tone of voice. They are useful for discussing sensitive issues and resolving misunderstandings, although they do not provide the visual cues present during face-to-face meetings. Be careful when using a cell phone in public places, and follow appropriate etiquette and organizational policies. See "Web Conferences and Videoconferences" on page 491.

Should you need to leave a voice-mail message, it should be clear and brief. ("I got your package, so you don't need to call the distributor.") For complicated messages, use another medium, such as e-mail.

Faxes

A fax is used when a document—like a drawing or a signed contract—must be viewed in its original form. Faxing is used when scanning is not an option or when a faxed document is requested. Fax machines are often located in shared areas, so let the intended recipient know before you send confidential or sensitive information. A cover sheet should include the name of the recipient and the number of pages in the document.

Meetings and Conference Calls

In-person **meetings** with individuals are most appropriate with an associate or a client with whom you intend to develop an important, long-term relationship. A face-to-face meeting may also be useful to help establish rapport, interview someone on a complex topic, solve a technical problem, or handle a controversial issue.

Group or committee meetings may be best for brainstorming, collaborating on a complex topic, and reaching decisions. A teleconference (or *conference call*) among three or more participants is an inexpensive alternative to face-to-face meetings requiring travel. The person coordinating the call should provide an agenda to all the participants and direct the discussion. For advice on how to record discussions and decisions, see **minutes of meetings**.

Web Conferences and Video Conferences

These conferences may be used for committee meetings when participants are geographically separated, for small groups working on a specific problem, for numerous participants in training, or for educational seminars (referred to as *webinars*). Participants can be connected through downloaded applications. Web conferences may be enhanced with phone connections and video applications, like Google Meet, GoToMeeting, or WebEx.

More formal videoconferences with high-end equipment often require professional services. These work best with participants who are at ease in front of the camera, and such conferences should be carefully planned, with technical support staff available.

Web Networking and Promotion

A company intranet Web site is ideal for sharing documents and files—including announcements and **policies and procedures**—within an organization. An intranet site can serve not only as a home base for resources like company directories and **newsletters** but also as a place where ideas can be developed through, for example, discussion boards and wikis.

A company's public Web site can provide sales and product information as well as information about an organization and opportunities to foster contacts with customers and clients. Such sites may include new-product announcements, **press releases**, **FAQs**, manuals, product or service reviews, **blogs and forums**, employment opportunities, and requests for proposals. See also **writing for the Web**.

Using **social media** sites can help individuals and organizations cultivate professional contacts and promote products and services. Networks for professionals, such as LinkedIn, aim to connect individuals and groups with common interests. Organizations may use social networking sites like Facebook to market their products and services as well as to enhance their brand identity. See also **job search**.

semicolons

The semicolon (;) links independent **clauses** or other sentence elements of equal weight and grammatical rank when they are not joined by a **comma** and a **conjunction**. The semicolon indicates a greater pause between clauses than does a comma but not as great a pause as a **period**.

Independent clauses joined by a semicolon should balance or contrast with each other, and the relationship between the two statements should be so clear that further explanation is not necessary.

▶ The new Web site was a success; every division reported increased online sales.

Do not use a semicolon between a dependent clause and its main clause.

▶ No one applied for the position; even though it was heavily advertised.

With Strong Connectives

In complicated sentences, a semicolon may be used before transitional words or **phrases** (*that is*, *for example*, *namely*) that introduce examples or further explanation. See also **transition**.

▶ The press understands Commissioner Curran's position on the issue; *that is*, local funds should not be used for the highway project.

A semicolon should also be used before conjunctive **adverbs** (*therefore*, *moreover*, *consequently*, *furthermore*, *indeed*, *in fact*, *however*) that connect independent clauses.

▶ The test results are not complete; *therefore*, I cannot make a recommendation. [The semicolon in the example shows that *therefore* belongs to the second clause.]

S

For Clarity in Long Sentences

Use a semicolon between two independent clauses connected by a coordinating conjunction (*and*, *but*, *for*, *or*, *nor*, *so*, *yet*) if the clauses are long and contain other **punctuation**.

▶ In most cases, these individuals are executives, bankers, or lawyers; *but* they do not, as the press seems to believe, simply push the button of their economic power to affect local politics.

A semicolon may also be used if any items in a series contain commas.

▶ Among those present were John Howard, president of the Omega Paper Company; Carol Delgado, president of Environex Corporation; and Larry Stanley, president of Stanley Papers.

Use **parentheses** or **dashes**, not semicolons, to enclose a parenthetical element that contains commas.

▶ All affected job classifications (receptionist, assistant, transcriptionist, and clerk) will be upgraded this month.

Use a **colon**, not a semicolon, as a mark of anticipation or enumeration.

▶ Three decontamination methods are under consideration; a zeolite-resin system, an evaporation system, and a filtration system.

The semicolon always appears outside closing **quotation marks**.

▶ The attorney said, "You must be accurate"; her client replied, "I will."

---

sentence construction

DIRECTORY

Subjects 494	Constructing Effective
Predicates 494	Sentences 496
Sentence Types 494	

S

A sentence is the most fundamental and versatile tool available to writers. Sentences generally flow from a subject to a **verb** to any **objects**, **complements**, or **modifiers**, but they can be ordered in a variety of ways to achieve **emphasis**. When shifting word order, however, be aware that it can make a big difference in the meaning of a sentence.

▶ He was *only* the accountant. [suggests importance]

▶ He was the *only* accountant. [defines the number]

The most basic components of sentences are subjects and predicates.

Subjects

The *subject* of a sentence is a **noun** or **pronoun** (and its modifiers) about which the predicate of the sentence makes a statement. Although a subject may appear anywhere in a sentence, it most often appears at the beginning: "*To increase sales* is our goal." Grammatically, every sentence, except commands, must have an explicit subject that agrees with its verb in **number**.

▶ *These departments have* much in common.

▶ *This department has* several functions.

The subject is the actor in sentences using the active **voice**.

▶ *The Webmaster reported* an increase in site visits for May.

A *compound subject* has two or more substantives (nouns or noun equivalents) as the subject of one verb.

▶ *The president* and *the treasurer* agreed to begin the audit.

Predicates

The *predicate* is the part of a sentence that makes an assertion about the subject and completes the thought of the sentence.

▶ Bill *has piloted the corporate jet.*

The *simple predicate* is the verb and any helping verbs (*has piloted*). The *complete predicate* is the verb and any modifiers, objects, or complements (*has piloted the corporate jet*). A *compound predicate* consists of two or more verbs with the same subject.

▶ The company *tried* but *did not succeed* in that field.

Such constructions help achieve **conciseness**. A *predicate nominative* is a noun construction that follows a linking verb and renames the subject.

▶ She is my *attorney*. [noun]

▶ His excuse was *that he had been sick*. [noun clause]

Sentence Types

Sentences may be classified according to *structure* (simple, compound, complex, or compound-complex); *intention* (declarative, interrogative, imperative, or exclamatory); and *stylistic use* (loose, periodic, or minor).

Structure. A *simple sentence* consists of one independent clause. At its most basic, a simple sentence contains only a subject and a predicate.

▶ Profits [subject] rose [predicate].

A *compound sentence* consists of two or more independent clauses connected by a comma and a coordinating **conjunction**, by a **semicolon**, or by a semicolon and a conjunctive **adverb**.

▶ Drilling is the only way to collect samples of the layers of sediment below the ocean floor, *but* it is not the only way to gather information about these strata. [comma and coordinating conjunction]

▶ The chemical composition of seawater bears little resemblance to that of river water; the various elements are present in entirely different proportions. [semicolon]

▶ It was 500 miles to the site; *therefore*, we made arrangements to fly. [semicolon and conjunctive adverb]

A *complex sentence* contains one independent clause and at least one dependent clause that expresses a subordinate idea.

▶ The generator will shut off automatically [independent clause] if the temperature rises above a specified point [dependent clause].

A *compound-complex sentence* consists of two or more independent clauses plus at least one dependent clause.

▶ Productivity is central to controlling inflation [independent clause]; when productivity rises [dependent clause], employers can raise wages without raising prices [independent clause].

Intention.   A *declarative sentence* conveys information or makes a factual statement. ("The motor powers the conveyor belt.") An *interrogative sentence* asks a direct question. ("Does the conveyor belt run constantly?") An *imperative sentence* issues a command. ("Restart in SAFE mode.") An *exclamatory sentence* is an emphatic expression of feeling, fact, or opinion. It is a declarative sentence that is stated with great feeling. ("The files were deleted!")

Stylistic Use.   A *loose sentence* makes its major point at the beginning and then adds subordinate phrases and clauses that develop or modify that major point. A loose sentence could end at one or more points before it actually does end, as the periods in brackets illustrate in the following sentence:

▶ It went up[.], a great ball of fire about a mile in diameter[.], an elemental force freed from its bonds[.] after being chained for billions of years.

A *periodic sentence* delays its main ideas until the end by presenting subordinate ideas or modifiers first.

S

▶ During the last century, the attitude of the American citizen toward automation underwent a profound change.

A *minor sentence* is an incomplete sentence that makes sense in its context because the missing element is clearly implied by the preceding sentence.

▶ In view of these facts, is the service contract really useful? *Or economical?*

Constructing Effective Sentences

The subject-verb-object pattern is effective because it is most familiar to **readers**. In "The company increased profits," we know the subject (*company*) and the object (*profits*) by their positions relative to the verb (*increased*).

An *inverted sentence* places the elements in an unexpected order, thus emphasizing the point by attracting the readers' attention.

▶ A better job I never had. [direct object-subject-verb]

▶ More optimistic I have never been. [subjective complement-subject-linking verb]

▶ A poor image we presented. [direct object-subject-verb]

Use uncomplicated sentences to state complex ideas. If readers have to cope with a complicated sentence in addition to a complex idea, they are likely to become confused. Just as simpler sentences make complex ideas more digestible, a complex sentence construction makes a series of simple ideas smoother and less choppy.

Avoid loading sentences with a number of thoughts carelessly tacked together. Such sentences are monotonous and hard to read because all the ideas seem to be of equal importance. Rather, distinguish the relative importance of sentence elements with **subordination**. See also **garbled sentences**.

LOADED   We started the program three years ago, only three members were on staff, and each member was responsible for a separate state, but it was not an efficient operation.

IMPROVED   When we started the program three years ago, only three members were on staff, each responsible for a separate state; however, that arrangement was not efficient.

Express coordinate or equivalent ideas in similar form. The structure of the sentence helps readers grasp the similarity of its components, as illustrated in **parallel structure**.

S

sentence faults

A number of problems can create sentence faults, including faulty **subordination**, **clauses** with no subjects, rambling sentences, omitted **verbs**, and illogical assertions.

Faulty subordination occurs when a grammatically subordinate element contains the main idea of the sentence or when a subordinate element is so long or detailed that it obscures the main idea. Both of the following sentences are logical, depending on what the writer intends as the main idea and as the subordinate element.

▶ Although the new filing system saves money, many of the staff are unhappy with it. [If the main point is that *many of the staff are unhappy*, this sentence is correct.]

▶ The new filing system saves money, although many of the staff are unhappy with it. [If the main point is that *the new filing system saves money*, this sentence is correct.]

In the following example, the subordinate element overwhelms the main point.

FAULTY   Because the noise level in the assembly area on a typical shift is as loud as a smoke detector's alarm ten feet away, employees often develop hearing problems.

IMPROVED   Employees in the assembly area often develop hearing problems because the noise level on a typical shift is as loud as a smoke detector's alarm ten feet away.

Missing subjects occur when writers inappropriately assume a subject that they do not state in the clause. See also **sentence fragments**.

INCOMPLETE   Your application program can request to end the session after the next command. [Your application program can request *who* or *what* to end the session?]

COMPLETE   Your application program can request *the host program* to end the session after the next command.

Rambling sentences contain more information than the reader can comfortably absorb. The obvious remedy for a rambling sentence is to divide it into two or more sentences. (See also **run-on sentences**.) When you do that, put the main message of the rambling sentence into the first of the revised sentences.

RAMBLING   The payment to which a subcontractor is entitled should be made promptly in order that in the event of a subsequent

S

contractual dispute we, as general contractors, may not be held in default of our contract by virtue of nonpayment.

DIRECT   Pay subcontractors promptly. Then, if a contractual dispute occurs, we cannot be held in default of our contract because of nonpayment.

Missing verbs produce some sentence faults.

▶ I never have *written* and probably never will write the annual report.

Faulty logic results when a predicate makes an illogical assertion about its subject. "Mr. Wilson's *job* is a sales representative" is not logical, but "*Mr. Wilson* is a sales representative" is logical. See also **logic errors**.

sentence fragments

A sentence fragment is an incomplete grammatical unit that is punctuated as a sentence.

FRAGMENT   And quit his job.
SENTENCE   He quit his job.

A sentence fragment lacks either a subject or a **verb** or is a subordinate **clause** or **phrase**. Sentence fragments are often introduced by relative **pronouns** (*who, whom, which, that*) or subordinating **conjunctions** (*although, because, if, when, while*).

▶ The new manager updated several personnel procedures*, although* ~~Although~~ she didn't clear them with Human Resources.

A sentence must contain a finite verb; **verbals** (nonfinite) do not function as verbs. The following sentence fragments use verbals (*providing, to work*) that cannot function as finite verbs.

FRAGMENT   *Providing* all employees with disability insurance.
SENTENCE   The company *provides* all employees with disability insurance.

FRAGMENT   *To work* a 40-hour week.
SENTENCE   Most of our employees *must work* a 40-hour week.

Explanatory phrases beginning with *such as, for example*, and similar terms often lead writers to create sentence fragments.

▶ The staff wants additional benefits*, such as* ~~For example,~~ the use of company cars.

A hopelessly snarled fragment simply must be rewritten. To rewrite such a fragment, pull the main points out of the fragment, list them in the proper sequence, and then rewrite the sentence as illustrated in **garbled sentences**. See also **sentence construction** and **sentence faults**.

sentence variety

Sentences can vary in length, structure, and complexity. As you revise, vary your sentences so that they do not become tiresomely alike. See also **sentence construction**.

Sentence Length

A series of sentences of the same length is monotonous, so varying sentence length makes writing less tedious to the **reader**. For example, avoid stringing together a number of short independent **clauses**. Either connect them with a subordinating connective, thereby creating a dependent clause, or turn some clauses into separate sentences.

STRING	The river is 63 miles long, and it averages 50 yards in width, and its depth averages 8 feet.
IMPROVED	The river, which is 63 miles long and averages 50 yards in width, has an average depth of 8 feet.
IMPROVED	The river is 63 miles long. It averages 50 yards in width and 8 feet in depth.

You can often effectively combine short sentences by converting **verbs** into **adjectives**.

▶ The digital shift indicator *failed.* ~~failed. It~~ was pulled from the market.

Although too many short sentences make your writing sound choppy and immature, a short sentence can be effective following a long one.

▶ During the past two decades, many changes have occurred in American life — the extent, durability, and significance of which no one has yet measured. *No one can.*

In general, short sentences are good for emphatic, memorable statements. Long sentences are good for detailed explanations and support. Nothing is inherently wrong with a long sentence, or even with a complicated one, as long as its meaning is clear and direct. Sentence length becomes an element of style when varied for **emphasis** or contrast; a conspicuously short or long sentence can be used to good effect.

S

Word Order

When a series of sentences all begin in exactly the same way (usually with an **article** and a **noun**), the result is likely to be monotonous. You can make your sentences more interesting by occasionally starting with a modifying word, **phrase**, or clause.

▶ *To salvage the project*, she presented alternatives when existing policies failed to produce results. [modifying phrase]

However, overuse of this technique can itself be monotonous, so use it in moderation.

Inverted word order can be an effective way to achieve variety, but be careful not to create an awkward construction.

AWKWARD   So good sales have never been.

EFFECTIVE   Never have sales been so good.

For variety, you can alter normal sentence order by inserting a phrase or clause.

▶ Titanium fills the gap, *both in weight and in strength*, between aluminum and steel.

The technique of inserting a phrase or clause is good for achieving emphasis, providing detail, breaking monotony, and regulating **pace**.

Loose and Periodic Sentences

A loose sentence makes its major point at the beginning and then adds subordinate phrases and clauses that develop or modify the point. A loose sentence could end at one or more points before it actually ends, as the periods in brackets illustrate in the following example:

▶ It went up[.], a great ball of fire about a mile in diameter[.], an elemental force freed from its bonds[.] after being chained for billions of years.

A periodic sentence delays its main idea until the end by presenting modifiers or subordinate ideas first, thus holding the readers' interest until the end.

▶ During the last century, the attitude of Americans toward technology underwent a profound change.

Experiment with shifts from loose sentences to periodic sentences in your own writing, especially during **revision**. Avoid the monotony of a long series of loose sentences, particularly a series containing coordinate clauses joined by **conjunctions**. Using **subordination** not only provides emphasis but also makes your sentences more interesting.

sequential method of development

The sequential, or *step-by-step*, **method of development** is especially effective for explaining a process or describing a mechanism in operation. (See **process explanation**.) It is also the logical method for writing **instructions**, as shown in Figure S–2 and Figure I–6 (page 266).

↗ Send   ✕ Cancel   ▤ Save Draft   ⌇ Add Attachment   ✉ Signature   Options ▸
TO All Hourly Employees <hourly@techline.org>
FROM Steven Scott <scott@techline.org>
CC _____   Show BCC
Subject Flextime Eligibility and Requests

Because Human Resources has received numerous calls about the approval process for using the new flextime schedule, this message outlines the eligibility requirements and the procedure for requesting flextime.

Eligibility
First, determine if you are eligible to use a flextime schedule. You are eligible if your job does not require you to answer telephones or to be available to the public between the hours of 8:00 a.m. and 5:00 p.m. In addition, you must meet with your department manager to ensure that any essential duties will be covered during those hours.

Request Procedure
After you have established your eligibility, submit a copy of Form FT, signed by your department manager, to Human Resources. We will send the form to your division manager for his or her approval.

Implementation
Human Resources will notify you when your request is approved or denied. If your request is approved, you may begin your new schedule on the first Monday thereafter. After three weeks, your manager must advise Human Resources in writing that your flextime schedule has not interfered with the smooth functioning of your department.

You may download copies of Form FT at techline.org/form/ft.pdf. If you have any questions, please contact Margaret Dienstein at extension 5648 or mld@techline.org.

> Transitions to emphasize steps in process

S

FIGURE S–2. Sequential Method of Development

The main advantage of the sequential method of development is that it is easy to follow because the steps correspond to the process or operation being described. The disadvantages are that it can become monotonous and does not lend itself well to achieving **emphasis**.

Most methods of development have elements of sequence to a greater or lesser extent. The **chronological method of development**, for example, is also sequential: To describe a trip chronologically, from beginning to end, is also to describe it sequentially. The **cause-and-effect method of development** may contain certain elements of sequence. For example, a report of the causes leading to an accident (the effect) might describe those causes in the order they occurred (or their sequence).

service

When used as a **verb**, *service* means "keep up or maintain" as well as "repair." ("Our company will *service* your equipment.") If you mean "provide a more general benefit," use *serve*.

▶ Our company ~~services~~ the northwest area of the state.
      serves

set / sit

Sit is an intransitive **verb**; it does not, therefore, require an **object**. ("I *sit* by a window in the office.") Its past **tense** is *sat*. ("We *sat* around the conference table.") *Set* is usually a transitive verb, meaning "put or place," "establish," or "harden." Its past tense is *set*.

▶ Please *set* the supplies on the shelf.

▶ The jeweler *set* the stone carefully.

▶ Can we *set* a date for the meeting?

▶ The high temperature *sets* the epoxy quickly.

Set is occasionally an intransitive verb.

▶ The new adhesive *sets* in five minutes.

shall / will

Traditionally, *shall* was used to express the future **tense** with *I* and *we*. Today, however, *will* is the generally accepted term. *Shall* is commonly used today only in questions requesting an opinion or a preference ("*Shall* we go?") rather than a prediction ("*Will* we go?"). It is also used in statements expressing determination ("I *shall* return!") or in formal regulations that express a requirement ("Applicants *shall* provide a proof of certification.").

slashes

The slash (/)—also called *slant line, diagonal, virgule, bar,* and *solidus*—both separates and shows omission. The slash can indicate alternatives ("*You may reach the customer service department at 515-678-2278/2279*") or combinations (*on/off switch*).

The slash often indicates omitted words and letters: miles/hour (miles per hour); w/o (without)

In fractions and mathematical expressions, the slash separates the numerator from the denominator (3/4 for three-fourths; *x/y* for *x* over *y*).

Although the slash is used informally with **dates** (*5/9/18*), avoid this form in business writing, especially in **international correspondence**.

The forward slash often separates items in URLs (uniform resource locators): inlandchorus.com/programs. The backward slash is used to separate parts of file names: *c:\myfiles\reports\annual18.doc.*

so / so that / such

Avoid *so* as a substitute for *because*. See also **as / because / since**.

> *Because she*
> ▸ ~~She~~ reads faster, ~~so~~ she finished before I did.

Do not replace the phrase *so that* with *so* or *such that*.

> *so that*
> ▸ The report should be written ~~such that~~ it can be widely understood.

Such, an **adjective** meaning "of this or that kind," should never be used as a **pronoun**.

> ▸ Our company provides on-site child care, but I do not anticipate
> *it.*
> using ~~such.~~

S

social media

Social media refers to Web sites or applications—such as Facebook, LinkedIn, Twitter, and Instagram—that allow the creation of online communities through which individuals and organizations can create content, interact, and share information. Accessed through Web browsers or mobile devices, social-media platforms often incorporate **instant messaging** and **e-mail** components, and many have **blogs and forums** that allow for comments, links to other Web sites, and the collection of information that is of interest to the community.

Social media plays several vital roles in professional communication. It can help job seekers establish a professional presence and network and help companies communicate more easily with stakeholders.

On an individual level, you can use accounts on sites such as LinkedIn and Twitter to develop your presence within your field to connect with colleagues. When you create accounts on these sites, your profile, including your profile picture, should be consistent to make it easier for potential employers and colleagues to find you. Your profile and postings should also be professional in tone; if you have used social media primarily for personal reasons, you may wish to create separate accounts that are focused on your work. You can also use social media for active networking. Many industries and professional organizations have established conversations around Twitter hashtags (such as #SmallBizChat, #IMCchat, and #womenintech) and meet at regularly scheduled times to discuss current events and mentoring needs.

Many organizations employ writers to maintain their social-media accounts in order to connect with their clients, share information about their products, and reach new customers. Social media can help organizations promote goodwill, resolve problems, and obtain near-instant feedback on their products and services.

Choosing the Appropriate Platforms

When you or your organization chooses which social-media platforms to join, consider both what you hope to accomplish and which platforms reach more of your target customers or contacts. For example, a manufacturing company might choose a platform that focuses on users of products similar to its own, whereas a service-oriented company might select a platform that allows users to request and receive immediate assistance. A small shop might choose several platforms for different purposes, such as advertising images of its products on a platform that is heavily image-based while participating in another platform that allows the owner to build a professional network.

Two social-media characteristics—status updates and networks—are particularly useful in the workplace. Status updates, which include posts on Facebook and tweets on Twitter, allow individuals or organizations to post brief announcements or responses to questions. Once these status updates are published, other accounts can immediately respond to them. Networks allow one individual or organization to link its company and products to another individual or organization. By doing so, the two entities become "connected" in the social-media community, allowing their posts to be intertwined into a type of ongoing conversation. Figure S–3 provides an overview of three popular social-media platforms of interest to businesses and professionals and shows how each uses status updates and networks to support its community.

Before selecting a specific social-media platform, consider the following:

- Conversations within social media are impossible to control or pause. You must be willing to respond to the inquiries and comments, positive and negative, of other community members.

- Social-media platforms may demand significant time from account holders. Users of many platforms expect quick, ongoing responses and updates. If a crisis occurs, you must be willing and able to monitor the account outside of normal business hours.

- Communications within a social-media platform might have a wider audience than you intend, even though most platforms allow accounts to limit their audiences.

Writing Style and Privacy Considerations

For writing style, follow both the practices of your organization and the requirements of the selected social-media platform. Pay close attention to the **context**, **purpose**, and **audience** of your message, ensuring that your message is clear, precise, and free of grammatical errors. See **proofreading**.

Posts in a social-media platform are immediately and often widely shared among other community participants and potentially on other, unassociated Web sites. For this reason, consider both the benefit of your post to your immediate audience and the potential implications of that post to those outside your social-media network. Although many platforms are considered "informal" and used primarily for personal communication, the ability of writing to be shared throughout a given network demands that you consider how your contributions represent you professionally. Organizations often review the social-media profiles of their applicants as part of the employment process. Other organizations employ services to monitor what is said about them online. Many organizations have policies that prohibit employees from discussing the workplace, even within a personal social-media account.

S

LinkedIn	Offers individuals opportunities to connect with others and to create a professional network or community.
	Provides a profile page that acts much like a **<u>résumé</u>** by highlighting an individual's work, education, skills, and experiences.
	Allows community members to participate in profession-specific discussion boards, as well as post and respond to employment ads.
	Allows people to follow specific businesses and organizations.
Facebook	Enables businesses to broaden their brand recognition and to interact with current and new customers.
	Provides insight about potential employees, vendors, and business associates.
	Assigns each individual or business a "wall," which can be used to post status updates, pictures, videos, or links to other Web sites.
	Allows users to "friend" or "like" other users, connecting the accounts and allowing interaction between each user.
Twitter	Allows users to follow a company or an individual who can keep clients and others aware of an organization's or individual's activities.
	Limits every message or "status update" to 140 characters; businesses and individuals can post timely updates or critical announcements.
	Allows organizations to enter near synchronous conversations with their clients and customers.

FIGURE S–3. Comparison of Social-Media Platforms

WRITER'S CHECKLIST   **Judicious Use of Social Media**

✔ Always consider the purpose and suitability of your contributions. Avoid contributions that publicly discuss topics better suited for one-on-one communication or that are considered divisive.

✔ Consider your posts to be available to everyone, and take into account how someone, such as your employer or school, might view your status update or shared picture.

✔ Follow your employer's policies regarding social media. Attempting to circumvent policies — by using a mobile device to access a blocked site, for example — could result in severe penalties or even termination.

(continued)

Judicious Use of Social Media (*continued*)

✔ Never comment about a job, an employer, or an instructor. Consider everything that you contribute to a social-media platform as available to the organization or individuals that you might be writing about.

✔ Carefully consider "friend" requests. Before establishing a connection, consider your organization's policy, your professional relationship, and any potential current or future conflicts of interest.

✔ Have at least one public, professional social-media account, especially if you are searching for jobs. Many employers now search job candidates' social-media accounts. If they cannot find you online, they may be suspicious that you are hiding something.

✔ Consider also the information in the Ethics Note in **blogs and forums** as you compose your message.

some / somewhat

When *some* functions as an indefinite **pronoun** for a plural count **noun** or as an indefinite **adjective** modifying a plural count noun, use a plural **verb**.

▶ *Some* of us *are* prepared to work overtime.

▶ *Some* people *are* more productive than others.

Some is singular, however, when used with mass nouns.

▶ *Some* sand *has* trickled through the crack.

When *some* is used as an adjective or a pronoun meaning "an undetermined quantity" or "certain unspecified persons," it should be replaced by the **adverb** *somewhat*, which means "to some extent."

▶ His writing has improved ~~some.~~ *somewhat.*

S

some time / sometime / sometimes

Some time refers to a duration of time. ("We waited for *some time* before making the decision.") *Sometime* refers to an unknown or unspecified time. ("We will visit with you *sometime*.") *Sometimes* refers to occasional occurrences at unspecified times. ("He *sometimes* visits the branch offices.")

spatial method of development

The spatial **method of development** describes an object or a process according to the physical arrangement of its features. Depending on the subject, you describe its features from bottom to top, side to side, east to west, outside to inside, and so on. Descriptions of this kind rely mainly on dimension (height, width, length), direction (up, down, north, south), shape (rectangular, square, semicircular), and proportion (one-half, two-thirds). Features are described in relation to one another or to their surroundings, as illustrated in Figure S–4, which provides the partial installation requirements for drinking fountains that comply with the Americans with Disabilities Act (ADA). Such descriptions often benefit from **visuals**, such as **drawings**, that can provide overviews and details, as is the case in Figure S–4.

Drinking Fountains and Water Coolers—Spout Height and Knee Clearance

In addition to clearances discussed in the text, the following knee clearance is required underneath the fountain: 27 inches (685 mm) minimum from the floor to the underside of the fountain, which extends 8 inches (205 mm) minimum measured from the front edge underneath the fountain back toward the wall; if a minimum 9 inches (230 mm) of toe clearance is provided, a maximum of 6 inches (150 mm) of the 48 inches (1,220 mm) of clear floor space required at the fixture may extend into the top space.

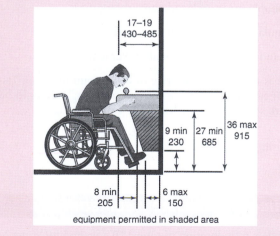

Figure 27a. Drinking Fountains and Water Coolers—Spout Height and Knee Clearance

FIGURE S–4. Spatial Description with Precise Measurements

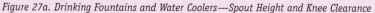

:cess-board.gov/ufas-html/fig27a.html. Accessed May 10, 2012.

The spatial method of development might be used for descriptions of warehouse inventory; **proposals** for landscape work; construction-site **progress and activity reports**; and, in combination with a step-by-step sequence, many types of **instructions**.

spelling

Because spelling errors in your documents can confuse readers and damage your credibility, careful **proofreading** is essential. The use of a spell checker is crucial; however, it will not catch all mistakes. A spell checker or an auto-correct function cannot detect a spelling error if the error results in a valid word (*to* inadvertently typed as *too*). If you are unsure about the spelling of a word, consult a dictionary.

spreadsheets

A spreadsheet is an interactive computer application for the organization, analysis, and storage of data in tabular form. (See also **tables**.) A typical spreadsheet in Microsoft Excel contains columns, rows, and cells, as shown in Figure S–5. The columns from left to right across the top of a spreadsheet are labeled with letters (A, B, C, and so on), and the rows at the far left of a spreadsheet are sequenced from top to bottom numerically (1, 2, 3, and so on). A cell is the point at which one column and one row meet, so it can be identified to match the column and the number in the row (A1, B2, and so on). The data in the columns and rows can be sorted (for example, A–Z or Z–A), manipulated with various mathematical operations, and formatted or printed as in a word-processing program.

Spreadsheet programs like Excel offer a wide variety of functions, options, and variations, so make use of the tutorials built into the

	A	B	C	D	E	F	G
1	Date	Company	State	Name	E-Mail	Source	Units
2	10/21/16	Company 1	NH	Allyson	Allyson@company1.com	Google search	100
3	10/21/16	Company 2	MA	John	John@company2.com	Referral from HR	250
4	10/22/16	Company 3	RI	Akram	Akram@company3.com	Met at convention	700
5	10/23/16	Company 4	CA	Hilary	Hilary@company4.com	Google search	430
6	10/24/16	Company 5	ME	Ming	Ming@company5.com	Contacted me	150
7	10/25/16	Company 6	MD	Sonia	Sonia@company6.com	Met at convention	75
8	10/25/16	Company 7	PA	Toby	Toby@company7.com	Contacted me	380
9						TOTAL	2085

FIGURE S–5. Spreadsheet

S

program for learning spreadsheet capabilities. Many colleges offer continuing education courses in the use of spreadsheets, and workplaces often provide courses or experts within the organization to help employees. The Web offers many videos and tutorials, but the Microsoft Office Web site for Excel is a useful starting point to connect with experts and other users via live chat and blogs (products.office.com/en-us/excel). Spreadsheets, or sections from them, can be printed and integrated into **reports** and other documents, as described in **visuals**. See also **graphs**.

style

A dictionary definition of *style* is "the way in which something is said or done, as distinguished from its substance." Writers' styles are determined by the way writers think and express their thoughts in writing—the way they use words, sentences, images, **figures of speech**, and so on.

A writer's style is the way his or her language functions in particular situations. For example, an **e-mail** to a friend would be relaxed, even chatty, in **tone**, whereas a job **application cover letter** would be more restrained and formal. Obviously, the style appropriate to one situation would not be appropriate to the other. In both situations, the **audience**, **purpose**, and **context** determine the manner or style the writer adopts. Beyond an individual's personal style, various kinds of writing have distinct stylistic traits, such as **business writing style**.

Standard English can be divided into two broad categories of style—formal and informal—according to how it functions in certain situations. Understanding the distinction between formal and informal writing styles helps writers use the appropriate style. However, no clear-cut line divides the two categories, and some writing may call for a combination of the two. See also **English, varieties of**.

Formal Writing Style

A formal writing style can perhaps best be defined by pointing to certain material that is clearly formal, such as scholarly and scientific articles in professional journals, lectures read at meetings of professional societies, and legal documents. Material written in a formal style is usually the work of a specialist writing to other specialists or writing that embodies laws or regulations. As a result, the vocabulary is specialized and precise. The writer's tone is impersonal and objective because the subject matter looms larger in the writing than does the author's personality. (See **point of view**.) A formal writing style does not use **contractions**, slang, or dialect. Because the material generally examines complex ideas, the **sentence construction** may also be complex.

Formal writing need not be dull and lifeless. By using such techniques as the active **voice** whenever possible, **sentence variety**, and **subordination**, a writer can make formal writing lively and interesting, especially if the subject matter is inherently interesting to **readers**. In the following conclusion to a historical study, a scholar reflects on **jargon** in business writing.

▶ Compared to some of the problems that afflict business and administrative writing—poor organization, obfuscation, and lack of consideration for the reader—phrases such as "as *per* your request" are a minor ill. It is my own view, however, that texts and teachers should continue to urge students to avoid jargon. People in organizations who face the same situation repeatedly will use similar language to different correspondents; however, the repeated language can be standard English that is friendly and that makes literal sense. Jargon that is not part of spoken English distances the writer from the reader; jargon that does not make literal sense devalues language as communication.

> —Kitty O. Locker, "'As *Per* Your Request':
> A History of Business Jargon,"
> *Journal of Business and Technical Communication* 1.1

Whether you should use a formal style in a particular instance depends on your readers and purpose. When writers attempt to force a formal style where it should not be used, their writing is likely to fall victim to **affectation**, **awkwardness**, and **gobbledygook**.

Informal Writing Style

An informal writing style is a relaxed and colloquial way of writing standard English. It is the style found in most personal e-mail and in some business **correspondence**, blogs, and **promotional writing**. (See also **blogs and forums**.) There is less distance between the writer and the reader because the tone is more personal than it is in formal writing. Consider the following passage, written in an informal style, from a nonfiction book on business management.

▶ Business, like art and science, has been revealed and conceived through the intellect and imagination of people, and it develops or declines because of the intellect and imagination of people.

In fact, there is no business; there are only people. Business exists only among people and for people.

Seems simple enough, and it applies to every aspect of business, but not enough businesspeople seem to get it.

Reading the economic forecasts and the indicators and the ratios and the rates of this or that, someone from another planet might

S

actually believe that there really are invisible hands at work in the marketplace.

It's easy to forget what the measurements are measuring. Every number—from productivity rates to salaries—is just a device contrived by people to measure the results of the enterprise of other people. For managers, the most important job is not measurement but motivation. And you can't motivate numbers.

— James A. Autry,
Love and Profit: The Art of Caring Leadership

As this example illustrates, the vocabulary of an informal writing style is made up of generally familiar rather than unfamiliar words and expressions, although slang and dialect are usually avoided. An informal style approximates the cadence and structure of spoken English while conforming to the grammatical conventions of written English.

◀ **PROFESSIONALISM NOTE** Writers who consciously attempt to create a distinctive style usually defeat their purpose. Attempting to impress readers with any specific style (casual, scientific, chatty, formal) can lead to affectation. Business writing need be neither affected nor dull. The key to a clear, direct, and even interesting style is to master basic writing skills and to keep your readers' needs in mind. What will be both informative and interesting to your readers? When that question is uppermost in your mind as you apply the steps of the writing process, you will achieve an interesting and informative writing style. See "Five Steps to Successful Writing" (page xvii). ▶

WRITER'S CHECKLIST   **Developing an Effective Style**

✔ Use the active voice — not exclusively but as much as possible without allowing your writing to become awkward or illogical.

✔ Use **parallel structure** whenever a sentence or **list** presents two or more thoughts of equal importance.

✔ Vary sentence structure to avoid a monotonous style.

✔ Avoid stating positive thoughts in negative terms (write "40 percent responded" instead of "60 percent failed to respond"). See also **ethics in writing**, **plain language**, and **positive writing**.

✔ Concentrate on achieving the proper balance between **emphasis** and subordination.

Style guides, such as *The Chicago Manual of Style* and the Associated Press *Stylebook and Briefing on Media Law*, provide specific and sometimes varied advice for handling issues of usage, style, and formats for citations, correspondence, and documents.

subordination

Subordination is the use of sentence structure to show the appropriate relationship between ideas of unequal importance.

▶ Envirex Systems now employs 500 people. It was founded just three years ago. [The two ideas are equally important.]

▶ Envirex Systems, *which now employs 500 people*, was founded just three years ago. [The number of employees is subordinated; the founding date is emphasized.]

▶ Envirex Systems, *which was founded just three years ago*, now employs 500 people. [The founding date is subordinated; the number of employees is emphasized.]

Subordination allows you to emphasize your main idea by putting less important ideas in subordinate **clauses** or **phrases**.

DEPENDENT CLAUSE	The regional manager's report, *which covered five pages*, was carefully illustrated.
PHRASE	The regional manager's report, *covering five pages*, was carefully illustrated.
SINGLE MODIFIER	The regional manager's *five-page* report was carefully illustrated.

Subordinating **conjunctions** (*because, if, while, when, although*) achieve subordination effectively.

▶ An increase in local sales is unlikely *because* the local population has declined.

You may use a coordinating conjunction (*and, but, for, nor, or, so,* or *yet*) to concede that an opposite or a balancing fact is true; however, a subordinating conjunction can often make the point more smoothly.

▶ *Although* their bank has a lower interest rate on loans, ours provides a wider range of essential services.

The relationship between a conditional statement and a statement of consequences is clearer if the condition is expressed as a subordinate clause.

▶ *Because* the bill was incorrect, the customer was angry.

Relative **pronouns** (*who, whom, which, that*) can be used effectively in subordinate clauses.

▶ OnlinePro, *which* protects computers from malicious programs, makes your system "invisible" to hackers.

S

Avoid subordinate constructions that overlap and depend on the preceding construction. Overlapping can make the relationship between a relative pronoun and its antecedent less clear.

OVERLAPPING   Shock, *which* often accompanies severe injuries and infections, is a failure of the circulation, *which* is marked by a fall in blood pressure *that* initially affects the skin (*which* explains pallor) and later the vital organs, such as the kidneys and brain.

CLEAR   Shock often accompanies severe injuries and infections. Marked by a fall in blood pressure, it is a failure of the circulation, initially to the skin (thus producing pallor) and later to the vital organs like the kidneys, and brain.

Effective subordination can be used to achieve **conciseness**, **emphasis**, and **sentence variety**.

suffixes

A suffix is a letter or letters added to the end of a word to change its meaning in some way. Suffixes can change the part of speech of a word.

NO SUFFIX   The proposal was *thorough*. [**adjective**]

SUFFIX   The *thoroughness* is obvious. [**noun**]

SUFFIX   The proposal *thoroughly* described the problem. [**adverb**]

The suffix *-like* is sometimes added to nouns to make them into adjectives. The resulting compound word is hyphenated only if it is unusual or might not immediately be clear (childlike, lifelike, *but* dictionary-like, Friedman-like). See **hyphens**.

S

surveys (*see* questionnaires)

synonyms

A synonym is a word that means nearly the same thing as another word does (*seller*, *vendor*, *supplier*). The dictionary definitions of synonyms are similar, but the connotations may differ. For example, a *seller* may be the same thing as a *supplier*, but the word *supplier* does not suggest a retail transaction as strongly as the word *seller* does.

Do not try to impress your **readers** by finding fancy or obscure synonyms in a **thesaurus**; the result is likely to be **affectation**. See also **connotation / denotation** and **antonyms**.

syntax

Syntax refers to the way words, phrases, and clauses are combined to form sentences. In English, the most common structure is the subject-verb-object pattern. For more information about the word order of sentences, see **sentence construction**, **sentence faults**, **sentence fragments**, and **sentence variety**.

S

T

tables

A table organizes numerical and verbal data, such as statistics, into parallel rows and columns that allow **readers** to make precise item-to-item comparisons. Overall data/trends, however, are more easily conveyed in **graphs** and other **visuals**.

Table Elements

Tables typically include the elements shown in Figure T–1.

Table Number. Table numbers should be placed above tables and assigned sequentially throughout the document.

Table Title. The title (or *caption*), which is normally placed just above the table, should describe concisely what the table represents.

Box Head. The box head contains the column headings, which should be brief but descriptive. Units of measurement should be either specified as part of the heading or enclosed in parentheses beneath it. Standard **abbreviations** and symbols are acceptable. Avoid vertical or diagonal lettering.

Stub. The stub, the left vertical column of a table, lists the items about which information is given in the body of the table.

Body. The body comprises the data below the column headings and to the right of the stub. Within the body, arrange columns so that the items to be compared appear in adjacent rows and columns for ease of comparison. (See Figure T–1.) Where no information exists for a specific item, substitute a row of dots or a dash to acknowledge the gap.

Rules. Rules are the lines (or *borders*) that separate the table into its various parts. Tables should include top and bottom borders. Tables often include right and left borders, although they may be open at the sides, as shown in Figure T–1. Generally, include a horizontal rule

FIGURE T–1. Elements of a Table

between the column headings and the body of the table. Separate the columns with vertical rules within a table only when they aid clarity.

Footnotes. Footnotes are used for explanations of individual items in the table. Symbols (such as * and †) or lowercase letters (sometimes in parentheses) rather than numbers are ordinarily used to indicate table footnotes. Otherwise, numbers might be mistaken for numerical data or could be confused with the numbering system for text footnotes. See also **documenting sources**.

Source Line. The source line identifies where the data originated. When a source line is appropriate, it appears below the table. Many organizations place the source line below the footnotes. See also **copyright** and **plagiarism**.

Continuing Tables. When a table must be divided so that it can be continued on another page, repeat the column headings and the table number and title on the new page with a "continued" label (for example, "Table 3. [title], *continued*").

Informal Tables

To list relatively few items that would be easier for the reader to grasp in tabular form than in running text, you can use an informal table, as long as you introduce it properly, as shown in Figure T–2. Although informal tables do not need titles or table numbers to identify them, they do require column headings that accurately describe the information listed.

T

Dear Customer:
To order replacement parts, use the following part numbers and prices:

Part	Part Number	Price ($)
Diverter valve	2-912	12.50
Gasket kit	2-776	0.95
Adapter	3-212	0.90

FIGURE T–2. Informal Table

tables of contents

A table of contents lists all the major sections of a long document or Web site in their order of appearance. Tables of contents allow **readers** to locate specific information quickly and easily by referencing section page numbers in printed documents or portable document format (PDF) files or by clicking hyperlinks in Web content.

When creating a table of contents, use the major **headings** and subheadings of your document exactly as they appear in the text, as shown in the entry **formal reports**. (See the table of contents in Figure F–6.) In print documents, the table of contents is placed in the front matter following the title page and **abstract**, and it precedes the list of tables or figures, the foreword, and the preface. On large or complex Web sites, the table of contents typically appears at the top of the first page.

telegraphic style

Telegraphic style condenses writing by omitting **articles**, **pronouns**, **conjunctions**, and **transitions**. Although **conciseness** is important, especially in **instructions**, writers sometimes try to achieve conciseness by omitting necessary words, thus producing misunderstandings. Compare the following two passages and notice how much clearer the revised version reads (the added words are italicized).

T

TELEGRAPHIC   Per 5/21 e-mail, 12 instruction booklets/questionnaire enclosed. Report can be complete when above materials received. July filling quickly, so let's set date. Pls advise.

CLEAR   *As promised in my May 21* e-mail, enclosed *are* 12 *copies of the* instruction booklet *and the* questionnaire. *We* can complete *the* report when *we* receive *the questionnaires.*

> *Our* July *calendar is* filling quickly, so *please call me to* set *a meeting* date *as soon as possible.*

Telegraphic style can also produce **ambiguity**, as the following example demonstrates.

AMBIGUOUS   The director wants report written by New York office. [Does the director want a report that the New York office *wrote in the past*, or does the director want the New York office *to write a report in the future*?]

CLEAR   The director wants the report *that was* written by the New York office.

CLEAR   The director wants the report *to be* written by the New York office.

◀ **PROFESSIONALISM NOTE** Although you may save yourself work by writing telegraphically, you may produce serious misunderstandings and make your readers work to decipher your meaning. Professional courtesy requires that you help your **reader**. Even when **text messaging**, make sure your reader will understand your meaning. ▶

tenant / tenet

A *tenant* is a person who holds or temporarily occupies a property owned by another person. ("The *tenant* was upset by the rent increase.") A *tenet* is an opinion or principle held by a person, an organization, or a system. ("Competition is a central *tenet* of capitalism.")

tense

DIRECTORY

Past Tense 520	Future Tense 521
Past Perfect Tense 520	Future Perfect Tense 521
Present Tense 520	Shift in Tense 521
Present Perfect Tense 521	

T

Tense is the grammatical term for **verb** forms that indicate time distinctions. The six tenses in English are past, past perfect, present, present perfect, future, and future perfect. Each tense also has a corresponding progressive form.

TENSE	BASIC FORM	PROGRESSIVE FORM
Past	I began	I was beginning
Past perfect	I had begun	I had been beginning
Present	I begin	I am beginning
Present perfect	I have begun	I have been beginning
Future	I will begin	I will be beginning
Future perfect	I will have begun	I will have been beginning

Perfect tenses allow you to express a prior action or condition that continues in a past, present, or future time.

PAST PERFECT   I *had begun* to read the manual when the fire alarm rang.

PRESENT PERFECT   I *have begun* to write the annual report and will continue for the rest of the month.

FUTURE PERFECT   I *will have begun* this project by the time funds are allocated.

Progressive tenses allow you to describe some ongoing action or condition in the past, present, or future.

PAST PROGRESSIVE   I *was beginning* to think we would not finish by the deadline.

PRESENT PROGRESSIVE   I *am beginning* to be concerned that we will not meet the deadline.

FUTURE PROGRESSIVE   I *will be requesting* a leave of absence when this project is finished.

Verbs that express mental activity (*believe, know, see,* and so on) are generally not used in the progressive.

> ▶ I ~~am believing~~ *believe* the defendant's testimony.

Past Tense

The simple past tense indicates that an action took place in its entirety in the past. The past tense is usually formed by adding *-d* or *-ed* to the root form of the verb. ("We *closed* the office early yesterday.")

Past Perfect Tense

The past perfect tense indicates that one past event preceded another. It is formed by combining the helping verb *had* with the past-participle form of the main verb. ("He *had finished* by the time I arrived.")

Present Tense

The simple present tense represents action occurring in the present, without any indication of time duration. ("I *ride* the train.")

A general truth is always expressed in the present tense. ("Time *heals* all wounds.") The present tense can be used to present actions or conditions that have no time restrictions. ("Water *boils* at 212 degrees Fahrenheit.") Similarly, the present tense can be used to indicate habitual action. ("I *pass* the coffee shop every day.") The present tense is also used for the "historical present," as in newspaper headlines ("Dow Jones *Reaches* a High for the Year") or references to an author's opinion or a work's contents—even if it was written in the past and the author is no longer living. ("Orwell argues for plain language in his 1946 essay.")

Present Perfect Tense

The present perfect tense describes something from the recent past that has a bearing on the present—a period of time before the present but after the simple past. The present perfect tense is formed by combining a form of the helping verb *have* with the past-participle form of the main verb. ("We *have finished* the draft and can now revise it.")

Future Tense

The simple future tense indicates a time that will occur after the present. It uses the helping verb *will* (or *shall*) plus the main verb. ("I *will finish* the job tomorrow.") Do not use the future tense needlessly; doing so merely adds complexity.

▶ This system ~~will be~~ *is* explained on page 3.

▶ When you press this button, the feeder ~~will move~~ *moves* the paper into position.

Future Perfect Tense

The future perfect tense indicates action that will have been completed at the time of or before another future action. It combines *will have* and the past participle of the main verb. ("She *will have driven* 1,400 miles by the time she returns.")

Shift in Tense

Be consistent in your use of tense. The only legitimate shift in tense records a real change in time. Illogical shifts in tense will only confuse your **readers**.

▶ Before he visited the facility, the manager ~~meets~~ *met* with the staff.

text messaging

Text messaging, or *texting*, refers to the delivery or exchange of brief written messages between mobile phones over cellular networks. Text messaging is effective for simple messages communicated between people on the move or in nontraditional workplaces. ("Client backup servers down.") Some text messages can include photographs, video, and other digital files. As with your workplace **e-mail**, consider carefully the content of your messages before sending them. For the real-time exchange of brief messages, the phone or **instant messaging** may be a better choice. See also **selecting the medium**.

that / which / who

The word *that* is often overused and can foster wordiness.

> ▶ ~~I think that when~~ this project is finished, ~~that~~ you should publish
> the results.
>
> *When* (above "I think that when")

However, include *that* in a sentence if it avoids ambiguity or improves the pace.

> ▶ Some designers fail to appreciate the workers who operate equip-
> ment constitute an important safety system.
>
> *that* (above "appreciate")

Use *which*, not *that*, with nonrestrictive clauses (clauses that do not change the meaning of the basic sentence).

NONRESTRICTIVE   After John left the law firm, *which* is the largest in the region, he started a private practice.

RESTRICTIVE   Companies *that* diversify usually succeed.

That and *which* should refer to animals and things; *who* should refer to people.

> ▶ Dr. Cynthia Winter, *who* recently joined the clinic, treated a dog
> *that* was severely burned.

there / their / they're

There is an **expletive** (a word that fills the position of another word, phrase, or clause) or an **adverb**.

EXPLETIVE   *There* were more than 1,500 people at the conference.

ADVERB   More than 1,500 people were *there*.

Their is the **possessive case** form of *they*. ("Managers check *their* e-mail regularly.") *They're* is a **contraction** of *they are*. ("Clients tell us *they're* pleased with our services.")

thesaurus

A thesaurus lists **synonyms** and **antonyms**, which are arranged alphabetically or retrievable by categories. Thoughtfully used, a thesaurus can help refine your **word choice** during **revision**. However, the variety of words it offers may tempt you to choose an inappropriate word for the **context** or to use an obscure synonym to impress your **readers**. (See **affectation**.) Never use a word unless you are sure of its meanings; its **connotations** might be unknown to you and could mislead your readers.

titles

Titles of documents are important because many **readers** decide whether to read a **report** or message, for example, based on its title. Titles are also crucial for filing and retrieving documents. For advice on creating and using titles for figures and tables, see **visuals**.

Reports and Long Documents

Titles for reports, **proposals**, articles, and similar documents should identify the document's topic, reflect its **tone**, and indicate its **scope** and **purpose**, as in the following:

▶ "Using Chaos Theory to Evaluate Small-Business Growth Management"

Such titles should be concise but not so short that they are not specific. For example, the title "Chaos Theory and Small Businesses" announces the topic and might be appropriate for a book, but it does not answer important questions that readers of an article would expect, such as "What does the article say about the relationship between chaos theory and small businesses?" and "What aspect of small businesses is related to chaos theory?"

Avoid titles with such redundancies as "Notes on," "Studies on," or "A Report on." However, works like annual reports or **feasibility reports**

T

should be identified as such in the title because this information specifies the purpose and scope of the report. For titles of **progress and activity reports**, indicate the dates in a subtitle ("Quarterly Report on Hospital Admission Rates: January–March 2018"). Avoid using technical shorthand, such as chemical formulas, and other **abbreviations** in your title unless the work is addressed exclusively to specialists in the field. For multivolume publications, repeat the title on each volume and include the subtitle and number of each volume.

Do not write titles in sentence form, except for titles of articles in **newsletters**, magazines, and similar publications that ask a **rhetorical question**: "Is Online Learning Right for You?"

E-mail, Memos, and Online Postings

Subject lines of **e-mail** messages, **memos**, and online postings function as titles and should concisely and accurately describe the topic of the message. Because recipients often use subject-line titles to prioritize and sort their **correspondence**, such titles must be specific.

VAGUE   Subject: Tuition Reimbursement

SPECIFIC   Subject: Tuition Reimbursement for Time-Management Seminar

Although the title in the subject line announces your topic, you should still develop an opening that provides **context** for the message. See **blogs and forums**.

Formatting Titles

Use the standards in this section for formatting titles unless you are following a style that recommends otherwise.

Capitalization.   Capitalize the initial letters of the first and last words of a title, as well as all major words in the title. Do not capitalize articles (*a, an, the*), coordinating conjunctions (*and, but*), or short prepositions (*at, in, on, of*) unless they begin or end the title (*The Lives of a Cell*). Capitalize prepositions in titles if they contain five or more letters (*Between, Since, Until, After*).

Italics.   Use **italics** or underlining when referring to titles of separately published works, such as a book, periodical, newspaper, pamphlet, brochure, legal case, movie, or television series.

▶ *Turning Workplace Conflict into Collaboration* [book] by Joyce Richards was reviewed in the *New York Times.*

Some style guides also recommend italicizing the titles of Web sites and blogs (but not URLs).

► We will include links to the blog *Gizmodo* (http://gizmodo.com/) and to *Consumer Reports Online* (www.consumerreports.org).

Abbreviations of such titles are italicized if their spelled-out forms would be italicized.

► *NEJM* stands for the *New England Journal of Medicine*.

Italicize the titles of CDs, DVDs, plays, long poems, paintings, sculptures, and long musical works.

Quotation Marks.   Use **quotation marks** when referring to parts of publications, such as chapters of books and articles or sections within periodicals or blogs.

► Her chapter titled "Effects of Government Regulations on Motorcycle Safety" in the book *Government Regulation and the Economy* was discussed in a recent article, "No-Fault Insurance and Motorcycles?" published on the blog *AmericanCycle*.

Titles of reports, essays, short poems, short musical works (including songs), short stories, and single episodes of radio and television programs are also enclosed in quotation marks.

Special Cases.   Some titles, by convention, are not set off by quotation marks, underlining, or italics. Such titles follow standard practice for capitalization and the practice of the organization.

► Microsoft.com [Web site], Business Writing [college course title], Old Testament, Magna Carta, the Constitution, Lincoln's Gettysburg Address, the Lands' End Catalog

The treatment for Internet content, such as individual YouTube videos, varies among documentation styles. See **documenting sources**.

to / too / two

T

To, *too*, and *two* are frequently confused because they sound alike. *To* is used as a **preposition** or to mark an infinitive. See **verbs**.

► Send the report *to* the district manager. [preposition]
► I do not wish *to* attend. [mark of the infinitive]

Too is an **adverb** meaning "excessively" or "also."

▶ The price was *too* high. [excessively]

▶ I, *too*, thought it was high. [also]

Two is a **number** (*two* buildings, *two* concepts).

tone

Tone is the attitude a writer expresses toward the subject and his or her readers. In workplace writing, tone may range widely—depending on the **purpose**, situation, **context**, **audience**, and even the medium of a communication. For example, in an **e-mail** message to be read only by an associate who is also a friend, your tone might be casual.

▶ Your proposal to Smith and Kline is super. We'll just need to hammer out the schedule. If we get the contract, I owe you lunch!

In a message to your manager or superior, however, your tone might be more formal.

▶ Your proposal to Smith and Kline is excellent. I have marked a couple of places where I'm concerned that we are committing ourselves to a schedule that we might not be able to keep. If I can help further, please let me know.

In a message that serves as a **report** to numerous readers, the tone would be professional, without the more personal **style** that you would use with an individual reader.

▶ The Smith and Kline proposal appears complete and thorough, based on our department's evaluation. Several small revisions, however, would ensure that the company is not committing itself to an unrealistic schedule. These revisions are marked on the copy of the report attached to this message.

The **word choice**, the **introduction**, and even the **title** contribute to the overall tone of your document. For instance, a title such as "Ecological Consequences of Diminishing Water Resources in California" clearly sets a different tone from "What Happens When We've Drained California Dry?" The first title would be appropriate for a report; the second title would be more appropriate for a popular blog or **newsletter article**. See also **blogs and forums**, **business writing style**, and **correspondence**.

transition

Transition is the means of achieving a smooth flow of ideas from sentence to sentence, **paragraph** to paragraph, and subject to subject. Transition is a two-way indicator of what has been said and what will be said; it provides **readers** with guideposts for linking ideas and clarifying the relationship between them.

Transition can be obvious.

▶ *Having considered* the benefits of a new facility, *we move next* to the question of adequate staffing.

Transition can be subtle.

▶ *Even if* this facility can be built at a reasonable cost, there *still remains* the issue of adequate staffing.

Either way, you now have your readers' attention fastened on the problem of adequate staffing, which is exactly what you set out to do.

Methods of Transition

Transition can be achieved in many ways: (1) using transitional words and phrases, (2) repeating keywords or key ideas, (3) using **pronouns** with clear antecedents, (4) using enumeration (1, 2, 3, or first, second, third), (5) summarizing a previous paragraph, (6) asking a question, and (7) using a transitional paragraph.

Certain words and phrases are inherently transitional. Consider the following terms and their functions:

FUNCTION	TERMS
Result	*therefore, as a result, consequently, thus, hence*
Example	*for example, for instance, specifically, as an illustration*
Comparison	*similarly, likewise, in comparison*
Contrast	*but, yet, still, however, nevertheless, on the other hand*
Addition	*moreover, furthermore, also, too, besides, in addition*
Time	*now, later, meanwhile, since then, after that, before that time*
Sequence	*first, second, third, initially, then, next, finally*

Within a paragraph, such transitional expressions clarify and smooth the movement from idea to idea. Conversely, the lack of transitional devices can make for disjointed reading. See also **telegraphic style**.

Transition Between Sentences

You can achieve effective transition between sentences by repeating keywords or key ideas from preceding sentences and by using pronouns that refer to antecedents in previous sentences. Consider the following short paragraph, which uses both of those means.

> ► Representative of many American university towns is Middletown. *This Midwestern town*, formerly *a small farming community*, is today the home of a large and vibrant *academic community*. Attracting students from all over the Midwest, *this university town* has grown very rapidly in the last ten years.

Enumeration is another device for achieving transition.

> ► The recommendation rests on *two conditions*. *First*, the department staff must be expanded to handle the increased workload. *Second*, sufficient time must be provided for training the new staff.

Transition Between Paragraphs

The means discussed so far for achieving transition between sentences can also be effective for achieving transition between paragraphs. For paragraphs, however, longer transitional elements are often required. One technique is to use an opening sentence that summarizes the preceding paragraph and then moves on to a new paragraph.

> ► One property of material considered for manufacturing processes is hardness. Hardness is the internal resistance of the material to the forcing apart or closing together of its molecules. Another property is ductility, the characteristic of material that permits it to be drawn into a wire. Material also may possess malleability, the property that makes it capable of being rolled or hammered into thin sheets of various shapes. Purchasing managers must consider these properties before selecting manufacturing materials for use in production.
>
> *The requirements of hardness, ductility, and malleability* account for the high cost of such materials.

Another technique is to ask a question at the end of one paragraph and answer it at the beginning of the next.

> ► New technology has always been feared because it has at times displaced some jobs. However, it invariably created many more jobs than it eliminated. Almost always, the jobs eliminated by technological advances have been unskilled jobs, and workers who have been displaced have been forced to increase their skills, which resulted in better and higher-paying jobs for them. *In view of this history, should we now uncritically embrace new technology?*
>
> Certainly technology has given us unparalleled access to information and created many new roles for employees.

A purely transitional paragraph may be inserted to aid readability.

▶   The problem of poor management was a key factor that caused the
weak performance of the company.
*Two other setbacks to the company's fortunes also marked
the company's decline: the loss of many skilled workers through
the early retirement program and the intensification of the rate of
employee turnover.*
The early retirement program resulted in engineering staff . . .

If you provide logical **organization** and have prepared an outline, your
transitional needs will easily be satisfied and your writing will have
unity and **coherence**. During **revision**, look for places where transition is
missing and add it. Look for places where it is weak and strengthen it.

trip reports

A trip report provides a permanent record of a business trip and its
accomplishments. It provides managers with essential information
about the results of the trip and can enable other staff members to benefit from the information. See also **reports**.

A trip report is normally written as a **memo** or an **e-mail** and
addressed to an immediate superior, as shown in Figure T–3 (page 530).
The subject line identifies the destination and dates of the trip. The body
of the report explains why you made the trip, whom you visited, and
what you accomplished. The report should devote a brief section to each
major activity and may include a **heading** for each section. You need
not give equal space to each activity—instead, elaborate on the more
important ones. Follow the body of the report with the appropriate
conclusions and recommendations. Finally, if required, attach a record of
expenses to the trip report.

trouble reports (*see* incident reports)

try to

The phrase *try and* is colloquial for *try to*. For business writing, use *try to*.

▶   Please try ~~and~~ to finish the report by next week.

T

Send   ✕ Cancel   ▤ Save Draft   ⏻ Add Attachment   ✉ Signature   Options ▶

TO	Roberto Camacho <rcamacho@psys.com>	
CC		Show BCC
Subject	Trip to Smith Electric Co., Huntington, West Virginia, January 4–5, 2018	

📄 Expense Report.xls (25 KB)   <u>Download</u>

Destination and dates

Purpose of trip

I visited the Smith Electric Company in Huntington, West Virginia, to determine the cause of a recurring failure in a Model 247 printer. Attached is my expense report.

Problem

The printer stopped printing periodically for no apparent reason. Repeated efforts to bring it back online eventually succeeded, but the problem recurred at irregular intervals. Neither customer personnel operating the printer nor the local maintenance specialist was able to solve the problem.

Action

On January 4, I met with Ms. Ruth Bernardi, the office manager, who explained the problem. My troubleshooting did not reveal the cause of the problem then or on January 5.

Summary of activities

Only when I tested the logic cable did I find that it contained a broken wire. I replaced the logic cable and then ran all the normal printer test patterns to make sure no other problems existed. All patterns were positive, so I turned the printer over to the customer.

Conclusion

Conclusion and implications

There are more than 12,000 of these printers in the field, and to my knowledge this is the first occurrence of a bad cable. I conclude that the logic cable problem at Smith Electric Company caused the recurring failures during 2017.

James D. Kerson, Product Analyst
Printer Systems, Inc.
1366 Federal St., Allentown, PA 18101
(610) 747-9955   Fax: (610) 747-9956
jdkerson@psys.com
www.psys.com

FIGURE T–3. Trip Report (Using E-mail Format)

T

U

unity

Unity is singleness of **purpose** and focus; a unified **paragraph** or document has a central idea and does not digress into unrelated topics.

The logical sequence provided through **outlining** is essential to achieving unity. An outline enables you to lay out the most direct route from **introduction** to **conclusion**, and it enables you to build each paragraph around a topic sentence that expresses a single idea. Effective **transition** helps build unity, as well as **coherence**, because transitional terms clarify the relationship of each part to what precedes it.

up

Adding the word *up* to **verbs** often creates a redundant phrase. See also **conciseness**.

▶ He quickly wrote ~~up~~ the report.

usage

Usage describes the choices we make among the various words and expressions available in our language. The lines between standard English and nonstandard English and between formal and informal English are determined by these choices. Your guideline in any situation requiring such choices should be appropriateness: Is the word or expression you use appropriate to your **audience** and your subject? When it is, you are practicing good usage.

This book contains many entries on specific usage questions. For a complete list of the usage entries in this book, see "Commonly Misused Words and Phrases" on pages 601–02. Usage entries are also distinguished by italicized titles (for example, see *utilize*). A reputable dictionary is also an invaluable aid in your selection of the right word.

U

utilize

Do not use *utilize* as a long variant of *use*, which is the general word for "employ for some purpose." *Use* will almost always be clearer and less pretentious. See **affectation** and **plain language**.

V

vague words

A vague word is one that is imprecise in the context in which it is used. Be concrete and specific.

VAGUE   It was a *good* meeting. [Why was it good?]

SPECIFIC   The meeting resolved three questions: pay scales, fringe benefits, and workloads.

Some words are vague because they encompass a broad range of meanings and interpretations (*good*, *bad*, *real*, *nice*, *important*, *thing*, *fine*). See also **abstract / concrete words** and **word choice**.

verbals

Verbals are **verbs** used as other parts of speech, such as **nouns**, **adjectives**, and **adverbs**. Depending on their function in sentences, verbals are identified as gerunds, infinitives, and participles.

Gerunds

A gerund is a verbal ending in *-ing* that is used as a noun. A gerund can be used as a subject, a direct **object**, the object of a **preposition**, a subjective **complement**, or an **appositive**.

▶ *Budgeting* is a useful managerial skill. [subject]

▶ I find *budgeting* difficult. [direct object]

▶ We were unprepared for their *coming*. [object of preposition]

▶ Seeing is *believing*. [subjective complement]

▶ My primary departmental function, *programming*, occupies about two-thirds of my time on the job. [appositive]

Only the possessive form of a noun or **pronoun** should precede a gerund.

> ▸ *John's* working has not affected his grades.

> ▸ *His* working has not affected his grades.

Infinitives

An infinitive is the bare, or uninflected, form of a verb (*go*, *run*, *fall*, *talk*, *dress*, *shout*), without the restrictions imposed by **person** and **number**. Along with the gerund and the participle, it is one of the nonfinite verb forms. The infinitive is generally preceded by the word *to*, which, although not an inherent part of the infinitive, is considered to be the sign of an infinitive. An infinitive is a verbal and can function as a noun, an adjective, or an adverb.

> ▸ *To expand* is not the only objective. [noun]

> ▸ These are the instructions *to follow*. [adjective]

> ▸ The company struggled *to survive*. [adverb]

The infinitive can reflect two **tenses**: the present and (with a helping verb) the present perfect.

> ▸ to go [present tense]

> ▸ to have gone [present perfect tense]

The most common mistake made with infinitives is using the present perfect tense when the simple present tense is sufficient.

> ▸ I should not have tried to ~~have gone~~ *go* so early.

Infinitives formed with the root form of transitive verbs can express both active and (with a helping verb) passive **voice**.

> ▸ to hit [present tense, active voice]

> ▸ to have hit [present perfect tense, active voice]

> ▸ to be hit [present tense, passive voice]

> ▸ to have been hit [present perfect tense, passive voice]

A split infinitive is one in which an adverb is placed between the sign of the infinitive, *to*, and the infinitive itself. Because they make up a grammatical unit, the infinitive and its sign are better left intact than separated by an intervening adverb.

V

> *initially*
> ▶ To ~~initially~~ build a client base, experts recommend networking ‸
>
> with friends and family.

However, it may occasionally be better to split an infinitive than to allow a sentence to become awkward, ambiguous, or incoherent.

AMBIGUOUS	She agreed immediately *to deliver* the specimen to the lab. [This sentence could be interpreted to mean that she agreed immediately.]
CLEAR	She agreed *to* immediately *deliver* the specimen to the lab. [This sentence is no longer ambiguous.]

Participles

A participle is a verb form that functions as an adjective. Present participles end in -*ing*.

> ▶ *Declining* sales forced us to close one branch office.

Past participles end in -*ed*, -*t*, -*en*, -*n*, or -*d*.

> ▶ What are the *estimated* costs?

> ▶ Repair the *bent* lever.

> ▶ Return the *broken* part.

> ▶ What are the metal's *known* properties?

> ▶ The story, *told* many times before, was still interesting.

The perfect participle is formed with the present participle of the helping verb *have* plus the past participle of the main verb.

> ▶ *Having gotten* [perfect participle] a large bonus, the *smiling* [present participle], *contented* [past participle] sales representative worked harder than ever.

A participle cannot be used as the verb of a sentence. Inexperienced writers sometimes make that mistake, and the result is a **sentence fragment**.

> *, his*
> ▶ The committee chair was responsible~~. His~~ vote being the ‸
>
> decisive one.

> *was*
> ▶ The committee chair was responsible. His vote ~~being~~ the ‸
>
> decisive one.

For information on participial and infinitive phrases, see **phrases**.

V

verbs

A verb is a word or group of words that describes an action ("The copier *jammed* at the beginning of the job"), states how something or someone is affected by an action ("He *was disappointed* that the proposal was rejected"), or affirms a state of existence ("She *is* a district manager now").

Types of Verbs

Verbs are either transitive or intransitive. A *transitive verb* requires a direct **object** to complete its meaning.

▶ They *laid* the foundation on October 26. [*Foundation* is the direct object of the transitive verb *laid*.]

▶ Rosalie Anderson *wrote* the treasurer a memo. [*Memo* is the direct object of the transitive verb *wrote*.]

An *intransitive verb* does not require an object to complete its meaning. It makes a full assertion about the subject without assistance (although it may have **modifiers**).

▶ The engine *ran*.

▶ The engine *ran* smoothly and quietly.

A *linking verb* is an intransitive verb that links a **complement** to the subject.

▶ The carpet *is* stained. [*Is* is a linking verb; *stained* is a subjective complement.]

Some intransitive verbs, such as *be*, *become*, *seem*, and *appear*, are almost always linking verbs. A number of others, such as *look*, *sound*, *taste*, *smell*, and *feel*, can function as either linking verbs or simple intransitive or transitive verbs. If you are unsure about whether one of those verbs is a linking verb, try substituting *seem*; if the sentence still makes sense, the verb is probably a linking verb.

▶ Their antennae *feel* delicate. [*Seem* can be substituted for *feel*—thus, *feel* is a linking verb.]

V

▶ Their antennae *feel* delicately for their prey. [*Seem* cannot be substituted for *feel*; in this case, *feel* is a simple intransitive verb.]

Forms of Verbs

Verbs are described as being either finite or nonfinite.

Finite Verbs.   A finite verb is the main verb of a **clause** or sentence. It makes an assertion about its subject and often serves as the only verb in its clause or sentence. ("The telephone *rang*, and the receptionist *answered* it.") See also **sentence construction**.

A helping verb (sometimes called an *auxiliary verb*) is used in a verb **phrase** to help indicate **mood**, **tense**, and **voice**. ("The phone *had* rung.") Phrases that function as helping verbs are often made up of combinations containing the sign of the infinitive, *to* (for example, *am going to*, *is about to*, *has to*, and *ought to*). The helping verb always precedes the main verb, although other words may intervene. ("Machines *will* never completely *replace* people.")

Nonfinite Verbs.   Nonfinite verbs are **verbals**—verb forms that function as **nouns**, **adjectives**, or **adverbs**.

A *gerund* is a noun that is derived from the *-ing* form of a verb. ("*Seeing* is *believing*.") An *infinitive*, which uses the root form of a verb (usually preceded by *to*), can function as a noun, an adverb, or an adjective.

▶ He hates *to complain*. [noun, direct object of *hates*]

▶ The valve closes *to stop* the flow. [adverb, modifies *closes*]

▶ This is the proposal *to consider*. [adjective, modifies *proposal*]

A *participle* is a verb form that can function as an adjective.

▶ The *rejected* proposal may be resubmitted when the client's concerns are addressed. [*Rejected* is a verb form that is used as an adjective modifying *proposal*.]

Properties of Verbs

Verbs must (1) agree in **person** with personal pronouns functioning as subjects, (2) agree in tense and **number** with their subjects, and (3) be in the appropriate voice. See also **agreement**.

Person is the term for the form of a personal pronoun that indicates whether the pronoun refers to the speaker, the person spoken to, or the person (or thing) spoken about. Verbs change their forms to agree in person with their subjects.

V

▶ I *see* [first person] a yellow tint, but she *sees* [third person] a yellow-green hue.

Tense refers to verb forms that indicate time distinctions. The six tenses are past, past perfect, present, present perfect, future, and future perfect.

Number refers to the two forms of a verb that indicate whether the subject of a verb is singular ("The copier *was* repaired") or plural ("The copiers *were* repaired").

Most verbs show the singular of the present tense by adding *-s* or *-es* (he *stands*, she *works*, it *goes*), and they show the plural without *-s* or *-es* (they *stand*, we *work*, they *go*). The verb *to be*, however, normally changes form to indicate the singular ("I *am* ready") or plural ("We *are* ready").

Voice refers to the two forms of a verb that indicate whether the subject of the verb acts or receives the action. The verb is in the *active voice* if the subject of the verb acts ("The bacteria *grow*"); the verb is in the *passive voice* if it receives the action ("The bacteria *are grown* in a petri dish").

very

The use of **intensifiers** like *very* is tempting, but the word can usually be deleted.

▶ The board was ~~very~~ worried about a possible product recall.

When you do use intensifiers, clarify their meaning.

▶ Web sales were *very* strong; they were up 43 percent this month.

via

Via is Latin for "by way of." The term should be used only in routing instructions.

▶ The package was shipped *via* FedEx.

▶ Her project was funded ~~via~~ *as a result of* the recent legislation.

V visuals

Visuals can express ideas or convey information in ways that words alone cannot by making abstract concepts and relationships concrete.

Visuals can show how things look (drawings, photographs, maps), represent numbers and quantities (graphs, tables), depict processes or relationships (flowcharts, Gantt charts, infographics, schematic diagrams), and show hierarchical relationships (organizational charts). They also highlight important information and emphasize key concepts.

Many qualities of good writing—simplicity, clarity, conciseness, directness—are equally important when creating and using visuals. Presented with clarity and consistency, visuals can help **readers** focus on key portions of your document, presentation, or Web site. Be aware, though, that even the best visual will not be effective without **context**, which is often provided by the text that introduces the visual and clarifies its purpose.

The following book entries are related to specific visuals and their use in printed and online documents, as well as in **presentations** (see that entry for presentation graphics).

Selecting Visuals

Consider your **audience** and your **purpose** carefully in selecting visuals. You would need different illustrations for an automobile owner's manual or an auto dealer's Web site, for example, than you would for a technician's diagnostic guide. Figure V–1 can help you select the most appropriate visuals, based on their purposes and special features. Jot down visual options as you consider your **scope** and **organization**.

❖ **ETHICS NOTE** Visuals have the potential for misleading readers when data are selectively omitted or distorted. For example, Figure G–8 (page 242) shows a graph that gives a misleading impression of investment returns because the scale is compressed, with some of the years selectively omitted. Visuals that mislead readers call the credibility of you and your organization into question—and they are unethical. The use of misleading visuals can even subject you and your organization to lawsuits. ❖

Integrating Visuals with Text

After selecting your visuals, carefully integrate them with your text. The following guidelines will improve the effectiveness of your visuals

V

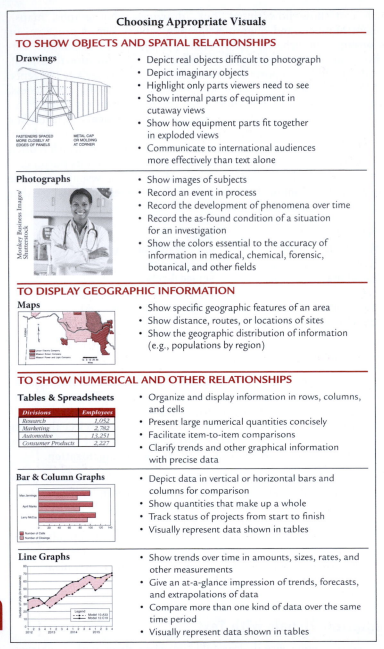

Choosing Appropriate Visuals

TO SHOW OBJECTS AND SPATIAL RELATIONSHIPS

Drawings

FASTENERS SPACED MORE CLOSELY AT EDGES OF PANELS   METAL CAP OR MOLDING AT CORNER

- Depict real objects difficult to photograph
- Depict imaginary objects
- Highlight only parts viewers need to see
- Show internal parts of equipment in cutaway views
- Show how equipment parts fit together in exploded views
- Communicate to international audiences more effectively than text alone

Photographs

Monkey Business Images/ Shutterstock

- Show images of subjects
- Record an event in process
- Record the development of phenomena over time
- Record the as-found condition of a situation for an investigation
- Show the colors essential to the accuracy of information in medical, chemical, forensic, botanical, and other fields

TO DISPLAY GEOGRAPHIC INFORMATION

Maps

Union Electric Company
Missouri Edison Company
Missouri Power and Light Company

- Show specific geographic features of an area
- Show distance, routes, or locations of sites
- Show the geographic distribution of information (e.g., populations by region)

TO SHOW NUMERICAL AND OTHER RELATIONSHIPS

Tables & Spreadsheets

Divisions	Employees
Research	1,052
Marketing	2,782
Automotive	13,251
Consumer Products	2,227

- Organize and display information in rows, columns, and cells
- Present large numerical quantities concisely
- Facilitate item-to-item comparisons
- Clarify trends and other graphical information with precise data

Bar & Column Graphs

Max Jennings
April Marks
Larry McCoy

0   20   40   60   80   100   120   140

Number of Calls
Number of Closings

- Depict data in vertical or horizontal bars and columns for comparison
- Show quantities that make up a whole
- Track status of projects from start to finish
- Visually represent data shown in tables

Line Graphs

Number of Units (in thousands)

Legend
Model 10.A33
Model 12.C19

2012   2013   2014   2015

- Show trends over time in amounts, sizes, rates, and other measurements
- Give an at-a-glance impression of trends, forecasts, and extrapolations of data
- Compare more than one kind of data over the same time period
- Visually represent data shown in tables

V

FIGURE V–1. Chart for Choosing Appropriate Visuals (continued)

Picture Graphs	• Use recognizable images to represent specific quantities
	• Help nonexpert readers grasp the information
	• Visually represent data shown in tables

Pie Graphs	• Show quantities that make up a whole
	• Give an immediate visual impression of the parts and their significance
	• Visually represent data shown in tables or lists

TO SHOW STEPS IN A PROCESS OR RELATIONSHIPS IN A SYSTEM

Flowcharts	• Show how the parts or steps in a process or system interact
	• Show the stages of an actual or a hypothetical process in the correct direction, including recursive steps

Schematic Diagrams	• Show how the components in electronic, chemical, electrical, and mechanical systems interact and are interrelated
	• Use standardized symbolic representations rather than realistic depictions of system components

TO GIVE AN OVERVIEW OF A COMPLEX PROCESS OR EVENT

Infographics	• Integrate text, graphs, images, and numbers to "tell a story"
	• Combine the communications advantages of text and graphics to give both an overview and a narrative explanation of a topic
	• Organize disparate facts, concepts, and images into an understandable whole

TO SHOW RELATIONSHIPS IN A HIERARCHY

Organizational Charts	• Give an overview of an organization's departmental components
	• Show how the components relate to one another
	• Depict lines of authority within an organization

TO SUPPLEMENT OR REPLACE WORDS

Symbols & Icons	• Convey ideas without words
	• Save space and add visual appeal
	• Transcend individual languages to communicate ideas effectively for international readers
	• Communicate culturally neutral images

V

FIGURE V–1. Chart for Choosing Appropriate Visuals

by describing how to position and identify them consistently and uniformly.

Begin by considering the best locations for visuals during the **outlining** stage of your draft. At appropriate points in your outline, either make a rough sketch of the visual, if you can, or write "illustration of . . . ," noting the source of the visual and enclosing each suggestion in a text box. You may also include sketches of visuals in your thumbnail pages, as discussed in **layout and design**. When **writing a draft**, place visuals as close as possible to—but following—the text where they are discussed; in fact, no visual should precede its first text mention. Refer to graphics (such as drawings and photographs) as "figures" and to tables as "tables." Clarify for readers why each visual is included in the text. The amount of description you should provide will vary, depending on your readers' backgrounds. For example, nonexperts may require lengthier explanations than experts need.

❖ **ETHICS NOTE** Obtain written permission to use copyrighted visuals in works that you intend to publish in print or online—including images and multimedia material from Web sites. Acknowledge all quoted or borrowed material in a source line below the caption for a figure and in a footnote at the bottom of a table. Use a site's "Contact Us" page to request approval. Acknowledge your use of any material from the public domain (thus uncopyrighted), such as demographic or economic data from government publications and Web sites, with a source line. See also **copyright**, **documenting sources**, and **plagiarism**. ❖

WRITER'S CHECKLIST   **Creating and Integrating Visuals**

CREATING VISUALS

✔ Keep visuals simple. Include only information needed for discussion in the text, and eliminate unneeded labels, arrows, boxes, and lines.

✔ Position the lettering of any explanatory text or labels horizontally; allow adequate white space within and around the visual.

✔ Specify the units of measurement used, make sure relative sizes are clear, and indicate distance with a scale when appropriate.

✔ Use consistent terminology; for example, do not refer to the same information as a "proportion" in the text and a "percentage" in the visual.

✔ Define **abbreviations** the first time they appear in the text and in figures and tables. If any symbols are not self-explanatory, label them, as in Figure G–13 (page 246).

(continued)

✔ Give each visual a caption or a concise **title** that clearly describes its content, and assign figure and table numbers if your document contains more than one illustration or table.

INTEGRATING VISUALS

✔ Clarify for readers why each visual is included in the text, and provide an appropriate description.

✔ Place visuals as close as possible to the text where they are discussed but always after their first text mention.

✔ Allow adequate white space around and within each illustration.

✔ Refer to visuals in the text of your document as "figures" or "tables" and by their figure or table numbers.

✔ Consider placing lengthy or detailed visuals in an **appendix**, which you refer to in the body of your document.

✔ In documents with more than five illustrations or tables, include a section following the **table of contents** titled "List of Figures" or "List of Tables," which identifies each by number, title, and page number.

✔ Follow the editorial guidelines or recommended style manual when preparing visuals for a publication.

voice

In grammar, *voice* indicates the relation of the subject to the action of the **verb**. When the verb is in the *active voice*, the subject acts; when it is in the *passive voice*, the subject is acted upon.

ACTIVE   David Cohen *wrote* the newsletter article. [The subject, *David Cohen*, performs the action; the verb, *wrote*, describes the action.]

PASSIVE   The newsletter article *was written* by David Cohen. [The subject, *the newsletter article*, is acted upon; the verb, *was written*, describes the action.]

The two sentences say the same thing, but each has a different emphasis: The first emphasizes the writer (*David Cohen*); the second emphasizes what was written (*the newsletter article*). In business writing, it is often important to emphasize who or what performs an action. Further, the passive-voice version is indirect because the performer of the action

V

generally follows the verb instead of preceding it. Because the active voice is more direct, more concise, and easier for readers to understand, use the active voice unless the passive voice is more appropriate, as described on pages 545–46. Whether you use the active voice or the passive voice, be careful not to shift voices within a sentence.

▶ David Cohen corrected the error as soon as ~~it was identified by~~
the editor. *identified it*

Using the Active Voice

Improving Clarity.   The active voice improves **clarity** and avoids confusion, especially in **instructions** and **policies and procedures**.

PASSIVE   Sections B and C *should be checked* for errors. [Have they been checked? Who should check them?]

ACTIVE   *Check* sections B and C for errors. [The performer of the action, *you*, is understood: (You) *Check* the sections.]

Active voice can also help avoid **dangling modifiers**.

PASSIVE   Hurrying to complete the work, the cables *were connected* improperly. [*Who* was hurrying? The implication is that the cables were hurrying.]

ACTIVE   Hurrying to complete the work, the technician *connected* the cables improperly. [Here, *hurrying to complete the work* properly modifies the performer of the action: *the technician.*]

Highlighting Subjects.   One difficulty with passive sentences is that they can bury the performer of the action within **expletives** and prepositional **phrases**.

PASSIVE   It *was reported by* the testing staff that the new model is defective.

ACTIVE   The testing staff *reported* that the new model is defective.

Sometimes writers using the passive voice fail to name the performer—information that might be missed.

PASSIVE   The error *was discovered* yesterday.

ACTIVE   The attending physician *discovered* the error yesterday.

Achieving Conciseness.   The active voice helps achieve **conciseness** because it eliminates the need for an additional helping verb as well as an extra **preposition** to identify the performer of the action.

PASSIVE   Arbitrary changes in policy *are resented by* employees.

ACTIVE   Employees *resent* arbitrary changes in policy.

The active-voice version takes one verb (*resent*); the passive-voice version takes two verbs (*are resented*) and an extra preposition (*by*).

Using the Passive Voice

The passive voice is sometimes effective or even necessary. Indeed, for reasons of tact and diplomacy, you might need to use the passive voice to avoid an implied accusation.

ACTIVE   Your staff *did not meet* the sales quota last month.

PASSIVE   The sales quota *was not met* last month.

❖ **ETHICS NOTE** Be careful not to use the passive voice to evade responsibility or to obscure an issue or information that readers should know, as in the following examples.

▶ Several mistakes *were made*. [*Who* made the mistakes?]

▶ It *has been decided*. [*Who* has decided?]

See also **ethics in writing**. ❖

When the performer of the action is either unknown or unimportant, use the passive voice. ("The copper mine *was discovered* in 1929.") When the performer of the action is less important than the receiver of that action, the passive voice is sometimes more appropriate. ("Ann Bryant *was presented* with a Sales Award by the president.") Even in such cases, another verb may enable you to use the active voice. ("Ann Bryant *received* a Sales Award from the president.")

When you explain an operation in which the reader is not actively involved or when you describe a process or a procedure, the passive voice may be more appropriate. In the following example, anyone—it really does not matter who—could be the performer of the action.

▶ Area strip mining *is used* in regions of flat to gently rolling terrain, like that found in the Midwest. Depending on applicable reclamation laws, the topsoil *may be removed* from the area *to be mined*, *stored*, and later *reapplied* as surface material during reclamation of the mined land. After the removal of the topsoil, a trench *is cut*

V

through the overburden to expose the upper surface of the coal to be mined. The overburden from the first cut *is placed* on the unmined land adjacent to the cut. After the first cut *has been completed*, the coal *is removed*.

Do not, however, simply assume that any such explanation should be in the passive voice; in fact, as in the following example, the active voice is often more effective.

▶ In the operation of an internal combustion engine, an explosion in the combustion chamber *forces* the pistons down in the cylinders. The movement of the pistons in the cylinders *turns* the crankshaft.

Ask yourself, "Would it be of any advantage to the reader to know the performer of the action?" If the answer is yes, use the active voice.

V

W

wait for / wait on

Wait on should refer to the activities of hospitality and service employees. ("We need extra staff to *wait on* customers.") Otherwise, use *wait for*. ("Be sure to *wait for* Ms. Garcia's approval.") See also **idioms**.

Web design (*see* writing for the Web)

when / where / that

When and if (or *if and when*) is a colloquial expression that should not be used in writing.

▶ When ~~and if~~ funding is approved, you will get the position.

▶ *If*
~~When and if~~ funding is approved, you will get the position.

In phrases using the *where . . . at* construction, *at* is unnecessary and should be omitted.

▶ Where is his office ~~at~~?

Do not substitute *where* for *that* to anticipate an idea or a fact to follow.

that
▶ I read in the newsletter ~~where~~ sales increased last quarter.

whether

Whether communicates the notion of a choice. The use of *whether or not* to indicate a choice between alternatives is often redundant.

▶ The client asked whether ~~or not~~ the proposal was finished.

The phrase *as to whether* is clumsy and redundant. Either use *whether* alone or omit it altogether.

> *We have decided to*   *contract.*
> ► ~~As to whether we will~~ commit to a long-term ~~contract, we have~~
>
> ~~decided to do so.~~

while

While, meaning "during an interval of time," is sometimes substituted for connectives like *and*, *but*, *although*, and *whereas*. Used as a connective in that way, *while* often causes ambiguity.

> *and*
> ► Ian Evans is a media director, ~~while~~ Joan Thomas is a vice president for research.

Do not use while to mean although or whereas.

> *Although*
> ► ~~While~~ Ryan Sims is retired, he serves as our financial consultant.

Restrict *while* to its meaning of "during the time that."

> ► I'll have to catch up on my reading *while* I am on vacation.

who / whom

Who is a subjective **case** pronoun, and *whom* is the objective case form of *who*. When in doubt about which form to use, substitute a personal pronoun to see which one fits. If *he*, *she*, or *they* fits, use *who*.

> ► *Who* is the training coordinator? [You would say, "*She* is the training coordinator."]

If him, her, or them fits, use whom.

> ► It depends on *whom*? [You would say, "It depends on *them*."]

who's / whose / of which

Who's is the contraction of *who is*. ("*Who's* scheduled today?") *Whose* is the possessive case of *who*. ("Consider *whose* budget should be cut.")

Normally, *whose* is used with persons, and *of which* is used with inanimate objects.

W

▶ The employee *whose* car had been towed away was angry.

▶ The report recommended over 100 changes, more than half *of which* the client approved.

If *of which* causes a sentence to sound awkward, *whose* may be used with inanimate objects. (Compare: "The business the profits *of which* steadily declined" versus "The business *whose* profits steadily declined.")

word choice

Mark Twain once said, "The difference between the almost right word and the right word is . . . the difference between the lightning-bug and the lightning." The most important goal in choosing the right word in business writing is the preciseness implied by Twain's comment. Vague words and abstract words defeat preciseness because they do not convey the writer's meaning directly and clearly.

VAGUE   It was a *productive* meeting.

PRECISE   The meeting resulted in the approval of the health-care benefits package.

In the first sentence, *productive* sounds specific but conveys little information; the revised sentence says specifically what made the meeting "productive." Although abstract words may at times be appropriate to your topic, using them unnecessarily will make your writing difficult to understand. See **abstract / concrete words**.

Being aware of the connotations and denotations of words will help you anticipate reactions of your audience to the words you choose. (See **connotation / denotation**.) Understanding **antonyms** (*fresh/stale*) and **synonyms** (*notorious/infamous*) will increase your ability to choose the proper word. Make other **usage** decisions carefully, especially in technical contexts, such as **average / median / mean** and **biannual / biennial**.

Although many entries throughout this book will help you improve your word choices and avoid impreciseness, the following entries should be particularly helpful:

affectation	21	**euphemisms**	181
biased language	49	**idioms**	254
buzzwords	64	**jargon**	291
clichés	76	**logic errors**	320
conciseness	97	**vague words**	533

A key to choosing the correct and precise word is to keep current in your reading and to be aware of new words in your profession and in

W

the language. In your quest for the right word, use a reputable and current dictionary. See also **English as a second language** and **plain language**.

writing a draft

You are well prepared to write a rough draft when you have established your **purpose** and readers' needs, considered the **context**, defined your **scope**, completed adequate **research**, and prepared an outline (whether rough or developed). (See also **audience** and **outlining**.) Writing a draft is simply transcribing and expanding the notes from your outline into **paragraphs**, without worrying about **grammar**, refinements of language, or **spelling**. Refinement will come with **revision** and **proofreading**. See also "Five Steps to Successful Writing" (page xvii).

Writing and revising are different activities. Do not let worrying about a good opening slow you down. Instead, concentrate on your ideas—now is not the time to polish or revise. Do not wait for inspiration—treat writing a draft as you would any other on-the-job task.

WRITER'S CHECKLIST   Writing a Rough Draft

✔ Resist the temptation of writing first drafts without planning.

✔ Use an outline (rough or developed) as a springboard to start and to write quickly.

✔ Give yourself a set time in which you write continuously, regardless of how good or bad your writing seems to be. But don't stop if you are rolling along easily—keep your momentum.

✔ Start with the section that seems easiest. Your readers will neither know nor care which section was written first.

✔ Keep in mind your readers' needs, expectations, and knowledge of the subject. Doing so will help you write directly to your readers and suggest which ideas need further development.

✔ When you come to something difficult to explain, try to relate the new concept to something familiar to readers, as discussed in **figures of speech**.

✔ Routinely save your draft to your local drive, a company network, an external hard drive, or the cloud.

✔ Give yourself a small reward—a short walk, a snack, a brief chat with a friend, an easy task—after you have finished a section.

✔ When you return to your writing, reread what you have written. Doing so can return you to a productive frame of mind.

W

writing for the Web

This entry is intended to help you contribute content for your company's or organization's Web site. For questions about the appropriateness of content you plan to post, check with your Webmaster or manager to determine if your content complies with your organization's Web policy. On campus, consult your instructor or campus computer support staff about standards for posting Web content. See also **blogs and forums**, content management, and **FAQs**.

Crafting Content for Your Site

Most **readers** scan Web pages for specific information, so state your important points first, before providing detailed supporting information. Keep your writing **style** straightforward and concise, and use **plain language** as much as possible. Use the following techniques to make your content more accessible to your audience. See also **conciseness**.

Text Content. Break up dense blocks of text by dividing them into short **paragraphs** so that they stand out and can be quickly scanned and absorbed. Focus each passage on one facet of your topic. Where necessary, include links to more detailed secondary information.

Headings. Use informative topic **headings** for paragraphs or sections to help readers decide at a glance whether to read a passage. Headings also clarify text by highlighting structure and organization. They signal breaks in coverage from one topic to the next as well as mark **transitions** between topics. Set off headings in boldface or another text style, such as a different color, on a separate line directly above the text they describe, or in the left margin directly across from the text. See also **layout and design**.

Lists. Use bulleted and numbered **lists** to break up dense paragraphs, reduce text length, and highlight important content. Do not overuse lists, however. Lists without supporting explanatory text lack **coherence**.

Keywords. To help search engines and your audience find your site, use terms that highlight content in the first 50 or so words of text for each new topic.

WITHOUT KEYWORDS	We are proud to introduce a new commemorative coin honoring our bank's founder and president. The item will be available on this Web site after December 3, 2018, which is the 100th anniversary of our first deposit.
WITH KEYWORDS	The new *Reynolds* commemorative coin features a portrait of *George G. Reynolds*, the founder

W

and president of *Reynolds Bank*. The coin can be purchased after December 3, 2018, in honor of the 100th anniversary of *Reynolds*'s first deposit.

For more about search engine optimization (SEO), Google AdWords, and Internet marketing tools, visit moz.com/beginners-guide-to-seo.

Directional Cues.   Avoid navigational cues, such as "on the next page," that make sense on the printed page but not online. Instead, position links so that they are tied directly to the content to which they pertain, such as the ***Back to Top*** links on pages that are several screens long.

Graphics.   Graphics provide information that text alone cannot; they also provide visual relief. Use only **visuals** that are appropriate for your audience and **purpose**. Avoid overusing complex graphs and animation that can clutter or slow access to your site. Work with the site Webmaster to optimize all graphics for speed of access. Ask about the preferred file-compression format for your visuals. Also consider giving visitors a graphics-free option for quicker access to your content.

Fonts.   Font sizes and styles affect screen legibility. Because screens display fonts at lower resolutions compared to printed text, sans serif fonts often work better for online text passages. Do not use ALL CAPITAL LETTERS or **boldface type** for blocks of text, because they slow the reader. For content that contains special characters (such as mathematical or chemical content), consult your Webmaster about the best way to submit the files for HTML (hypertext markup language) coding, or post them as portable document format (PDF) files.

Using Links

Use *internal links* to help readers navigate the information on your site. If text is longer than two or three screens, create a **table of contents** of links at the top of the Web page, and link each item to the relevant content further down the page. Use *external links* to enrich coverage of your topic with information from outside your site and to help reduce content on your page. When you do, consider placing an icon or a text label next to the link to inform users that they are leaving the host site. Avoid too many links within text paragraphs because they can distract readers, make scanning the text difficult, and tempt readers to leave your site before reaching the end of your page.

Links to outside sites can expand your content. However, *review such sites carefully before linking to them*. Is the site's author or sponsoring organization reputable? Is its content accurate, current, and unbiased? Does the site date-stamp its content with notices such as, "This page was last updated on January 1, 2018"? Link directly to the page or specific

W

area of an outside site that is relevant to your users, and be sure that you provide a clear **context** for why you are sending your readers there. For more advice on evaluating Web sites, see page 461.

Posting an Existing Document

If you post an existing document to a Web site, try to retain the original sequence and layout of the document. If, for example, you shorten or revise an existing document for posting to the Web, add a notice informing readers how it differs from the original.

Before posting the document publicly, review it offline to ensure that it is the correct version and that all links work and go to the right places. Consider creating a "single-file version" of the content (a version formatted as a single, long Web page) for readers who will print the content to read offline. See also **proofreading** and **repurposing**.

Convert documents such as reports, flyers, and brochures to PDF files to make sure your electronic documents look identical to your printed documents. Readers can view a PDF file online, download it, or print it in whole or in part. Using specialized PDF software, you can create sophisticated forms, add signatures and watermarks to documents, and password-protect sensitive files.

❖ **ETHICS NOTE** Keep a record of how and where you find content online, be it text, images, tables, streaming video, or other material. Seek approval from the copyright holder before using any such information. Besides being legally—and ethically—required, documenting your sources bolsters the credibility of your site. To document your sources, either provide links to your source or use a citation, as described in **documenting sources**. See also **copyrights, patents, and trademarks** and **plagiarism**. ❖

Protecting User Privacy

Ensure that your content is consistent with your site's privacy policies for site users. A site's privacy statement informs visitors about how the site sponsor handles solicited and unsolicited information, its policy on the use of cookies, and its policy on handling security breaches.

Writing for a Global Audience

When you write for an international audience, eliminate expressions and references that make sense only to someone familiar with American English. Express **dates**, clock times, and measurements consistent with international practices. For visuals, choose symbols and icons, colors, representations of human beings, and captions that can be easily understood, as described in **global communication** and **global graphics**. See also **biased language**, **English as a second language**, and **idioms**.

W

Y

"you" viewpoint

The "you" viewpoint places the reader's interest and perspective foremost. It is based on the principle that most readers are naturally more concerned about their own needs than they are about those of a writer or a writer's organization. See **audience** and **persuasion**.

Using the words *you* and *your* rather than *we*, *our*, *I*, and *mine* can help convey the "you" viewpoint. Consider the following sentence.

▶ *We must receive* your signed approval before *we can process* your payment.

Even though the sentence uses *your* twice, the words in italics suggest that the **point of view** centers on the writer's need to receive the signed approval in order to process the payment. (See also **refusal letters**.) Consider the following revision, written with the "you" viewpoint.

▶ *So you can receive* your payment promptly, please send your signed approval.

In some instances, you may need to avoid using the **pronouns** *you* and *your* to achieve a positive **tone** and maintain goodwill. Notice how the first of the following examples (with *your*) seems to accuse the reader; the second (without *your*) uses **positive writing** to emphasize a shared goal—meeting the client's needs.

ACCUSATORY   *Your* budget makes no allowance for setup costs.

POSITIVE   The budget should include an allowance for setup costs to meet all the concerns of our client.

By considering the readers' interests as you write, you can achieve your **purpose** not only in **correspondence** but also in **proposals**, **reports**, and **presentations**.

your / you're

Your is a possessive **pronoun** ("*your* wallet"); *you're* is the contraction of *you are* ("*You're* late for the meeting").

Index

Words and phrases in **bold type** indicate main alphabetical entries. Usage terms appear in *italic type*.

Commonly Misused Words and Phrases

Model Documents and Figures by Topic

Use the following list as a quick reference for finding selected samples of business writing and visuals by topic. See also the complete Contents by Topic on the inside front cover of this book. For additional models, see the LaunchPad Solo for Professional Writers at *launchpadworks.com/*.